GW00901580

The

Great

Divorce

Controversy

Edward S Williams

Belmont House Publishing
London

The Great Divorce Controversy is published by Belmont House Publishing

First published 2000

ISBN 0 9529939 3 7

Copyright © Edward S Williams 2000. All rights reserved. No part of this publication may be reproduced, stored on a retrieval system, or transmitted in any form, or by any means, electronic, mechanical, photocopying, recording or otherwise without prior permission of the publisher.

The right of Edward S Williams to be identified as the author of this work has been asserted by him in accordance with the Copyright, Designs and Patents Act 1988.

Unless otherwise stated, scriptural quotations are taken from the HOLY BIBLE, New International Version. Copyright © 1973, 1978, and 1984 by the International Bible Society. Used by permission.

Published by Belmont House Publishing
36 The Crescent
Belmont
SUTTON
Surrey SM2 6BJ

A Catalogue record for this book is available from the British Library.

Printed by Redwood Books, Trowbridge, Wiltshire.

Typeset by Ted Williams

Cover design by Ted Williams and Gwyn Williams

To my wife Eileen and family

Two people provided advice, encouragment and practical help with the writing of this book. Audrey Williams, my sister, gave great help with preparing the manuscript and worked tirelessly on the references. My friend Jack Proom spent endless hours reading the text and suggesting improvements. My thanks also to Anna White for help with proofing reading.

Contents

Preface

Divorce, with the resulting breakdown in families, is one of the great moral issues of our time. It is now so widespread that there are few people who are not is some way affected. And because it affects people in such an intimate way it is difficult to discuss and many prefer to avoid the subject. Moreover, there is now a consensus that divorce is necessary in a modern society. But the appalling consequences of broken families mean that the issue will not go away—too many people are being hurt. Many feel instinctively that mass divorce, a relatively new phenomenon, is bad for society. The aim of this book is to explore the ideas and beliefs that have allowed it to come about.

My interest was initially aroused through my work in public health. Divorce was the major social change affecting family structure, and the continual flow of information that came across my desk seemed to show that the children of divorce – and the adults, for that matter – did not do well from a health point of view. All the evidence pointed in the same direction, and so my original intention was simply to document the obvious—to show the health consequences of family breakdown. As a child of divorce (my parents divorced when I was eight years old) I already knew, at first hand, the negative effects of divorce and that they were long lasting.

But as I read into the subject I was surprised at the controversial nature of the issue. Not only was the interpretation of the scientific information open to dispute, there was also disagreement in the Church over the grounds for divorce. On the one side were those who believed that the Bible allows divorce with the freedom to remarry. Some believed that adultery and desertion are biblical grounds for divorce, and that the innocent party is free to remarry in church. Others believed that as marriages can 'die', divorce with the right to remarry is necessary to allow a fresh start.

On the other side of the dispute were those who believed that divorce is against the teachings of Christ. They argue that marriage is a lifelong union – one wife at a time, and that wife till death – and therefore even a legal divorce does not break the marriage bond. This means that remarriage following divorce is not permitted. And here is the conundrum—both sides claimed that their position was based on Scripture.

And this ongoing scriptural controversy has been raging for nearly four centuries, and there is no sign that the theologians are about to agree. Although a large number of books have been written on the subject the dispute remains unresolved. Two recent books illustrate the depth of the division. In his book *Putting Asunder* (1999) Stephen Clark shows from the Bible that divorce is permissible for marital unfaithfulness and so the innocent party is free to remarry. On the other side of the debate, Andrew Cornes in *Divorce and Remarriage* (1993) shows from the Bible that marriage is an indissoluble bond that can only be broken by the death of one of the marriage partners, and therefore remarriage is impossible. So which side is right?

It occurred to me that simply looking at the Scriptures would not provide a definitive answer, for even leading theologians could not agree. To understand the issues I needed to dig deeper. I therefore decided to examine the arguments that had been used to justify the respective positions to see if they would throw further light on the controversy. How did the dispute arise? Who were the people behind the controversy? What were the underlying ideologies?

I was surprised to find that the controversy flowed from the Reformation, and that the great reformers Martin Luther and John Calvin, under the influence of Erasmus, a Renaissance humanist 'par excellence', were the first to discover grounds for divorce in the Bible. As I traced the divorce debate through the Church of England, through the English parliament, and in Protestant America, it gradually became clear that at the heart of the controversy was the issue of the indissolubility of marriage. The arguments were passionate, and at times, heated and bitter.

You will read the views of many prominent people from both sides of the dispute: bishops and archbishops, theologians and reformers, statesmen and politicians, sociologists, psychologists and feminists. As far as is possible I have attempted to let people present their case in their own words, so there are many direct quotes. This should help you to test the validity of the arguments. And while human arguments have limited value, it is nevertheless useful to see the views of those who have shaped Western thought on divorce. But the ultimate appeal must be to the Bible, and, having examined the arguments I present my own interpretation of biblical teaching on marriage and divorce. My position will become clear as you read the book. My hope is that you will examine the evidence and decide for yourself what is the true biblical position on marriage, divorce and remarriage. We have nothing to fear from examining the controversy, for it is the truth that sets us free—it is ignorance and error that can harm us.

Chapter 1

The phenomenon of mass divorce

Controversy in society and confusion in the Church

Family breakdown has reached epidemic proportions in most countries of the Western world. The leading nation of the West, the United States of America, has the highest divorce rate in the civilised world, and England the highest rate in Europe. In the past decade almost 12 million American and one and a half million English families have experienced divorce, involving countless millions of children in the heartbreak of a broken home. It is estimated that at current divorce rates almost half of all marriages in America, and four out of ten in England will end in divorce. The numbers are now so great that the phenomenon can be referred to as mass divorce, and there is hardly a family that is not in some way affected. Grandparents are witnessing the break-up of the marriages of their sons and daughters, watching in despair as their grandchildren suffer the trauma of a broken home. Other members of the wider family, like aunts and uncles, are affected as family relationships become strained by the recriminations that follow divorce. The ripple effects have spread through the whole of society, from the highest in the land to the lowest, and few families have escaped the hurt caused by divorce.

A new perspective has begun to dawn as many people grasp the fact that divorce is not merely an event, but rather a process with long-term consequences. It has profound effects for the husband and wife, for their parents and their children, and for other members of the wider family. Clearly divorce has social, emotional and profound economic consequences.[1] Indeed, a major consequence of mass divorce has been the feminisation of poverty. Economic analysis indicates that after divorce the standard of living of husbands and fathers tends to remain the same or improve, while wives and children slip below the poverty line.[2]

DIVORCE NUMBERS IN ENGLAND

There is no doubt that the effects of divorce have produced enormous social change in both America and Britain. The remarkable transformation of England from a society with virtually no divorce in the 19th century, to a society with mass divorce in the last decades of the 20th century is one of the most important social changes to occur in the last hundred years. Divorce numbers have increased from a few hundred per year in the last decade of the 19th century to over 150 thousand per year in the 1990s – a five-hundredfold increase. **Figure 1** shows the rise in divorce since statistics were first collected in 1858.

An increase in divorce numbers occurred in the immediate aftermath of both world wars. After the First World War the numbers peaked at three and a half thousand in 1921, while the peak following the Second World War in 1946 was 60 thousand. In 1957, the first year for which figures were collected on children, just over 30 thousand were affected by the divorce of their parents. During the next three decades the number of children involved increased almost eightfold, to 228 thousand in 1996. During the 25 years from 1971 to 1995 almost five million English children have experienced the break-up of their families.[3] The metamorphosis of England from a society with no divorce to one with mass divorce has not occurred by chance, but as the result of changes in the ideas and beliefs that influence social policy. In this book we shall examine the thinking behind the transformation of England into a society that readily accepts divorce.

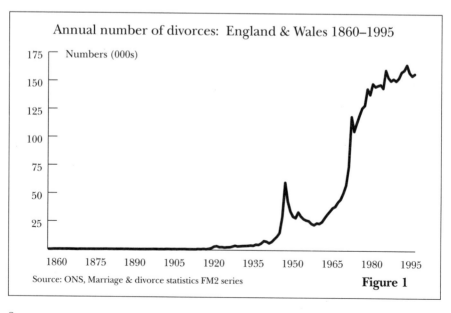

Annual number of divorces: England & Wales 1860–1995

Source: ONS, Marriage & divorce statistics FM2 series

Figure 1

MASS DIVORCE IN AMERICA

American society embraced divorce from the earliest colonial times, and was the first modern nation to experience mass divorce. In her book on the history of divorce in America, *Divorce: An American Tradition* (1991), Glenda Riley makes the point that people all over the world have expressed astonishment at the spread of divorce in the United States. Divorce has been examined from every angle, and Americans often reproach themselves and their tension laden society for making it a widespread American phenomenon. 'The historical record, however, indicates that contemporary American divorce is more than a recent outgrowth of a troubled modern society. American divorce has a long and venerable history: Puritan settlers first introduced it in the American colonies during the early 1620s. The resulting institution of American divorce was vital, and growing, long before late 20th century Americans carried it to its current state.'[4] In his book, *Divorce – the American experience* (1975), Joseph Epstein notes that few Americans remain untouched by divorce. 'If they have not themselves been divorced, the probability is great that they are married to someone who has been divorced, or have a brother or sister or son or daughter or parents who have been divorced, or close friends who have been through a divorce... In a way that was not true thirty or twenty or even ten years ago. In America divorce has become a serious alternative to a marriage that has fallen short of expectations. As more and more people divorce, the social disgrace that used to be so prominently associated with divorce lessens, with the consequence that divorce itself becomes a more real possibility for an ever greater number of people.' He makes the point that far from being a socially radical act it has become an almost regular experience. 'Novels and movies and television make free and easy use of divorce as a subject matter; jokes are made of it; news of it among friends no longer makes for very delicious gossip. All of which attests that divorce is becoming socially commonplace, humdrum almost.'[5]

The move towards mass divorce really started after the American Civil War in the 1860s when it became increasingly common. The rate more than doubled in the thirty years between 1870 and 1900, rising from 29 to 73 per hundred thousand population. Concern in the 1890s about what was regarded as the growing evil of divorce led to a national debate, many people wanting to limit the growth in divorce. During the 20th century numbers increased inexorably, although mass divorce only became a feature of American life in the 1960s as the rising trend accelerated at an unprecedented rate with numbers doubling between 1965 and 1975. The numbers peaked in the 1980s at over one million divorces per year. The growth in American divorce numbers since reliable figures became available in the 1860s is charted in **figure 2**. In every year since 1975 over one million American families have been broken by divorce, half of which occurred within the first seven years of marriage. The average divorce involves one child, and in the three decades since 1960 about 26 million American children have experienced the break-up of their families.[6]

The mass divorce phenomenon of the last three decades has had a major impact on American children. In 1990, there were 64 million American children under 18, of whom 37 million (57.8 per cent) were living with both of their natural parents, 7.2 million (11.3 per cent) in a stepfamily, 15.8 million (24.7 per cent) in a single-parent arrangement, 3 million (4.6 per cent) in a home with no parent present, and 1 million (1.5 per cent) were living with adoptive parents.

Turning to the 15.8 million children living with a single parent, we see that 6 million were living with a divorced single parent, and 4.9 million with a separated (or rarely widowed) single parent. The remaining 4.9 million children were living with a single parent who had never married.[7] Altogether then, the home circumstances of at least 18.1 million children had been affected by the divorce of their parents.

Many social commentators believe that the rise in divorce has contributed to the severe social problems that are a feature of contemporary American life. Over the last 35 years, while the divorce rate has doubled, the number of crimes have increased threefold, violent crimes fivefold, illegitimate births have risen by 400 per cent and teenage suicide rates have tripled.[8] A nationwide survey of 16 thousand American schoolchildren showed that 20.5 per cent had seriously considered attempting suicide during the 12 months preceding the survey, with female students (27 per cent) being

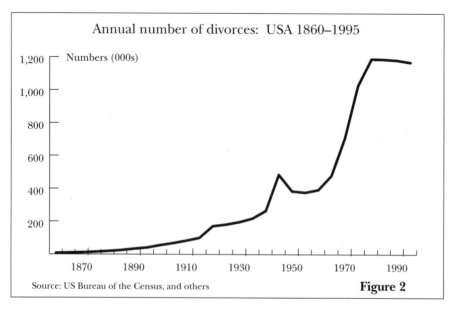

Annual number of divorces: USA 1860–1995

Numbers (000s)

Source: US Bureau of the Census, and others

Figure 2

significantly more likely than male students (15 per cent) to have done so. An alarming finding was that 7.7 per cent of students had actually attempted suicide during the previous year.[9] At the National Violence Prevention Conference in 1995 delegates were informed that the increasing suicide rates among young men was a major concern, and Senator Tom Harkin declared 'a stunning simultaneous breakdown of community, family, and work has created a vacuum which has been filled by violence, drugs and gangs'.[10] David Blankenhorn, the President of the Institute for American Values in New York, has argued that fatherlessness, which results from divorce and illegitimacy, is the engine that drives many of America's worst social problems. 'The most important predictor of juvenile delinquency is not race or income. It is the absence of a father. For teenage pregnancy it is a similar story. Young fatherless women are twice as likely to get pregnant outside marriage. The explosion of juvenile crime and teenage pregnancy tracks the increase in fatherless homes with eerie precision.'[11]

Comparing divorce in England and America

America has always had a higher divorce rate than England, although since the 1960s the differential has started to disappear. In 1906 there were 72 thousand divorces in America (population around 85 million) compared to only 546 in England (population around 35 million). By 1910 the American divorce rate was forty-five times higher than the English rate; the next four decades saw a dramatic decline in the divorce differential due to the large increase in English numbers, and in the 1950s the American rate was only three and a half times higher than the English rate.[12] The two decades following the 1960s were characterised by a steep rise in both countries with the American figures peaking in the 1980s, while the English rate continued rising into the 1990s, leading to a further reduction in the divorce gap. One of the questions that we will address is why America has always had higher divorce rates than England. In the 1990s the American divorce rate was about 30 per cent higher than the English rate.

Another way of illustrating the magnitude of family breakdown is to look at the numbers by decade. In England in the first decade of the century there were less than six thousand divorces. In the 1920s there were 31 thousand, a fivefold increase. During the decade of the Second World War (1940s) the numbers increased to 251 thousand, largely as a result of the many post-war divorces. A phenomenal increase occurred in the 1970s when over 1.2 million divorces were recorded, and in the 1980s there were 1.5 million. In the thirty years since 1965 there have been 3.6 million divorces in England & Wales.[13,14] In America, during the 1920s there were around 500 thousand divorces; in the 1950s around 1.1 million. During the decade of the sixties, 4.7 million divorces were recorded, the numbers doubling to 9.6 million in the 1970s, and increasing to 11.7 million in the 1980s.[15] An inevitable question is—what proportion of current marriages will end in divorce? In England it is predicted that at current divorce rates, after four years of marriage 10 per cent of couples will have divorced, after 10 years 25 per cent and after thirty years 40 per cent. At current divorce rates almost half American marriages will end in divorce.

EMOTIONAL DEVASTATION

These statistics tell little of the reality of divorce. Those who have experienced the break-up of their family know that it is usually associated with intense emotional pain. Later in this book we shall examine the evidence which shows that in most divorces both husband and wife suffer severe mental anguish. In some cases the emotional pain is similar to, or even worse than bereavement. The intensity of the mental suffering is far greater than most people thought possible. Frequently both partners suffer intense feelings of rejection, become very angry, and go through a period of inexpressible sadness and depression.

The following personal account of divorce will probably strike a chord with many people. The author is very honest about his feelings, and writes, 'I know about wrecked families and wrecked lives. I know about solicitors, about broken hearts, broken dreams and tears; I know about the questions you have asked yourself countless times... I know how much it hurts when you think about the person who was once your best friend...' He goes on to describe how the sense of loss in divorce is almost the same as bereavement, but with divorce the emotions rapidly alternate between a whole gamut of feelings. 'Intense bouts of anger are often interlaced with hatred, self-reproach or even self-pity, because divorce is not only about the loss of a partner. It is about the humiliation of rejection, of failure. It is about possible financial ruin or even being made to feel a social leper. The bereaved spouse will have some consolation in not having to deal with that.'[16]

The children involved usually suffer just as much as their parents—sometimes even more. For children a divorce is often worse than the death of one of their parents. In her book, *Caught in the Middle* (1997), Anne Charlish comments that the 'conflicts and anxieties created by the loss of a parent through divorce are practically unbearable for a child. Research going back some twenty years confirms that divorce is, indeed, worse for children than bereavement.'[17] They suffer because they lose the security of their home and family, but even more because they witness the sadness and suffering of their parents. Sometimes they are forced to choose between their parents, the two people in the world they love most of all.

The depth of feeling aroused by divorce is illustrated by an exercise in a school that asked children to make up their own Ten Commandments. The first two commandments of the children dealt with the issue of marriage and divorce. The first was—'You should not be allowed to get married unless you are really sure'. The second dealt with the same issue—'You should not be allowed to leave your children'. Note that both commands have a message for their parents. The Rev James Jones, commenting on the reaction of the children, writes, 'These schoolchildren spoke out of their own pain. Divorcing adults often remark on how well the children are coping. It is more likely that they hide their feelings from their parents and cry into their pillows. The break-up of marriages and the consequent divorce of families are having disastrous social consequences which politicians are at last recognising. Every study shows that children brought up in stable relationships are more likely to flourish and less likely to offend against society.'[18] A particularly sad aspect of the suffering is that children are the innocent victims. They have done no wrong and, as we shall see later, invariably do not wish their parents to divorce. But they have no say in the matter. It is the parents who choose to divorce—and they could have done otherwise. Children have no such choice, but are fully embroiled in the situation of spiralling sadness and distress.[19]

THE ECONOMICS OF DIVORCE

The costs of single parenthood affect society in many ways. Politicians are starting to recognise the economic consequences, as expenditure on social security grows to support the huge and increasing number of single mothers created by divorce. One of the fastest growing groups of welfare claimants are unsupported mothers and their children. Research in America has shown that divorced women suffer an average decline of about 30 per cent in their incomes the year after their marriage breaks up.[20] Indeed for many women and children divorce is the start of a struggle against poverty. In 1990 the British Government was spending over three billion pounds supporting lone-parent families, and 80 per cent of lone mothers received no maintenance support from the fathers of their children. Clearly a large proportion of fathers feel that divorce ends not only their relationship with their wife, but also their duty to support their children. Further evidence of political concern about the economic burden imposed on the state is an attempt by the British Government to force absent fathers to support their children by setting up a Child Support Agency. The Agency, which came into operation in 1993, aims to pursue absent fathers to recoup some of the costs of state support. It has proved to be a highly controversial operation, causing considerable dissatisfaction among remarried men and their second wives.

Another sobering fact is that today's divorcee will become tomorrow's poor elderly, as most will not share in the pension of their former husbands. The children of divorce also cost the state. According to an article in *The Economist*, children who experience the break-up of their parents' marriage are 'at greater risk than children from intact homes of becoming the next generation of badly educated low earners and single parents'.[21] Yet another economic consequence is the need for more housing to accommodate the increasing numbers of households that result from divorce. Research by the Joseph Rowntree Foundation has shown that divorce triggers a decline in housing standards. Although about a third of those who leave the matrimonial home move in with relatives or friends, research suggests that for every hundred divorces, fifty-three new households are created. Divorcing couples tend to move out of owner-occupation and into rented or council housing. Divorced mothers with their children and lone fathers tend to fare worst. According to the Foundation divorce has triggered a downward spiral for both partners—from owner-occupied to rented housing; from detached houses to semi-detached; from houses to flats with fewer and smaller rooms.[22] Government planners have recently estimated that about five million new homes will be needed in Britain by the year 2016, mainly because divorce divides existing households.

A remedy for unhappy marriages

There is now a public debate about the scale of divorce and its consequences for society. In many ways society is ambivalent in its reaction. While there is some concern about the large number of divorces, many believe that divorce is a legitimate part of modern life, a means of rescue – especially for women – from marriages in which love has faded. Some people even regard divorce as an adult entitlement that should not be challenged.[23] Others see divorce as a human right that offers protection from the tyranny of an unhappy marriage. They argue that making divorce a right would allow the family reorganisation to be dealt with in a more wholesome climate.[24] The idea that children have a stake in their parents' marriage, and that divorce causes children to suffer, is seldom mentioned. Indeed, many influential voices have sought to justify divorce by suggesting that the break-up of an unhappy marriage actually improves the well-being of children.[25] As the incidence of divorce has grown, becoming common among the intelligentsia and opinion formers, the social stigma has all but disappeared. It has become increasingly accepted as the remedy for unhappy marriages.

CRISIS OR MORAL PANIC?

The trends described above are seen by many as evidence that the traditional family, the foundation on which Western Christian civilisation has been built, is in a state of serious decline. A growing number of social commentators now argue that the current trends in family breakdown are causing a serious social crisis in Britain and America. According to the historian Lawrence Stone the transformation of England from a largely non-divorcing society in the Middle Ages to a divorcing one in the second half of the 20th century 'is perhaps the most profound and far reaching social change to have occurred in the last five hundred years'.[26] In previous centuries both England and America accepted marriage and stable family life as the norms of a good society. In a sermon in St Paul's Cathedral in 1908 the Archbishop of York (Cosmo Gordon Lang) highlighted the importance of the family to the well-being of the nation. 'The great alternative between national efficiency and national degeneracy revolves around the strength or weakness of the home. Now the basis on which this family life rests is obviously the relationship between husband and wife. It is a relationship so important to the whole progress of humanity that it was the one object upon which our Lord laid down a definite and detailed social law. It was a law based on the oneness of man and wife. "Therefore whom God hath joined together let no man put asunder. They twain shall be one flesh." It was in loyalty to this law that Christian society set about its mission to restore and purify family life in the midst of a pagan world in which the marriage tie was loose, and therefore, the family life disordered and weak.'[27]

Commenting on marriage discipline in America at the end of the 19th century, the Bishop of Vermont (Arthur Hall) emphasised the link between the family and marriage. 'The family is God's first institution upon earth, the cradle of the Church and state alike; marriage is the foundation of the family. Where family life is dishonoured, wedded unfaithfulness lightly regarded, parental responsibilities neglected, filial respect and obedience slighted, then we may be sure society is rotten at the core. One trembles for the future of a state or nation where lax theories concerning domestic life gain ground.'[28]

Melanie Phillips, a columnist for the *Observer*, believes that the progressive collapse of the intact family is bringing about a set of social changes which is taking Britain into uncharted and terrifying waters. She writes, 'there are now whole communities, framed by structural unemployment, in which fatherlessness has become the norm. These communities are truly alarming because children are being brought up with dysfunctional and often antisocial attitudes as a direct result of the fragmentation and emotional chaos of households in which sexual libertarianism provides a stream of transient and unattached men servicing their mothers.' Phillips points out that children whose families are broken do relatively worse in virtually every area of life than children from intact families brought up by their own father and mother. 'Children's problems are by no means confined to those brought up by single parents. Stepparents often create worse problems. The distress and damage done to a middle-class child shunted around between stephouseholds may take the form of depression, eating disorders, educational under-achievement and an inability to form lasting adult relationships... Our whole culture has devalued marriage to a breakable contract of little intrinsic worth, and children to merely another set of consumer commodities.'[29]

Commenting on the divorce situation in America, Barbara Dafoe Whitehead, in her book *The Divorce Culture* (1997), concludes that a high-divorce society 'is a society marked by growing division and separation in its social arrangements, a society of single mothers and vanished fathers, of divided households and split parenting, of fractured parent-child bonds and fragmented families, of broken links between marriage and parenthood. The shift from a family world governed by the institution of marriage to one ruled by divorce has brought a steady weakening of primary human relationships and bonds. Men's and women's relationships are becoming more fleeting and unreliable. Children are losing their ties to their fathers. Even a mother's love is not forever, as the growing number of throwaway kids suggests.'[30]

In his book, *Life Without Father* (1996), David Popenoe writes that 'father absence is a major force lying behind many of the attention grabbing issues that dominate the news: crime and delinquency; premature sexuality and out-of-wedlock teen births; deteriorating educational achievement; depression, substance abuse, and alienation among teenagers; and the growing number of women and children in poverty. These issues all point to a profound deterioration in the well-being of children.'[31] There is evidence that the widespread incidence of divorce is a major factor behind the economic insecurity of women and children. The majority of children from divorced families have lost any meaningful contact with their fathers. It is not surprising that the evidence shows that divorce is one of the factors spawning a generation of angry and deprived children who are not achieving at school, as we shall see in chapter 17.

In her book, *Second Chances* (1990), divorce researcher Judith Wallerstein makes the point that in the 1980s people had the comfortable illusion that divorce was a time limited crisis. Children were resilient and soon after the divorce everything would settle down and life would improve for all. Divorce would allow the adults to undo the mistakes of their youth, and the children would be better off because their parents were happier. 'But that is not what our research revealed. The men, women and children whom we interviewed were still deeply affected by the divorce ten and fifteen years later. For them, the break-up and its aftermath were life-shaping events.'[32]

In an essay which deals with the lawlessness prevalent within some British schools, Bruce Anderson writes, 'Discipline and education are non-existent, while bullying and truancy are rampant.' He mentions one school in which the 'children are being trained for only two careers – the dole or jail – and the horrifying truth is that most of their parents could not care less'. And the situation in this particularly poor school is in no way unique in its awfulness as up and down the country tens of thousands of children are being mis-educated. According to Anderson the root cause of most current social problems 'is the breakdown of family life, plus declining standards in parenting. There is no easy way of tackling this problem.'[33] In an article in the *Sunday Telegraph*, Leo McKinstry argues that the government is right when it says action is urgently needed to prop up the institution of marriage in Great Britain. 'For family life in modern Britain is beleaguered... The effects of the breakdown of family life can be seen all around us: delinquency of young men growing up in fatherless families; the explosion in the costs of social security, now reaching a third of all state spending; in the neglect of the elderly; and child abuse and bullying.'[34]

The most serious concern is expressed by those who believe that the collapse of marriage and the family is endangering the survival of Western civilisation. Canon Michael Harper in his book *Equal and Different* (1994) warns that today 'the family is again in serious crisis. If we fail to find a solution we will be plunged into a new dark age of lawlessness and chaos, which could destroy our civilisation... Just when people need clear guidelines on taking moral decisions on family matters, such as cohabitation, abortion, birth control, divorce, most of the churches fudge the issues and offer people little or confusing advice.'[35]

On the other side of the debate are those who disagree that mass divorce is causing a crisis and warn of the danger of moral panic, arguing that the family is not declining but changing to suit modern lifestyles. According to Sue Slipman, a member of a governmental Advisory Committee on Women's Issues, 'the 1990s have given rise to the growth of a breed of moral panickers who are alarmed at the changes wrought within the social fabric and in particular within the institution of the family and who now wish to reassert a new agenda that is based on duties not rights... Unlike the panickers I do not believe that all the changes over these twenty years have been deleterious.'[36]

In an essay that describes changes to the family in recent decades, John Haskey notes that the diversity of family forms has increased, with 'traditional' families in relative numerical decline. He concludes that the changing patterns of marriage, divorce and cohabitation means that family structures have become more diverse, and also that individuals are more likely to experience living in a greater variety of types of families during their lifetimes. 'Of course, exercising choice, or the growing emphasis upon individual development and fulfilment, is much easier in a society if different patterns of demographic behaviour are generally accepted as valid alternatives, and the trend towards a variety of norms is perhaps the most significant of post-war social change.'[37] Those who hold the view that the family is simply changing, adapting to the modern world, believe that talk of a national crisis is scaremongering by people wishing to mount a moral crusade. David Popenoe comments that for ideological reasons, 'even though the empirical data to support the trend are now overwhelming, the notion of "family decline" remains steeped in controversy'.[38] So, right at the beginning of the debate we are entering controversial territory, for when it comes to family breakdown even the most straightforward facts are open to dispute.

CONFUSION IN THE CHURCHES

In the midst of this major debate about the welfare of the family and the consequences of mass divorce, the Christian Church has been strangely silent. Instead, the current debate in Christian circles over the remarriage of divorcees in church confuses many people about the Church's teaching on divorce. Almost everybody is familiar with the words of the traditional marriage service, 'till death us do part', and assumes that the Christian message is that marriage is for life. Yet most Christian denominations, with the notable exception of the Roman Catholic Church, are increasingly willing to remarry divorcees in church—something that was almost unheard of in previous generations. Despite the growth in the number of church remarriages, most denominations have different rules about this. To add to the confusion there are different shades of opinion within denominations. Some ministers believe that the words of Christ do not allow any remarriage at all, while others believe that Christ permitted remarriage following divorce under certain circumstances. The overall impression is that in recent years churches have become lax in their application of the marriage vows and, in certain circumstances, even condone divorce.

According to Stanley Ellisen, a Baptist theologian, there are few issues on which the Church is so confused and uncertain as on the problem of divorce and remarriage. 'Small wonder, since so many pastors also share that confusion. Some pastors will marry divorced people; some will marry some, but not others; and yet others will not pronounce a pastor's blessing on any second-go-round of marriage apart from the death of one of the partners. With that confusion, what is a church member to do or believe on the subject?'[39] Ellisen goes on to make the point that in the last thirty years most Protestant church bodies, because of the increased influx of divorcees into the Church, have begun to rethink and revise their views on the remarriage of the so-called 'guilty party' in church. 'Thus the Church is in the throes of a revolution in its thinking on divorce and remarriage which the social environment has forced upon it... Theology ought to be on the leading edge of our social thinking, not dragged into the arena by it. This evidently has not been the case on this crying social issue of our time.'[40]

Church of England

For centuries the Church accepted that marriage was a lifelong union of one man with one woman until they were parted by death. According to canon law expert, Norman Doe, 'in the Church of England one basic understanding is that, short of annulment, a remarriage is contrary to

Scripture'.[41] In 1957 the Church reaffirmed a resolution that marriage is indissoluble save by death, and another made it clear that the Church should not allow the use of the marriage service in the case of anyone who has a former living partner.[42] There is little doubt that prior to the 1960s the Church took a strong line against divorce and would not approve the remarriage of divorcees in church.

But a change of outlook has occurred in the last three decades. With the growth of mass divorce, the Church has felt the need to modify its position to deal with the thousands of divorcees who are seeking remarriage. Accordingly, in 1981 the General Synod passed a motion 'that there are circumstances in which a divorced person may be married in church during the lifetime of a former spouse'. However, in 1984 a large majority of diocesan synods voted down draft marriage regulations produced by the House of Bishops.[43] The effect was to leave the marriage discipline of the Church of England in confusion. It has affirmed two resolutions that are diametrically opposed to each other – an Act of Convocation, which makes it clear that the Church should not use the marriage service to remarry anyone who has a former partner still living, and a General Synod resolution, which has agreed that there are circumstances in which a divorced person may be remarried in church during the lifetime of a former spouse. The current situation is that those clergy who believe in good conscience that a second marriage is possible, are free under the provision of civil law to allow second marriages and a number are doing so. While the ultimate decision to remarry a divorcee in church is a matter for the clergyman concerned, the House of Bishops has expressed the hope that clergy would seek the advice of their bishop before allowing a remarriage to take place in church.

Not surprisingly, there are now different rules in the various dioceses, depending upon the views of the bishop. Some bishops permit remarriage of divorcees, others do not. The difficult position of the Church was illustrated by the marriage of an ordained woman priest in a registry office because the man she chose to marry was a divorcee. The couple did not request a church wedding because they knew the bishop would refuse. The Rev Paul Needle, who introduced a motion on remarriage to the General Synod in 1994, said 'this is the sort of thing I want sorted out. If she was a curate in another diocese, she would not have this problem. It is total anarchy.'[44]

The Church now accepts divorced clergy, and a confidential report has found that parish priests increasingly flout the Church's official line. The Bishop of Doncaster (Michael Gear) is quoted, 'It really is important that we find a way to identify the occasions where it is appropriate for a divorced person who has a living partner to remarry in church. I'm sure there are cases where it is right, without saying we are undermining those who stick with the commitment.' The Archdeacon of York (George Austin) disagreed, fearing that remarriage would become a free-for-all. 'You could have a situation where a man had abused his wife, she was terribly hurt and he remarried in church, which is not compassionate as it makes her feel God has turned against her. We must look with compassion at the hurt family, the people who are left.'[45] Another worry for the Church is that marriage breakdown among the clergy has reached record levels. Whereas a few decades ago divorce among vicars was rare, recent figures suggest that now there may be up to 50 a year.[46] The remarriage debate in the Church of England is discussed in more detail in chapter 11.

Methodist Church

As a church in the Protestant tradition the Methodists have always believed that the Bible, in certain circumstances, allows divorce and remarriage. In recent years, with the advent of mass divorce, the numbers of divorced people who seek marriage in a Methodist church has risen rapidly. By 1994, 64 per cent of all marriages involved at least one divorced person, compared with 34 per cent in 1974.[47]

In 1946 the Methodist Conference adopted a statement on *The Law of Marriage and Divorce* which accepted that, first, a member of the Church who was an innocent party in a case of adultery is permitted to sue for divorce; second, it is permissible for a member of the Church who is an innocent party in an action in which divorce has been granted to marry again. A procedure was developed for the way ministers should consider requests from divorced persons for remarriage.[48] Under this procedure, when a divorced person sought remarriage, a minister was responsible for determining what went wrong in the previous marriage, thereby making the distinction between the innocent and guilty party in a divorce.

Over the years, however, it became apparent how extraordinarily difficult it was to unravel responsibilities and to apportion blame. In addition, the advent of no-fault divorce has made the distinction between innocent and guilty less clear cut and in most cases irrelevant.[49] This procedure, in which each minister seems to do what is right in his or her own eyes when couples seek to be remarried, produced a huge variety of responses and unpredictable advice. 'Diverse judgements about the principle of marriage after divorce, about the appropriateness in particular circumstances of a couple marrying in church and about the moral significance of cohabitation lead to inconsistency of approach. Sometimes one minister's opinion is played off against another's.'[50]

The Church published a new set of pastoral guidelines in 1996 on how all requests for marriage, including remarriages, should be dealt with by Methodist churches. The guidance was developed after a long process of consultation that sought to make a judgement about the suitability of a

Christian marriage ceremony in particular cases. *Christian Preparation for Marriage* explains that, while respecting the views of those who believe that a marriage in church of a divorced person whose former spouse is still alive contradicts the will of God, pastoral considerations lead to the judgement that in a large number of situations it is justifiable for divorced persons to marry in church.[51]

The report describes marriage in terms of friendship and love which brings into focus the vulnerability of contemporary marriages. Because our knowledge of each other is limited, it is inevitable that mistakes are sometimes made. 'When one or both partners decide that their relationship has come to an end as a creative, life-giving experience, this may signal the end of the marriage. Each partner needs to test this daunting prospect as thoroughly and seriously as possible with the other. They are wise, individually and together, to check their perceptions against the insights of their close families and friends. The judgement may have to be made, however, that their marriage has broken down irretrievably.'[52] Nevertheless, 'the whole process of love celebrated, of love damaged beyond repair, of grief and penitence, and of new love discovered can be one in which those involved learn a great deal about themselves. People may grow and mature through the experience, though many regret what it has cost – to others as much as themselves – to become more aware of themselves and of the transforming mercy of God.'[53]

The new policy of the Methodist Church is to welcome everyone who enquires about an intended marriage service, and to ensure at the moment of enquiry, that each couple is directed to a minister who is not prevented by conscience from considering their request for remarriage.[54] The couple is engaged in a process of marriage preparation, after which they reach a clear decision relating to their request for remarriage in a Methodist Church. 'At the conclusion of a marriage preparation course, the minister must meet each couple and hear from them whether they still wish to be married in a Methodist Church. If the couple reaffirm their request for marriage, the minister shall normally honour this request.'

Occasionally, a provisional pastoral judgement is made that a particular marriage in a particular church may have a destructive impact on the unity of the congregation or the good name of the Methodist Church in the community. In these cases the advice will be 'that they may wish to pursue their request in another circuit; on rare occasions, the advice may be that they should not pursue their request in any Methodist Church'.[55] The essence of the policy of the Methodist Church, therefore, appears to be not to distinguish between first marriages and remarriages. All are welcome, irrespective of whether they have been divorced or not. The policy does not comment on the number of times that the Church is willing to remarry an individual.

15

Baptist Union

The Baptist Union of churches also has difficulty with the issue. Marriage and divorce is discussed in the booklet *Belonging* (1994), a resource for the Christian family, published by the Baptist Union. It starts by recognising that the interpretation of the biblical material is not easy. 'Christians who differ, sometimes quite fundamentally, on this issue are all sure that they have biblical support for their views... Concerning matters relating to divorce and remarriages, Christians are not always agreed, either about the meaning of the biblical material or its application to our society and culture.'[56] The issue of remarriage is a particular problem for Baptist churches because local Anglican and Catholic churches often have a policy which does not permit remarriage in church, and this leads to people approaching Baptist pastors as a last resort. 'Many Baptist churches refuse to remarry divorcees on the basis of Scripture. Others who feel the biblical material is ambiguous also refuse out of respect for the other denominations in the local area. Still others will marry divorcees depending upon the specific circumstances.'[57]

Belonging proposes that churches may explore ways of offering those about to divorce an appropriate form of words to mark the end of the marriage. Some of the issues raised by a rite for divorce are discussed. 'If divorce is seen as freedom from an oppressive relationship, there is the fear that the Church should not be seen to "celebrate" a divorce. If the emphasis is upon repentance and grace, this takes care of the moral dimension that a covenant has been broken. But why should divorce be singled out as an area of moral failure, over and against other "sins"? If the emphasis is upon death and resurrection, this takes away the heavy moralisation, and the analogy of a funeral avoids appearing to celebrate a divorce. The death of a marriage with all its hopes and dreams is acknowledged and mourned, and a resurrection of a new life and fresh start is prayed for.' According to the booklet the advantages of a divorce rite are that it responds to the needs of the couple and their children for a sense of closure, forgiveness, healing. It provides an opportunity for the community to acknowledge the divorce and pledge support for them as individuals. It also helps to define their new status after divorce.[58] So while the Baptist denomination appears to be sympathetic to remarriage, its position lacks conviction.

United Reformed Church

In principle the United Reformed Church has no objection to the remarriage of divorcees in church when the circumstances are right. If a marriage breaks down, and reconciliation proves impossible and the marriage ends in divorce, the Church has a pastoral role. 'Christ taught the ideal in all aspects of human life but he had a deep compassion for those who failed to attain the ideal, and who recognised and regretted their failure. The Church also needs to show compassion for those who fail to maintain the ideal in a marriage relationship but who still hold a Christian view of marriage. Since the Church upholds the ideal of Christian marriage as a lifelong relationship, requests for remarriage after divorce are given prayerful consideration.'[59] The minister will usually discuss the circumstances surrounding the breakdown of the previous marriage and the satisfactory resolution of any resulting problems, particularly the care of children. Some divorcees and some ministers may wish to have a service in which penitence can be expressed for the failure of the previous marriage, recognition be given that the relationship is now ended and the desire to seek a new beginning made explicit. The service of 'prayer for release from vows' is available for those who wish to make use of it. When the minister and the Church are satisfied that the circumstances are right, divorcees may be married in church. It will be made clear that the service is a Christian marriage service and therefore the ideal of a lifelong union is involved. Where the local minister cannot consider remarriage on grounds of conscience, arrangements are made within the Province to enable the couple to be interviewed and married within the United Reformed Church.

THE GREAT CONTROVERSY

There is no doubt that divorce remains one of the most controversial issues of our time. Despite its apparent social acceptance many people are deeply disturbed by its effects on family life and the hurt it causes to children. Many find it surprising that in the face of the ominous warnings of the serious social dangers associated with widespread family breakdown, the Church's preoccupation is with making remarriage in church more widely available. While most Protestant denominations readily accept divorce and remarriage, the consciences of many Christians warn them that something is profoundly wrong with the Church's lax attitude. In the Church of England the issue of remarriage remains controversial, and recent events show that, despite an intensive debate that has lasted for almost three decades, the Church is split right down the middle.

At the heart of the divorce controversy is the apparent contradiction between the words of Christ and the teaching of the Church. Almost everybody knows that Christ spoke out strongly against divorce and took an uncompromising position on remarriage, calling it adultery. He said, 'anyone who divorces his wife and marries another woman commits adultery against her. And if she divorces her husband and marries another man, she commits adultery' (Mark 10:11,12). And so a central issue is whether the Church is being faithful to the teaching of Christ. We need answers to two crucial questions: first, why are the Protestant denominations so free and easy in their acceptance of divorce and remarriage? And second, why has the Church of England, which for centuries taught that marriage is indissoluble, recently changed its mind by accepting that there are circumstances in which divorcees may be remarried in church during the lifetime of their former partners? These questions lie at the centre of the controversy that has raged in the Church and society over the centuries. The plan of this book is to uncover the issues at stake by providing information and comment, so that readers can make up their own minds as to where the truth lies in one of the great controversies of our time.

Chapter 2

Marriage under challenge

The decline of traditional marriage and the ideas
behind modern secular marriage

Divorce numbers have risen in a climate of growing hostility to marriage and the traditional family. Marriage rates in Great Britain and America have declined dramatically over the last twenty years, and in England marriage rates are at their lowest point since records were first kept in 1838. Recent market research, which questioned 1,500 people on their attitude to marriage, found that half thought it was not as important as it used to be, with only four out of ten regarding marriage as the ultimate commitment.[1] Coinciding with the decline in marriage is an increase in cohabitation as many couples are now choosing to live together, some before marriage, and some with no intention of ever marrying. A fundamental argument against marriage is that it is an outdated institution which needs to be replaced by more suitable and sensible arrangements. It is now commonly believed that cohabitation allows a greater sense of freedom, offering sexual and emotional closeness without the restrictions imposed by marriage.

MARRIAGE TRENDS IN ENGLAND

In 1836 an Act of Parliament introduced civil marriage into England for the first time. Religious marriages were conducted in a church and civil marriages by a registrar of marriages in a registry office. A consequence of the changes introduced by this Act was that marriage statistics became available from 1838. The earliest records show that during the 1840s almost 98 per cent of marriages were solemnized by a religious ceremony, and 92 per cent of all marriages took place in the Church of England. The proportion of civil marriages gradually increased during the 19th century to reach 15 per cent by 1900, doubled over the next 60 years to 30 per cent in 1962, before doubling again in the next three decades, reaching almost 60 per cent by 1996.[2]

In order to describe trends in marriage rates we need to distinguish between first marriages and remarriages. This distinction is important for much of the theological debate revolves around the legitimacy, in the eyes of the Church, of remarriage. Moreover, the marital status of people who are entering into marriage has changed over the last three decades. In 1961, for example, 85 per cent of marriages were first marriages (between a bachelor and a spinster), 10 per cent involved the remarriage of one partner and 5 per cent the remarriage of both partners. Just three decades later, in 1996, only 58 per cent were first marriages, 23 per cent involved the remarriage of one partner and 19 per cent the remarriage of both partners.[3]

During the 1960s the first marriage rate was fairly stable, before peaking in 1972 at 100 per thousand eligible population for spinsters and 86 for bachelors. The next two decades were characterised by a steady decline in the rate, as shown in **figure 3**. Among bachelors, for example, the rate fell by 65 per cent in the twenty-five years after 1971, and in 1997 the rate of 28 per thousand is the lowest since records have been kept. Among women the first marriage rate declined by 63 per cent over the same period, to a rate of 35 per thousand in 1997.[4]

A remarriage involves the second or subsequent marriage of one or both partners following the dissolution of a previous marriage through either death or divorce. As we have already seen, the proportion of all marriages that are remarriages has increased dramatically over the last few decades. When the rates were at a peak following the Second World War, about 300 per thousand divorced men and 150 per thousand divorced women were remarrying each year, as shown in **figure 4**. During the 1960s rates stabilised

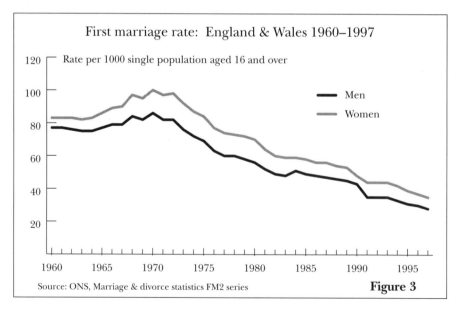

First marriage rate: England & Wales 1960–1997

Source: ONS, Marriage & divorce statistics FM2 series

Figure 3

for a time, before peaking again in 1972. Since then rates have declined steeply, the male rate falling from 284 per thousand divorced men in 1972 to a rate of 48 in 1997 – a reduction of over 80 per cent in just 25 years. The rate among females, which was lower than that of males in the 1950s and 60s, declined less steeply and is now almost similar to the rate among men. The annual remarriage rate of widowed men and women has followed a trend similar to that among divorced people.[4]

These figures confirm a dramatic decline in marriage rates across the board, with the greatest decline occurring among people remarrying. The effect of these trends is that the number of divorced people in the population has grown, and in 1996 one in 13 men and one in 12 women were divorced.[5] There is a strong association between the type of marriage ceremony and remarriage, with 80 per cent of remarriages in 1996 involving a civil ceremony, compared to 43 per cent of first marriages. In 1996, 11 per cent of Church of England marriages, and 37 per cent of marriages in other Christian churches, were remarriages.

MARRIAGE TRENDS IN AMERICA

The latter half of the 1960s saw major changes in the social landscape of the United States. We have already seen that the divorce rate doubled in the ten years after 1965. Coinciding with the growth of divorce were changing patterns of marriage and alterations in family structure.

First marriage rates reached an all time high immediately after the Second World War as many eligible young men returned to civilian life. Following the post-war peak there was a gradual decline in rates during the 1950s, while

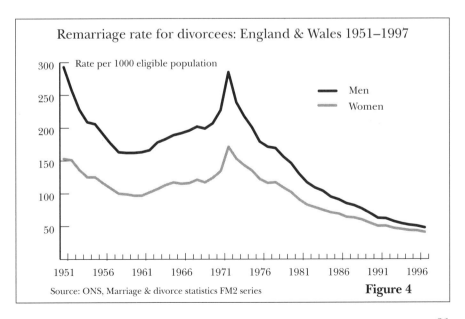

Remarriage rate for divorcees: England & Wales 1951–1997

Source: ONS, Marriage & divorce statistics FM2 series

Figure 4

in the 1960s rates remained fairly constant. By 1970 the rate was 93 per thousand single women aged 15 and over. During the next two decades there was a steep decline as the rate fell to 58 per thousand, a decrease of 38 per cent in just twenty years. Among single men the marriage rate has declined by 42 per cent over the same period. This sharp decrease in marriage has been somewhat offset by increasing rates of cohabitation.[6] During the 1970s and 80s the proportion of all marriages that were first marriages decreased from 69 per cent to 54 per cent.[7]

Another significant change has been the older age at which women marry for the first time. In 1970, among women aged under 25, 88 per cent had married compared to 57 per cent in 1990. During the same period the median age of first marriages increased from 20.4 years to 24 years. Although the average age of first marriage has increased, around 95 per cent of women still eventually marry.

High divorce rates have created a large pool of people eligible for remarriage. In 1970 the remarriage rate for divorced women was 123 per thousand; two decades later in 1990 the rate had declined to 76, a fall of 38 per cent. The remarriage rate of divorced men almost halved over the same period. During the heyday of remarriage in the 1960s almost 90 per cent of divorced women would remarry, 33 per cent within a year of their divorce, and around 60 per cent within three years. Of the women who divorced in the early 1980s, only 16 per cent had remarried within a year of their divorce, and 36 per cent within three years.[8]

However, despite the decline in remarriage rates, the proportions of all marriages that were remarriages increased from 31 per cent in 1970 to 46 per cent in 1988. It has been suggested that the recent levels of remarriage after divorce may be more close to two-thirds than the three-quarters often cited.[9] Nevertheless, remarriage will remain relatively widespread, resulting in a continued increase in the number of reconstituted, blended, and stepfamilies.[10] According to a Bureau of Census Report the data show that divorce has peaked and, although it will decline slightly, remains high enough to merit attention as a major social and economic issue. 'In addition, the data show that, although remarriage rates have fallen, the growth of consequent stepfamilies is significant, and that a large segment of the United States adult population flows into and out of several marital categories during their life course. The societal changes have led to American children today living in increasingly varied and complex living arrangements.'[11]

THE IDEOLOGICAL CHALLENGE TO MARRIAGE

Behind the decline in numbers is a serious and ongoing ideological challenge to the relevance and meaning of marriage. Over the last three decades the institution of marriage has come under a sustained attack from the intelligentsia and opinion formers in Britain and America. A growing body of literature, both academic and popular, has challenged the relevance of marriage in the modern world. The thinking behind the ideological challenge is important for it has influenced the way society views both marriage and divorce. As long as society held a high view of marriage, mass divorce could not take root. However, when marriage became devalued in the eyes of society, the gateway to mass divorce opened wide. If marriage is a flawed, irrelevant institution then divorce becomes a sensible option for those who are in unhappy marriages. After all, what sense is there in trying to save a marriage if the institution is basically flawed and bad for women? To comprehend the move to mass divorce we need to understand the thinking that has portrayed the institution of marriage as no longer relevant to the modern world.

Many commentators have claimed that marriage is a cause of women's oppression, and an institution that inhibits psychological growth. It has been portrayed as the foundation of a patriarchal society. A further criticism is that marriage is based on sexual inequality, and is therefore a form of bondage for both husband and wife.[12] Another point of view is that marriage turns a woman into a wife and expects the wife's place to be in the home. This limits a woman's horizons and inevitably relegates her to domestic duties.[13] The terms 'man and wife' are a terminology that reflects the innate inequality of the marriage situation, for the wife has lost her identity as a woman. Marriage becomes a battlefield, with both sides engaged in a war neither can win: for the partner who wins the power play inevitably loses the respect and love of his or her mate.[14]

World famous feminist author Germaine Greer ridiculed marriage in her best seller *The Female Eunuch* (1970). She asserted, 'if independence is a necessary concomitant of freedom, women must refuse to marry'.[15] She provided detailed reasons why 'women ought not to enter into socially sanctioned relationships, like marriage, and that once unhappily in they ought not to scruple to run away'.[16] She mocked the idea that a woman might find love and security in marriage, and advised married women, if not entirely satisfied with their lot, to consider abandoning the marriage.[17] *The Female Eunuch* undoubtedly had a major impact on the lives of many women. Its powerful rhetoric persuaded women to see marriage in a different light—to see themselves as the victims trapped in oppressive marriages. Undoubtedly many women were encouraged to view their marriages with scepticism, and to accept divorce as a sensible means of escape from the oppressive situation in which they found themselves.

Another criticism of marriage is that it destroys individuality, independence, self-confidence and self-respect.[18] Because marriage is so patently a patriarchal institution ordained by men it has become an anachronism and irrelevant to our society.[19] Following this line of reasoning, Law Commissioner and distinguished family lawyer, Brenda Hoggett, expressed the view, 'Family law no longer makes any attempt to buttress the stability of marriage or any other union… Logically we have already reached a point at which, rather than discussing which remedies should now be extended to the unmarried, we should be considering whether the legal institution of marriage continues to serve any useful purpose.'[20]

Modern secular marriage

Clifford Longley provides a perceptive comment on the feminist attitude towards marriage. 'The feminist critique of traditional marriage describes it as a focus for the oppression of women. Pressure from women, and many men, to undo this sense of oppression has been the motivating force for marriage reform this century. Now the campaigners have driven the reform so far that modern marriage and traditional marriage are two different things. Modern marriage is totally secular, an institution with no apparent roots in religion at all. The guardians of traditional marriage, the churches, have coped with the feminists by merely denying that oppression exists in marriage.'[21] The distinction between traditional marriage and secular marriage is important, because these two notions of marriage are based on entirely different premises. Traditional marriage is founded on the biblical idea of a covenant relationship between a man and his wife, in which they promise to live together, whatever the circumstances, for life. Modern secular marriage, on the other hand, is regarded as little more than a temporary contract that may be terminated when it no longer suits either partner.

Despite the continuing ideological challenge to marriage, most men and women still have an innate desire to marry and the majority will eventually do so. A recent Mori poll showed that 77 per cent of the British population disagreed with the statement that marriage is dead, and for 71 per cent of women the preferred lifestyle was one of being married and having children.[22] But the way society at large views marriage has undergone a fundamental change during the last century, and especially during the last three decades. In many Western countries, according to the *Encyclopedia Americana*, the concept of marriage as a permanent commitment has been abandoned and does not form part of society's cultural values. 'Marriage is in the process of being defined as a temporary relationship, to be maintained only as long as it helps both partners get what they want out of life.'[23] An illustration of the secularisation of marriage in England has been the steady decline in the proportion of church marriages, the steepest decline occurring during the last three decades. However the statistics do not tell the whole story, for even some of those who marry in church have a secular attitude towards their marriage.

The notion that marriage has a religious or moral dimension is debunked by modern secular thought. Modern marriage is a union of convenience for those who want something more than is offered by cohabitation, which, despite all the gloss, creates a great sense of insecurity. So a loving couple joins in marriage for their mutual happiness and benefit. While both partners are happy with the relationship, the marriage is valid; when one or both partners tire of the relationship, or when the relationship does not meet their inner needs, then the marriage has lost its meaning and should come to an end. Indeed, it is wrong for a couple no longer in love to stay married; the idea that parents should stay together for the sake of their children is a nonsense based on the old-fashioned ideas of duty and responsibility. Modern secular marriage lasts only while it fulfils its primary purpose of making the couple happy. In their book, *The Divorce Experience* (1977), Morton and Bernice Hunt describe how the changes wrought by technology, the women's movement, the sexual revolution, and the redefining of the roles of men and women have all made it impossible for marriage to survive as it was, for it could not meet the needs of modern men and women. 'And therefore it has changed in its internal structure, its balance of power, its allocation of roles, and above all in its expected duration – formerly a lifetime, now only as long as it fulfils its proper contemporary functions. Divorce has thus become not the antithesis of marriage but an essential aspect of the marriage system. It is the only way an individual can remain happily married – by changing partners – as his or her needs change in the course of a lifetime.'[24] According to this view, marriage is a temporary arrangement, with the expectation that partner change will be essential to remain happy.

Because modern marriage is so uncertain, couples are being encouraged to draw up prenuptial agreements to protect themselves in the eventuality of a future divorce. According to the Law Society, requests for prenuptial agreements are increasing, as some couples now feel it is wise to draw up such an agreement. Another feature of modern marriage is that some women choose to retain their maiden name because they do not want to give the impression that they are dependent on their husband. For example, a recently-married woman was so incensed at receiving Christmas cards addressed to 'Mr and Mrs' that she placed an advertisement in the local paper stating that she wished be known by her maiden name, not by her husband's name. In the advertisement she made it clear that although she was married she had not changed her name. Instead she would continue to be known personally and professionally by her maiden name, making no apology to the misguided fuddy-duddies who believe this to be strange or unconventional. Her reason was that she believed a woman should be able to retain her identity when she marries. Commenting on the issue, the author of *Modern Manners* said that it was perfectly acceptable for women to keep the name by which they were known before marriage.[25] Another newly-married young woman tells in a feature article how she felt obliged to explain to countless people in the workplace why she chose to change her name after her marriage. She explained that most disapproval came from middle aged women in senior positions.[26]

The contemporary view is that modern secular marriage should not interfere with the career aspirations of the wife, who goes out to work in order to maintain her financial independence. The expectation is that housekeeping duties will be shared between husband and wife, and should the wife have a baby, it is important that she returns to work as soon as possible so as not to damage her career prospects. Children are cared for in childcare as the modern wife and mother is out competing in the workplace. Should the marriage fail, as many do, divorce is the legal mechanism used to terminate a relationship that has already ended. For this reason divorce needs to be cheap and easy to obtain. It is, of course, nobody's fault that a marriage breaks down because one cannot be blamed for falling out of love— it is something that just happens. And should they love again, they always have the option of remarrying.

The Proposal: giving marriage back to the people

The report on modernising marriage by the British Labour Party's influential think-tank Demos is an important document because it recognises the secularisation of marriage that has taken place in society and proposes changes to the legal framework to accommodate secular marriage. In an open and honest way, *The Proposal* (1997) presents the logical implications that follow from the move towards the secularisation of marriage. The ambition of *The Proposal* is to revitalise marriage and give it a new lease of life by putting it 'in the hands of the people for whom it exists – the couples who wish to make commitments to each other, and who wish to choose their own rituals – *but in the context of a legal framework*'.[27]

The marriage of the future should be based on three guiding principles. The first is that church and state should be separated and all ceremonial privileges of religious denominations removed. The effect will be to remove the distinction between religious and civil marriage, allowing people to choose a ceremony that reflects their own belief system. 'The second principle is that society has an interest in encouraging couples to make commitments to one another through the life course. Couples who wish to marry – including same-sex couples – should be free to do so and to make a legal commitment to one another. The third principle is that the wishes of the couple who marry are all-important. This is why we need a comprehensive deregulation of the rules and regulations concerning the marriage ceremony allowing freedom of choice of celebrant, place and time and vows.'[28] According to Demos, these principles would underpin a changed culture of marriage, based on choice, and making an ancient ritual relevant, modern and meaningful. Encouraging people to write their own vows, and to devise their own ceremonies would emphasise communications within relationships, and encourage the development of life skills and interpersonal skills that are invaluable in negotiating successful and durable marriages. What sort of marriages would result from these changes? There would be 'imaginative and creative uses of different places for marriage ceremonies; everything from supermarkets to nightclubs, from planes to hilltops, from ancient burial sites to churches, from restaurants to people's own homes, from street ceremonies even to cemeteries.'[29]

The report goes on, 'the most important culture shift that we are edging uncertainly towards is the recognition that the institution of marriage cannot be rebuilt if people continue to make commitments they cannot sustain. In turn, this may lead to a recognition by some people that they cannot commit to lifelong marriage, but do feel they can commit for a specific time period at the end of which they can renew and renegotiate their marriage vows. Individuals and couples who do not have children may wish to experiment with time-limited marriages, perhaps typically for ten years. These would explicitly reject the idea of marriage as indissoluble but would emphasize the importance of renewing, reaffirming and even renegotiating marriage vows in recognition of the fact that over the course of a lifetime, people are bound to change. However, serial marriage would be encouraged.'[30]

The importance of vows is recognised. Those who marry in a church 'may find that they have less flexibility than other people to rewrite their vows. The implication is that the more traditional or inflexible religious denominations who insist on the commitment to vows such as "till death us do part" may well find themselves losing out to other religious ceremonies such as those conducted by Unitarians or by humanist celebrants. This is the logic of the democratisation of the system which this proposal opens up.'[31] *The Proposal* is based on the idea that modern secular marriage is usually a temporary arrangement. This is why the vow 'till death us do part' is seen as optional, and only for those who abide by the inflexible rules of the church. It is not difficult to appreciate that the concepts that underpin modern secular marriage are very different from the biblical view of lifelong marriage, which is discussed in chapter 15.

Opposition to marriage

In tune with the ideology described above, it has become fashionable for articles in women's magazines, feature articles in newspapers and comments on radio and television to adopt a position that is sceptical about marriage. An article in the *Guardian*, under the headline 'Till disillusion and failure do us part', claims that an examination of divorce figures show that 'marriage in Britain is already halfway to obsolescence. For many people it differs from other long-term relationships only in that you must first wait and then be fined in order to get out of it.'[32] It is common for celebrities to openly express their opposition to marriage, and many choose to live with their lover without being married. An article in *The Sunday Times* comments on a number of celebrities who are living together. A well-known actor who has been living with his girlfriend for seven years is quoted, 'Thank God I'm finally U. Obviously, we have both talked about marriage, but we figured, if it ain't broke don't fix it. I once read an article by Donald Sutherland who believed marriage changes relationships inside and outside the union... If anyone out there has bought us a wedding present tell them to give it to someone else.'[33] In an article in *Vanity Fair*, Madonna, the world-famous film star who recently gave birth to her first child without being married to the father, admitted that she and the baby's father are no longer together. She complains that people are extremely judgemental of her and her choice to become a mother while not married. She says, 'I know lots of married people who have terrible unhealthy relationships; marriage isn't a guarantee of anything.'[34] Speaking to *Vanity Fair*, unmarried Ms Michelle Pfeiffer, who has just embarked on a new relationship after ending a three-year affair, is quoted, 'I thought, I don't want some guy in my life forever who's going to be driving me nuts.'[35]

A young woman expresses her view of marriage in a feature article in *Vogue*. She writes, 'Indeed, for those of us born in the sixties marriage is more often thought of as the final aria of a Wagner opera, while our twenties, traditionally the time of matrimony, are filled with serious, committed, monogamous "trial marriages" typically lasting three to five years. The logic behind these domestic arrangements is that being free of state-sanctified covenants, we avoid tying ourselves down to relationships we may ultimately outgrow.'[36] A feature article in *The Sunday Times* asks why romantic novels always end with marriage. 'Because the people who write them know that that's the end of the really good stuff, all the juice has been squeezed. And it's high time that the rest of us admitted that marriage is the boring and unworkable institution that it is. Let's stop pretending that marriages are made in heaven, that they signify perfect love and that they last forever... Everybody who is married or has ever been married knows that marriage breeds contempt, children and divorce. But if you say it out aloud it seems to upset people terribly. The messenger is blamed... Let's face it, married people are unutterably dull. Their souls denuded of hope, their sex lives denuded of interest and, worst of all, their fridges are stuffed with food not champagne.'[37]

The eminent presenter of Women's Hour, a mainline programme on BBC Radio 4, caused a major stir by arguing that marriage is licensed prostitution. In a feature article in *Options* magazine entitled 'Why no woman should marry' Jenni Murray, a divorced mother living with a partner, says that marriage enhances a man's status but robs a woman of her self-respect and independence, officially stamping her a legal prostitute. She relates how she felt a niggling sense of self-betrayal as one man, her father, gave her into the custody of another man. When she was refused unemployment benefit because she was a married woman, she concludes, 'So with the best intentions, I had become a kept woman—officially stamped a legal prostitute. I believe that marriage is an insult and that women shouldn't touch it.' She notes that things have changed since she walked down the aisle. 'Some women choose not to be "given away". Many keep their own names and almost all their jobs. In some ways it makes me feel proud: what a lot my generation of feminists has achieved in only 20 years. But I can't shake off a deep sense of unease about the marriage trap.' Murray asserts that the pressure to conform still sends women up the aisle in droves, and that couples who have lived together happily for years decide to marry because they want to have children. 'Why? Will a simple certificate of law provide so much extra security? And does the nuclear family really provide the most stable environment in which to bring up children? Rather, in many families, marriage is a licence to exercise power behind closed doors.' Murray believes there is a strong argument for remaining an unmarried mother. 'There's no stigma attached any more—you can, if you're lucky, still raise your children in a loving family. But should it all go disastrously wrong, you're more likely to have retained your job, your name and your independence.'[38]

The British actress and star of the TV series *Prime Suspect*, Helen Mirren, 'has spent years explaining to *People, Hello!* and *OK* and other journals of record why she doesn't believe in marriage, while simultaneously flaunting the robustness of her own arrangements'.[39] Cherie Lunghi, a well-known actress and the strong woman of the Kenco television commercial, is a single mother who cannot believe that 'people are still bandying these happy-ever-after ideas around when we know from the statistics that marriage as a convention is well and truly on the rocks. I'm doing what everybody else does: living my life according to what suits me, not according to the rules laid down by society, rules that have fallen apart.'[40]

The film *Four Weddings and a Funeral* ends with the leading man (Hugh Grant) and woman (Andie MacDowell), after a long love affair reaching the deal, 'Will you promise *not* to marry me?' They want the audience to know that having witnessed four marriages they have chosen to live together without marriage. The film *Sliding Doors* tells the story of a tender love affair between a cohabiting young woman (her partner is having an affair) and a charming hero who does not bother to tell her that he is a married man. The young woman is slightly disconcerted when she discovers her new lover has a wife, but instantly reassured when he tells her he is separated and plans a divorce.

Writing in *The Times*, Polly Toynbee expresses the view that 'every girl has to be taught that she may or may not marry, she may or may not stay married but the odds are now weighted against her finding a man who will support her and her children for ever. Her life has to be her own destiny. Any man who might attach himself for part or all of the journey is not her destiny. There is no point in moralising about it, or mourning the passing of family values; that is how life is now.'[41] An anti-marriage sentiment is common among British politicians, and many members of the Parliament 'have long-standing live-in relationships with men and women whom they have no intention of marrying'.[42]

Mary Ann Glendon, in her book *Abortion and Divorce in Western Law* (1987), describes the way many Americans think about marriage and divorce. 'The American story about marriage, as told in the law and in much popular literature, goes something like this: marriage is a relationship that exists primarily for the fulfillment of the individual spouses. If it ceases to perform this function, no one is to blame and either spouse may terminate it at will. After divorce, each spouse is expected to be self-sufficient... Children hardly appear in the story; at most they are rather shadowy characters in the background... In the continuing cultural conversation about marriage and family life, American law has weighed in heavily on the side of individual self-fulfillment. It tells us that if a marriage no longer suits our needs or if the continuation of a pregnancy would not fit in with our plans just now, we can choose to sever the relationship.'[43]

THE RISE IN COHABITATION AND BIRTHS OUTSIDE MARRIAGE

A consequence of the widespread scepticism towards marriage is that couples are choosing to cohabit as the social stigma associated with living together has all but disappeared over the last three decades. In an article in *Population Trends*, demographer John Haskey demonstrates this change in social attitudes by the type of questions used in surveys on cohabitation. In the 1970s couples were asked whether they were 'living as married', while surveys in the early 1980s used the words living as 'man and wife' to ascertain rates of cohabitation. In more recent surveys people were asked whether they are 'living together as a couple'. Haskey makes the point that the use of language in these social surveys reflects the changing social attitude towards marriage. 'That is, first the pretence of, and then all reference to, marriage was finally dropped; informal unions have become recognised as a social institution in their own right.'[44]

During the last three decades the proportion of cohabiting couples has increased dramatically. Information from the General Household Survey, a continuous survey of private households in Great Britain, showed that in the early 1960s around 5 per cent of single women lived with their future husbands before marriage. By the 1990s about 70 per cent were doing so, and in the case of women marrying a second time around 90 per cent cohabit before their second marriage. Divorced people are now less likely to remarry and many choose to live with a partner; in 1993 over 40 per cent of divorced men and 27 per cent of divorced women were living in a cohabiting relationship.[45] The main argument put forward by those who favour premarital cohabitation is that it is wise for a couple to live together before getting married so that they can have a trial period to test their compatibility and commitment. Should the trial fail then it is easy to end the relationship and move on to the next one without experiencing the trauma of the divorce courts. While it is commonly believed that a trial marriage will reduce the likelihood of a marriage breaking down later, the opposite is true. Those who cohabit before marriage have double the divorce rate of those who do not live together before marriage.

Some celebrities choose to publicise their cohabitation as a statement of their rejection of marriage, others see little point in getting married. Actress Juliet Stevenson described her relationship with partner Hugh Brody, the father of her four-year-old daughter, in a feature article in the *Mail on Sunday*. 'What really annoys me about being described as a single mother is that it diminishes my partner. What's he suppose to think when he hears or reads that? It's as if he doesn't exist and yet he is at home more than I am.' She explained that she and her partner have a completely standard, ordinary relationship. 'I really don't see any difference between having children with somebody you live with and being married to them. I can't understand what all the fuss is about. I have loads of friends among the mothers at Rosalind's school and I wouldn't have a clue whether they are married to their partners or not. It's just not important.' She said that when she and her partner first got together 'we did talk about it (marriage) and we may still get married. I'm not at all anti-marriage, it's just that I've never quite seen the point of it myself.'[46]

It is not overstating the case to say that in today's world the distinction between legal marriage and informal cohabitation has become blurred as many people claim that there is no essential difference. The way language is used supports the idea that marriage and cohabitation are equivalent relationships. The word 'partner' is now used to refer to couples who are living together, whether or not they are married. Accordingly, the words 'husband and wife' are falling into disuse; they are no longer used in polite conversation for fear of causing offence to couples who are not married. Official government publications use the word 'partner' in place of husband or wife. For example, pregnant women are encouraged to invite their 'partners', not their husbands, to attend antenatal sessions. It is now usual practice for invitations to be addressed to an individual and their 'partner'. Furthermore, most social surveys combine married and cohabiting couples together into one category, as if they make up the same marital group. In many social surveys mothers are categorized as 'supported' or 'unsupported', rather than as married, cohabiting or single mothers. This classification assumes there is no distinction between married mothers who are living with their husband, and single mothers living with a male partner; the husband and cohabiting 'partner' are seen as equivalent—they are assumed to provide an equivalent amount of emotional, economic and social support.

(The relationship between cohabitation and child abuse is discussed in chapter 17). To keep pace with contemporary thinking the British Government is considering setting up a register of cohabitation to protect the rights of cohabitees when they end their relationship. There is little doubt that the spread of cohabitation, once termed 'living in sin', is changing the traditional social and moral patterns of behaviour in society.

Births outside marriage

Another significant trend linked to the decline in marriage and rise in cohabitation is the increasing number of children born outside marriage. In England, at the beginning of the 1960s, around 6 per cent of births were to unmarried mothers. The proportion of babies born outside marriage increased gradually during the 60s, doubled during the 70s, doubled again during the 1980s, and by the 1990s over one-third of all births were to unmarried mothers. Thus, the proportion of births outside marriage had increased almost fivefold in three decades. The annual number of children born outside marriage reached 200 thousand for the first time in 1990, and increased to 220 thousand in 1995. Just over half of these babies were born to mothers who were probably in a cohabiting arrangement.[47] In the last decade just less than two million children have been born to unmarried parents. The proportion of families in Great Britain headed by a lone parent increased from around 8 per cent in 1971 to 22 per cent in 1993. This increase in lone-parent families is related to the numbers of divorces and births to single mothers that have occurred during this period. There were about half a million stepfamilies in Great Britain in 1991, corresponding to one million children living in stepfamilies.[48]

In America one-third of births are to unmarried mothers. Each year over one million babies are born to unmarried mothers, and approximately one-third of these are born to teenage mothers. A new study by the Census Bureau has found that, in 1991, only 58 per cent of all children still lived in an intact family with their own married biological parents. That means that 42 per cent of children live in some alternative family arrangement; that is, with single parents or stepparents, as we saw in chapter 1.[49] In many American neighbourhoods the family has collapsed. Among households with children in poor inner cities, fewer than one in ten has a father in the home. Many argue that the plight of the inner cities reflects a wider social malaise, one caused by the profound changes in the structure of the family—the result of increased divorces and births outside marriage.[50]

REDEFINING THE FAMILY

The last two decades have witnessed an unprecedented debate on the meaning of the family. Mass divorce has had a dramatic effect on the way society thinks about the family. Following a divorce, father, mother and children no longer live in the same home and the family is thought of as broken. Accordingly the term 'broken family' was coined to describe the family structure that resulted from divorce. However, many people argue that the term 'broken family' is inappropriate as divorce does not break a family, but simply changes its form. In their book, *Divorced Families* (1987), Constance Ahrons and Roy Rodgers explain that the common term 'broken family' has become a synonym for divorced families. 'In practice this usually means that children lose their fathers, and without a father and a mother in one household a child is labelled as coming from a broken home. What is really conveyed, however, is that divorce severs parenting. Not only do we have to rid ourselves of the myth of the predominance of the traditional nuclear family, but we also have to rid ourselves of the myth that it is exclusively the best way to rear children.'[51] The family is not broken by divorce, according to this line of reasoning, but transformed into a different type of family. Divorce provides the opportunity of replacing the original family with a stepfamily. Children benefit by being removed from a high conflict natural family and re-established in a happy stepfamily. But as remarriage has fallen out of favour and increasing numbers of children are living only with their mother, the concept of the single-parent family has come into being. So divorce does not break a family but creates a single-parent family. The next step in the evolution of the family was for the single mother to live with a boyfriend, commonly referred to as her 'partner', to form a cohabiting family. Experience has proved these relationships to be short-lived and some divorced women and their children are involved in a sequence of such relationships.

The problem facing society today has been to describe these new living arrangements, which were once considered immoral and socially unacceptable, in terms of the family. In order to do so, it has been necessary to claim that all lifestyles are equally valid and to deny any moral imperative. Those who point to the moral dimension are seen as judgemental, forcing their unwelcome moral views on others. Rather, couples should be allowed to choose the family arrangement that suits them, free from restrictive moral laws. Increasingly the concept of the family has become separated from marriage, while the idea that there are many different, equally valid, types of family has gained acceptance. Much of the debate on the family is an attempt to justify mass divorcing by denying that divorce breaks families. This justification has been achieved by redefining the family and claiming that divorce creates different types of family.

Legitimising the single-parent family

The growing army of unmarried mothers added another dimension to the debate. For centuries it was believed in Western society that procreation should take place only in marriage. It was widely recognised that the care and attention of both parents was best for children. Illegitimacy, therefore, was frowned upon as immoral and universally condemned. According to the *Encyclopaedia Britannica*, 'not to condemn illegitimacy would be to attach no special significance to marriage. Recognising the great importance of marriage for social responsibility and stability, and the corresponding dangers of nonmarriage, the state makes marriage easy, the requirements being few and simple.'[52]

Examining the issue of illegitimacy, the Royal Commission on Marriage and Divorce (1956) made the following comment: 'Legitimacy is the status held by a lawful child of a marriage. Any departure from that conception can only be made by ignoring the essential moral principle that a man cannot, during the subsistence of his marriage beget children by another woman. It is unthinkable that the state should lend its sanction to such a step, for it could not fail to result in a blurring of moral values in the public mind. A powerful deterrent to illicit relationships would be removed, with disastrous results for the status of marriage as at present understood. The issue is fundamental but perfectly plain. If children born in adultery may subsequently acquire the status of legitimate children, an essential distinction between lawful marriage and illicit unions disappears.'[53]

However, during the decades of the permissive society, as the number of illegitimate children grew exponentially, the old-fashioned idea of defining children born to unmarried women as illegitimate became socially inconvenient. Accordingly, in the early 1980s the British Government dispensed with the concept of illegitimate births, and removed the tag *illegitimate* from children born outside marriage. By this action the government gave official recognition to the single-parent family, thereby accepting that a father was not an essential part of the family. The crucial link between marriage, children and the family had been fractured. The government had struck a terrible blow against marriage. It was no longer essential for a family to be composed of both mother and father, joined together by lawful marriage. Instead, a new modern type of 'family', made up of a single mother and her children, had gained the official recognition of the state. The British Government saw the father's role in the family as a non-essential, optional extra. Moreover, it demonstrated its commitment to single-parent families by providing financial support to them, thereby taking over the responsibility that had traditionally belonged to the father.

Criticism of the traditional family

A large literature has accumulated as sociologists, psychologists, politicians, theologians and family therapists, among others, express their views on the future of the family. Much of the debate is extremely critical of the traditional two-parent family, arguing that it is only one of a number of equally relevant family types. Over the last three decades many intellectuals, academics and media personalities have been extremely contemptuous of the traditional family, condemning it as a patriarchal institution that represses women and children. Jon Davies, a lecturer at the University of Newcastle upon Tyne, writes of a 'culture which is quite profoundly sceptical about and hostile to the very notion of the stable nuclear family. Our culture seems to be casually experimenting with a wide range of procreational, familial, and nurturing practices.'[54] A classic example of the hostility of the British establishment is demonstrated by the surprising attack of the Mothers' Union, a traditional supporter of the Christian view of marriage. A former vice-president of the Union, Christine McMullen, wrote in its journal that the nuclear family 'is seen by many as too stifling, secretive and imprisoning'. She argued that there is a multiplicity of family styles around today, and all need to be considered as valid. 'We can think of a family in terms of who is in it—a mother, father and two children, or a single parent and some children, or an elderly couple being looked after by a son or daughter. A family may be a mother and father who each bring up children from a former marriage; or the adults may live together and the children move between their natural parents and stepparents, with a variety of natural and stepbrothers and sisters. A family can be people joined by blood ties, or joined by promises to each other'[55]

The report of the National Forum for Values in Education and the Community is another example of the confusion that abounds in Britain around the family. This high-powered committee was given the task of defining the core spiritual and moral values shared by society that should be taught to schoolchildren. While the final report contained several references to the importance of the family, marriage was not specifically promoted. Marriage was neither mentioned in the main statement, nor in the ten principles for action, that made only one mention of families, suggesting that society should support families in raising children and caring for dependants.[56] Following criticism, the forum agreed to compromise by inserting a point supporting marriage, but with a subsequent paragraph that recognised that the love and commitment required for a secure and happy childhood could be found in families of different kinds.[57] This example illustrates the antipathy towards marriage displayed by a national forum supposedly representing the people. In the popular mind no link now exists between marriage and family.

A leading article in *The Sunday Times* made an interesting observation: 'The family has not been fashionable for at least a generation. The British intelligentsia has long derided it as at best a hindrance to progressive lifestyles, at worst a form of bourgeois repression. The insidious climate and politics which undermined the nuclear family has produced a popular culture which went out of its way to disparage it (when did you last see a British television series lauding traditional family values?). Now the nation has to deal with the consequences in the form of soaring crime, increasing squalor, widespread welfare dependency, the spread of the yob culture and crumbling communities. And, suddenly, the family is back in fashion. It is becoming increasingly clear to all but the most blinkered of social scientists that the disintegration of the nuclear family is the principal source of so much social unrest and misery.'[58]

The Family Research Council, an American conservative think-tank, commented, 'As we enter the final decade of the 20th century, we find ourselves embroiled in a second civil war. A civil war of values that will likely determine the future of the family in our society... from Congress to the Supreme Court, two value systems are clashing in a great struggle over family, faith and freedom, with our children as the ultimate prize.'[59]

A view that is gathering pace is that the traditional family of father, mother and children living together in one household is a thing of the past. The large number of homes broken by divorce and the one-third of births that take place outside marriage, with many fathers showing no further interest in their offspring, are seen as evidence to support this view. A report of the Church of England, *Something to Celebrate* (1995), claims that 'the two-parent family with children, a breadwinning husband and a wife who stays at home with the children now make up only a small minority of all households in the UK at any one time... the family portrayed on the front of a cereal packet in the 1950s now barely exists.'[60] A book in a series of Pastoral Care handbooks, *Happy Families?* (1995), believes the concept of the traditional family was built on romantic idealism that is out of place in a modern world.[61] 'Some Christians might make the effort to recreate the images and social structures of yesteryear, but in striving to do so most only succeed in adding to the burden of guilt that already oppresses the lives of so many within the Church.'[62] Moreover, the notion of what constitutes a family is in a state of so much flux and redefinition, that 'it is little wonder that there is so much disagreement as to what the family really is'.[63] A former director of the Family Policies Studies Centre believes that the traditional family is in terminal decline. 'There are fewer marriages, more cohabitation, more children born out of wedlock, high divorce rates and more one-parent families. These are powerful forces and, faced with them, the governments are relatively powerless. The trends of the last 12 years were not for turning.'[64] The traditional family, we are encouraged to accept, has had its day as the new family arrangements become increasingly popular.

Moreover, many influential sociologists have reached the conclusion that the demise of the traditional family is no bad thing, for it has been a major cause of social problems. *Understanding the Family*, published by the Open

University in 1995, is but one example of this way of reasoning. Based on an extensive academic review of sociological literature, the authors write, 'the family has been described as a place of male dominance, oppression of women and denial of children's freedom and individuality. It has also been viewed as an active agency in reproducing social inequalities, isolating individuals from each other and eroding a broader sense of community.'[65] Having reviewed the evidence, the authors conclude that the reality of the nuclear family is 'quite a disturbing picture if we consider the exploitation of women, abuses of children, not to mention the isolation of families that are likely to occur'.[66] This negative view of the traditional family is the orthodox sociological view taught to students by colleges and universities.

There is no longer a consensus around the definition of what constitutes a family. *Something to Celebrate* makes it clear that 'we cannot assume that a particular shape of family, to the exclusion of all others, is God-given. To suggest that belonging to a nuclear family is the only real way in which human beings can find fulfilment, and then to compare every other kind of family with that, seems to us to be unhelpful.'[67] The notion of family is elastic, and because diversity is the key, we must put aside our desire for certainty. In other words the authors of *Something to Celebrate* are unable to define the family. They are sure of one thing, however, and that is that 'families exist where marriage may not (or cannot) and we should not treat them as if they were one and the same thing'.[68] With this statement, as we shall see later, they reject biblical teaching that marriage is the basis of the family. *Something to Celebrate* concludes that there is no one form of family, but rather a diverse choice of arrangements.

Following a similar line of thinking, the authors of *Happy Families?* believe that 'today's families are striving to redefine what it means to be a family'.[69] They identify at least seven quite distinct types of family in Western culture, including husband and wife families, single-parent families, changing families, blended families, cohabiting families and an emerging family model based on gay relationships, both between homosexual men and lesbian women.[70] They conclude their analysis, 'The family is clearly in the midst of enormous upheaval and change… It might well be that new versions of the extended family of the past could provide a new way forward for the future, this time not based on kinship in the strict sense, but on networks of unrelated friends and associates as well as those bound together by genetic links. Whatever the future may hold, the redesigned family will certainly feature in it.'[71]

The final step in the redefinition of the family is to dispense with the idea that parenting is necessarily associated with marriage. Clearly people become parents without being married, and clearly children do not need to be brought up by their biological parents. Indeed, many children are brought up in childcare or by foster parents. Ahrons and Rodgers explain that with 'a slight shift in our thinking – and one much more in touch with the reality rather than the mythology of nuclear families – would permit us to expand our definitions of parenting. First, we need to separate marriage from parenting. Biological parenting can and does occur irrespective of marriage. Second, we need to expand our definition of parenting. Sociological parenting does occur whenever an adult assumes responsibility for childrearing. This expanded definition of parenting would allow us to hold a view of families in which children may be reared successfully in one- or two-parent households, in families which span more than one household, and in families which may include more than two parents. Children then may have one, two, three, or more parents, sociological and biological parents, and parents of one or both genders.'[72]

It is interesting to note that all political parties are keen to be seen supporting the family, for they sense that the ideal of the family still has a lot of popular support. Responding to public concern, the new Labour Government has set up a Committee on Family Policy to oversee the welfare of the family. However, it has been widely noted that the terms of reference of this committee do not mention marriage. A feature article in the *Daily Telegraph* comments, 'The status to be given to marriage in government policy is turning into one of the great hidden debates of our time... Among ministers and civil servants, the use of the m-word has become contentious.'[73] Taking a lead from the Church of England report, most political parties are nervous of coming out in unequivocal support of the traditional family. Ideological considerations have made many politicians fear 'that if they accept that marriage is a good thing, they will be locked into that most forbidden of modern heresies, intolerance of alternative lifestyles'.[74] Few are prepared to make the link between the family and marriage, for they no longer consider it to be politically safe to do so. Furthermore, most official government publications avoid the words husband and wife for fear of causing offence—the word 'partner' is used instead.

A CLIMATE HOSTILE TO TRADITIONAL MARRIAGE

The move to mass divorce has occurred in a climate of open hostility to traditional marriage and the family. It has become politically correct to challenge marriage, which is portrayed as an institution that is hardly relevant in a modern democratic society. Attacks on marriage in films, TV chat shows, magazines and the popular press are commonplace. Few politicians are prepared to openly support marriage for fear of being labelled as those who discriminate against single mothers. The continuous campaign of ridicule has made marriage socially undesirable, and those who decide to marry feel obliged to make their excuses for going against the trend. Another strand in the attack on traditional lifelong marriage is the promotion of modern secular marriage. For those who choose to marry the ideas of modern secular marriage are presented as the ideal. This means that the moral and religious component of marriage is rapidly disappearing, many couples seeing marriage as a temporary arrangement that lasts only so long as both partners are satisfied with the relationship.

The sociological attempt to redefine the family is essential to the success of those who promote divorce as the remedy for unhappy marriages. For many people the thought that divorce breaks the family causes them to have second thoughts. This is because the family is fundamental to the human condition and all people, parents and especially children, have an innate need to be part of a family. In order to justify divorce as the remedy for unhappy marriages it is necessary to convince people that by divorcing they do not break their family, but rather create a new reconstituted family. This has been achieved by redefining the family and removing its link to marriage. Showing that there are many different types of family has made marriage incidental to family life. So the family of father, mother and children based on marriage is portrayed as only one of a number of equally valid options. Divorce simply creates a different type of family and usually one that is less stifling than the traditional family.

Nevertheless, the views presented in this chapter remain highly contro-versial for they are diametrically opposed to the views of marriage and the family that have for centuries formed the cornerstone of Western society. As traditional views have become devalued, so many people have been prepared to accept the concepts of secular marriage and mass divorce, thereby rejecting the values upon which our civilization has been built. But how have these ideas, which were once anathema to the Western mind, gained such wide acceptance? The story of mass divorce in England and America should help answer this question.

Chapter 3

Divorce and the Reformation

Erasmus, Luther, Calvin and other reformers on divorce

The story of divorce in England and America starts with the Reformation of the Christian Church in the 16th century. The ideas developed by the reformers were to have a massive influence on what the Church and society believed about divorce. Indeed, it is impossible to understand the history of divorce without recognising the influence of reformation thought, for, as we shall see, the seeds of mass divorce were sown at the time of the Protestant Reformation. The great reformers, Martin Luther and John Calvin, developed ideas that led to the legalisation of divorce, first, in Protestant Europe, then in colonial America and eventually in England. In many ways the Reformation was a watershed in the history of divorce.

ST AUGUSTINE'S TEACHING ON DIVORCE

Prior to the Reformation most of Christendom believed that marriage was an indissoluble bond and there was no legal provision for divorce. As early as the 4th century after the birth of Christ, St Augustine of Hippo outlined the Christian doctrine on divorce. In his treatise, *The Good of Marriage*, he writes, 'Once, however, marriage is entered upon in the City of our God, where also from the first union of the two human beings marriage bears a kind of sacred bond, it can be dissolved in no way except by the death of one of the parties.' He goes on to explain, 'The good, therefore, of marriage among all nations and all men is in the cause of generation and in the fidelity of chastity; in the case of the people of God, however, the good is also in the sanctity of the sacrament. Because of this sanctity it is wrong for a woman, leaving with a divorce, to marry another man while her husband still lives, even if she does this for the sake of having children.'[1] There is no doubt that the greatest theologian of the early Church believed in the absolute indissolubility of marriage and this belief denied remarriage even to the innocent party after divorce. Augustine viewed marriage as a sacrament because he believed it symbolised the unity of Christ and his Church.[2] The common definition of sacrament, accepted by both the Roman Catholic and Reformed Churches, is that of an outward and visible sign, ordained by Christ, of an inward spiritual blessing. This definition owes much to the teaching and language of Augustine, who wrote of the visible form which bore some likeness to the thing invisible.[3] Marriage was believed to be the outward sign which symbolised the unity of Christ with his Church, 'a bride, beautifully dressed for her husband' (Revelation 21:2). Augustine recognised that marriage was for the good of all nations and people, and not only those who embraced the Christian faith. In his book, *Christian Marriage* (1948), George Hayward Joyce shows that Augustine was unhesitatingly firm on the absolute indissolubility of Christian marriage. 'He (Augustine) discusses the relevant passages of the New Testament, and shows that they admit of no other interpretation than that marriage once contracted can never under any circumstances be dissolved: that though separation may be necessary, the tie which binds the partners remains unbroken.'[4]

THE ROMAN CATHOLIC POSITION ON DIVORCE

At the start of the 16th century the position of the Catholic Church on divorce was widely accepted in most European countries. Stated simply, the teaching of the Catholic Church was that a valid marriage formed an indissoluble bond between husband and wife. It followed that a married person could not enter into another marriage during the lifetime of their spouse. Church doctrine taught that the marriage bond (*a vinculo matrimonii*) was broken only by the death of a marriage partner, and for this reason remarriage during the lifetime of either spouse was impossible.

Here a word of explanation is necessary. The word 'divorce' has been used to describe both a complete divorce that dissolves the marriage bond (*a vinculo matrimonii*) and allows a remarriage, and to describe a separation from bed and board (*a mensa et thoro*), or a judicial separation. In this legal arrangement, husband and wife lived apart, but the marriage bond was still intact and they were not free to remarry. The doctrine of the indissolubility of marriage holds that the marriage bond cannot be broken during the lifetime of a partner to allow a remarriage. So strong was this belief that not even King Henry VIII of England contemplated divorcing his first wife Catherine of Aragon when she was unable to give him a male heir.

George Hayward Joyce provides a Catholic view of marriage. 'The civilisation of Christendom – the civilisation of which we are the heirs – was founded on Christian marriage. The religion of Christ had lifted life on to a new plane. It taught that marriage is sacred, God being the agent who establishes and ratifies the union between husband and wife: that the bond thus divinely blessed is indissoluble until death: that the wife is no mere chattel, but a party to a contract between equals; and that all sexual relations outside marriage, whether on the part of the husband or wife, are grievously sinful. These truths gave to the union a dignity, a purity, and a sanctity hitherto undreamed of. Where they held sway in men's minds the foundations of society were secure: it could never suffer complete ruin. For in the social organism the true units are not isolated individuals, but families. And where the Christian ideal of marriage prevails, the family, strengthened by super-natural sanctions, will hold good through every crisis, and even in the greatest political convulsions provides the principle of eventual recovery.'[5]

Although the Catholic Church stood firm on the doctrine of the indis-solubility of marriage it made provision for annulling invalid marriages. The provision for annulment rested upon impediments to marriage laid down by the Church. The purpose was to prohibit people closely related by blood (consanguinity) or marriage (affinity) from marrying each other. However, the Church extended the grounds of impediments well beyond those outlined in Scripture and by the 12th century marriage was forbidden to the seventh degree. This meant a man could not marry a woman who was his sixth cousin. In the 13th century the prohibition was reduced to the fourth degree, permitting the marriage of couples more distantly related than third cousins. Other impediments included spiritual affinity, which meant that marriage was forbidden between members of a family and any of the active participants at one of its baptisms or confirmations. Impotence was also considered an impediment. Despite the long list of impediments the ecclesiastical courts were reluctant to grant annulments. Although, at times, annulments were used as a convenient means for getting around the indissolubility of marriage the evidence shows that marriages were rarely annulled.[6]

ERASMUS' CHALLENGE TO THE INDISSOLUBILITY OF MARRIAGE

The first few decades of the 16th century saw the first serious theological challenge to the doctrine of the indissolubility of marriage. Desiderius Erasmus, a Renaissance humanist *par excellence*, was aware of the problems caused by a doctrine that did not allow remarriage. As a humanist he attached primary importance to man and his faculties, aspirations and well-being. He believed that human beings had great potential for improvement and solving human problems. The motive of Erasmus, like all those who promote the idea of remarriage after divorce, was to help those trapped in unhappy marriages.

Writing in *The New Testament Logia on Divorce* (1971), Norskov Olsen makes the point, 'Erasmus brings the reader face to face with the problems of the many thousands who are unhappily coupled together, with the result that both parties thereby perish. They could be saved if they were divorced and able to marry someone else. If this were possible without doing injury to the word of God, then it ought to delight all godly men. Furthermore, charity sometimes does what it legally is not able to do, and it is justified in doing so.'[7] What Erasmus is saying is that in order to solve a human problem, love is justified in turning a blind eye to a divine law that seems to be unduly harsh. It follows that divorce, because it produces a happy outcome, is justifiable on the basis of love, even although technically it may be against the law.

Erasmus' line of reasoning to justify divorce was popularised by Joseph Fletcher in his book *Situation Ethics* (1966). The fundamental principle is that there are no moral absolutes that cannot be modified, in the name of love, to suit the circumstances of the time. Only love is intrinsically good, nothing else. For the situational ethicist something that is technically labelled as wrong, in certain circumstances can be the only right way. So Erasmus, by justifying divorce in the name of love, although conceding it to be technically against the law, was following the principles of situation ethics. The chapters that follow show that in the debates on the issue of divorce and remarriage, the most persistent argument advanced for divorce is that it allows a couple to escape an unhappy, miserable marriage and find happiness in a second or subsequent marriage.

Erasmus' approach was characterised by a conviction 'that enlightenment would usher in a new era and bring reform within the Church. Two basic propositions are laid down. It should be permissible to dissolve certain marriages, not fortuitously but for very serious reasons, by the ecclesiastical authorities or recognised judges, and to give the innocent party the freedom to marry again.'[8] Erasmus protested that a man separated from an unfaithful wife is excluded from entering the honours and privileges of the marriage relationship by human laws, but not by the law of the gospel. In his opinion it was cruel not to come to the rescue of these sufferers. Because divorce without the right of remarriage seemed against the equity of nature, Erasmus believed 'it should be looked into if there may not be other interpretations which are to be read in the gospels and epistles'.[9]

His starting point was the belief that there must be a human solution to the problem of unhappy marriages. On the basis of that humanist presupposition, Erasmus set about finding a scriptural justification for his belief. This point must be underlined because it is fundamental to the debate. Erasmus' starting point was not the Scriptures, but his presupposition that divorce was the remedy for unhappy marriages. Erasmus believed that the teaching of Jesus in Matthew chapter 19 permitted divorce and remarriage to the innocent party in the case of marital unfaithfulness. According to Olsen, 'Erasmus clearly states that Christ made one exception for divorce, namely adultery. On the other hand he also seems to imply that there could be other reasons.'[10]

Joyce notes that Erasmus contends that Christ's words should not be taken as a strict command, but rather as an ideal at which Christians should aim.

Erasmus concluded that there did not seem to be any reason why the Pope should not allow a divorce in cases where the continuance of the marriage bond was nothing but an evil. 'He had seen, he assures us, many cases, especially during his stay in England, in which men who had previously lived virtuously, had nevertheless, since the Church could not help them to escape from an intolerable yoke, simply set God's laws at defiance.'[11] Erasmus, interpreting 1 Corinthians chapter 7, comments on the example of a youth caught in an unhappy marriage through being drunk. In such a marriage there may be hatred, dread of poisoning and murder. As such a couple cannot live together and be faithful to each other they are likely to perish. However, if the marriage is dissolved by a divorce and they are allowed to marry again, it is hoped that they will both be saved.[12]

In making this suggestion Erasmus assures his reader that he does not want to open the window to repeated divorces, but rather in the hope that divorce might be a remedy for an unfortunate marriage.[13] In other words, it was Erasmus' belief that divorce was a remedy that allowed a second chance for happiness. The results of Erasmus' interpretation of the Scriptures on divorce found an eager audience among the reformers. 'Indeed, the Protestant reformers latched on to Erasmus' interpretation of the divorce texts and defended his exegesis from the moment they became known.'[14] Erasmus' views are important for they are the foundation of the Protestant position on divorce which has persisted until today. He can be regarded as the spiritual father of the crusade to liberalise divorce.

JOHN CALVIN'S VIEWS ON DIVORCE

Calvin believed that God instituted marriage during the time of man's innocence in order that a man and woman might be united as perpetual and undivided companions for life.[15] There are two conditions for Christian marriage. The first is that marriage is the union of one man and woman. The second condition is 'that the bond of marriage, once formed between two, is no more dissolved by any divorce, but only by the death of either. For in regard to the intimation by Christ, that the wife may be put away for fornication, this makes the spouses cease to live together at bed and board, but does not dissolve the bond of marriage; so that he commits adultery who marries one thus put away, just as he does who has intercourse with another man's wife.

Since Christ then made marriage both by his own grace, and bound it, as it were, with a faster chain, as Christ is the one spouse of one Church, and that by an indissoluble tie, so a man is the one husband of one wife, and that by perpetual union, in like manner as Christ is perpetually joined with his spouse the Church.'[16]

In his exposition of Matthew chapter 19, Calvin explains that 'from the beginning God joined the husband to the woman and the two became a complete man. Therefore he who divorces his wife tears from himself half of himself. And it is quite against nature for a man to tear his body asunder.'[17] Calvin argues that the bond that binds husband and wife is holier than that which binds children to their parents. It is therefore unthinkable that a man can renounce his wife. The Creator of the human race made male and female so that each should be content with a single wife and not desire others. Christ emphasised the dual number, two become one. 'Therefore from creation is proved the indivisible society of one man and one woman.' Commenting on the phrase 'one flesh', Calvin writes, 'anyone who divorces his wife tears himself asunder because the force of holy marriage is that the husband and wife join together to make one man'.[18]

Christ's statement 'what God has joined together' is meant to bridle men's lusts so that they will not break their marriage by divorcing their wives. The magistrate who gives a man permission to divorce is abusing his power. Commenting on Matthew 19:9, Calvin says that although the law does not punish divorces yet he who rejects his wife and takes another is adulterous. 'For it lies not in a man's will to dissolve the bond of marriage, which the Lord wishes to remain settled; and thus she who occupies the bed of a lawful wife is a concubine.' But an exception is added. 'A woman who commits adultery sets her husband free, for she cuts herself off from him *as a rotten member* [my italics]. Those who think out other reasons for divorce, and want to be wiser than the heavenly Master, are rightly to be rejected.'[19]

Calvin explains the exception clause in Matthew 5:31, 'For a woman who treacherously violates her marriage, may well be cast out, as the bond is broken by her fault and the man gains his liberty.'[20] He explains that the man who divorces his adulterous wife is free to remarry. 'Christ releases from his bond the husband who convicts his wife of adultery.' Similarly if a man commits adultery he has defected from marriage and the wife is given freedom. It follows that 'when Christ accuses of adultery the man who marries a divorced woman, it is certain that he is restricting it to unlawful and frivolous divorces.'[21]

Calvin makes it clear that he does not permit divorce for leprosy or any other grave illness. His strong dislike of divorce is apparent from his writings on marriage as described in Ephesians. 'The husband may plead, "I have a dreadful and stubborn wife; or else she is proud, or has a wicked head, or else is too talkative". Again, another perhaps is a drunkard, another is idle… Although the men misbehave themselves on the one hand, and the women on the other, yet God will not have the marriage to be broken or dissolved thereby, except (I say) in the case of the divorce of which our Lord Jesus speaks.'[22]

Comment

So we see that Calvin held a high view of marriage, believing it to be an indissoluble union. He placed heavy emphasis on the fact that at marriage, a man and a woman become one flesh, joined by God. Consequently he rejected divorce absolutely, with one exception—adultery of the husband or wife, which he regarded as a ground for lawful divorce. It seems remarkable that he was able to reconcile the two positions that he seemed to hold. Marriage is an indissoluble union, yet it can be dissolved by adultery. He does not make it clear whether adultery automatically (in God's eyes) dissolved the marriage, or whether it was up to the wronged party to decide whether they wished to dissolve the marriage. Calvin seemed to imply that the innocent spouse had the right of deciding whether the marriage should be dissolved or not. Yet Calvin's teaching leaves a number of unanswered questions. What of the children who want their mother and father to stay together? What about the family? Is adultery the one sin that breaks a family no matter what? And what happens to the children when the innocent parent remarries having divorced their adulterous spouse? Who cares for the children? Do they remain with the adulterous, disgraced divorcee (who is not permitted to remarry), or do they live with a stepmother or stepfather? Calvin says nothing about the effect of divorce on the family and nothing about the consequences for the children.

Nevertheless, Calvin's teachings are crucially important because they form the thin edge of the wedge in the challenge to the indissolubility of the marriage bond. The first step was to argue that the marriage bond was broken by adultery. Once this ground was conceded it was easy to extend the argument by claiming that, as marriage was not indissoluble, but dissolved by adultery, there may be other grounds for divorce. The other reformers were not slow in finding the other grounds.

MARTIN LUTHER'S VIEWS ON DIVORCE

After his split with Rome, Luther left the monastic way of life and was married. In his voluminous writings he had much to say on the issue of marriage and divorce. In his treatise on *The Babylonian Captivity* of the Church he denounced the idea that marriage was a sacrament. He argued that marriage did not meet the criteria, for it was not instituted by Christ, it did not impart grace and it was not necessary for salvation. He believed that the theological claims could not be justified from Scripture, but had grown out of the tyrannical impulses of the papacy. The consequence of Luther's fierce attack on the sacramental nature of marriage was that, in the mind of the average Christian, he seemed to be denying the importance of marriage.

In *The Christian in Society*, in a chapter entitled 'The Estate of Marriage', he wrote, 'How I dread preaching on the estate of marriage! I am reluctant to do it because I am afraid if I once get really involved in the subject it will make a lot of work for me and for others. The shameful confusion wrought by the accursed papal law has occasioned so much distress...'[23] He deals with the issue of celibacy and the validity of cloister vows, concluding that priests, monks and nuns are duty-bound to forsake their vows whenever they find that God's ordinance to produce children is strong within them. He deals with the eighteen impediments of the Catholic Church to valid marriage and finds that the only sound reason for dissolving a marriage is when a husband or wife is unfit for marriage.[24]

Luther identified three grounds for divorce. The first is the situation in which the husband or wife is not equipped for marriage. The second is adultery, and the third is that in which one of the parties deprives and avoids the other, refusing to fulfil the conjugal duty or to live with the other person.[25] In the case of adultery, Luther believed that Christ permitted the divorce of husband and wife so that the innocent person may remarry; that Christ makes it quite clear that he who divorces his wife on account of unchastity and then marries another does not commit adultery. In discussing the example of Joseph and Mary, Luther says 'we are told plainly enough that it is praiseworthy to divorce an adulterous wife. If the adultery is clandestine, of course, the husband had the right to follow either of two courses. First, he may rebuke his wife privately and in a brotherly fashion, and keep her if she will mend her ways. Second, he may divorce her, as Joseph wished to do. The same principle applies in the case of a wife with an adulterous husband.'[26] With regard to the guilty party, Luther believed that 'the temporal sword and government should therefore still put adulterers to death, for whoever commits adultery has in fact himself already departed and is *considered as one dead* [my italics]. Therefore the other may remarry just as though his spouse had died, if it is his intention to insist on his rights and not show mercy to the guilty party. Where the government is negligent and lax, however, and fails to inflict the death penalty, the adulterer may take himself to a far country and there remarry if he is unable to remain continent.' Luther acknowledged that some might find fault with his proposed solution, 'Can I help it? The blame lies with the government. Why do they not put adulterers to death? Then I would not need to give such advice. Between two evils one is always the lesser, in this case allowing the adulterer to remarry in a distant land in order to avoid fornication.'[27]

In his exposition of Matthew's gospel, Luther found that Christ sets down only one legitimate cause for the divorce and remarriage of a man and his wife. 'Since it is only death that can dissolve a marriage and set you free, an adulterer has already been divorced, not by men but by God himself, and separated not only from his wife but from his very life. By his adultery he has divorced himself from his wife and has dissolved his marriage… he has brought on his own death, in the sense that before God he is already dead even though the judge may not have executed him. Because it is God that is doing the divorcing here, the other partner is set completely free and is not obliged, unless he chooses to do so, to keep the spouse that has broken the marriage vow. We neither commend nor forbid such divorces, but leave it to the government to act here; and we submit to whatever the secular law prescribes in this matter.'[28]

Another reason for divorce was when 'one of the parties deprives and avoids the other, refusing to fulfil the conjugal duty or to live with the other person. For example, one finds many a stubborn wife like that who will not give in, and who cares not a whit whether her husband falls into the sin of unchastity ten times over. Here it is time for the husband to say, "If you will not, another will; the maid will come if the wife will not".'[29] In addition to the three grounds for divorce with the right to remarry, Luther also believed that a man and wife might live apart where the husband and wife cannot get along together for some reason other than the matter of conjugal duty. However, they should not have the right to remarry, and reconciliation should be attempted.[30]

Luther believed that the proper procedures for marriage and divorce should be left to the lawyers and made subject to the secular government. 'For marriage is a rather secular and outward thing, having to do with wife and children, house and home, and with other matters that belong to the realm of government, all of which have been completely subjected to reason. Therefore we should not tamper with what the government and wise men decide and prescribe with regard to these questions on the basis of the laws and of reason.'[31] According to Luther Christ was not functioning as a lawyer or a governor, to set down or prescribe any regulations for outward conduct, but as a preacher to instruct consciences about using the divorce law properly, rather than wickedly and capriciously, contrary to God's commandment. As far as non-Christians are concerned, Luther saw them of no concern to the Church, 'since they must be governed not with the gospel, but with compulsion and punishment'.[32]

In response to the question why Moses permitted divorces, Luther says that it was better to grant wicked people divorce 'than to let you do worse by vexing or murdering each other or by living together in incessant hate, discord and hostility'. And Luther goes on, 'this might be advisable nowadays, if the secular government prescribed it, that certain queer, stubborn, and obstinate people, who have no capacity for toleration and are not suited for married life at all, should be permitted to get a divorce.' Having given his reasons for divorce, he then concludes that 'those who want to be Christians should not be divorced, but every man should keep his own spouse, sustaining and bearing good and ill with her, even though she may have her oddities, peculiarities and faults. If he does get a divorce, he should remain unmarried. We have no right to make marriage a free thing, as though it was in our power to do with as we please, changing and exchanging. But the rule is the one Christ pronounces: What God has joined together let no man put asunder.'[33]

Luther says that he has been accused of 'teaching that when a husband is unable to satisfy his wife's sexual desire she should run to someone else.

Let the topsy-turvy liars spread their lies... What I said was this: if a woman who is fit for marriage has a husband who is not, and she is unable openly to take unto herself another – and unwilling, too, to do anything dishonourable – since the pope in such a case demands without cause abundant testimony and evidence, she should say to her husband, "Look, my dear husband, you are unable to fulfil your conjugal duty toward me; you have cheated me out of my maidenhood and even imperilled my honour and my soul's salvation; in the sight of God there is no real marriage between us. Grant me the privilege of contracting a secret marriage with your brother or closest relative, and you retain the title of husband so that your property will not fall to strangers. Consent to being betrayed voluntarily by me, as you have betrayed me without my consent." I stated further that the husband is obliged to consent to such an arrangement and thus to provide for her the conjugal duty and children, and that if he refuses to do so she should secretly flee from him to some other country and there contract a marriage.'[34]

Comment

The church historian, Professor JP Whitney made comments on Luther's teachings in his evidence to the British Royal Commission into divorce of 1912. 'Luther's idea of marriage has caused much discussion; in some passages he seems to regard it as existing merely for physical reasons; elsewhere, as in treating cases of prolonged sickness, his view is on a higher plane. Here, as elsewhere, his language is unbalanced and variable. A question of much importance is his view of the state and its power over marriage and divorce... In practice Luther allowed almost free divorce. The treatment of an adulterer as dead through his adultery (being liable to stoning under the Old Testament) should be noted. The suggestion of emigration to another state with easier laws, for an adulterer who could not amend himself is characteristic of Germany with its many states. Luther's writings would justify the drawing of a parallel between the marriage vow and the vow of celibacy, which was not only treated as undesirable, but as breakable with impunity. The frequent sermons against regarding marriage as a sacrament would also seem to have lowered its status in public esteem.'[35]

It is difficult to believe that Luther's views are based on a sound interpretation of the Scriptures. It seems, instead, that they were influenced by his opposition to the doctrines of the Catholic Church. It is surprising that he placed so much faith in secular lawyers to formulate divorce laws, which he believed the Church should obey without question. Perhaps he was conceding, having rejected the doctrine of the indissolubility of marriage, the impossibility of formulating workable divorce laws. His teaching that when a husband is unable to satisfy his wife's sexual desire she should run to someone else hardly seems to be consistent with the code of sexual behaviour taught in the Bible. It would seem to condone sexual immorality. Was he unaware the Bible says there should not be even a hint of sexual immorality among Christians?

The idea that a marriage is ended because 'by his adultery he has divorced himself from his wife and has dissolved his marriage... because it is God that is doing the divorcing here' has no scriptural basis. It would surely mean that some couples could be divorced without being aware of the fact. The idea that a man who commits adultery is dead in God's eyes is doctrinal nonsense. Was King David dead in God's eyes after he committed adultery with Uriah's wife, Bathsheba? Indeed not. David repented and God forgave his sin. And furthermore, David and Bathsheba's son Solomon was in the line of Christ. God in his mercy was able to forgive and restore the adulterer and adulteress. So the notion that adultery leads to the end of a marriage because the adulterer is dead not only has no basis in Scripture, but is an intellectual fallacy. Worse, it suggests that adultery is a sin that is beyond the mercy of God.

Luther's teaching that the adulterous party is 'as good as dead' raises many difficult questions. Is the husband who does not know that his wife has committed adultery married to a dead woman? Does the wife, who is also a mother, become dead as both wife and mother when she commits adultery? Or does a wife only become dead in God's eyes if the husband decides to exercise his right to a divorce? What if an adulterous wife repents of her sin and asks God and her husband for forgiveness? What if her husband refuses forgiveness? Is she dead or alive? It seems hard to believe that the Protestant position on divorce is based on such a nonsensical interpretation of the Scriptures. Surely Luther was a man who wanted to prove the Catholic Church wrong and used the Scriptures in an attempt to justify his position on divorce. How he arrived at three grounds for divorce from the Scriptures is difficult to understand, or was he conceding that it was up to human wisdom, and not divine law, to decide the grounds of divorce? No matter how we look at Luther's views, it is inescapable that they are not based on a sound interpretation of the Scriptures, and do not form a Christian view of marriage. Notwithstanding, it is important to for us to understand that the teachings of Luther are the fragile foundation on which the Protestant doctrine of divorce is built.

BUCER'S VIEWS ON DIVORCE

Martin Bucer, the Strasbourg reformer who ended his days as the King's reader of the Holy Scriptures at Cambridge, had by far the most radical opinions on divorce encountered in the main currents of the Reformation. He believed that the emotional relationship between husband and wife was the most important aspect of marriage. Husband and wife should live together in a relationship based on mutual love and sexual faithfulness. Should these qualities be missing from a relationship, there is no true marriage. Christ taught that 'the woman in the beginning was so joined to the man, that there should be a perpetual union both in body and spirit: where this is not, the matrimony is already broke, before there be yet any divorce made or second marriage.'[36] Indeed, it is God who separates through the law those who in their hearts are already parted. This is permitted in order that greater evil may be avoided.[37] Implicit throughout Bucer's teaching is the notion that incompatibility of mind is a legitimate cause for divorce. Accordingly, divorce was permitted not only for adultery and desertion, but also for emotional incompatibility and by mutual consent if the marriage was not working.[38] In effect Bucer was proposing divorce not for a marital offence but for the breakdown of the marriage relationship, thereby allowing the freedom to establish a new and more satisfying marriage. Bucer concluded that all he had written on divorce was in harmony with God's law and the teachings of Christ. In particular, he believed there was no disagreement between divorce for mental incompatibility, as mentioned in his writing, and Christ's words stating that adultery was the only cause of divorce.[39]

Bucer's idea of marriage was revolutionary for the time. While there was almost universal agreement that the prime purpose of marriage was procreation, Bucer argued for a form of marriage where companionship and the emotional love between husband and wife were the primary purpose. When the emotional relationship breaks down then 'there is no true marriage' and divorce is the remedy. The happiness and emotional satisfaction of each individual is paramount. This view denies the biblical picture of marriage as a relationship based on the union between Christ and his Church; it also rejects the concept of love based in sacrifice and self-denial. Christ loved the Church and gave himself for the Church. He denied himself for the sake of the Church. Bucer seemed not to grasp the link between marriage and the family. Was he really saying that the teaching of Christ permitted parents to desert their children when they were no longer emotionally compatible? We shall see later that Bucer's views have a lot in common with modern secular psychotherapy. The ideas that he planted would grow to fruition in the 20th century.

ZWINGLI'S VIEWS ON DIVORCE

Along with the other reformers, Huldreich Zwingli believed in the secularisation of marriage and the legalisation of divorce. He understood the Bible to teach that adultery was the most minor ground for which divorce was permissible. When Christ mentioned adultery as a reason for divorce, he did not exclude other reasons.[40] Zwingli reasoned that if adultery was a biblical ground for divorce, then so were 'greater reasons' that endangered the marriage bond. It should be noted that in Zwingli's opinion 'greater reasons' covers not only impotence but also what would now be called incompatibility.[41] In the case of an unsuitable marriage, the couple were to live together for a year at least so that the intercessions of their friends might bring about a better understanding. If the state of things was the same at the end of a year they might separate and remarry.

In a document which outlines his view on divorce, Zwingli mentions that divorce is allowed in the case of public adultery, and the innocent party is allowed to remarry. Other reasons given are impotence or other bodily weaknesses, but only after a year's probation during which time the body's weakness is made evident. For other situations, like threatening of life, mental sickness and desertion there are no definite rules and the judge has the discretion to decide each case on its merits. In line with his belief in the secularisation of marriage, divorce was to be granted by the secular authorities since they alone could make a legal marriage.[42]

THE COUNCIL OF TRENT: 1560–63

The response of the Catholic Church to the reformers' powerful attack on the indissolubility of marriage was to restate the Church's position on divorce at the Council of Trent (1560–63), and introduce it into canon law. The teachings of the Lutherans and Calvinists were condemned as heretical. The seventh canon, as finally accepted by the Council, read:

> If anyone shall say that the Church is in error, when it taught and still teaches, in accordance with the teaching of the Gospels and the Apostles, that the bond of marriage cannot be dissolved by reason of the adultery of one of the partners, and that neither of them, not even the innocent one who gave no cause to the adultery, can contract another marriage while the other partner is alive: and that the man who dismisses his adulterous wife and marries another, and the woman who dismisses her adulterous husband and marries another, are guilty of adultery – let him be anathema.

The character of the canon admits of no question. It is a dogmatic definition of the indissolubility of marriage.[43] This statement set out in sharp relief the gap between the doctrinal position of the Catholic Church and the reformers.

THE REFORMERS' INFLUENCE ON DIVORCE

There is no doubt that the Protestant Reformation had a major impact on the religious life of Europe and America. Martin Luther, the great theologian, drew attention to the need for salvation through justification by faith alone, and John Calvin placed great emphasis on the Scriptures as the source of God's revelation to man. The religious map of Europe was redrawn as many nations, including Germany, England, Scotland, Holland, Switzerland and Scandinavia embraced the new reformed teachings. The reformers rejected virtually all aspects of the Catholic doctrine of marriage including the concept of marriage indissolubility. Calvin in the *Institutes of the Christian Religion*, argued that the Catholic Church was mistaken in believing that marriage was a sacrament. He went on, 'But, having graced marriage with the title of sacrament, to call it afterwards uncleanness and pollution and carnal filth – what giddy levity is this? How absurd to bar priests from this sacrament!' Having made marriage a sacrament the Church took over the hearing of matrimonial cases, which were not to be handled by secular judges. Calvin concludes his discourse, 'At length, we must extricate ourselves from their mire, in which our discourse has already stuck longer than I should have wished.'[44]

The views of the Protestant reformers on divorce were to a large degree a reaction against the teachings of the Church of Rome. According to Professor Whitney many continental reformers wrote extensively on marriage and divorce. 'So far as their treatment was founded upon the New Testament they were greatly influenced by Erasmus… But their treatment was also largely affected by the course of events. In the outburst of individualism, and the reaction against existing Church authority, these writers gave undue prominence to points of the controversy with Rome: these received naturally more attention than was proportionately their share… The magnitude of the revolution attempted by the continental reformers should not be overlooked. Existing marriage laws were overturned; the share of the state and the Church in the new system was not only important theoretically but practically; the difficulty of determining these respective shares increased disorder.'[45]

Their position on marriage and divorce differed from the traditional view in two fundamental respects. The first was their emphasis on the secular nature of marriage; the reformers made it abundantly clear that marriage was not only not a sacrament, but that it was 'a rather secular and outward thing'. It should be left largely to the secular authorities to administer marriage law and even the marriage ceremony should be of a civil nature. This line of thinking was to have far-reaching effects on the way marriage was viewed in Protestant communities. Some Puritans went so far as to forbid a religious marriage service. We should remember this teaching as we observe the influence of the Protestant doctrine of divorce in the USA. The second respect in which Protestant thought differed from the traditional view was to regard the marriage bond as being dissolved by adultery and desertion, among other things. Divorce with the right of the innocent party to remarry was seen to be consistent with the teachings of Christ. The position of the guilty party to a divorce was less clear. There is little doubt that the Protestant reformers went beyond the teachings of Scripture in their attempt to justify divorce.

Nevertheless, the teachings of Calvin and Luther had enormous influence and became the foundation for divorce legislation in Europe, and later in

America. Their teachings were also the main plank of the arguments used to legalise divorce in England in 1857. Professor Whitney said in evidence to the 1912 Royal Commission, 'Liberty of divorce, it has been said, was a product of the Reformation. The views of the continental reformers have great historical interest, apart from their merits or demerits. The course of marriage legislation in Germany, and the extension of divorce in America, has been plausibly ascribed to their influence. Further, the height of continental influence upon the English Reformation is marked by the production of the *Reformatio Legum Ecclesiasticarum*, [discussed later in this chapter] which in its proposed legislation upon marriage and divorce resembled the continental schemes. On the other hand, the very definite position taken by the Church of England was marked by its rejection of the *Reformatio Legum.*'[45]

The outcome of Calvin's teaching was that the law of Geneva permitted divorce for reason of adultery, but only if the petitioner was clearly not guilty of any offence. Wilful desertion was also a ground for divorce. Scotland, under the influence of John Knox, followed the doctrinal position of Calvin and introduced divorce legislation in 1563 with adultery as the main ground. Malicious desertion for four or more years was added in 1573.[46] Other Protestant states, such as Germany, Switzerland, Holland, Denmark, Norway and Sweden introduced legal divorce in the 16th century, usually for the classic Protestant grounds of adultery and desertion. Some Protestant territories developed divorce laws based on the views of reformers such as Bucer and Zwingli, whose opinions were even more liberal than those of Calvin and Luther. In Zurich, for example, under the influence of Huldreich Zwingli, the marriage ordinance of 1525 permitted divorce for adultery, malicious desertion, and plotting against the life of the other partner. The judges also had discretion to consider other causes such as cruelty, insanity and leprosy.

THE ENGLISH POSITION ON DIVORCE

The first time the Church of England met in Synod in the 8th century at the Council of Hertford, canon law made it clear that divorce with remarriage was not permitted;

> Let no man relinquish his own wife, but for fornication, as the gospel teaches. But if any man divorce a wife, to whom he has been lawfully married, let him not be coupled to another, but remain as he is, or be reconciled to his wife if he will be a right good Christian.[47]

An investigation of marriage in medieval England showed that according to 13th century canon law, a valid and indissoluble marriage was effected when a man and a woman who were free to do so exchanged words in the present tense indicating their consent to be husband and wife. There was no necessity for any ceremony, publicity, witnesses or consent by any other parties such as parents. Gratian added that the exchange of consent had to be ratified by sexual intercourse, for in his view the exchange of consent alone had not created an indissoluble bond.[48] The problem with clandestine marriages was that they made the legitimacy of offspring uncertain, thereby clouding and confusing inheritance. Canon law made it clear that there were certain impediments to marriage, such as a pre-existing marriage, near kin by blood or marriage (the Church spelt out the prohibited degrees), impotency, a marriage contracted before the age of seven, and forced consent. The law also made provision for the church courts to grant a divorce *a mensa et thoro*, or judicial separation, in cases of adultery, spiritual fornication and abuse. This procedure released a couple from the obligation of living together under certain circumstances, although the marriage bond was not dissolved, and so remarriage was not permitted for either party. The hope of the courts was that the erring partner would reform his or her way so that reconciliation was possible.[49]

In his book, *Marriage and the English Reformation* (1994), Eric Carlson concluded that the overarching goal of the canon law was 'the right ordering of Christian society, a goal shared with secular governments, and in their minds no society was orderly in which couples married willy-nilly without a care for their families' interests, their feudal responsibilities, or the health of their souls'.[50] According to Carlson, the church courts pointed the way which the secular courts followed: marriages arranged and effected without the consent of feudal lords could not be dissolved because they were binding in the eyes of God, but they could be punished and were. And so secular courts did not attempt to dissolve marriages. They accepted absolutely the doctrine that consent alone made a marriage valid in the eyes of God, and therefore unbreakable.[51] This position was accepted by the Church and taught to the people, and there was no challenge to the idea that marriage was an indissoluble bond until the Reformation in the 16th century.

In England the debate on the sacramental nature of marriage was more restrained than it was on the continent, where Martin Luther denounced the idea of marriage as a sacrament. King Henry VIII felt certain that marriage was a sacrament because the Church said it was, and Thomas More ridiculed the teaching of Luther as vulgar nonsense. Nevertheless, when the Ten Articles appeared in July 1536, matrimony had quietly dropped from the list of the sacraments. *The Bishop's Book* of 1537 referred to marriage as being instituted by God for several good ends and that marriage 'like as the other sacraments do' consisted of both an outward sign and an inward grace.[52] But marriage was no longer listed among the sacraments for it was not instituted by Jesus and was not necessary for salvation.

The Reformation in England followed a different course from the continent, and this was particularly true when it came to divorce. The marital problems of the young Henry VIII, who sought grounds for annulling the marriage with his first wife, Catherine of Aragon, became a major dispute with the Church of Rome. At issue was the fact that Catherine was the widow of Henry's brother Arthur. Henry wanted the marriage to be annulled by the Pope on the grounds that it was invalid. The King's marital problem focussed attention on the issue of divorce as learned theologians all over Europe gave their opinion on how the matter should be resolved. Thomas Cranmer, Archbishop of Canterbury, was opposed to divorce at that time, and undoubtedly had a strong influence on the young King, and also on the thinking of the English Church. It was significant that Henry VIII did not seek a divorce from Catherine, but rather to have the marriage annulled, although the new teachings on divorce were already having a profound effect on the divorce laws in other Protestant countries.

The King's Book, published in 1543 after the English Church had seceded from Rome, aimed at helping the clergy understand the deep truths of the Christian faith. While conceding that marriage was not a sacrament, it recognised that one of the benefits of marriage was that 'the persons so lawfully conjoined be bound to conceive certain trust and confidence, and certainly to believe, not only that their said state and manner of living in wedlock is honourable, acceptable, and meritorious before God; but also that the knot and bond of matrimony contracted between the said persons is made thereby to be indissoluble.'[53] In lawful marriage 'according to the ordinances of matrimony prescribed by God and holy church the bond thereof can by no means be dissolved during the lives of the parties between whom such matrimony is contracted. And in this also the people be taught, that whosoever goeth about to dissever himself from the bond of lawful marriage, he goeth about, so much as in him lieth, to divorce Christ from his Church.'[54]

In the first half of the 16th century a variety of marriage ceremonies had been used in England until Archbishop Cranmer provided the Church with its first official and uniform marriage service in 1549. The opening statement of the service set out to explain the dignity and purpose of marriage. 'Dearly beloved friends, we are gathered here in the sight of God, and in the face of this congregation to join together this man and this woman in holy matrimony, which is an honourable estate instituted by God in paradise, in the time of man's innocency, signifying unto us the mystical union that is betwixt Christ and his Church; which holy estate Christ adorned and beautified with his presence, and first miracle that he wrought, in Cana of Galilee, and is commended of Saint Paul to be honourable among all men...' Marriage was not to be undertaken lightly, but reverently, discreetly, advisedly, soberly and in the fear of God, considering the causes for which marriage was ordained. One cause was 'the procreation of children, to be brought up in the fear and nurture of the Lord, and praise of God. Secondly, it was ordained for a remedy against sin, and to avoid fornication, that such persons as be married, might live chastely in matrimony, and keep themselves undefiled members of Christ's body. Thirdly for the mutual society, help, and comfort, that the one ought to have of the other, both in prosperity and adversity.' The English church had made it clear that marriage, although not a sacrament, is an honourable estate, ordained by God. And so the sacramental argument had now become irrelevant to the dignity of marriage. The marriage service was a witness to the fact that the indissolubility of the marriage bond was not dependent upon its sacramental nature. The prayer book of 1552 incorporated the words of the marriage service as designed by Thomas Cranmer.

Reformatio Legum Ecclesiasticarum

The teaching of the reformers on divorce was having a disturbing influence in the Church. Some of those who were sympathetic to the new ideas flowing from the continent were questioning whether England too should follow the example of their continental brothers and legalise divorce. To help clarify the situation, Henry VIII set up a commission in 1543 under the leadership of Thomas Cranmer, composed of bishops, clergymen, lawyers and laymen, to propose a canon law for the Church of England. But Henry died before the commission had finished its work. During the reign of Edward VI free discussion and publication of the Scriptures was allowed, and foreign reformers, such as Martin Bucer and Peter Martyr flocked to England. Peter Martyr actually lived with Cranmer, and was one of the 32 commissioners working on the *Reformatio Legum*. It was a time of great religious debate and it seems that Cranmer, probably influenced by the approach of the continental reformers, changed his view on divorce, which he now believed was permitted for adultery. The Rev John Keble described the influence of reformation thought on the work of the committee. 'In April 1549 Bucer came over to England, and was the archbishop's visitor for some time, before he settled in Cambridge. His views on divorce are well known; and by way of enforcing them, he made it one of the topics of his book *De Regno Christi*, which he wrote by special desire for the young King, and transmitted it to him though this tutor. The book having had the oversight of Peter Martyr, may be considered as the formal expression of the mind of the foreign reformers, so far as it was brought to bear upon England. It recommends dissolution of marriage not only for adultery, but for desertion also, and cruelty...' Keble believed that many of the arguments were similar to those used almost a century later by Milton in his writings on divorce. Indeed, so great were the similarities with Milton's writings that 'much of the *Reformatio Legum* appears very much as if they were adopted from his [Milton's] book'. In October 1551 a commission had been issued to Cranmer, Ridley, Peter Martyr and five others to complete the revisal and report to the King. Ridley and two others withdrew, but the report was completed and ready for King Edward's approval when he died in July 1553.[55]

The *Reformatio Legum Ecclesiasticarum* proposed that divorce should be legalised on the grounds of adultery, desertion or prolonged absence without news, deadly hostility, or violence by a husband against his wife unless it were justified by his need to punish her. In effect, it was proposing the most liberal divorce law in Europe. However, the proposals met opposition in the House of Commons and were opposed by the ordinary clergy of the Church of England. In all likelihood the proposals were also opposed by Queen Elizabeth I and her advisers. According to Keble, 'it pleased God to put a stop to the contemplated change, when all seemed ripe for it'.[56] And so the Church of England, despite the upheavals on the continent, remained theologically committed to the indissolubility of marriage and the *Reformatio Legum* was never implemented.

Church reaffirms the indissolubility of marriage

Following the failure of the *Reformatio Legum* to change marriage discipline, the Church again affirmed its belief in the indissolubility of the marriage bond. In 1597, under Archbishop John Whitgift, the Provincial Synod of Canterbury promulgated canons under the Great Seal of England stating the Church's position. 'Let those persons who have separated from each other be directed by monition and prohibition to live in chastity, and not to have recourse to other marriages so long as the other lives.'[57]

At the end of the Elizabethan era, in 1603, the canon laws of the Church of England were revised to make it absolutely clear that the Church did not recognise a full divorce with the right of remarriage. Canon 107 stated the Church's position on divorce:

> In all sentences pronounced only for divorce and separation *a thoro et mensa*, there shall be a caution and restraint inserted in the act of the said sentence, that the parties so separated shall live chastely and continently; neither shall they, during each other's life, contract matrimony with any other person. And, for the better observation of this clause, the said sentence of divorce shall not be pronounced until the party or parties requiring the same have given good and sufficient caution and security into the court, that they will not any way break or transgress the said restraint or prohibition.[58]

During the reign of Elizabeth 1 there was no divorce in England. It was now clear that the matter of divorce was settled in the mind of the Church of England, and divorce *a vinculo matrimonii* was not permitted by the ecclesiastical courts. By the beginning of the 17th century the Church of England and continental Protestantism had parted ways with regard to their position on divorce.

The Book of Common Prayer, which became spiritually binding as the law of the Church in 1662, incorporated the concept of indissolubility into the marriage service. Those who were wed, in the presence of God, took the vow, 'I take thee to my wedded wife (husband), to have and to hold from this day forward, for better for worse, for richer for poorer, in sickness and in health, to love and to cherish, till death us do part, according to God's holy ordinance; and thereto I plight thee my troth.' The priest, joining their hands together, says solemnly, 'Those whom God hath joined together let no man put asunder.' The pre-reformation prayer was 'O God, who didst teach that it should never be lawful to put asunder those whom thou by matrimony hadst made one.' In his closing words the priest quotes, 'For this cause shall a man leave his father and his mother, and shall be joined to his wife, and they two shall be one flesh.' The marriage service makes it clear that marriage is for life, no matter what the circumstances. The words of this service were, and still are, deeply ingrained into the mind of the people of England.

THE WESTMINSTER CONFESSION OF FAITH

Meanwhile in 1648 the Westminster Confession of Faith, which was dominated by Presbyterians and the conservative wing of the Puritan movement, outlined reformed doctrine on marriage and divorce. The doctrinal statement made it clear that 'marriage is an ordinance of God, designed for the mutual help of husband and wife, for the honourable propagation of the human race, and for other important purposes connected with the comfort and improvement of the species'.[59] With regard to divorce, the Confession says:

> In the case of adultery after marriage, it is lawful for the innocent party to sue out a divorce, and, after the divorce, to marry another, *as if the offending party were dead* [my italics]. Although the corruption of man be such as is apt to study arguments unduly to put asunder those whom God hath joined together in marriage; yet nothing but adultery, or such wilful desertion as can no way be remedied by the Church or civil magistrate, is cause sufficient of dissolving the bond of marriage.[60]

Clearly the doctrinal position of nonconformist England was strongly influenced by the teachings of Calvin and Luther.

TWO DOCTRINES ON DIVORCE

Following the Reformation the Christian Church was split in its interpretation of what the Bible taught about divorce, and the disagreement was fuelled by the views of Erasmus, Luther and Calvin. Nevertheless, the teachings on divorce were among the most important to emerge from the Reformation and had an enormous influence on legislation in Europe. While Protestant

Europe legalised divorce for adultery and desertion in the 16th century, the effect of legalisation was relatively small, for most people still believed that marriage was for life and were against divorce. But the seeds of a greater liberalism had been sown and the harvest of easy divorce lay in future generations. The Church of England, on the other hand, after the unsuccessful attempt to introduce the ideas of the continental reformers through the *Reformatio Legum Ecclesiasticarum*, was resolute in its stand against divorce *a vinculo matrimonii*, believing that the Scriptures taught that marriage was an indissoluble bond. These ideas were cemented into church discipline through the canon law of 1603 and the marriage service.

So England alone of the countries that embraced the Reformation retained the concept of the indissolubility of marriage, while the other Protestant countries moved to legalise divorce. While both camps claimed that their position was based on Scripture, they were diametrically opposed to each other. Clearly it was impossible for both sets of belief to be based on biblical truth—the Bible teaches either that marriage is dissoluble or that it is indissoluble; it either permits divorce with the right to remarry or it does not. It follows that one side in the dispute had fallen into error. The great debate in the English Parliament and Church in the second half of the 19th century, discussed in the next chapter, revolved around the question of the indissolubility of marriage.

Chapter 4

Divorce in England – the first step

House of Lords debates in 1856 and 1857

During the 18th and 19th centuries England had the lowest divorce rate in the civilised world. William Gladstone, in his speech to the House of Commons opposing the Divorce Reform Act of 1857, said that no single age, or country, or period had ever known such a low level of divorce as that in England.[1] In the country at large marriage was held to be a sacred lifelong union. Most people took seriously the marriage vows they made in the presence of God as binding for life. The ideas conveyed in the old familiar words 'for better for worse, for richer for poorer, till death us do part' was a part of the common conscience of the community. According to the Archbishop of York (Cosmo Lang) the words of the marriage service emphasised a notion of marriage that was not primarily a mutual arrangement for happiness, but an obligation of lifelong and faithful service.[2] In the House of Lords, Lord Redesdale explained that the reason the marriage law was held more sacred in England than in any other country was because divorce had been withheld from the people at large.[3] The Bishop of Oxford (Samuel Wilberforce) maintained that there was a feeling among the people of England that marriage with any other person was impossible.[4] The idea that marriage was for life was widely believed and accepted as the basis of a good society, and divorce was an alien concept to ordinary Englishmen and women.

The transformation of England from a non-divorcing society to one with mass divorce has occurred not by chance, but as the result of changes in the ideas and beliefs that surround marriage and divorce. This chapter discusses the first step along the path to mass divorce. The parliamentary debates around the Divorce Reform Act of 1857 are significant for they illustrate the ideas behind the struggle to legalise divorce in England. At the heart of the debates was the Christian understanding of the meaning of marriage, and biblical teaching on divorce and remarriage.

THE INDISSOLUBILITY OF MARRIAGE: 1600–1857

At the beginning of the 17th century England stood in a unique position among the countries that had embraced the Reformation. Under the influence of Thomas Cranmer, William Tyndale and the Puritans, the Christian faith in England had been truly reformed. The Bible had been translated into English and was available to the ordinary man; the doctrine of salvation by faith alone was widely taught and believed. Scripture alone was the source of God's revealed truth, and there was a hunger in the country to study the Bible. England unique among the Protestant countries had no provision for legal divorce, and the Church of England remained firmly committed to the doctrine of the indissolubility of marriage.

As we noted in chapter 3, there were no recorded divorces during the reign of Elizabeth I, and the Church's canon law expressly forbade divorce *a vinculo*. Ecclesiastic courts regulated all matters relating to marriage and divorce. In accordance with canon law these courts did not permit legal divorce with the right to remarry, although they did permit separation of bed and board on grounds of adultery and excessive cruelty. As marriage was considered indissoluble the separated parties were not permitted to remarry. The Church's belief in the doctrine of the indissolubility of marriage was based on Scripture, and most churchmen were sure that the words of Christ did not allow remarriage under any circumstances. According to historian Roderick Phillips, 'one characteristic of the anti-divorce literature of the first half of the 17th century is that it appealed almost entirely to scriptural interpretation. There were long discussions of the biblical texts and other ecclesiastical authorities, but there was virtually none of the social theology of the pro-divorce writers, who tended to give more emphasis to the conceptions of justice and the right ordering of morality and society.'[5]

So the Church stood firm in not granting divorces with the right to remarry, even in the case of adultery. The unequivocal doctrinal position was that marriage could only be ended by the death of one of the marriage partners, for according to Scripture, 'by law a married woman is bound to her husband as long as he is alive, but if her husband dies, she is released from the law of marriage' (Romans 7:2). The family was seen as the basic social unit, and stability within the family was essential for the good of society. Because marriage was ordained by God, any behaviour that threatened the integrity of marriage and the family was seen as contrary to divine law.[6] Social historian Eric Carlson makes the point in *Marriage and the English Reformation* that 'popular belief in the indissolubility of betrothal was practically universal and unshakeable' in 16th century England.[7] Within the Church of England the issue was settled and, according to Roderick Phillips, 'no bishop, archbishop or incumbent of high Anglican office in the first half of the 17th century supported the legalisation of divorce'.[8]

Even among the judiciary the essential indissoluble nature of the marriage contract was clearly recognised. A well-known judgement given in 1790 by Lord William Edward Stowell, who stands in the front rank of English judges, illustrates the standpoint of the older jurisprudence. In his judgement Lord Stowell made the point, 'Marriage is the most solemn engagement which one human being can contract with another. It is a contract formed with a view, not only to the benefit of the parties themselves, but to the benefit of third parties; to the benefit of their common offspring, and to the moral order of civil society. To this contract is superadded the sanctity of a religious vow. Mr Evans must be told that the obligations of this contract are not to be relaxed at the pleasure of one party. I may go further: they are not to be lightly relaxed even at the pleasure of both parties. For the two persons have pledged themselves at the altar of God to spend their lives for purposes that reach much beyond themselves: it is a doctrine to which the morality of the law gives no countenance, that they may by private contract, dissolve the bonds of this solemn tie, and throw themselves upon society in the undefined and dangerous character of a wife without a husband and a husband without a wife.'[9]

The historian Gertrude Himmelfarb in her book on Victorian England, concludes that among middle-class England the family was 'not only revered but sentimentalised to a degree never known before or since'.[10] The family was a domestic unit and the home the exclusive and private domain of the family. Not only were middle-class women kept out of the labour market, the men themselves retreated to the bosom of their family as if to escape from the harsh world of moneymaking, for the nuclear family had become the dominant form.[11] She notes that Victorians of many different religious persuasions agreed that family and home were the keystones of society and the country.[12] Marriage was regarded with such profound respect that even in private conversation among men, adultery was regarded as a crime.[13]

In 1830 a commission was appointed to consider the divorce law and in particular the expediency of obtaining a legal divorce in cases of adultery. A large majority in the House of Lords were against the motion. Addressing the House of Commons, Dr Robert Phillimore said that marriage was looked upon by the law of the country as an indissoluble contract; and though some great individual hardships might arise from viewing it in that light, he believed that experience showed that the general happiness of the married life was best promoted by considering marriage generally speaking as an indissoluble contract. He mentioned that it was possible for Parliament to permit divorce for adultery by special legislation. However, Dr Phillimore informed the House, 'I wish to have it understood distinctly, that it ought to be the principle of the law that marriage is indissoluble. The interests of families—of the whole community, composed of families, demand that marriage should be declared indissoluble.'[14]

DIVORCE BY PRIVATE ACTS OF PARLIAMENT: 1670–1857

The principle of the indissolubility of marriage could be extremely inconvenient at times and a cause of real hardship to some individuals. In particular the landed aristocracy found it difficult to accept that they were unable to rid themselves of an adulterous wife and remarry in order to perpetuate the family name. Between 1670 and 1857 a small number of individuals, mainly among the aristocracy, used a private Act of Parliament as means for circumventing the principle of marriage indissolubility to obtain a legal divorce.

The first such divorce was passed in 1670 during the time of Charles II. Lord Roos – a man by the name of John Manners – had separated from his wife who was guilty of blatant adultery and had borne children by her lover. Lord Roos first obtained an Act bastardising the children of his adulteress wife, Lady Ann, and then a divorce from the ecclesiastical court. This did not allow for remarriage as the marriage bond was still intact. As the Lord wanted the right to remarry in the hope of producing a legitimate heir, he proceeded with a private Act of Parliament to legally dissolve the marriage. The King attended the House of Lords as they passed a bill permitting Lord Roos to remarry. It seems that the House of Lords passed this bill to establish a precedent that would enable King Charles II to divorce his wife, by whom he had no children, to marry a second time and so to exclude the Duke of York from the throne. The bill excited great discussion in the House and all the Roman Catholic peers and fourteen of the seventeen Anglican prelates were against it. On a vote it was carried with a small majority.[15]

This case provided a precedent and in the future a small number of the aristocracy were to use private Acts of Parliament to obtain a divorce. At first these divorces were used in the interest of property descent. Later they were used as a matter of convenience to enable remarriages in the pursuit of marital happiness.[16] During the period 1670 to 1857, 325 parliamentary divorces were granted, of which only four were to women. It was a difficult and expensive procedure, and, not surprisingly, parliamentary divorce was a rare event, averaging about two per year.

IDEOLOGICAL BACKGROUND TO DIVORCE LIBERALISATION

Despite the strong stand of the Church of England there were others in society who opposed the indissolubility of marriage on religious or ideological grounds. Religious opposition was led by the Puritans who were sympathetic to the views of the Protestant reformers and not content with the conservative approach of the Church. In particular, they attacked the ecclesiastical courts and demanded that civil magistrates should handle the decision of matrimonial cases. Ideological opposition came from the ideas of socialism and liberalism.

Milton on divorce

John Milton, the famous English poet, Puritan and Renaissance humanist, took up the cause of divorce in the 1640s. He wrote his pamphlets *The Doctrine and Discipline of Divorce* in 1643, and *The Judgement of Martin Bucer concerning Divorce* in 1644, as an appeal to the Westminster Assembly of Divines and to the Long Parliament. He informed his readers that he was addressing an issue of great and powerful importance to the governing of mankind. In the tracts Milton argued that adultery should not be the sole cause for divorce. Rather, incompatibility of mind was a more valid cause because the forced yoke of a loveless marriage was a crime against human dignity.[17] Milton believed that the chief end of marriage was the mutual love, society, help and comfort of the husband and wife. The second end of marriage was procreation.

The failure to fulfil either of these two objectives constituted grounds for divorce. The law should not force a marriage to continue where no mutual affection binds the partners together. Where the spiritual bond was lacking, such a marriage was already more disrupted than if the couple were divorced, and was unpleasing to God. For such a couple to remain married was a form of hypocrisy.[18] Milton believed that the teaching of Christ allowed divorce by mutual consent. Christ did not condemn all divorce but all injury and violence in divorce. But no injury could be done to those who mutually consent to divorce.[19] Milton's views were strongly criticised at the time and he was regarded as a new libertine. His arguments were later to be repeated by those who promoted the liberalisation of divorce laws.

Robert Owen – the father of socialism

In the first half of the 19th century there was increasing political agitation for the legalisation of divorce. Robert Owen, generally regarded as the founder of British socialism, was a strong advocate for legalisation.[20] From an early age Owen had rejected the Christian faith, although he believed in a supreme being and in later life followed spiritualism. He developed a rationalist philosophy for improving society, which perceived established religion as a singularly vicious opponent. The main point in Owen's philosophy was that man's character was formed by circumstances over which he had no control. It followed that education and social amelioration could help solve man's problems. His vision was of a new society with a new system of morality. He had an intense dislike for the values of what he referred to as the old moral order that he wanted to destroy.

Owen denounced the institution of marriage and the existence of private property. He believed that the human race needed to be liberated from a trinity of monstrous evils; private property, irrational religion and marriage.[21] In *Eve and the New Jerusalem* (1983), Barbara Taylor comments that at the heart of the analysis of the Owenites was a systematic critique of what they called the marriage system, that is, patriarchal marriage and the nuclear family (single-family arrangements). 'It was as fathers and husbands that men oppressed women; it was as daughters, wives and mothers that women experienced their most subjugation. Sexual subordination was basically a family affair. The inequities of marriage had been a major theme of feminist writers from the 17th century onward.'[22]

Marriage was an 'unnatural crime which destroys the finest feelings and best powers of the species, by changing sincerity, kindness, affection, sympathy and pure love into deception, envy, jealousy, hatred, and revenge. It is a Satanic device of the Priesthood to place and keep mankind within their slavish superstitions, and to render them subservient to all purposes.' It bred unhappiness through its stress on the family. Indeed, the concept of the family was rooted in the values of the old immoral world and constituted a serious stumbling block to man's achievement.[23] Owen identified the family as a cause of crime, tyranny and oppression, particularly of women, which produced widespread misery.[24]

After 1834 Owen devoted himself to preaching his moral, rationalist and divorce reform ideas around Britain. In 1835 he published the most influential Owenite text on the marriage question, *Lectures on the Marriages of the Priesthood in the Old Immoral World*, in which he argued for civil marriage and cheap, easy divorce – both demands which were also being raised by certain liberal nonconformists at the time. 'Owen's writings – and those of other Socialist propagandists who wrote on the issues – can be seen as part of a growing movement for the liberalisation of marriage. But they also led in a far more radical direction, towards a repudiation of the entire system of single-family arrangements... For Owen, it is the existence of the bourgeois family unit – the little commonwealth which looks only to its own interests and ignores those of its neighbours – which is the real barrier to social reform, rather than the power of the husband/father within the family.'[25]

He took part in public debates on marriage and divorce, which caught the popular imagination, and attracted large crowds. Claiming that both the individual and society were more important than the family, he taught that the family was a divisive social unit and advocated the need for divorce law reform.[26] 'Throughout the late 1830's and early 1840's a continual stream of publications poured from the pens of Socialist ideologues, defending, reinterpreting and occasionally even wholly revising Owen's proposals. Lectures were great crowd-catchers, attracting audiences of up to five or six thousand people.'[27] It is not difficult to see that the new British socialist movement was founded on ideas that were hostile to marriage and the family.

John Stuart Mill – the philosophy of utilitarianism

Liberalism, the growing political ideology of 19th century society, held that divorce was necessary for the achievement of individual freedom and happiness. A basic assumption of liberal thinkers was that man is endowed with reason and goodness, and it was only the institutional frame into which he was born that corrupts and enslaves him. The enemy of progress was custom, tradition, institutions and social habit.[28] To the liberal mind, marriage was an institution from the past based on the subjection of women. Rigid marriage laws were the means of entrapping a man or woman with no hope of freedom from an unhappy marriage.

The liberal philosopher, John Stuart Mill argued for the legalisation of divorce. Mill, who had always been indifferent towards the Christian faith, developed a philosophy of utilitarianism, which asserted that the goal of ethics is to achieve the greatest happiness for the greatest number. In his essay on *The Subjection of Women*, Mill discussed the legal servitude into which women are plunged upon getting married. Even women who are well looked after by their husbands have sold their freedom in exchange for board and lodging. His view was that people who had failed in one attempt at happiness ought to be allowed a second try. Mill proposed that a marriage between equals is likely to be happier than one in which men hold all the power. He believed that women should demand greater freedom and equality in marriage.[29]

The political ideas of the 19th century were associated with a growing secularisation of life. As more members of Parliament were adopting a secular attitude towards divorce, in 1850 there was political pressure to set up a Royal Commission to inquire into the state of the law relating to divorce. Other factors that persuaded Parliament to set up a commission were dissatisfaction with the running of the church courts, and a growing criticism of the divorce procedure by the middle class.[30] The commission, which reported in 1853, proposed a reconstruction of the court system to provide for divorce through a secular court, but made no recommendation to change the law on divorce.[31] The commission did not express a view on whether the lower income groups in society should have reasonable access to secular divorce. One of the commissioners, Lord Redesdale, dissented from the majority recommendation for he was against the idea of making divorce widely available. He warned that the proposed change in the court system would create an appetite for licence, which would lead to an irresistible demand for more divorce.

THE DIVORCE REFORM ACT OF 1857

Based on the findings of the commission the government, of which Mr William Gladstone was a member, introduced a bill in 1854. The original intention was to remove legal action for separation (about twenty a year) from the ecclesiastical courts, and legislative action for divorce (about three a year) from Parliament and transfer these powers to a new civil court. After a short debate in the House of Lords the bill was withdrawn and reintroduced in 1856. Mr Gladstone was now the leader of the opposition and Viscount Henry John Palmerston the Prime Minister.

The chief aim of the new bill was to legalise divorce on the ground of adultery. This would make divorce more widely available to the people of England. It soon became clear that the main issue at stake for the Parliament of Christian England revolved around the question of whether marriage was dissoluble or indissoluble. At the heart of the debate was the central question—what did the Scriptures teach regarding divorce? The debate was passionate and aroused profound feelings. So contentious was the issue that the bill was withdrawn on a number of occasions before finally passing through the parliamentary process. Supporters of the bill claimed that according to the law of England marriage was dissoluble, as evidenced by the divorces granted by private Acts of Parliament. They argued that marriage was dissolved by adultery and proposed that those who were divorced should be entitled to remarry. A key proposal was that the adulterer and adulteress could be legally married following a divorce from their first marriages. Many believed that divorce was a remedy for unhappy marriages, allowing unfortunate couples a second chance of happiness. Opponents argued that it would cause great damage to the future well-being of the nation, warning that once a country embarked on the road of divorce legalisation, one law would lead to another and the end would be divorce on demand. Another concern was that liberalising divorce would weaken society's view of marriage.

The following selection from Hansard of the parliamentary speeches gives an idea of the arguments on both sides of the debate, reveals the feelings aroused, and shows how both sides believed the issue was of paramount importance for the future welfare of the nation.

Debate in the House of Lords: April–June 1856

The Divorce Reform Act, introduced to the Lords in April 1856, had the two main objectives of legalising divorce for adultery, and transferring the jurisdiction in matrimonial cases from ecclesiastical courts to a new Court of Divorce. A husband might present a petition to dissolve his marriage on the ground of his wife's adultery, and a wife might petition on the ground of her husband's aggravated adultery. The court would pronounce a decree dissolving the marriage, permitting the parties to marry again. *The Times* in a leading article wrote that in England the law of husband and wife 'is based on the fiction that they make up between them but one person, the existence of the woman being to all intents and for all purposes utterly absorbed and swallowed up in that of the man'. This fact led to the unfair distinction in the matter of divorce. It hoped that the bill would 'do away with the crying injustice and inequality of the law, to give to the poor the same remedies as the rich, and to work this out through simple rules and cheap but efficient machinery'.[32]

Lord John Campbell said it was a most anomalous state of things that a marriage could not be dissolved in England without an Act of Parliament. However he cautioned their Lordships against giving too great facilities for divorce. Such a course would be attended with unhappy consequences. It was only in cases of adultery that divorce could be safely given, and this was the line pointed out by the divine founder of Christianity. The question arose as to whether the wife should be given the same right of divorce as the husband. No doubt the crime in both cases was the same, but the consequences were not the same. When adultery was committed the woman forever annulled all the purposes of the marriage, and there could be no condonation on the part of the husband. He would therefore not go to the length of giving the woman the same rights as the man.[33]

The Bishop of Oxford (Samuel Wilberforce) said that after deep and mature consideration he was unable to consent to the fundamental part of the bill, which was to facilitate divorce in all cases of adultery upon the part of the wife, and in cases of adultery with certain aggravations on the part of the husband. Although he conceded that his honest opinion was that marriage might lawfully be dissolved for the act of adultery, he was doubtful that 'the morality of the nation would be promoted by affording such facilities'. He feared that 'the consequences would be the wide spread of the master evil, collusion, which would by degrees sap the sanctity of married life among the lower classes'.

 He argued that there was no outcry among the poor for more access to divorce, and warned that whenever relaxation of the marriage tie had been introduced it commenced 'by giving facility for dissolution only on ground of adultery; but never had relaxation stopped there. Other cases of hardship had soon been suggested until, for incompatibility of temper, and at last for mutual dislike, divorce had in some countries been allowed.' The consequences of the bill 'would be the opening of the floodgates of licence upon the hitherto blessed purity of English life'. Among the people of England there was a 'feeling that marriage with any other person was impossible, and the removal of that check would have the effect of unsettling altogether the present estimate which the masses formed of the sacredness of holy matrimony'. He implored their lordships not to hurry a measure through the House which, whether for good or for evil, touched the foundations of the whole family life of the people.[34]

The Duke of Argyll pointed out the apparent inconsistency of the bishop's position. Although he did not claim that marriage was indissoluble, or that divorce for adultery was against divine law, the bishop wished to neutralise the divine permission, which he admitted had been given to divorces in certain cases.[35] The Duke was, of course, right to identify the inconsistency in the bishop's position. This criticism undoubtedly struck home, for the bishop was to give a great deal of thought to the issue, and would inform the House at a later stage in the debate that the Scriptures did not permit divorce with the right to remarry, even in the case of adultery. But the failure to base his opposition to the bill on the biblical doctrine of the indissolubility of marriage had seriously weakened his position.

The Bishop of St David's (Connop Thirlwall), supporting the Bishop of Oxford, expressed the view that if the legislation were carried it would not stop there, but would lead to demands for more changes to the law. Indeed he saw no limit to their legislation on this subject until divorce was made cheaper and easier of access.[36] But the position of the Bishop of Oxford was again challenged. Lord Cranworth, the Lord Chancellor, pointed out that as the bishop started from the assumption that there was nothing in the Scriptures that forbade divorce for adultery, surely he must give the person complaining of adultery the facility for divorce as it was not inconsistent with divine law.[37] Lord Campbell supported the Lord Chancellor, and said that the Bishop of Oxford did not consider the marriage tie indissoluble – nor indeed could he for he was not a Roman Catholic, and did not regard marriage as a sacrament. Accordingly the bishop would allow marriage to be dissolved for the adultery of the wife.[38] The Bishop of Oxford responded to these criticisms later in the debate.

Lord Redesdale declared his belief in the indissolubility of marriage, and therefore divorce with the right to remarry was not permitted. With regard to the consequences of divorce, he doubted whether they produced happy results, and questioned the social benefits which would flow from an extension of the law.[39] Divorce had been a thing withheld from the people at large, and the consequence was that the marriage law was held more sacred than in any other country in the world. 'At present where tempers differed, the parties felt that they must nevertheless remain together and accommodate themselves to each other, and this knowledge had caused the marriage state to be so happy in this country.' Who would be adversely affected by the bill? 'Why, every single marriage was touched more or less by the principle of the present change in the law... If their Lordships were to examine the history of twenty or thirty divorces, they would find no more than two or three instances in which the parties who had obtained a divorce had enjoyed anything like happiness. In numberless cases no remarriage took place, and where there were children the greatest distress and inconvenience were experienced.'[40]

70

The Bishop of Salisbury agreed with the position of Lord Redesdale. The purpose of his speech was to show that the bill was against the most fundamental teaching of the Bible. He believed that it was his duty to vindicate in the House of Lords what he believed to be the truth of God's most Holy Word. He started by discussing the teaching of Christ on divorce in the gospels of St Mark and St Matthew. He argued that although the writing of divorcement permitted by Moses provided both for separation and remarriage, the Lord cancelled these provisions, and made separation and remarriage impossible. Thus it was recorded by St Mark that the Lord said, 'if a woman put away her husband and be married to another, she committeth adultery' and in St Matthew the same judgement of the Lord was recorded, though in a different way. The Lord's words in the fifth chapter of St Matthew were, 'Whosoever shall marry her that is divorced committeth adultery' and his words in chapter 19 were almost the same; and in both these passages it was observable that in speaking of the woman divorced the article was omitted, which would include every woman, whatever was the reason of her divorce. These passages made plain the Lord's mind with regard to the woman—separation so as to remarry was impossible. Nor was it less clear with regard to the man. The Lord said in St Mark, 'Whosoever shall put away his wife and marry another, committeth adultery against her' and in St Luke, 'Whosoever putteth away his wife and marrieth another, committeth adultery.' The bishop said no teaching could be plainer than this, and he could come to only one conclusion—that the Lord had annulled the provisions of Moses for granting divorce and that divorce and remarriage were, according to the law of Christ, impossible.

The bishop then dealt with the exception clause of St Matthew. He admitted that there was one exception for divorce – not for divorce and remarriage, but for separation without the power of remarrying – and that was in the case of adultery. He quoted from Matthew chapter 5, 'Whosoever putteth away his wife, saving for the cause of fornication, causeth her to commit adultery' and chapter 19, 'Whosoever shall put away his wife, except it be for fornication, and shall marry another, committeth adultery.' He noted that this relaxation was not confined to one sex, for the Lord made man and woman entirely equal in this matter. The words of St Paul, in I Corinthians chapter 7, 'if she depart' implied that it was possible for the woman in the case of adultery to get a divorce from her husband; not such a divorce as to be remarried, but only such as would enable her to act upon the revelation of God's mind given by the Apostle, 'let her remain unmarried, or be reconciled to her husband'. And even this one relaxation was further guarded through the words of the Apostle Paul, 'Let not the wife depart from her husband. Let not the husband put away his wife.'

The Bishop of Salisbury concluded that it was contrary to the teaching of the Lord for a husband to put away his wife, or a wife to put away her husband,

and marry again. He entreated their Lordships to weigh well what they were doing, because it was his most solemn conviction that they were not, as had been said, about to sweep away one of the relics of the Roman Catholic religion, but were going against the plain letter of Holy Scripture. He entreated them to pause before they arrayed all those who adhered to the Word of God against any decree which man might make on the subject; he entreated them not to give their verdict against what had been the law of England for centuries, and which he believed was the true interpretation of Holy Writ.[41]

The proponents of the bill were able to make much of the fact that there was an apparent disagreement in the interpretation of the Scriptures, and especially the fact that the Bishop of Oxford, in his first speech, did not support the position that the marriage bond was indissoluble. There was an unwillingness to accept the Christian view, so powerfully expressed by the Bishop of Salisbury, and the Earl of Derby was able to say, 'I cannot help observing that even among those who opposed the bill there was a very considerable opinion on the subject.' He mentioned that the Bishop of Oxford did not contend for the indissolubility of the marriage tie, and asserted that under certain conditions the marriage tie is dissoluble. 'I am therefore altogether favourable to the principle of this bill, and I confess I have been unable to hear from the authorities quoted tonight anything in Scripture or anything in reason which should prevent the Legislature from dealing with this question.'[42]

Viscount Dungannon feared that the remedy proposed was far worse than the disease, and that if divorce was once made a part of the law of the land it would be the means of introducing great unhappiness to the community. The difficulty in obtaining divorce was in a great degree the cause of the morality which existed in England with regard to the marriage state. That morality would be shaken to its very foundations by the present bill, which was fraught with danger to the morality, the well-being, the order of society and the happiness of the community at large.[43]

The Bishop of Oxford was unsuccessful with an amendment that would have removed the clauses that allowed divorce with the right to remarry. He then introduced a motion to insert the following words into the bill. 'Provided always that it shall not be lawful for a husband or wife who shall have been found guilty of adultery to intermarry with any woman or man with whom the adultery has been proved to have been committed.' This motion was agreed with little opposition, and soon afterwards the government withdrew the bill. It was introduced for a third time in February 1957 and during the second reading, the Bishop of Exeter (Henry Phillpotts) moved that the bill should be postponed so that a commission might be appointed to examine the doctrine of the Church concerning marriage and divorce. Although the motion for postponement was defeated the bill was again withdrawn.

Debate in the House of Lords: May–June 1857

For the fourth time, on 19 May 1857, the government introduced the bill to the House of Lords. The Lord Chancellor invited their lordships to consider a subject of the utmost importance, a measure that was of the very deepest interest to society in general. He assured the House that nothing would induce him to submit a bill which he believed would have the slightest tendency to shake the confidence of the country in the permanency, if not the absolute indissolubility, of the marriage tie. He acknowledged that before the Reformation marriage was considered as being absolutely indissoluble and was regarded as a sacrament of the Church. However, the Reformation had changed the feelings of the community upon this subject. The opinion of the reformers was that there was nothing of a sacramental nature connected with marriage, which they thought to be a mere civil contract which ought to be dealt with in the same way as other civil contracts—by considering what was in the best interests of the parties concerned. He argued that 'if it be right that marriage should be dissolved in the case of adultery, and no one denies the right – surely such dissolution should not take place by occasional measures, but through the intervention of a public tribunal, open to all – to the poor as well as the rich.' He proposed that on the husband complaining that his wife had been unfaithful he might come before the new tribunal, and on establishing his case, on showing no improper conduct on his part, he should be entitled to obtain at once a full divorce which entitled him to remarry. But the same rule had not applied to the wife complaining of the adultery of her husband. It had always been the feeling of the House that the effect of adultery on the part of the husband was very different from that of adultery on the part of the wife.

The Lord Chancellor reminded the House that when the bill was last before the House, the Bishop of Oxford had introduced a clause to the effect that in the case of the dissolution of the marriage, the adulterer should never be at liberty to marry the adulteress. When that proposition was made he had raised his solitary voice against it. It was carried nevertheless by acclamation – as if such a proposition was ever likely to have a moral or useful tendency. The Lord Chancellor, however, 'thought it was a great blot on the bill, and would be fraught with unmixed evil instead of good, because he believed that such an enactment would be the means of removing that which in every honourable mind must be the great check to the commission of adultery.' For that reason he had not thought fit to reintroduce the clause into the present bill.[44]

The Archbishop of Canterbury (John Sumner) made the point that it was impossible to foresee the consequences which might result from the legislation. He warned, 'there was great danger, lest in endeavouring to apply a remedy to an existing and acknowledged evil they opened the way to greater evils than those which they desired to remove. The facilities of divorce which had been admitted in many of the Protestant states on the Continent, were no doubt intended not to injure morality but to obviate existing inconveniences: but those facilities had ended in so gross a laxity of morals that it was notorious that there was a strong desire in those countries to remove them, and to return to a state of things more in accordance with the system which happily in this country had never been set aside.'

He thought that no one could deny that, according to the general tenor of divine law, marriage, once contracted, was designed to be indissoluble – indissoluble saving for one cause, a cause which destroyed the purpose and intent of marriage – saving for the cause of unfaithfulness. For that cause it was declared lawful for a man to put away his wife, and, by parity of reasoning, it would be lawful for a woman to put away her husband. But here he stopped. He regretted that the bill did not stop here. But the bill permitted the parties whose guilt had occasioned the dissolution of the first marriage to form afterwards a legal union, whereas the divine law said, 'Whosoever shall marry her that is put away commits adultery.' He appealed to the divine law and informed the House that while he was prepared to vote for the second reading, he would oppose in committee the clause which permitted the guilty parties to be united in legal marriage.[45]

Lord Lyndhurst, one of the promoters of the bill, could not disguise from himself that both in the House and out of doors there was very considerable opposition to the measure. It was opposed both on social and religious grounds. While he did not wish to enter into any scriptural argument, he considered conclusive the scriptural doctrine that marriage might be dissolved in case of adultery. He maintained that was the principle of the whole Protestant Church, over and over again declared to be sanctioned by the express terms of the Scriptures. He admitted, however, that according to the law of England, as it at present existed, marriage was indissoluble by any legal tribunal. He advocated protecting the rights of women and believed they were sometimes the victims of the laws made by men. One of the objections to the principles of the bill, as it stood, was the great inequality between the sexes. He begged the House to consider that when a man maliciously deserted his wife, that should be ground for a divorce. In commercial contracts if one party violated the agreement the other was released from it. Why should not the same principle be extended to a deserted wife?[46] Lord Lyndhurst made no secret that he was committed to extending the grounds for divorce beyond the present bill. He saw it as only the first step in a campaign to liberalise the divorce laws.

Lord Wensleydale said that the law of England, notwithstanding the attempt to change it in the *Reformatio Legum,* was and always had been that a marriage once made was indissoluble, and he could not therefore look without great misgivings upon the proposal which made such a sweeping alteration in the law of the land, and made it dissoluble by legal right. He argued that although the bill aimed to set up a divorce tribunal in London, it would be impossible to prevent extending divorce facilities to inferior courts. The consequence would be that 'the poor would have an easy mode of putting an end to a connection which had become irksome to them by the commission of adultery, and this facility appeared to him to threaten consequences extremely prejudicial to morality, and be likely to lead to an extensive corruption of manners amongst those classes where public opinion has not so much influence to prevent the commission of such crimes, as in the higher walks of life. He therefore looked upon the principal clause of the bill with great alarm as to its probable consequences.'[47]

The Earl of Malmesbury argued that the liberty of remarrying ought to be restricted, for nothing could be more injurious to the interests of morality than to allow a man to marry after he had divorced his wife for adultery. He mentioned the case of two adulterous persons having obtained a divorce and afterwards marrying one another. 'Suppose they again committed adultery and come before the Court for a second divorce, surely it would not be contended by the noble Lord on the woolsack that it would be for the benefit of morality or of society that those persons should be able to obtain a second and perhaps third divorce, as was the case in Saxony and other parts of Germany?'[48] In other words, how many times may a person divorce on grounds of adultery and remarry? The Earl of Malmesbury was raising an awkward question that no one tried to answer.

The Duke of Norfolk responded to Lord Lyndhurst's assertion that popes had been constantly in the habit of granting dissolutions of marriage. He challenged Lord Lyndhurst to put his finger on a single case in which a pope had dissolved any valid marriage. It was the universal feeling of the Roman Catholic Church that marriage was indissoluble. He would oppose the bill in any way that he could.[49]

Lord Campbell clarified the main issue at stake in the debate. According to Roman Catholic doctrine, marriage was a sacrament and could not be dissolved, but all Protestant churches believed, according to the precepts of their divine founder, that marriage might be dissolved for adultery, and it seemed to him to be straining and quibbling when any other interpretation was attempted to be put on the words of our Lord.[50] The real question was whether England was going to follow the Protestant position on divorce.

Viscount Dungannon felt extremely strongly on the issue which he believed struck at the very root of the best interests of society—civil, moral and religious. The moment it was known that greater facilities existed for divorce the result would be an encouragement to the indulgence of illicit desires, and 'the happiness which had up to this time generally characterised our social relations in this country would be materially impaired'. He thought that the introduction of the bill would prove a source of misery among the poorer classes of people that was painful to contemplate.[51] According to Lord Redesdale the declarations contained in Scripture for the indissolubility of the marriage tie were far stronger than the single passage quoted against it. Even the passage cited as sanctioning the dissolution of marriage contained the strongest possible injunction against it. The Scriptures said a man and wife were one flesh, and that he who married a divorced woman committed adultery. How could he commit adultery unless the woman was still a wife? He contended on moral grounds that the strongest possible arguments existed against the principle on which the bill was founded. There was no country in the world, looking at all classes of the population from the highest to the lowest, where married life had been held so sacred or had produced so much happiness as in England, and that had mainly arisen from the obstacles to obtaining a legal dissolution of the marriage tie.[52]

The Bishop of Salisbury responded to the statement of Lord Lyndhurst that no scriptural authority could be cited against the bill. The testimony of the blessed Lord on the subject was most distinct and emphatic; the Saviour most clearly prohibited any remarriage. While he permitted separation under particular circumstances, no sanction was given in the New Testament for divorce with the right to remarry. The strongest assertions were given by great authorities in every century of the Christian Church, including St Augustine, that it was not lawful to separate husband and wife that they might remarry. There could be no question that the law of England before the Reformation was in agreement with the rule plainly expounded by Augustine. All the authorities he had consulted made it clear that according to the law of England no divorce was allowed. The bishop thanked God that 'he had hitherto providentially prevented us from altering this law, because the law enshrined the principle that, as we believe there were no limits to the forgiveness of our sins by our heavenly Father, so there was no limit to the forgiveness – let the sin have been ever so grievous, let the adultery have been committed under every possible aggravation – which any Christian man ought to be ready, if circumstances permitted it, to extend to a penitent wife.' He knew that the general opinion was against him, but as a minister of Christ, standing not merely as a peer of Parliament, but as an ambassador of the great head of the Church, he was anxious to testify his solemn conviction that there was no possible offence of which a wife could be guilty that the husband – if he hoped for forgiveness himself – should not be willing as a Christian to place within the limits of forgiveness. There might of course be considerations which might prevent the exercise of such a forgiving Christian spirit, but the law should never allow either party to be placed beyond the limits of the hope of such pardon and reconciliation.

The divorces that had been granted by Acts of Parliament had, he believed, been attended with the worst results, and if they extended them to the poor man, far from giving him a blessing, they would give him that which would poison the happiness of his home. He would not withhold a benefit from the poor, but he would not inflict on them a curse. The laws of the Church did not recognise the dissolubility of marriage, and their Lordships should consider the difficult position in which they would place ministers of religion if they passed the present bill. At present the law of the land and the law of the Church were in harmony on this subject. The bill, however, would place them at variance and in the event of it passing he did not see how ministers of religion could act equally with loyalty to the law of the land and to the law of Jesus. The final point of the bishop was that if they once opened the door, they could not easily close it again. He protested against the bill.[53]

The Bishop of Oxford addressed the House explaining that since the last debate, when he stated that he felt a difficulty in resting his opposition to this bill on the understanding that the word of the blessed Lord distinctly settled the question, he had made a careful study of the matter. The charge of quibbling had been directed against Christian men who endeavoured to give an unpopular interpretation to God's word, without one earthly motive except their single desire to clear their consciences from sin. The quibble was this—Matthew recorded the Lord speaking on the subject of divorce. The Lord at that time was speaking to the Jews on two matters. In this case the Lord was speaking to the Jewish race and he said, 'You have here, through the glosses of the scribes and Pharisees, come to an understanding that you may for every cause give your wife a writing of divorce and put her away.' Then he added, 'but Moses never gave you any such authority; he only permitted you to put away your wife when you found uncleanness in her.' The evangelist who recorded this passage added that afterwards the Lord retired into the house, and that the disciples went and asked him what was the law of the new kingdom on the subject of marriage. 'Now here we were clearly to look for an explanation of the whole matter; and then what did our blessed Lord say? He said that in the new kingdom there could be no such divorce of those whom God had joined as would permit either, in the life of the other, to marry.' The bishop posed the question. 'Was the woman who had committed adultery to be entitled, by reason of her sin, to greater privilege than those extended to other women—was the woman who had broken the *vinculum* by her adultery to be free to marry again, while the woman who had been unjustly put away was not to marry again?' He then quoted St Augustine upon this point, 'It is lawful, therefore, for a man to dismiss his wife for the cause of fornication, but the *vinculum* of the marriage lasts on, and it is not lawful for him to marry.'

Lord Lyndhurst (who had told the House that St Augustine supported the view that adultery permitted divorce and remarriage) interjected that in the early part of his works St Augustine did not say so, though towards the close of his works he might have. The bishop responded that his friend

Lord Lyndhurst had fallen into considerable error on this point, as any great man might when he did not thoroughly understand his subject. He went on that St Augustine laid down the indissolubility of marriage in every part of his writings and especially in his commentary upon the fifth chapter of St Matthew. It must be borne in mind that St Augustine did not rest this question upon any notion of sacramental evidence. Lord Lyndhurst responded that he had said that St Augustine holds distinctly that adultery, whether committed by a man or woman, is a justifiable cause of divorce. He affirmed that St Augustine was not sure whether the parties should have the right to remarry. The Bishop of Oxford remarked that the whole question depended upon the right of the parties to marry again. All he desired to press upon their lordships was that his most learned friend had not shown from St Augustine that adultery was a justifiable ground for remarriage.

The Bishop of Oxford reminded their Lordships that 'through God's blessing they had inherited a nation and society in which, with all its many faults, it could truly be said that there was no nation in Europe in which family purity was so much prized as among the mass of the people of these islands'. That was the case under the existing law, and he asked whether it was the course of wise and prudent men to rashly change a system in order to introduce one, the consequence of which they could not entirely foresee? The history of every nation which had pursued that course showed that increased facility produced increased occasion for divorces, while at the same time morals were lowered, purity sullied and the honour of married life invaded. The Church taught the people that marriage was indissoluble except by death; but they were now to be told that they might take one another, not for better or worse, but until the sin of one might enable him or her to put the other away and marry again. It might be long before the people would take advantage of the new law, for such changes seldom appeared in their full effects at once; but slowly, step by step, it might change the whole moral aspect of the nation and deteriorate the temper of the people.

The bishop said he must, of course, vote against the second reading, which he believed justified and legalised the marriage of the divorced woman, undeniably forbidden by our Lord. This should settle the question for those who received the word of revelation. What hope would there be for the prosperity of the country if the law of Christian Britain was made at variance with the law of Christ?[54]

The bishop, of course, was speaking prophetically about the likely long-term effects of a bill that he believed was against divine law. It is remarkable that he was able to foresee the consequences from where he stood in history. From his knowledge of the Scriptures, and with the gift of spiritual insight, he was able to warn that slowly, step by step the moral condition of the nation would change, and that the honour of marriage would be invaded.

The Bishop of London (Archibald Tait) supported the bill, because the Sermon on the Mount contained an assertion which every Protestant church regarded as decisive upon the question of divorce. General propositions were seldom unqualified. If they were told that there should be no separation between husband and wife, there might still be cases of such foul iniquity as to effect the utter disruption of the marriage tie. 'It was said that the law of the Church of England was that marriage was indissoluble. Of course there was no provision for the dissolution of marriage, but he was not aware of any authority for this broad statement.' He maintained that the universal opinion of Protestant churches was that in some grave cases marriages might be dissolved, and in those cases he thought it better that the dissolution should be pronounced by such a court as was proposed by the bill. The present system was likely to do far more harm than good, and an opportunity now opened of satisfactorily setting the question upon an intelligible and religious basis. He hoped the Lordships would read the bill a second time.[55]

The Duke of Argyll claimed a decided majority of the Bench of Bishops was in favour of the bill. He asked the House to do two things—first, to grant the remedy of divorce on the ground permitted by the Scriptures, and, second, not to extend the ground of divorce beyond that clear point.[56] The Bishop of Lincoln (John Jackson) said nearly all their lordships agreed that our Lord's words did allow a separation on the ground of adultery, but did not permit the remarriage of the woman put away from her husband with the adulterer.[57]

After this lengthy debate the House divided and the contents won the division by 47 votes to 18. Nine bishops voted for the bill: The Archbishop of Canterbury, the Bishops of London, Winchester (Charles Sumner), Bangor (Christopher Bethell), Bath and Wells (Robert Eden), Carlisle (Henry Villiers), Kilmore (Marcus Beresford), Llandaff (Alfred Ollivant), Ripon (Robert Bickersteth), St Asaph (Thomas Short). The five against were; the Bishops of Chichester (Ashurst Gilbert), Durham (Charles Longley), Lincoln (John Jackson), Oxford and Salisbury.

Third reading: June 1857

During the third reading of the bill, the Earl of Malmesbury said that every word he had heard in relation to the bill only tended to prove to him that the difficulty of legislation upon divorce was much greater than he had at first believed. All that he had seen and heard convinced him that they were very far from finding a solution to the difficulty in the measure before the House.[58]

The Earl of Wicklow said that the arguments urged against the bill were infinitely stronger than the single one in favour, namely of giving the poor man the same facility for divorce as the rich man. The moment the bill stepped out of the preamble it was opposed to the existing law of the land

and to the law of God. By both of these marriage was indissoluble, and this bill, if passed into law, would be the first great inroad on that principle. If this bill was passed and the principle of the indissolubility of marriage was once broken through, Parliament would be asked before long to go further in the same direction.[59]

The Bishop of Oxford offered a last protest to the passing of the measure. He believed it was contrary to the law of God, contrary to the law of the Church of England, and fruitful in future crime and misery to the people of England. He believed that in passing the bill they were dealing a more fatal blow to family purity than was possible by any other act. He could not let the bill pass without dividing the House in order that the names of those who opposed it to its last stage might stand on record to posterity.

It was passed by a majority of 46 to 25. Significantly, seven bishops now voted against the third reading and five in favour.[60] The Bishops of Exeter, Llandaff, Rochester, Chichester, Durham, Oxford and Salisbury voted against the bill.

PROTESTS AGAINST THE ACT

Following the passage of the bill through the House of Lords a number of protests were issued. The Bishop of Exeter protested because the bill authorised the intermarriage of the adulterous parties, but did not relieve the clergy from the legal obligation of celebrating marriage in such cases with the office of the church. The bishop noted that adultery was constantly spoken of in Scripture as symbolising apostasy from the Church, and as the violation of the marriage union. 'In contempt of this sacred truth the bill not only sanctions the marriage of parties whose ability to marry is founded altogether on their being adulterers, but it also compels the clergy to marry them in profanation of the most sacred words of Scripture, and with perversion of the most solemn truths of the gospel.'[61]

Lords Lyndhurst and Hutchinson protested because the bill did not permit divorce for wilful desertion. They argued that wilful desertion violated the purpose for which marriage was instituted. 'Even in the most ordinary contract, the breach of it on the one side puts an end to the obligation on the other, and we see no reason why a different rule should be applied to the contract of marriage, and more especially in a case destructive of the entire object of the union.' Moreover, they claimed that desertion was justified from Scripture by the highest ecclesiastical authority. 'It is well known that at the Reformation the subject was anxiously and carefully considered by prelates and divines eminent for learning and piety, and that they came to the conclusion that wilful desertion was a scriptural ground for divorce. We find the names of Archbishop Cranmer, of the Bishops of London, Winchester, Ely, Exeter and others; of Latimer, Parker and of Peter Martyr, Martin Bucer, Beza, Luther, Melancthon, Calvin among those who maintained this opinion, and which was adopted by the whole body of Protestants on the continent of Europe. Accordingly it has been the acknowledged doctrine of all their churches to the present day.'[62]

The Bishops of Oxford and Salisbury, together with Lord Nelson and Lord Redesdale, and with qualifications, the Duke of Leeds and Lord Dungannon, issued a protest because, in opposition to the Word of God, embodied in the law of the Church, the bill sanctioned the remarriage of a divorced husband or wife during the lifetime of the divorced wife or husband. 'Because, in direct contradiction to the plain teaching of our Saviour Christ, the divorced adulteress is permitted to remarry during the lifetime of her husband.' They saw the Court of Divorce provided by the bill as being accessible only to the rich. The effect of this legislation 'will almost inevitably lead to committing the decision of causes involving the sentence of divorce *a vinculo matrimonii* to many and inferior local courts, and so to the risk of widespread collusive adultery'. They objected because the 'permission of inter-marriage, as granted in the bill to the parties through whose adultery the divorce has been caused, tends to produce a dissolution of manners throughout that large class of society in which no conventional law severely punishes the divorced woman'.

They believed that the whole tendency of the bill was to dissolve the sanctity and endanger the purity of God's great institution of family life throughout this land. Finally they protested 'because it will lead to the clergy of the Church of England being required to pronounce the blessing of Almighty God on unions condemned by their Church and repugnant, as many of them believe, to the direct letter of Holy Writ, and to employ at unions founded on dissolved marriages, from the marriage service of the Church of England, language which is in its plain sense inconsistent with the dissolubility of marriage'.[63]

Comment

The debate of 1857 in the House of Lords was a watershed in that the battle lines over divorce were clearly drawn. On the one side of the controversy were those who understood the crucial importance of the teaching of the indissolubility of marriage and were therefore opposed to divorce with the right of remarriage. They argued that once this absolute principle was breached, it would be impossible to hold the position that adultery was the only ground for divorce. Breach the principle of indissolubility and the trickle of divorces permitted for adultery would slowly but inevitably become a flood as other grounds were discovered. On the other side were those who wished to introduce divorce with the right of remarriage. They were divided into those who supported the Protestant doctrine of divorce and were content with divorce on grounds of adultery alone, and those who saw the bill as simply the first step in an ongoing campaign to liberalise the divorce laws in England.

The debate is important for it introduced the idea of divorce into the national consciousness and demonstrated a clear difference of opinion among the bishops. At this crucial time they were unable to speak with a united voice, some arguing that marriage was indissoluble and others, accepting the Protestant doctrine of divorce, arguing that marriage was permitted for adultery. While a majority of the bishops in the House of Lords appeared to support the Divorce Act, there is little doubt that this view was not held by the majority of the clergy, and certainly not by the majority of the people. In other words, the bishops were speaking for themselves, and their ideas were not in tune with the wishes of the vast majority of the Church. A petition against the Act signed by nine thousand clergy suggested that the dominant view in the Church was that marriage was indissoluble, and many felt that the bishops had not faithfully represented the position of the Church of England.

Chapter 5

Yes, it is a Protestant doctrine!

House of Commons debate of 1857 and its aftermath

The debate moved to the House of Commons during a warm summer in late July, at the same time as many members were eager to leave London for the holiday season. The government, however, was determined to use its large majority to force the bill through during the current session of Parliament, while those opposed to the legislation felt that there was insufficient time for the debate. Led by William Gladstone a group of Christian parliamentarians did all they could to oppose the passage of the bill. After a determined attempt to delay the debate until a future session, it took place in late July and August, when many were away on summer holidays.

DEBATE IN THE HOUSE OF COMMONS: JULY AND AUGUST 1857

Presenting the bill to the House the Attorney General (Sir Richard Bethell) claimed that the main purpose was simply to alter the procedures for the legal process of divorce. He was happy to say that concern about the bill was unfounded, and he wished to make it plain that the bill made no material alteration in the existing law of divorce. The bill involved only long existing rules and long established principles, and it was intended to change the way in which the law was administered. He claimed that the law of England for the last two hundred years was that marriage was dissoluble and had permitted divorce for adultery. That, after all, is what over three hundred private Acts of Parliament had achieved. He said that Christ had re-established the original solemnity of the marriage institution and quoted from Matthew's gospel chapter 19:4–6 regarding the meaning of marriage. He argued, 'If man and wife were thus mystically incorporated, what was it that severed and destroyed the continuance of that mysterious union? Was it not adultery? If such were the sacred character of the marriage vow did not those words of Christ bring with them this conclusion, that that which severed the mysterious bond was the most effectual means according to the letter and spirit of Scripture, of dissolving marriage. This was written in Scripture, and it was written in the heart, for every human being capable of appreciating the sanctity of marriage must feel that when one party to the marriage was guilty of that sin which struck the very soul of the contract, the holy character of the union could never again be restored.' He explained that the bill would permit the adulterer and adulteress to be lawfully married following divorce. The Attorney General based his vindication of the main principle of the bill upon two grounds. First, that the human dissolubility of marriage had been received as the law of the Church and of the state ever since the Reformation; and, second, that it was rightly the law of the Church and of the state, inasmuch as it was strictly in conformity with the express declaration of Holy Writ.[1]

Sir William Heathcote pointed out that the Attorney General attempted to establish two principles which were entirely contradictory and destructive of each other. At one time he treated marriage as generally dissoluble, subject only to the regulations and restrictions of human legislation; at another time he treated it as indissoluble, subject to certain exceptions imposed, not by human legislation, but by Holy Scripture. Sir William explained that for the first 300 years of the Christian era there never was the smallest doubt in the whole Christian world in giving an interpretation of the exception clause in Matthew's gospel opposite to that which the House was now told to accept. If the so-called exception had the tendency of allowing a divorced person to marry again it would have occurred to the Christians of that period. But such a course was never suggested until the Christian Church had entered into an intimate relationship with the corrupt Roman Empire, which introduced pagan laxity. After a time, however, the Church righted itself entirely, and had continued from that day to this without any doubt upon the subject. Despite what the Attorney General had said, Sir Heathcote maintained that both the law and the Church of England had rejected the course proposed by this bill.

If the bill passed into law, persons would be as freed from the marriage bond as if it had been dissolved by death, and they would be entitled to call upon any clergyman of the Church of England under pains and penalties to marry them according to the rites of the Church. It was well known that the great majority of the clergy believed that it would be their duty to refuse to give the sanction of a religious service to the remarriage of a divorced person, and although the Attorney General knew that, and that remarriages might be performed at a registrar's office, he had not inserted any protection in the bill to save those clergymen from the pains and penalties to which they might be subjected for refusing to marry a divorced person. It was impossible that this measure could lead to a permanent settlement of the law of marriage, either in respect of the court which it proposed to institute, or in respect of the limits which it prescribed for divorce. 'Once fairly embarked in its dangerous course, we must advance step by step until we found ourselves in the deplorable situation in which the Prussians stood at the moment – a position from which the best men were now recoiling with horror, and in which they were vainly endeavouring to obtain the alteration of a law that reduced marriage to the level of the most ordinary contract, capable of being put to an end without difficulty by the consent of the parties.'

In his opinion the introduction of the bill was an indication of a major national crisis. The sanctity of the family home, the purity of the woman and her equal position in the social scale were now at stake. He asked them to look around before taking a step which once taken would be impossible to retrace. At the very moment in which they were carrying on this discussion the flame had burst forth and the plague begun to show itself. He knew that at this very time a body of dissolute and depraved men was already exulting over the licence that they expected to receive at the hands of the Legislature.[2]

Mr Henry Drummond rose and pointed out that when the Attorney General quoted from the Scriptures he made a very remarkable omission, for he left out the words, 'Therefore what God had joined together man must not put asunder.' That was the original idea of marriage. That was God's law, God's way of regarding the marriage relationship. He pointed out that from the first chapter of Genesis to the last chapter of Malachi, marriage was assumed to be indissoluble. The whole groundwork of the expostulations of the prophets to the rebellious nation rested on this foundation. The day of the choosing of Israel to be a separate people from the rest of mankind was called the day of their espousals. The principle recurred continually throughout the prophets: 'Only return to me, and you shall be again as the one betrothed in your youth, for I hate putting away; and I will be a husband to you again.'

He said a man could not be judged as a bachelor having once been married. 'You are judged and are responsible for the care of her to whom you have been united. The oath taken in marriage is the most solemn that can be taken. Do you think, after taking such an oath, whereby you swear to protect a woman until death does you part, that you can qualify that oath by saying, "until the House of Lords shall us part" or "until an Act of Parliament shall us part?"' Mr Drummond confirmed that the doctrine of divorce was a Protestant doctrine, and issued this challenge, 'Yes, it is a Protestant doctrine! Do you think that by an Act of Parliament you can do what you like? Everyone in the insolence of absolute authority has thought so… You may, in your pride, decree the dissolution of marriage, but woe to those who put confidence in your decision and reject the universal testimony of Scripture from the first chapter in Genesis down to the last in Revelation.'[3]

Mr Frederick Lygon said that experience taught that increased facilities of divorce only increased the tendency to divorce, and the House would do well not to break hastily, in a few weeks, the most precious link in the chain of social order that bound society together. If the House weakened the sacredness of the marriage tie by admitting its dissolubility in cases of adultery, they could not stop there, but must allow divorce for the most trivial of reasons. That was the case in Prussia, and if the same assertion could not be made of America it was because the facility of divorce had not prevailed there long enough to develop its natural tendency. He ended his speech by quoting the words of Edmund Burke, 'the Christian religion by rendering the relation of marriage indissoluble has done more towards the peace, happiness, settlement, and civilisation of the world than by any other part in the whole scheme of divine wisdom'.[4]

Mr Christopher Puller was concerned about the obligation that the bill placed on the clergymen to remarry the guilty parties. He thought when some seven thousand clergymen had signed a declaration that it would be a violation of their consciences to have to pronounce the benediction of the Church on parties guilty of adultery, it was no answer to them to say that for 200 years past there had been annually two or three divorces passed by Parliament. To him a key question was whether the act of adultery did not altogether do away with the one flesh union spoken of in Scripture. Was the reality not that adultery put asunder a husband and wife? Was it the duty of a Christian man to cleave to an adulteress? Yet he felt bound to admit that considerable alarm prevailed throughout the country in consequence of a feeling that the operation of the bill before the House would be to impair the sanctity of the marriage vow. He, however, did not share in that alarm.[5]

Mr Loftus Wigram objected to the way the bill, which dealt with a question that awakened the liveliest emotion in every domestic circle, was being rushed through Parliament. It should be given more time, for the measure before Parliament would have an enormous influence on the characters and prospects of the rising generation.[6] Mr John Hatchell warned that increasing the facilities of divorce would produce, in the course of time, an enormous increase in the number of divorces. If they once passed this law they could never go back, but must continue in the same course, however terrible the evils that would flow from it. If it were once found that marriages could be dissolved with ease, numbers of persons would enter into the state of matrimony with the detestable intention of committing a crime for the purpose of dissolving it. He called upon the House to pause before they passed a bill which was exceeding likely to prove disastrous to the country.[7]

Mr George Bowyer said the bill came before the House with the pretence of justice and fair play. It was pretended that it was a poor man's bill. But if this were a poor man's bill, it was remarkable that petitions signed by as many as 90 thousand persons should be presented against the bill, and none in favour of it. The key question was whether the divine law allowed any divorce; that is, whether the divine law allowed the bond of marriage to be so broken that the parties might marry other persons. A large body of the English clergy declared that divorce with the right to remarry was contrary to the Christian religion. He said they were treating the Church very badly, in that they were not willing to give the Church time to consider this great question. It was a theological question and yet they were asked to deal with it as if it were mere ordinary legislation based on temporal principles. It was a bill involving the very foundation of society and the fundamental principles of the divine law. If they facilitated divorce for adultery it would soon be urged that such divorce be granted even in cases where adultery had not been committed. If they once broke in upon the salutary principle of the common and ecclesiastical law of England, they would not know where to stop. They would give rise to a universal immorality.[8]

Mr Richard Malins objected to the bill because he believed that marriage once entered into should last for the life of the parties. Now it was to be understood in every case where a marriage was solemnised, that a law court might at some future day dissolve that marriage. He looked upon such a proposal with the greatest apprehension. He objected to the bill on the higher ground that it was best for the interest of society that marriage should last for the life of the parties. He quoted the words of Lord Stowell in the first report of the Royal Commission, 'For though in particular cases the repugnance of the law to dissolve the obligations of matrimonial cohabitation may operate with great severity upon individuals, yet it must be carefully remembered that the general happiness of the married life is secured by its indissolubility.'

Mr Malins continued, 'The question is whether, by taking an extended view of human society, it is not for the happiness of the greater number that marriage should be regarded as indissoluble. Suppose a woman prefers another man to her husband, if there were no possibility of divorce, she would know that by giving way to that attachment she would condemn herself to disgrace and misery for the rest of her life. But by this bill, and even under the present system, the prospect of divorce is open to her and she knows that by going through a certain process she might become the wife of the man whom she prefers to her husband.' He said the government had certainly no reason to be satisfied with the course which the debate had taken for out of the seven honourable members who had preceded him six had opposed the bill, and the seventh had only spoken of it with faint praise.[9]

Lord John Manners said that the Attorney General based his vindication of the main principle of the bill upon two grounds. First, he said that the human dissolubility of marriage had been received as the law of the Church and of the state ever since the Reformation; and, secondly, he said that it was rightly the law of the Church and of the state, inasmuch as it was strictly in conformity with the express declaration of Holy Writ. He claimed that the Attorney General's argument that divorces by private Acts of Parliament had the force of law was totally and entirely erroneous. He then stated his deliberate opinion that the bill violated both Scripture and the settled law of the land. If it only proposed to allow the remarriage of the innocent sufferer it ought to be supported by the most irrefutable scriptural arguments; but when it gave to guilty persons the privilege of enjoying through life the fruits of their sin it was not only opposed to the best interpretations of the Word of God, but struck a blow at the foundation of all human law. The inevitable effect of the bill was to smooth the path before the adulterer's feet, and to teach the disappointed wife that if she had only the bad courage to sin blindly and boldly, to violate at once the command of God and her own solemn vows, years of worldly happiness and, if they might judge from the experience of other countries, years of worldly respectability would yet be in store for her under the same solemn sanction and with the same nuptial benediction as were at present reserved for the innocent and the pure. He opposed the bill because of the inevitable effect which the loosening of the marriage tie must have upon the masses.

He had heard with regret, bordering on astonishment, the Attorney General's declaration that under no circumstances would the government consent to relieve the clergy from the monstrous oppression to which the bill proposed to subject them. The Attorney General regarded it of the essence of the bill that the clergy should not escape from its nefarious operation. Agitating clergymen must be brought to know that they, like other men, were subject to the common law. The clergy had, however, distinctly stated in their petitions their belief that the bill was opposed to the Word of God and to the social and domestic happiness and welfare of the people. They had good reason to believe that their views and claims were not listened to in the House with the respect to which they thought they were entitled. They prayed that if the bill should become law they might be exempted from all penalties for not obeying a law clearly inconsistent with the spirit and letter of the vows which they had taken and the dictates of their consciences. The question was merely whether as conscientious, learned, pious, laborious a body of men as had ever preached the glad tidings of the gospel, should be bound to give way to the lust of adulterers and the tyranny of Parliament. Under any circumstances he should oppose this bill which, if passed, would lead to the most momentous and fatal consequences. So spoke Lord Manners on the 30 July 1857 in the House of Commons.[10]

Mr William Gladstone, the future Prime Minister and greatest politician of Victorian England, now arose to address the House. He pointed out that after the speech of the Attorney General introducing the bill, with a single exception, eight gentlemen in succession – a circumstance unparalleled in his experience – spoke on the same side of the question. Mr Gladstone mentioned letters he had received on the subject, one man writing that the labouring classes are against the bill to a man, and also a large proportion of the middle classes. Another wrote that the bill, as it came down from the Lords, was thoroughly hateful in the eyes of the great mass of middle classes and the poor, eminently so amongst all Church people. Yet another poor man wrote that instead of the marriage vow running 'until death us do part' it should be 'until we do quarrel'. Mr Gladstone continued, 'The feeling of the country may be, as I believe from the very imperfect evidence which we have been allowed to collect, against this measure; but if the bill be passed, although an overwhelming majority of Christian husbands and wives may be against it, you will have constituted an interest in behalf of certain parties who will become, as it were, an entire sect in favour of such laws, both for their maintenance and for their extension... I conceive it to be one of the most degrading doctrines that can be propounded to civilised men—namely, that the legislature has power to absolve a man from spiritual vows taken before God.'

Mr Gladstone said that the Attorney General had invited them to accept his interpretation in preference to that of the 17 thousand clergymen of the kingdom. The Attorney General said that by the fact of adultery the bond of marriage is broken. 'Now is that the sense of Scripture? He wishes us to accept his arbitrary, capricious, self-willed construction of Holy Scripture and to consent to his bill founded thereon, whereby 19 out of every 20 of the adulterers in the land will be protected and saved harmless.'

Reviewing the history of Christendom, Gladstone made the point that for the first three centuries after Christ they found no trace of divorce for remarriage. In the West, the law of the Church, after some struggles, remained unbroken and it was triumphantly established that a Christian marriage, once validly contracted, ought not to be dissolved. 'All Englishmen and all Englishwomen – all Irishmen and all Irishwomen – and in Ireland the observance of the marriage vow is still more exemplary than in this country – know that on entering into the marriage state they contract an indissoluble tie... The union has been absolute and total. The whole course of desire, thought, purpose, will and habit has adapted itself to the entireness of that union. The marriage state is a total and absolute change. You pass over a gulf which you know you cannot repass; you enter upon a new state, and you adopt all its obligations; but you are now going to make that gulf which has hitherto been impassable, passable; you are going to say to the woman who has sinned, although she may have sinned under the

89

strongest temptation, 'Your sins shall be unpardoned; you shall be divorced, and nothing shall reconcile you to the man from whom you have been divorced. You may marry again, and you may offend again; your sin shall be unpardonable by the person you have offended, though with his whole heart and soul he may be desirous to forgive you.'

'This indissolubility of English marriage is an idea which has never been shaken in the mind of England (cheers). At no time have the middle and lower classes of the English people known what it was to have marriage dissoluble. Take care, then, how you damage the character of your country-men. You know how apt the English nature is to escape from restraint and control: but here is a great feeling of restraint observed among your population, and which has prevailed ever since England was England, that the marriage tie is indissoluble. And is there any adequate reason for giving a shake to this notion? Are you quite sure, when you have shaken the feelings of the people on this vital point, that they will settle down again upon a basis defined for them by my learned friend the Attorney General by an Act of Parliament? As I have said, you are bringing in a system entirely novel – not novel, perhaps, as regards that small class of persons who have from time to time been divorced through the intervention of private Acts of Parliament – but perfectly novel as regards the great bulk of the community, and the great precedents of human history. No single age, or country, or period has ever known a low of divorce like this. None have ever gone so far, without going further... It is most material that we should bear in mind the arbitrary and novel character of this plan, with respect to which I regret that I cannot regard it in any other light except one – namely, as the first instalment of change (cheers) – the first stage on a road of which we know nothing, except that it is different from that of our forefathers, and that it is a road which leads from the point to which Christianity has brought us and carries us back towards the state in which Christianity found the heathenism of man (cheers).' 'If I have spoken warmly on the subject, it is because it has offended my own conscientious feelings. I resist this measure because I believe it to be a retrograde step, and pregnant with the most dangerous consequences to our social interests, in that it tends to bring us back again towards a state of laxity which Christianity does not recognise. I resist this measure because I believe it is not desired by the people of this country (cheers). I admit that the indications we have before us of the manner in which the bill is regarded out of doors are imperfect, but they all go to prove that the feeling of the country is hostile towards it. I object because it contains a proposal harsh and unjust towards the ministers of religion, but still more because the assumption of this function by Parliament involves an insult to what is far higher than the ministers of religion—namely to religion itself. Lastly, I must be permitted to renew the objection that it is introduced at a time when it is impossible to bring the general mind of the country and the House to an adequate consideration of its magnitude and importance; and, although I may be utterly powerless in arresting its progress, at least I am determined, so far as it depends on me, that I will be responsible for no part of the consequences that may result from a measure fraught, as I believe it to be, with danger to the highest interests of the people (loud and prolonged cheers).'[11]

Sir George Grey (Secretary for the Home Department) reminded the House that Mr Gladstone had been a member of the government of 1854, which had introduced a similar bill to Parliament. He heard none of the conscientious scruples from Mr Gladstone at the time. In reply to this accusation Gladstone pointed out that it was not a bill for which he was responsible and that at that time he had not given the subject the attention that it deserved due to the pressure of his position. With regard to remarriage and the clergy, Sir George Grey's main line of argument was that those who opposed the bill were inconsistent in their position in that they had not opposed the private Acts of Parliament which dissolved marriage for adultery. 'Assuming, of course, that there is no scriptural prohibition binding on our consciences, I think it idle to discuss whether marriage is dissoluble or not. We have the authority of the whole human race in opposition to this alleged indissolubility of marriage.' His main objection to the bill was that it did not go far enough in making divorce available to those suffering from deficiency of means. It may be true that when the bill is passed into law clergymen may be called upon more frequently than at present to pronounce the blessing of the Church upon the marriage of persons who have been divorced; but that was only a question of degree—not of principle.[12]

The Solicitor General (Sir Henry Keating) said that the weight of authority was in favour of the marriage tie being dissoluble in certain cases. He admitted that the bill did not go as far or bring divorce as low as it might. However it was easier to extend the provisions of such a measure than to abridge them. With regard to the clergy they had no more right to complain of this bill than of the system which had existed for the last one hundred and fifty years.[13]

Mr Spencer Walpole spoke as one of the commissioners. He made the point that there was only one cause of divorce – and it ought to go from the one end of the country to the other that there was but one ground for divorce – and that was adultery. The consequence of the divorce was, since the marriage vow was broken by that act, that the tie which held the parties together was gone and, both by the bill and by the law, the parties were remitted to their single state, and being remitted to the single state they were both allowed to marry again. Marriage was dissoluble for the one great offence, the sin of adultery, and that when that happened there was nothing in Scripture prohibiting recourse to second nuptials. In his view Scripture was silent on the question of remarriage, and, being so silent, it was in the power of every state to deal with the subject in the way most conducive to public morals and most beneficial to the community at large. 'There being no scriptural prohibition of divorce on the ground of adultery, but, on the contrary, an allowance of it, and there being no prohibition of the remarriage of parties so divorced, the social question immediately arises—ought the state to allow or to prohibit these remarriages?

'I believe that Scripture allows divorce both to the man and the woman on the ground of adultery; but, examining the question socially, I find a broad distinction between the consequences of this sin as committed by the husband or the wife. On the one hand, the adultery of the wife necessarily breaks asunder all family ties, and may introduce into the family circle a spurious offspring. On the other hand, the adultery of the husband has no such consequences, and for these reasons I doubt whether we ought to allow the woman to obtain divorce equally with the man.' He explained that if adultery committed by the man were to be a ground of divorce on the application of the woman, it would probably encourage collusion where the parties mutually desire a separation, and in fact, would enable them to obtain divorces almost at their pleasure. 'I fear there are many men who would not scruple to adopt this method of ridding themselves from the shackles which bind them to one whom they have ceased to care for. Hence by collusion their object might be obtained.' He accepted the bill because he believed 'it would tend to uphold the sacredness of the marriage tie, to discourage the inducements to sin… and preserve that blessed security and peace which now constitute – as God grant they may ever constitute – the charm, the happiness, and the unspeakable blessing which now surrounds an English home.'[14] Mr Walpole was, in effect, defending the Protestant doctrine of divorce, except that he wanted the doctrine to be applied differentially between men and women.

In response Mr Joseph Napier said that the cardinal blemish was the provision for the remarriage of the adulterer and adulteress. The bill required them to make such unions not only legal but Christian marriages. This was not only changing the law of the land, but was going in the very teeth of the divine law. He asked Mr Walpole whether his mind was so clear of all doubt that he could give his sanction to the principle involved in the bill, that if a woman married her adulterer during the life of her husband, the guilty parties were as fully married as if the first marriage had been dissolved by death? If the bill were adopted a clergyman who had married a woman, and made during the ceremony the declaration contained in one of the prayers in the office for the solemnisation of matrimony, that it should never be lawful to put asunder those who matrimony had made one, may, after that woman had committed adultery and been divorced, be called upon to marry her again, and to repeat the solemn declaration. In his opinion, the clergyman would be the instrument of prostituting the holy service of the Church by converting an adulteress into a bride.[15]

The Attorney General responded that there were many instances of adultery followed by marriage in the Scriptures. There was certainly a remarkable one of adultery and murder combined (King David committed adultery with Bathsheba) followed by the remarriage of the parties. He then taunted Gladstone by reminding the House that Gladstone had been a member of the Cabinet that had introduced a bill to Parliament in 1854. 'Was not the duty of a Cabinet Minister plainly this, to be no party to any measure that was opposed to religious obligations, the duties of morality, or the interests of the Church of England?' He said that the difficult question of the clergy could be dealt with in committee, but he saw no reason why one particular class should be exempted from the obligations which that law involved.[16] The second reading of the bill was passed with a majority of 208 ayes and 97 noes.

In the first week of August, Mr Samuel Warren QC addressed the House of Commons in an attempt to delay the bill going into the committee stage. He regarded the bill as one of enormous importance, permanently affecting the social and moral welfare on the country. 'Why such a measure should be thus relentlessly thrust through the legislature, with such heedless haste, at this period of the session, when we are exhausted – when everybody is sighing to be somewhere else than here – I cannot comprehend… And yet the government persists, in spite of protests, in going on, under such unfavourable auspices, with a bill of greater real importance than will perhaps be before Parliament in our time—one universally and permanently affecting the national interests for good or for evil, but for evil, as I verily believe.' He then quoted many authorities to show that the law of England was that marriage was indissoluble. 'Well, sir, I contend that I have established by irrefutable authority – on testimony of eminent practical statesmen, of great judges, of distinguished moralists and divines – that the law of England has always regarded marriage as indissoluble, and has done this in accordance with the teaching of Christian morality. I say that it is a doctrine of incalculable importance for the highest interests of society, that marriage should be indissoluble, and yet the Attorney General spoke of it with a sort of subdued contempt, as that unreasonable law of the indissolubility of marriage: and he said the law will remain as before, but the mode of getting at it will be divested of existing objections.' Mr Warren then drew the attention of the House to a declaration on the part of the clergy with nine thousand signatures. The declaration read:

We the undersigned clergy of the united Church of England and Ireland, being mindful of the vow made by us at our ordination, that we would 'give faithful diligence always, so to minister the Doctrine, and Sacraments, and Discipline of Christ, as the Lord hath commanded, and as this Church and realm hath received the same' hereby express our earnest desire that facilities, unauthorised by Holy Scripture, and by the law and ritual of the united Church of which we are ministers, may not be given to the dissolution of Holy Matrimony. Remembering, also, that it is declared in the Word of God that marriage with a divorced woman is adulterous, we fervently pray that the clergy of this realm may never be reduced to the painful necessity of withholding the obedience which they must always desire to pay to the law of the land, or else of sinning against their own consciences, and violating the law of God by solemnising such marriages as are condemned as adulterous in his Holy Word.

He argued that the very words of the marriage ceremony would be at variance with the law of the land if the bill became law. The marriage vow contained the words: forsaking all other, keep thee only unto her, so long as ye both shall live. 'Remove this element of indissolubility, and how much of hallowed and hallowing character of matrimony vanishes! Depend upon it, sir, with that attribute of indissolubility are linked inestimable and incalculable blessings; it extinguishes at once and for ever all unholy and vicious hopes and prospects; it makes each party become everything to each other. Sir, the effect of this bill will be to put an end to this state of things – to make the hallowed tie severable on the impulse of guilty caprice and passion – to propose illicit objects for contemplation.' He implored the noble Lord not to hurry it on.[17]

Mr Alexander Beresford-Hope said that at the end of the session, with one half of the House gone out of town and the other wearied and fatigued, members were required to deliberate upon the momentous question whether they should, by a single hasty Act of Parliament, alter the law regulating one of the most important and sacred of social and political contracts which had existed in England for 1,200 years – since Christianity was first spread among the Saxon race – and make marriage legally dissoluble, which for twelve centuries had been indissoluble by the laws of the land. It was true that a few marriages had been for the last century and a half dissolved by a clumsy roundabout expedient. Once the law changed the principle would be asserted that marriages might be dissolved. He pointed out that in the American town, San Francisco, no fewer than 130 divorces had taken place in one year.

He warned that they would be taking the first step – although it might take some time – towards such a state. He believed they might not see the fruits of their legislation for many years to come. The growth of such vicious weeds would become ranker and ranker as fresh generations sprang up, which had not been educated in the belief of 1,200 years, that God's own ordinance of marriage was only to be dissolved by God's own act of death. Only then would be seen the error of this legislation. He noted that marriage chastity was greatly observed in England. However, if the bill were passed an evil spirit would eat into the minds of the people, and their established mode of viewing things would be gradually warped and distorted. Some years in the future 'we should perceive the mischief that had been wrought, when the opinion had become prevalent through the towns and villages of the land, that the solemn vow made before the altar of the Most High – when Christian men and women took each other for better for worse, for richer for poorer, in sickness and in health, till death did them part – meant only that they took each other until they tired of one another's society, till one or other of them seduced or was seduced, and till the magistrate wrote for them the bill of divorce... It might be that the future historian of the decline and fall of the British Empire would trace the first dawning of our decadence to the insidious weakening of those moral ties which had hitherto preserved us earnest in our work, and determined in what we undertook to do.'[18]

Mr Thomas Collins said that a measure more repugnant to the general feeling of the country, more distasteful to the masses of the community had hardly ever been laid upon the table of that House. He protested not only against the principle on which the bill was based, but also against the want of principle it exhibited. If this bill passed they would be compelled to give the sanction of a religious rite to what the clergy regarded as legalised bigamy. But no Act of Parliament could separate a man and his wife. The boasted omnipotence of Parliament was not able to destroy the law of God, or to declare authoritatively what was and what was not constant with the Word of God.[19]

Mr Gladstone responded to the accusation of hypocrisy levelled against him by the Attorney General. He pleaded guilty of having been a consenting party in the year 1854 to the introduction of a bill that involved the principle of the dissolution of marriage for adultery. 'But I told the House myself that it was but recently – that it was only during the present year – that I had been able to make the investigations which led me to form the opinion which I expressed a few nights ago.'[20]

In response to protests from the clergy the bill was amended in the Commons to make provision that 'no clergyman in holy orders to the United Church of England and Ireland shall be compelled to solemnise the marriage of any person whose former marriage may have been dissolved on the ground of his or her adultery'. But the amendment contained a proviso that in the event of the incumbent refusing to solemnise such a marriage, any other minister of the Church of England licensed within the diocese must be allowed to officiate.[21] So a concession was made to the clergy in that they were not compelled to perform the marriage service over persons who had been divorced on grounds of their adultery.[22] But an innocent divorcee had the right to be married in a church of the Church of England, provided the couple could find a minister to perform the marriage service. This amendment was strongly opposed by the Bishop of Salisbury because the teaching of the Church was made to appear to be a mere moral scruple on the part of the clergy. The Bishop of Oxford commented that the clause made no reference to the bishop, and indicated that if he knew of a hired interloper coming to remarry a divorcee he would meet him at the church door with an inhibition and suspend him from office. The Bishop of London supported the amendment because it made a concession to the consciences of the clergy, and because the church belonged to the laity as well as the clergy.[23]

During the third reading of the bill in the House of Commons, Lord John Manners entered a last protest against the principle on which the measure was based. He objected to the manner in which the bill had been forced through Parliament. He also protested against the conduct of business by the noble Lord at the head of the government, Viscount Palmerston. He took leave of the ill-omened, anomalous and inconsistent bill, raising again what he knew was a vain protest.[24]

Viscount Palmerston, the Prime Minister, said that it was not his intention to hurry the bill through Parliament. He referred to the exemption given to clergymen who may object to celebrating the remarriage of persons whose marriage has been dissolved by reason of their own offence. 'I can truly say I never gave a more reluctant consent to anything than I did to the concession made in this matter. I did it solely in deference to the feelings of a large body of clergymen, whose feelings even though wrong, were in my opinion entitled to respect. With regard to the question of the indissolubility of marriage, it was impossible for the government to admit that plea. I deny that there is anything in the teaching of the Church of England to justify the opinion that marriage is indissoluble… It was simply, then, on the ground of their conscientious objection to marry persons who had been guilty of a great moral offence, that I consented to the concession on behalf of the clergy.'[25]

Comment – A good or bad tree?

And so the controversial debate ended. Support for the bill had come from two distinct groups. First, were those who saw legalisation as the first step in a campaign to bring the freedom of divorce within reach of the ordinary man. In this group were secular humanists and liberals who rejected biblical teaching on marriage, believing that divorce was the remedy for unhappy marriages. They regarded with subdued contempt the doctrine of the indissolubility of marriage, referring to it as a relic from the dark ages. Nevertheless, despite their rejection of the Christian faith many still paid lip service to the Scriptures.

The second group were those who supported the Protestant doctrine of divorce, such as Mr Walpole and a number of the bishops, including the Bishop of London. These men believed that adultery broke the marriage tie. It was wrong, in their minds, to deny those affected by adultery the remedy of divorce provided by Christ, and the right to find happiness in a second marriage. They saw the Divorce Act of 1857 as simply implementing the Protestant doctrine of divorce. Once this law was in place the law of England would be consistent with the teachings of Scripture and that would be the end of the matter. They believed it was possible to legislate for divorce on grounds of adultery without going any further. Society would accept the justice of the new law and only genuine cases of adultery would be granted a divorce. The new divorce law would benefit the innocent party and was for the greater good of society. According to this line of reasoning the Act of 1857 was based on the teachings of Christ, and consistent with the theology of the great reformers. So it was a good tree, planted in the firm ground of biblical truth. They predicted that the bill would produce a harvest of good fruit, helping to maintain the sanctity of marriage and family life in England. The validity of this view needs to be tested against the results that flowed from the Act of 1857.

Because the views of this group were contrary to the orthodox teaching of the Church of England that marriage was an indissoluble bond, there was a serious division in the witness of the Church. A diary entry of the Bishop of Oxford illustrated the depth of feeling aroused by this division; he wrote following the second debate in the House of Lords, in which the Bishop of London supported the bill, 'Sad, the debate last night. The division of the bishops, and especially the Bishop of London's tone pained me deeply. What is to be the end of it but that of a house divided against itself?'[26] This comment appreciated the significance of division within the Church on such a crucial issue, and expressed a sense of foreboding for the consequences for a Church divided against itself on such an important moral issue.

Opposed to the bill were those who believed that marriage was indissoluble and, therefore, divorce with the right to remarry was not permissible. Prominent among those who held this position were the Bishops of Salisbury and Oxford, Lord Redesdale, Lord John Manners, William Gladstone, Samuel Warren, George Bowyer, Richard Malins, Alexander Beresford-Hope and Henry Drummond. They did not believe that the so-called exception clause in Matthew's gospel allowed divorce with the right to remarry for adultery. They warned that the divorce legalisation for adultery was but the thin edge of the wedge; it was only the first instalment in an ongoing campaign to liberalise divorce. With great foresight they saw that this would be only the beginning—it was the first step. Once the principle of the indissolubility of marriage was lost, it was inevitable that the demand for more divorce would grow. As a consequence the marriage tie would be weakened as it became little more than a contract that was dissoluble when one of the parties failed to keep their side of the agreement. They warned of the social and moral consequences for society. It would take a long time before the full effect of the legislation was felt, for the vast majority of the population still believed in the indissolubility of marriage, and were unlikely to make use of the legal provision. The danger, therefore, lay in the future generations that would no longer believe that marriage was indissoluble. As we shall see, their insight proved to be remarkably accurate. After this tremendous struggle, England had embarked on the pathway to divorce. The first and most crucial step had been taken.

The Bishop of Oxford, one of the strongest opponents of divorce legislation, made a cardinal error by basing his initial opposition on the likely social consequences of the legislation, and not on the Scriptures. The proponents of the bill used the fact that he did not initially support the indissolubility of marriage to weaken his position. Later in the debate, having appreciated the importance of this point, the Bishop of Oxford made clear his belief that the Scriptures taught that marriage is indissoluble. And herein lies an important principle. Arguments based on social reasons are always a matter of opinion. And in human debates the majority opinion is likely to hold sway. The Bishop of Oxford's opinion on the social outcome of divorce was only as good as the next man's. The position of the Bishop of Salisbury, who based his opposition almost entirely on the Scriptures, was impregnable and no one was able to counter his arguments.

AFTERMATH OF THE ACT

The Divorce Act, which became law in January 1858, made it legally possible for the first time in Christian England for a civil court to grant a legal divorce with a licence to remarry a third party. In other words, a court now had the power to dissolve marriage absolutely. There was, however, an important distinction in the way a husband and wife could use the law on adultery. While a husband could petition for divorce on grounds of his wife's adultery, a wife could only do so if her husband's adultery was compounded by other marital transgressions – that is, the husband needed to be guilty of what was known as 'aggravated' adultery. The effect of introducing legal divorce was immediate as numbers increased substantially, as shown in **figure 5**, from around 150 per year in the 1860s to around 500 per year at the turn of the century.

Although the Act of 1857 gave little hint of the avalanche that was to come in the next century, there were early signs that caused concern. An American lawyer who observed the working of the new Divorce Court expressed his opinion: 'The Court, daily crowded as it is with anxious litigants of both sexes, presents a scene at once entertaining and alarming. The marvellous rapidity of its proceedings and the facility with which the matrimonial knot is untied – sometimes by the single judge alone, and sometimes by the full Court – form, indeed, a rare contrast to the tediousness and fatiguing deliberation so much complained of by suitors for the like remedy in other countries... Forensic argument there is none; judicial exposition there is none, or scarcely any; so the points affecting the dearest interests of families – the protection of married women, and the custody of children, are peremptorily disposed of in two or three minutes. Hence, the parties are dissatisfied, the practitioners puzzled, and the reporters bewildered... As you have no public officer to check collusion, and as these suits, in the great majority of cases are *ex parte*, it follows that if the plaintiff is to be permitted to keep back material facts affecting his own conduct, the Court is not very likely to hear of them, and must often decide in the dark.'[27]

Lord John Campbell, who was President of the Royal Commission of 1850 and played a prominent role in the parliamentary debates, wrote in January 1859, 'I have been sitting two days in the Divorce Court and like Frankenstein, I am afraid of the monster I have called into existence... Upon an average, I believe there were in England about three divorces a year *a vinculo matrimonii*, and I had no idea that the number would be materially increased if the dissolution were judiciously decreed by a court of justice, instead of being enacted by the legislature. But I understand that there are now three hundred cases of divorce pending before the new Court... there seems some reason to dread that the prophecies of those who opposed the change may be fulfilled by a lamentable multiplication of divorces and by the corruption of public morals.'[28] Sir Cresswell Cresswell, divorce court judge, commented, 'The opposition to the Divorce Act of 1857 was well-founded. I have been

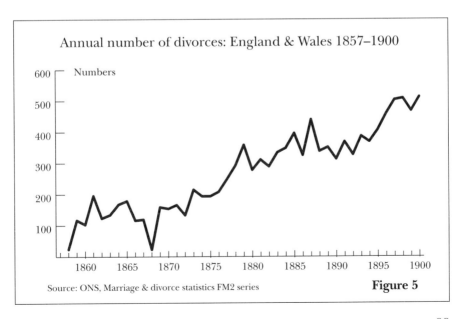

Annual number of divorces: England & Wales 1857–1900

Source: ONS, Marriage & divorce statistics FM2 series

Figure 5

taught the lesson of experience, and have come to the conclusion that it would be better for society to treat marriage as indissoluble, considering it merely as a social question.'[29]

Queen Victoria was not pleased with the consequences of the Act and wrote to her Lord Chancellor asking whether steps could be taken to prevent the proceedings of the Divorce Court receiving publicity. 'These cases, which must necessarily increase when the new law becomes more and more known, fill now almost daily a large portion of the newspapers, and are of so scandalous a character that it makes it almost impossible for a paper to be trusted in the hands of a young lady or boy. None of the worst French novels from which careful parents would try to protect their children can be as bad as what is daily brought and laid upon the breakfast table of every educated family in England, and its effect must be most pernicious to the public morals of the country.' Lord Campbell replied that having been unsuccessful in introducing a parliamentary bill to give effect to the Queen's wishes, he was helpless in preventing the evil.[30] In a sermon preached at Archbishop Tenison's Chapel entitled *Christian Marriage Indissoluble*, James Cowan warned of the future consequences of the Divorce Reform Act, 'Let the state utter with her whole strength and voice that the marriage bond can be easily cancelled and fresh unions formed... this favouring of adulterers to the encouragement they already derive from knowing that the state does not regard their sin as a crime, though God calls it a deadly one, and, not all at once – because English decency will long delay it – but ultimately the Word of God will be made of none effect, married life will lose all its privileges and safeguards and charms; morality will be outraged, evil called good and good evil.'[31]

An article in the *Church Quarterly* of 1896 noted the evil consequences of the Divorce Act. 'Since that Act has been in full operation testimony has come from those who have had knowledge of its working to show its evil results. The strongest language might be used without exaggeration of the iniquities which, in spite of attempted safeguards and the control of able judges, have become associated with the Court which the Act created. If experience is to be our teacher and expediency our aim, we are led again in the direction of affirming the necessity of maintaining the indissolubility of the marriage tie.'[32]

DISSATISFACTION AMONG THE CLERGY

There is no doubt that the Divorce Act was a cause of real unhappiness to the clergy. The Lower House of the Convocation of Canterbury discussed the Act in 1858 and made petitions to the House of Bishops encouraging them to try and obtain an amendment to the law, because the Act had 'filled the minds of your petitioners with the deepest grief and most serious harm'. One of the main causes of unhappiness was that for the first time the law of

England recognised the principle of the dissolubility of Christian marriage. And worst, 'it even permits the marriage of the parties guilty of adultery, during the lifetime of the innocent husband or wife, thus virtually encouraging the commission of crime'. Another petition drew attention to the canon of 1603 which specifically forbade the parties separated by a divorce from remarrying during each other's life. 'So that your petitioners when called upon to remarry even the innocent party during the life of the partner from whom he or she has been divorced, will be compelled to transgress either the law of the Church or the law of the state.'[33] The Lower House implored the Upper House to use their endeavours in Parliament to procure the amendment of the Act, but the bishops did not respond.

In the Upper House of the Convocation of Canterbury, in February 1859, the Bishop of Salisbury expressed the opinion that Parliament, in passing the Divorce Bill, did that which would equally justify them in making a new article of the creed. 'Whatever may be the true interpretation of Scripture, there can be no question as to the teaching of the Church on the subject. It was said that the change would not affect more than some half-dozen cases, but almost 400 marriages have been dissolved, and the clergy may be called upon to marry persons who are already married. Now, I should advise my clergy to run all risks rather than to marry one of these people. The law of the Church of England on this subject was fully recognised by Lord Wensleydale and other eminent lawyers, that marriage is indissoluble; but Parliament has changed that law, and now the law of the state is at variance with the law of the Church. I am extremely glad that the other House has expressed its opinion on this matter.'[34] The Bishop of London, however, regretted the use of expressions which cast aspersions on the legislature of the country. 'If it be said this is a hardship pressing on the conscience of individual clergymen, the reply is, there is nothing to compel them to violate their consciences, because they need not marry divorced people unless they choose to do so. It is said they are obliged to permit these marriages to be celebrated in their churches. No doubt that is so. But then the serious question arises whether the church belongs to the clergymen or to the parish. I think we ought to endeavour to soothe down any irritation which exists, and I regret the strong expressions which have been used on this occasion.' He foresaw great harm being done to the convocation if it took a hostile attitude to Parliament.[35]

Debate in Convocation: 1865

In 1865 the issue was still exercising the convocation. The Lower House passed yet another resolution inviting the House of Bishops to take into early consideration the subject of the Divorce Act, reminding the bishops that they had failed to respond to a number of similar resolutions from the Lower House. In the Upper House the Bishop of Oxford said that few of his fellow bishops would affirm that the present state of the law was satisfactory. Although the dissatisfaction in some minds was greater than in others, he believed it to be universal. Many of those who at the time of the alteration of the law of marriage, and the formation of that unhappy Court of Divorce, had supported the change, had expressed their deep regret at what had resulted from the establishment of that Court. 'They were forewarned that it would seriously affect the moral purity of the country – that it would afford an almost unlimited facility for raising the question of the dissolution of marriage – for making public all the shameful details which day by day when the Court is sitting appear in the papers, shocking every Christian family – and for shaking the sacredness of the marriage contract. All this has been already produced, and consequences are likely to follow from which even the warmest supporters of the Court at its formation would have recoiled, and are now recoiling. That the clergy, who find the law of the Church standing one way and the law of the realm standing another way, should feel aggrieved at the present state of things appears to me to be inevitable.'[36] The Bishop of Oxford proposed a resolution that the House sympathise with those clergymen whose consciences were aggrieved by the present state of the law of marriage.

The Bishop of Lincoln (John Jackson) agreed that all the evils that they anticipated from the Act of Parliament had been realised. They had been told that the number of divorces in a year would probably be seventeen or eighteen, whereas they amounted to hundreds. They had been told that the judge of the Court would have time at his disposal which could be devoted to other purposes, but it was now necessary to appoint another judge. 'We were told that those painful disclosures which had appeared from time to time in the newspapers would disappear. Instead, it has become a matter of grave question whether it is right to allow even the leading newspapers to lie about on one's table. And there is great reason to fear that the unhappy clause which allows the intermarriage of both the guilty parties has proved, as it was naturally expected it would, a very powerful instrument in the hands of the seducer.'[37]

The Bishop of Salisbury gave his final comment on the issue that he cared about so deeply: 'The Lower House express an earnest desire to get some amendment to the present law, and they request that we assist them... I agree with the Bishop of Oxford that the present state of the law is highly unsatisfactory, and undoubtedly that dissatisfaction has in a great measure arisen from the results which have followed the change in the law of marriage. I cannot but believe that the reports of the Divorce Court, with which the papers almost daily teem, are a fruitful source of immorality... I certainly feel myself that I have not the slightest responsibility with regard to any results of this change of the law. I from the first to the last did my utmost, by voting in every division against the alteration of the law, to avert the evil results which

I believe to have occurred, in great measure, from the change in the law. Not that I justified my opposition by any mere forecast of what the results might be; but I rested it on my clear conviction that divorce *a vinculo* is contrary to the law of the Church of God; that, according to the doctrine of the Church of England, marriage is indissoluble, and that this doctrine of the Church of England is justified by the teaching of God's Holy Word. This is my clear conviction, and it was that conviction that led me to vote against the change in the law.'[38]

The Bishop of London defended the 1857 Act. He made a distinction between the law of the Church and its doctrine. Although the law of the Church expressed in her canons had excluded divorce *a vinculo*, it had never been the doctrine of the Church of England that to dissolve a marriage was in every case contrary to the law of God. He was uncertain about the consequences of the Divorce Act. 'There certainly is a great grievance which every person must feel who reads the newspaper reports of these abominable cases, and if there were any means of putting a stop to them I think it would be a great blessing. Many persons think that as there is this festering sore in society it is better that it should be dealt with in the way in which the present Divorce Court deals with it, than that the evil should be hushed up as it was before. On that I express no opinion. It is quite possible that the facility of divorce may have increased this evil in society, but it is of course also quite possible that it may have diminished it, making people more cautious as to how they behave themselves, seeing that the punishment of divorce is now capable of being inflicted on persons whom it could not reach before. It is a difficult thing to express an opinion about.' The bishop had little sympathy for the resolution proposed by the Bishop of Oxford. 'If a man's conscience is hurt by the fact of any of the canons of 1603 are being overridden by the statute law of the land, I am not in a position at present, without legal advice, to say whether that is a grievance in which I sympathise or not.'[39]

The Bishop of Ely (Edward Browne) was not prepared to support the view that all divorce and remarriage was contrary to the law of God, or that the Act had placed the law of the land in opposition to that of the Church. 'I should be very sorry if any expression went from us in this House that the law of the state had been put in antagonism with the law of the Church.' But a still more difficult question perhaps was, 'is the law of God – not the law of the Church, but the law of God, as revealed in Holy Scripture – in any manner contravened by the new legislation? For my own part I do not think it is.' He could not support the resolution proposed by the Bishop of Oxford. 'It might be construed as expressing our feeling that we believe that the law of God distinctly forbids all divorce whatever, or at all events distinctly forbids the remarriage of the parties. Now, as an individual member of this House, I am not prepared to express that opinion.'[40]

The Bishop of Peterborough (Francis Jeune) deeply deplored some of the results of the present state of the law. 'It is a gross and grievous scandal that these cases should be made known over the length and breadth of the land; that they should be made the subject of profit by prurient newspapers, for I am told that the accounts found in the respectable papers are chastened down; but it is grievous that, under colour of law, such obscene publications should be freely circulated. The results to which I have alluded are evil results.'[41]

The Archbishop of Canterbury (Charles Longley) not only lamented the consequences of the Act, but regarded the permission for the remarriage of the guilty party as a violation of the Word of God. 'In comparing the two resolutions, certainly that of the Bishop of Ely appears to me but feebly to express my feelings on the subject of the present law; and I could not be content to let it go forth to the world that I only "lament some of the consequences" of recent legislation, and feel no aversion to the principle of that legislation on one or two very important points. The all important point, however, which is here at issue is the question of the remarriage of the guilty parties; and that is to my mind most contrary to the Word of God. In the course of the debates which took place in 1857, I for one used my most strenuous endeavours to prevent the passing of the new Act.

'I did feel the measure was a violation of my own conscience; and I am not surprised at finding that it is also felt to be a violation of the consciences of the clergy. The resolution of the Bishop of Oxford, therefore, comes more nearly to my own feelings, in declaring that we lament the present state of the law of marriage in this country. My aversion to the law as enacted in the year 1858 depended principally upon my believing it to be a violation of the Word of God; but I also anticipated most fully the grievous results which have since taken place. I think it has produced the evil which is flowing over the country, and is tending to demoralise society more than anything of which I have any recollection... My principal reason is that in the sight of God I believe our law of divorce to be contrary to God's law.'[42]

After a long debate the House of Bishops, with the support of the Archbishop of Canterbury, passed a resolution which lamented the state of the law of marriage in England.

Debate in Convocation in the 1880s

In 1883 the Lower House of Convocation of Canterbury again discussed the issue. Prebendary Brook said the Divorce Acts had acted most injuriously on the spiritual condition of the people, and brought the marriage vow into disregard. He had no doubt these Acts would lower the sanctity of marriage.[43] Canon Hopkins supposed that none of them could help deploring and regretting the anomalies that had arisen from the Divorce Acts. 'The officers of the Court themselves mourned over the necessity which was laid upon them to carry on the work put before them. Day after day miserable, horrible revelations of collusion, and deliberate immorality merely to satisfy carnal lust like brute beasts were made, and the officers of the court were distressed, they felt humiliated by them. The Church ought to give some advice to the people to stand firm on the old Church ground and hold fast to the truth, that those whom God had joined together no man could put asunder, and they should act on that.'[44] The Lower House passed the following resolution:

> That this House deeply regrets the existence of the Divorce Acts and the liberty which they grant for the remarriage of divorced persons, as tending to lower both the public estimate of the indissolubleness of the marriage bond and the tone of public morals.

The second part of the resolution dealt with the embarrassment to the clergy in publishing banns of civilly divorced persons and to admitting those who had contracted a civil remarriage to the Holy Communion.[45]

In February 1885 the Lower House wanted a public statement from the bishops on how the clergy should act with regard to divorce in order to prevent breaches of Church law through ignorance. Canon Lowe said that looking at the present state of morals that prevailed in the country, and seeing the perplexity upon this subject which prevailed in the minds of the laity, 'the Church was brought into very grave difficulties which they could not dispose of by half considered measures, or by gentle appeals to quietness, or by saying, "Peace, peace!" when there was no peace...' Meanwhile, when the country at large, and their fellow churchmen who had grown up in respect for the law of the land, learned that the law of the land allowed divorced persons to marry, and more than that, sanctioned the use of the church for the blessing of such marriages, and as far as possible restrained the bishop from prohibiting the celebration of them, then the puzzled and perplexed laity asked the question, 'Is it unlawful for divorced persons to marry'?[46]

All that was wanted from the bishops was for them to clarify the law of marriage. 'A statement from the bishops as to what was the law of the Church, so far as they understood it, would be a great help to the clergy and laity, and would be very useful in the present emergency. If, after that, persons chose to go against the law they must take their own course. It was proposed to ask the advice of the bishops as to how the clergy should act in the difficulties which might arise from a divergence between the law of the realm and the law of the Church in respect to marriage.'[47]

In response to the unrest among the clergy the bishops set up a committee to examine the issues raised by the Lower House. But the report of the committee, presented to the Upper House in July 1885, remained ambiguous on the question of remarriage, for 'in regard of the question of remarriage, the teaching of Holy Scripture cannot be pronounced to be perfectly clear'. Nevertheless, the House was advised to make the following declaration: 'That in the case where the sin of adultery shall have been fully proved before a competent court, and a decree of divorce shall have been obtained, the innocent party so set free, ought to be advised not to remarry during the lifetime of the guilty party.'[48] However the subject was so sensitive that the president ordered that the report should remain on the table and so it was not discussed and there was no declaration from the bishops on the question of remarriage.

REMARRIAGE OF AN ADULTERER IN CHURCH

The remarriage of a divorced man, guilty of adultery, in St Mark's Church, North Audley Street in London, brought the issue to public notice in 1895. The Lower House was outraged and brought the facts of the case to the attention of the Upper House. There 'was celebrated with the rites of the Church, by licence from the Chancellor of the diocese of London, in the name of the bishop, a marriage in which the bridegroom had been the respondent in an undefended suit in the Divorce Court, and had been divorced from his wife on the ground of adultery.

'The Lower House humbly request their Lordships in the Upper House to take such steps as they think best for preserving the Church from the repetition of so grave a scandal, by which the consciences of Christian people are wounded, the standard of morality in the country is lowered, the sanctity of family life sapped, and the blessing of the Church given to persons intending to live in a state which the Lord of the Church has, directly or implicitly, condemned. This House therefore entreats your Lordships to do whatever can be done to prevent such unions being ever solemnised in church.'[49]

Even the bishops were outraged at this scandal. 'There can be no question at all', said the Bishop of London (Frederick Temple), 'of the very serious mischief that is done by such a scandal as that of the celebration in a church of a marriage between two parties one of whom has been lately guilty of gross acts of adultery, and had been divorced in consequence of his guilt. I do not speak of it as a scandal that there should be a remarriage of divorced persons so that an innocent party is in any way to be prevented from such remarriage. I think that the old rules, which certainly tended in the direction of advising innocent persons not to remarry, were sound and good rules; but I should not be prepared to go so far as to say that such marriages ought to be stopped.

'But the guilty party stands on a totally different footing. At present he is allowed to come into the church in defiance of the incumbent's rights, and there to have his marriage celebrated by any clergyman who is willing to celebrate it, although he has given absolutely no proof whatever of anything like repentance for the wickedness of which he has been guilty... it is monstrous that a person who has been guilty of such an offence as that should be admitted to the Holy Communion, and that without anything whatever being done to remove the scandal that he has brought upon the whole Church by his conduct... I am clear about it that we ought to do our very best to show that the Church, at any rate, will have nothing whatever to do with the marriage of any man or any woman who, having committed so dreadful a crime, comes and asks for the blessing of the Church on the formation of another union.'[50]

The Bishop of Chichester (Richard Durnford) was equally upset. He questioned whether, looking at the course of divorce cases in which the guilt is not always one-sided and in which there is often a very culpable, though obscure, connivance on the part of the party who is pronounced to be innocent, it may be better with regard to divorced persons that no licence should be issued at all in the case of either guilty or innocent parties. 'It is a safer course as the divorced parties have a clear remedy. They can go to the registry and there obtain the sanction of the civil law to their union.'[51]

The Bishop of Salisbury (John Wordsworth) observed that social reformers thought that the Divorce Act would be a kind of regenerating influence in society. But they were wrong. 'We have found that the Divorce Act has not brought the social reform which some people imagined, and that it has not brought happiness, but untold misery, and I believe that the time is now ripe for such a change as is in prospect.'[52]

Comment

The public focus on divorce and remarriage, and the continual pressure for the Church to clarify its position, placed the bishops in an extremely difficult position. There was little doubt that the Lower House, which was predominantly in support of the absolute indissolubility of marriage, spoke for the grass roots of the Church. But the law of the state had made it clear that marriage was dissoluble and that the innocent divorcee had the right to be remarried in church. Herein lay the potential for a major conflict between state and Church, which might go so far as to raise the question of the disestablishment of the Church.

Debate in Convocation: 1897

A committee of the Lower House on the laws of marriage produced a report in 1897 which contained a resolution:

> that in the opinion of this House the law of the Church of England recognises no *divorce a vinculo*, and has never sanctioned the dissolution, save by death, of a marriage duly solemnised and consummated.[53]

Following a debate in which different views were expressed, the resolution was accepted and referred to the Upper House. In response the Upper House produced a report on the laws of marriage which attempted to placate the different constituencies within the Church. 'It ought, in our judgement, to be clearly and strongly impressed upon the clergy as their advisers in matters of discipline and conduct, that the Christian ideal is that of indissoluble marriage; and that the most dutiful and loyal course, even in the case of the innocent party, is to put aside any thought of remarriage after divorce. But if any Christian, conscientiously believing himself or herself to be permitted by our Lord's words to remarry, determines to do so, then endeavour should be made to dissuade such a person from seeking marriage with the rites of the Church, legal provision having been made by civil process; the language of the marriage service is unsuitable for repetition, except in cases where the marriage tie has been dissolved by death, or the marriage proved to have been invalid from the beginning.'[54]

The report received the overwhelming support of the House of Bishops, and clearly represented their thinking. The statement was worded in such a way that it could mean different things to different people. It was an attempt to keep happy those who supported the indissolubility of marriage, without actually saying that marriage was indissoluble. It supported remarriage of the innocent party, but preferably not in church. So both sides of the argument should be satisfied. The indissolubleness of marriage was an ideal, something to strive for, but not an absolute estate. While remarriage of the innocent party was not very nice, the bishops were not prepared to say that it was morally wrong, and therefore left it to the conscience of the individual. In effect the bishops were trying to face both ways at once. They could not take an unequivocal position that remarriage was against the Word of God, because 'the teaching of the Holy Scripture cannot be pronounced perfectly clear'.

CONVOCATION OF YORK REPORT ON DIVORCE

Meanwhile the Convocation of York had set up a committee of the Lower House in 1893 to consider the difficulties that were being created for the clergy by the rising number of divorces. After a thorough examination of the subject, the committee produced a comprehensive report of over a hundred pages which discussed the historical, theological and legal aspects of divorce. The report stated that no member of the committee who took an active part in its work 'now doubts that the law of Christ, which has been for centuries the expressed law of the whole Western Church, and had been unswervingly applied by the Church Courts so long as they had jurisdiction in matrimonial causes—*is one wife at a time, and that wife till death.* There is to be found only one reason for separation; for dissolution of marriage not one.'[55] The report noted that those who concede a right of *divorce a vinculo* (that is, full divorce with the right to remarry), strictly limited to the case of adultery and to the so-called innocent party, 'have never been able to escape the logical conclusion that if remarriage is to be admitted to one party, it can only be so because the original marriage is at an end; and if that marriage be at an end then not one but both are free. But in truth, if divine law be once dismissed, there is no other guide than human passion or supposed expediency.'[56] While the report received strong support in the Lower House of the Convocation, the Upper House expressed no opinion.

Following a complaint that the report contained some inaccuracies, it was revised and the final version received by the Lower House in June 1896. The following resolutions were carried:

> that the marriage law of the English Church is that to which those who are members of it must look, and by which they must abide.
>
> that this law is clearly set forth in the marriage service, namely, that the sanctity of marriage as a Christian obligation consists in the faithful union of one man with one woman until the union is severed by death.
>
> that this law is in accordance with Holy Scripture and has the support of the vast majority of Councils and of Fathers and these the most weighty.
>
> that this law does not permit the marriage of any person separated by divorce so long as the former partner is living.
>
> that it is therefore inconsistent to issue any marriage licence, or to allow banns to be published, or a marriage solemnised with the rites of the Church for any such person.[57]

Of significance was the fourth resolution, which did not make a distinction between the innocent and guilty parties. Because the marriage bond was still intact neither of the parties, innocent or guilty, were permitted remarriage. The debate in the Lower House gave strong support to the resolutions, which were passed unanimously. The Upper House, however, was not impressed and they were not willing to express an opinion on the report, or take any action as a result.

And so as the Church of England moved into the 20th century there was a clear divide on the issue of divorce between the grass roots of the church and the bishops. The predominant view among the ordinary clergy, as expressed by the Lower Houses of the Convocations of Canterbury and York, supported the absolute indissolubility of the marriage union. An article in the *Church Quarterly Review* in 1895, written by the editor Darwell Stone, concluded after a detailed consideration of Church history and an examination of the Scriptures, that 'the existing law of the Church of England, then, as stated in the prayer book in the natural sense of the words of the marriage service, as indicated in the canons of 1603, and as illustrated by the traditional teaching of representative divines, is that the bond of Christian marriage is indissoluble, and that if married persons are separated, even for adultery, neither party may contract a fresh marriage in the lifetime of the other.'[58]

Among the bishops, on the other hand, the majority view was not in favour of the indissolubility of marriage. Most bishops accepted the Protestant doctrine of divorce, believing that there was a distinction between the guilty and innocent parties with regard to divorce and remarriage, many supporting the right of the innocent party to remarry. Darwell Stone highlighted the reluctance of the bishops to take a stand on the issue. 'There are indications that our English bishops are disposed to allow under certain conditions the "marriage" in church of divorced persons and the admission to the Holy Communion of those who after divorce have been "married" in church or before a registrar. We trust that the Providence of God may avert any formal action giving effect to such a tendency. In our judgement it would result in evils of which it is not easy to see the end. We do not think some who are high in office in the Church have fully estimated the distress that is being caused to many churchmen.' Stone reminded his readers that the utterances of the bishops were not the voice of the Church of England. 'But we cannot refrain, even at the risk of seeming presumptuous, from expressing our opinion that our rulers would do well to give not a little thought to the unsettlement of many minds. It is possible for us to know, what perhaps the very dignity of their position makes it difficult for them to adequately realise, that some recent utterances have made sad the hearts of loyal sons of the Church of England, and have played into the hands of those who are wishful to discredit her claims.'[59]

So at the end of the 19th century the bishops were careful to make no statement that could be construed as giving unequivocal support to the indissolubility of marriage. It should not escape our notice that their view conveniently avoided bringing the Church into conflict with the divorce laws of the state. As a consequence of the Act of 1857 divorces were now counted in the hundreds, rather than the few dozen predicted by the proponents of the legislation.

Chapter 6

Discovering more grave matrimonial offences

The Royal Commission of 1912 and the divorce debate
in the first decades of the 20th century

At the turn of the century, despite the increasing numbers, divorce was still a relatively rare occurrence in England. Divorce facilities were only available in the Divorce Court in London, and so to most ordinary English people divorce was something that they only read about in the newspapers. It had little relevance to their daily lives. Within society, however, a number of factors were encouraging a more liberal approach to divorce. The growing mood of secularism meant that divorce and remarriage were increasingly seen in purely secular terms.[1] Another influence was the increasing strength of the women's movement, which was pressing for equality within marriage. On the political front, the Divorce Law Reform Union had recently been formed and was agitating, in the interests of morality so it claimed, for a wide extension of the laws of divorce. The Union was receiving promises of support from many influential members of Parliament, and the introduction of a bill to allow the wives of long-term convicts to obtain a divorce illustrated the way political opinion was moving.[2] The government, in responding to what it saw as the growing dissatisfaction with the divorce laws, especially among the legal profession, decided to set up a Royal Commission to investigate the matter.

Within the Church of England divorce remained a highly controversial issue and there was no clear statement as to where the Church stood. There was a feeling of uneasiness about the spreading campaign to liberalise divorce, and in 1910 a thousand delegates at the annual conference of the Church of England Men's Society resolved unanimously to do their utmost to resist the liberalisation of divorce.[3] Adding to the controversy was a sharp division of opinion within theological circles over what the Bible taught about marriage and divorce. Canon William Knox-Little defended the traditional view of marriage in the book *Holy Matrimony* (1900). He described marriage as a new relationship constituted by God that was as close as that between 'brother and sister, or parent and child—a relationship, therefore, which it is as impossible for man to break in the one case as the other. Whatever else may come between them, father is father, son is son, brother is brother, and sister is sister, while the world stands. And husband is husband, and wife is wife, till death us do part. To put away a wife and marry another is to attempt to break what man cannot break. It is adultery. To put away a husband and marry another is to attempt to do what man cannot do. It is adultery. To marry a divorced woman, and, by parity of reasoning, to marry a divorced man, is to simulate a bond that cannot bind. It is adultery.'[4]

A growing number of Anglican bishops and theologians were against this view, and openly supported the campaign to make divorce more widely available. The basic argument was that Christ's teaching on marriage stated an ideal rather than a law. While Jesus had made it clear that adultery was a cause for divorce, other things that really destroyed the marriage bond, like desertion, cruelty and not showing love to one's partner, may be other causes for divorce. The Canon of Westminster, Hensley Henson, a leading exponent of this view expounded his ideas on divorce in a book, *Christian Marriage* (1907). He mentioned the grave difficulties that confronted the Church in trying to ascertain the actual teaching of Christ on the subject. 'Even in the crucial matter of marriage we shall find that our Lord's recorded teaching is not free from ambiguity. Either the different statements of the Evangelists are not wholly harmonious, or the text of the crucial passages is uncertain, or, finally, the passages themselves are capable of more than one rendering.'[5] A second difficulty was that the circumstances at the beginning of the 20th century were extremely remote from those which conditioned the teaching of Christ. 'We cannot fairly separate his pronouncements on marriage from the situation, social and political, which originally called them forth.'[6] True to the Protestant view of divorce, Henson believed that adultery 'by its own mere force, cancelled and destroyed the natural union. Precisely as divorce does not break the marriage tie, adultery does break it.'[7] Divorce was but the legal declaration of an accomplished fact—the marriage bond had already been dissolved by the act of infidelity.[8] Canon Hensley Henson and other like-minded theologians would be given ample opportunity to express their ideas to the forthcoming Royal Commission.

DEBATES IN THE CANTERBURY CONVOCATION: 1910–1911

During the working of the Royal Commission the issue of divorce was debated in the Lower House of Canterbury Convocation. In April 1910 the Archdeacon of Oxford informed the House that the Committee on Marriage Laws took the position that marriage was indissoluble save by death. 'It was greatly to be desired that this synod should utter no uncertain sound in the great controversy now before them, but plainly declare what the law of the Church of England had ever been, in accordance with the standard which our Lord laid down for Christians. To keep this before themselves and others must be the chief business of this synod at the present time.'[9]

The Bishop of Southampton (James Macarthur) commented on the idea that the present divorce law discriminated against the poor. He said that the House should not give its approval to proposals which would make divorce easier for the poor, but rather should endeavour to make divorce more difficult for the rich. It was gratifying to find some leading lawyers giving expression to the view that divorce applications were too frequent, and that churchmen were not alone in feeling very strongly that the Act of 1857 was a great mistake. It had been said by some that the passages of Scripture bearing upon the subject were of doubtful interpretation, and that there had been always a difference of opinion in the Church, but he thought the great majority of the members of the House believed there was no doubt whatever that Christ did not really intend to make any exception in the words reported in the gospel of St Matthew. The Church wanted people to feel that if they had been divorced by sentence of a civil court they were not in a position to marry again. 'The whole circumstances of the Divorce Court were most depraving, leading to much perjury and degradation of character. For that reason the House should do everything possible to discourage divorce and if possible put an end to it and revert to that former plan under which no one could obtain a divorce except by special Act of Parliament.'[10]

The author of *Christian Marriage*, Hensley Henson, the Canon of Westminster, strongly opposed the position taken by the Committee. He thought they were in some danger of mistaking the gravity of the multiplication of divorces. 'It was not necessarily the case that the multiplication of divorce argued moral declension in the community. It might be the case that a community with numerous divorces was morally sounder than a community in which divorce was prohibited altogether, for what they did by prohibiting divorce altogether was not to prevent misconduct, not to prevent widespread immorality, but to drive it more or less under the surface.'[11]

Canon Williams Newbolt declared that the function of the Convocation was to reassure the public mind. The attitude that the House ought to take up was the absolute impossibility of dissolving the marriage tie. 'It was often said that marriage was a contract entered into by two parties, and that it was perfectly possible for the contracting parties to dissolve that contract. But marriage is not a contract. Marriage was a state entered into by contract, which was a different thing altogether. It was a state, which could not be altered, except by death... Whatever expediency might direct, they had nothing to do with expediency. Divorce was an evil thing in itself, and if it was an evil thing, let it go forth that the House would have nothing to do with it.'[12] After the debate the Lower House passed the following resolution:

> That in the social, moral and spiritual interests of the people, it is desirable that the Divorce Act of 1857 should be repealed, and that accordingly every effort should be made by Clergy and Laity alike so to influence public opinion as to bring about the possibility of such repeal.[13]

The Upper House of Canterbury Convocation debated the issue in 1911. The Bishop of London (Arthur Winnington-Ingram) said that the real happiness of the country depended upon the purity and sanctity of its home life. He noted that there was an increasing loosening of the marriage bond which was affecting the spirit in which persons entered the marriage state. Some people had the idea, 'Well, we will try how we can get on, and if we cannot get on together we can always have a divorce and marry again.' The bishop thought that the country had come to the parting of the ways in this matter, and that unless the Church took a very firm stand, then the same things would happen in England as were occurring on the other side of the Atlantic. It was not too late for the Church to take action, and he asked the Church to speak with a decided voice before it was too late. It might be argued that it was better to wait for the Royal Commission to report, but he did not agree with that view. If there was any body that ought to pronounce on the matter before the report came up, it was the national Church. He protested against any increase in the facilities for divorce. He viewed with the gravest concern the establishment of divorce courts up and down the country. He also protested against any increase in the grounds upon which divorce would be granted.

He was familiar with the argument about 'one law for the rich and another for the poor', but he did not agree with it. The increase in the facilities for divorce had really been a curse to the rich, and had not been a blessing, and, therefore, the argument about 'one law for the rich and another for the poor' did not apply at all. It seemed to him that while, as citizens, they were bound to try to prevent the country making a great mistake, they had a further duty as churchmen. He did not agree that churchmen ought to look at the matter only from the point of view of the Church. They had to look at it from the point of view of the country, and, therefore, as citizens, they were bound to exercise every effort to prevent the country making a mistake. Beyond that it seemed to him they had the right to demand that the consciences of church people should not be offended as they were at the present time.[14]

The Archbishop of Canterbury (Randall Davidson) spoke out strongly against those who claimed that the law of the Church of Christ was that marriage was absolutely indissoluble. 'We have all seen leaflets and resolutions which state quite bluntly that the absolute indissolubility of marriage, in any circumstances whatever, has been "the law of the Church of Christ from the first". So expressed these words do, in my judgement, gravely mislead people who are unfamiliar with Church history... I am not at this moment expressing any opinion on either side in that great question.'[15] The Bishop of Birmingham (Charles Gore) responded that he believed the phrase to which the archbishop had taken such strenuous exception – the phrase 'the law of the Church of Christ from the first' accepted the absolute indissolubility of marriage – to be precisely true. He said that having given his best attention to the matter he believed that particular phrase to be precisely and exactly true. He believed that it was the Lord's intention to make marriage indissoluble and that if they examined the gospels critically and precisely that intention emerged. Moreover, the earliest statements of the law of the Church, both East and West, maintained that indissolubility absolutely.[16] The Upper House duly passed the resolution:

> That this House opposed, as detrimental to the social, moral and religious interest of the nation, any extension of the grounds on which divorce can now be legally granted.[17]

Comment

The tone of the debate shows the strength of feeling within the Church against the changes that were being contemplated by the Royal Commission. The Bishop of London made a critical point, noting that the Church had a prophetic responsibility to the whole nation and not only to the Christian community. The Church ought to do everything possible to prevent the nation from making a mistake by ignoring the laws of God with regard to marriage. As the light of the world and the salt of the earth the Church has an interest in the social, moral and religious well-being of the nation. It should, therefore, do all it can to preserve the moral standards of society. Extending the grounds of divorce would be detrimental to national well-being and therefore the Church ought to oppose such an extension.

THE ROYAL COMMISSION ON DIVORCE: 1912

Criticism by prominent members of the legal profession of the law that was the result of the Divorce Reform Act of 1857 persuaded the government to set up a Royal Commission. It was common knowledge that the law had opened the way for collusion between husband and wife who wanted a divorce. A husband would stay overnight in a seaside hotel with a woman of ill repute to provide bogus evidence of adultery. The law was not working well in practice and many in the legal profession pointed to procedural flaws in the Divorce Court. Under the chairmanship of a prominent high court judge, Lord John Gorell, a commission was set up in 1909, with the task of enquiring into the state of the divorce laws, paying special regard to the position of the poorer classes. The commission undertook a massive investigation, holding seventy-one sittings and taking evidence from 246 witnesses.

Theological evidence

Many liberal theologians were invited to give evidence to the commission, while the views of those who supported the indissolubility of marriage were poorly represented. In his evidence Hensley Henson asserted that the passages in the gospels that dealt with divorce 'are not really either clear in meaning or harmonious in doctrine'. He explained that 'most Protestant Christians agree in the principle that whatever can be shown to render impossible the primary objects of marriage is *prima facie* a sufficient ground for divorce. If it be rightly contended that there is nothing in the gospels which can fairly be described as "a definite and detailed social law", and if it is not the case that Christ's words with respect to marriage are in such sense "plain and direct" as to close the question for his disciples, then it would seem to follow that the conditions of divorce are properly to be determined by the state in the light of Christian principles with reference to the actual necessities and circumstances of men.'[18]

Rev William Sanday, Professor of Divinity at Oxford, asserted that the words of Christ express a moral ideal rather than a positive rule. The words of Christ did not exclude the possibility of exceptions, and the one exception stated in the New Testament need not be treated as necessarily excluding all others. The recognition 'by Christians of a lofty and unqualified moral ideal does not of necessity prevent a Christian state from legislating upon a lower level, and that in determining what other exceptions may legitimately be made to our Lord's ideal, there is room for a statesman at the present day to consider what is best in the interests of the higher expediency'.[19]

Rev Canon Hastings Rashdall, Fellow and Lecturer of New College Oxford, found it difficult to regard a saying of Christ as absolutely and permanently binding upon his followers if it collided with the dictates of the moral consciousness in the present. It was only for general principles and not for details of morality, which must necessarily vary with changing circumstances, that Christians can look for guidance to the dicta of the Master. In his teaching on divorce Jesus attacked 'the idea that a husband had the right to divorce his wife for mere caprice – for any cause… Against such a view he set forth that the true ideal of marriage was a permanent monogamous union. No one should enter upon a marriage union without intending to make it so. That adultery on the part of the wife, which *ipso facto* destroys such a union, was an exception would go without saying.' Rashdall concluded that the only principle that is absolutely binding upon Christians for all time is that the ideal of marriage is lifelong. 'I am quite clear that no principle of religion or morality forbids divorce with liberty of remarriage if a sufficient social advantage can thereby be secured, including the notion of social advantage, a strong public opinion in favour of permanent marriage and fidelity to marriage bonds and a generally healthy state of feeling as to sexual relations.'[20] Others to give evidence from the same point of view were Dr WR Inge, Dean of St Paul's, and the Rev CW Emmet.

Rev EG Wood, vicar of St Clement's, Cambridge, and a member of the English Church Union, defended the view that marriage was indissoluble. He said that the theory of the indissolubility of marriage was based on the fact that marriage was divinely instituted in the time of man's innocence. The words of Christ all pointed to the idea of a divine institution. The Church doctrine of indissolubility did not arise out of any sacramental theory; the Church held marriage to be indissoluble not only in the case of Christians, but of non-Christians also. He said that the law of the Church of England was that marriage is indissoluble and that the remarriage of the divorced person was not allowed. His arguments also dealt with the scriptural proof of indissolubility.[21] The Bishop of Birmingham (Charles Gore) supported the indissolubility of marriage. 'I should say that the original mind of Christ was that marriage was entirely indissoluble, and for that reason the early Church started out with that view with great unanimity and absence of hesitation.' He believed that all marriages should be treated as indissoluble in the Church, but this was limited to Christian marriages, though he believed that all marriages in England, with the exception of Jewish marriages, should be treated as Christian.[22]

After a thorough examination of the evidence a fundamental, unbridgeable division emerged between the commissioners. At the heart of the disagreement was the issue of the grounds for divorce. While the majority was in favour of extending the grounds, three commissioners, including the Archbishop of York, Cosmo Lang, strenuously opposed any extension. So irreconcilable was the division within the commission that each side felt obliged to produce its own report.

The Majority Report

The Majority commissioners agreed that the central question was, 'Should the law be amended so as to permit of divorce being obtained on any, and, if any, what grounds other than those at present allowed?' According to the report, the evidence from a range of theologians revealed a wide difference of opinion upon the important question of the indissolubility of marriage. The range of views was summarised as follows;

- That all marriages are indissoluble.
- That all Christian marriages are indissoluble.
- That marriage is dissoluble on the ground of adultery only.
- That marriage is dissoluble on the grounds of adultery or desertion.
- That marriage is dissoluble on other serious grounds based on the necessities of human life.[23]

The report noted that 'differing opinions have resulted in the acceptance by Roman Catholics of the doctrine of the indissolubility of marriage, while

Protestant communities have generally treated the tie as dissoluble but have differed as to the grounds upon which it might be dissolved'.[24] In view of the conflict of opinion the commissioners concluded that 'we must proceed to recommend the Legislature to act upon an unfettered consideration of what is best for the interest of the state, society, and morality, and that of the parties to [law] suits and their families'. The basic starting point of the Majority report, therefore, was that 'the state should not regard the marriage tie as necessarily indissoluble in its nature, or dissoluble only on the ground of adultery, but, regarding the dissolubility of the tie as not limited to the ground of adultery, may allow other grave causes'.[25] Although a few of the witnesses would have liked to see the Act of 1857 repealed on religious grounds, such a course was not practicable, and the suggestion that the Legislature should consider marriages absolutely indissoluble was dismissed from consideration.[26] They acknowledged that those who objected to any extension of the grounds for divorce did so because they believed that any such extension would be contrary to Christian principles.[27] However, the commission did not mention the resolution that had just been passed by the convocation of the national Church, opposing as detrimental to the social and moral interests of the nation any extension of the grounds for divorce.

It was necessary to reform both the procedure and the law to remove the serious grievances that existed, and to provide opportunities of obtaining justice within the reach of the poorer classes. 'We consider that reform is necessary in the interests of morality, as well as in the interests of justice, and in the general interests of society and the state.' However, the commission did not believe that it should attempt to express an opinion as to the true Christian principles applicable to the subject.

'If we start with the fact that the Western world has recognised that the union between man and woman in marriage should in the best interests of all concerned be monogamous, and that a monogamous union ought to be continuous until the death of one of the parties, yet experience teaches that causes other than death do in fact intervene to make continuous married life practically impossible and to frustrate the object with which the union was formed. We have to deal with human nature as it always has been, and as it is: and it is established beyond all question that for various reasons, amongst others improvident, reckless and early marriages, drunkenness, sensuality, brutality, immorality, lunacy, and crime, many marriages become absolute failures, and married life becomes either morally or physically, or both morally and physically, impossible. We have had before us a great body of evidence from witnesses, and a large number of letters which show that, unless the union formed by marriages which have already ceased in fact, can be dissolved by law, lives become hopelessly miserable, illegal unions are formed, immorality results, and illegitimate children are born.

'The fear of those who would treat the marriage tie as indissoluble, or would oppose any extension of the present grounds for divorce, is that the stability of the marriage tie in general would be adversely affected and that there would be a general lowering of the standard of morality. We believe that this fear is groundless, that it ignores the actual experiences of life, and that, if it were strictly acted on, it would perpetuate the evil results produced by the present state of the law. The remedy of divorce is at present, as we have shown, practically inaccessible to the poorer classes and the evidence before the commission shows that this state of things does not tend to develop due regard for marriage, but the reverse.'[28]

The Majority commissioners laid down two guiding principles for the state to use in considering the best interests of the whole community. First, no law should be so harsh as to lead to its common disregard, and second, no law should be so lax as to lessen the regard for the sanctity of marriage. 'It appears to us that those who allow the vague fear of possible injury to morality to exclude all other considerations act in conflict with the first principle. The alternative is to *recognise human needs* [my italics], that divorce is not a disease but a remedy for a disease, that homes are not broken up by a Court, but by causes to which we have already sufficiently referred, and that the law should be such as would give relief where serious causes intervene which are generally and properly recognised as leading to the break-up of married life. If *a reasonable law based upon human needs* [my italics] be adopted we think that the standard of morality will be raised and regard for the sanctity of marriage increased. Public opinion will be far more severe upon those who refuse to conform to a reasonable law than it is when that law is generally regarded as too harsh and as not meeting the necessities of life.'[29] Having decided to extend the grounds they saw no serious difficulty in determining what should be regarded as such causes. The Majority report recommended an extension of matrimonial offences to include the new grounds of cruelty, desertion of at least three years, incurable insanity, and incurable drunkenness. It also found that adultery by the husband was no less excusable than that committed by the wife, and concluded that the grounds for divorce should be similar for both sexes.

Comment

The effect of the Majority report was to remove the debate from the framework of biblical teaching because there was no agreement between theologians regarding the biblical grounds for divorce. Moreover, because they believed that the biblical view was no longer relevant in a secular society, they felt justified in disregarding the biblical principles of marriage and divorce. The Majority report was quite explicit in making it clear that their proposals were not based on Christian principles. They claimed that the best interests of the state, society, and morality and families were served by ignoring the teaching of Christ. Having sidelined divine truth they proposed their own 'reasonable' divorce law that, in their view, society needed. They actually claimed that to make divorce more widely available would increase the moral standards of society.

The philosophical basis of the Majority report is similar to that expounded by Erasmus, the Renaissance humanist. Having identified the problem of unhappy marriages, the remedy is, in their opinion, divorce. It offers relief to those in unfortunate marriages and satisfies human need. On the basis of their understanding of human need, the Majority report went on to argue that there was no logical reason why adultery should remain the only recognised offence for divorce. Of course this was precisely what the opponents of the 1857 Divorce Reform Act had predicted. Once the indissolubility of marriage was rejected there was no logical reason to limit the ground of divorce to adultery. Those who oppose extending the grounds are regarded as harsh and unreasonable. According to the Majority commissioners it is those who treat the marriage tie as indissoluble who may be responsible for the evil results produced by the present law. Thus the divorce law of England, which affected every family in the nation, was to be based on the opinions of a group of men rather than on biblical truth.

The Minority Report

The commissioners, Cosmo Gordon Lang (Archbishop of York), Sir William Anson (MP) and Sir Lewis Diblin (Judge of the Court of Arches), started their report by outlining the English law with regard to marriage. 'In England marriage is recognised by law to be monogamous, so that the special rights and duties of each spouse with regard to the other are shared by no-one else; and, further, the law contemplates that it will be lifelong, that is to say, will normally endure during the joint lives of the parties.' Most marriages in England are solemnised in Church with the promises to maintain the marriage relation during their joint lives, notwithstanding the vicissitudes of health, fortune and other circumstances.[30]

'The state is sometimes called the third party to the marriage contract because it not only lays down the conditions which must be satisfied both as to personal qualifications, and as to the incidents of the contract, but it also gives to the union of those who have been legally married special and definite recognition. The state protects family life, it defines and defends the authority of parents over their children, the rights of children to the care of their parents, and to a certain limited extent, the obligation of husband and wife towards each other. But apart from any share which the state can claim in a marriage contract by reason of what it confers, it has a concern of its own in the peace of the community, the welfare of the family, the rearing of healthy children, and the training of good citizens, which renders it imperative that the making and breaking of marriage contracts should be treated as a matter of public importance touching the commonwealth itself, and not as merely private transactions only affecting the parties. The permanence of the nuptial tie is all but universally admitted to be of advantage to the state. The preservation of that union, so long as it can be secured is manifestly essential to the best interests of society. The advantage to the state and the interests of society are thus brought into emphatic prominence at the outset of this report because they indicate what, in our opinion, is the only correct point of view from which a Royal Commission can regard the subject of divorce.'[31]

Commenting on the excessive prevalence of divorce in the Americas, the report draws attention to the fact that in the United States for many years there has been in operation a system not unlike, so far as the grounds of divorce are concerned, that which the Majority would impose on England. 'The outstanding fact is that in the case of the great English-speaking American people, which has, and for many years has had, a divorce law largely similar to that which our colleagues would see established in this country, the number of divorces has grown rapidly year by year. It has now reached a figure which in proportion to population, is now considerably more than double that of the number of divorces in any other country of the world except Japan.' The report reaches the conclusion that as the two countries have so much in common 'that if we in England adopt what are substantially the American grounds for divorce, we shall not escape the grave disasters which have followed their adoption in the United States'.[32]

The claim that there was a strong demand for more access to divorce by the poorer classes was challenged. 'The evidence, so far from showing any great or general demand on the part of the poorer classes for divorce on other grounds besides that of misconduct, clearly proves the absence of any such demand.' The report observes that an organisation like the Mothers' Union, which consists of almost 300 thousand wives and mothers, would be aware of any general demand by the poor for wider powers of divorce. But on the contrary, a number of meetings of the branches of the Union have passed resolutions rejecting the need for any extension to the grounds of divorce. Yet the Chairman of the Commission deemed the views of the Mothers' Union to be of little value because some of those who collected the information themselves believed that marriage is indissoluble.[33] On the other hand, the Majority were sympathetic to the evidence produced by the Women's Co-operative Guild, an organisation that advocated extending the grounds of divorce. A witness from the Guild expressed strong views, 'Wherever there are two people joined together and they find their whole interests are quite opposed to each other... that should be grounds for divorce.'[34]

Criticising the proposed new grounds for divorce, the Minority commissioners point out that they are 'purely empirical in the sense that they are tentative, experimental, dependent upon qualification and degree… They are frankly opportunist, designed to meet what are supposed to be the practical needs of the moment, and capable of expansion in any direction under the pressure for further facilities which concession is almost certain to produce. They must be judged, not only by their immediate and intended results, but by their inevitable sequel. If the state is to maintain any clear attitude as to divorce, it must take its stand upon some guiding principle.' The principle on which the Majority report appears to be based is that 'divorce should be permitted for causes which are generally and properly recognised as leading to the break-up of married life'.[35]

'The dilemma that presents itself is this. On the one hand, it is in the final degree dangerous and unstatesmanlike to deal with so momentous a matter as marriage and divorce on notions of present expediency, without any governing principle to guide us; on the other hand, the only principle suggested is one which requires that divorce should be granted on the mutual consent of both parties, and on proof of the invincible aversion of either of them for the other.'[36] The Majority report does not recommend divorce for incompatibility and divorce by mutual consent, not because they violate any principle, 'but merely because for the moment no effective demand for them can be discerned. But the inevitable conclusion of the premises adopted by our colleagues cannot be evaded.' The evidence of many distinguished witnesses showed that they were in favour of divorce for marital breakdown. The secretary of the Women's Co-operative Guild is quoted as an example, 'When man and wife agree to part, I feel it would be much better for the morals of both to grant a divorce. All our members are most emphatic that where husband and wife could not live happily together it was no real marriage, it was a life of fraud without love. Nothing but love should hold two together in this most sacred of bonds.' The suggested remedy is divorce. Indeed, 'divorce should be granted whenever there was a serious desire on the part of either of the parties not to live with the other', and this would apply 'to the case of a man who wanted to be freed from his wife in order that he might live with another woman'.[37]

The Minority commissioners make the point, 'One of the strongest reasons for not allowing desertion and cruelty as good causes of divorce is the ease with which they may be utilised for the dissolution of marriages of which the parties have simply grown tired, and the mutual desire to make an end. The danger lies not merely in the risk of a misuse of law in individual cases, but in the creation of a habit of mind in the people; for there is evidently a tendency in the United States for husbands and wives and their friends in certain classes of society to see no discredit in divorce based on allegations of cruelty or desertion, while judges make no effort to detect collusion, but consider it to be their duty to facilitate divorce whenever the parties are obviously tired of one another.' They submit that the proposals of the Majority report 'would lead the nation to a downward incline on which it would be vain to expect to be able to stop half way. It is idle to imagine that in a matter where great forces of human passion must always be pressing with all their might against whatever barriers are set up, those barriers can be permanently maintained in a position arbitrarily chosen, with no better reason to support them than the supposed condition of public opinion at the moment of their creation. But if the principle which lies behind the proposals of the Majority report be once admitted, with all that it necessarily implies, the result would be practically to abrogate the principle of monogamous lifelong union.'[38]

Discussing the proposals in relation to the Christian faith, the Minority report makes the point that it is 'the duty of the state to legislate for the general good of the whole nation'. To those who profess allegiance to the Christian faith it is almost axiomatic that the teachings of Christ as to the true conditions of family and social life were intended to promote the general welfare of the world. All witnesses that gave evidence to the commission, 'upon the fact and nature of our Lord's teaching to the world on marriage and divorce, are agreed that Christ intended to proclaim the great principle that marriage ought to be indissoluble... When we compare the principle thus enunciated and vouched for by this remarkable consensus of authority truly representing our Lord's teaching, with the principle, if there be any, which underlies the recommendations of the Majority report, we find them irreconcilable. If the one is calculated to promote the public good the other cannot be so. That marriage should be normally lifelong and indissoluble, and that marriage should be dissoluble on grounds which lend themselves to the easiest collusion, and which seem necessarily to involve the right of either partner to put an end to it all at will, are contradictory propositions. If the nation desires, as we believe it does, to maintain the ideal of lifelong obligation, it cannot permit Parliament to lay down a long and increasing list of statutory exceptions, some of them dependent for their effect upon the construction of terms, which do not admit of precise definition, by judges who may well vary in their intellectual and moral attitude towards these questions of divorce.'[39]

Commenting on the proposals in relation to family life, the Minority commissioners made the observation that the strength and continuity of the family are threatened by two counter-forces, namely the assertion of individual liberty and the claims of logical Socialism. 'As to the former there is a very widespread claim on the part of individuals for liberty from the restraints of marriage whenever they become difficult and irksome. As to the latter, logical Socialism is contending that the family stands in the way of the solidarity of the state, and this tendency is operative in many continental countries and in some of our own colonies.' The report makes the point that the strength of English social life has been the family, the home. 'The evidence is reassuring that among the great bulk of the people, especially among the middle class and artisans, the obligations of marriage are respected, and home life is pure and consistent. There can be little question that the reason for this state of things is the general social conviction that marriage binds those who enter it for better or for worse. It is a lifelong obligation with all the sacrifice which such an obligation involves. Our contention, therefore, is that the state, in its own interest, should maintain and not relax the standard of its present marriage law.'[40]

DEBATE IN THE CHURCH

Within a fortnight of publication the Archbishop of Canterbury commented on the report of the Royal Commission in the Upper House of Convocation. He said it would be misleading if the Church were to pass its publication over in silence. The great division of opinion between the two reports was reducible to one single large substantial question—should there or should there not be an extension of the grounds on which divorce can be granted in England? The Majority report recommended a very considerable extension of the grounds on which divorce could be granted. The Minority report, which deprecated extending the grounds, was speaking on behalf of the public interest of England as a whole. 'The report deals, not with what churchmen want as such, but with what the nation needs, the nation including churchmen, nonconformists, and non-Christians... the commissioners, Minority as well as Majority, have spoken as to what would, in their judgement, be to the advantage of the nation as a whole.'

He said that the Majority report, stirred by the stories of hard cases, desired on that ground to depart from the principle which had always governed these matters. The real line of divergence between the two was, on the one side, the hard cases justifying departure from principle; on the other, retention of the principle, notwithstanding the admission that there were hard cases. He complimented *The Times* for producing both reports for the public to read, and noted that they supported the Minority report. 'We believe that the lines upon which the Church of Christ and the Church of England has acted and spoken in the matter are drawn upon large principles of the common well-being, as well as upon the guidance and direction which come from above.'

Those who advised these changes recognised that they would be contrary to the tradition, rule, and principles of the Church. The Archbishop pointed out that the chairman of the commission, Lord John Gorell, went so far as to say that, 'if the changes he recommends were to be accepted, the marriage service seems to be out of keeping with modern thought, and would need reconstruction'. He noted that such a declaration, coming from the chairman of the commission, was of extreme importance. He said that the Church was 'looking at the well-being of the English people, religiously, morally, and socially, and to their life as a whole. And it is because I believe that the recommendations which are contained in the Minority report bring out what would be for the well-being of the people as a whole, and deprecate what be for the ill-being and for the disadvantage and the ruin of the people as a whole, that I welcome the publication of the Minority report.'[41]

The Bishop of London (Winnington-Ingram) said that it was of the greatest help that at the commencement of the struggle *The Times* had taken such a definite stand on the right side. The real distinction between the two reports was that the Minority report was based on principle, while the Majority report was founded on the argument for expediency. The new grounds suggested for divorce would gradually come round to collusion, and divorce by mutual consent. He said that during the last eleven years he had had a very unpopular fight in London to prevent the marriage of divorced persons, and their membership of the Church. The people who during that time had most backed him up by their advice and brotherly commendation had been the American bishops, because they had seen what had happened when the grounds of divorce had been extended. The bishops of America had seen the mischief which came about as a result. They said that they could not stop divorce in their country, but they could say, 'For heaven's sake stop it over in England.' He mentioned that the Church ought to bring home to the great masses of men the actual position of affairs. That evening he would address a huge meeting in Hammersmith for men, and would try to explain the points in dispute. He did not think that there was any popular movement behind the Majority report, though it would not be safe to take that for granted.[42]

At a meeting of the English Church Union in November 1912 to consider the report of the Royal Commission, Darwell Stone, Principal of Pusey House, Oxford, said the Church looked upon divorce and remarriage as an evil thing, and the Church would not tolerate it. 'There can be no true justice in adding to that degree of toleration which unhappily it has already received... if we who are here tonight had been engaged in public affairs in the year 1857, we should, I hope, have been found among those who offered the most strenuous opposition to the bill which then became an Act. At that time the claims of what I have called the higher justice demanded that the evil of divorce and remarriage should not be extended from those who could afford to obtain Acts of Parliament to those who could afford suits in the present Divorce Court. That same justice now demands that the evil of divorce and remarriage be not extended from those who can afford suits in the present Divorce Court to those who can afford suits in local courts. The reasons which were strong and urgent in 1857 for resistance to the bill of that year are strong and urgent also for resistance to what is now proposed.'[43]

At the same meeting, Lord Halifax said that the recommendations of the Majority report could be shown to be a danger to morality, the security of family life, and the well-being and happiness of individuals, and, so far as they were founded on any principle at all, would lead to the spread and promotion of divorce by mutual consent, which did not differ from the promotion of free love. If desertion was made a ground for divorce, it would greatly facilitate the opportunities for collusion. He strongly objected to insanity and imprisonment as grounds for divorce.[44]

Rev FB Meyer, an eminent Baptist minister, author of many Christian devotional books and member of the Free Council of Churches, gave a personal view. 'As a Christian minister and in dealing with the professing members of the Church, I should certainly incline to hold with the Minority report, but on broad public grounds, and as one who has been for a long time familiarised with the wrongs which women suffer through inability to rid themselves of worthless husbands and which men have to bear through inability to be free from drunken and dissolute women, I certainly think that we should do wisely to adopt the suggestions of the Majority report. It is clear that though the ideal of indissolubility of marriage save for the one act of adultery is the supreme ideal that should govern the Church we must remember that the immense mass of the people are outside the Church organisation and do not acknowledge the rule of Christ's legislation. I have seen such intolerable wrong borne through long years by men and women that I favour the proposals which would somewhat relax this unbearable burden, whilst leaving intact all that is high and best in wedlock.'[45]

Strongest opposition came from the Catholic Church. Monsignor Moyes wrote, 'The Catholic Church cannot approve of the recommendations of the commission, which go to extend the reasons and facilities for granting divorce, for the plain reason that she can never approve of divorce at all... The Catholic Church can see in the report of the commission only a further capitulation to the moral laxity of the age. She holds that the evil of divorce, as contrary to the divine ideal of marriage, is one which cannot be palliated by reasons of so-called expediency. At present, if a man has become tired of his own wife and covets the wife of his neighbour, he has only to consummate his guilt, and then ask the injured party to "set him free" (furnishing, if need be, evidence for the purpose) and the law of the land will become the helper of his purpose by setting the seal of its sanction upon the union of the guilty parties. That is the naked moral evil, and people do not cure a moral evil by legalising it. Between the Majority and the Minority reports the Catholic Church finds little to choose. The latter seems to be a well meant but futile effort to arrest in its logical path a principle which it has already surrendered. The former regrettably but consistently proceeds to carry the rejection of the principle to its wider and further application. Once it was conceded that the bond of valid marriage could be dissolved at all, it was only a question of time before men would discover that there were many other plausible reasons, equivalent as justifying causes to that of adultery. Having yielded the principle of indissolubility, it is utterly vain for the Minority to attempt to set limits to the area of surrender, and to say to this, or to a coming generation, thus far and no further. The evidence given by the report will only serve more than ever to convince Catholics – and I may hope many sincere Anglicans – that the dignity and sanctity of marriage are entrenched in its indissolubility. We believe that it is God who joins together the bride and the bridegroom in a sacramental covenant, and unites them as the foundation of the Christian family, and believing that we can never bring ourselves to think that because either has proved unfaithful to their vows, God will consent to undo his own bond and break up his own work, and gratify unlawful love by blessing the union of an adulterer and adulteress. If we could accept such a degrading concept of God and of Christian marriage there would be no reason why we should not accept at the same time the commission's report and its recommendations.'[46]

Comment

Clearly, the divisions, which appeared at the time of the Reformation, were still as wide as ever. The Protestant view remained sympathetic to divorce, and saw no reason for not extending the grounds, while the Catholic Church stood firm on the indissolubility of marriage. Between them stood the Church of England, which was being pulled in both directions. Because of the internal struggle the Church of England remained unsure of which way to move.

Debate in Convocation: 1914

The Lower House of Canterbury Convocation spent two days debating the reports of the Royal Commission, including a number of resolutions which expressed opposition to its proposals. The general tone was critical of the findings of the Majority report and even the Minority report did not find universal approval. The Bishop of Southampton (Macarthur), for example, did not feel satisfied with the language used by the Minority commissioners with reference to the repeal of the 1857 Act—he vigorously dissented from the idea that the repeal of that Act must be considered impossible. A resolution opposing the remarriage of all divorced persons, both guilty and innocent, in church during the lifetime of their former spouse gained solid support, although there was an unsuccessful attempt to remove reference to the innocent party. Supporting such an amendment, Canon Aitken argued that the infidelity of one party to the marriage contract would seem to dissolve the true matrimonial relationship. To put the person who had been sinned against in such a position that denied them all future possibility of getting married seemed to be a grave injustice. The Archdeacon of Stow asked whether there was an entirely innocent party, for the term referred to the one who had not been found guilty in a court. The amendment to remove reference to the innocent party was defeated.

The Lower House passed a number of resolutions condemning the recommendations of the Royal Commission, including:

> that this House considers the proposals of the Majority of the Royal commissioners, for providing additional grounds for divorce, inadmissible on any interpretation of the teaching of Christ which has been accepted by the Church, and would feel bound to oppose legislation to give effect to these proposals.

The resolution on remarriage stated:

> that the provision of the law of 1857 enjoining or permitting the solemnisation of remarriage in church, or by clergymen of the Church of England, of divorced persons, whether guilty or innocent, during the lifetime of the other party, should be repealed.[47]

The Upper House of the Convocation considered the resolutions in April 1915, when England had embarked on the First World War. The bishops felt that it was an inappropriate time to debate each resolution in detail, as the nation was focused on other issues. While the tone of the debate suggested that the Upper House had reservations about some of the resolutions, the bishops nevertheless reassured the Lower House that the resolutions had their sympathy.[48]

Comment

There was no doubt that the grassroots of the Church of England, as represented by the Lower House of Convocation, were outraged at the proposals of the Majority report. There was a massive gulf between the Christian view of marriage, which was still widely accepted by the population at large, and the views expressed by the Majority commissioners. So there was little popular support for the Majority report and even press comment was not favourable. A leading article in *The Times* noted that while the Majority advised that divorce and remarriage be made lawful upon five new grounds in addition to the present ground of adultery, the Minority recommended that valid marriages continue to be indissoluble except for adultery. 'We desire to affirm at once in the clearest and most comprehensive terms our approval of the views of the Minority, and our dissent from those of the Majority upon this vital issue… The common good, by the general consent and experience of all European peoples, is best promoted by the lifelong union of one husband to one wife. That is the one sure basis on which the family, society and the state can be reared… But while the Majority conceive that the legalisation of divorce on the grounds set out in their report would tend to preserve the ideal, the Minority are convinced that it would inevitably weaken the moral habit which is the chief safeguard of marriage. That is the real controversy between them. The case which the Minority makes upon it seems to us irresistible... There is no halfway house between marriage indissoluble except for adultery and marriage dissoluble at pleasure... Divorce on some such grounds as are advised by the Majority is of course no new experiment. It has been tried in other lands, and the social conditions which have arisen under it deserve attention. The Minority rightly lays stress upon the consequences of divorce in the United States... The evidence shows that in America two at least of the grounds for divorce which the Majority would recognise – desertion, namely, and cruelty – not only tend to make collusive divorces common, but also tend to create in certain kinds of public opinion an easy tolerance for such divorces.'[49]

The editorial was remarkable for its strong condemnation of the Majority report. It was also perceptive in noting that there is no halfway ground between marriage indissolubility (except for adultery) and divorce on demand. However, it is worth noting that those who supported the Minority report now generally conceded the dissolution of marriage for adultery. In other words, the Minority report was basically supporting the Protestant doctrine of divorce. Because the commission was split, and because of determined opposition from the Church and the press, the government decided not to try and implement the recommendations of the commission. So why was the Majority report so out of touch with the feeling of the country? Many of its ideas had been lifted from the American experience of divorce. Introducing American grounds for divorce into conservative England was likely to be a difficult task, and not surprisingly there was little popular support for the proposals.

However, the important point is that the agenda for future changes to the law had been set. It was unlikely that England, where marriage was so much part of the culture of the country, would be moved so easily to the new liberal grounds for divorce. But the ideas had been floated—and with time, slowly but surely, the unthinkable would become acceptable. There is no doubt that the commission was a major step forward for the divorce campaign. It was now firmly driving the agenda. Within seven short years the recommendations of the Majority report, so roundly condemned as contrary to the principles of the Christian faith and so obviously against the best interests of society in general, would gain the support of the House of Lords, and within 25 years would become the law of England.

During the first decade of the 20th century there were on average less than 600 divorces per year, and the trend remained fairly stable until the advent of the First World War. A large increase in divorce occurred at the end of the War as a number of returning soldiers divorced their wives for adultery, and in 1920 men initiated 77 per cent of the 3090 divorces. It is important to bear in mind that the law on adultery still differentiated between men and women; wives could only divorce their husbands for aggravated adultery.

Chapter 7

The slippery slope

The parliamentary struggles of the 1920s

The First World War was hardly finished before the campaign to liberalise divorce was again on the move. Although the influence of secular humanism had grown in strength, its arguments had only a limited influence on a society in which many people still accepted the traditional Christian view of marriage. The advent of a theology that allowed a more liberal approach to divorce provided a major boost to the campaign. Many churchmen of the Modernist school of theology supported the view that marriage was dissoluble, and advocated more liberal divorce laws.[1] In 1920 Archdeacon Robert Charles preached a sermon on divorce in Westminster Abbey that was published in the *Guardian.* In his sermon Charles said that the gospels of both St Matthew and St Mark dealt with the question of divorce for offences less than that of adultery. Although he pointed out that in the gospel of St Matthew a clause was inserted to guard against any misinterpretation of St Mark, he had not succeeded in convincing the Church because a large body of Anglicans believed that divorce was forbidden in all circumstances. Charles's views were published in *The Teaching of the New Testament on Divorce* (1921). The book was a direct attack on the doctrine of the indissolubility of marriage. 'It is now being taught in many places that marriage is wholly indissoluble, however flagrant may be the guilt of the husband or wife, and that consequently, should a man divorce his wife or a wife her husband on the ground of adultery and marry again, such a person is guilty of breaking an unquestionable law of Christ, and excludes himself or herself thereby from the communion of the faithful. As for these three statements, I hope to prove that they are mere human traditions based on a complete mis-interpretation of Christ's teaching, and without an atom of authority in the gospels.'[2] Charles asserted that Christ taught that the marriage bond was effectually dissolved by adultery, and so remarriage following divorce was permissible. He also believed that the Bible allowed divorce to the believing husband or wife who is deserted by an unbelieving partner.

Extending the argument, Charles noted that as some couples marry for the wrong reasons, not every marriage celebrated in Church could be regarded as a joining of man and woman by God.[3] If a marriage is 'not in accordance with God's will, not all the Churches in the world can make it so'. The Church cannot by its blessing transform marriages which are entered into irresponsibly, and make them into marriages such as God would have them. As examples, he refers to marriages that result from some transitory attraction, or passing passion, or sheer vanity, or greed of gain, or power, or caprice.[4]

Charles asks whether divorce is justifiable for certain grave offences short of unfaithfulness. 'Should, then, the state intervene and grant divorce on certain definite grounds other than unfaithfulness? If hardness of heart warranted a relaxation of the marriage law under the Mosaic dispensation, it is reasonably asked if the hardness of heart so prevalent in the present day does not warrant some relaxation of a marriage law which presupposes an ideal state of society? There are many husbands and wives who are separated, not by any decree of the state, but by grave offences such as desertion, or by irremediable evils such as habitual intoxication or hopeless insanity. In the case of deliberate desertion extending into many years, it seems not unreasonable that the Church should legislate specially for such cases, as did St Paul, and release the believer from the yoke of bondage. Adequate grounds could be adduced for like action on the part of the state.'[5]

Charles concluded that those who deny the right of divorce and remarriage confuse the essence of marriage with its public recognition by the Church or state. 'They do not care how often the essential principle of marriage is outraged and destroyed, so long as the outer and lifeless husk of it is preserved.'[6]

Comment

Although Charles's book was challenged, it was a devastating attack from within the Church on the indissolubility of marriage. The apparent biblical justification for extending the grounds of divorce was an encouragement for those who were intent on achieving greater liberalisation of the laws. It was now possible to claim that the Bible not only permitted but also encouraged divorce for those who had married contrary to the will of God. The proponents of divorce liberalisation were confident that the tide was flowing in their direction and no longer felt constrained by religious opposition. It was no surprise that the divorce movement thought the time was ripe to change the law through a Private Member's bill.

Modern proponents of divorce believed that a doctrine was necessary which addressed human needs. Because Christ's teachings are ambiguous there was little point in pursuing the Scriptures for it is impossible to be sure what they really mean. The notion that lifelong marriage is but an ideal, largely unattainable in the modern world, characterised the modern approach to divorce. As Christ did not legislate against divorce, modern divorce laws should be adapted to suit the age in which we live. The teachings of Jesus must be interpreted in the light of sociological perceptions of human need. When the primary objects of marriage are rendered impossible, the relationship is dead, and the parties are free to divorce and remarry. Modern supporters of the Protestant doctrine of divorce base their arguments less on the ideas of Luther and Calvin, who attempted to support their views with the Scriptures, and more on the need for social expediency.

LORD BUCKMASTER'S DIVORCE BILL: 1920

Lord Stanley Buckmaster introduced a Private Member's bill in March 1920, reminding the House of Lords of his failed attempt in 1918 to make desertion a ground for divorce. On that occasion the bill was lost upon a division by 10 votes. He had received letters from all classes of people 'pointing out the undeniable sufferings and difficulties of their lives, and entreating him to make one more effort to see if their lot could not be lightened'. The bill he was now introducing contained all the recommendations of the Royal Commission, although in many cases he would have liked to go far further than the Royal Commission thought wise.

To maintain justice and morality in England the reforms recommended by the Majority report of the Royal Commission should be passed into law. 'I feel certain you will be in agreement that it is impossible that a report of such value, signed by such men, should simply be thrown into the rubbish heap, and that no steps whatever should be taken to test the opinion of the Houses of Parliament as to whether or not the recommendations should be carried.' The grounds for divorce would be adultery, desertion for three years, cruelty, habitual drunkenness, and imprisonment under a commuted life sentence. 'If the marriage tie is broken in fact by the desertion of one spouse from the other, people who are left derelict in these circumstances are under a temptation to form irregular unions which frequently proves too great for even a strong character to resist; and when these unions are formed either the unhappy children are to be branded as bastards during the whole of their lives, or they take steps to sterilise their union and, though they are living together in common adultery, they take care that the curse of illegitimacy shall not descend upon their children.' He went on, 'Some there may be among your Lordships who think that divorce on any ground is wrong, who regard the marriage tie as so permeated and interpenetrated with divine sanction and authority that to dissolve it under any circumstances is to cause offence against something higher than earthly laws. I sincerely respect and reverence those views, which I find myself wholly unable to share. I know that against such a position no argument and no persuasion can by any possibility avail. Though the tide of human unhappiness were multiplied in strength a thousand times it would still beat in vain against the rock of that defence.' He concluded, 'The bill attempts to afford some relief for people who through no fault of their own have been left desolate and derelict upon the world, and to dissolve a union which binds a person to another in a living death where the spouse is cursed with habitual drunkenness or is under the misfortune of incurable insanity or the stain of inexpiable crime.'[7]

Lord Braye reminded the House that in 1914, only a few hours before the outbreak of war, a similar measure was before the Lords. 'Those who think with me on this matter hold the view that it is one upon which we differ from the promoters of the bill absolutely. There is, in fact, no common ground whatsoever for rapprochement or approximation to agreement… The object of the bill is nothing more than this—to facilitate the opportunities for divorce; to extend the courts of divorce all over the country, and therefore to make it easy for people in the country who are not able to come to London to get their matrimonial affairs settled there… I say that we absolutely disagree with the principle of the bill, because we look upon marriage as a divine institution, and we know that the Founder of Christianity laid down the law against which there is no kind of dispute or contradiction: "Whosoever shall marry a divorced woman commits adultery." Therefore this bill, although it looks as if it was doing a great deal of good and was prompted, as no doubt it was, by the most humanitarian of motives, is in our view doing the reverse and facilitating the commission of the crime which the Decalogue condemns… It seems a waste of time to consider any portion of the bill when you totally and absolutely disagree with the principle.'

He reminded the House that he was speaking as a Catholic. He believed the bill would loosen the marriage bond. 'It overthrows the whole foundations of our social system. It interferes with and overthrows the family. It overthrows the idea of paternity, and it separates man from woman… Wider and wider every year the doors of the Divorce Court in this country are opened. The crowds that wait at those doors are increasing, and the people who are advocating the facilitating of divorce are growing in number in the critical times in which we live. I do not conceal from myself that the time may not be far distant when the marriage bond will be almost completely dissolved in this country… Where it will end we cannot tell, but it is the duty of those who are believers in the Christian faith, to do all they can to retard this direction of public feeling and of public morals.'[8]

The Archbishop of York (Cosmo Lang) spoke as a member of the Royal Commission. He did not think it was necessary to constitute the sittings of Divorce Courts in eighty-nine towns in the country. It would mean reporting these cases, often sordid and unsavoury, in immense detail in all the local newspapers, and bring the suggestions, the traditions, and the associations of divorce right down to the very doors and homes of people who until now had little familiarity with divorce. The archbishop then explained his belief about marriage, 'To me the conception of marriage as dissoluble only by death, which has been so impressively sustained by the Christian Church, especially in the West, during all these centuries, is the conception which answers to the mind and teaching of its divine Founder and Head... I do not think anyone could maintain that the proposals which are contained in this bill are consistent with any interpretation of the words of Christ, if they are regarded as still binding upon the Christian conscience.'

He noted that the principle of the Majority report was that causes that led to the break-up of married life ought to be regarded as sufficient for justifying divorce. But where will that principle lead? The only way of dealing justly with the hardships was to permit divorce by mutual consent. 'The pressure of emotion caused by the individual cases of hardship must be balanced by care for the general welfare. The whole basis of any marriage law is, of course, that the making and breaking of the marriage contract is a matter which concerns the whole community and is not merely a private transaction which concerns the individuals themselves. The aim of our marriage law, as of all marriage laws, ought to be to make the institution of marriage as stable as possible and to make it lifelong in its obligations.

'The stability of the institution of marriage is therefore of more importance than the relief of individuals. Hitherto in this country the law has been supported in its efforts by public opinion. And why? Because the conception conveyed in the old familiar words, "For better for worse, for richer for poorer, until death us do part" has become part of the common conscience of the community... They import a conception of marriage as not primarily a mutual arrangement for happiness but an obligation of lifelong and faithful service. I suggest that it is taking a very strong step for the legislature to disturb the strength of that common conscience upon which its own desire to maintain the strength of the institution of matrimony so largely depends... In the effort to redress the failure of individual marriages you may run the risk of undermining the basis of marriage itself, upon which, after all, the home life of the people depends.'

In conclusion the archbishop returned to his main point. 'The object of the marriage law is not to relieve individuals or to promote their happiness, but to protect and safeguard the security and continuity of marriage itself. We are living at a time of manifold restlessness which infects body and mind and the whole field of social life. Is it not well at such a time to keep the homes of the country stable and steadfast? It is a time when men are more clamorous for rights than mindful of duties. Is it not well at such a time to maintain an ideal of marriage as something that confers, not the rights of happiness, but the duties of patient forgiveness and loyal service?' Because he believed the main provisions of the bill would weaken the stability of marriage and lower its ideal he requested their Lordships to withhold it from a second reading.[9]

Lord Phillimore said the main objective of the promoters was to facilitate and increase divorce. 'Our civilisation is, after all, based upon Christianity, and if we depart from Christianity we run a great risk of losing the touchstone of our civilisation, and if there is a thing which the Christian Church has taught it has been that marriage is either wholly or, at any rate, almost wholly a contract for life, indissoluble "till death us do part". I say almost because there is one tradition which has run through parts of the Church and which has found its place in some Protestant bodies which has made adultery a cause for divorce, and, in rare instances, desertion. The main body of Christian teaching has been that nothing is to separate people who are once married. If I could I would go back to the state of things which existed before 1857, and I would have no divorce at all. I am not speaking merely as a Christian, and as a believer, and as a member of the Church of England; I am looking at this matter from the point of view of social order and the prosperity of the country and the maintenance of the English home. And I submit that it is desirable by every means in our power to buttress and support the sanctity and permanence of marriage...

'Nobody in this debate has mentioned those who have more claim to our consideration than anybody, and they are the children. What about them? What about the child which finds its father or mother leaving or being left by the other spouse, and introducing a new father or mother into the household? The children are at least innocent. Children cannot protest themselves, and it is the children above all others we ought to consider. The parties have brought the children into being by their marriage, and they must keep their responsibilities for the children intact... With regard to the so-called equality of the sexes, let it pass. We all know that adultery on the part of the woman is not the same thing as adultery on the part of the man, that it involves a greater moral fall, and that it produces more practical mischief. But if the ardent advocates of femininity want that, and if they would be content with that alone, I would offer little opposition to such a proposal.'

In conclusion Lord Phillimore said, 'It has been prophesied earlier that if you once begin granting divorces the appetite would become more and more frequent. The promoters of the original bill (1857) expected their judge to have so little to do that he was not only to do Divorce and Probate, but he was to be prepared if necessary to fill the place of a Judge of the Court of Admiralty... Now we have three judges at least trying to cope with the number of divorces which have flowed upon us.'[10]

The Lord Chancellor, Lord Frederick Birkenhead, said that the real controversy in the House was between those who believe that marriage ought to be indissoluble for any reason and those who do not hold that belief. 'This is the only controversy on principle. You can create any number of controversies on points of detail, but the only controversy on principle is between those who – and they told you openly and plainly that which they thought and that which they would secure if they had the power – say that for no reason should marriage, which is a sacrament, be dissolved, and those who do not take this view.' After briefly outlining the history of divorce in England he said, 'today we approach it on the basis that marriage is not, and ought not to be, treated as being indissoluble; and I say – I hope without giving offence – that those who take and attempt to advocate the other view do not live in this world; their arguments are the whisperings of the abandoned superstitions of the Middle Ages... I think that 90 per cent of the population of these islands are agreed that upon some grounds marriage ought to be dissoluble. That means – and let us never forget this – the definitive rejection of the ecclesiastical view. When once that conclusion is reached, on what other principle must we proceed? The commission indicated the principle. I accept it. I recommend it to the consideration of the House. They lay down that marriage ought to be dissoluble upon any grounds which have frustrated what by universal admission are the fundamental purposes of marriage.'

He gave a detailed justification of each new ground for divorce, and then he mentioned children. 'I say boldly that the case of children is the strongest part of our proposals, and if you compare their state under the system which exists today and the state of the children as it would be if these proposals were accepted, no reasonable man could doubt as to where the balance of advantage lies. We shall remove, under this proposal, the children from contact with the spouse who from moral or physical taint is unfit to sustain the obligation of marriage. Their plastic and impressionable minds will be withdrawn from squalor and immorality, from drunkenness and crime, and afforded a chance at least of happy homes and useful citizenship. Who would dare to maintain that it is good for a child to live in a house in which its mother spends a life of open adultery and in which its brothers and sisters, if such are born, must be named bastards. Such surroundings are to be found in thousands of houses all over the country today.' He concluded with this exhortation to the House, 'I would most earnestly implore your Lordships to be the pioneers in this great reform, and if it should prove so to be, I believe that daily and nightly your Lordships' names will be breathed with unspeakable gratitude by thousands of the most unhappy of your fellow subjects, and by generations yet to be you will be acclaimed for the wisdom and humanity of the decision taken tonight.'[11]

The Archbishop of Canterbury (Davidson) approached the issue on social grounds, rather than on religious grounds as he would have more to say on that in another assembly. He said that it was the horrible and often cruel

136

complications in family life, especially for children, which the tangle of easy divorce brought about – the testimony from over the Atlantic was absolutely overwhelming – which moved most people in their votes on the subject. The archbishop then challenged the so-called demand for more divorce, and in particular that there were tens of thousands of deserted wives who were bearing illegitimate children. His enquiries found that in the East End of London, that out of six and a half thousand babies and children under observation, there were practically none born to deserted wives. He acknowledged that there were many hard cases. 'I ask you, with all the earnestness I can command, to take care to proceed with caution and with accurate knowledge. Remember that what you do in this matter you do irrevocably. There can be no going back. You can never retrace the step you take in the direction of laxity. You open a door and, however wrongly that door may be used or however freely it may be entered by the wrong people, you are helpless, you cannot shut it again. Experience shows that.

'In many parts of America there is no doubt at all of the desire to stiffen the laws laid down some time ago which allowed divorce in insanity cases. It has been found that the laws will not answer, but the Americans cannot go back. On every side evidence is coming forward that they wished they had not done it… Not only are you taking an irrevocable step, but you are dealing with a very sacred thing touching the home life of England. You are – I do not scruple to say it – on holy ground.'

The archbishop said that the whole of life in Europe was seething and the wildest proposals for social change were in the air. He mentioned that a scheme for new laws of marriage and the family was being officially circulated through eastern and north-eastern Europe. 'In a careful and thoughtful document it is said how marriage laws must be tolerated for a time until fuller liberty can be brought about; and meanwhile what they say is that all they can do is to establish complete freedom of divorce thus refraining from making marriage a lifelong institution.' He concluded with the warning, 'We are setting our feet upon a slippery slope if we touch this matter in the way that is now suggested.'[12]

Lord Parmoor said the Lord Chancellor issued a challenge that he was quite willing to take up. 'It seems to me quite impossible to discuss this question if you eliminate the religious and Christian aspect. That is an essential and fundamental matter which cannot be eliminated. At any rate, no layman can eliminate it when dealing with the great question of the stability and sanctity of marriage. In answer to the Lord Chancellor I will only quote one passage from the marriage service, which no doubt was read at his marriage, as explaining my view of what is meant by the sanctity of marriage. "Marriage is an honourable estate instituted of God in the time of man's innocency, signifying to us the mystical union that is betwixt Christ and his Church".' He went on to make the point that there ought to be no difference between the public welfare view and the Christian view. 'Christianity has been the morality on which our doctrines of public welfare are founded, and if you trace the influence of Christianity, it has always appealed to the highest moral ideals of humanity, and it is because it has done so that Christianity has maintained its position as the great teacher of moral truths to mankind.'[13]

The Marquess of Salisbury responded to the Lord Chancellor's comment that the basis of the marriage law in England rested upon a medieval superstition. 'Ultimately it rests on the gospel... All our civilised notions of marriage have grown up under the sanction of these doctrines of the Christian Church.' He then challenged the basis for extending the grounds of divorce. 'If disease, for example, is to be a reason for divorce, why take one particular disease? Is it not as difficult and objectionable for a woman to cohabit with a man who has consumption? Why not admit all communicable diseases such as consumption? I turn to desertion. Why three years? What is there in three years? Why not two years, or one year, or three months? There is no ground upon which you can stand in these arbitrary figures. Indeed, in taking all these grounds together, a man can come to the Court and say, "This woman whom I have married is repulsive to me; I cannot live with her; I have a physical dislike of her; I cannot endure the married state along with her" – that is a slight extension of the argument of the noble and learned Lord – that ought to be good enough for the divorce.'[14]

There was now a large majority in the House of Lords in favour of extending the grounds of divorce. On division the second reading was passed by 93 votes to 45 and the bill passed to the committee stage. In committee, when it became clear that it would not be possible to make any changes to the essence of the bill, the Archbishop of Canterbury introduced the following amendment:

> The marriage of a person whose previous marriage has been dissolved under the provisions of this Act, and whose former husband or wife is still living, shall not be solemnised in any church or chapel of the Church of England.

He said, 'Well, we have been beaten on clause after clause. The noble and learned Lord Buckmaster has had his way; but he has treated us with perfect considerateness and courtesy at every turn... How ought the Church to regard the new plan? Some of the new enactments can by no stretch of language be brought within our Lord's own words.' The archbishop quoted from Matthew's gospel, 'But I say unto you, that whosoever shall put away his wife, saving for the cause of fornication, causes her to commit adultery, and whosoever shall marry her that is divorced commits adultery.' He said that the state desired to change its law on the ground of what is believed to be a wide desire for change on the part of those who do not regard Christ's word as authoritative or binding. If the bill became law, the state would allow divorce for causes which the whole Church of the West had quite invariably repudiated.

The archbishop quoted a few examples to illustrate the impossible position in which the Church would find itself under the proposed new law. 'A country parson may find a man coming to him and saying, "I want remarriage because my wife, whom I married years ago for better or worse, is mentally afflicted and has long been under restraint. I want to take another wife and the Court of Law says I may. Please marry me."' The archbishop continued, 'Is it contended that in order to meet these cases which you have decided against our strong protest to be, as you think, for the public good, that the Church must alter its law… What we want, and what we firmly claim, is that we may as a body be allowed to be loyal to Christ's teaching as we understand it. You must not say to the Church, "We have changed your rules for you; your parsons may now do as they please in these matters." We claim the right to say that if people demand this sort of marriage they must seek the solemnisation of it outside the Church.' The archbishop reiterated his point that to leave remarriage 'to the clergy would be chaotic, to enforce it would be intolerable tyranny, and the only alternative, and the true one, is to keep it outside the Church whose rules you have decided to ignore or reverse'.[15]

Lord Buckmaster said he found it difficult to accept the amendment, because he understood that the Church accepted divorce for adultery. The archbishop responded, 'I want to make it perfectly clear that the Church's law has never sanctioned the marriage of an innocent divorcee.'

The Bishop of Ely (Frederick Chase) strongly supported the amendment. 'Our opposition is primarily based upon our loyalty to Christ and the words of Christ. The great majority of Christians, I believe, are convinced that our Lord delivered a judgement on the matter of divorce… To a very large proportion of earnest Christians it would be a matter of the keenest distress if the marriages now made for the first time legal were solemnised by the service of the Church.' Lord Selborne warned that if the House decided against this amendment, 'you are beginning a trouble which will last till it is settled by accepting the amendment or by the severance of the present connection of the Church and state'. The Archbishop of York read from the marriage service, 'in sickness and in health, to love and to cherish, till death us do part, according to God's holy ordinance; and thereto I plight thee my troth'. He said that remarriages which used these words must be unreal, and in some cases they would be a mockery.[16] After further discussion the amendment was rejected by one vote, 51 to 50.

Third reading in the Lords

In the third reading of the bill, Viscount Halifax came to the House from a sick bed to make a speech on the subject about which he felt passionately.

He said that the matter was of supreme importance to the interest not merely of England but to the whole English-speaking race. 'I think the struggle is between those who believe in the indissolubility of marriage and those who think, with whatever reservations they may favour, that it is not much more than a contract made between two people. The extensions of divorce made in this bill lead, quite as naturally as water runs down hill, to the bottom of the slippery slope which is divorce by mutual consent. We can almost hear now what will be said on the subject – that incompatibility of temper is inconsistent with the true spiritual union of souls, and as such ought to provide grounds for divorce... It is quite impossible for any one who recognises the authority and teaching of our Lord not to deplore the position that divorce has obtained on the Statute Book, and it is equally impossible for them to agree to any extension of divorce.'[17]

The archbishop responded on behalf of the bishops. He noted that the subject affected the life of the whole country. He said that it was not the occasion for going over each item of the controversy as they had had their say about the wrongs which the bill made for the first time operative as ground for divorce—desertion, drunkenness, mental illness, and the rest. They had also discussed the question of the ministry of the Church in regard to persons who desire remarriage. 'We deprecate wholesale extensions because we believe in their detrimental effects on the morals of the English people and on the tone of English married life... It has been said in these debates that we are showing some strange, novel, unnatural narrowness or bigotry when we remind the House of Lords, and remind the country of the Church's rules in this matter.' There was a broad line of divergence between those who supported the bill and those who did not. 'We on our side believe unhesitatingly in the great principle of the Christian marriage law, the bond unbreakable – some say absolutely unbreakable; I, with others, would say unbreakable save for unfaithfulness, or, as it is called in St Matthew, fornication, which is given there as our Lord's own exception.'

The archbishop then referred to the sermon preached in Westminster Abbey by Canon Robert Charles. 'Some people supposed that Canon Charles had said that the provisions suggested in the bill would be legitimate under true religious law. Certainly some of the newspapers had given that impression.' The archbishop claimed, however, that a careful reading of the sermon showed that the Canon believed that Jesus forbade divorce on lesser grounds than adultery. The archbishop was convinced that relief from the marriage bond was allowed by the teaching of Christ only in the case of unfaithfulness. 'We believe that this principle is sound and conducive to the well-being of the people. It is the principle laid down by our Master in the Sermon on the Mount. We have for long centuries made those principles our own, and by them we stand. That is our side.'

Referring to the arguments of Lord Buckmaster the archbishop said that he (Buckmaster) came to break down that position. 'He introduces other reasons for divorce that cannot possibly be brought within Christ's word or within the Church's definite teaching.' He said that once they had made the changes proposed it was impossible to change back. 'Start on that slope and you will find it not only slippery but to climb back absolutely impossible.' He then gave his final warning of the consequences of the bill. 'If you bring about the change you are proposing now, you will have its fruits to deal with in the future, and I venture to prophesy that, just as you prize the purity and simplicity of the average English home, you will then rue bitterly the initial vote you gave tonight. You will be powerless to go back. I ask you to pause while you still can. We who oppose this bill at all events are resolved that our voice and vote shall be recorded in favour of maintaining in its essence unimpaired the old law, the Christian law, the law which has helped to make and keep England strong.'[18]

Lord Selborne said that 'a fundamental issue, which the Lord Chancellor had tried to evade, was whether the new causes of divorce in the bill are compatible with the teaching of Jesus Christ. Whatever view was taken of the disputed chapters in St Matthew, nobody could say that the causes of divorce to be enacted in this bill were compatible with the teaching of Christ. The real issue as stated by the Lord Chancellor was this—the authority of the report of the Royal Commission against the authority of the New Testament. But whether it be the opinion of the Royal Commission or the Lord Chancellor each ground is nothing whatever but a matter of opinion, and I want to emphasise with all the force at my command what I believe to be an absolute fact—that there is no logical stopping point until you come to dissolution by mutual consent.' The Earl said that the two great lawyers, the Lord Chancellor and Lord Buckmaster were both sincerely desirous of promoting human happiness. 'But then the question must be asked—which knows most about human happiness, these two great lawyers or their Creator?' To answer that question he appealed to the experience of those countries which had departed most widely from the Christian position about marriage. 'I take the United States as typical, and would ask your Lordships who are in favour of this bill this question: Is married life on the whole happier in the United States than in England? Can anybody even suggest that?' He said that President Roosevelt was so concerned about the terrible state of affairs with regard to divorce that he had called a national conference to examine the issue.[19]

Lord Buckmaster said that the real objection to the bill was based on religious grounds. 'I do not think I should be doing my duty if I let this bill pass without expressing my own strong individual protest against the view that the introduction of this bill is contrary to the teachings of Christianity.' He said that Lord Braye stood in an impregnable position. 'He represents the Roman Catholic faith, which, from the earliest days, has declared that marriage can never be dissolved by the act of man. To him, therefore, I make no answer for no answer can be made.' Referring to the speech of Viscount Halifax, Lord Buckmaster noted that he (Viscount Halifax) spoke on behalf of the Church of England, and said that according to their law marriage is indissoluble, and that the conflict today was 'between the indissolubility of marriage and this bill. I think he is right. But the indissolubility of marriage has been abandoned this afternoon by the most reverend Primate who has admitted that for adultery marriage can be dissolved; and no one can doubt that the Church of England is bitterly divided upon this question. Some hold the views of Viscount Halifax and Lord Phillimore. There are others who hold different opinions... I am simply saying that it impossible for anyone to speak with the undivided authority of the members of the Church of England behind him in this matter, because they are not united and they are not agreed.'[20] On a division the bill passed with a majority of 154 to 107.

After their defeat in the House of Lords the church leaders issued a public statement warning of the moral dangers inherent in the bill. 'The Matrimonial Causes Bill, extending the grounds of divorce to include desertion for three years, cruelty, habitual drunkenness and incurable insanity, has passed the House of Lords. In those countries where such facilities have been granted, reaction against this legislation, which is generally recognised as being disastrous to the welfare of society, has already made itself felt and efforts are being made to restrict the facility of divorce... There are the gravest reasons for fearing that this bill is only an instalment, which will be followed by far more drastic measures, for not only does the bill draw purely arbitrary and illogical distinctions as to what shall or shall not constitute grounds for divorce, but its author has admitted that he himself would like to go much further. This impression is heightened by a sinister and rather ridiculous feature of the support given to these proposals in the House of Lords—namely, the profession on the part of the promoters that they based themselves on a higher moral and religious standard than that hitherto professed by organised Christianity. The assumption of many of the promoters during the debates has been that the Christian Churches are obstacles in the path of progress and morality.' Signatories included the Archbishop of Canterbury and prominent church leaders from other denominations.[21]

The Divorce Law Reform Union issued a reply through the columns of *The Times*. They made the point that the bill would only bring the law somewhat into line with that of 14 other countries, as well as 7 colonies. 'We contend that so far from the recommendations of the Majority report of the Royal Commission, as embodied in Lord Buckmaster's Bill, tending to injure the interests of numberless men, women and especially children, they will, if the bill is passed, not only give relief, not to a small number of hard cases, but to many thousands of persons who have been waiting many years for their release. It is quite certain that if there is to be no other way of escape from a miserable marriage than by committing the act of adultery – the most recent records of the Divorce Court prove this – more and more people will avail themselves of that ground... The country has now to make up its mind whether it will have perpetuated the existing system of permanent separation without the power to remarry – resulting in a larger and larger increase in the number of irregular unions and illegitimate children, or none – or whether it will recognise the justifiable needs of the people, and make it possible for them to contract legal unions and have legitimate children.'[22]

Comment

The vigour of this public exchange demonstrated the strong feelings on both sides of the debate, as well as the large gulf in principle between the two sides. The divorce campaign was being thrust forward by a group of men who were deeply antagonistic to the Christian faith. Proponents of divorce reform regarded the teachings of Christ on divorce as an irrelevant relic from the dark ages, and saw the Church as an obstacle to progressive thought. They made plain their rejection of marriage as an institution ordained by God, and believed that the marriage bond could be dissolved for what they called 'grave reasons'. To them it was self-evident that divorce liberalisation was a good thing. They believed passionately that divorce opened the gateway to future happiness, especially for children who would be saved from their parents' immoral behaviour.

Those who opposed extending the grounds of divorce believed that Christian marriage was the rock on which Western civilisation had been built. The Archbishop of York emphasised that the marriage law was for the good of the whole community and not a private transaction of individuals. Lord Parmoor supported the belief that there was no difference between the Christian view and the public welfare view. In his challenge to the bill, the Marquess of Salisbury noted the arbitrary nature of the reasons given for extending the grounds of divorce. Subsequent events have proved the soundness of the Marquess of Salisbury's argument. Once the foundation of Christian truth is set aside, then there is no ethical or logical reason why divorce should not be granted for any and every reason.

The major weakness in the Christian position was the division on whether or not marriage was an indissoluble bond. While the Archbishop of Canterbury and a number of other bishops were committed to the Protestant doctrine of divorce, others in the debate, like Lord Phillimore and Viscount

Halifax, supported the view that marriage was an indissoluble bond. With the skill of a forensic lawyer, Lord Buckmaster exposed this division, and ridiculed the lack of agreement within the Church of England. If they could not even agree between themselves, how could anybody believe their witness? Because of this division the Church was unable to speak with authority. The theological dispute around the Protestant doctrine of divorce, which had raged in the Church for decades, was having a major influence on the outcome of the debate. It was now abundantly clear that the Church's inability to clarify its position on divorce was having an impact on the way marriage was viewed in England.

While the Church was not agreed on the indissolubility of the marriage bond, they were at least united in opposition to the remarriage of divorcees in church. The Archbishop of Canterbury, supported by other bishops, argued that, out of loyalty to the teachings of Christ, the Church could not accept that the remarriage of divorcees, whose former partner was still living, should be solemnised in the Church of England. The position taken by the Archbishop of Canterbury, with the full support of the bishops, is highly significant to the present unresolved debate regarding the remarriage of divorcees in church. Is the Church now saying that those who defended the Christian position against remarriage with such conviction were wrong, and lacking in compassion, and that Lord Buckmaster and his friends were right?

OPPOSITION IN THE HOUSE OF COMMONS

The victory gained in the House of Lords was short-lived, for the bill met determined opposition in the House of Commons; in a free vote the bill was voted down in the proportion of three votes to two. *The Times* commented, 'The division on the divorce motion last night showed the House of Commons for what it is, the most medieval Chamber in living memory. The weight of the argument was overwhelmingly in favour of the enactment of the recommendations of the Majority report of the Royal Commission... Yet the House of Commons is so far behind the spirit of the age that it cannot even countenance a pious resolution in favour of a very restricted extension of the grounds of and facilities for divorce.'[23] This comment was in stark contrast to *The Times* editorial of 12 November 1912 (quoted in chapter 6) which asserted that the proposals of the Majority report would lead to an easy tolerance for divorce.

THE EQUALISATION OF DIVORCE FOR ADULTERY: 1923

The divorce campaign learned from the reverse of 1920. It had been a tactical mistake to try and move conservative England too far in one giant step. A more sensible approach, which aimed to keep public sentiment on their side, would be to move one step at a time—and the next logical step would be to achieve the equalisation of the grounds of divorce for women. Accordingly in 1923, Major Cyril Entwistle introduced a Private Member's bill into the House of Commons with the single objective of equalising access to divorce on the grounds of adultery. There is little doubt that the proponents saw equalisation of the law as another small but necessary step along the pathway. There was little opposition to the bill in the House of Commons. Many members believed that there was no real issue of principle. Moreover, it was now widely accepted that the sex differential in divorce was unjust. In the 1920 debate few people had opposed the clause that proposed equal access for men and women, and the Church had not objected.

In the House of Commons Mr Francis Blundell opposed the bill as a Catholic. He believed the bill to be bad, immoral, and likely to have a most deleterious effect on the public morals of the country. 'I know enough to see that this bill may be a very easy way of procuring collusion. This bill introduces quite a new principle and one cannot see how far it is going to lead one, nor can one see any limit to collusive action which might be started if this bill passed... It is said we should pass this bill because the women want it, and I think many honourable gentlemen consider the new electorate composed largely of women as a strange and unknown thing, and seem to be not quite sure what they had better do in order to conciliate them... I have not had a single communication from my own constituency except from the Mothers' Union, which invited me to oppose this bill, and thanked me for voting against it on the second reading.'[24]

Rev Henry Dunnico said that in so far as the bill sought to lay down a common standard of morality for both sexes he was in entire agreement. Adultery whether committed by the man or woman deserved to be deprecated. However he did not believe that the act of adultery on the part of the man, generally speaking, was as serious in its consequences and as disastrous in its results as adultery on the part of the woman. 'There are several reasons for that. In the first place, the mother occupies a place in the home that the father does not. The idea of motherhood is an indispensable factor in the idea of the home. Any act of adultery of the part of the woman must affect the home to a degree and extent that it does not when committed by the father... I believe the bill to be the first step in a powerful campaign to make the dissolution of the marriage tie easier, and whatever tends to make the dissolution of marriage easier strikes a fatal blow at the very foundation of national greatness and the fabric of the home... I believe the real secret of England's greatness is that in no other land on the face of the earth does the home count for so much and play so large a part in shaping and moulding the national character.'[25]

The bill passed the third reading by a massive majority of 257 votes to 26. *The Times* leader of 9th June 1923 commented, 'Though various attempts have been made at different stages to amend the bill and to enlarge its scope, it leaves the House in the same simple shape in which it was introduced. Its simplicity has been its salvation, and in the House of Lords it will be introduced by Lord Buckmaster, with whose much wider proposals for reforming the marriage laws it does not conflict. It has met with little opposition on religious grounds... For our own part we believe that the bill expresses a principle on social and moral justice to which there can be no objection. It brings the law of England and Wales into conformity with that of Scotland and nearly all other civilised and Christian nations. It can hardly, therefore, be regarded as the beginning of a descent down a "slippery slope".'[26]

Second reading in the Lords

Lord Buckmaster introducing the second reading in the House of Lords said the bill left untouched the wider questions of divorce. 'Its aims are confined within narrow limits. It is not designed in any way to alter the existing grounds upon which divorce can be obtained. It does not attempt to explore once more that large disputed area upon which your Lordships entered with such patience and industry when I introduced my bill for matrimonial reform more than two sessions ago. It has this purpose and this purpose alone: to secure that whatever may be the grounds of divorce they shall be the same for both women and men.'

He appealed to Lord Birkenhead to help secure the passage of the present bill. Afterwards they could see if they could not work together for greater and more liberal measures. He then turned to the current position of the law. 'At this moment cruelty, however gross, however prolonged, however degrading and insulting, gives a woman no right to liberty at all. Then insanity. Even though her husband be shut up for ever in a lunatic asylum she must stay outside, and if he be liberated, our law declares that she must submit herself to his embraces and transmit to the third and fourth generation the taint of insanity by which her husband has been affected. Drunkenness gives her no right of relief... There is no liberty granted today for any of the horrible degrading relationships that arise when men and women are married and have physical repulsion from each other... The law says, "Hate each other as much as you like, let the act of married relationship be to each of you an infinite degradation; debase and degrade a thing which may be made the most beautiful and high communication. The law says you must go on until the end of time and you shall never know what it is to be able to enjoy the free and happy companionship that men and women experience who are bound together in the bonds of affection." The feelings that I express about these things have caused people to say that I have been obsessed with this question.' He reminded the House that work on the divorce issue would not end with this bill. 'No one can doubt that the change is coming fast, that the minds

146

of men and women are being influenced by the ever moving conditions of society and the swift procession of the years. The change will come. I cannot say whether it will be our hands or the hands of those who follow us by which the harvest is gathered, but it will be you, my Lords, who have sown the seed.'[27]

Lord Braye opposed the bill on the sole ground of opposing the extension of divorce. 'We have had many discussions in this House on the question of divorce, in general – very long and, indeed, embittered debates. Divorce is in the air. It has come to stay in this country in all probability. Since 1857 it has certainly been acknowledged by the law of the land.' He wished to stop the spread of divorce and to prevent the facilities for divorce from becoming larger and wider than they were at the present time. 'The cry still is for facilities, "Give us divorce. The principle of divorce is recognised by the country and we want facilities. We want to get divorces more quickly and more easily!"'

He predicted that those who supported the bill were only too anxious to find other and better reasons for extending the power of obtaining divorce. 'The opponents of marriage in this country, and many other countries, are marching on. It is terrible to think of the goal towards which they are marching because once the divine law is forsaken, as it was to a large extent at the Reformation, there is no possible stopping place.' He mentioned that they heard continually of women wishing to get their freedom, and men who wished to be free from their wives. 'If you pursue this matter in some portions of the press you might imagine, from the words that are used, that the yoke of marriage is regarded as the most intolerable thing that was ever imposed upon any civilised community.' He made the point that the doctrine of the sanctity and indissolubility of marriage was believed by millions of Catholics. 'It is a doctrine which is the foundation of all civilisation, because if you dissolve marriage you dissolve the family, and you put an end to all idea of property passing from father to son.' He said, 'It is urged that a bill like this is only a mere extension of divorce, but it is by multiplying these extensions for divorce that you will lay siege to the citadel, and finally, entirely obliterate in this country the idea of marriage. Sanctity of marriage holds good now in this country and I believe the majority of people are opposed to the facilitating of divorce.'

He then mentioned that in a debate Lord Buckmaster said that his (Lord Braye's) position was impregnable. 'But he added that the position of those who maintained that a marriage might be dissolved for one reason, and then opposed such measures as this, was incomprehensible. Such a position, which is the Protestant position, is incomprehensible. The contract of marriage is unbreakable and can admit of no exceptions whatever… But this country goes halfway, believes in marriage as a holy thing and then sets forth the grounds on which a marriage can be dissolved.'[28]

The Archbishop of Canterbury (Davidson) said that they had been reminded of the debates of the last few years and the formidable effort made by the two noble Lords to facilitate divorce by multiplying the grounds on which it could be claimed. They had failed due to lack of parliamentary time and failure of opportunity in the House of Commons. He again stated his own position on the matter. 'I believe, as we all do, in the lifelong obligation of a marriage contract, but we all admit, and are bound to admit – even the noble Lord who moved the rejection of the bill would be bound to admit – that there are occasions upon which public interest seems to require that there should be some modification of the original contract.'

He would vote for the bill simply because it confined itself entirely to a dissolution of marriage for one specific ground of adultery and nothing else. 'Had it gone on, as the previous Bill when modified by this House went on, to extend and multiply the grounds of divorce I should have felt bound to do all I could to prevent its becoming law... But we believe that there is one principle by which we must stand, and that principle is that the sole ground upon which a marriage can be dissolved is to be found in our Lord's own words in the gospel according to St Matthew, namely, that it should be on the ground of unfaithfulness to the marriage vow, in the sense of fornication and adultery alone. That we know to be the principle which is in accord with the Christian faith; I believe it to be most firmly the principle which, on social grounds, is accepted by the people of this country as a whole.'[29]

Earl Russell said that a grave disadvantage of the bill was that they would have to wait ten or twenty years to see how it worked before any further reform was granted. Those interested in divorce reform regarded it as nothing but a paper change and only useful to a small extent. The right to remarry was the crux of the whole question.[30] The bill was read a second time and passed by 95 votes to 8.

Comment

Lord Buckmaster made clear the crusading nature of the divorce campaign. Work would be ongoing and he was sure that change was coming fast—the seeds had been sown and soon the harvest would be gathered. What was the harvest to which he so looked forward? Did he foresee the harvest of mass divorce that lay in the future? The strongest opposition to the bill came from Lord Braye, who as a Catholic was fundamentally opposed to the principle of the bill. His aim was to reduce, rather than increase, the facilities for divorce. He believed that each extension to the grounds of divorce affected the ideal of marriage. He identified the weakness of the Protestant position, which wanted divorce for one or two reasons, and then wanted to stop. But that position was untenable for there was no halfway position. The Archbishop of Canterbury supported the bill because he believed that divorce for adultery was permissible. But he opposed extending the grounds beyond adultery.

And so the Matrimonial Causes Act, which became law in 1923, removed the additional burden imposed on women and gave them equal access to divorce for reason of simple adultery. The new law led to an increase in the number of divorces that were initiated by women which from 1924 onward exceeded those initiated by men. There was a further gradual increase during the 1930s, the numbers between 1926 and 1935 averaging 3,700 per year. Compared to the divorce rate before the First World War, there was a fourfold increase by the 1930s, as shown in the figure in chapter 8.

Chapter 8

Increasing the sum of human happiness

AP Herbert's bill extends the grounds for divorce – 1937

Clearly those who desired more liberal divorce laws were not content with the small gains of 1923 and continued the campaign. The determination of the proponents of divorce liberalisation was supported by a flow of press comment on the unsatisfactory nature of the law. Meanwhile the issue of divorce remained controversial in the Church as a growing school of thought, which included a number of Modernist theologians, was now openly supporting the crusade for more liberal laws. The Archdeacon of Coventry, at a diocesan conference, provided an example of this strand of thinking. 'The limitation of the grounds of divorce to the one ground of adultery has resulted in a state of affairs which is disastrously prejudicial to public morality. As the law stands at present those who wish to bring an end to the marriage are forced to take one of two alternatives – either one must commit adultery or one must commit perjury. The law as it stands is a definite incitement to immorality. It was the duty of the Church to press for, and not merely to acquiesce in, reform of the existing marriage law; reform could be found in an extension of the grounds of divorce which did not necessarily mean making divorce more easy.'[1]

However, a large body of opinion within the Church did not agree with the views being expressed by the Archdeacon and some Modernist theologians. There was a deep sense of frustration that the mainline views of the Church were not being adequately presented to the world at large. This sense was compounded by the inability of the church leadership, which was divided on the issue, to make a clear statement on the position of the Church of England.

THE LAMBETH CONFERENCES: 1920 AND 1930

Meanwhile the issue of marriage and divorce had been on the agenda of the Lambeth Conferences. The Encyclical Letter of 1920 dealt with the indissoluble nature of marriage. According to the Encyclical, the fellowship between man and woman in marriage was the earliest which God gave to the human race. The Lord reminded them that from the beginning of creation God made them male and female. The words of Christ declared God's original purpose of marriage. The man and his wife are no longer two, but one flesh, and those whom God has joined together man is not to put asunder. 'This revelation about God's purpose gives the keynote to all that the Church has to teach about marriage... But marriage is not ordained only to give opportunity for the development of those two lives in unity. It has essentially the aim of bringing other lives into the world. Its indis- solubility should secure to the children the continued care and love of both their parents, so long as they live.'[2] A resolution passed by the 1920 Conference affirmed,

> as our Lord's principle and standard of marriage, a lifelong and indissoluble union, for better, for worse, of one man and one woman, to the exclusion of all others on either side, and calls on all Christian people to maintain and bear witness to this standard.

The resolution accepted the right of a national or regional church within the Communion to deal with cases which fell within the exception men- tioned in Matthew's gospel. While recognising the extreme difficulty of governments in framing marriage laws for citizens, many of whom do not accept the Christian standard, a further resolution expressed its firm belief that in every country the Church should be free to bear witness to that standard through its power of administration and discipline exercised in relation to its own members.[3]

In 1930 the Lambeth Conference again dealt with the issue of divorce. The Encyclical Letter, in its comments on the life and witness of the Christian community, reminded the Church that Christ's community had been commissioned to set a standard of life which was not that of the world. It said that too often the standard of Christians had been assimilated to that of the surrounding society, or the spirit of the age. 'But the tremendous commission of the head of the Church confronts us. "Ye are the salt of the earth," and "Ye are the light of the world." No metaphors could be more searching. Salt and light, he says, and that in every place and relationship of life—first and foremost, in all that concerns the family. The beauty of family life is one of God's most precious gifts, and its preservation is a paramount responsibility of the Church. Its foundation is the lifelong union of husband and wife on which our Lord decisively sets his seal. One flesh he said they were to be. Holy marriage is part of God's plan for mankind. It follows that any community disregards this at its peril. Empires have perished before now because the dry rot of laxity and corruption in home life set in. To maintain the ideal of marriage is therefore to preserve the social health of the community. It is a national interest of supreme value. It follows that divorce is unnatural. It destroys the security of the nation and the stability of the family. If there are children, they are deprived of the guardianship to which God called both their parents. To the defence of Christ's standard of marriage we summon the members of the Church, for on it depends all that makes the magic of the word home.' The Lambeth Conference resolved that in cases of divorce,

> while passing no judgement on the practice of regional or national churches within our Communion, recommends that the marriage of one whose former partner is still living shall not be celebrated according to the rites of the Church.[4]

THE CHURCH OF ENGLAND EXAMINES DIVORCE

As a consequence of the Lambeth Conference's strong call for the Church to witness before the world to Christ's standard for marriage, there was again pressure on the Church of England to clarify its position. Responding to the call the Bishop of Salisbury (George Donaldson) proposed in 1931 that a joint committee of both Convocations should be set up to examine the implications of the Lambeth resolutions for the Church of England. The bishop emphasised the urgency of the situation and said that while the Church had been unable to agree about Christ's teaching on marriage the situation had gone from bad to worse. The main reason for the disturbing situation was to be found in the new views of marriage which were prevalent in society. A change in the spiritual outlook of the nation had led to increasing impatience with the bondage of the marriage tie. Against the Christian view of marriage was the modern secular view, according to which it was a contract, entered into with the understanding that the marriage tie was not necessarily a lifelong contract.

He argued that they should aim to establish a rule throughout the Church of England that no marriage should be celebrated in church of a person whose former partner in marriage was still living. At present the Church's practical attitude was ambiguous. While some bishops and clergy took that line, others were prepared to solemnise a second marriage in the case of what was called the innocent party. But who was the innocent party? He referred to the confusion and mischief caused by the modern system that encouraged collusion between the husband and wife in securing a divorce. 'In these cases the distinction between the innocent and guilty party was utterly and contemptibly false. No, it was really not possible for the Church to distinguish in that way between the innocent and guilty.'[5]

The Bishop of St Albans (Michael Furse) felt strongly with the Bishop of Salisbury that this was a matter of great urgency. There were a great number of people both in England and in other parts of the world that were looking for a definite lead on the question of marriage. In his judgement the position of the Church had been greatly complicated by certain pronouncements from individual bishops with reference to the question of marriage not only of the innocent but also of the guilty parties. It seemed to him quite intolerable that they should go on with divided views on such a fundamental issue as Christian marriage. He believed there was no halfway house between the strict view of the lifelong, indissoluble tie, and that of allowing practically any causes for the dissolution of marriage. The reason 'the Church had refused to admit divorce with the possibility of remarriage, was that if one did remarry, in the eyes of the Church one was continuing the sin which one had committed, which was adultery. The fact that one had legal sanction for doing what in the view of the Church was adultery, did not alter the position; or make it less a sin because one lived in that state.'[6]

The joint committee, which held twenty-two sessions, gathering evidence from experts and leading authorities, produced a report entitled *The Church and Marriage*. Because of fundamental differences in belief, there was a majority report, supported by most of the committee, and two minority reports.

The Church and Marriage: the majority report

The majority report noted that throughout the present century new views had become prevalent with regard to the married state. 'There is in many quarters a revolt against any view of marriage which emphasises its social aspects and obligations, and an increasing tendency to regard it as a purely individual affair.' The report also drew attention to a growing tendency to regard marriage as a purely human and civil contract that ought not to be allowed to remain binding when its terms have become unwelcome.[7] A widespread inarticulate revolt against the experience of unhappy marriage was identified. Behind the revolt was the 'active propaganda of a minority pressing with reasoned arguments for a definite policy of reform, and the situation generally, and not least among Church people, was one of bewilderment and distress'.

The report restated the essential principles of marriage as a lifelong and indissoluble union between one man and one woman to the exclusion of all others, as indicated by both experience of the natural order and by the teaching of the New Testament. The first and natural purpose of marriage is the maintenance of the race, and, therefore, the procreation and nurture of children. 'The child must be tended and reared; he must be trained and prepared for life – a process which must continue until he approaches manhood. Moreover, in the natural course children will be born through a period of years, and the parents' obligation towards them will not cease until their own youth has passed away.' Parental affection and the fond attachment of a child for its parents are fundamental instincts of human nature, and any separation of children from their parents, inevitable as it must occasionally be, is in some sense an interference with the natural course. As the primary object of marriage is the maintenance of the race, the rearing of children and the stability of the home preclude the idea of marriage as a transitory relation.[8]

Another purpose of marriage is a spiritual relationship of which sexual intercourse is only the outward sign. 'The sexes are complementary to each other. Each supplies what is wanting in the other, and the experiences of life bind the two partners together in a permanent spiritual union, which in happy marriages endures and develops long after the fires of youth have died down.'[9] Some were suggesting, in view of the emancipation of women, the mitigation of the old rigours of parental authority, and the increased knowledge of birth control, that the family as an institution was falling into decay, and that the state would increasingly take over its functions. 'We believe, on the contrary, that the family is based upon deep rooted instincts of the human race, and that in fact the ethical value of the family has not been impaired by recent changes, but its necessity for man's moral welfare made more plain.'[10]

The report defined divorce as a complete putting away of a former spouse, with the right to remarriage. It also noted that 'the view of marriage as a lifelong and exclusive union of one man and one woman was in fact very much of a novelty in the world into which Christianity brought it. Not only did the Romans accept divorce, but the Jews allowed it for various causes, and even (some scholars maintain) required a man to divorce his wife if she were adulterous. The doctrine that neither party may put away the other, and marry another, on pain of being guilty of adultery, is directly due to Christ.'[11] The Church must hold fast to this teaching. Where there has been full consent and the marriage has been consummated, the marriage is for life, and it is against the will of God for Christian men and women to remarry during the lifetime of the former spouse.[12]

Discussing the Church's responsibility with regard to state legislation, the report concluded that, in view of the present condition of society, it must be conceded that, so far as secular legislation was concerned, some provision for dissolving the legal bond is inevitable. Because England was not wholly Christian, but included large numbers of people who definitely rejected the obligations of the Christian religion, 'the question – on what grounds a marriage may be dissolved – must be faced in the light of existing circumstances'. The report made the point that the Church ought not to oppose every suggested modification of the present law, without carefully considering each suggestion upon its merits.[13]

The report reached the firm conclusion 'that in no circumstances should the "second marriage" in the lifetime of the former partner be solemnised with the rites of the Church: because the refusal of such solemnisation will be the way in which the Church will testify to the lifelong character of the marriage bond, and to its belief that a divorce *a vinculo* is wrong'.[14]

The Church and Marriage: the minority reports

The Bishops of Birmingham (Ernest Barnes) and Barking (James Inskip) and the Dean of Hereford (Dr Waterfield) and Canon Guy Rogers were unable to sign the majority report. Their basic argument was that Christ had laid down an ideal for marriage and not a definite law. The Church was free to legislate for divorce, bearing the ideal in mind, and taking account of changing conditions in society. Christ had left men to legislate for themselves, for he had set before them the supreme ideal. 'We believe that the mind of Christ would approve of legislation on the part of his Church which, while keeping ever in view the divine ideal, had compassionate consideration for the troubles arising from failures to live up to that ideal, and might be changed from time to time to meet the requirements of changing conditions.' For these reasons they could not agree with the unqualified statement that the Church must regard marriage as an indissoluble union. They believed that the state was right to provide legislation for divorce under certain circumstances, and thought that it was a mistake on the part of the Church to maintain the attitude that the state had done wrong. They believed that there were cases of unhappy marriages when advice to divorce 'for your sake and the sake of the children' was in tune with the mind of Christ.[15]

They were not prepared to deny to a genuinely innocent person the privilege of having their second marriage blessed by being celebrated in church. They recognised the strength of the argument that in the case of one who had already taken the vow of a lifelong obligation, and had failed to keep it, the sincerity with which the same obligation could be assumed a second time was open to question. 'But we press our contention that the first vow was, in intention, sincere, and we submit that the second vow may be the same. In every vow sincerity of intention is all that can be demanded of human nature.'[16]

In conclusion the minority report quoted *The Modern Churchman*: 'The question to be asked and answered in connection with any proposed alteration in our marriage laws is whether such alteration will promote the Christian ideal of marriage. This, social experience has taught us, is not best secured in all cases by literal obedience to a principle of Christ as though that principle were a legal precept, but by the application of the whole body of Christian principles to the complexities of an ever changing situation, with the definite purpose of advancing in practice to the Christian ideal.'[17]

The second minority report, signed by the Bishop of Norwich (Bertram Pollock), proposed the adoption of universal civil preliminaries to marriage, allowing the Church to provide a religious marriage service for those who wanted a church wedding.[18]

DEBATE IN CONVOCATION: 1935

When the Bishop of Salisbury presented the majority report to the Upper House in 1935, he emphasised that the Church should not oppose every proposal that the state may have for extending the grounds of divorce. He said that it was neither wise nor right to seek to impose by legislation their Christian views upon those who did not share their faith. Further, if they withdrew their opposition to any moderate and carefully drawn legislation for extending the grounds of divorce, they might actually help the state in resisting the more extreme proposals for the relaxation of the marriage law. As two standards of marriage were already in existence in England they could not at present bring the whole nation to the Christian view of marriage, although their attitude towards secular proposals for marriage reform must always be subject to their Christian ideal. 'It must be the attitude best calculated to bring the nation ultimately to accept the Christian ideal, and allowance must be made for the fact that rigid opposition by the Church might result in an increased unwillingness to listen to its message.'[19]

The Archbishop of Canterbury (Cosmo Lang) disagreed with the view of the minority report concerning the nature of Christ's teaching on marriage. He believed that Christ laid down a definite standard by which the institution of marriage should be regulated. He agreed with the Bishop of Salisbury that the Church should not oppose reasonable legislation to extend the grounds for divorce. He said that in previous parliamentary debates the question had been argued simply on the grounds of public welfare, simply whether or not any particular proposal would be for the good of the community and for the stabilising rather than the weakening of the marriage vow. 'The same attitude was taken up by my revered predecessor and myself in the long debates which took place from time to time in the House of Lords on the bills which the late Lord Buckmaster so passionately urged. The point was always made by him and by Lord Birkenhead with great force and vigour in those debates that the arguments which I had continually put before the House of Lords about the public disadvantage of these proposals were of little value because they were urged by persons who were committed to the view that in all circumstances any kind of divorce was wrong. If this report is published and Resolution 10 were approved, it would show that members of the Church were not blind to the position of the state in this matter, that they had regard to the difficulties created where a public opinion which is not wholly Christian was held by multitudes of citizens, and that it might be difficult to impose a strict adherence to Christian principles by law upon persons who do not hold or follow the Christian faith. But even in admitting that I am sure we must adhere to the position that each particular proposal must be judged upon its own merits.'[20] Resolution 10 stated that the Church should be prepared to give consideration to proposals to amend the divorce laws, provided only that any proposed amendment did not tend to make marriage a temporary alliance or to undermine the foundation of family life. The acceptance of this resolution by Convocation made it clear that the Church of England would not oppose the legislation for extending the grounds of divorce that was soon to be debated in Parliament.

Having examined the divorce issue in great detail, both Houses of the Canterbury Convocation accepted the following resolutions, although there was some support for the minority report:

> That this House affirms as our Lord's principle and standard of marriage a lifelong and indissoluble union, for better or for worse, of one man with one woman, to the exclusion of all others on either side.

> That this House also affirms its belief that, as a consequence, in no circumstances can Christian men or women remarry during the lifetime of a wife or husband without a breach of the moral principles by which the institution of marriage is governed according to Christ's teaching.

> That in order to maintain the principle of a lifelong obligation clearly expressed in the marriage service, the Church should not allow the use of that service in the case of anyone who has a partner still living; any person who remarried contrary to the second of the above resolutions ought not to be admitted to the Sacraments and privileges of the Church except on such conditions as the Church may require.[21]

The Convocation of York accepted a similar set of resolutions although there were differences in the wording. For example, the first resolution, as accepted by the Upper House, avoided the word indissoluble, describing marriage as a union continuing till the parties were parted by death. A number of other resolutions were passed which dealt with issues such as the competence of the Church to enact its own discipline in regard to marriage, the question of admission to communion of remarried persons, and recommendations concerning nullity.

In *Divorce and Remarriage in Anglicanism*, AR Winnett points out that refusal to solemnise the remarriage of any divorced persons had the support of all the Church's representative bodies and concluded, 'It may be therefore said to represent the considered judgement of the Church and to possess a spiritual authority which cannot lightly be set aside.'[22]

At last the Church had stated its position in clear terms, even although a minority of the clergy did not support the resolutions. Of significance was the resolution that the Church should not interfere with the right of the state to legislature for a secular society. This view would become important in the parliamentary debates to extend the grounds of divorce.

———————

A feature of the divorce crusade was that it always claimed public support for what it was trying to achieve. It was no surprise, then, that the introduction of the Private Member's bill to Parliament in 1936 was supported by a letter from a number of women's organisations, including the National Council for Equal Citizenship, the National Council of Women of Great Britain and the Women's Liberal Federation, which claimed to speak on behalf of the vast majority of women. They were convinced that in providing for a moderate extension of the grounds for divorce the parliamentary bill had the support in principle not only of those for whom they spoke but of the mass of women and indeed of public opinion in general. 'The organisations which we represent feel that the reforms provided for in this bill are long overdue, and, if carried out, will do much to enhance public respect for the institution of marriage. By providing for relief in cases where the union has ceased to be a marriage in any real sense of the term, the bill, we are confident, will discourage extramarital relationships, and can only strengthen the ideal of marriage as a union designed for the mutual society, help and comfort that the one ought to have to the other.'[23]

However, the Mothers' Union, an organisation that represented over half a million women, was opposed to the bill. They wrote in *The Times*, 'The Mothers' Union has always opposed any bill which provided increased facilities for divorce, and in 1931 and 1935 the central council, which is a body representative of the members throughout the country, reaffirmed this position. We should deeply regret the bill as it stands becoming law as we believe that ultimately none but Christian standards can be for the well-being of the nation.'[24]

AP HERBERT'S DIVORCE BILL: 1936–37

The Private Member's bill to extend the grounds of divorce was introduced in the House of Commons in November 1936. Euphemistically referred to as the Marriage Bill its primary intention was, in line with the recommendations of the Gorell Commission, to extend the grounds for divorce beyond adultery for the first time. The preamble to the bill stated that its purpose was 'for the true support of marriage, the protection of children, the removal of hardship, the reduction of illicit unions and unseemly litigation, the relief of conscience among the clergy, and the restoration of due respect for the law'.[25]

Debate in the House of Commons: November 1936 to May 1937

Mr Rupert De la Bere introduced the bill to the House with the hope that it 'may be possible to bring happiness to those who have been crushed by the severity of our present system of marriage law'. He supported it because of the misery and distress which have been caused in so many homes, because the Act of 1857 had created a situation in which, as many judges had asserted, the existing law was ineffective and farcical. It was the direct cause of many virtuous couples living in sin. He noted that the Archbishop of Canterbury and the Lord Chief Justice had expressed the opinion that reform must come, and the Modern Churchmen's Union had promised their general support for the bill. He said that almost everybody would agree that an act of infidelity is very far from being the only or the most important breach of marriage obligations. 'It is a single act as opposed to desertion, but in our law many persons whose marriage has broken down from other causes are compelled either to commit, or to pretend to commit, adultery in order to obtain release.'[26]

Mr AP Herbert, the real architect of the bill, told the House that he believed that the bill would bring new strength to institutions which they valued—the Church, the law, the relation between Church and state, and marriage and the family. 'At the moment the law is mocked not only in words but in deeds. There is collusion and perjury, and it is sufficient to say that the wrong people get what they want and the right people cannot.' The Archbishop of Canterbury had said that the time had come when Parliament could no longer resist the growing public demand for some extension of the grounds of divorce. The Modern Churchmen's Union had given general support to the bill. Mr Herbert reminded the House that he represented more clergymen of the Church of England than any other member, but he had not received a single protest since he entered the House though he had made no secret of his intention. 'There is not the slightest doubt that there has been a great change in the attitude of the Church during the last few years (cheers). There is no doubt that most reasonable churchmen are not only ready but eager for some reasonable reform of the law.' He then referred to the resolution passed in the Upper House of Canterbury Convocation stating that the Church would not oppose any reasonable legislation for extending the grounds of divorce.

Mr Herbert agreed that extending the grounds was controversial. 'Not long ago a divorce judge said that it would be incredible to future generations that divorce should be granted for a single act of adultery while it is denied when the whole purpose of marriage has been frustrated by deliberate and permanent desertion. If a man goes to America or Australia and carelessly omits to commit adultery or keeps quiet about it if he does, who can say it is in the interests of the state, the children, marriage or anything else that the woman shall permanently be tied to nothing at all, and unable to build up a new home with someone who would protect her and her children?' With regard to the criticism that the bill would lead to divorce by consent, he reminded the House that 'at this moment we have divorce by consent, and divorce by consent in the most shameful and degrading form, by means of arranged adultery, whether bogus or genuine; a method of divorce by consent which is shameful and degrading not only to every individual who takes part in it, but to every institution it touches.' He went on, 'The intention of the bill is not that there should be more divorce, but easier divorce in the right cases and for the right people, and, wherever possible, more conciliation. It is not true that divorce reform need always mean more divorce.' He concluded by arguing that the divorce laws of England could not be defended by reference to divine sanction, nor on the grounds of human reason. 'They are based in the main on historical accident, on antique prejudice, and upon the strange and almost bestial notion that the one thing which matters in married life is the sexual act and that the only breach of the marriage obligation which really matters is a breach of sexual fidelity. They are like some architectural monstrosity, which stands upon a hill and offends the eye of all beholders year after year, and yet, because it is so familiar, if anybody tries to pull it down, there arises a great outcry. These laws are the cause of great, unnecessary and unjustifiable unhappiness, and, apart from that, they are a danger to our institutions. Twenty-four years ago a Royal Commission worked for three years and condemned them, but nothing has been done. Since then the Press has never ceased to support the demand for reform. I am sure we have the bulk of the people behind us, and now, I believe we have the churches as well. It remains for this House at last to rise up and tackle and settle this problem.'[27]

Sir Francis Acland said that opposition to the bill came mainly from those with strong religious convictions. But he reminded them that the Majority report of the Royal Commission recommended that the legislature should be unfettered by any consideration other than 'the interests of the state, society, morality, the parties and the children'. In his opinion, 'The sanctity of marriage is rather better upheld by those who wish to reform the divorce laws than by many, I do not say all, of the representatives of the Christian churches.' He observed that it was curious that people should not only accept for themselves, but should desire to enforce on the state the teachings they found in the gospel concerning divorce. 'Nearly all of us agree that the Founder of the Christian religion, at the least, was the greatest moral teacher of all time. Let us think of his teaching in relation to the place and time in which he taught... Is it not natural that the great teacher, who watched the life he knew so well with his all-seeing and all-pitying eyes, was bound to teach, in cases where there now are great state services for the custody and treatment of the mentally deranged, of the inebriates or of the prisoners,

160

and was bound to feel that, for the Galilean villager, there was no alternative but continuance of life in the home and therefore the maintenance of the marriage bond. There must be evidence in the House today that the fires of religious feeling on this subject are not burning so strongly as they did 20 or even 10 years ago.' He informed the House that a great deal of the best religious opinion, represented by the views of the Modern Churchmen's Union, was remarkably in line with the proposals of the bill.[28]

Mr Reginald Sorensen said that the children could not benefit from a home where the parents were not living happily. He was anxious to place the interests of the children before everything else. 'I have seen children who have lived for many years in homes which bear the semblance of unity but underneath are full of poison and canker, and of all that which destroys the best interests of the children themselves... Children come to know subconsciously, if they do not know consciously, when there is no real union between their parents. It is not long before children of average intelligence know whether the atmosphere in which they live is one which can be called a home or precisely the reverse. For that reason I plead most earnestly that those of us who are happily married, should, for the sake of the children, not condone homes which are not in the best interests of those children, morally and spiritually.'

He implored the House not to be intimidated by any ecclesiastical body. 'All of us may lose votes over this, but what does it matter? In the long run what we have to do is to try to serve humanity and the best interest of humanity from the standpoint which we think is right.' He asked the House to remember that 'there is still this great army of men and women who are living, not in a world that is fine, but in a world that they think is black, in a world that they feel is a prison, that is taking the soul out of all that they once called life, and is therefore reducing them to the position of disguised hypocrites. We do not want more hypocrites; we want more men and women whose union is based on honesty, more who are bound together, not because they are afraid of their neighbours, not because they are compelled by law, but because the partnership between them is based upon inherent merit and will last through all the stresses and strains of time.' He wanted to see real marriage saved from the attack being made upon it by the inner inconsistencies of life. He begged the House to pass the bill and thereby do something to lift a little darkness from the lives of thousands of their fellow human beings (cheers).[29]

Mrs Mavis Tate said it was not possible to hide mutual hatred between married partners from children, no matter now sincerely they might wish to do so. 'But it is not only the children of unhappy marriages where the parents are living together whom we have to consider. What of the children being brought up today with the stigma of illegitimacy because the parents have been able to find no relief in divorce and have taken unto themselves

what is known as a lover or a mistress, children who are being brought up in
what would be a happy and healthy home life if they were not living under
the stigma of illegitimacy.' She argued that it was the duty of the House to
do everything they could to safeguard the rising generation and to see that
children grew up in healthy, happy and moral homes, but it was not possible
where they had a wife trying to bring up children on small sums of money
under a maintenance order and unable to marry a man who was willing to
marry her because she was tied to a man who was nominally her partner.[30]

Mr Ernest Thurtle said it was a grave reflection on the House that after
26 years the recommendations of the very authoritative Royal Commission
had still not been put into effect. Those who had opposed reform in the
past have, therefore, been responsible for a great deal of avoidable human
misery and suffering. It was time that marriage laws were made to approximate
much more closely to the opinion of the age. At the present time marriage
laws were an archaic survival from distant days. They were very largely based
on the doctrines of the Church. 'Whether we like it or not, it is true that the
conception of the state of marriage is not now in conformity with the
conception held by the great majority of the citizens of this country.' The
Church should not seek to prevent the state making special legislation for
the benefit of all sections of the community irrespective of their religious
belief. He went on, 'If the bill passes into law it will not make our marriage
laws ideal. I would go very much further than these proposals. I would like
to see marriage a free voluntary association which might be terminated by
the mutual consent of the parties concerned.' He concluded, 'The bill
would undoubtedly tend to strengthen the institution of marriage in a very
real sense. It would bring to many thousands of men and women a happiness
which is now denied them. It would rescue thousands of unfortunate
children from a cruel and anomalous position.'[31]

The Attorney General (Donald Somervell) then praised Mr Herbert for
introducing the bill in exactly the manner and the temper in which the
House desired it to be presented. 'If speeches are an index of the mind of
the House, it is quite clear that the House desires this bill to get a second
reading. I think there has been only one speech from an honourable
Member opposed to the second reading, and the other speeches which have
dealt with points of detail have expressed the desire that it should get a second
reading.'[32] The bill was read a second time and passed by 78 votes to 12.
The result was received with cheers. Only 90 Members of the House of
Commons, out of 600, had bothered to vote in the debate.

Responding to the letter of the Mothers' Union four supporters of the bill
wrote to *The Times*, 'As backers of the Marriage Bill, may we beg the Council
of the Mothers' Union, to believe that we are not less concerned than they
to uphold the sanctity of marriage, to strengthen the bonds of matrimony,

and to diminish the number of irregular unions which, in the present state of the law, are inevitably and probably increasingly numerous.'[33] The Mothers' Union replied, 'We have examined the bill carefully, but feel impelled to point out that in spite of some clauses aimed at rectifying existing abuses the most obvious result of the proposed Marriage Bill would be largely to increase the number of divorces in this country. It is difficult to see how this would "uphold the sanctity of marriage and strengthen the bonds of matrimony" as its supporters claim. To make divorce easier so that the parents of children who would otherwise be illegitimate might marry is to treat the symptoms of a disease and not the disease itself. A large increase in the number of divorces can have no other effect than to alter the whole conception of marriage in the eyes of the young and of future generations. They will inevitably cease to regard it as a permanent union with grave responsibilities, and believe that marriage is only to be looked upon as permanent by those whose marriages prove satisfactory.'[34]

The third reading

The third reading of the bill was held on 28 May 1937. In many ways it was the real debate in the Commons, and for the first time those who opposed the bill expressed their opposition in clear terms. The debate, which up till now had been all in one direction, drew some passion from the participants.

Sir Patrick Hannon attempted to delay the passage of the bill by introducing an amendment that the bill 'be read upon this day three months'. He questioned how much public support there was for the bill. 'Those of us who are in contact with a great variety of local organised opinion in this country must have felt, since the bill was introduced, a steady current growing, indicating a deep seated objection to the measure... It strikes, in the judgement of many of us, at the very superstructure of family life, and in a land like this, which has been attached to high Christian principles for nearly 2000 years, and where the family has been the unit of society, we cannot introduce legislation of this kind without danger of serious injury to the whole of our national life.' He regretted very much that certain distinguished churchmen had registered their view in favour of the bill. 'I venture to suggest that in our great national Church and in the Catholic Church and among much of the nonconformist opinion in this country, there is strong feeling against this bill.' He concluded, 'We have felt a deep-seated spiritual obligation to oppose the measure, and I would like to say that as long as I am in this House, or take any part in public life, I shall never be a party to an extension of the means by which family life can be broken up or the sanctity of family life assaulted by legislation in this House; and in the strong feeling which I have expressed I think that I have been giving expression to the deep-seated convictions of millions of people in this country.'[35]

Commander Robert Bower spoke in opposition to the bill. 'I wish to make it as clear as I can that we continue to oppose the bill, and must reaffirm our absolutely uncompromising hostility to any attempt to extend the grounds for divorce, which this bill does, despite the wording of its preamble. The fundamental principle to which we adhere is the complete indissolubility of Christian marriage, which was accepted, practically universally, for 1800 years as one of the foundation stones of our Christian civilisation... it is a view which was definitely accepted by the very great majority of our people until quite recent times.' He complained about the whole idea of the secularisation of the question of marriage and divorce. 'We base our case on the maintenance of the old, well tried and well established system of Christian ethics upon which the whole of our Western civilisation is based. The honourable Member for Shoreditch stated the other day that the more enlightened opinion of the country called for the bill. We may then regard the honourable Member as the spearhead of enlightened opinion in the country, and behind him what do we get? We get a motley crew of Communists, Atheists, Agnostics, and modernistic churchmen and the most ghastly of present day phenomena, the journalist churchman. A canon of St Paul's the other day wrote an article in a newspaper, which has a large circulation, entitled *I believe in Divorce...* We have a right to ask the motley crew who support this bill upon what they base their outlook on life. If they want to do away with Christian marriage, what are they going to put in its place? We believe that the family, not the state, not the individual, is the unit of Christian civilisation, and that all legislation of this kind tends to destroy the unit of the family and break down Christian civilisation.' Mr Bower then quoted from a letter that he had received from an elderly ex-Member of Parliament, Sir Alfred Pease, who wrote:

> In every case of maintaining morality and in securing human happiness there must be vicarious sacrifice, voluntary or imposed—the few must sacrifice themselves, or be sacrificed in the interests of society in general. If the inviolable sanctity of marriage is upheld it makes the entry into matrimony serious, it induces effort to make the best of things if things do not go smoothly and it is a protection for the children. It surprised me to see so many members of the Church of England, to which I belong, and even members of the clergy and of the bench of bishops supporting the loosening of the marriage ties, the breaking of the solemn vows made at its altars, sacrificing the interests of the majority for the minority and lowering the sanctity of family.

The reading of the letter was greeted with derisory laughter that spurred a response from Commander Bower. 'How can any decent Christian find anything funny at all in such a letter? The attitude of honourable Members who laugh is rather like the attitude they showed on the report stage. When an honourable Member mentioned the Mothers' Union there was at once great guffaws of laughter, until another Member pointed out that there were many thousands of members in the Mothers' Union all of whom had votes. Then the laughter turned into sympathetic cheers, the sincerity of which was probably in inverse proportion to their volume.' Commander Bower concluded his deeply unpopular speech, 'This is a matter which deals with the basis of Christian life, and if the bill is passed it will simply have the effect of removing one more of the all too few remaining sheet anchors which prevent our civilisation from drifting into chaos.'[36]

Mr Sorensen chided Commander Bower for not exhibiting a more Christian spirit in his speech. He pointed out that the existence of many thousands of broken homes were not due to this bill. 'We are anxious that this bill should pass in order that family life in the real sense of the word might have a better and finer chance of being successful.' He then urged those who opposed the bill to realise that an attempt to impose their particular religious convictions upon others that do not accept those convictions is not in the interest of mankind. The bill places marriage on a higher plane because where a marriage has ceased to exist it will be brought to an end on the application of the innocent party. 'Therefore, I urge upon those who oppose this bill an appreciation of the fact that we are desirous of seeing marriage placed upon a higher plane altogether, in the interests of the parties concerned, in the interests of the country and in the interests of the children... I do not wish to see the shadow of the handcuffs over marriage. I do not see anything sacred or holy in two people being handcuffed together when they despise one another. I want to see people who are joined together in matrimony remain so as long as they possibly can.'[37]

Mr Thurtle accused the opposition of intolerance. 'They seek to impose their point of views on others. That is why I said they were intolerant. It is the most presumptuous form of intolerance, the intolerance of the minority. They are in a very marked minority in this country, and they have no right to seek to impose upon the great mass of British people the views which they hold.' He supported the bill because it would do something to bring relief to people who 'are at present suffering through no fault of their own cruel hardships; and it will also do something to bring the law of this country in regard to marriage to a more enlightened level than that on which it is at the present time'.[38]

In winding up the debate Mr Herbert said they had struck a good blow for democracy, because they had shown that given a good cause, a good heart and goodwill it was possible for the humblest and newest private Member to bring a self-appointed task to a third reading in the House of Commons. They believed they were doing some good to the most valuable institutions of the Church, the law and to marriage itself. The bill would help to discourage rash marriages and rash divorces. To those who opposed the bill on religious grounds he would say that he wondered whether they were truly interpreting the message of Christ. 'They take the view that we should abide by the words, "Whom God hath joined let no man put asunder", and leave it at that. I am and have been most anxious to avoid saying anything which would wound anybody, but I would like to say to those who genuinely feel in the way I have indicated that I wonder whether they can be sure that in taking that attitude, they are truly interpreting the message of Christ. Christ, after all, was a Christian; he was, I think, a realist; he liked to tear away the shams and subterfuges and to get down to the heart of things. I am very sure he did not say to the woman taken in adultery that "hard cases make bad law". I do not say this to raise a laugh or to cause a wound, but I wonder what he would have said to the General Council of the Mothers' Union. I wonder what he would have said to any happily married mother and wife who is so confident that her happiness is due to her own virtue and the misfortunes of others are due to their own fault, that she will not accede to any alteration in the law even to lessen the unhappiness of those others. I maintain with all solemnity and reverence that there is not a single word in this bill of which he [Christ] would not approve. I say, on the other hand, that there are many deplorable things in the present situation which he would resent. I hope that I shall not be thought to have done wrong in saying this, but that, after all, is the assumption, in some of the letters we receive, that we are breaking God's law.'

He concluded his speech, 'We say that this is a bill that not only will increase the sum of human happiness, but that will be of great benefit to many valued institutions. Finally, if I may use again that Name which I have dared to use already, we say that above all, in the finest sense of the word, this is a Christian bill, and I hope the House will give it its third reading by a very large majority (cheers).[39] The bill was passed with a majority of 153–190 votes to 37.

Debate in House of Lords: June 1937

Introducing the bill to the Lords, Lord Eltisley said that the bill was undoubtedly a controversial and contentious measure. After much time in committee there was some agreement between its promoters and those who were the most severe critics. However, there was not full agreement. The bill attempted not only to deal with individual cases of hardship and unhappiness, but above all, it strove to maintain and preserve the great institution of marriage. Its aim was to strengthen and not to relax the marriage tie.[40]

Viscount FitzAlan responded to the claim by Mr AP Herbert that Christ would approve of every word in the bill. 'He used these words – I think I have got them accurately – that there is not a single word in the bill of which

Christ would not approve. Considering that almost every word in this bill is contrary to the doctrines and teachings held by the vast majority of Christians throughout the world, I would think that was a rather absurd statement and also rather a lapse from good taste.' This bill treated marriage as a question of convenience and sentiment. 'It ignores the fact that in the minds and hearts of the vast majority of Christians throughout the world marriage was a sacrament ordained by God; that it is not to be treated according to the whims and fancies of popular opinion that change from time to time.' They shared the opinion of other denominations who regarded this bill as interfering gravely with the sanctity of marriage and they joined with those people of other denominations in doing all that they thought right and proper in opposing this bill. 'I cannot help feeling that more noise had been made with regard to this bill, both in Parliament and in certain sections of the Press, with regard to this bill than was warranted by public opinion outside... Also, I think, that amongst the people of this country, especially among the middle classes and to a large extent among the poor, there is a feeling that the sanctity of marriage ought not to be interfered with, that quite enough has been done already in that direction, and that it is deteriorating the character of the people to weaken in any degree the marriage tie... The promoters of this bill seem to think that it is going to settle the question for a long time, perhaps for a quarter of a century. What was going to happen then? The slippery slope is again going to be greased and where it would lead them, God only knows. I cannot help feeling that the time has come when we should check this tendency. What about the children? We people in England are very fond of our children. The increased number of divorces must be doing a great deal of harm to the children. It creates an atmosphere which they cannot get clear of, and that must familiarise them with the idea of divorce. Again, take those cases where there are already children of parents seeking divorce. It entirely deprives those children of any proper idea of home or family life. Sometimes I wonder whether, if this tendency to divorce continues to increase, there may not be revulsion of opinion on account of the effect it is having on the character of the nation through the children deteriorating because of it. I only hope and pray that something may happen in the future that will cause this tendency for divorce to diminish.'[41]

The Archbishop of Canterbury (Cosmo Lang) outlined his position on the bill. 'The existing law of the state in the matter of divorce had proved, and was proving, very unsatisfactory in its operation and had given rise to grave abuses detrimental not only to marriage itself but to public morality. The bill proposes some timely and valuable remedies against these abuses. It had other useful provisions, including relief to the conscience of the clergy. For those reasons, although I hope it may be amended in various respects in committee, I think as a citizen and a Member of the House of Parliament, that it is entitled to the careful consideration by your Lordship's House. I cannot, therefore, honestly vote against the second reading of the bill. On the other hand, I cannot divest myself of my responsibility as a representative and officer of the Church. In my judgement divorce, and certainly remarriage after divorce, is inconsistent with the principles laid down by Christ and accepted in its own law and formularies by the Church. It may be that the state is unable to impose the Christian principles of marriage by law upon a population which is only partially or imperfectly Christian, but for that very reason it is of the greater importance that the Church should maintain those principles for its own members and uphold its own standard for the good of the whole community. In view, therefore, of the position which I hold in the Church, I cannot take the responsibility of seeming to promote legislation which in some of its principal proposals is inconsistent with those principles and with that standard. Thus I cannot give a vote for the second reading of the bill. In those circumstances if a division is challenged on the second reading, in that division I can take no part.'

'Our belief as Christians, or churchmen, that divorce and remarriage after divorce are inconsistent with the principles laid down by Christ and accepted by the Church, cannot preclude us as citizens from the right or even the duty to improve the existing law where it demands improvement, or to remedy abuses which have been disclosed… Now the proof of a single act of adultery by a man or woman is sufficient as a ground of divorce. Now it is the actual operation of this change that has led to the abuses which cry for remedy.' Turning to a clause in the bill which dealt with the relief of the clergy, the archbishop said that the last Lambeth Conference, representing the bishops of the whole Anglican Communion throughout the world, recommended that the marriage of one whose former partner is still living should not be celebrated according to the rites of the Church. Here in England both Convocations have decided that in order to maintain the principle of a lifelong obligation, which is clearly expressed in the marriage service, the Church should not allow the use of that service to anyone who has a partner still living. The archbishop then informed the House that the Convocations of the Church had recently affirmed 'as our Lord's principle and standard of marriage a lifelong and indissoluble union for better or for worse of one man with one woman to the exclusion of all others on either side. And they have laid down the consequences that a Christian man or woman cannot remarry during the lifetime of a former wife or husband without a breach of this Christian principle, and the further consequence which I have already mentioned, that the marriage service, which explicitly embodies that principle, cannot be used in any such remarriage.'

The archbishop said that the stability of marriage and family life could only be strengthened if the Church, which still has some considerable influence within the community, asserts and upholds the witness of a high standard. 'Without some such witness, strenuously and consistently upheld, the danger may be, not of the dissolution of individual marriages, but of the gradual dissolution of the institution of marriage itself. In these circumstances how can I resist the conclusion that I might be contributing to that danger if, as the chief officer of the Church, and therefore in a sense its representative, I were by formal vote in this House to associate myself with the promotion of a bill which, whatever merits it may have, contains proposals which are inconsistent with the specifically Christian principles of marriage? I cannot take that responsibility (cheers).' For these reasons, he explained to the House, that if the motion went to a division he must stand aside.[42]

Lord Snell said that those who opposed the bill appeared to be willing to let the past decide the issues of the present. Lord FitzAlan had said that the measure struck at the root of the doctrine of marriage as a sacrament. 'Put in the crudest form, the reply would be that we are to be relieved of our responsibility for our domestic institutions, in our own country in our own time, by the views of marriage that have come down to us from other, and not too intelligent ages. To bind changing human nature to the standards of bygone ages, or even to ignore the facts of the present situation, is to justify ancient theories, but not to help our present needs... By all that we know of present circumstances, by our best solemn judgement, we believe that this reform is very much overdue, that it is urgent, and that it cannot, with safety be longer denied. It is nearly thirty years since the famous Royal Commission was appointed. Ever since that time these questions have been canvassed by thinkers, by moralists and by statesmen, and from every point of view they come to us with a great record of thought behind them... I would like to justify the bill by the relief that it will give to individuals, and also by the moral renewal that it will give to the state. In every part of the community there are many thousands of unhappy individuals who are looking to the House to give them the chance of a new and happier life... To take the view that there can be no relief from a vow once made, that a promise made under certain conditions is irrevocable, seems to many of us to mock human tragedy and human suffering... I have heard the argument that the safest thing on the whole would be to leave things as they are. But to do nothing would in reality be to do a great deal; it would be to do the wrong thing in the wrong way at the wrong time, and if that course were followed it might be that the very institution of marriage itself would break down, for sensible people will not put upon themselves eternal fetters— fetters from which there was no chance of relief.' He concluded, 'I believe finally that this bill deals with a great human, moral and social problem. It offers hope of a new life in the shape of a home and family. It at the same time serves one of the highest purposes of the state; first, by striking a blow at promiscuous relationships; secondly, by giving to decent people a chance to rear a family; and thirdly, to make marriage a desirable and revered institution rather than, as it was in too many cases at present, a degraded, dreaded prison from which there was no escape.'[43]

The Bishop of St Albans (Michael Furse) said that he believed that the bill would weaken instead of strengthen the institution of marriage, lead to an increasing number of divorces, and, quite obviously, expose more children to the danger and ill consequences that come from broken homes. 'I know that it has been said that it is better to break up a home that is unhappy, but I have been very much struck by what is said by some headmasters and headmistresses of schools... They maintain that they would far rather have to deal with boys and girls who come from homes, however unhappy those homes had been and are, than with those who come from homes broken up by divorce. They say that has a worse moral effect on boys and girls.'

The bishop continued, 'The Christian view of marriage as a lifelong, indissoluble union between one man and one woman to the exclusion of all others, is not merely based on a text or two taken from the New Testament, but I suggest is part and parcel of the original plan of the Creator in bringing men into the world and in fulfilling his purpose that the whole of the human race should have the fullest possible life... Marriage is, I submit, fundamental not only to the well-being of this nation but to the well-being of all the nations, of the whole of the human race. Marriage, we believe, is not primarily for self-gratification or merely to produce the happiness of one man or one woman. It is a vocation for service of a threefold character... The making of a home is the first object of marriage. That depends on the husband and the wife loving each other. Yes, and we believe that love really means primarily not to get but to give. It means the highest form of mutual service one to the other, to create a home where children can be brought up in the proper environment. The procreation of children is the next object; and thirdly, the education of them in the problem of living together.' He went on, 'We think we can play about with the institution of marriage as if it were something that man has made... Here is something fundamental which we are trying to bring up to date... I submit that this is no time to be trifling with such a fundamental thing with almost total disregard of the meaning of marriage.' Then he made the point that the bill would have a great influence in forming public opinion. 'In passing this bill your Lordships are letting it be known to young and old that marriage has got to last five years, but after that they can get out. You are weakening public opinion, the one stronghold which is upholding hundreds and thousands of men and women who are gallantly holding on for the sake of other people. Do not despise them. They are the finest people in the world. You know perfectly well that people have felt there is a way of escape, and you are making more ways of escape. This is the education that you are giving, and we have been educating the country in this way since 1857. What is happening today? Fewer and fewer people care a snap of the fingers about the sanctity of marriage.'

The bishop concluded his speech with the observation that they were suffering from an overdose of sentimentality which had been dressed up as Christian charity. 'Two things have made this country great through the character of its people—standing by your word when you have given it, even when it is to your own cost to keep it, and seeing a difficult situation through and not whining about it.'[44]

The Bishop of Durham (Hensley Henson) was dismissive of the speech by the Bishop of St Albans. 'He will not think me discourteous if I refer to him in a phrase often used in the 17th century. He talked at large without addressing himself to the bill, which I strongly suspect he has not read.' The bishop said that he believed that this bill, if it were passed into law, 'so far from bringing the law of England into conflict with the law of Christ, would bring the law of England into deeper and truer harmony with that law. I believe that the law of England as it is at present is in some conspicuous particulars inequitable, and I believe that this bill will remedy a great many hard cases which a just law ought to be able to remedy.' He believed that the four gospels taught 'with every adequate reason that the marriage union is dissoluble'. He heartily commended the bill to the House. He then issued this plea, 'I do hope it will not go out from this Chamber that this great House is consciously and deliberately setting itself against the Christian law of marriage'. They had no ground for withholding the liberty of divorce.

He concluded his speech by expressing his support for the bill. 'I support this bill because I believe it will strengthen the hands of those of us who are seriously perturbed by the wave of licentiousness which has swept over the Western world in the wake of the Great War... I believe if we pass this bill we shall rebuild a great many broken homes, and shall once more enable many children to have strength and comfort in an ordered domestic life, and shall strengthen the state by helping to rebuild it.'[45]

The Marquess of Reading said it was 'both a tragedy and a scandal that people should be driven to commit a sort of synthetic adultery in order to bring themselves within the scope of the existing law, and to escape from a marriage which had become either a mockery or a martyrdom'. Introducing some ground for divorce other than adultery would at least cleanse the courts of some of the accumulation of horror and of filth that abounded. 'It will at least, perhaps, stop the procession of hotel porters remembering a particular petitioner after a period of years and a succession of some thousands of guests, and of hotel chambermaids opportunely arriving with the morning coffee when the couple was still in bed.' He said it would save the self-respect of some of the people who have to go through these revolting machinations in order to get their freedom under the present law. It was because he believed that the bill would introduce temperate, beneficent and long overdue reforms, go far to alleviate a great volume of human unhappiness, and do much to restore dignity and reality to the law, that he offered his sincere and convinced support.[46]

The Archbishop of York (William Temple) said that while he believed it was desirable that the bill should pass into law, he did not think it was appropriate that an occupant of the Bishop's Bench should vote for it. 'We have, for a long time past, acted on the assumption that the law of the state and the law of the Church in this matter should be the same. What I desire to suggest is the grounds on which the law of the state and the Church should be determined should certainly be different, and it is at least possible that the difference in grounds may lead to a different law itself. The function of Church and state in relation to the promotion of human welfare at large are not the same... If it were true that the passing of this bill would lead to the damage of public morals, no doubt it would be our duty to resist it, but, as I have indicated, I am persuaded that it ought to be passed, and for the reason that I believe it will improve rather than damage public morals.' He concluded 'it seems to me quite necessary that the state, in the interest of public morals, should adopt some action which secures wider possibilities of divorce than exist now. That view, however, must not be held in any way to modify the right and the obligation of the Church to uphold its own ideal and to require the conformity to that ideal of those who would be its full members.'[47]

The Bishop of Birmingham (Ernest Barnes) said that he was convinced that the bill was a careful attempt to bring the marriage law into harmony with opinions long held by an overwhelming majority of enlightened Christian people in the country. One of the greatest merits of the bill was that it would promote morality by lessening the number of irregular unions among working people. He hoped that it would lessen the number of collusive divorces. 'For me a marriage should never be dissolved unless, owing to the misfortune and still more the wrongdoing of one of the partners, it has already ceased to exist except in name... Some think the bill is too severe. Others regard it with active or passive disapproval because they think that remarriage after divorce is inconsistent with principles laid down by Christ and accepted by the Church.' He was convinced that those who maintained this view were wrong, in so far as they assume that the Founder of Christianity was a lawgiver rather than a prophet. Christ indeed set forth with impressive emphasis his ideal of the lifelong union of one man and woman to the exclusion of all others. But he left his followers free to legislate for men and women living in a world where wrongdoing is all too common.

He also claimed that bishops in the Church of England had always permitted divorce. He quoted as evidence the fact that the bishops had not opposed parliamentary divorces in the House of Lords, and that nine bishops had supported the Divorce Bill of 1857. 'In the face of such evidence I must emphatically challenge the suggestion that as a bishop of the Church of England I ought not to vote for the present bill because remarriage after divorce is contrary to the traditions of the Church of England. On the one hand, I am convinced that Christ set forth an ideal and left his followers free to legislate so as to give relief from intolerable unions if thereby they did not harm social morality. On the other hand, there is conclusive evidence that this view was at the Reformation accepted by some of the most representative bishops of the Church. In fact, the grounds on which divorce with the right of remarriage shall be allowed must be determined by the conditions of the time. Every effort should be made to preserve the stability of family life, to keep the home inviolate so that children may thrive in its wholesome shelter. But when the marriage tie has become unbearable through the wrongdoing or, in very rare cases, the misfortune of one of the partners the Church should acquiesce in the ending of the union and may rightly bless the other partner's attempt to make a new home.' He concluded, 'I will merely add that I give general support to this bill, not as a concession to be made to a semi-pagan community, but because it seems to me to be legislation in accordance with the spirit of Christ'.[48]

The Marquess of Salisbury could not support the bill. To him the vital thing was the stability of marriage. 'Anything else inevitably leads to disaster. Once there is a doubt about the foundation upon which the law stands, there is unrest at once. Everyone who was a little uneasy in his marriage thinks— a little more political agitation and we may get the law modified again. There is no fundamental reason for a great many of the provisions of this new bill. They may be good or they may be bad, but many of them are only questions of degree.' One of the most notable things was that the bill had no definition clause. Yet nearly all bills had one. The bill originally had a definition clause, but it had disappeared. 'We do not know what desertion is. Not absolutely… Take insanity. Is that the only misfortune that can happen to a married person which makes marital relations impossible? All sorts of diseases make marital relations impossible. Why then is insanity picked out, and how long do your Lordships think you are going to stand upon a ledge so frail as that? If insanity is to be a reason, why not other diseases which befall mankind and prevent marital relations? Of course they must all follow in due course, and when they come the Bishop of Birmingham will defend them… Insanity is only a question of degree. Take such a pitiful form of insanity as melancholia. I suppose you can have incurable melancholia; yet think of the cruelty of adding to the wretched man's anguish of mind, profoundly depressed as he is, the knowledge that divorce is hanging over him. How can that be defended? How different that is from the conception of marriage as the Church of England teaches it: "For better for worse, for richer for poorer, in sickness and in health." That is the real bond. A partner to a marriage is melancholy, frightfully depressed, and the spouse is encouraged by this bill to add to all the terrible weight of the burden of depression that he or she would be absolutely deserted.' He concluded by saying that he could not support the bill. The foundation of the bill seemed to be utterly unreliable. It made the marriage law unstable, and opened the door henceforward to repeated change. He was anxious that 'this House should realise how grave a matter this bill is, what a great departure it is from our hitherto received practice, and how it launches the marriage law of England upon a path of which I do not see the end'.[49]

Lord Henry Gorell acknowledged the tributes to the work of his father. 'Tonight we are concluding a debate which is different from all the others. In no other case have we had these reforms, so long discussed, brought up to your Lordships from another place, nor have we had in any of those long discussions such an overwhelming expression of opinion all on one side. In the whole course of the debate there have been only three Members of your Lordships' House who have spoken against the bill, and all three have based themselves upon their opposition entirely to divorce of any kind whatsoever. We may profoundly respect their views, but I think the whole consensus of opinion shows clearly that your Lordships' House no longer feels that the legislature is bound to accept that point of view. To those who have followed this controversy from the very start nothing has been so remarkable as the extraordinary change in public opinion. The press, at any rate, is very indicative of what the public is thinking, and some of the major organs of the press, which were pronouncedly against the majority proposals in 1912, have now thrown their whole weight upon the side of this bill.'

He noted that there were three distinct and different Christian opinions— that marriage is indissoluble, that it is dissoluble only on the ground of adultery, and the growing weight of opinion that marriage is dissoluble wherever in fact the ideal had broken down. Only three of their Lordships had spoken against the bill, and all three of them had based themselves on their opposition to divorce of any kind whatsoever. They should not lose the chance, after a quarter of a century, of passing into law reforms upon which, with almost no exception, their Lordships seemed to be in hearty agreement.[50] The bill passed without a division and England had its bill that would increase the sum of human happiness.

EFFECT OF THE NEW ACT

The Matrimonial Causes Act of 1937, which came into force in 1938, extended the legal grounds for divorce beyond the sole ground of adultery for the first time; the additional grounds included three years' desertion, cruelty and insanity. The Act also included a new restriction that, except in cases of extreme hardship, no petition for divorce could be filed during the first three years of marriage. Because the Act did not explain how these terms were to be defined and interpreted the judges had wide discretion in their interpretation of the law. For the first time in a thousand years it was possible to gain a divorce for reasons that had no possible biblical justification.

The enactment of the new grounds was followed by an immediate rise and divorce numbers almost doubled from 4,886 in 1937 to 8,254 in 1939, as shown in the **figure 6**. Moreover, to a large degree the increase in divorces in 1938 and 1939 were due to the new ground of desertion as the number of petitions for adultery remained more or less constant. In 1949 the government made legal aid for divorce proceedings widely available to the poor. After that, legal aid funded half the divorce cases.[51] The gateway to mass divorce was now wide open.

THE CHURCH OF ENGLAND RESOLUTIONS ON MARRIAGE: 1938

A remarkable irony was that in 1938, the year in which the new grounds for divorce were introduced into England, both the Canterbury and York Convocations formally adopted the first four resolutions of the *Church and Marriage Report* as the marriage discipline of the Church. At long last the Church had produced a public statement on its beliefs on marriage and divorce. By affirming these resolutions the Church had made a public declaration that it believed that marriage was indissoluble save by death, and therefore remarriage during the lifetime of a former partner was not permissible in church. It was now clear that the views expressed by the liberal bishops were inconsistent with the doctrinal position of the Church. These resolutions, at the time of writing, are still in force and remain the official position of the Church of England. The first four resolutions affirm:

> That this House affirms that according to God's will, declared by our Lord, marriage is in its true principle a personal union, for better or for worse, of one man with one woman, exclusive of all others on either side, and indissoluble save by death.

> That this House also affirms as a consequence that both divorce itself and re-marriage after divorce during the lifetime of a former partner always involves a departure from the true principle of marriage as declared by our Lord.

> That in order to maintain the principle of lifelong obligation which is inherent in every legally contracted marriage and is expressed in plainest terms in the Marriage Service, the Church should not allow the use of that service in the case of anyone who has a former partner still living.

> That while affirming its adherence to our Lord's principle and standard of marriage as stated in the first and second of the above resolutions, this House recognises that the actual discipline of particular Christian

Communions in this matter has varied widely from time to time and place to place, and holds that the Church of England is competent to enact such a discipline of its own in regard to marriage as may from time to time appear most salutary and efficacious.[52]

Comment – A Divided Church

In the parliamentary debates of the 1930s the division among the bishops had seriously damaged the Church's witness to the nation. England had eagerly accepted an extension of the grounds for divorce that went well beyond the teaching of Christ with hardly a word of warning from the Church of the moral and social consequences that would follow. The two overriding reasons for the failure of the Christian witness were, first, the decision taken by the Church not to oppose 'reasonable' legislation to extend the grounds of divorce, and second, the growing influence of the liberal bishops.

At the end of the debate it was not at all clear whether the Church was opposed to divorce or not. The decision taken by Convocation not to oppose any 'reasonable' extension to the grounds for divorce had now borne its fruit as the state introduced new grounds for divorce, claiming that it had the support of the Church. The Church justified its position by claiming that it was inappropriate to try and impose its moral standards on the population of England. But the weakness of this position is apparent from the fact that it was in direct opposition to a resolution affirmed by the Church just two short decades before. Indeed, in 1911 the Church had declared publicly that extending the grounds of divorce was detrimental to

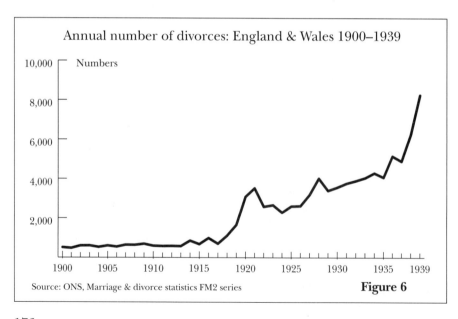

Annual number of divorces: England & Wales 1900–1939

Source: ONS, Marriage & divorce statistics FM2 series   **Figure 6**

the social, moral and religious interests of the nation. For this reason the Church had opposed such an extension. At that time the Bishop of London (Winnington-Ingram) had reminded his fellow bishops of the Church's prophetic responsibility to the whole nation, and not only to the Christians in society. It was the responsibility of the Church to do everything possible to prevent the nation from making the mistake of increasing the facilities for divorce.

Times had changed and the Church had succumbed to the argument that as a minority it had no right to foist its morality on the majority. Accordingly, the Archbishop of Canterbury (Lang), while acknowledging that the essence of the bill was against the words of Christ, felt unable to argue that it was harmful to the wider interests of society. Instead he agreed that it provided a valuable remedy for many abuses. He felt obliged to maintain a neutral position to the bill and later left a note that explained his action. 'Rightly or wrongly, I came to the conclusion that it was no longer possible to impose the full Christian standard by law on a largely non-Christian population, but that the witness to that standard, and consequent disciplinary action towards its own members or persons who sought to be married by its rites, must be left to the Church.'[53]

It was desperately sad that the Church, although it knew that the standards of Christ were for the good of the whole of society, fell into the trap of not taking a public stand against the evil of extending the facilities of divorce. Having just affirmed the Church's belief in the lifelong nature of marriage, they had lost sight of their responsibility to speak to the nation—whether or not it listened. The Church had forgotten that Christ was a light to the nations, and that his followers were the light of the world and the salt of the earth. The Church had lost its saltiness.

The second reason for the dismal witness of the Church was the influence of the liberal bishops. Although the main body of the Church did not accept their views, as shown by the debates in Convocation, the bishops had the effrontery to argue that extending the grounds of divorce would bring the law of England into harmony with the law of Christ. As an ardent supporter of the divorce campaign the Bishop of Durham (Henson) claimed that the bill would help rebuild broken homes and bring comfort to children. The Bishop of Birmingham (Barnes) believed the bill was consistent with the opinions of enlightened Christians and in accordance with the spirit of Christ. It would promote morality by reducing the number of irregular unions. Both bishops believed that a tolerant divorce law would allow people to find real happiness and build genuine relationships. They saw it as their Christian responsibility to legislate in a way that would promote human happiness and had popular support. However, their opinions were not based on the Scriptures, and their reasoning was consistent with the ideology of secular humanism.

The classic Protestant position that adultery is the only ground for divorce, which dominated all the previous debates, was strangely missing. Both the Divorce Acts of 1857 and 1923 were based on the Protestant doctrine of divorce. But after eighty years, no one was prepared to defend it. By common consent it had proved unworkable in practice and had led to collusion between parties determined to get a divorce. Even the Archbishop of Canterbury admitted that the existing law of divorce had proved very unsatisfactory in its operation and had given rise to grave abuses detrimental not only to marriage itself but to public morality. Where did this debate leave those who supported the Protestant doctrine of divorce? They believed that Scripture taught that adultery dissolved the marriage bond and permitted divorce with the right to remarry. Why did they not defend that position in the 1937 debate? Why were they not fighting to defend the divorce law, which according to their beliefs was based on the teachings of Christ? Why were they not arguing that the only permissible ground for divorce was marital unfaithfulness? The answer is that the Protestant doctrine of divorce had been discredited by history. Surely those who claim that the Scriptures allow divorce for adultery need to re-examine their theology.

Those who opposed the 1857 Divorce Reform Act predicted that divorce for adultery was only the thin edge of the wedge that would inevitably lead to demands for more grounds for divorce, and their prediction was now being fulfilled. However, those who supported the Protestant doctrine were not true to their convictions. Having used the argument that adultery dissolved the marriage bond to undermine the indissolubility of marriage in England, they now found that there were also other causes for divorce. And so there was the strange sight of those who supported the Protestant position on divorce siding with the secular humanists in the struggle to extend the grounds of divorce.

The only opposition to the bill came from those who believed that marriage was indissoluble. They alone witnessed to the lifelong nature of marriage and warned of the dangers that lay ahead. The Bishop of St Albans reminded the House that marriage was ordained by God the Creator and was therefore indissoluble, and not something with which they should be trifling. Marriage was fundamental to the well-being of the nation and for the good of the whole of society. It created a home where the children could be brought up in a secure environment. He warned of the dangers mass divorce created for children. He also warned that by making mass divorce available they were creating a low view of marriage.

Comment – The arguments of the secular humanists

The serious division of opinion among the bishops who spoke in the House of Lords revealed a weak and divided Church that had lost its influence.

The Christian witness had become confused and irrelevant. Consequently, the secular humanists were free to make divorce laws consistent with their ideology. With hindsight their arguments seem amazingly naïve and lacking in intellectual vigour. It seems remarkable that the proponents of divorce were so sure that extending the availability of divorce to ordinary men and women would increase the sum of human happiness for parents and children alike. They claimed that divorce would rescue children from cruelty and abuse, and that parents should divorce for the sake of their children. Divorce was presented as something that offered the hope of a new home and family. They were confident that there were many good men eager to remarry divorcees and bring up other men's children. They assumed that children thrived in stepfamilies which were invariably happy, healthy, moral homes. Such was the understanding of the secular humanists. It was on the strength of these arguments that England exchanged the words of Christ for divorce laws based on human wisdom.

Chapter 9

A new principle in divorce

The struggle for a divorce law based on the irretrievable breakdown of marriage: 1950–63

After the Second World War over half of the divorce petitions by women cited the new grounds of desertion and cruelty. While the real effect of the change in legislation is difficult to judge as the Second World War led to a massive increase in divorces, with numbers peaking at 60 thousand in the immediate post-war period, there is no doubt that in the early 1950s after the post-war peak in divorces had subsided, there were six times as many divorces as in 1937, the year before the latest Act came into force (see **figure 7** on page 192). The increase in divorce associated with the aftermath of war is a well-known phenomenon, and the reasons probably include hastily arranged wartime marriages, and a rise in adultery associated with the prolonged separations that occur during a time of war.

This post-war deluge of divorce was having an influence on public opinion, and the social stigma that had once accompanied divorce was starting to fade—it was no longer the social disgrace that it once had been. Yet there was concern that all was not right and many in society still viewed divorce as a tragedy, especially for the children. Some saw the high divorce numbers as a symptom of a sick society. Archbishop Geoffrey Fisher cited growing divorce numbers as one of the reasons for the movement of official opinion in the Church of England against the remarriage of a divorced person in church during the lifetime of the other party. Proponents of divorce liberalisation, however, were still not satisfied for their aim was to make divorce on demand available to the whole of society.

EIRENE WHITE'S PRIVATE MEMBER'S BILL: 1951

In March 1951 a Labour Member of Parliament (Eirene White) introduced a Private Member's bill to the House of Commons with the aim of making divorce more widely available. Her bill aimed to introduce a new principle into divorce legislation which would make divorce available after a period of separation although no marital offence had been committed. It would now be possible for the guilty party to divorce an innocent spouse against their will. In other words, it would be possible for a husband guilty of adultery to divorce his wife against her will, although she had committed no marital offence, after a period of separation. Although the bill proposed a period of separation of seven years, this period was arbitrary, and once the principle was agreed, there would soon be convincing arguments that seven years was too long to wait for this new freedom.

Mrs White told the House of Commons that her bill would allow the dissolution of marriages which had broken down and in which none of the purposes of marriage were being served. The social purpose of the bill was to meet the situation in which many thousands of men and women were living apart in a state which was not marriage, but in which they were unable legally to form another union. She estimated that the number of those separated was at least 100 thousand and might be much higher, and it was an important social problem because of the number of illegitimate children involved. She mentioned the moral defects of the existing law. It was based on the assumption that a marriage could be terminated only if one partner had committed a legally proven offence against the other. The legal verdict, which declared one party innocent and the other guilty, was confined to a particular offence which had to be proved. To insist that the whole divorce procedure should be based upon the distinction between the guilty and the innocent was wrong. She was profoundly convinced that the present law was unjust and detrimental to public interest.[1] Seconding the bill, Mr Martin Lindsay said that the purpose of the bill was to deal with those marriages which were already dead. He asked if it was in the true interests of any of the parties that marriages, which were marriages only in name and which were pure shams should be kept inviolate. When marriages broke up, in about half the cases the so-called innocent person in law was more responsible for the marriage having broken up. He said that if the bill passed into law it would bring to scores of thousands of people the happiness which was at present denied them.[2]

Opposing the bill, Mr Richard Wood asked why the figure of seven years had been chosen. If they agreed to the principle of seven years' separation being a ground for divorce, they would open themselves to the very greatest pressure from all kinds of organisations to reduce the period to two years or even less. He suggested that the bill, which proposed to relieve unhappiness, would have the opposite effect and would weaken the contract of marriage, and therefore produce more unhappiness in the future. He said that the bill introduced a principle of divorce, not by consent, but by unilateral compulsion. This was an entirely new and a very dangerous principle.[3]

Mr Cyril Black said that a new principle would be established and it would be only a relatively short time before they faced a public demand for the period to be reduced to something much shorter. He made the point that divorce legislation had increased the number of divorces, and when he quoted figures to support his contention, Mrs White intervened to say that he was giving a misleading picture. While it was true that legislation had increased the number of legal divorces, it was entirely misleading to infer from that that legislation had increased the number of broken marriages. Mr Black retorted that there were no statistics on broken marriages, only on divorces.[4]

Mr David Weitzman said that many of them remembered with gratitude the Act of 1937, which brought relief to both sexes on a number of grounds, including desertion. They had travelled slowly but surely, and he hoped that they had reached the stage when they could, by this bill, give relief to many more deserving cases. 'There are thousands of cases which will be remedied under the bill. There are men and women who have been voluntarily separated for many years, and there is no question whatever of their coming together again. There are men and women living apart one or other of whom could bring divorce proceedings, but such a person refuses to do so and prefers to keep alive a bond which means nothing but enslavement. There are men and women in such conditions who have found others whom they could marry, and with whom they could be happy, but legitimate union is denied them. They must live alone or they must live in sin. If they live in sin they must either not have children, or, if they do, those children must bear the brand of illegitimacy.' He said that this was a good bill, which would not weaken marriage, and would not adversely affect the interests of children. It would bring happiness to thousands who had suffered for years.[5]

Mr Sorensen said that if the parties to a marriage had come to the stage where they could no longer tolerate each other and in consequence were separated, the marriage had in essence broken down. He submitted that it was in the best interests of marriage itself to recognise the fact, and give opportunity for men and women thus separated from true marriage to start afresh and, if possible, to build up their mutual lives more successfully than before.[6]

Mr Bell said that the bill abandoned the last restriction on divorce. They were dealing not with the thin end of the wedge but the thick end. 'This is the end of marriage. This bill, in fact, is going to abolish marriage. I have here a document which has been sent out by a body calling itself the Marriage Law Reform Committee, and that committee has been behind all the agitation over this bill. They are the propagandists of the bill, and they have pressed forward their particular views and sent around a circular which has been addressed to all members of the Bar concerning the bill now before the House.' He said that the whole object of having a marriage bond was to confer permanency upon the marriage relationship. The formal bond performed a vital function by giving stability and security to the people who were within it. It strengthened them in difficult times. He was convinced that if they weakened the formal bond of marriage they would not only increase the number of divorces, but they would also increase the number of broken homes.[7]

The Attorney General (Sir Hartley Shawcross) advised Parliament that he thought it unwise to legislate in isolation, indicating that the best way to proceed would be to appoint a Royal Commission to examine the whole field of marital law. He noted that an unhappy commentary on the existing state of the law was that the vast mass of the people considered that in practice divorce by consent was possible. He said that a vote on the bill before the House would prejudice the findings of a commission and suggested that the bill be withdrawn.[8] Mrs White reluctantly offered in the interests of future law reform to withdraw the bill, but some Members of Parliament were so determined to proceed with the proposals that they forced a vote. The debate ended in farce, as Members were not sure what the vote was about.

PUBLIC DEBATE ON DIVORCE

The parliamentary shenanigans forced the issue of divorce legislation yet again into the public arena. The Mothers' Union, an organisation with a large membership of Christian wives and mothers, expressed their opposition to this new crusade in a letter to *The Times*, 'This Bill would introduce entirely new principles into the divorce legislation of this country because, first, it would enable the guilty partner in an unhappy marriage to become the petitioner in a divorce suit, and an innocent party might find himself or herself in the position of being divorced against his or her will. Secondly, it would open the door to divorce by mutual consent. Thirdly, it would penalise those who for honest conscientious scruples refuse to divorce their guilty spouses, because of their belief in the lifelong character of the marriage bond. The Mothers' Union has for 75 years upheld the Christian principle of lifelong marriage between one man and one woman, and it has taken part, in the past, in upholding this principle by vigorous protests against any weakening of the marriage laws in this country. Unfortunately in recent years its members have seen a gradual decline in public opinion with regard to marriage and divorce.'[9]

The Ethical Union responded, 'There is no probability that the provisions of the bill would weaken the marriage law, lower standards of conduct in marriage, or open the door to dangerous possibilities. The intention of its sponsors is not only to bring open and honourable relief in many thousands of cases of unnecessary suffering, but also to encourage strictness in the observance of the law by taking away excuse for present evasions and infractions. It is for the sake of sound and honest monogamous marriage that the bill has been devised and is needed; and those who are behind it have been over a long period familiar with the facts in cases where marriage has broken down.' Referring to the specific points raised by the Mothers' Union, the letter continued, 'First, it is not necessarily in the public interest that the innocent party who will not divorce an offending partner shall be protected in this attitude at whatever cost. Second, seven years' delay and the examination and decision of a competent court are conditions which distinguish the proposals from what is usually known as divorce by mutual consent, and offer an alternative which may be preferable to committing a matrimonial offence. Third, belief in the lifelong character of the marriage bond is certainly to be respected as a personal view and self-imposed rule, but in this country there are already legal grounds for divorce and the provision of the bill cannot properly offend any conscience since it does not propose to enforce any view or any act.'[10]

In response the Bishop of Monmouth (Alfred Edwin Morris) made the point that 'although the Registrar General has recently ordered registrars to inform the contracting parties that the law of England is that marriage is a lifelong union of one man with one woman to the exclusion of all others, the law also says that in certain circumstances the state will dissolve the marriage. The truth is that in the eyes of the state marriage is a lifelong union only in the sense that the parties cannot themselves dissolve the marriage, but are bound by their contract until the state says they are free. The Church, on the other hand, says that what it means by marriage is a union that cannot be dissolved. What is needed is a frank recognition that the Church and the state do not mean the same thing when they speak of marriage. A marriage entered into on the understanding that it is dissoluble is not the same thing as a marriage that is regarded by both parties *ab initio* as indissoluble, and the state, having to legislate for all its citizens, may enact with regard to the former what it would be improper for it to enact with regard to the latter. People should be free, as they are in fact at present free, to contract an indissoluble marriage, and the state should not try to take away this freedom by presuming to dissolve such a union at the will of one of the parties.'[11]

A letter supporting the Bishop of Monmouth maintained that there was a common assumption that divorce wipes out all bonds, spiritual as well as legal. But this view is certainly wrong for the divorce court does not absolve from their vows those who have taken them. 'It follows that the question upon what grounds should the legal obligations of marriage be dissolved is merely one of public expedience. Up to now, the permanence of marriage has been considered as a principle of basic importance to the community, and so the law has never permitted divorce either by consent or contrivance; but this latter is what is now proposed. Dissolution by consent is but a very short step farther. Has the framework of society so changed as to require this great and dangerous erosion of the basic principle?'[12]

Another letter in *The Times* predicted that the arguments in favour of the bill 'will no doubt be those which have been put forward in favour of every extension of the grounds of divorce—the marriage is a mockery, the parties are unhappy, no purpose is served by keeping them legally tied. These arguments utterly ignore the lessons we have learned since 1857. Every extension of the grounds of divorce has increased the number of marriages which have broken down, and the institution of marriage itself has been increasingly weakened. The actual parties to the divorce, or more often one of them, may purchase a little happiness, generally transitory; but it is at the expense of the happiness of many others who, in a climate of opinion where marriage is a respected institution and divorce reprobate, would make a success of their lives together. Any schoolmaster, social worker, or practitioner in the Divorce Court will tell you that it is the children who suffer from the divorce. One sees them every day—a subject of contention, playing off one parent against the other, distraught, insecure, neurotic. Generally, even a bad home is better than no home. But, in fact, if the parties make the best of a bad job, they will frequently find in the end that they have made quite a good job of it. The bill, however, does far more than merely extend the grounds of divorce, it introduces a fundamentally new principle in the matrimonial law. Here, for the first time, the law sanctions divorce by mutual consent, or even without the consent of the wronged spouse. The court, no matter what infamy has been perpetrated by the petitioner, has no discretion to withhold its decree; its function is merely to register the divorce. Further, there is no argument in favour of divorce after seven years' separation, which would not equally apply to five years, or two years, or even three months, if the court is satisfied that there is no prospect of reconciliation. Indeed, on the arguments in favour of the bill, the sooner the farce is ended the better.'[13]

The Marriage Law Reform Society admitted that Mrs White's Bill would introduce a new principle into English divorce law. 'This principle is that when a marriage has obviously failed and come to an end in fact, it is public policy to end its nominal existence in law… It is correct that the new bill would enable divorce to be obtained, even if one party objected on religious grounds. The objector need not recognise the divorce but, more important, it is submitted, it is in the interests of public morality that the minority who object to divorce should not be permitted to force their views on other people. When a person refuses a divorce, whether from spite or religious conviction, the other partner is left married but separated, and with no choice but celibacy or an extramarital union. As much as the Mothers' Union, the Marriage Law Reform Society believes that marriage should be permanent, but we do not see why people should be penalised all their lives because of a mistake they may have made in youth.'[14]

The Archbishop of Canterbury (Geoffrey Fisher) wrote in his diocesan letter, 'Thinking people of all kinds are well aware that the nation is suffering in its deepest springs of life from the disregard of monogamy, the multiplication of divorces and consequent remarriages – which are by their nature, though not in law, correctly described as bigamous – and the evil of broken homes. It is well known that children of such homes, deprived of the proper security of the home, are specially liable to become neurotic, unstable and psychologically unbalanced. Exactly the same results are produced in the general psychology of a nation when its homes become insecure... The Matrimonial Causes Bill is at best a palliative which seeks to conceal the real disease. It rests on the supposition that by enabling an illegitimate union to become a legal marriage you have made things better. You have, in fact, merely depressed further the meaning of marriage... Are we to be guided by the desires of man as he is, or are we to shape our steps as far as is possible by what man should be and can be? Along one line, all the disabilities will be removed and marriage become a matter of personal convenience terminable at will; on the other, everything possible will be done to support the true principles of marriage as essential to a healthy nation, let alone a Christian nation.'[15]

The Archbishop of York (Cyril Garbett) warned about the dangers inherent in the bill which would further undermine the Christian home. He believed that the bill would be a long step towards divorce by consent. He wrote, 'Unless a resolute stand is taken against these new proposals within a few years marriage will be treated as a temporary contract which can be broken after a brief experiment. There are hard cases for which we should have every sympathy; but this new bill would increase hard cases, for the more easy divorce becomes the more light-heartedly will many enter into marriage. Instead of reducing unhappiness, it is more likely to increase it through the greater ease with which marriages will be dissolved.'[16]

Concerned about the public opposition to her bill, Mrs White considered it wrong for the Church to try and impose its view of marriage on all citizens, whether they were Church members or not. She wrote in a letter to *The Times*, 'We are entitled to hear from the Archbishops of Canterbury and York whether they wish to have a clause added to exclude their members from the provisions of the bill. That is the only logical way to meet the views recently expressed by the two archbishops... It is not enough for Dr Fisher to declare that marriages which Parliament has sanctioned as legal are bigamous. This view is not supported by many sincere citizens who have an equal right to consideration and who, accepting divorce as a necessary remedy for human error, are anxious to remove the anomalies of the existing law. The Church would not wish to obstruct the reform of the civil law. If it wants legal exemption for its members it should say so.'[17]

ARCHBISHOP GEOFFREY FISHER ON DIVORCE: 1955

In 1955 the Archbishop of Canterbury (Geoffrey Fisher) addressed a group of city men on the problems of marriage and divorce. Discussing the meaning of marriage the archbishop noted that the Church required for a true marriage the intention of lifelong union as expressed in the marriage service. What happens to a couple when they are married? 'One answer is that they have merely entered into a legal contract, which is valid so long, but only so long, as both sides keep the bargain. If one fails, the other can sue for restitution of rights or for release from the contract with compensation. It is difficult to resist the further conclusion that, if it is a legal contract only, then it can freely be ended by the mutual desire of the contracting parties.' However, such a theory of contract would change the whole conception of marriage and would substitute for it a view which in many ways offends the deepest instincts of mankind. 'It subordinates the idea of a stable home, and the interests of children, to the personal choices of the parents. By reducing the status of the home and family to a contract open to revision at will, it disturbs and demoralises society. It is repugnant to religion.' Commenting on the belief that the 'ideal' of marriage was a lifelong union, Dr Fisher said that it must be remembered that Christ spoke with great emphasis about this 'ideal'; that he spoke of it not as an ideal but as what marriage, in fact, by its nature *is*. He drew attention to the tremendous emphasis Christ placed on the definition of marriage. 'Consider the gospels of St Matthew and St Mark; "From the beginning of the creation God made them male and female. For this cause [of mutual need] shall a man leave his father and mother and cleave to his wife; and they shall be one flesh: so that they are no more two, but one flesh. What therefore [not whom, but what] God hath joined together, let not man put asunder." This, according to these gospels, is what marriage is; factually, not ideally.'[18]

Commenting on the early history of divorce, Fisher referred to the influence of the first Christians, a small group of believers fighting for their existence. At the time the Jews allowed 'divorce for every cause' and permitted remarriage; even bad housework or a preference for someone else was judged sufficient, and a woman so divorced could marry again. The Romans and Greeks were even laxer; either partner could divorce the other on the slightest pretext and marry again. Fisher explained that the Church went directly against these universal social practices with the flat demand of the gospel statements and the practice of the Church. The tiny group of believers in the end revolutionised marriage. They routed the whole practice of the contemporary world. They created a new belief in monogamous lifelong marriage as a duty to God, and imposed it upon their members and in the end on the civilised world. 'Surely the impetus for such an assault and victory must have come from our Lord. It could not have happened otherwise. It is not, therefore, surprising that the Church in the West has put such an emphasis on the lifelong and indissoluble character of marriage. Plainly the thing of lasting importance is to preserve this victory of Christ.'[19]

Fisher said that the reason why the Church had taken such a strong stand against divorce and remarriage in the 1930s was because it 'realised that the mounting tide of divorces was threatening to overthrow the whole Christian conception of marriage. It was no longer a question of deciding about exceptions to our Lord's standard but of preserving that standard itself for the nation.' The social evils springing from broken homes became more evident as their numbers increased. In particular, evidence accumulated from all sides of the dreadful harm done to the children of broken homes. As the social evils were mounting, it was becoming clear that 'the moral grounds on which divorce rested were also alarmingly unsatisfactory. Adultery had once been the only ground of divorce and could claim some kind of recognition as such in the gospels. But while continuous adultery was one thing, a single act of adultery was not a good ground on which to break up a marriage for life. And adulteries could be 'arranged'. There was no longer any security that the 'innocent party' really was the innocent party, and in any case the line between innocence and guilt in breaking up a marriage is rarely so clear-cut as a divorce decree might suggest. In short, the moral basis of divorce could hardly be regarded as satisfactory.'[20]

The archbishop also discussed the controversial issue of remarriage in his talk. He believed that the way of the Church of England was nearest to Christ's will, because it dealt as much as possible in terms of moral and spiritual truth. 'The attitude of the Church, shortly put, is:

> No marriage in church of any divorced person with a partner still living, since the solemnising of a marriage is a formal and official act of the Church, and the Church must not give its official recognition to a marriage which (for whatever cause) falls below our Lord's definition of what marriage is.
>
> But the relation of such people to the Church or their admission to communion is another matter: one of pastoral care for the sinner, and properly a matter of pastoral discretion.'[21]

Fisher concluded that the Church corporately should not marry below Christ's standard. 'It stands before the world to proclaim that this is what Christ means marriage to be and what he says it is.'[22]

THE ROYAL COMMISSION ON DIVORCE: 1956

Aware of the contentious nature of the proposal in the Private Member's bill sponsored by Mrs White, the government effectively sidelined the issue by setting up yet another Royal Commission in 1951 to inquire into marriage and divorce. The commission, comprising 13 men and 8 women, worked for four years, held 102 meetings, received over two thousand letters and 250 memoranda, and heard oral evidence from 67 organisations and 48 individual witnesses.

Reporting in 1956 the commission gave its view on the reasons for the rise in divorce. It noted that there had been a large increase in numbers since the Herbert Act of 1937, and felt that 'the divorce figures must give rise to grave concern. We are satisfied that marriages are now breaking up which in the past would have held together.' The commission concluded that a number of factors were contributing to the rising figures. 'The complexity of modern life multiplies the potential of disagreement and possibilities of friction between husband and wife.'

Earlier marriage was another factor, and 'the greater demands now being made on marriage, consequent on the spread of education, higher standards of living and the social and economic emancipation of women. The last is probably the most important. Women are no longer content to endure the treatment which in past times their inferior position obliged them to suffer. They expect of marriage that it shall be an equal partnership; and rightly so.'[23] The report continues, 'Old restraints, such as social penalties on sexual relations outside marriage have been weakened, and new ideals to take their place are still in process of formation. It is perhaps inevitable that at such a time there should be a tendency to regard the assertion of one's own individuality as a right, and to pursue one's personal satisfaction, reckless of the consequences to others... The wider spread of knowledge in matters of sex is of great value, but may have produced in the popular mind an undue emphasis on the overriding importance of a satisfactory sexual relationship without a similar emphasis on the other stable and enduring factors of a lasting marriage. There is a further factor in the problem of marriage breakdown which is more dangerous, because more insidious in its effects, than any of the others. In fact, we believe it lies at the root of the problem. There is a tendency to take the duties and responsibilities of marriage less seriously than formerly... The result of this outlook is that there is less disposition to overcome difficulties and to put up with the rubs of daily life and, in consequence, there is an increasing disposition to regard divorce, not as the last resort, but as the obvious way out when things begin to go wrong.'[24]

There was nothing in the commission's findings to support the argument that divorce legislation would heighten society's view of marriage. On the contrary, easy divorce appeared to have cheapened the marriage bond, as suggested by the opponents of divorce liberalisation. The change in the community's attitude to divorce is to some extent responsible for this situation. The pendulum has swung very far to the side of tolerance, and consequently relatives and friends may be inclined to acquiesce too readily, if not to encourage, divorce as a way out when marriage failure threatens.[25]

189

Some members of the commission proposed an entirely new basis for divorce. 'They recommended that the existing grounds of divorce should be abolished and their place taken by a single, comprehensive ground which would allow divorce to be granted if it could be proved that the marriage had irretrievably broken down.'[26] They argued that it was illogical to grant a divorce for an isolated act of adultery, which may have been repented of, but not for a marriage that is completely at an end. Those who supported the doctrine of breakdown favoured the addition of two new grounds: divorce by mutual consent and divorce at the option of either spouse after a period of separation. All commissioners, with one exception, agreed that the doctrine of marital offence should be retained. However, nine members were in favour of introducing an additional ground—that there should be dissolution of a marriage which has irretrievably broken down.[27]

Another nine members were opposed to the introduction of the doctrine of breakdown of marriage, because they considered it would be gravely detrimental to the well-being of the community. Those who opposed the doctrine of breakdown of marriage recognised that it would entail divorce by consent, and 'in its more fully developed forms it would also entail the recognition of divorce against the will of a spouse who had committed no recognised marital offence'. The introduction of either of these elements was regarded 'as fundamentally objectionable and as containing the seeds of grave damage to marriage as an institution. We believe that the consequences of providing the "easy way out" afforded by divorce by consent would be disastrous to stability in marriage... People would come to look upon marriage less and less as a lifelong union and more and more as one to be ended if things begin to go wrong, and there would be a very real risk that in the end widespread divorce would come to be an accepted feature of our society. As those attitudes spread they would undermine, and ultimately destroy, the concept of lifelong marriage.'[28]

They highlighted the evils which would result if the community were to come to accept divorce as the obvious way out of all marriage difficulties. 'We are deeply concerned about the effect on children of the present divorce rate; their suffering would be multiplied if divorce were to become more widespread. The best home for children is of course a happy home, but in our opinion (and most expert witnesses confirmed this) children can put up with a good deal of friction between their parents so long as the home remains intact.'[29]

Commenting on Mrs White's Bill the commissioners pointed out that it would introduce into the law 'a new principle which would have even more damaging consequences for the institution of marriage than divorce by consent, since it would mean that either spouse would be free to terminate the marriage at pleasure. In other words, people would enter marriage knowing that no matter what they did or how their partner felt, they could always get free. No married person could ever be sure that he would not be divorced. The introduction into marriage of this sense of insecurity and uncertainty would have a most disturbing effect on family life, which would ultimately react on all members of the community.'

Those who supported the concept of marriage breakdown argued that under the stress of changes in society and the waning influence of religious thought, divorce has tended to be regarded as a measure of relief from individual hardship. The notion of matrimonial offences, in which one party to the divorce is treated as guilty and the other as innocent, can be traced to the conception of divorce as a penalty for the breach of marriage obligations. 'We think the law of divorce as it at present exists is indeed weighted in favour of the least scrupulous, the least honourable and the least sensitive; and that nobody who is ready to provide a ground of divorce, who is careful to avoid any suggestion of connivance or collusion and who has a co-operative spouse, has any difficulty in securing a dissolution of the marriage.'[30]

The Archbishop of Canterbury, however, told the commission that it should not feel constrained by the Christian doctrine on marriage. He said, 'In the nation there are those who hold and apply the Christian standard of marriage. But there are very many, perhaps a majority, who do not hold it on Christian grounds or do not hold it at all. That being so, the Royal Commission could not base its recommendations solely on the grounds of Christian doctrine.'[31] With this statement the Church was again making it quite clear that it no longer believed that the biblical view of marriage was relevant for the whole of society, but only for those who followed the Christian faith.

The commission was overwhelmingly of the opinion that the present law based on the idea of the matrimonial offence should be retained. However, on the principle that a marriage should be dissolved if it has irretrievably broken down, the commission was split down the middle. Nevertheless, the notion of the irretrievable breakdown of marriage had been placed firmly on the agenda and would come to fruition within less than two decades.

The response to the commission was surprisingly muted. This was probably because it provided little to support those who wanted to introduce divorce for the irretrievable breakdown of marriage. The Bishop of London (Henry Campbell) expressed surprise that there was so little debate about the findings of the commission. Addressing the London Diocesan Conference he said that there could be no remarriage in church when one or other of the parties had a living partner. In his view, the growing numbers of divorce were cause for lamentation and shame. 'The teaching of modern psychology, which vaguely but markedly influences the minds of the people, tends towards self-expression regardless of others and suggests the harmfulness of repression, which again tends to a "go as you please" attitude to life. The Church has to be firm in her witness to the God-given theory of marriage, an indissoluble union of one man and one woman. Therefore we have to stand to our resolution that there can be no remarriage in church when one or other of the parties has a partner living.' At the same meeting the Bishop of Willesden (George Ingle) pointed out that 20 thousand children were affected every year by divorce and said that if this went on we would be creating a 'divorcing society—a society in which it became habitually easy to seek the dissolution of marriage, and the whole thing would have a snowball effect.'[32]

ATTEMPTS TO EXTEND GROUNDS OF DIVORCE: 1958

Despite the failure of Mrs White's Bill and the inconclusive recommendations of the Royal Commission, the passion to liberalise divorce still burned strong among many politicians and intellectuals. The Archbishop of York (Arthur Ramsey) drew attention to the moral crisis caused by the growing number of divorces – in 1910 there were 596 divorces compared to 30 thousand in 1953 – and mentioned that one of the causes was the divorce-mindedness of the community.[33] (**Figure 7** describes the divorce numbers between 1937 and 1961.) His view was challenged by the Marriage Reform Society. 'But is it right to draw the inference that more divorce is evidence of divorce-mindedness, which might lead one to the view that the ties of family life are being seriously weakened? It is thought that from such statistics as are available – and admittedly they are scant but none the less informative – there are no more, in fact probably fewer, broken homes today than there were at the turn of the century. It is surely the number of broken homes in

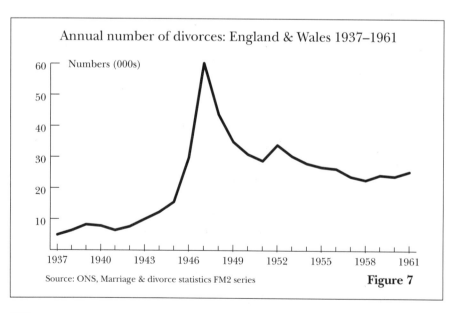

Annual number of divorces: England & Wales 1937–1961

Source: ONS, Marriage & divorce statistics FM2 series

Figure 7

1910 compared with 1953 that will provide the answer to family stability. Divorce figures on their own will supply no such information.'[34] The Marriage Reform Society was concerned at the disastrous consequences of the present arrangements, and especially 'the squalor and perjury which results from the retention of the legal concept of the matrimonial offence which flies in the face of mid-20th century realities and leads to a high proportion of collusive divorces and widespread contempt for the law'.[34] They were determined to promote a parliamentary bill to bring about urgently needed divorce law liberalisation. The purpose of the bill would be to establish divorce by mutual agreement when a marriage has irretrievably broken down, where the spouses are childless, or in the case of those whose children have reached maturity. The Society was seeking MPs to sponsor their bill.[35] A private member's bill introduced in 1958, sponsored by Mr William Deedes, met with little success.

LEO ABSE'S PRIVATE MEMBER'S BILL: 1963

Five years later in 1963 a further attempt was made to extend the grounds of divorce. Mr Leo Abse, a Labour Member of Parliament and a passionate supporter of the divorce campaign, introduced another Private Member's bill, entitled the Matrimonial Causes and Reconciliation Bill. Its sponsors claimed that the prime aim was to 'amend the law so as to encourage the estranged to make a bid for happiness'. This would be done by allowing couples to reunite for a trial period of one month, without prejudicing the grounds for divorce if the reconciliation failed. However, hidden within the bill was a clause similar to that in Mrs White's Bill that allowed a spouse to be divorced against their will, having committed no marital offence, after seven years separation. In effect this clause would allow the husband who had committed a marital offence, such as adultery, to divorce his wife against her wishes.[36]

The second reading passed without a division, but a fierce debate took place in the Commons standing committee. Mr Dick Taverne said that many of the illicit unions which existed, and which inevitably took place when people no longer lived with their legal wives or husbands for a period of five or seven years, could be legitimised. The more illicit unions that existed, the more the institution of marriage was undermined and the less respect there was for marriage.

Mr Charles Doughty said that even before the bill had become law, there were proposals for reducing the period from seven to five years—and if it was five years, why should it not be three years? Mr John Parker claimed that changing the law would not weaken marriage. They had to take account of the enormous growth in what might be called *de facto* marriages. 'That is when, because one or other of the parties is not free under the present law, two people form a union which is a stable union and which has children setting up what to all intents and purposes is a new family.' He pointed out that 39 per cent of illegitimate births in Birmingham were to parents living in stable family units who would marry if they could. He did not think that those who held particular religious views had the right to force those views upon another person whose views were different. However, a number of Conservative Members argued that divorce should not be permitted where one of the parties objected on religious, sociological or ethical grounds.

Mr David Weitzman asked whether they wanted one party to commit adultery in order to get a divorce. 'Is that what righteous people want, people committing matrimonial offences in order to get a divorce? Or are people to act honestly in this way and make living separately after the marriage has irretrievably broken down grounds for divorce after a number of years?'[37] Following a narrow vote, an amendment was added to the bill that a court must take account of any genuinely held religious, ethical or sociological objections to the divorce. A move to reduce the separation period from seven to five years was rejected by 15 votes to 7.

Leaders of the Church of England, the Roman Catholic Church, the Established Church of Wales and the Free Church Federal Council were united in opposition to the proposed changes in the divorce law, and took the unusual step of issuing a joint statement. 'There is great concern about one clause which would add a new ground for divorce of such a kind as to introduce a dangerous new principle into our marriage laws. It is the clause which would allow divorce after seven years' separation, whether or not a matrimonial offence has been committed against the petitioner... we believe that it would help to undermine the basic understanding of marriage as a lifelong union if the principle were introduced that a marriage could be terminated by the desire of the partners to terminate it. In the fulfilment of our duty to uphold the Christian meaning of marriage we are concerned for the welfare of the state and the people. At present both a church marriage and even a registry office marriage are at one in affirming that the two partners enter upon a lifelong covenant. We think that there would be an increasing tendency to enter upon this covenant less seriously if the law allowed it to be ended on the principle of the partners' own desire to end it. Furthermore, if once the principle of divorce by consent after separation were admitted by the law, the pressure would arise (as the debate on this bill confirmed) to make the period shorter.'[38]

But not all Christians were happy with this statement. A letter to *The Times* claimed that neither the British Council of Churches nor the Christian Citizenship departments of at least some Free Church denominations would have set their names to a pronouncement of this nature. 'Besides, the actual practice of Free Churches up and down the land is at variance with the whole tone of yesterday's statement. It has been estimated that nearly a fifth of all marriages celebrated in Congregational Churches, and nearly an eighth of those celebrated in Methodist Churches are of divorced persons.' The writer made it clear that there was 'a genuine and deeply felt difference between the pastoral approach of Free Church ministers and that of their Anglican or Roman Catholic counterparts. Lastly, on general social and theological grounds, yesterday's statement was regrettable. The legalism of the official Anglican attitude to divorce and other sexual matters is at present being strongly criticised by distinguished Anglican theologians, in Cambridge and elsewhere. And even if we could all be quite certain what Christian marriage discipline should be, we should now be most reluctant to impose it on a society which does not, by and large, share the presuppositions on which that discipline has to be based.'[39]

Speaking at a rally of the Union of Catholic Mothers, the Roman Catholic Archbishop of Liverpool said that the joint public pronouncement of the Christian leaders against the proposed new divorce legislation was greeted in many sections of the press as the tactics of a pressure group. 'Once you agree that for those good reasons divorce should be allowed there is no reason whatever why divorce should not be granted for any reason under the sun. Once you attempt to improve on the law of God, once you tinker with the eternal law, there is no end and no more security.'[40] The bishop drew attention to the fundamental truth that it is not possible for human wisdom to improve on God's law for marriage and divorce.

Five Members of Parliament, including the Rev Llewelyn Williams and John Morris, wrote to *The Times* objecting to the statement of the churches, for 'they have never stated clearly what they mean by marriage. To us it means setting up a joint home and living together in companionship, love and affection and, if possible, bringing up a family happily together. Without at least some of these characteristics it is an empty symbol. After seven years' separation it is dead. We believe that in such circumstances it is in the public interest that the legal fiction should be ended and each party set free to try to make a happy second marriage, if they so desire... We take strong objection to persons using the law of the land to veto a second marriage of an ex-spouse who does not share their religious views. Too often such a veto is motivated by a malicious desire for revenge; if due to genuine religious convictions, it smacks of religious persecution. Already a large number of *de facto* marriages have come into existence where one spouse is denied the freedom to make a second legal marriage. For public opinion does not accept the right of veto as being fair or right. It is difficult to obtain accurate figures but there is strong evidence that the number of illegitimate children living with their parents in stable *de facto* marriages is now probably greater than the number of children of divorced and separated persons. Such love marriages seem to be particularly fruitful. Fortunately divorcees frequently have no children, or only one: sexual incompatibility being a frequent cause of the breakdown of a marriage... We believe the bill will strengthen marriage by increasing the number of legal happy marriages.'[41]

The MPs letter produced a strong response. One correspondent expressed surprise that the reverend gentleman who signed the letter, 'did not tell his co-signatories what was the teaching of Jesus Christ about marriage. It is this teaching, and this teaching alone, that should determine what Christians mean by marriage. The terminable contract, which your correspondents would substitute for this, is totally different, and it is strange to see a Christian minister supporting this idea of the nature of marriage.'[42]

The Canon of Windsor (Geoffrey Bentley) responded that the letter 'gave an admirably clear account of the humanist doctrine of marriage. According to this doctrine the substance of marriage is the common life of man and wife; if therefore the common life comes irreparably to grief, marriage is really at an end, and subsequent divorce is merely legal confirmation of the empirical fact. Refusal of divorce in such circumstances can only perpetuate a legal set up which has no basis in reality. In view of our own conception of marriage as lifelong we Christians are bound to reject the humanist doctrine; but we have to face the fact that it is not easy to refute with arguments on the common sense level... By and large we must allow that the conception of marriage as essentially lifelong stands or falls with the authority of Christ. In other words, it depends upon faith and cannot be adequately substantiated by common sense reasoning alone.

'What, then, is the duty of Christians in a mixed society? It should be clear to us that we are ourselves called to lifelong fidelity in marriage, no matter what the matrimonial law of the society in which we live may be; but it is not so clear what we ought to do when changes in the law are being canvassed. Since Christ has taught us that union for life is proper to man as man and not just a special rule for his own disciples, we cannot simply wash our hands of the matter; love for our neighbour seems to demand not only that we should try to commend lifelong fidelity to unbelievers as well as to believers, but also that we should oppose legislation which would withdraw legal support from such fidelity.'[43]

When it became clear that the bill was likely to fail due to lack of parliamentary time, AP Herbert, the hero of the 1937 legislation, wrote to *The Times* imploring the government to make time available for the passage of the bill. He mentioned that when his bill stood in danger because 'Private Members time' was exhausted, 'Mr Baldwin's Government graciously gave us a government day for the completion of the report stage and the third reading. I hope that, if the need arises, this course will be favourably considered by the present government.'[44] This was a remarkable intervention by the architect of the 1937 Divorce Act. He was admitting that his bill had been only an instalment in an ongoing campaign to achieve divorce on demand. But had Herbert not solemnly maintained that not a single word in his bill was against the teaching of Christ, suggesting a Christian justification for his views on divorce?

However, parliamentary opposition during the third reading meant that the bill would be lost because of lack of time, and Leo Abse had no option but to withdraw the contentious clause. He admitted that his mild reform had aroused the most formidable opposition. The real reason for all the clamour was that the clause, if it became law, was the first attempt to emancipate the divorce law and rid it of the humbug and pretence that now existed. In his opinion the divorce law was choked by the doctrine of the matrimonial offence. The clamour existed to maintain the fiction that in every divorce there must be a so-called guilty and innocent party. 'At present the law directs that if two parties want a divorce, then to maintain the myth that divorce can never be obtained by consent in this country, one of the parties must affect to commit adultery or must commit adultery or must declare that the matrimonial home has been quit without the consent of the other or must not defend extravagant allegations of cruelty. Nothing but honesty can prevent two parties to a marriage at this moment in this country who want a divorce, from obtaining one. Solicitors and judges are deceived regularly. How many of the decrees in undefended cases of desertion and cruelty could possibly be granted if they were defended?' He assured the House that he and the other sponsors of the bill would continue their campaign to change the law.[45] Miss Joan Vickers congratulated Mr Abse on the courage he had shown, and said that he had started something in England which would continue. He had put down a stepping stone and in the future he would get everything he had requested in his bill.[46] Mr John Parker, a sponsor of the bill, said there was strong resentment among many people at the attitude of the churches. No section of the population had the right to try to force their views on marriage and divorce on the great majority. If the churches persisted in their opposition to changes of this kind there would be a strong wave of anti-clericalism in Britain; the churches would have deserved it, and they would suffer from it.[47]

Debate in House of Lords: 1963

In the House of Lords, Lord Silkin expressed regret that the seven-year clause had been removed and tried to reintroduce it by way of an amendment. He said the clause would give a chance to start a new married life to the hundreds of thousands of couples who were living in a state of 'unmarriage', and would thus help to stabilise the marriage institution. It would enable parents of the estimated 200 thousand illegitimate children to marry and legitimise their children.[48] Meanwhile, Mr Abse had a letter published in *The Times* in which he pointed out that the opportunity for a full debate in the Commons was prevented by shabby procedural stratagems. Now that there was an opportunity for it to be debated in the Lords he hoped that it would be used for an objective sociological appraisement. He noted that Archbishop Ramsey had expressed the view in a television transmission that the opinion expressed by the representatives of the Anglican Church was 'due to the fact that they are sociologists not theologians'. He hoped, therefore, that the bishops would at last put forward the sociological grounds upon which their opposition was based, so that it may be tested. He wrote, 'The sociologist regards marriage as an institution whose *raison d'être* is the foundation and maintenance of the family and the seven year clause takes this wholly into account. When husband and wife have not seen each other for seven years – whatever the validity of Christian theology for the committed Christian – how can such a marriage be regarded as rooted in the family; and equally how can remarriage be forbidden on sociological grounds, to the parents of some 200 thousand illegitimate children now being denied a family life with married parents because of insistence that only an innocent party may petition for a divorce... If the Anglican opposition is not based on dogma, then we need to know the sociological arguments against the bill which has these objectives.'[49] In effect, the Church was claiming that its opposition to the bill was based on sociological grounds and not dogma, and Mr Abse had challenged the Church to justify their opposition to his bill on those grounds.

The Archbishop of Canterbury made a landmark speech in the House of Lords which was to have enormous consequences for the future of divorce legislation. He said that it had been suggested that the Church wished to impose its views upon the law of the country. 'While the churches have their beliefs and standards which they urge their members to follow, and teach that they can follow with the help of God's grace, they accept the fact that a great many citizens do not share their beliefs and that this is reflected in the divorce laws of the country. However, the churches are concerned with what is likely to be good and right for the country as a whole, and it is from that concern that I, for one, express my views about the new clause now before us. We have the problem before us now, the problem concerning divorce; because there is something very wrong in the country, and this has been growing. Too many marriages break down. There are too many strains in families; too many illicit unions, both before and after marriage.

'In a letter in *The Times* yesterday (he was referring to the letter by Mr Abse) it was asked whether the case of the churchmen who oppose the clause was based only on dogma or on sociological considerations. I would say that the considerations which I have been putting before your Lordships are indeed sociological considerations concerning the deep well-being of society. But as to dogma—this is a word which arouses prejudice so let me use the word belief. In this matter the churches are not asking to impose their belief on those who do not accept it, for churchmen have already accepted that there is a divergence between their belief and the state's law on divorce… And we have our terrible problems largely because the status of marriage is weakened and the approach of so many people to it is wrong. Do not, my Lords, weaken this status further… My Lords, this is not to say that I am content with the present law on divorce and the operation of the divorce courts. When the recent statement by a number of church leaders in this country ended with the words; "We are anxious to examine any measures for reducing the hardships which would not affect the foundations of marriage" we meant what we said. It is very difficult to see what can be done, but I am concerned that we should try. Is it not, for instance, worth while asking for further examination of the word illegitimate? Is it necessary for all purposes – for instance, for the purpose of bequests – that there should be the present distinction at all? Again, if it were possible to find a principle at law of breakdown of marriage which was free from any trace of the idea of consent, which conserved the point that offences and not only wishes were the basis of the breakdown, and which was protected by a far more thorough insistence on reconciliation procedure first, then I would wish to consider it. Indeed, I am asking some of my fellow churchmen to see whether it is possible to work at this idea, sociologically as well as doctrinally, to discover if anything can be produced… Do not let us undermine what is not only the belief of the churches, but the meaning of marriage as one of the bases of our society.'[50]

Lord Morton of Henryton spoke as the Chairman of the Royal Commission on Marriage and Divorce (1956). He pointed out that the commission had firmly rejected by 14 votes to 4 the proposal now before the House. He quoted from the commission: 'To vest in a husband or wife the right to divorce a spouse who had committed no recognised matrimonial offence and who did not want a divorce would result in a great injustice. It would, for example, allow a man who had committed adultery or had been cruel to his wife to leave her and subsequently to divorce her against her will. This would violate a principle which has been long established in the law—namely, that a man shall not be allowed to take advantage of his own wrong.'[51]

Lord Gladwin spoke with the greatest diffidence although he was one of the sponsors of the new clause. As a humble but sincere member of the Church of England he doubted 'whether the rules governing the conduct of monogamy in our modern society should be approached altogether from a religious point of view. I rather think that in that particular assertion I have the support of the most reverend Primate himself – in his remarks about dogma, for instance. I think we ought, therefore, to regard divorce primarily as a social problem on which all who have thought about the matter at all are fully entitled to express a view.'[52] The amendment to reinstate the seven year clause was lost on a vote.

Comment

In effect Archbishop Ramsey had conceded that biblical teaching (dogma) was no longer relevant to the divorce debate in England. From then on the issue would be approached on the basis of sociological principles. The leadership of the Church of England believed that the teaching of the Scriptures had little to offer in trying to improve the divorce laws—a sociological approach was likely to prove more fruitful. So the problem of divorce was to be solved by human reason alone and any and all opinions based in sociological thought were equally valid. Effectively the Christian position was being sidelined as a minority view based on an unacceptable dogma. The Scriptures had become irrelevant in the debate and the appeal was to human wisdom guided by the spirit of the age.

Chapter 10

A divorce bill full of tears

The Divorce Reform Act of 1969 and the move

to no-fault divorce

The permissive 1960s were a time of moral uncertainty when many traditional values were questioned. Writing at the end of the decade, William
Barclay observed that in the past thirty years the Christian ethic had come
under serious challenge. 'Thirty years ago no one ever doubted that divorce
was disgraceful; that illegitimate babies were a disaster; that chastity was a
good thing; that a honest day's work was part of the duty of any respectable
and responsible man; that honesty ought to be part of life. But today, for
the first time in history, the whole Christian ethic is under attack. It is not
only the theology that people want to abandon—it is the ethic as well.'[1]
Behind the permissive society was a headlong charge to be free from the
restraints of Christian moral standards. Those who led the charge portrayed
Christian morality as repressive and judgemental, something which prevented people from really expressing themselves. Real freedom meant
freedom from outdated moral laws that belonged to another age; freedom
from a morality that inhibited people from enjoying their natural sexual
desires. 'Free love' became the slogan as the rules of the old sexual morality
were abandoned. Love was the only value that mattered, nothing else. So
long as people acted from a motive of love then everything was permissible.
Society no longer accepted the concepts of absolute right or wrong. The
advent of oral contraceptives encouraged the belief that men and women
were free to indulge in sexual relationships without the danger of pregnancy.
Free love meant that marriage had been devalued for it was possible to have
a loving sexual relationship without getting married. For those who did

marry, divorce was seen as the means of liberation from an unhappy situation. When married couples are no longer in love they have the right to search elsewhere for happiness. Divorce was merely the legal mechanism which provided freedom from inconvenient, unwanted marriages. It is not surprising that the decade of the sixties was an era that yearned for divorce laws in keeping with the mores of the permissive society.

PUTTING ASUNDER – A REPORT OF THE CHURCH OF ENGLAND: 1966

In 1964 the Church of England set up a working group under the chairman-ship of the Bishop of Exeter (Robert Mortimer) to advise the state on divorce law reform. The Archbishop of Canterbury, following his speech in the House of Lords, encouraged the group to investigate the issue from a sociological as well as a doctrinal perspective. The aim was to 'consider whether the inclusion of any new principle or procedure in the law of the state would be likely to operate more justly and with greater assistance to the stability of marriage and the happiness of all concerned including children than at present; and in such a way as to do nothing to undermine the approach of couples to marriage as a lifelong covenant'. They acknow-ledged the need to consider 'not only what the Church is bound to require of its own members but also what the Church thinks should be the law of the land in the 20th century. These two aspects of the Church's duty should be carefully distinguished.' This point is emphasised. 'How the doctrine of Christ concerning marriage should be interpreted and applied within the Christian Church is one question. What the Church ought to say and do about secular laws of marriage and divorce is another question altogether. This can hardly be repeated too often.' It follows that 'any advice that the Church tenders to the state must rest, not upon doctrines that only Christians accept, but upon premises that enjoy wide acknowledgement in the nation as a whole'.[2]

What troubled the committee was the generally low opinion of the current divorce law, which had been passed by Parliament with so much acclaim less than 30 years earlier. The main recommendation of *Putting Asunder* was controversial in that it moved away from the principle of marital offences as the grounds for divorce, and supported the idea of the irretrievable breakdown of the marriage, the concept that had been rejected by the previous Royal Commission in 1956. 'We came to the conclusion that whatever the legal theory might be, legal practice was moving, in company with the mind of society, towards the concept of breakdown of marriage.'[3] They found no reason to suppose that the doctrine of breakdown of marriage would favour divorce by consent in the objectionable sense of those words. Nor did they find the concept of marriage breakdown to be unworthy or incompatible with a covenant of lifelong intention. 'Indeed, we were persuaded that a divorce law founded on the doctrine of breakdown would not only accord better with social realities than the present law does but would have the merit of showing up divorce for what it is – not a reward for marital virtue on the one side and a penalty for marital delinquency on the other; not a victory for one spouse and a reverse for the other; but a defeat for both, a failure of the marital "two-in-oneship" in which both its members, however unequal their responsibility, are inevitably involved together.'[4]

Conceding that a spouse who has committed a marital offence, such as adultery, might take advantage of his or her own wrongdoing to get the marriage dissolved against the will of the innocent party, the report comments that 'divorce is a drastic piece of surgery, the unnatural severing of what should be one and indissoluble. As such it is bound to cause pain and loss and leave lasting scars. To demand that a divorce law shall let no one be hurt is therefore to ask the impossible.'[5]

Comment

It seems remarkable that a Church group believed that a law which permitted a husband or wife to take advantage of their own wrongdoing would be more just, and would promote the happiness of all concerned, including the children. Were they unaware of the basic biblical principle that a man reaps what he sows? In effect, *Putting Asunder* was proposing a law that would make it possible for either spouse to claim a divorce when they believed their marriage to be at an end, irrespective of the opinion of their partner, or whether their partner wanted a divorce or not. It also rejected the traditional Protestant doctrine of divorce that marital offences, such as adultery and desertion, were the only biblical grounds for divorce.

According to an editorial in *The Times*, 'The report of Exeter's committee on the law of divorce is bound to colour all future discussion of the subject. It will, of course, arouse great passion among Christians in Britain... The Exeter committee has unanimously pronounced itself in favour of divorce on the grounds of breakdown of marriage. It follows that the new report will not lack for critics, some of whom will want to know how a committee appointed by the Archbishop of Canterbury can come to a conclusion which – many may think – would tend to loosen the bonds of Christian marriage.'[6] Another article described the report as 'one of the most controversial of its kind published and could well lead to allegations against the Church of England that it is setting double standards if not actually facing both ways. It emphasises that the group was concerned solely with the secular side of marriage; that it is advice to the secular society for the secular law; and that secular legislation on divorce must not derogate from the church's freedom to treat the marriages of its own members in accordance with its doctrines and rules, upon which no recommendations are made.'[7] But the editorial was wrong for there was hardly a voice raised in opposition.

CHURCH ASSEMBLY DEBATE: 1967

Opening the debate on *Putting Asunder*, Mr Richard Gooch asked the Church Assembly to recognise the unsatisfactory state of the present law, and to view sympathetically any attempt to improve the law which would have the effect of increasing the stability of marriage. He explained that although Parliament might legislate particularly for those who owed no allegiance to the Church, the law should not override the Church's rules for its members.[8] The Bishop of Southwell (Gordon Savage) said that the Church must demonstrate throughout every parish that it does not close its eyes to the fact that a marriage can die, and that problems confront all those involved. He said that they needed to let it be seen that they cared deeply. Sometimes the clergy were blamed for the apparent hardness of the Church's discipline.[9]

Professor James Anderson, who was a member of the working group, said that the suggestions made in *Putting Asunder* would not widen the gulf between the law of the Church and the law of the state. 'On the contrary, we think they would lead to a great improvement in the civil law of divorce—which would not be something that the Church would ever want a committed Christian to avail himself or herself of. Our own attitude to divorce is quite plain. But the state does allow divorce, and our proposals are designed to suggest a civil law of divorce, better for the people and the nation.' He was convinced that changes in the law of divorce would come. There was mounting pressure in many different areas and among many different groups. 'In the past, the bishops in the House of Lords, and other Church leaders have stood rather like Canute trying to prevent the tide coming in. I am sure that changes in the law are going to be imposed on us, and it therefore seems to me to be imperative that the Church, instead of merely saying no, no, no, should apply its mind to what would be a more satisfactory civil law of divorce than the present law—I am not pleading for any change in our own attitude to divorce, but that we should realise that we have a responsibility to the nation not merely to say no and then accept any law that comes, but to make constructive and suitable suggestions.'

He said that the principle of a matrimonial offence had broken down and lacked logic. One could get a divorce for insanity, and no sane person could call that a matrimonial offence. One could get a divorce for cruelty, and by the interpretation of the courts this really meant little more than an intolerable situation. 'Not only has the logic gone, but the whole idea that one gives divorce to an innocent party because of the appalling behaviour of the other is hopelessly compromised if one gives divorce after discretionary statements which show that both parties are equally to blame. But the matrimonial offence has virtually no connection with reality. It has to be determined that one party is guilty and one is innocent. This does not happen in more than about 5 per cent of cases.' He urged the Assembly to affirm that the breakdown of marriage should be the sole ground of civil divorce.[10]

The Archbishop of Canterbury spoke in favour of the report. He repudiated the idea that the proposals were favouring divorce by consent, and said that if he thought that *Putting Asunder* involved divorce by consent, he would show not the slightest sympathy or favour with it. 'I believe that if the Assembly were to vote commending the *Putting Asunder* proposals, it would be voting for something of service to the community, and something which would leave unaltered the relationship between the Church's law and standard of marriage, and the state's law of marriage.'[11]

Yet there was a lone dissenting voice. The Rev Henry Cooper believed that the Church had a prophetic responsibility to the nation. He reminded the Assembly that the Church had the duty to advise the community about morals, and the state about the way in which moral principles were embodied in the law. He said most emphatically that they did not believe in two standards, one for Christians and one for mere human beings. The gospel was not preached to Christians; it was preached to men. Christ did not say, 'If you become a Christian then you must not remarry after divorce.' He made an absolute statement—whosoever. The Rev Henry Cooper accepted that absolutes were not popular because the changing climate of philosophical opinion was against them. He thought that most moral theologians would argue that there were very few, if any, absolute principles in moral theology, that almost all admitted exceptions. But Christ had made no exception at all. He said that the Church should not give the impression that evil was not evil, or that men at large were exempt from the natural law of creation. The marriage service referred to marriage as an act of God—those whom God has joined together. When they talked about a marriage dying they were speaking subjectively. He said that the Church had always taught that the *vinculum* was a reality. 'I fear the effect of this report may be that the nation will think that the Church has now gone back on that, and the breakdown of marriage is something which is real, objectively, and not merely in the minds of the parties concerned... The gospel is for all men, and is the fulfilment of God's law; this must be made clear, whatever further advice is given, either to the state officials or to individuals.'[12]

Comment

The general tenor of the debate was supportive of the report, for the idea that the Church should not try and impose its views on society was widely accepted. Biblical moral standards were for Christian people only, those who felt an allegiance to Christ. But the majority should not to be burdened by the harsh Christian laws on divorce. Instead, the Church would help secular society find divorce laws that were compassionate, just and for the good of all. This was the consensus view in the Church Assembly and was consistent with the position taken by Archbishop Lang in 1937. But a dissenting voice reminded the Church of its prophetic responsibility to the nation. The gospel of Christ is not for Christians only, but for all men and women. Christ's teaching on divorce was not directed at Christians only, but at all people—whosoever. Yet the overwhelming endorsement of the report by the General Assembly meant that the Church was accepting that the marriages of non-Christians could be dissolved if either husband or wife chose to end the marriage. And of course it was possible for Christians to use the law to get a divorce if they so wished. Parliament was now free to make major changes to divorce legislation, free from the constraints of biblical teaching and with the full blessing of the Church.

At the conclusion of the debate on *Putting Asunder* the Assembly looked at the controversial subject of remarriage. After a short debate a resolution was passed that requested the Convocations to give fresh consideration to the question of the marriage in Church of persons who have been divorced. And so started the campaign, which is still ongoing, to change the marriage discipline of the Church.[13]

THE FIELD OF CHOICE – A REPORT OF THE LAW COMMISSION: 1966

In 1965 the Law Commission Act set up a body to promote reform of the divorce laws. The commission, under the chairmanship of Mr Justice Leslie Scarman, acknowledged that it was not for them but for Parliament to settle such controversial social issues as the advisability of extending the present grounds for divorce. Their function was to advise Parliament and the general public by pointing out the implications of various courses of action.

The report of the commission, *Reform of the grounds of Divorce, The Field of Choice*, presented to Parliament in November 1966, identified two objectives of a good divorce law. First, it seeks 'to buttress, rather than to undermine, the stability of marriages which have a chance of survival'. Second, 'when, regrettably, a marriage has irretrievably broken down, to enable the empty legal shell to be destroyed with the maximum fairness, and the minimum bitterness, distress and humiliation'. According to the commission the law should make it possible to dissolve the legal tie once that had become irretrievably broken down in fact. 'If the marriage is dead, the object of the law should be to afford it a decent burial. It should achieve this in a way that is just to all concerned, including the children as well as the spouses, and which causes them the minimum of embarrassment and humiliation. Above all, it should seek to take the heat out of the disputes between husband and wife and certainly not further embitter the relationship between them or between them and their children. It should not merely bury the marriage, but do so with decency and dignity and in a way which will encourage harmonious relationships between the parties and their children in the future.'[14]

The report was highly critical of the existing law and argued fiercely against retaining a law based on the principle of the matrimonial offence. In the majority of divorces both parties were at fault in varying degrees. 'The idea that marriages break up because one party has committed an offence against the other is unreal. Moreover, the issues tried by the court are superficial; in consequence the court never gets at the root of the trouble in the marriage.' To prove that a matrimonial offence had been committed involved a hostile form of litigation, which branded one spouse as guilty. 'This leads to bitterness and frequently has harmful effects on the children, who may well love both parents.' The elaborate parade of hostility that occurred during the court proceedings brought 'the law and the whole administration of justice into disrepute, and encourages the giving of hypocritical evidence at best and perjury at worst'.[15] The existing law did not aid the stability of marriage, but tended to discourage attempts at reconciliation. 'It does not enable dead marriages to be buried, and those that it buries are not always interred with the minimum of distress and humiliation. It does not achieve the maximum fairness to all concerned, for a spouse may be branded as guilty in law though not the more blameworthy in fact. The insistence on guilt and innocence tends to embitter relationships, with particularly damaging results to the children, rather than to promote future harmony. Its principles are widely regarded as hypocritical.'[16]

The commissioners noted that while it had been suggested that divorce inevitably has adverse consequences for children, 'it can be argued that what causes the major disturbance to the children is the break-up of the home and the quarrels that preceded it, and that once a break-up has occurred a subsequent legal recognition that the marriage is dead can do little more harm and may indeed do good. The final break may lead to a lessening of the bitterness between the parents and may facilitate the establishment of a new stable environment which is the children's greatest need.'[17]

According to the commission, the proposals of the archbishop's group on divorce made in *Putting Asunder* were procedurally impracticable. It would not be feasible, even if desirable, to undertake an inquest in every divorce case because of the time and the costs involved. *The Field of Choice* suggested the following alternative proposals. First, divorce for marriage breakdown, but without the inquest suggested in *Putting Asunder*. Second, divorce by consent as an additional ground, especially in the case of marriages in which there are no dependent children. Third, divorce after a period of separation should be a ground irrespective of which party was at fault. Either a husband or wife should be allowed to ask for a divorce on the ground that the marriage has broken down irrespective of whether he or she is the innocent or guilty party.[18]

DIVORCE LAW REFORM BILL: 1968

With the backing of two authoritative reports those campaigning for no-fault divorce were now confident of success. The Divorce Law Reform Bill, sponsored by Mr William Wilson (Labour MP for Coventry) was introduced to the Commons in January 1968. It provided for divorce by consent after a two-year period of separation. Provision was also made for unilateral divorce, without the consent of both parties, after a separation of five years. At a press conference Mr Leo Abse said that the objectives of the bill were to buttress rather than undermine the stability of marriage, and to enable the 'empty legal shell' to be destroyed with the maximum of fairness and the minimum of distress, when marriage has irretrievably broken down. The only ground for divorce under the bill was that the marriage had irretrievably broken down. The parties must live apart for at least two years and either both want a divorce, or one does and the other offers no objection. 'The effect of this is that for the first time two people, believing their marriage has broken down, will be able to end it with dignity. There would be no need to hurl accusations against each other and display their private life and indiscretions to public view. This clause will civilise our divorce law.' A second ground for divorce would be if the parties had lived apart for at least five years, one party can petition for divorce even though the other objects.[19]

Controversy followed when the Archbishop of Canterbury deplored the proposal for divorce by consent and the shortening of the period of separation. He did not believe that the bill provided sufficient protection for the innocent party or the children. Mr Abse accused the archbishop of breaking faith with an agreement reached between the archbishop's own committee, chaired by the Bishop of Exeter, and the law commissioners. According to Mr Abse these two bodies had reached an agreement that a marriage could be deemed to have irretrievably broken down if the parties had been apart for two years and both parties wanted a divorce.[20] The archbishop denied that he had repudiated an agreement on the proposals contained in the Divorce Bill. He had told the Law Commission that there were parts of the proposed compromise that he could not support. At a question and answer session with students from Manchester University Dr Ramsey said, 'Our present laws are very bad. The bill that appeared this week is a kind of compromise. As usually happens in a compromise, it contains bits that are very good and bits that are very bad. I think it is rather a muddle.'[21]

An editorial in *The Times* supported the bill. It posed the obvious question, 'If marriage breakdown is really to be the criterion surely there is no need to wait for a separation of five years even when one of the partners does not wish a divorce. It is right to make a divorce rather more difficult in these circumstances, but a marriage cannot have much of a chance after a separation of three years.'[22]

An eminent barrister, Mr Geoffrey Crispin QC, who had practised for many years in the Divorce Division of the High Court, expressed his views on the bill in a forceful letter in *The Times*. 'The changes are not concerned with divorce by consent at all: divorce by consent has been with us for many years, for any two spouses who want a divorce have been able to get it, and have got it. What is now proposed once again, as it was proposed in Mr Leo Abse's Bill (of 1963), is that divorce should be granted to an offending spouse against the consent of the innocent spouse. My experience satisfies me that the vast majority of petitioners will be men: that women who have committed no other offence than giving up a career, growing older and bearing children will be 'put asunder' against their wish if this bill ever becomes law. It is idle to talk of safeguards; they simply cannot be devised, and more and more women and children will be left to the indignity of state assistance… If the country really wants this kind of loose relationship, terminable almost at the will of one spouse, then the solution might be to give up the institution of marriage altogether, and to cease to distinguish between legitimacy and illegitimacy. I am appalled that the churches and the many women's organisations do not appear to have appreciated the implications of this thoroughly bad bill or to have made themselves heard.'[23] Another letter made the rather obvious point that 'only a few rich husbands can really afford to keep more than one wife, and that for most other men it is virtually impossible to maintain two families without privation of one or the other'.[24]

The bill was debated in the House of Commons on 9 February 1968, and the second reading was passed with a large majority of 159 votes to 63. However, due to lack of parliamentary time it was unable to make progress. Following the failure of Mr Wilson's private member's bill, Mr Alec Jones introduced a similar bill in December 1968. This time a sympathetic Labour Government would provide time for the bill to pass through the parliamentary process.

THE DIVORCE REFORM ACT: 1969

Mr Alec Jones reminded the House of previous attempts in 1951 (Eirene White, Labour Member for Flint East), 1963 (Leo Abse, Labour Member for Pontypool) and February 1968 (William Wilson, Labour Member for Coventry South) to reform the divorce laws. The present basis of the law, based on marital offences, had stood for 110 years but there was growing dissatisfaction. 'To continue in legal being a marriage which has irretrievably broken down hardly seems to be a means of witnessing to the sanctity of marriage or of upholding its public repute.' He noted that individual cases highlight tragedies caused, not by divorce, but by the irretrievable breakdown of marriage. These empty marriages did increasing harm to the community and injury to the idea of marriage itself. 'The result of keeping in being these empty marriages is a large number of illicit unions, which cannot be regularised, and a still larger number of illegitimate children who cannot be legitimated. The law commissioners estimated that if the law were changed as we suggest it could be by this bill, about 180 thousand illegitimate children could be legitimated.' Mr Jones said that the bill recognised that the irretrievable breakdown of a marriage and not the matrimonial offence would be a ground for divorce. Divorce would no longer be regarded as the punishment of one party to a marriage and the relief of the other. The bill took the line that if irretrievable breakdown was established the marriage should be dissolved notwithstanding the objection of one party, but only so long as disproportionate hardship was not caused to the party. The structure and fine balance of the bill were the result of discussions between churchmen, lawyers and politicians. It was a sincere and practical attempt to overcome the deficiencies of the present divorce law without weakening the institution of marriage.[25]

Mr Bruce Campbell predicted that the bill would give another surge forward to the disintegration of family life, which had been going on for the last 20 to 25 years. The time must soon come when they must ask themselves whether the institution of marriage was worth bothering about any more, because each time divorce was made easier, marriage was made cheaper. People tended to enter into marriage as a sort of experiment, and if it did not work out, there was always the divorce court at the end of it. 'Every time that marriage is weakened and made a more precarious partnership, the family life of the nation is weakened. If divorce is made easy, marriage is cheapened, so that people enter into marriage lightly and because they enter marriage lightly, such a marriage will probably reach the divorce court much sooner than others, and so the vicious circle grows.'[26]

Mr Marcus Worsley said that people get divorced for quite inadequate reasons. 'Easy and acceptable divorce encourages people to divorce as an apparently easy option, whereas in reality nothing is solved by a divorce of that character. I further believe that divorce nearly always puts the supposed happiness of the parents before the actual happiness of the children. I believe, finally, that divorce is contagious and that the contagion is often handed on to later generations.' He said that the bill aimed to make divorce easier. It contained a new concept which was to introduce a divorce against the wishes and without the agreement of wholly innocent people, who wish to maintain their marriages while their partners did not. 'I hope that we shall not accept what I regard as this monstrous proposition as part of a package deal under the general heading of divorce reform.'[27]

Mr David Weitzman regarded the bill as a long overdue measure which 'will not undermine the sanctity of marriage, but on the contrary, will help to make it more of a reality and will bring happiness and relief to thousands of couples who are living in so-called sin, as well as the blessings, such as they are, of legitimacy, to many children'. He asked, 'if a marriage has irretrievably broken down why should it be allowed to continue? Should it be allowed to continue for the sake of either party? That would surely mean a life of unhappiness for both, chained together and chafing at the links. Should it be allowed to continue for the sake of the children? What could be worse for the upbringing of children than the obvious discontent and strife between parents who could not get on—their glaring distaste and dislike for each other, the very negation of family life? Should it be allowed to continue on the ground of sanctity of the marriage life? Surely that would mean sacrificing the happiness of people to a false belief, for how can there be sanctity when any belief in it has departed?'

He pointed out that 75 per cent of divorces were obtained by consent. The bill would help to get rid of hypocrisy and perjury which undoubtedly attended divorce petitions under the present law. 'It is said that it is wrong to give relief to a guilty person against an innocent spouse. In how many cases can it be said that one party is wholly guilty and the other wholly innocent? What is the sense of keeping a party tied to something which does not exist in reality with the other party being condemned to live in sin, often with children who are illegitimate?'[28]

Sir Lionel Heald had hoped that they could approach the bill on the basis of widespread agreement on the principle of some degree of divorce by consent, combined with the concept of irretrievable breakdown. The bill contained 'not only divorce by consent, but the very opposite, divorce against the will of one spouse, however innocent, at the request and for the benefit of the other spouse, however guilty'. He said it would be a bad day for Britain when the 'law not only permits, but actually encourages, a man to force his wife into a divorce for the sole purpose of allowing him to marry another woman, and to do so every five years without making proper provision for the wives and children'.[29]

The Solicitor General (Sir Arthur Irvine) said that there were signs of widespread agreement that reform was called for, and so it was right for the government to make time available for the House to reach a decision. The bill bore the imprint of the recommendations of both the report of the Archbishop of Canterbury's Committee and the Law Commission's report. On the general point of legal aid he said that if Parliament decided that the law of divorce needed to be reformed, 'I suggest that it is hardly fair that the reform should be resisted and people denied their rights in the courts on the sole ground that it would put additional expenditure on the Legal Aid Fund.'[30]

Mr Kenneth Lewis asked if the government had taken fully into account that this would mean a great increase in divorce and therefore a considerable increase in cost to the welfare state? It would, he predicted, create a new arm to the welfare state.[31]

Dame Joan Vickers, one of the sponsors of the bill, said that women were not worried so much about themselves as about the maintenance of their children. 'I have one proposal to make about financial security which I do not think requires legal action. A deserted woman, particularly one in the lower income group, must immediately go to social security for help.' She concluded, 'I am certain that the bill will create more happiness for many people than do the present conditions and that it will enable them to lead more honest lives than they may now do when separated.'[32]

Mr Simon Mahon said that the honourable lady (Joan Vickers) told the House that the bill would bring more happiness into the lives of families and homes and marriages. 'I believe that the bill is full of tears. Any extension of the divorce laws on the lines proposed would undermine family life and marriage more than anything we have done before.' The people of Wales were not demanding the bill. It was not a priority and the people were not clamouring for the bill. 'I have been filled with sadness by some of the attitudes of the Labour Government. I have reported it to the highest authorities in the Labour Government. They are doing things which they should not be doing and they have done things which they should not have done. If the government were adopting a position of neutrality, how is it that they have spent so much time looking into the provisions which will have to be made if the bill becomes law? Surely they have prejudged the issue. I am putting myself right if the government will not put themselves right and I am saying that this is a government sponsored bill just as the Abortion Bill was a government sponsored bill... Who is it who is so powerful that he can ignore the traditional postures of the Labour Party and bring pressure to bear on the government even to make time available and even to make plans? Was it the Liaison Committee? Was it the Divorce Reform Association? Was it the Humanist Society? Do the government themselves want the permissive society?'

Mr Donald Dewar intervened to say that many members of the Labour Party felt very strongly that they wanted to see progressive and humane social change. He pointed out that Mr Mahon's views were based on his religious faith. Mr Mahon responded, 'Of course I am a Catholic, but my reason, apart from my faith, tells me that this is a bad bill... I want to know what the government intend. What is their next ambition? Is it to destroy religion in voluntary schools, or take religion out of all schools in the country... The bill is the sort of thing that will undermine the country. This is what will put us at the bottom of the league table of nations. I believe that with all my heart and soul, otherwise I would not say so.'[33]

Mr Daniel Awdry was an enthusiastic supporter of divorce law reform. 'The present divorce laws contain a great deal of hypocrisy and cause unnecessary bitterness and unhappiness between the parties. Secondly, it is deeply distressing that about 200 thousand children have been born in this country as illegitimate and they will never be made legitimate unless this change is made in the law.' He said that he had had meetings with the clergy in his area and almost all supported the ideas in the bill. Practically all the clergymen agreed that the concept of matrimonial offence was out of date. 'I am of course concerned that one marriage in 13 ends in divorce. However, I believe that the bill will not weaken the institution of marriage but strengthen it. That is why I support it.' He mentioned two safeguards in the bill. First, the court may refuse a divorce if it would result in grave financial or other hardship. Second, the court would not grant a divorce unless the financial provision made by the petitioner for the respondent was reasonable or the best which could be arranged in the circumstances. 'It would enable a court to withhold a divorce unless a very large proportion of the husband's capital was transferred to the wife. I can envisage cases in which the court would refuse a decree unless the husband was literally stripped of all his capital.'[34]

Mr Ian Percival said that the government was using the parliamentary procedures to advance the bill. That was why the second reading debate was continuing on a Tuesday morning. He referred to the financial safeguards of the bill and said that the promoters must face up fairly and squarely to one simple fact that the words, 'or the best that can be made in the circumstances', are utterly useless as any form of safeguard for the financial position of the respondent.

Mr Richard Wood said, 'I think that most of us felt that the Solicitor General must have had his tongue in his cheek when he was talking about neutrality… It is no longer a Private Member's bill for which the government can disclaim responsibility. The government are actively helping to get it through, and I therefore hope that we shall be assured of two things: first, that the government clearly recognise the financial and other consequences of making the bill law; and, secondly, that they accept the obligation to take steps to relieve the hardship which, without their intervention, will certainly be suffered.'[35]

Mr Donald Dewar said he wanted to make it perfectly clear that he did not regard the bill as being an attack on marriage. 'I believe that the bill is a contribution to a sane and humane attitude to the law of divorce, and I congratulate the government on providing time for it.'[36]

Mr Leo Abse rose to make the final speech in the debate. In response to Mr Mahon he said, 'Let him remember that for some of us who are socialists there are no boundaries to our compassion. We do not limit our compassion to the sick, the unemployed and the disabled. We believe that we should extend it to those who are illegitimate and those who are in deep and distressing marital woe.' He said that the bill sought to hack a way through the jungle of lies, half-truths, miserable stratagems and ugly publicity that the doctrine of matrimonial offences had proliferated. Only when they were emancipated from this doctrine could they begin to move forward to considering how the courts and the lawyers could be deployed as marriage menders and not marriage breakers. Parliament could affirm its intention not to have an easier divorce law, 'but to have a more rational one that is more humane, more compassionate, and, in my view, more in keeping with the civilised feelings of our people'.[37] The bill was read a second time and passed by 183 votes to 106.

Debate in the House of Lords

Lord Stow Hill pointed out that the bill was 'the final end-thinking of years of consideration by parliamentarians, churchmen, academics and practising lawyers'. He said the bill did not open the door to easy divorce, that door was already open under the existing law and it would be hard to open it wider. Nine out of ten divorce suits were not contested. The bill was designed to support and strengthen the institution of marriage by ensuring that before divorce was granted the parties had ample time for reflection and reconciliation in all cases where that was possible. It would bring relief to many unfortunate and blameless people to whom the existing law denied it.[38]

Lady Summerskill said the main purpose of the bill was to make marriage more easily dissoluble without proper consideration being given to the consequences for the wife and children. 'Most men could not afford two wives. That, shortly, is why I said that this is a "Casanova's charter". None of the arguments that I am giving now applies to the rich man. The best provision, according to this bill, that can be made in the circumstances could mean that the first wife would receive £1 a week after the second family had been taken into account. I do not think that this is an exaggeration.'[39]

The Archbishop of Canterbury said that as the starting point of the Church's belief was that marriage is the lifelong union of a man and woman, the very idea of divorce is something which should evoke horror. He asked the question, 'Does the proposal tend to weaken the institution of marriage in the eyes of those who are approaching marriage, or does it encourage those who are approaching marriage to have a lower view of its lifelong obligation? This aspect of the matter – let me call it the educative effect of the law – of the approach to marriage, has been very little emphasised in the discussion, and I make no apology for recalling it.' He noted that a law based on the doctrine of matrimonial offences 'often leads to acrimonious disputes between the parties as to which of them is in the wrong, so hinders reconciliation in cases where reconciliation might be possible, and encourages a degree of collusion so that divorce by consent is virtually what happens in the present system'.

The archbishop said that he was hopeful that a sound law based on breakdown might be formulated to replace totally the present law. But there was still the difficulty of framing a law based on breakdown that avoided injustice towards a man or woman who had been the victim of really scandalous conduct. 'So, my Lords, I ask: Does the present law achieve a law of breakdown which would be sufficient to protect the institution of marriage and avoid flagrant injustice?' He was anxious about three points in the bill. First, was it axiomatic that separation for two years had proved irretrievable breakdown? Second, he viewed the treatment of financial provision in the bill with real anxiety. Thirdly, he asked whether the bill safeguarded the public interest in the institution of marriage in the case of a petitioner who had treated the spouse in a manner which was appalling and flouted the public's respect for the institution of marriage. 'So, my Lords, I wish that the bill could be rid of what I believe to be its blemishes. The existing law is bad, and I would gladly see it replaced—and there was evidence that many of my fellow churchmen, with me, would be glad to see it replaced by a law based on breakdown.' He could not vote for the bill as it stood, as the things he had criticised were for him matters of justice and principle.[40]

Lord Ilford said it was grossly unjust that a man or woman should have a divorce forced on them against their wish when they had been guilty of no misconduct or error. Few men had the means of supporting two families. It was the lack of support which would in the majority of cases produce the gravest financial hardship among abandoned women.[41]

The Earl of Longford said he regarded certain essential features of the bill as utterly evil. Catholics looked on marriage as a divine institution, instituted by God as a permanent union between one man and one woman. The Earl referred to one provision in the bill, 'which is the most horrible provision that has come forward in any measure brought before Parliament since the War. I need hardly say that I am referring to the permission that will be given to the man who has left his wife to kick her out after five years.' He then reminded the House what the Bishop of Exeter had said six years ago as he suspected that the bishop had ratted on his first view. In those days the bishop had said, 'We believe that once it is established by law that marriage can be brought to an end either by the mutual consent of both parties or even by a single unilateral act of will of one, you strike a grave blow at the stability of marriage and thereby run the risk of creating far more unhappiness than this clause would cure.'[42]

The Bishop of Exeter (Mortimer) said the Earl had just reminded him of something he (the bishop) had said on a former occasion. 'But I would point out to him that the former occasion was the former occasion, and that the occasions are quite different.' He shared the noble Earl's puzzlement and surprise 'that a person like myself, who some twenty or thirty years ago spent so much time in writing and speaking in defence of the principle of the indissolubility of marriage, in favour of the proposition that strict monogamy is a precept of the natural law, should now support this or indeed any other divorce reform bill. I still believe that the best ordered society is that one in which all the members observe a strict rule of monogamy; and I still believe, if not in the metaphysical doctrine of the indissolubility of marriage, at least that the obligations of a marriage, duly contracted, are lifelong, and that it is wrong and cynical for either party to ignore or evade them or seek by means of a civil divorce to be totally rid of them.' He could scarcely take any other view when he considered the plain, direct teaching which is contained in the Scripture: 'Whosoever shall put away his wife and marry another committeth adultery against her.'

After discussing some of the clauses in the bill, the bishop concluded, 'When all is said and done, the great question is this: will this bill weaken the institution of marriage and thereby damage society? I do not think it will. With or without the bill there will be desertions and irregular unions. With or without the bill there will be arranged divorces, by or with the consent of both parties. With this bill there will be, first, a greater emphasis on the duty of both parties to seek outside help for the purpose of reconciliation before they admit defeat. Secondly, there will be a strengthened power of the court to protect the interests of children and wives. Thirdly, there will be a greater freedom for the parties to agree between themselves on an equitable sharing of the family assets. Fourthly, and most important of all, there will be a greater possibility of signalling the end of a marriage, if that is what it has to come to, with dignity, mutual respect and honesty. For these reasons I shall vote for the second reading of the bill.'[43]

Baroness Emmet of Amberley spoke about the cost of divorce. 'In the case of matrimonial offence, if you cannot afford to pay the penalty it is paid for you by your neighbour.' They ought to bear in mind the cost of all these things. That year the cost of legal aid was over £6.75 million, of which 83 per cent was spent on matrimonial cases. They must foresee that they shall have to support most of the deserted wives in a certain income group. 'Probably we shall have to recover children who lose their homes; we shall have to look forward to looking after them when they become delinquent.' She was concerned about the effect that the bill would have on the character of the British people. 'If our British character is allowed to break down and slip away, then our place in the world will go also.'[44]

Lord Hodson made the point that the average man in the country could not pay to support two wives because the wage was not enough to keep two homes. Nobody seemed to be prepared to deal with this. All speakers in the Lordships' House shook their heads sadly and said, 'We are very sorry; we will think about it. Something must be done.' But nothing can be done except by national assistance, which means that their neighbour pays. 'When the man marries the paramour (if he does) he will be under an obligation to that woman which will come before the obligation to the first wife; and not only will she get the money on Friday night but she will have the right to it. So the taxpayer will have to pay. I do not want my card to have on it another stamp for the discarded wives' tax, to cover the expense of keeping these unfortunate women who have been discarded by their husbands.' Lord Hodson concluded, 'If this bill is passed and either party is able to end the marriage whether or not the other spouse agrees, it will, I think, bring about a major change in the nature of marriage. And the Christian concept of marriage as a voluntary union for life, already weakened by successive moves towards easier divorce, will be given a further, perhaps final, blow.'[45]

Lord Denning supported the bill on the simple ground that the present law was based on a wrong theory, the so-called principle of matrimonial offences. The present law was out of date and should be replaced by a better principle, which was stated in the Archbishop's Commission, namely, the irretrievable breakdown of marriage. He argued that 'if the court sees that the marriage has irretrievably broken down, discretion is always exercised. So in point of practice the judges have introduced the principle of the irretrievable breakdown of marriage into our law, and we all know that there is no real inquiry into the guilt or innocence. If one side wants a divorce and the other does not object, you can always find grounds. You need not go so far as adultery – cruelty we have extended far enough – and there can be constructive desertion and the like. It can always be done when the other side does not object. So we have introduced the irretrievable breakdown of marriage, and this bill substantially states the existing practice whereby the courts do grant a divorce when there has been an irretrievable breakdown. Get away from the old fiction, from the out of date theory of the matrimonial offence.'[46]

The Bishop of Leicester (Ronald Williams) spoke in opposition to the bill. He began his opposition by guarding himself from the propaganda implied by the title of the bill. 'Divorce Reform Bill' was a title which, in itself, made it difficult for anyone to oppose it, because one was immediately put into the position of appearing to oppose something that was quite obviously good. One could hardly have expected it to be described as the 'Easier Divorce Bill'. He was not entirely converted to the idea of the breakdown of marriage as the principle ground for divorce. 'This idea has swept through the thoughtful world almost like an epidemic. I think it began in what we used to call the Dominions, and it has won very great support in this country... The fact remains that the word breakdown is a word which we usually apply to mechanical objects, and we have the idea that if a car, for instance, breaks down that is not our fault. I am not at all sure whether we are helping the cause of marriage, in the best sense, by suggesting that it is just a lucky chance whether or not it breaks down. We surely have to do everything to keep before people's minds that it is a matter of personal behaviour, attitudes, loyalty and self-discipline; and these are not things that are necessarily conveyed by the word "breakdown" of marriage.' He could not square his conscience with voting in favour of the bill.[47]

After a prolonged debate, in which almost all agreed that the existing divorce laws were unsatisfactory, the bill was read a second time by 122 votes to 34. Four bishops voted in favour of the bill and three voted against. The Archbishop of Canterbury abstained.[48]

Comment

The 1969 Divorce Reform Act, which came into force in 1971, introduced a new philosophy that aimed to remove the concept of blame from divorce. Heavily influenced by *Putting Asunder*, the legislation changed fundamentally the way divorce was to be regulated. Terms such as 'guilty party' and 'matrimonial offence' were removed and replaced by a solitary ground, namely, the irretrievable breakdown of marriage. However, the petitioning partner still needed to establish one of five 'facts' as evidence that such an irretrievable breakdown had occurred. The five 'facts' included the three former marital offences of adultery, unreasonable behaviour and desertion, and two new separation criteria—which allowed divorce either by mutual consent after two years' separation, or by the sole wish of the petitioning party after five years' separation. An editorial in *The Times*, 'Divorce on Demand' identified two broad objections to the bill as it stood, 'that it provides for easier divorce because it does not rigorously apply the new doctrine that a marriage should be dissolved only when it has irretrievably broken down; and that there are not sufficient financial safeguards for deserted wives, who will find themselves for the first time liable to be divorced without having committed any matrimonial offence.'[49]

The concept of the so-called 'no-fault' divorce shifted responsibility for defining marriage breakdown to the individual, for it was now possible for a couple to separate for any reason of their choice. As long as they lived apart for the required period, then either the husband or wife could claim a divorce. For the first time in England it became possible for a legal divorce to be obtained on the evidence of a couple's separation. Moreover, it was now possible for a husband or wife to be legally divorced by their spouse against their will, even although they had committed no marital offence and wished the marriage to continue. Procedural changes meant that the details of most petitions could be dealt with by post, and there was no proper inquiry into the facts. In effect, England now had divorce on demand with the full blessing of the Church. The emphasis was on giving the individual what they wanted; individual contentment and happiness were the paramount considerations. Recognition that the institution of marriage was important for the well-being of society was given lip service but was scarcely apparent in the legislation.

During the permissive 1960s, the role and meaning of marriage came under serious challenge and divorce numbers took off, doubling to reach 58 thousand by 1970 as shown in **figure 8**. The introduction of no-fault divorce legislation ushered in a truly phenomenal rise, numbers escalating to 74 thousand in 1971 and 119 thousand in 1972. A further steady increase occurred in the decade of the seventies reaching 138 thousand by 1979. Following the introduction of the Matrimonial and Family Proceeding Act of 1984, which allowed a couple to file for divorce after their first wedding anniversary, the numbers continued to climb and peaked in 1985 at 160 thousand.

FAMILY LAW ACT: 1996

Even the divorce law of 1969, introduced with so much acclaim, proved unsatisfactory. Within two decades the Law Commission, under the chairmanship of Mr Justice Peter Gibson, produced a report entitled *The Ground for Divorce*, which argued yet again for the need to reform the divorce laws. The commission had done a great deal of research in an effort to understand the problems with the current law. This included a study of divorce files in courts across the country to discover more about the working of the system. They also surveyed a representative sample of a thousand members of the general public to ascertain what they saw as the good and bad features of the law. Wide ranging discussions were held with many organisations.[50] Having completed its research, the commission concluded that there was widespread concern about the consequences of divorce both for the couple concerned and their children. There was also concern that the present divorce process was making the situation worse, and they noted that there were many calls for the reform of the law.

On the basis of their investigations the commission argued that the present law was confusing and misleading, for there was a considerable gap

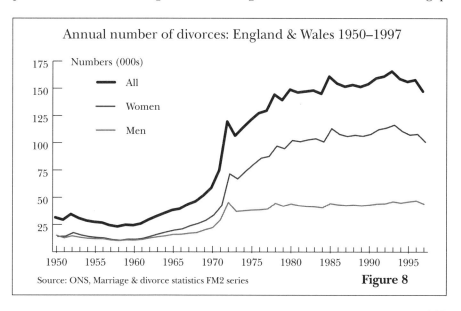

Annual number of divorces: England & Wales 1950–1997

Source: ONS, Marriage & divorce statistics FM2 series

Figure 8

219

between theory and practice, which led to a lack of respect for the law. While the law pretended that the court would conduct an inquiry into the facts of the matter, in the vast majority of cases it did no such thing. Parties were encouraged to lie, or at least to exaggerate, in order to get what they wanted.[51] A system that required fault-based facts such as adultery, desertion or unreasonable behaviour as evidence that the marriage had broken down could be intrinsically unjust. 'The fault-based facts can also be intrinsically unjust... If one has committed adultery or behaved intolerably there is usually nothing to stop the other obtaining a divorce based upon it, even though that other may have committed far more adulteries or behaved much more intolerably himself or herself. Nor does the behaviour fact always involve blame; it may well be unreasonable to expect a petitioner to live with a spouse who is mentally ill or disabled or has totally incompatible values or lifestyle.'[52]

The current law provoked unnecessary hostility and bitterness. 'A law which is arbitrary or unjust can exacerbate the feelings of bitterness, distress and humiliation so often experienced at the time of separation and divorce. Even if the couple has agreed that their marriage cannot be saved, it must make matters between them worse if the system encourages one to make allegations against the other. The incidents relied on have to be set out in the petition. Sometimes they are exaggerated, one-sided or even untrue. Allegations of behaviour or adultery can provoke resentment and hostility in a respondent who is unable to put his own side of the story on the record.'[53] The law did little to support those marriages which had a chance of survival, and could make things worse for the children. 'It is not known whether children suffer more from their parents' separation or from living in a household in conflict where they may be blamed for the couple's inability to part.'[54]

In the face of these arguments the commission concluded that there was a formidable case for reform. It proposed that using 'facts', such as adultery, to establish that a marriage had broken down caused problems and should be removed from the arena of divorce legislation. Instead, irretrievable breakdown would remain the sole ground for divorce, and one or both parties filing a statement and waiting for one year would be sufficient to establish that such a breakdown had occurred. No facts would be required, only a declaration that the marriage was at an end.[55] Mediation would be offered in the hope that the waiting period would be used constructively to sort out financial matters and other problems. Everyone seeking a divorce would attend an initial personal interview, where they would be given information about the law, marriage guidance and mediation. The effect of these proposals would be to make unilateral divorce available after waiting for one year. The commission claimed that by reducing conflict the reforms would minimise the harm to children, and encourage parents to consider how they would meet their responsibilities in the future, rather than dwelling on the unhappiness of the past. According to a leading article in *The Sunday Times*, 'The Law Commission, quite simply, has produced a method of ending marriages efficiently, cheaply and with as little bloodletting as possible. Swift conciliation is the aim. The new proposals are not intended to help persuade warring married couples to rebuild their marriage. Such an ambition could not be further from the official mind.'[56]

Based on the proposals of the Law Commission, the Lord Chancellor published a consultation paper in 1993 proposing yet another alteration to the divorce law. The prime purpose of the Family Law Act of 1996 was to make the divorce procedure easier still by removing the need for the petitioning party to prove any 'facts' as evidence that the marriage had broken down. The party wishing to get divorced, after attending an initial information meeting with a properly qualified independent person and following a three month cooling off period, is able to make a statement of marriage breakdown. Couples on legal aid will be entitled to state funded marriage counselling. The time required for a couple to live apart before making a statement that the marriage has broken down was increased from 12 to 18 months by a vote in Parliament.

And so the campaign to legalise divorce in England had finally achieved its objectives. It was now clear that the state regarded marriage as little more than a temporary arrangement, the law doing everything possible to assist couples to end their marriages as easily as possible. The way marriage was viewed had changed to such a degree that no-fault divorce was accepted with almost no opposition. According to the Law Commission the object of the law was to afford a decent burial to those marriages that had 'died'. It was now generally agreed that there was no moral imperative involved in divorce. Because marriages just 'died', both state and Church accepted that the law must 'bury' them with as little fuss and aggravation as possible. At the time of writing the Lord Chancellor has announced that the Family Law Act, that was due to come into effect in 2000, was not to be implemented because initial pilots had proved disappointing.

Comment

Having traced the history of divorce in England over a century and a half, we can now draw some conclusions. Significantly, a number of people who took part in the prolonged and controversial debate which started in 1857, predicted that the road to divorce was also the road that led to national ruin. They spoke of a slippery slope, and warned that once England embarked on the legalisation of divorce there would be no stopping place; the inevitable slide would lead to divorce on demand. In 1857 Mr Beresford-Hope predicted that the future historian would trace the first dawning of the decline of the British Empire to moral weakening that resulted from lax divorce laws.[57] In 1920 Lord Halifax remarked that the divorce debate was one of supreme importance to the national interests of England.[58] Commander Bower expressed the view that divorce liberalisation would destroy the English family. He said the 'Herbert Bill' of 1937 would remove one of the sheet-anchors that prevented Western civilisation from drifting into chaos.[59] Lord Hodson concluded that the divorce law of 1969 would bring about a major change in the nature of marriage. He predicted that the Christian concept of marriage as a voluntary union for life, already weakened by successive moves towards easier divorce, would be given a further, perhaps final, blow.[60] At the dawn of the 21st century the Church of England is locked in the last great struggle over the marriage question. The Church, which has for centuries witnessed to the indissolubility of the marriage bond, is seriously considering a U-turn in marriage discipline which will allow divorcees with a living former partner to remarry in church.

It has not been difficult to see that the ideology underpinning the divorce campaign was hostile to biblical Christianity. Many promoters of the campaign based their arguments on the tenets of secular humanism, believing that man's supreme aim is to attain happiness in this world. They were confident that by reason alone, freed from the prejudices of Christian moral teaching, human beings could comprehend the world and solve its problems. Marriage was portrayed as a particularly bad institution for it trapped people in unhappy relationships from which there was no escape. Divorce was a valuable resource because it freed people from unhappy marriages and offered another chance of happiness. The major obstacle in the way of the campaign was Christ's teaching on the indissoluble nature of marriage.

The Majority report of the Royal Commission of 1912 responded by simply disregarding biblical principles in drawing up its recommendations, on the pretext that there was no agreement about what the Scriptures taught. Lord Gorrel went so far as to suggest that if the proposals of the commission were implemented, then the Christian marriage service would be out of keeping with modern thought and would need to be reconstructed.[61] Lord Birkenhead said that those who believed in the indissolubility of marriage did not live in this world; their arguments were the whisperings of the abandoned superstitions of the Middle Ages.[62] Sir Francis Acland argued that it was the promoters of divorce, and not the Christian church, who upheld the sanctity of marriage.[63] Mr Thurtle asserted that the Church should not try to impose its archaic moral laws on the nation, and prevent the state from passing divorce laws that would be for the benefit of all.[64] It seems surprising that some churchmen were prepared to be part of a campaign that was so fundamentally antagonistic to the message of the Bible.

Moving the debate away from the Scriptures and into the social arena was crucial to the success of the campaign. A feature of the debates during the 20th century was the way in which biblical teaching increasingly gave way to sociological reasoning. The climax to this process was the Archbishop of Canterbury's decision to encourage a group of churchmen to examine the issue of divorce from a sociological perspective. Sociological theory became the intellectual justification for divorce by providing evidence of the apparent benefits for women and children trapped in unhappy marriages. A standard argument for extending the grounds of divorce was that it would lead to future happiness, and there were even murmurs that parents should divorce for the sake of their children. Mr AP Herbert went so far as to say that his divorce bill would increase the sum of human happiness. It was usually assumed that divorced women would find ideal new husbands who were eager to support them and their children. Another strand of the sociological argument was that restrictive divorce laws were a cause of illegitimate births, as men and women who had left unsatisfactory marriages were having children in their new relationships. Making divorce easier would enable such couples to divorce and be remarried, thereby reducing the incidence of children born outside wedlock. The falseness of this argument is apparent from the record levels of illegitimate births that have accompanied the move to mass divorce. Indeed the highest levels of cohabitation are among divorcees, many of whom seem to prefer to live with a new partner without being married.

What seems remarkable is that the finest legal brains and the greatest theologians in England were unable to find grounds for divorce that worked in practice. Each new law was heralded as a breakthrough that would do away with past injustice and promote marriage stability. Yet in every debate the existing laws were heavily criticised, sometimes by the people who had initiated the change in the first place. The concept of the 'matrimonial offence', developed by the Protestant reformers as the grounds for divorce, was based on a wrong theory according to Lord Denning, and has been completely discredited from a legal point of view. The failure of the 'matrimonial offence' concept to produce just divorce legislation must cast considerable doubt on the thinking that lay behind the concept. When the lawmakers moved away from the principle of marriage indissolubility there was no other guiding principle, and so each new law was based on human expediency. All extensions to the grounds for divorce were invariably based on arbitrary decisions without any reference to a moral standard. For example, the length of separation proposed for unilateral divorce was first seven years, then five, then three and finally 18 months. When each new law was put to the test it proved to be unsatisfactory, the cause of collusion and injustice. Once divine law was set aside, the best that human wisdom could devise was a law which allowed divorce on demand. It has proved to be beyond human ingenuity to discover grounds for divorce that worked in practice. The choice, then, was between the indissolubility of marriage as taught in the Bible or unilateral no-fault divorce as promoted by the ideology of secular humanism. The halfway ground suggested by the Protestant doctrine of divorce has proved to be an illusion. And so England concluded, after an extended debate that has lasted since 1857, that it preferred divorce laws based on the ideas of secular humanism. God's moral law was not good enough.

Chapter 11

Confusion over remarriage

Remarriage debate in the Church of England: 1971–2000

With the enactment of the no-fault legislation the divorce campaign had achieved its objective with regard to the law. Clearly the state now regarded marriage as little more than a temporary arrangement, the law doing everything it could to assist divorcing couples to end their marriages as easily and quickly as possible. The resulting growth of divorce meant more people would be requesting a second marriage according to the rites of the Church, and the question was how church discipline would respond to the new situation? While those who supported the traditional view of marriage as an indissoluble bond believed that remarriage in church was wrong, others believed that it was unreasonable for the Church to refuse remarriage for those who had been lawfully divorced. Some even argued that allowing remarriage in church would strengthen the institution of marriage. They believed that the reluctance of the Church to allow remarriage was hurtful, and discriminated against those who, although they were divorced, were not to blame for the breakdown of their marriage. In a speech to the Church Assembly in 1967 dealing with the remarriage issue, Canon Desmond Dean of Southwark said that thousands of people were tired of being treated as second-class citizens and third-class Christians. He pleaded for a thoughtful look at the attitude which automatically shut the door to remarriage in church irrespective of every other consideration. He did not mean that the Church should follow the prevailing fashion of each generation, but that as fresh problems arose new thought should be given to ways of meeting them. He did not believe that the final word had been spoken, or that the Church had closed its mind.[1]

The obstacle in the way of church remarriage was the resolution passed in 1938, and made an Act of Convocation in 1957, which stated in clear, unequivocal terms that marriage was an indissoluble union and therefore remarriage in church was not permitted. In an attempt to find a way around this obstacle a commission was set up in 1968 under the chairmanship of Professor Root of Southampton University. Its main purpose was to prepare a statement on the Christian doctrine of marriage, and to enquire 'whether there might be occasions for relaxing the present rule of the Convocations whereby a divorced person with a former partner living may not have on remarrying a marriage service in Church'.[2]

MARRIAGE, DIVORCE AND THE CHURCH – THE ROOT REPORT

The commission's report *Marriage, Divorce and the Church,* which was published in 1971, suggested that a full investigation into marriage required the assistance, among others, of an anthropologist, a sociologist and a lawyer. The commissioners claimed that many regarded the replacement of the concept of irretrievable breakdown for that of matrimonial offence as a great gain from the Christian point of view.[3] 'Just as it is possible for any organism to wither and die before it has grown into its full nature, so too marriage may break down before it has grown into what it should become.'[4]

The report adopted a modern, contextual approach to the theology of marriage and divorce. 'The final and definitive "meaning" of passages in Scripture can never be attained, nor are the words of the New Testament self-evident and timelessly clear, precisely because they cannot be abstracted from their temporal and spatial context, any more than the life of Jesus can be abstracted from its context. Thus, although to some it seems to be the case that Jesus affirmed the indissolubility of marriage in such sayings as "What God hath joined together, let not man put asunder", and "Whosoever shall put away his wife, and marry another, commiteth adultery against her", the fact remains that this is not the only possible, or the only defensible, meaning of these texts. Equally, there is no doubt that what Jesus is recorded as having taught about marriage and divorce, and what he demanded of his followers as the standards of marriage, left them amazed. This is not to say, however, that he meant that marriage cannot be dissolved, or that in every conceivable circumstance it would be wrong to remarry. The fact that there can be much genuine uncertainty and disagreement among biblical exegetes on these points is of profound importance. It is a direct consequence of the way in which God reveals himself to the world in the realities of time and space. Scripture, equally, is offered to us as a means of grace in the conditions in which we are.'[5]

From this theological position it followed that an appropriate way of developing the Church's discipline on remarriage would be to find the majority opinion—the moral consensus. 'But the question needs to be asked whether there is the moral consensus. It is not for the commission to attempt to determine the answer to this question; but there is sufficient evidence to oblige us to raise this question and others, which follow from it. Is there a growing consensus among Christian people, both clerical and lay, first, that some marriages, however well-intentioned, do break down; secondly, that some divorced partners enter into new unions in good faith and that some of these new unions show such evident features of stability, complementarity, fruitfulness, and growth as to make them comparable with satisfactory first marriages; and thirdly, that Christian congregations are not scandalised, in the theological sense of the word, by the presence of such persons in their midst or by their participation in the Holy Communion? If an affirmative answer is given to these questions, then we are bound to raise the question that naturally follows from such an answer. Is there also a growing moral consensus that such persons, with due safeguards, may properly have their marriages solemnised according to the rites of the Church? Indeed, it may well turn out on inquiry that a moral judgement on this matter has already formed itself within the Church of England... in the belief that remarriage in church would be not a weakening but a strengthening of marriage. It is possible that those who say that to remarry in church would cause offence to the Christian conscience may find that failure to do so causes greater offence.[6]

'If it were to be found that a moral consensus in favour of remarriage in church (with due safeguards) does exist, then it would be the duty of the bishops in Synod to determine whether this consensus is theologically well founded. *It is the unanimous conviction of this Commission that this is the case.* Such a moral judgement would not be inconsistent with the witness and teaching of the New Testament as a whole...'[7]

The report suggested that a discreet inquiry should be made into three aspects before a remarriage could be solemnised. First, the inquiry should establish that all possible obligations remaining from the first marriage have been discharged, such as the economic needs of the former spouse and her children. Second, an inquiry into the character and dispositions of the two persons seeking remarriage, including an investigation into the circumstances of the previous divorce. Thirdly, assurance would be required of the same intention of lifelong fidelity.

Comment

The essence of the report was that it is not possible from the Scriptures to know what Jesus was actually teaching, and in any case the interpretation needs to change according to the circumstances of the time. If we cannot be sure that Jesus taught that marriage was indissoluble, remarriage becomes a possibility, in certain circumstances. Because of this uncertainty, the Church should decide its position on remarriage according to the majority view. Whether it was right or wrong to remarry divorcees in church would be decided by consensus. If the majority view was in favour, then the theologians would seek scriptural justification for the Church's position. In other words, the Church's teaching on marriage would flow from the view of the majority. When the majority view changed, then so should the marriage discipline of the Church. Furthermore, the suggestion that the Church's acceptance of remarriage during the lifetime of a former partner would strengthen marriage is very different from Christ's teaching—he referred to remarriage following divorce as adultery. Effectively the Church would be supporting the view that marriage is a temporary relationship which can die and be replaced by another.

GENERAL SYNOD DEBATES: 1972–1974

The Root report was debated in Synod on three occasions. When Canon Herbert Waddams introduced the report in 1972, he said the commission was of the opinion that the words attributed to Jesus about divorce could not be taken out of the context of his other sayings, and could not be treated as legislative and binding when other parallel sayings were not regarded in that sense. The commission considered that true Christian attitudes should combine the highest doctrine of marriage with a practice which gave adequate attention to the needs of personal fulfilment. To take the words of the New Testament text and apply them literally and legalistically to conditions in the second half of the 20th century was not the best way of fulfilling the teaching of Jesus. For these reasons the commission had come to the conclusion that there were no simple definitive answers to be found in the text of the New Testament to the personal questions of the day, but that the teaching of the New Testament, as expressed by Jesus, had to be taken in conjunction with the examination of moral, theological, and practical issues, and a choice had to be made in the light of all those.[8]

He said there could hardly be doubt that marriages do in fact irretrievably break down, and asked whether the Church had to continue to stand aside when people, perhaps sincere Christians, wanted to enter into a new Christian partnership and to remarry. Or was the Church to temper judgement with mercy in suitable cases and proclaim by its action that God welcomes those, as he welcomes all repentant sinners, and offers them a new life of creative and fulfilling love?[9]

In the first debate in February 1972 the report was not well received in Synod. Many voices were highly critical although there was also a fair amount of support. Rev David Stevens believed the commission had made a disastrous mistake. It had come up with the disastrous idea that the Church of England ought to reconsider its attitude to the remarriage of divorcees during the lifetime of a previous partner and so reverse the Church's true moral consensus on a point arrived at after many years of thought and not taken in hand unadvisedly, lightly or wantonly. He had been investigating the matter for some years among the ordinary parish clergymen, and five years ago had consulted a hundred clergymen, the majority of whom wanted to keep the present regulations.[10]

Mrs Catharina Lucas asserted that if the commission truly felt that the remarriage of divorced persons in church was theologically well founded, then it should have said so. It should have said, 'There it is, take it or leave it. In the past the teaching and practice of the Church has been wrong; now we know better.' What the conclusion seemed to say was: 'If this is what you want to satisfy what society feels you ought to be offering in 1972, then we will cook the books for you.' She mentioned that someone facing a similar ethical problem had said, 'Get thee behind me Satan.' She asked whether the Church could formulate and change its doctrine on the basis of the moral consensus of a particular era.[11]

The Bishop of Lichfield (Arthur Reeve) refuted the unworthy suggestion that by maintaining church discipline on marriage they were being unkind and uncharitable. He said that the Church believed that the institution of marriage was vital for the true health of the nation. They believed that in maintaining that principle they were doing something that was of the greatest value to the greatest number of people. That was what they ought to go on doing and in so doing would be showing true charity.[12]

Mr John Easton expressed the opinion that if the commission's proposal was accepted, even if parish priests and bishops showed all the discretion they could in operating the distinctions that would be required, the hard cases would re-emerge, and the Church would be forced into indiscriminate remarriage.[13] The Bishop of Norwich (Maurice Wood) referred to a sentence in the report that said, 'And there is an increasing number of responsible church people, clerical and lay, who in conscience find themselves unable to deny that remarriage can be the will of God.' The bishop believed that a sentence like that was designed to lessen the unpopular, but right, standard of Christian marriage.[14]

A further debate was held in November 1973 when the Synod was asked to consider three resolutions. The first, proposed by the Bishop of Leicester (Ronald Williams), recommended that there should be no change to the current rules of the Church. The second, proposed by the Bishop of Worcester (Robert Woods), recommended that the Church change its rule to allow the remarriage of divorcees in church during the lifetime of their former partner, and the third resolution proposed that the Synod should refer the matter to the dioceses to see if there was support for the proposals, and whether there was theological justification for the remarriage of divorcees. After a vigorous debate, and numerous amendments to each resolution the matter ended in some confusion.

By the time of the third debate, held in November 1974, the report *Marriage, Divorce and the Church* was clearly under heavy criticism. The Bishop of Truro (Graham Leonard) gave the view that the report was based on an inversion of the New Testament order about morals and theology. He said that as he read the New Testament it seemed abundantly clear that moral action was derived from God's revelation in Christ. Man sees what God is like and what he has done for us. Man sees that God wants us to respond to his love and walk worthily. But the report put it the other way around. The commission said, 'This is the way we want to go; let us look for theological reasons to justify it.'[15] It was now clear that the heavily criticised Root report was not the vehicle to achieve change in the marriage discipline of the Church of England.

MARRIAGE AND THE CHURCH'S TASK – THE LICHFIELD REPORT

But the issue would not go away. Those who promoted remarriage continued to argue that the Church needed to reform its marriage discipline. They claimed that even after a decade of debate the Church of England remained the most rigorist of all churches in its pastoral practice. Although in 1975 there were just fewer than five hundred remarriages of divorcees out of 133 thousand marriages in the Church of England the promoters of remarriage asserted that there was widespread dissatisfaction with the existing marriage discipline. Many church leaders were determined that the Church should change its view on remarriage.

Accordingly in October 1975 the Archbishops of Canterbury and York set up another commission under the chairmanship of the Bishop of Lichfield (Kenneth Skelton). The aim was to examine afresh the Christian doctrine of marriage and the marriage discipline of the Church of England, especially in the light of recent debates in the General Synod and elsewhere, and to report on the courses of action open to the Church in seeking to promote in contemporary society the Christian ideal of marriage as a lifelong union between husband and wife.

The commission published its report, entitled *Marriage and the Church's Task*, in 1978. It argued that although the figures showed remarriage in church was not a pressing problem for the Church of England, this did not dispose of the matter. Differences in practice between the Church of England and the Free Churches had led to a position where the Church of England appeared to have the strictest marriage discipline of all the churches in the country. Moreover, the last decade had been marked by an increasing impatience among some clergy with the present rules. Evidence received from one diocese in the Midlands indicated that half of the clergy were dissatisfied with the present discipline of the Church which disallowed the remarriage of divorcees. 'In two dioceses the diocesan bishop has made it known that he regards his clergy as free to marry divorced people in appropriate cases. In dioceses where the bishop continues to base his practice on the convocation regulations some clergy are willing "to take the law into their own hands" or to exercise the right which the law of the state gives them. It would be misleading to suggest that the clergy were as a whole dissatisfied with the present situation.'[16]

The report observed that the extension of nullity (of marriage) and the provision of a public service of prayer and dedication were both, in their different ways, an attempt to meet a particular problem by bypassing the convocation regulations. 'We have come to the conclusion that a solution is not to be sought along those lines. In our view the Church is faced with a choice between two possible courses of action:

to maintain the present official position that divorced persons should in no circumstances be married in church; and

to adopt a system whereby, without conceding a general right of remarriage in church, divorced persons were in certain cases permitted to be married in church following a pastoral enquiry.'

Regarding the first option the report comments, 'If the Church decided after debate to maintain the position that divorced people should not be married in church it would not be sufficient to do nothing, since it is dissatisfaction with the existing system which has caused two successive enquiries to be set up. It would therefore be necessary for that decision to be formally affirmed by the General Synod, and embodied as an Act of Synod.' In the opinion of the authors, the second option of remarriage in church in certain cases was the preferred one. At that time the parish priest was free in law to marry divorced people at his discretion. 'In our judgement the use of this liberty is inconsistent with the maintenance of a clear witness to the Church's general teaching on the permanence of marriage. For any scheme of selective remarriage to work, it must be clear that the occasions when remarriage in church occur are exceptional and determined by a consistent policy. The only way to ensure that this happens is to require that the decision in each case be taken by the bishop, or by members of a small panel nominated by the bishop to act on his behalf.'[17]

Although the Church's witness to the true character of marriage fell on ears ready to hear, its refusal to remarry created a barrier to understanding, 'and a sense of injustice, which on occasion leads to permanent alienation from the Church and, in general, perpetuates a belief that it is out of touch with the reality of married people's lives'.[18] Another advantage of selective remarriage, from the point of view of the witness of the Church in society, was that 'the dangerous impression of pharisaism and unrealism, which attends the existing discipline, would be dispelled. It would be apparent that the Church's concerns for the stability and permanence of people's actual marriages was being affirmed in a way that could have a stabilising effect on the institution of marriage itself. Instead of standing apart from men and women marrying after divorce and thus being unable to influence their attitude and intentions as at present, the Church would be in a position to meet them where they are and to emphasise their need for a realistic awareness of the past and of a mutual commitment for the future.'[19]

The commission, however, was not able to come to a common mind in regard to remarriage in church. Although all on the commission took a 'high view' of marriage, the majority considered that the best witness to that view of marriage would be offered by a pastoral ministry which includes, in particular circumstances, the marriage of some divorced persons in church. 'We believe that the Church of England ought now to be prepared, in appropriate cases and on the basis of a diocesan decision, to allow this. A minority of us consider that the Church should continue to refuse to marry divorced people, believing that to depart now from a long held position would compromise the Church in its witness to the society in which we live.'[20] The report recommended – by majority – that:

> The Church of England should now take steps to revise its regulations to permit a divorced person with the permission of the bishop to be married in church during the lifetime of a former spouse.

> The marriage of divorced persons in church should be solemnised by the use of one or other of the existing permitted orders for the solemnisation of marriage, with the addition of an appropriate invariable Preface.[21]

Comment

The basic argument of *Marriage and the Church's Task* was that current church discipline is over-rigorous, legalistic, unreal, and not meeting people at their point of need; it causes a sense of injustice and alienation from the Church. The inference was that divorcees were being deprived of their rights, unjustly treated by being denied a second church wedding. Remarriage in church, on the other hand, would soften the hardline image of the Church, meet the needs of people and give them what they wanted. The best way for the Church to witness to a 'high view' of marriage was to allow the selective remarriage of divorcees in church. The arguments were purely pragmatic, and concerned about what was likely to be popular.

Results of diocesan synod voting: 1979–1980

The report was referred to the 43 diocesan synods to gauge the response. Debate in the synods focused on the remarriage question. While eighteen dioceses carried motions in favour of remarriage in church in certain circumstances, seventeen dioceses voted against the remarriage motion, and another three confirmed their opposition to remarriage by carrying motions to the effect that no change should be made to the marriage discipline of the Church. One diocese defeated a motion that no change should be made.[22] In most dioceses the vote was close. Even the dioceses that voted in favour had a division of opinion, with a sizeable minority opposing remarriage in church. From the point of view of those who advocated remarriage the response could not have been worse. The Church was split down the middle, with an equal number of dioceses being for and against the remarriage of divorcees in church. It was inescapable that the Church was divided. The split was not just down the middle, but also between the leadership and the grass roots.

GENERAL SYNOD DEBATE: 1981

The first debate on the Lichfield report took place early in February 1981, following the diocesan votes. The Archbishop of Canterbury (Arthur Ramsey), who had set up the commission, gave the report his firm support. He said that he did not deviate from what he had said several times before in Synod. In the present circumstances and as a matter of personal experience, some of the strongest marriages he had known had been second marriages, because the teaching about marriage as a lifelong bond was communicated in the most fertile soil, that was people who came to the Church with a sense of failure, longing for forgiveness and with a hope of building on realistic foundations. He believed that if the Church had a strong and firm doctrine of marriage, it could afford to be generous about the occasional exceptions which would need special treatment. He still held to the recommendations of the Lichfield Commission and so was disappointed that there was a lack of consensus and agreement. He hoped that they could at least agree on the sort of service of thanksgiving for a remarriage.[23]

The Archdeacon of Doncaster (Ian Harland) expressed his concern that the man in the street believed that the words 'till death us do part' actually meant physical death. They had a difficult educational task helping the man in the street understand that marriages did, in fact, die before physical death, and that it was perfectly proper that the Church should find a known way of pronouncing them dead. Secondly, the man in the street did not understand how it was possible for those already bound by marriage vows to take them again. He said that to provide some sort of release from vows might strike the man in the street as the means of doing that with integrity, so that the Church was not departing from its conception of the marriage as lifelong.[24]

The Bishop of Durham (John Habgood) said that Synod needed to recognise that they were in a double impasse. They were in an impasse because of the divisions within the Church of England, and any decision to go forward on remarriage of divorced persons would be deeply divisive and lead to different disciplines being exercised in different dioceses. The second element in the impasse was that they genuinely wanted to do two different things, and it was because of that fundamental impasse that they found themselves divided as people. They all wanted to support the stability of marriage, but they also all wanted some means of exercising pastoral care and showing the love and compassion and forgiveness of Christ to those whose marriages had died or come unstuck, and their problem was how to do both of those things.[25]

Debate in July 1981

The remarriage debate continued during the summer meeting of the General Synod in York in July 1981. Despite the deep division within the Church, the Bishop of Winchester (John Taylor) introduced a motion proposing that there may be grounds for remarriage in church during the lifetime of a former spouse. He said they could not go on pretending that their present method of witnessing to the Lord's teaching about marriage was the last brake holding society from rushing down the divorce slope. The rush was on, and if the brake had not held, they had to do something other than stamp wildly on the foot pedal.[26]

The Archbishop of Canterbury (Ramsey) spoke in support of the resolution, saying that he had not changed his mind, but rather been fortified in the stance which he had always taken in the discussion, which started in the Synod in 1972, as to whether the Church could maintain its commitment to Christian marriage as a lifelong relationship in good times and in bad and yet afford to be generous to those who genuinely seek a second chance.[27] The archbishop said there was very little hard evidence, as far as people thinking about divorce, that religious sanctions had any impact on either individual conduct or collective trends. What they knew was that at present, the Church's most positive role lay, not in reinforcing individuals against divorce, but tragically in reinforcing the stigma of divorce.[28]

He noted that for a great majority remarriage was not a second chance but a first chance, based on a maturer understanding of what marriage involved and approached with every intention of constructing, after a previous failure, a lifelong lasting relationship.[29] He said that it was now self-evident to those outside the Church, as well as to many within it, that the Church's corporate attitude remained confused and confusing. There was as yet no visible consensus over remarriage. Yet in its complexities and pastoral consequences it was not a matter that could go on being left to individual clergy. More was now demanded of the Synod than finely-tuned expressions of intent.[30]

Mrs Nancy Wilkinson argued that the Church was in danger of creating a two-tier system. That was proper marriage for first-timers, and what she called 'an inferior and rather shaming sort of sinners wedlock for the naughty ones, only to be entered into by means of a special service or a penitential preface, after negotiating various hoops set up by the bishop or the priest'. If they wanted such a dual system of marriage then they should say so openly. But as she understood it, what was being asked for was just one sort of sanctified cohabitation, and that was marriage. If that was so, then surely it was only logical to marry all comers on the same basis, and with the same service.[31]

Rev David Holloway reminded the Synod that they were all trying to find an acceptable solution to the problem. They had to face the reality that there was a serious division of opinion in the Synod. They had the straight-forward question: Is it right to remarry divorced people in church while a former partner is still living? But on that there was a division of opinion. On the one side were those who want forgiveness, and on the other those who hear Jesus' words 'whoever divorces his wife and remarries another commits adultery against her'. He made the point that they should only move forward with consensus. A small majority did not work. Three years ago they voted by a small majority against remarriage in church, but they were again reopening the whole issue on that small majority. He asked how Synod could say to the world that they considered one way or another was right when they had a close vote. He reminded them that Synod meant going together. 'We are not Parliament, we are the Church of Jesus Christ, and the biblical way of deciding is that it seems good to the Holy Spirit and to us.' He reminded Synod that they were dealing with people's lives. He did not want to see splashed over the *Sun* or the *Daily Mirror* or *The Times* that the Synod agreed to divorce and remarriage unless the Synod as a body was sure that it was right.[32]

Rev Brian Brindley said he belonged to that half of the Church who did not accept the Lichfield proposal. He proposed an amendment to remove the word 'remarried' from the resolution before Synod, and replace it with 'married'. He argued that many found it extremely difficult to accept the notion implied by the word 'remarriage'. He was also fearful that if this motion was passed it would appear in the press that Synod agreed to remarriage.[33] The amendment was accepted by Synod and the word 'remarried' was replaced, so the resolution read;

> that there are circumstances in which a divorced person may be married [not remarried] in church during the lifetime of a former partner.

Rev Peter Peterken said he was mindful that the Church outside the Synod was split right down the middle on the main issue of remarriage in church. The fact was that, whatever they decided, they were likely to leave half the Church feeling that a victory had been won and half the Church feeling that they had been unfaithful to the Lord Jesus Christ. He did not believe that division and hurt were what the Lord wanted for his Church, but he was sure it would please Satan very much to see them tearing the bride of Christ apart while they were discussing the question of Christian marriage.[34]

The Archdeacon of Leicester reminded the Synod that it must keep faith with the dioceses and send concrete proposals down to them. He said that without solid backing at the grass roots of the Church, what they proposed would be quite unworkable and would only cause bitterness, a black market in second marriages, and all sorts of rackets.[35] After a prolonged debate it was resolved on 7 July 1981 'that this Synod:

> believes that marriage should always be undertaken as a lifelong commitment;
>
> considers that there are circumstances in which a divorced person may be married in church during the lifetime of a former partner; and
>
> asks the Standing Committee to prepare a report setting out a range of procedures for cases where it is appropriate for a divorced person to marry in church in a former partner's lifetime, for consideration by the Synod before any action is taken to repeal or modify the relevant existing regulations and resolutions of the convocations.'[36]

And so the General Synod had made the momentous decision that a divorced person may be married in church during the lifetime of a former partner under certain, as yet undefined, circumstances. The voting in Synod was as follows: House of Bishops, 27 in favour and 7 against; House of Clergy, 134 in favour and 58 against; House of Laity, 135 versus 49.

Comment

This decision of the Synod was taken in the face of centuries of church discipline that had made it crystal clear that the words of Christ did not permit remarriage. The presumption that underlies the Synod's resolution is that marriage is not necessarily lifelong, for marriages can die. Consistent with this belief, the Synod voted to dispense with the word remarriage, suggesting that there was no difference between a first marriage and a remarriage following divorce. In the eyes of the General Synod a first marriage is essentially the same as a second, third or subsequent remarriage. The implication is that divorce has no moral consequences.

The General Synod, it appears, had made the remarkable discovery that the Church had been wrong all the time; the Church fathers had misinterpreted the teachings of Christ and misled the world. In its wisdom Synod would now correct this false teaching, which for centuries had denied divorcees the right to be married in church. The consequence of this decision was that the Church had changed its message to the world; it was now saying that the teaching on remarriage had been in error, harsh and lacking in compassion, for in truth the words of Christ had all along permitted selected divorcees to remarry.

REPORT OF STANDING COMMITTEE ON MARRIAGE DISCIPLINE: 1983

The Standing Committee on Marriage Discipline produced a report in April 1983 entitled *Marriage – and the Standing Committee's Task*.[37] The Standing Committee was aware of the need to move as quickly as possible, for it was now important for the Church to institute changes so that its marriage discipline was consistent with the recent Synod vote. In a wide-ranging investigation the committee considered virtually all the known procedures for church remarriage, including: the Canon Law Nullity procedure, an Eastern Orthodox Church type procedure, the Scottish Episcopal procedure, other Anglican Communion procedures, the Parish priest's sole discretion procedure, and another possible Pastoral procedure. After considerable thought the committee finally came down in favour of what was called 'Option G' as the preferred method for handling requests for second marriages in the Church of England.

The essence of 'Option G' was that the circumstances of each application for a church wedding should be examined sensitively and with proper thoroughness. Applications for remarriage would be made in the first instance to the incumbent. The incumbent would be assisted by a green book which gave guidance as to the extent and nature of the enquiries which should be made. On completion of his initial enquiries the incumbent would fill out an application form and submit it to the bishop. The bishop would add his comments before passing the application to a panel of advisers. The panels would be multi-diocesan as this would promote consistency across the country. The Standing Committee were of the 'unanimous conviction that if permission for marriage in church is duly given, that marriage should be solemnized according to one of the currently authorised marriage services. There should be no question of a different type of – or second class – marriage service for second marriage occasions.'[38]

The report concluded that any acceptable procedure must include provision for a release from marriage vows. There are two reasons for such a release. First, to assure the individual that he is no longer obliged to keep vows previously so solemnly made (whether or not he sees them as being still operative) and to remove all hesitancy, and perhaps even guilt, about making identical vows a second time, and second, 'to assure the Church, both locally and generally, that the second marriage is not being undertaken lightly and that what is being done is being done advisedly, openly and officially with the Church's approval and that what is proposed in the second marriage is marriage according to the Church's understanding and law, and nothing less.'[39]

GENERAL SYNOD DEBATE: JULY 1983

The report of the Standing Committee was considered by the General Synod in July 1983. When Mr Oswald Clark introduced the report he reminded the Synod that they needed to make a decision. He said that something had to be done by the General Synod if the present unsatisfactory situation was not to subside into utter chaos with every bishop and priest going their own way to the public disrepute of the Church of England and the further undermining of the permanence of the institution of marriage. The Standing Committee pleaded for a decisive answer that week. Moreover, whatever the popular press might choose to say, the subject before the Synod was 'marriage' and not 'remarriage', for the Synod motion of 1981 was specifically amended to make that plain.[40]

But not everybody was satisfied with the proposals before Synod. Mrs Katherine O'Hanlon spoke as a former national Chairman of Young Wives' Groups and vice chairman of the Mothers' Union. She said that the report and its bureaucratic procedures did not uphold Christian marriage. She raised the question of compassion for the wounded person who saw their spouse lusting after another, and rushing off to the nearest church to have another Christian marriage. She wanted to know how many times a person could be absolved from their vows. A couple could marry and in just over three years come back with a different partner, taking the same marriage vows. She reiterated her question—how many times could they take the marriage vow?[41]

The Archbishop of Canterbury (Robert Runcie) was a keen supporter of the proposals. He observed that it might be impossible to persuade some people outside the Church that it was not a step in the direction of laxity. The Synod ought to be clear that what they were doing was no retreat from the highest possible view of marriage. Moreover, he did not believe that the proposals embodied in 'Option G' were excessively bureaucratic. He did not believe that they should dismiss them as such without having some experience of them. He urged the Synod to support the proposals because it was becoming increasingly difficult to explain to couples that the Church had agreed to something in principle but had not devised a means of putting that principle into practice.[42]

Mrs Joyce Coombs was scathing about the procedure for investigating the circumstances of a previous marriage. She asked where the information would be obtained—from the former spouse, from mothers, from fathers, from mothers-in-law and fathers-in-law, from sisters and sisters-in-law, from neighbours on the one side and neighbours on the other side, from parochial church councillors? She thought the whole thing was revolting and shame-making and humiliating. She was entirely opposed to the malevolent bureaucracy. She hoped that some other and better system would come to light.[43]

On July 14 1983 the Synod carried a motion adopting 'Option G' as the procedure for consideration as to whether a divorced person may be permitted to marry according to the rites of the Church. It also requested the Standing Committee to bring forward as quickly as possible such proposals as were necessary to rescind the existing resolutions which prevented the remarriage of divorcees in church. The motion was carried with two-thirds of the Synod voting in favour. The voting went as follows: House of Bishops, 33 for and 10 against; House of Clergy, 131 for and 64 against; House of Laity, 120 for and 69 against.

REMARRIAGE PROCEDURES (OPTION G) UNACCEPTABLE: MARCH 1984

But the dioceses were not willing to accept 'Option G'. The General Synod received a report from the House of Bishops in March 1984 stating that the bishops had run into a serious problem in the dioceses.[44] Diocesan discussions had made it clear that 'Option G', which had been approved by a two-third majority in Synod, was not the way forward. The bishops' report hastened to reassure Synod that although 'Option G' was unacceptable there was strong support for the principle of the selective remarriage of divorcees in church. It was just the procedures that the dioceses did not like. 'In the light of the consultations in dioceses, the House (of Bishops) has come to believe that the elements of a new, more generally acceptable, approach might start with placing the responsibility for the decision firmly upon the bishop of a diocese in consultation with the parish priest, and, in difficult cases, with a panel of diocesan advisers. It would be necessary to establish generally agreed criteria endorsed by the General Synod for the guidance of diocesan bishops and of the clergy and lay people concerned.' The bishops wished to test the opinion of the General Synod on whether their approach would have the Synod's support. The House of Bishops hoped that the Synod would be able to consider the new proposals in November 1984 for final approval, so that they could take effect from early 1985.[45]

The Bishop of Winchester (John Taylor) told the Synod that in view of the overwhelming dissatisfaction with 'Option G', the House of Bishops had decided unanimously that it should not return the report of the Standing Committee to the Synod. The Synod was asked to entrust to the bishops the drafting of a fresh regulation that would take account of the main criticisms of the 'Option G' procedures and be more widely acceptable. The bishop said that a straw poll among the clergy revealed strong support for some change. He argued that the House of Bishops was ideally placed to produce a more generally acceptable procedure. He said that since there was wide agreement that the diocesan bishop should be the final arbiter when any couple sought permission for a church wedding in those circumstances, the bishops would inevitably judge each suggestion with their eye on its practicality for themselves and their priests.[46]

The Bishop of London (Graham Leonard) spoke a word of warning. He made the point that they lived at a time when the state had been steadily eroding not only the Christian understanding of marriage, but marriage as a fundamental human institution. He said that the marriage union of one man to one woman for life to the exclusion of all others was now treated in the law and in the courts as no more than a temporary contract terminable at will. The Law Society said that it had no obligation to uphold Christian marriage and family life. In his judgement the administration of the law as it stood had in effect removed any moral content to the understanding of marriage by the law. It was against that background that the Church had to determine its policy on the marriage of divorced persons.

He reminded the Synod of Article 21 of the Thirty-nine Articles: that Councils of the Church 'forasmuch as they be an assembly of men, whereof all be not governed with the Spirit and Word of God, may err, and sometimes have erred, even in things pertaining unto God'. He asked the Synod, whether they had not erred in one respect. He asked, in view of the difficulties the Synod was experiencing, whether the right and sensible thing to do was to stop and ask themselves whether they had not erred. He was referring not just to the York resolution but to the thrust of their concern ever since the Root report.

The Bishop of London did not believe that the great majority of those seeking the best for the country were primarily concerned with the issue of marriage in church for the divorced. He believed that to offer simply repetition of the marriage service with its vows as they stood would inevitably be taken by the country at large with deep disappointment and with sadness, if not anger, as no more than the Church coming along to endorse what the state had done. He believed that many in the country were now looking for a bold affirmation by the Church of the meaning of true marriage, of the responsibilities which it brings; of the care for children which it lays upon those who undertake it; of the virtues of loyalty and faithfulness. The Synod should have the humility and the courage to say that they had isolated one issue and had failed to emphasise their positive responsibilities; that they believed that the institution of marriage was not merely for Christians, though Christians were given the grace to fulfil it; that they believed that it was an institution given by God in creation and the Church therefore had the responsibility to speak to all men.[47]

The Archbishop of Canterbury spoke in support of the proposal that the bishops be asked to produce draft marriage regulations for the Church. He said they should not forget that they were concerned with ministering an act of divine generosity. That was always open to misunderstanding by those who had been faithful to the rules.[48] In March 1984 two-thirds of the General

Synod voted for a resolution inviting the House of Bishops to produce draft regulations for the remarriage of divorcees in church.

THE DRAFT MARRIAGE REGULATIONS

A report of the House of Bishops, which introduced the draft *Marriage Regulations*, explained that a division existed within the Church. 'In the Church of England some, who hold that marriage is a divinely sealed contract or an eternal bond of a sacramental character, regard the marriage in church of a divorced person whose former partner is still living as either not permissible, or as not possible, except where it can be shown that the previous marriage was not a true marriage. Others in the Church of England, who regard marriage as a permanent covenant, sacramental in character, through which two people become one in the fidelity of love, hold that marriage can be dissolved if the bonds of love and mutual commitment have been totally broken down. This view is based on an understanding of the character and teaching of Christ as revealed in the gospels in upholding God's law yet ministering his grace (or on the Matthean exception in Matthew 19 or on the Pauline privilege in Corinthians.) In the light of this, new marriage in church may be permissible despite the fact that the former spouse is still living. All believe that their views are rooted in Scripture and found in the practice of the Church from the earliest times.'[49]

The draft regulations, entitled *Marriage in church after divorce*, proposed that the divorced person may be free to marry in church under the following conditions:

if the relationship now dissolved by divorce was, either in its original intention, or as it developed, one which clearly failed to aspire to the nature and purpose of marriage as taught by our Lord

where the prime reason for the breakdown of the former marriage was arbitrary action by the other party of that marriage or where the applicant was divorced against his or her will

where a turning to or from Christ by one partner of the former marriage caused an incompatibility of spirit that love could not overcome.[50]

Comment

According to the bishops' proposals a marriage can be dissolved if the bonds of love and mutual commitment have been totally broken down. In other words, marriage lasts only as long as a husband and wife are in love. Should they fall out of love, or should either's commitment wane, the marriage bond is dissolved and they are free to divorce. The marriage is said to have died, and so the parties are free to marry again. The bishops claim that this view of marriage is rooted in Scripture. But it is not difficult to see that this view will condone divorce on demand, for anyone who out of their selfish desires wants a divorce in order to marry someone else, can declare that they are no longer in love with their marriage partner. Anyone can assert that they are no longer committed to their marriage and claim the right to a divorce. This is the very attitude to marriage that Christ called adultery. The view of marriage held by the bishops has more in common with the ideals of secular humanism than the teachings of Christ. The biblical view of marriage will be discussed in chapter 15.

Result of diocesan synod voting: 1985

In 1985 the diocesan synods were again asked to respond—this time to the draft Marriage Regulations produced by the House of Bishops. They were asked to vote on the motion 'that this synod approves the terms of the draft Regulations referred by the General Synod following its July 1984 group of sessions'. Diocesan synods were requested to respond by January 1985 so that the draft regulations could be taken to the General Synod for final approval.

Once again the dioceses voted down the proposals by a decisive majority; the official motion was rejected in 31 diocesan synods and approved in only 12. Voting by houses within the diocesan synods was as follows: bishops in favour 31, against 12; clergy in favour 15, against 28; laity in favour 12, against 31.[51] Clearly there was a large difference of opinion between the bishops on the one hand, and the clergy and laity on the other hand.

GENERAL SYNOD DEBATE: 1985

There is little doubt that the promoters of remarriage were hoping to achieve a successful outcome to their campaign in 1985. They had the support of most bishops and a majority in the General Synod; all that they needed was a majority vote in the dioceses, and the battle would be won. But the decisive diocesan vote made it clear that the grassroots did not support the campaign to change the marriage discipline of the Church. Moreover, the fact that the dioceses had now, on two occasions, decisively rejected proposals for introducing remarriage in church raised serious doubts about the frequent claims that there was strong support for change. Instead, it seemed that the push for change was coming from the bishops and the General Synod against the wishes of the body of the Church.

It was now impossible for the bishops to take their discredited draft Marriage Regulations to the Synod for final approval. Once again the House of Bishops prepared a paper for Synod reporting the defeat of their draft Marriage Regulations in the diocesan Synods. 'Despite the general principle agreed by the General Synod in July 1981 that "there are circumstances in which a divorced person may be married in church during the lifetime of a former partner", the attempts to reach a consensus on an appropriate procedure to implement that decision have failed. In these circumstances the House (of Bishops) has resolved not to refer the draft Marriage Regulations to the General Synod for approval. This means that the present convocation resolutions remain in force. The House agrees however:

> that there is a substantial number of those in the Church who believe in good conscience that a "second" marriage is possible in some cases

> that those clergy who take this considered view are free under the provision of civil law to allow such "second" marriages and that a number are already doing so

> the ultimate decision in such cases must be a matter for the clergyman concerned.

The House of Bishops hoped that those clergy who wished to allow a "second" marriage to take place in church would seek the advice of their bishops. The overall desire was to achieve as much pastoral consistency and fairness as was possible in the present circumstances.'[52]

The Bishop of Guildford (Michael Adie), introducing the bishops' paper, informed the General Synod that there was clearly not a sufficient majority for change. He said that although the draft Marriage Regulations had been proposed by the House of Bishops and accepted by the Synod, the House did not bring it back. The substantial view of the House was that they must come to terms with the fact that there were significant numbers on both sides of the debate. To try to move firmly in either direction seemed inappropriate. The bishops therefore advised that there should be no further formal action on the matter. Rather they must face the realities which were:

> The convocation resolutions of 1957 (Canterbury) and 1938 (York) still stand. These resolutions state clearly: 'The Church should not allow the use of the (marriage) service in the case of anyone who has a former partner still living.' In Canterbury in October 1957 the resolutions were declared to be an Act of Convocation, and, unless and until rescinded, have the force that belongs to such an Act. That statement therefore remains the primary statement of the position of the Church of England on this matter.

> In July 1981 the Synod passed a resolution, 'that there are circumstances in which a divorced person may be married in church', but that statement was a prelude to asking for a report on procedures to make that principle operative....

> Clergy have had since 1857 freedom to refuse to marry the divorced, but of course they have had also freedom at law to marry such people. A number of clergy use that freedom to solemnise the weddings of divorced people. They have not needed the permission of the bishop to undertake such

weddings and most bishops have not hitherto thought it right to be involved in that decision.

The clergy were asked to seek the advice of their bishop in order to ensure that any priest who intended to marry divorced people had taken all the factors into account in reaching that decision in principle. The priest would, for his own satisfaction, need to justify his decision to act contrary to the primary regulations of the Church. The bishops' concern was to secure responsible decisions, and to achieve such consistency between one parish and another, and between one diocese and another, as circumstances allowed. But the House of Bishops was not giving a green light to 'second' marriages, as had been suggested. They were not advocating that every man should do that which was right in his own eyes. They were recognising the division of view in the Church; they were aware of the strain that this would impose on many, and were ready to face their responsibilities and give advice and leadership in a situation which had to be described as unsatisfactory.[53]

Canon Douglas Rhymes said that if they sought the advice of one bishop they would get one kind of advice, and if they sought the advice of another they would get different advice. They could not have a doctrine of marriage which is indissoluble, and then marry again, unless and until they could in some way declare the previous marriage defective and therefore dead, because it was just a theological impossibility. He gave the opinion that probably more than half the Church, looking at the statistics and the voting in Synod, believed that there was a real and profound theological case in many cases for the remarriage of those who had been married and whose partners were still alive, not out of convenience, not to follow the spirit of the times, but because of the doctrine of grace and forgiveness. For that very positive reason, many in the Church believed that a second marriage was the will of God, when the first had failed, when there was real penitence, when forgiveness had been received and when a new start could be made with the blessing of the Church.[54]

The Archbishop of Canterbury said that in the report before the Synod it would be thought that two contradictory methods have been put down side by side. Some will appeal to the convocation regulations as their authority, while others will appeal to the 1981 resolution of the Synod which can be implemented at the parish priest's discretion. He did not believe that to be an entirely fair or constructive impression. There were clearly those, like himself, who had argued for a consistent pastoral discipline to allow for some second marriages to be solemnised in church, and in Synod they had not carried the day.

The Synod should recognise why it had not been possible despite prolonged consultation to implement the 1981 resolution. First, the repetition of the marriage vows in church was an offence to many people.

Second, a belief that in days of rising divorce figures and rising unease as to whether recent legislation had seriously undermined the principle of marriage as lifelong in intention, the Church should not even seem to be departing from it. Third, the real pastoral problem of discriminating between the deserving and the undeserving by some general rules; and, fourth, reluctance on the part of a majority to go down the road of extended nullity. He said that there came a time when he must agree that there is no real consensus in his favour, and that the peace of the Church demanded that they cease this endless wrangling over a question on which they were so divided.

It is much more important that they concentrate on the immense pastoral need for preparing and sustaining people in their marriages, and recognising the plight in which they were placing the parish priest by speaking with a divided voice. Their failure to agree had put the responsibility of judgement clearly back where it belonged—the parish priest in consultation with his bishop.[55]

Comment

It was now abundantly clear that despite two commissions and a prolonged debate, the grassroots of the Church of England remained unconvinced that it was right to remarry divorcees in church.

There is no doubt that the driving force behind the campaign for remarriage was the House of Bishops, that was using the General Synod to impose its views on the Church. Decisive votes against its proposals in the dioceses surely represented a massive vote of no confidence in the leadership of those who were promoting remarriage in church. But the promoters of remarriage were not prepared to accept defeat. They were quite prepared to play a waiting game. All that they had to do was wait until the views in the dioceses changed and they would be assured of success. It was essential to keep the issue on the agenda, and to keep pushing the idea that those who opposed remarriage were hardliners who lacked compassion. Within less than a decade the remarriage issue was again on the agenda of the General Synod.

GENERAL SYNOD DEBATE: 1994

In December 1994 a private motion was introduced in the Synod by the Rev Paul Needle;

> that this Synod request the Standing Committee to bring forward proposals to allow divorcees to be remarried in the Church of England.

His aim was to get the issue back on to the agenda as soon as possible. He noted that it was now politically correct to refer to remarriage as the 'further marriage of divorcees'. He pointed out the inconsistency in church discipline. He said that if someone lived in some dioceses an incumbent might allow them to marry, with the support and the permission of the diocesan bishop. In other parishes individual incumbents assumed the right to set the law of the land over the Act of Convocation which governed present church thinking. In the rest a request to a bishop was likely to be met with a refusal for such a ceremony.[56]

The Archdeacon of York (George Austin) said they had heard a good deal about compassion. He wanted to make a plea for compassion for those who were hurt by the breakdown of marriage and who were not necessarily seeking remarriage, the children of a broken home, the divorced wife or sometimes husband left to bring up the children alone, who then find, in all their pain and hurt, that the Church was going to remarry the spouse who had treated them like that. He said that compassion should be for everybody, not just for the person coming along for the second marriage. He was concerned that the Church of England was beginning to be held in contempt by many people because they seemed ready to cast aside their principles at the drop of a hat.[57] The following motion was carried;

that this Synod request the House of Bishops to consider the present practice of marriage in the Church after divorce and to report.[58]

The issue was once again referred back to the bishops to make proposals for the remarriage of divorced people in church.

MARRIAGE – A TEACHING DOCUMENT: 1999

Five years later the House of Bishops published a teaching document which was clearly meant to prepare the ground for the long-awaited report on remarriage. According to the document, 'Marriage is a pattern that God has given in creation, deeply rooted in social instincts, through which a man and woman may learn love together over the course of their lives. We marry not only because we love, but to help love. Without the practice and disciplines of marriage, our love will be exhausted and fail us, perhaps very harmfully to ourselves and others. When publicly and lawfully we enter into marriage, we commit ourselves to live and grow together in this love.'[59] And marriage helps each partner grow in maturity, and overcome personal failings and inadequacies. Continuing on the theme of love, the report says that for love in marriage to grow, it must develop in a number of ways. 'The emotional failure of a marriage may indicate that one or both partners have not recognised the need for growth, and are looking simply to repeat the same kind of emotional satisfactions with which their love began.'[60]

Comment

It is significant that this view of marriage is not based in biblical truth, but rather on the secular humanist notion that the essence of marriage is love. The key verse from Genesis, which forms the foundation of the biblical view of marriage – 'for this reason a man will leave his father and mother and be united to his wife, and they will become one flesh' – is not mentioned. And this is a remarkable omission for it was this verse that both Jesus and the apostle Paul used when they taught about marriage and divorce, as we shall see in chapter 15.

How do the bishops understand marriage breakdown? *Marriage* claims that from the time of the Reformation the Church of England has rejected its belief in the indissolubility of marriage. 'All Christians believe that marriage is "indissoluble" in the sense that the promises are made unconditionally for life. "For better for worse, for richer for poorer, in sickness and in health, to love and to cherish, till death us do part, according to God's holy ordinance": these well-known words, used for many centuries, are decisive for what it means to undertake marriage. Some strands of the Western Church have concluded from this that a divorce decree is ineffective and a subsequent marriage invalid in the eyes of God. The reformers of the Church of England did not believe that this was taught in Scripture, and they did not teach it in the Book of Common Prayer. In this respect they came closer to the understanding of the Eastern Church, which allows for the possibility of the "death" of a marriage. Yet from the seventeenth century until the present century English Church law made no allowance for a second marriage in the lifetime of a previous partner; and some Anglican Christians have believed, and still do, that such a marriage is, strictly speaking, impossible.'[61]

Comment

There are two problems with this paragraph. The first problem is the suggestion that the Church of England did not believe that Scripture or the Book of Common Prayer taught that a subsequent marriage [following divorce] is invalid in the eyes of God. The inference that flows from this statement is that the vows of the marriage service do not mean that marriage is for life. We have already heard the Archdeacon of Doncaster's (Ian Harland) dismay at the fact that the man in the street believes that the words 'till death us do part' actually means physical death. The Church 'had a difficult educational task helping the man in the street understand that marriages did, in fact, die before physical death, and it was perfectly proper that the Church should find a known way of pronouncing them dead'.[62] And so we are asked to believe that the vow 'till death us do part' refers not to the death of one of the marriage partners, as most people have believed through the centuries, but to the death of the marriage. The difficulty with this 'spin' is that we are expected to believe that the words do not mean what they appear to mean, but rather that they are meant to convey the metaphysical notion that a marriage may die. How many people who have taken their marriage vows in the Church of England would accept this interpretation?

Second, the claim that the reformers of the Church of England did not believe in the indissolubility of marriage is inconsistent with the historical facts. As we have already seen in chapter 3, the continental reformers, strongly influenced by the writings of the Renaissance humanist Erasmus, developed what has come to be called the Protestant doctrine of divorce. The continental reformers, led by Martin Luther, claimed to find grounds for divorce in the Scriptures. But what was the response of the Church of England to the teachings of the continental reformers? In 1543 Henry VIII set up a commission under Archbishop Thomas Cranmer to examine the issue. Strongly influenced by the continental reformers Peter Martyr and Martin Bucer, the commission eventually produced the *Reformatio Legum Ecclesiasticarum* in 1552 which proposed that divorce should be legalised in England on the grounds of adultery, desertion, deadly hostility, and unjustifiable violence by a husband against his wife. However, these proposals met opposition in the House of Commons and were rejected by the clergy of the Church of England. According to John Keble, 'it pleased God to put a stop to the contemplated change, when all seemed ripe for it'.[63] And so the Church of England, despite the upheavals on the continent, remained theologically and pastorally committed to the indissolubility of marriage and the *Reformatio Legum* was never implemented.

In 1597 the Provincial Synod of Canterbury, under Archbishop John Whitgift, promulgated canons stating the Church's position. 'Let those persons who have separated from each other be directed by monition and prohibition to live in chastity, and not to have recourse to other marriages so long as the other lives.'[64] At the end of the Elizabethan era, in 1603, the canon laws of the Church of England were revised to make it absolutely clear that the Church did not recognise a full divorce with the right of remarriage. It was now clear that the matter of divorce was settled in the mind of the Church of England, and divorce *a vinculo matrimonii* was not permitted by the ecclesiastical courts. By the beginning of the 17th century the Church of England and continental Protestantism had parted ways with regard to their position on divorce. According to historian Roderick Phillips, 'no bishop, archbishop or incumbent of high Anglican office in the first half of the 17th century supported the legalisation of divorce'.[65]

Historically the Church of England has always believed that marriage is an indissoluble union and therefore that divorce with the right to remarry is contrary to the teaching of the Church. What is true is that there has always been a minority within the Church of England, usually well represented among the bishops, that has sought to undermine this teaching and introduce divorce with the right to remarry into the marriage discipline of the Church. Undoubtedly, the document *Marriage* is yet another attempt to justify this position.

And does the Church believe that a further marriage is possible after divorce? According to *Marriage*, 'in some circumstances to marry again after divorce may compound the wrong that one has done, for example when obligations to the partner or children of the first marriage are not being met'. But in other circumstances remarriage 'may be responsible, prudent (for example in the care of young children) and emotionally wise. There is no simple rule for discerning this, for each case is different.' The Church has to decide whether the remarriage ought to be carried out in church. In the past, the Church met this responsibility by refusing to remarry a person with a still living former partner in church. The report mentions that the Church has been discussing changes to its policy on remarriage in response to changing pastoral needs. However, should the Church decide to change its marriage discipline to allow remarriage, 'it will be on precisely the same principles that have guided it up to this point: that marriage is an unconditional commitment for life; that a further marriage after divorce is an exceptional act…'[66]

And how do we know God in marriage breakdown? God meets 'us as free and generous mercy, and as demanding holiness; these two characteristics are not in tension or contradiction, but complementary. The scope of God's holiness is the scope of his mercy, and the more we are ready to open ourselves to the demand, the more we will know of his generosity, forgiving us where we have failed and granting us success where we thought we were bound to fail.'[67] And so for those who are seeking a second marriage the Church advises not to hurry into a new marriage, and makes the point that a church marriage may currently be possible if one lives in a parish where experimental diocesan guidelines are being followed. But the church remarriage is dependent upon an honest discussion of the past, and a willingness to allow the minister, in discussion with the bishop, 'to reach a decision about the appropriateness of your marrying in church'.[68]

MARRIAGE IN CHURCH AFTER DIVORCE – A DISCUSSION DOCUMENT: 2000

A discussion document from a working party commissioned by the House of Bishops was finally published in January 2000. The report acknowledges that marriage should always be undertaken as a lifelong commitment and says that nothing in the report should be taken to imply any change in the Church of England's teaching on marriage.

The report holds the view that 'it can be said in a literal sense of two people that they were married and are no longer married'.[69] Where there is honesty to the work of the Holy Spirit 'the Church's duty and privilege is to assure the believer of forgiveness and acceptance in Christ. This *may* take the form of supporting him or her in a new marriage.'[70] Discernment is required in deciding each particular case. The report believes that remarriage should take place in accordance with a nationally agreed set of pastoral criteria, principles and procedures which will need to be implemented with care and precision.[71]

The pastoral criteria suggest that the following areas should be explored:

the couple should clearly understand the purpose of marriage (i.e. that it should be faithful and lifelong);

they should have come to terms with the breakdown of the previous marriage and should show sufficient readiness to enter wholeheartedly into the new relationship, with evidence of repentance, forgiveness and generosity of spirit regarding the previous relationship;

adequate provision must have been made for any children and for the former spouse;

a reasonable time should have elapsed since the divorce: the further the divorce lies in the past, the less personal and social 'baggage' is likely to be carried into the new relationship;

the new marriage should not be such as to give rise to hostile public comment or scandal;

the relationship between the applicants should not have been a direct cause of the breakdown of the former marriage;

neither of the partners should have been married and divorced more than once;

there should be evidence of receptiveness to the Christian faith.[72]

This report has been sent to diocesan synods, which are being asked to respond by March 2001, with a view to reporting to the General Synod before the end of 2001.

Comment

It is worth recording the shift in the public position of the leadership of the Church on the issue of remarriage. In the 1920s, during the acrimonious debates in the House of Lords, the bishops were united in their public opposition to the remarriage of divorcees in church. So strong was this opposition that the Archbishop of Canterbury (Randall Davidson) introduced an amendment, with the full support of the bishops in the House of Lords, that the marriage of a divorcee 'whose former husband or wife is still living, shall not be solemnised in any church or chapel of the Church of England'. The Bishop of Ely (Frederick Chase) explained that their opposition was based on loyalty to the words of Christ. He said that a very large number of Christians would be distressed if remarriages were solemnised by the marriage service of the Church. The Archbishop of York (Cosmo Lang), quoting from the marriage service, said that a remarriage, which used the words of the marriage service, must be unreal, and in some cases would be a mockery. In 1938 the Church of England accepted the recommendations of the *Church and Marriage* report and resolved that 'remarriage after divorce during the lifetime of a former partner always involves a departure from the true principle of marriage as declared by our Lord'.[73]

In 1955 Archbishop Geoffrey Fisher wrote in *Problems of Marriage and Divorce* that 'there are a number of reasons why the Church is right to exclude from marriage in church all, without exception, who have a former partner still living… The Church has its duty to Christ and to society to bear witness to what he said marriage is. It cannot, least of all in present circumstances, make exceptions in its public solemnisation of marriage without compromising its witness.'[74]

In direct opposition to the public witness outline above, there is a group within the Church of England that is determined to allow the remarriage of divorcees in church. This public shift in the position of the Church requires an explanation. The public is entitled to know on what basis the Church has changed its position. Was the Church wrong in the past not to allow the remarriage of divorcees in church? The bishops need to explain how is it possible for the Church, which in the past took such a strong public stand against the remarriage of divorcees in church, to claim in the 1990s that such remarriages are in line with the teaching of Christ.

Chapter 12

The American divorce habit

Divorce in America from colonial times to the end of the 19th century

America's road to mass divorce was very different from that chosen by England. While England accepted divorce reluctantly and only after a fierce struggle, the American people right from the beginning yearned after divorce. Whereas in England the debate revolved around the indissolubility of marriage, the American debate was more concerned with finding the right grounds for divorce. So it is no surprise that the divorce rate in the USA is the highest in the world. Divorce has become so ingrained into the social fabric that it is an accepted component of American culture. In *The Divorce Culture*, Barbara Dafoe Whitehead writes, 'Divorce is now part of everyday American life. It is embedded in our laws and institutions, our manners and mores, our movies and television shows, our novels and children's storybooks, and our closest and most important relationships.'[1] A consequence of the divorce culture is that in the last quarter of the 20th century American fathers are living apart from their children more than ever before in the nation's history. A growing body of evidence shows that the massive erosion of fatherhood, caused mainly by divorce, is contributing to many of the major social problems of contemporary life.[2]

DIVORCE DURING COLONIAL TIMES

The roots of the American divorce culture go right back to the earliest colonial times. Early in the 17th century a small number of English settlers successfully established a colony in Virginia, taking with them their English culture, laws and religion. With the advent of James I to the English throne in 1603 the Puritans were becoming increasingly discontented with the theology and worship of the established Church. Although James was an ardent Calvinist, he was scornful of the Puritans' plan for reforming the established Church. The King was not willing to restrict the power of the bishops, hence his dictum, 'No bishop, no king'. One consequence of the King's repression of Puritanism was to drive some into exile. The prospect of religious freedom provided powerful motivation for colonisation of the New World.

In 1620 a group of Puritans set sail for America to establish the colony of Plymouth. The original colonists who settled New England were devout Puritans seeking freedom to practice their religion unhindered from what they considered to be the restrictive rites of the Anglican Church. A real cause of dissension was that the Church of England retained what the Puritans believed was the Roman Catholic doctrine of the indissolubility of marriage. They saw the conduct of marriage ceremonies by priests as savouring of the papist belief in the sacramental character of the relationship. In their eyes marriage was not a sacrament but a civil contract, and so only magistrates were allowed to marry a couple. The founders of the church and commonwealth in New England shared this Puritan idea of marriage as a purely civil contract.[3] Accordingly, in the early 1620s Plymouth officials declared marriage to be a civil rather than an ecclesiastical matter. As keen followers of Calvin's theological teachings they broke free from the influence of the Anglican Church and from the English legal position on divorce, and made provision for granting divorces, although the causes were not codified. So from the earliest times most New England colonies granted divorce for adultery, desertion and irremediable cruelty.[4] There were no divorce laws as such and the authority to grant divorce was vested in the provincial statute. The first American couple to divorce obtained their decree in 1639 from a Puritan court in Massachusetts. In her book *Divorce: an American Tradition*, Glenda Riley makes the point that by permitting divorce, Puritan leaders initiated a democratic innovation with far-reaching effects. They offered American colonists, whatever their station in life, the possibility of remedying excessive marital incompatibility and changing their lives.[5] Yet it is doubtful if the masses of the people sympathised with this complete secularisation of marriage, which was in such pronounced opposition to the sentiment of the Christian Church throughout its history.[6]

Early on in the southern colonies the situation was different, for the Anglican influence was strong and remained so for many generations. In Virginia, for example, because of the customs and doctrine of the prevailing Anglicanism, there was no divorce.[7] As in England, marriage and divorce were based on ecclesiastical law, which did not permit divorce with the right to remarry for any cause, although separation from bed and board were permissible for adultery and extreme cruelty. In the early days, however, there were no ecclesiastical courts because there were no bishops, so even separations were not possible. But this hardly mattered, for most colonists were faithful to the teachings of the Church and divorce was not really an issue. Other southern colonies, such as Maryland, North and South Carolina and Georgia followed the pattern set in Virginia and made no provision for divorce.[8] It was not until 1848 that Virginia granted divorce with the right to remarry, and in South Carolina no divorces were granted until 1868.

In the 18th century divorce was much easier to obtain in the New England colony of Massachusetts than in England. During the period 1692 to 1782 over a hundred divorces were granted for grounds not considered legitimate in England.[9] Moreover, in the later decades of the century the divorce trend showed a rise that was far steeper than the increase in population, indicating a real rise in the rate of divorce. The upward trend was illustrated by the fact that in the first few decades of the 18th century there were around 5 petitions for divorce per decade, compared with around 90 by the end of the century. Other New England colonies each pursued their own divorce policies. The Massachusetts Bay Colony, for example, permitted divorce from a civil court from 1629 on the grounds of the wife's adultery, the desertion of either spouse or 'the cruel usage of the husband'. Connecticut had the most liberal provision and by 1666, the law permitted divorce on such grounds as adultery, desertion, fraudulent contract, or seven years' absence.[10] The English Government, as can be imagined, was not pleased with the situation in the colonies and in 1773 sent a directive to all Royal Governors instructing them to withhold consent from any divorce act passed by a colonial legislature. This effectively halted divorce in the colonies, with the exception of Massachusetts, until the Revolution of 1775.

Pennsylvania followed some of the laws and practices of England during the first part of the 18th century with regard to divorce, which was granted through the state legislature. The grounds for divorce were adultery, bigamy and homosexuality. Divorce was rare in the colony and none were granted between 1728 and 1766; between 1767 and 1773 there were only two successful legislative divorces out of five applications. In the decade before 1785, when the Divorce Act was passed, there were eleven divorces. The colony of New Netherlands, which was neither Puritan nor Anglican, adopted a conservative approach and permitted divorce only on grounds of adultery. For many years New York had one of the most conservative divorce laws in the USA.

Undoubtedly the religious beliefs of Anglican England, Calvinist Holland and Lutheran Germany all had a major influence on the way divorce was viewed in the different states.[11] And so colonial America of the 18th century constituted a patchwork of the different divorce laws and policies created by each state that reflected the ideas of the Old World from which the colonists had come.

DIVORCE AFTER THE WAR OF INDEPENDENCE

After the War of Independence many of the states took advantage of their new freedom to pass divorce legislation. In Pennsylvania, for example, the Divorce Act of 1785 was established on the principle that marriage was a lifelong union based upon mutual affection between husband and wife. The intention of the legislature was to grant men and women freedom from marriages that caused them moral or physical harm.[12] Grounds for divorce were adultery, bigamy, desertion for more than four years, and impotence or inability to procreate at the time of the marriage. The Act was revised in 1815, when the period for desertion was reduced from four to two years, and in 1817 cruelty was added to the grounds.[13]

During the early 19th century there was a general move to liberalise the grounds for divorce. In Connecticut the law was extended to include divorce for reason of 'any such misconduct as permanently destroys the happiness of the petitioner and defeats the purpose of the marriage relation'.[14] Many of the other states in the north-east introduced liberal laws which included general clauses that allowed divorce for intolerable hardship and offences against marriage. The state of New York was an exception in that it permitted divorce only on the grounds of adultery and resisted attempts to liberalise the law.

Until about the 1830s, while American divorce laws were more liberal than those of other western countries, they were not so liberal as to make divorce a real alternative to marital unhappiness. But in the 1830s and 1840s many states generously amended their divorce statutes. Slowly the southern states followed the pattern set by the North, and by 1850 nearly all had liberalised their laws. The western states introduced the most liberal laws in the country, although they differed from state to state. Many states included an omnibus clause, which gave the courts extremely wide discretionary powers in granting divorce.

The *Cincinnati Gazette*, commenting on the diverse nature of the divorce system, pointed out that there were thirty-two states, and almost as many different laws of divorce as there were states.[15] A letter in *The Times* (London) made the point, 'I am scarcely overstating the real facts of the case when I say that there are almost as many varieties (of divorce systems) as there are Stars and Stripes. In North Carolina, by the Act of 1827, the courts have unlimited discretion to grant divorces "whenever the courts shall be satisfied that justice requires it". And in Illinois, by the Act of 1833, "whenever the courts shall be satisfied of the expediency of making such a decree". In South Carolina there was no instance of a divorce, either by the sentence of a court, or by Act of the Legislature, up to 1840; while, on the other hand, in New Hampshire, the continuing as "a Shaker" for three years is ground for divorce.'[16]

Eighteenth century view of marriage

The growing divorce culture was undoubtedly having an effect on the way marriage was viewed. Towards the end of the 18th century a new way of thinking, which believed that the purpose of marriage was companionship and to make the couple happy, was becoming increasingly widespread in society. The traditional belief that the prime purpose of marriage was to have children and raise a family was being replaced with the idea that love and companionship were the essence of marriage. Consequently women increasingly began to expect love in their marriages. Coinciding with the notion of a loving marriage was the belief in the happy marriage. In his book *Breaking the Bonds*, Merril D Smith writes, 'Many of the 18th century essayists writing in magazines, as well as in newspapers and pamphlets, believed that an individual had a right to freedom and happiness in and of itself.'[17]

An article in the *North American Review* describes a modern view of a true marriage as 'a natural concord of and agreement of souls, a harmony in which discord is not even imagined. When two beings unite in love, this is the true marriage of soul and soul'.[18] Husbands and wives were supposed to be partners linked by mutual affection rather than by duty, as in previous decades. Although love within marriage was not a new idea, during the mid-18th century a new emphasis was placed on the 'companionate' marriage.[19]

This view of marriage, especially prominent among Pennsylvania Quakers, spread throughout the country with the American Revolution. The consequence was that men and women searched for the ideal partner—one who would not only fulfil the role of husband or wife, but who would also be a companion, and one they could love and who would love them in return. Marriage was a relationship in which 'each has found the ideal; the man has found the one woman of all the world—impersonation of affection, purity, passion, love, beauty and grace. The woman has found the one man of all the world, her ideal, and all that she knows of romance, of art, courage, heroism, honesty is realised in him. The idea of contract is loose. Duty and obligation are instantly changed into desire and joy, and two lives, like uniting two streams, flow on as one.'[20] Women, moreover, wanted an equal partnership, while their husbands continued to see marriage in patriarchal terms.[21] As this idealistic view of marriage took root it was inevitable that the dreams of many women would not be met, as their husbands failed to come up to expectations as romantic heroes. It is perhaps not surprising, then, that women instituted a relatively large proportion of divorces.

DIVORCE AFTER THE CIVIL WAR

The divorce rate increased rapidly after the Civil War as Americans began to take advantage of the new opportunities offered by easy divorce. Consequently, throughout the 19th century Americans annually obtained more divorces than were given in all Europe.[22] The ease with which the marriage tie could be dissolved in some parts of the United States was illustrated by a story in the *Cleveland Herald*. The newspaper chronicles the marital history of a woman who married for the first time in 1861. Her first husband was killed in the War, and her second husband in a street brawl. 'As she returned home from the funeral, much admiring her good fortune, No 3 proposed to her, and the next day they were married. She did not like this one, and as he seemed to be rather tardy in following the example of his predecessors, she sued for divorce and gained it. A few months passed and she married again, but once more the Courts were invoked to dissolve the tie. This brings the romance of love down to May 1867, when No 5 married the experienced wife, but after two months she disposed of him with the aid of the friendly Divorce Court. She remarried, was again divorced, and in February 1868, married No 7. This union lasted a year, when she is now anxiously waiting for No 8.'[23]

In 1869 another divorce drama gripped the nation and illustrated the American approach to marriage in the second half of the 19th century. A prominent journalist connected with the *New York Tribune*, Mr Albert Richardson, fell in love with a married woman, Mrs M'Farland who had two children. She returned the journalist's passion and quarrelled with her undependable husband, who had a reputation of being rather fond of his drink. Mr M'Farland became jealous of his wife's liaison and shot and slightly wounded her lover. The wounded Mr Richardson was not put off by this turn of events and promptly announced in public his intention of marrying M'Farland's wife as soon as she could procure a divorce. Mrs M'Farland took up temporary residence in the state of Indiana in order to make use of their generous divorce laws. After the required 16 months the divorce was obtained without any difficulty. The furious husband, deeply upset by the actions of his wife, confronted Richardson in the offices of the *New York Tribune* and shot him again, delivering a near fatal wound. A report in *The Times* (London) continues the story, 'What followed was peculiarly American. M'Farland was dragged to a felon's cell, while Richardson was taken to the Astor-house, and on his deathbed held a levee. Interviewing reporters chronicled to the minutest details the sayings and doings, the agonies and anguish of both. Bulletins of Richardson's condition and M'Farland's ravings filled columns of the New York papers, and were sent all over the country by telegraph. Mrs M'Farland sat by the side – not of her husband – but of her lover; finally Richardson, on the threshold of eternity, was married to the woman by a ceremony which deserves reporting.' The marriage ceremony went as follows:

Marriage officer to Richardson—Do you take the woman whom you have by your side now, in this hour, standing near the heavenly land, and renew

257

to her the pledges of your love? Do you give your heart to her, and your
name? Is she, before God and before these witnesses, your beloved, your
honoured, and your lawful wife?

Marriage officer to Mrs M'Farland—And do you accept him as your head
in the Lord? And are you now to him a wife sacred and honoured, bearing
his name? And will you love him to the end of your life?

The marriage officer—Then, by the authority given me by the Church of
Christ, I do pronounce you husband and wife; and may the blessing of
Almighty God, the Father, the Son, and the Holy Spirit, rest upon you and
abide with you.

Later, when the ceremony was reported to M'Farland in his cell, his comment
was—he married my wife! Mr Richardson died the next day.[24] At his
subsequent trial, M'Farland was acquitted of murder, and walked out of the
court not only a free man but with the custody of the elder son, to the great
anger of the women's movement. While this may be an unusual case, it is
important because it gives insight into the prevailing attitude to marriage
and divorce.

The outcome of this infamous case forced the whole issue of divorce into
the public eye. Meetings were held to protest against the decision of the
court and the feminist advocate of divorce liberalisation, Mrs Elizabeth Cady
Stanton, was given an opportunity to air her views. In a series of lectures
she dealt with the social problems caused by marriage. She asserted that
the concept of indissoluble marriage was slavery for the woman; there was
no other human slavery that knew such depths of degradation as a wife
chained to a man whom she neither loves nor respects. Mrs Stanton had
numerous opportunities to present her views on marriage and divorce at
public meetings across the country.[25]

By the early 1880s the ease and frequency of divorce, especially in the
eastern states, was a cause of growing concern. The Divorce Reform League
was formed in 1881 by the Reverend Samuel Dike with the aim of reducing
the frequency of divorce. He drew attention to the alarming increase in
divorce numbers, showing that while the population of the USA had
increased by 70 per cent in 30 years, the number of divorces had increased
500 per cent. However, because of the diversity of the divorce laws and
practice in the various states, there was little reliable information on divorce
numbers. In early 1884 many influential petitions were sent to Congress
requesting that some action be taken to improve the collection of facts
surrounding marriage and divorce. Included among the petitioners were
Samuel Dike, Theodore D Woolsey, ex-president of Yale College, many
prominent judges, and some of the most influential citizens of the states
involved—governors, legislators, jurists, divines and prominent educators.

The petitions drew attention to the wide differences between the laws of the several states as to the cause of divorce, and the confusion over divorce suits involving residents from different states, which led to many distressing legal conflicts. Marriage was often treated at the same time in one state as dissolved and in another as subsisting.[26] In other words, a man might be convicted of bigamy in one state while in another he would be considered as lawfully remarried. The period of residence required before instituting divorce proceedings varied from three months to five years, although in the majority of states the time limit was one year. A grave scandal was that an advertisement in a distant newspaper was often accepted by the courts as sufficient notification to the other side in a divorce action, even though it was clear that the defendant had almost no possibility of seeing the advertisement. In effect, a husband or wife could be divorced without being aware of the fact, and with no opportunity to contest the case.

The Protestant Episcopal Church called the attention of Congress to the great importance of collecting reliable statistics on the subject of divorce. In view of the great laxity in the present divorce laws some reform was needed, such as uniformity of the law and increased stringency in defining the proper grounds for a divorce.[27] The petition from the Episcopal Church gave added weight to the call for a national inquiry, and in 1887 Congress authorised an investigation into divorce and marriage.

CONGRESS REPORT ON DIVORCE: 1889

The Department of Labour undertook the official congressional study. Colonel Carrol D Wright, Commissioner of Labour at Washington, issued the official report in 1889, over a thousand pages in length, providing a detailed statistical analysis of divorce over a period of 20 years for several states. The report confirmed that divorce numbers in the USA were growing at an alarming rate. It commented on the wide range of causes for divorce, 42 in all being specified for absolute divorce. The most common causes were adultery, physical incapacity, cruelty or apprehension of violence, and inhuman treatment. Less common causes included failure or neglect of a husband to provide for his wife, habitual indulgence in a violent or ungovernable temper, gross neglect of duty, habitual drunkenness, incurable chronic mania, indignities rendering cohabitation intolerable or life burdensome, and the catch-all cause 'any other cause deemed by the court sufficient, and when the court is satisfied that the parties can no longer live together'. The report gave examples, taken from court records, of the reasons for which divorces had been granted. In one case the wife alleged that her husband did not come home until 10 o'clock at night, and when he did come home he kept his wife awake talking. Divorce was awarded for mental cruelty. In another case the wife complained that 'my husband would never cut his toenails, and I was scratched very severely every night, especially as he was very restless'. Again the application for divorce was successful. In another example, after twenty-seven years of marriage a husband said to his wife. 'You are old and worn out; I do not want you any longer.' This remark caused his wife mental anguish and she was granted a divorce. Court records showed that men were less likely to be granted divorces for cruelty. An example of a woman being found guilty of extreme cruelty was a wife who habitually neglected and refused to cook for her husband, and had spat in his face on several occasions. Her husband was successful in his petition for divorce.[28]

The Times (London), in its review of the report, made the rather obvious point that divorces were much easier to obtain in America than in England, and that the growing laxity augured ill for domestic peace. 'It now remains to be seen whether the respective state Legislatures, overcoming their mutual jealousies and their extreme independence, will take concerted action to provide a remedy for a condition of things that is a blot upon civilisation.'[29] An international comparison of divorce numbers showed that in 1888 there were 23,472 divorces in the United States, which was nearly four thousand more than in France, England, Italy, Germany, Holland, Sweden, Norway, Austria, Romania and Canada put together.[30] The relative frequency of divorce is illustrated by the fact that in 1901 there were around 500 divorces in England compared to 20 thousand in the USA. According to William O'Neill in *Divorce in the Progressive Era*, the law played a crucial role, because divorce was itself a creature of the law. 'If divorce is prohibited, as it was in South Carolina for most of the century, or limited to a single cause, as in New York, where until 1966 adultery was the only ground, then no divorce problem exists.'[31] The rate of increase was alarming as divorce numbers increased at about five times the rate of population increase. The rapid escalation of divorce numbers in the final decades of the 19th century was a cause of concern to all society, and especially to Christians who could remember a time when divorce was rare.

The rise in divorce, which followed the civil war, had taken society by surprise. The Protestant mind, while convinced that divorce rested on perfectly sound theological grounds, was not at all comfortable with the situation. Although most Protestant denominations permitted divorce, they still felt that it represented moral failure and should only be used as a very last resort. Moreover, the weight of public opinion was strongly against divorce. William O'Neill identified the inconsistency of the Christian opposition to mass divorce. He writes, 'The early opponents of mass divorce were, therefore, baffled by the contradiction between theology and morality. In consequence their first responses to the divorce movement were fitful, sporadic and ineffective.'[32] Because of the concern about the damage of easy divorce, many states adjusted their laws to make it harder to get. Some states made the residential requirements more rigorous, some forbade remarriage for one or two years following divorce and some refused to accept divorces granted out of state for grounds which they did not recognise. A few states even repealed their omnibus clauses that allowed the courts great discretion in granting divorce. As a consequence of these changes divorces were harder to get than at any time since the Civil War.[33]

The publication of the US Bureau of Census statistics again raised alarm over divorce. These showed that in the two decades up to 1907 there were 1.4 million divorce applications, and one million final divorces were granted. A comparison of the divorce statistics of England and America illustrates the extent of the American divorce problem. Over the period 1866 to 1905, there were 1,328,000 divorces in the USA, compared with 13,428 divorces in England.

NINETEENTH CENTURY VIEWS ON THE DIVORCE PROBLEM

The American fascination with divorce meant that almost everybody had an opinion on the social issue of the times. Many books and articles dealt with the subject and there was a continuous flow of press comment. An examination of a selection of views illustrates the nature of the divorce controversy. It is interesting to note that much of the American debate revolved around the reasons for divorce, and many of the arguments were based on the premise that is was pointless for a couple to stay together when their marriage had become dysfunctional.

In 1881, in the two volume *Commentaries on the Law of Marriage and Divorce*, Joel Bishop gave his views on American divorce legislation. He took a rationalist approach, believing that divorce was necessary for the good of society. He contended that if the Christian Church were not so divided on the subject of divorce, then its teaching would undoubtedly be followed by every state legislature. Since men and religious bodies differed as to what the Scriptures taught, and as there was no common Christian theology, the legislatures must act from a viewpoint that took political and social interests into account.[34]

Bishop believed that the state had an interest in private morals and the public happiness and general virtue of the community. For this reason a sound divorce policy demanded 'the dissolution of marriages which have failed to accomplish substantially the ends for which they were created. By their dissolution the state obtains the benefit of the fruits of such new alliances as the parties may choose to enter into, with the advantage of having the children trained under those better influences which harmony and matrimonial concord in the parents produce.'[35]

According to Bishop there were two alternatives. Either permit divorce with the privilege of remarrying to all that cannot or will not live together, or accept illegitimate sexual relationships 'and the bringing into the world of innocent children under the burdens and disgrace of bastardy'.[36] He illustrated this point by referring to the situation in South Carolina where divorce was not permitted even for adultery. 'Where divorces are not allowed for any cause whatever, we sometimes see men of excellent character unfortunate in their marriages, and virtuous women abandoned or driven away houseless by their husbands, who would be doomed to celibacy and solitude if they did not form connections which the law does not allow, and who make excellent husbands and virtuous wives still. Yet they are considered living in adultery, because a rigorous and unyielding law, from motives of policy alone, has ordained it so.'[37]

He acknowledged that the causes of divorce were not easy to define. 'Clearly adultery; desertion, which practically breaks up the relationship, and is by many deemed a greater offence against the marriage than even adultery; extreme cruelty, which renders cohabitation unsafe; perpetual, perhaps temporary imprisonment for crime; drunkenness, when it is confirmed, habitual and beastly – are completely destructive of the ends of marriage, therefore they should severally be made causes for its legal dissolution. Beyond this line, we come to grounds uncertain and shadowy. There are smothered hatred, love turned to the reverse, jealousies which no reason can allay, an indefinite jarring of natures in collision, and other purely mental causes, which render marriage burdensome, and destroy its higher and holier purposes.'[38]

Bishop's analysis was a devastating rebuke on the witness of the Church. The reason America was forced to use a rational approach to divorce was because the Church was unable to agree on the reasons for divorce. He also made the point that while most state legislatures were sympathetic to the Christian faith, confusion in the Church meant they were unable to base their laws on Christian principles.

During the 1850s feminist leaders became increasingly involved in the marriage question and advocated the need for divorce reform. Susan Anthony, Elizabeth Cady Stanton and Amelia Bloomer were three of the more prominent feminists who crusaded for easier divorce laws as a necessary condition for the improvement in women's position within marriage.[39] Mrs Stanton was the most vocal advocate in the cause of liberal divorce. At an early age she was convinced of the wisdom of making divorce available to women trapped in unsatisfactory marriages. Having read Milton she concluded that absolute divorce was both a right and a duty.[40] 'Are not the very letter and spirit of the marriage contract based on the idea of the supremacy of man as the keeper of woman's virtue – her sole protector and supporter?' She believed that the Bible had for two thousand years been the greatest block in the way of women's progress. It had given divine authority to men's demands for women's subjection. For thousands of years God had given anti-feminism its cloak of respectability. In her mind Christianity was a problem for it had created a low view of women which placed them in subjugation to men.[41]

Mrs Stanton took every opportunity to propagate her views. In her opinion, marriage was degrading to women who were always the victims of the institution.[42] A true marriage was marked by the loving companionship of man and woman, 'their capacity for mutual help and happiness and for the development of all that is noblest in each other'.[43] It was folly to talk of the sacredness of marriage and motherhood, 'while the wife is practically regarded as an inferior, a subject, a slave. Having decided that companionship and conscientious parenthood are the only true grounds for marriage, if the relation brings out the worst characteristics of each party, or if the home atmosphere is unwholesome for children, is not the very *raison d'être* of the union wanting, and the marriage practically annulled? It cannot be called a holy relation – no, not a desirable one – when love and mutual respect are wanting.' She believed that the question of divorce should be settled by the parties themselves, without interference from either the state or the Church.[44] 'If divorce were made respectable, and recognised by society as a duty, as well as a right, reasonable men and women could arrange all the preliminaries, often, even, the division of property and guardianship of children, quite as satisfactorily as it could be done in the courts.'[45]

In a letter to the Seventh National Women's Convention in 1856 Mrs Stanton wrote, 'How can women devoutly subscribe to a theology which makes her the conscientious victim of another's will, forever subject to the triple bondage of the man, the priest, and the law? How can she tolerate our social customs, by which womankind is stripped of all true virtue, dignity and nobility? How can she endure our present marriage relations by which woman's life, health and happiness are held so cheap, that she herself feels that God has given her no charter of rights, no individuality of her own? I answer that she bears all this because in her blindness she sees no way of escape. Her bondage, though it differs from that of the Negro slave, frets and chafes her just the same.' She continued, 'Marriage as we now have it is opposed to all God's law. It is by no means an equal partnership. The silent partner loses everything... She is nameless, for a woman has no name! She is Mrs John or James, Peter or Paul, just as she changes masters; like the southern slave, she take the name of her owner.'[46]

Historian Nelson Blake makes the point in *The Road to Reno*, that the determination shown by Mrs Stanton in pushing the divorce question to a place of high priority in the women's rights movement was highly significant. 'Whereas divorce in earlier periods of history had been primarily a prerogative demanded by men to rid themselves of unwanted wives and open the way for new marriages, 19th century American divorce was becoming more and more a right demanded by women on humanitarian grounds. The day was passing when wives would meekly submit to all kinds of abuse from brutal husbands.'[47] Mrs Stanton was a significant figure for she was setting the agenda for the future feminist onslaught against marriage, and encouraging the idea that divorce was an important aspect of women's true emancipation. Although at the time she was regarded as a radical with outlandish ideas, there is no doubt that she was a prophetess of the women's movement whose ideas were to bear fruit in the mainstream of feminism.

Mrs Stanton's views illustrated the hostility of the feminist position to the biblical teaching on marriage. According to this early feminist analysis, marriage was an equal partnership for the mutual help and happiness of the partners. If a marriage failed to fulfil these needs then it ceased to have any reason for existing. However, because women had no rights in marriage they were subject to male exploitation, which was a form of bondage. Divorce was seen as a means of liberating women from the bondage of marriages that had ceased to fulfil the needs of the wife. It followed that divorce should be made respectable and recognised by society as a duty.

In 1860 Horace Greeley, editor of the *New York Tribune*, challenged attempts to liberalise the laws in New York. A serious debate ensued in the pages of the *New York Daily Tribune*, between Greeley and Robert Dale Owen, the son of the utopian reformer. Greeley wrote that the state of Indiana was 'the paradise of free-lovers' as its divorce laws enabled men and women to get unmarried nearly at pleasure. Owen objected, arguing that it was in New York and New England where reasonable divorce was refused that free love prevailed, not in Indiana. 'I regard the marriage relation as the holiest of earthly institutions. It is for that very reason that I seek to preserve its purity, when other expedients fail, by the besom of divorce... Marriage fulfils God's intention so long as the domestic home is the abode of purity, of noble sentiment, of loving-kindness, or, at least, of mutual forbearance... The question remains whether it be more pleasing in the sight of God and more conducive to virtue in the man, to part decently in peace, or to live on in shameful discord.' According to Owen, the chief purpose of marriage was to nurture love in the broadest meaning to the word. Therefore, when love ceased so should the marriage.[48]

Greeley responded that the very essence of marriage is that the couple should cleave to each other till death. 'I dissent entirely from your dictum that the words of Jesus relative to marriage and divorce may have been intended to have a local and temporary application. On the contrary, I believe he, unlike Moses, promulgated the eternal and universal law, founded not in accommodation to special circumstances, but in the essential nature of God and man.' He went on, 'The divine end of marriage is parentage or the perpetuation and increase of the human race. To this end, it is indispensable – at least eminently desirable – that each child should enjoy protection, nurture, sustenance, at the hands of a mother not only but of a father also.'[49] Owen restated his belief that a marriage without love, defiled by evil passions, was an outrage that ought to be dissolved for the good of mankind.[50] Greeley retorted that the main vice of the age was a morbid egotism, which overrode the gravest social necessities in its mad pursuit of individual personal ends. 'But to the libertine, the egotist, the selfish sensual seeker of personal and present enjoyment at whatever cost to others, the indissolubility of marriage is an obstacle, a restraint, a terror; and God forbid that it should ever cease to be.'[51]

This debate is significant for it illustrates the two opposing views of marriage that were struggling for the mind of America. Greeley adopted a biblical view of marriage, holding that a couple should cleave to each until death because the divine end of marriage is that husband and wife should have children and become parents. Owen, on the other hand, saw the chief purpose of marriage as nurturing a loving relationship. It followed that a marriage without love was an outrage that should be ended for the good of the individuals and society.

The president of Yale University, Theodore Woolsey, published a series of articles in 1867 in which he described the history of divorce, and denounced the moral decay in America that was responsible for the increase in divorce numbers. He claimed that the Scriptures taught that marriage was virtually indissoluble, except for the one reason given in Scripture. Having reviewed biblical teaching, Woolsey found a general principle that 'legal divorce does not in the view of God and according to the correct rule of morals authorise either husband or wife thus separated to marry again, with the single exception that when the divorce occurs on account of a sexual crime the innocent party may without guilt contract a second marriage'.[52]

Woolsey, therefore concluded that the Scriptures forbade divorce for desertion. He nevertheless remained convinced that adultery broke the marriage bond and this made remarriage for the innocent party permissible. 'There is nothing in these passages, nor in our Saviour's principle in regard to marriage, nor in other passages of the New Testament, that can fairly be regarded as forbidding the innocent party, against whom the crime of adultery has been committed, to contract a second marriage.'[53]

Woolsey's essays provided a classical defence of the Protestant position on divorce. While he recognised the moral decadence of the divorce culture, and had a strong dislike for divorce, he was unable to take a stand against it because he believed that the Bible permitted divorce for one cause. And herein lay the dilemma of the Protestant position. Although they disapproved of divorce, and recognised that it was a cause of serious social problems, they were unable to witness against it because of their theological position.

In 1887 Charles and Carries Thwing published *The Family: An Historical and Social Study* which analysed the divorce situation from a Christian perspective. According to the Thwings' understanding, the institution of the family has its basis in marriage, so that without marriage the family cannot exist.[54] The divine purpose of marriage is to be discovered in the Bible, which was a revelation of the divine will. They saw marriage as far more than a contract, for it forms relationships which no contract, as such, can create, and which no dissolution of the contract can annul. They also believed that the state had an interest in marriage and the family, which formed the best basis of social order. 'In every marriage the state may be said to be one of the parties, and in every divorce it has an interest. Perhaps the most important element in marriage is not the relation of the contract to the parties themselves, but its relation to the state; and certainly the effect of divorce upon society is more important than its effect upon the parties themselves.'[55] The family appears to be a type of divine government. 'In its narrowest, as well as its broadest sense, the family is the medium of a divine revelation. Into the family was Christ born, in a family Christ lived; from the family, also, we receive those conceptions of God, as Father, Brother, and Friend, which we believe most truly represent his character.'[56]

The Thwings believed that among the fruits of the Reformation were 'seeds which have been rich in the depreciation of the family and in the appreciation of the individual. The Reformation has profoundly modified the thought and social life of the last three hundred and fifty years. It gave lasting impulses to the growth of individualism.' They recognised the growth in individualism in the larger rights given to women, and in all the discussions regarding their 'rights'.[57]

During the last five decades the marriage relationship had changed from a permanent and lifelong state to a union existing for the pleasure of the parties. 'The change thus swiftly wrought is so revolutionary, involving the very foundations of human society, that we must believe it to be the result not of any temporary conditions, but of causes which have been long and silently at work. The cause underlying, and in a sense including all other causes, is the growth of individualism which is the direct product of the Reformation.' However, they felt that the right of individual liberty was in danger of being pressed so far that the counterbalancing truth of individual responsibility would cease to act. And they identified this tendency in the marriage relationship. 'The belief is prevalent, and seems to be growing, that marriage is a civil contract, and a civil contract only. Like other contracts, it is entered into for the pleasure and convenience of the parties, and like other contracts, may be terminated when pleasure and convenience are no longer served.'[58]

The Puritan protest against the Church of England, no less than the protest against the Church of Rome, had its effect upon the popular conception of marriage. 'The conception of marriage as a relation purely secular has been at the basis of our modern divorce legislation. This legislation recognises the right of the individual and the right of the state to an interest in the dissolution of the marriage tie. It does not in the least recognise any peculiarly sacred character in the institution. The growth, moreover, of atheistic and socialistic principles in society has weakened in the popular mind the conception of marriage as a divine ordinance, and therefore as a tie of binding force. To those who eliminate God from the world it becomes an easy task to rob marriage of its sacred character.'[59] In the Thwings' view the established Church in England and the Episcopal Church in the United States had done well in following the spirit of the Catholic doctrine. The dissenting churches, the Congregationalists, Baptists, Methodists and other American churches should no longer hesitate to emphasise the religious elements of marriage.[60]

This analysis was accurate in identifying the role of the Reformation in changing society's view towards marriage and divorce. Unlike Woolsey, the Thwings recognised that Protestant theology had an enormous influence on the way society viewed marriage, and was the starting point for the secularisation of marriage that had become the platform for the mass divorce movement. They also understood the link between marriage and the family and insisted that without marriage there could be no family. But the tide was moving rapidly against the biblical view, and the ideas of sociology would soon present an interpretation that would be more acceptable to the spirit of the age.

The *North American Review* started a drive against divorce in 1889 with a series of articles which asked the question 'Is divorce wrong?' The main divisions of American thought were covered in the articles. Colonel Robert Ingersoll gave a secular humanist view of free divorce. In his view a true marriage is a natural harmony in which there is no discord. 'When two beings thus love, thus unite, this is the true marriage of soul and soul... Each has found the ideal.' But the death of love is the end of the marriage. 'When love is dead, when husband and wife abhor each other, they are divorced. Indeed, upon what principle can a woman continue to sustain the relation of wife after love is dead? It is immoral for a husband to insist on living with a wife who has no love for him. Marriages are made by men and women; not by society, not by the church and certainly not by supernatural beings. Few people have an adequate idea of the suffering of women and children, of the number of wives who tremble when they hear the footsteps of a returning husband, of the number of children who hide when they hear the voice of a father... It is not in the interests of society that good women should be enslaved, that they should live in fear, or that they should become mothers by husbands whom they hate.'[61] (It is important to note that the views of marriage held by secular humanists Robert Dale Owen and Robert Ingersoll, and feminist Mrs Elizabeth Stanton, are remarkably similar to those of the English bishops, as we saw in the previous chapter. They all believe that the essence of marriage is love, and that when love ceases the marriage is effectively dead and divorce is the way out.)

Henry C Potter spoke for the Protestant Episcopal Church. As a rule no minister was allowed to solemnise the marriage of any man or woman who had a divorced wife or husband still living. But if the person seeking to be married is the innocent party in a divorce for adultery, that person, whether man or woman, may be married by a minister of the Church. Obviously the Protestant Episcopal Church allowed the complete validity of a divorce in the case of adultery, and the right of remarriage to the innocent party. But the Church had not determined in what manner either the grounds of the divorce or the 'innocence' of either party was to be ascertained. He pointed out that divorce among church members was very rare; that it was regarded with extreme aversion. Public opinion in the Church maintained the law as it was, but could not be trusted to execute more stringent laws.[62] Potter was making it plain that majority opinion in the Protestant Episcopal Church was sympathetic to the Protestant doctrine of divorce, and therefore would not accept a more rigorous marriage discipline that disallowed all divorce.

Cardinal Gibbons wrote from the Roman Catholic view. He observed that 'upon marriage rests the family, and upon the family rests society, civilisation and the higher interests of religion and the state. Yet divorce, the deadly enemy of marriage, stalks abroad today bold and unblushing, a monster licensed by the laws of Christian states to break hearts, wreck homes and ruin souls.' God in Paradise instituted marriage. Christ came to restore things that were perishing, and he reasserted in clear and unequivocal terms the sanctity, unity and indissolubility of marriage. But the Protestant reformers from the very beginning made out new laws of marriage and divorce. The new doctrine, pleasing as it was to sensual man, was speedily learned and speedily put into practice. Divorce promised freedom for newer joys. But the Catholic Church said no to divorce. As time goes on the wisdom of the Church in absolutely forbidding divorce grows more and more plain. And nowhere was this truer than in America. The Catholic Church had always allowed a separation from bed and board for adultery.[63]

Also contributing to the series, Mr William Gladstone supported the view that he had argued so forcefully in the debate in the House of Commons. 'Remarriage is not admissible under any circumstances or conditions whatsoever. Not that the difficulties arising from incongruous marriage are to be denied or extenuated. They are insoluble. But the remedy is worse than the disease.' Gladstone observed that divorce with the liberty to remarry altered the character of marriage. Marriage is essentially a contract for life, and only expires when life itself expires. The Christian marriage involves a vow before God. No authority has been given to the Christian Church to cancel such a vow. 'While divorce of any kind impairs the integrity of the family, divorce with remarriage destroys it root and branch. The parental and the conjugal relations are joined together by the hand of the Almighty no less than the persons united by the marriage tie to one another. Marriage contemplates not only an absolute identity of interests and affections, but also the creation of new, joint and independent obligations stretching into the future and limited only by the stroke of death.' Gladstone observed that since the English Divorce Act was passed in 1857 the standard of marriage morality had perceptibly declined among the higher classes, and divorce scandals had become more frequent.[64]

Opinions on the American system of divorce

Around the turn of the century there was a great deal of criticism of the divorce system. Some people were highly critical of the patchwork of divorce laws and the trivialisation of marriage, which they believed represented a major failure of public policy. The American Minister to Great Britain expressed his views in an article in *Forum* published in 1889. Approaching the issue from the point of view of public policy, Mr Phelps regarded the interests of society as more important than individual rights. He asserted 'the whole business (divorce) is a disgrace to our country and an alarming menace to social order'. He gave many reasons why he believed that the facility of divorce and of remarriage subsequent to divorce was the real cause and source of mischief. 'It is remarkable that divorce is most frequent in the states where churches are most numerous, educational machinery most elaborate, and the theory of morality maintained at its highest point.' The institution of the family was the beginning of government and the foundation of society, and free divorce coupled with liberty of remarriage impaired the family and thereby undermined the whole fabric of society. Phelps concluded that the remedy was to be found in the entire abolition of the sort of divorce that allowed the parties, or either one of them, to marry again.[65]

The President of the Bar Association of Missouri, Professor JD Lawson, explained the situation in the USA to the British Royal Commission on divorce in 1912. He said that if one of the parties was within the state the court could proceed to hear the case and render judgement. In some states divorces were often obtained without the other party knowing or even suspecting that such a suit has been brought. 'The husband deserts his wife and goes to another state, brings a suit for divorce, notice is given by publication in some newspaper, which he selects, and which satisfies the law, but which he is certain she will never see... Later, when the husband marries again, he has a lawful wife in his new state, and yet in the state which he left he has another lawful wife. If subsequently there is property to be divided, if there are children of both marriages, think of the confusion there will be.'[66]

Mr Robert Crane, an American lawyer of great experience also gave evidence to the British Royal Commission on divorce. He said that as a result of nearly forty years' observation and professional experience of the laws of divorce in the United States, in his opinion the frequency of divorce and the growing indifference to the duty and obligations of marriage, were primarily due to the fact that marriage in America was defined by statute to be merely a civil contract, and that no form of solemnising the ceremony was provided or required. In several of the states the law specifically declared that the parties might marry without the intervention of anyone. All that was required is that they make a written declaration setting forth their names, ages, places of residence, and the date, place, and fact of their marital union. He noted that justices of the peace, clerks of courts, police, magistrates and the leaders of a multiplicity of sects and of ethical societies, were empowered to perform the rites of marriage. 'In America, justices of the peace, in the Western states, are commonly the proprietors or keepers of a public house. His court is usually held in an apartment over or adjoining his bar. As the state requires no form of marriage he is left free to exercise his fancy as to the time and manner in which he shall perform the rite. It is no unusual experience for him to repair from his bar to his court to declare, amidst the levity of the loafers and the hangers-on about the premises, that the couple arraigned before him is man and wife. Persons thus married can, naturally, have no comprehension of the solemnity of their engagement. God has not joined them together and they are quite willing, if circumstances suggest the desirability of a release from their contract, to invoke the aid of the most convenient and pliable court to put them asunder. Aside from all questions of religious belief, a marriage which has no better sanctity than attends the making of a promissory note, or a bargain for the purchase and sale of produce, cannot, in the very nature of things, be more highly regarded by the majority of thoughtless persons than the obligations of an ordinary commercial transaction.'[67]

These accounts by eminent lawyers illustrate the low view of marriage that was prevalent in America at the turn of the century. To most people marriage was little more than a civil contract, like any other, and there was little realization that marriage was meant to be a lifelong union. The implications for divorce are obvious.

DIVORCE AND THE CHURCH

The Christian voice in the debate was confused. While the Protestant Episcopal Church was conservative on the issue of divorce, most Protestant denominations such as the Methodists, Congregationalists, Presbyterians, Lutherans and Baptists accepted the Protestant doctrine that divorce was permitted for certain reasons. All these denominations allowed remarriage after divorce under certain circumstances, although there was no agreement on what the circumstances were. Moreover, within the denominations there were various shades of opinion about whether the Bible permitted divorce or not. There were also different views on remarriage; some pastors had conscientious objections against remarrying divorcees in church, while others were quite happy to do so.

The conservatism of the Episcopal Church, inherited from its roots in Anglicanism, was demonstrated by a proposal in 1808 that the Church should prohibit the clergy from remarrying divorced persons under any circumstances. Although the House of Bishops rejected the proposal, it showed that many among the clergy and laity supported the indissolubility of marriage. The official position was that it was inconsistent with the law of God that the ministers of the Church should marry any person who was divorced unless they were the innocent party in a divorce caused by adultery. This resolution was introduced into canon law in 1868.[68] However, a number of clergy within the Church were committed to the indissolubility of marriage and disapproved of the remarriage of the so-called innocent party in cases involving adultery. Experience told them that many of the innocent parties were not innocent at all, and they were convinced that because of collusion between husband and wife it was often not possible to establish that one party was truly innocent. The General Convention of 1877 reaffirmed the canon that remarriage was only available to 'the innocent party in a divorce for the cause of adultery, or to parties once divorced seeking to be united again'.[69]

In 1904 the House of Bishops passed an amendment that aimed at forbidding the remarriage of all divorcees, both guilty and innocent. The Chamber of Deputies rejected the amendment because they believed it was too far in advance of the spirit of the country.[70] The Convention, however, accepted a compromise measure that would not compel ministers to remarry divorced persons. Commenting on the decision of the Convention, the *New York Times* said that the Church had gone as far as it could towards asserting and enforcing the indissolubility of marriage, and as far as other Protestant bodies could be expected to follow. 'To go further and say that in no case shall a minister of the Episcopal Church give the sanction of that Church to the remarriage of the innocent party to a suit of divorce is to lead whither there is no chance that any other Christian body or any secular Legislature will follow... But that is a position which the Episcopal Church has thus far distinctly refused to take, and which, we repeat, it would pretty clearly lose valuable influence in taking.'[71]

Not all the clergy, however, were satisfied with the position of the Church, and some clergy announced their intention not to remarry any divorced person, not even the innocent party in a divorce for adultery. This was seen as an implied criticism of the proceedings of the Church. Those clergy who refused remarriage to divorcees were interpreted by some to 'have proceeded on the idea of the absolute indissolubility of marriage, a Roman idea'.[72] Despite the confused position within the Church many people believed that the laws on divorce, in which most states allowed different grounds for divorce, were a national scandal. An editorial in the *New York Times* made the point, 'It is not tolerable that a man and a woman should be recognised by the law of one state as living in lawful wedlock, while in another they would be, if they should move to it, living in unlawful cohabitation... The working of the present chaos of laws will have the effect of shaming those states of which the laws are distinguished by their laxity.'[73]

The Presbyterians expressed concern about the growing divorce numbers and the General Assembly in 1883 deplored the fact that the divorce laws in many states were in direct contravention to the laws of God. At subsequent assemblies attempts were made to withdraw the Church's historic recognition of wilful desertion as a legitimate ground for divorce.[74] Although these attempts were unsuccessful, it showed that some within the Church were questioning the biblical basis for permitting divorce for desertion. In 1884 the Methodists moved to a position that recognised adultery as the only ground for divorce, while the Baptist Church favoured a uniform divorce law based on the Scriptures.[75] The Evangelical Lutheran Church reaffirmed its traditional stand, allowing divorce for adultery and desertion. In an effort to develop a Christian consensus that would enable the Church to present a united front to the secular world, an Interchurch Conference on Marriage and Divorce was set up, with Episcopal Bishop William Doane taking a lead. Twenty-five Protestant denominations attended the first meeting in 1903, at which there was considerable discussion on the issue of remarriage after divorce. A recommendation that ministers refuse remarriage to people who divorced for reasons forbidden under the rules of their church was hotly debated. But this proposal did not gain the support of the Presbyterians because they opposed any recommendation that would prevent divorced Roman Catholics from being allowed remarriage in a Protestant Church. The argument was that while the Catholic Church did not recognise divorce, Jesus Christ and the Presbyterian Church did. After a close vote the proposal was rejected and a compromise agreed that ministers should be advised not to marry persons whose marriage was prohibited by the laws of their own church, unless the minister believed that there were special circumstances in a particular case in which his refusal would do an injustice to an innocent person who had been divorced for scriptural reasons.[76]

William O'Neill made the following assessment of the Christian position with regard to divorce. 'From about 1898 to 1907 the churches lavished attention on the question, but their labours were productive of more discourse than action. Almost every denomination discovered that no significant changes in any direction could be effected. Liberals, conservatives, and the merely confused pulled in so many directions that they cancelled each other out, and a policy of inaction was literally forced upon the churches. Thus conservatives, far from being able to form a united Christian front against divorce, could not move even a single denomination.'[77]

ATTEMPT TO FIND A UNIFIED DIVORCE LAW

A National Congress on Uniform Divorce Laws was held in 1906 with the full support of President Theodore Roosevelt. The President spoke of the 'widespread conviction that the divorce laws are dangerously lax and indifferently administered in some of the states, resulting in a diminishing regard for the sanctity of the marriage relation. The hope is entertained that co-operation amongst the several states can be secured to the end that there may be enacted upon the subject of marriage and divorce uniform laws, containing all possible safeguards for the security of the family.'[78] The objective of the Divorce Congress, which was the most ambitious attempt to unify divorce laws, was to consider the practicability and desirability of having a uniform law throughout the United States. The great dilemma facing the Congress, which was attended by 42 of the 45 states in the Union, was to find common ground. 'The problem,' said the *New York Times*, 'is to propound some project of divorce which on account of its intrinsic reasonableness and equity, shall commend itself to the sense of equity and to the sense of reasonableness of all the representatives of all the states of this Union. But the existing differences in the statutes of the different states show that they have taken widely differing views upon the question. It indicates that there is no common denominator... At present a man or woman may be a malefactor or malefactress in one state and a blameless citizen in another. But the effort to find a common standard which shall "impose itself" is at all events laudable.'[79] The *New York Times* had correctly identified the widely different views held by the states as a major obstacle. When the representatives from Pennsylvania proposed five causes for divorce, five grounds for annulment and four for legal separation, claiming they were in accordance with modern views, they produced a strong reaction from the New York delegates who objected to the inference that their law was out of date.[80] One Christian delegate argued that the aim should be to prevent people from getting divorces who ought not to have divorces, and not to put endless obstacles in the way of those who have a moral right to freedom from the bonds of marriage. Another argued that it was pointless to suspend divorce laws until there was an understanding that the chief purpose was to increase the sum total of human happiness in the country.[81]

Because the views of the states were so widely divergent it proved impossible to achieve a consensus on the grounds for divorce. The Congress Report of 1906 'recognised that entire uniformity was not now attainable. The sovereign right of each state to the exercise of its judgement in the passage of laws relating to the statutes of its own citizens, and the conflicts of views in the communities of the different states, on the dissolubility of the marriage tie, and the grounds for such dissolution, preclude the possibility of any universal agreement, at the present time, upon the causes for absolute divorce.'[82] In the face of this reality, the Congress made it clear that the aim should be to reduce rather than increase the number of causes, and recommended that no state should recognise additional causes. After an intensive study of the issue by eminent lawyers and jurists and prominent churchmen, the Divorce Congress found that there was an agreement among a large number of states in regard to the causes of divorce. The six grounds for divorce generally recognised were: adultery, bigamy, conviction and sentence for crime followed by two years' continual imprisonment, extreme cruelty, wilful desertion for two years and habitual drunkenness.

Another issue which exercised the Congress was 'a general conviction, that the growing increase of divorces, with their attendant evils, was due to the misuse or fraudulent use made by the resident of one state of the laws and courts of a sister state, for the sole purpose of obtaining divorces which could not be secured under the laws of their own state'.[83] One of the main objects of the Congress was to root out what they saw as the scandal of migratory divorces. But a major obstacle was the so-called 'American doctrine', which allowed 'the wife to acquire a separate domicile when the husband had been guilty of a matrimonial offence entitling her to a divorce'. The Congress decided that this doctrine was 'too firmly rooted in American jurisprudence to be disturbed, even though it has brought in its train as a logical result inconvenience and uncertainty, arising from the diverse effect accorded to such decrees outside of the state which granted them, where the defendant was not served within its jurisdiction'.[84] In an attempt to deal with this problem the Congress decided that a non-resident defendant should be given notice of a divorce suit, where practicable, and an opportunity to defend the action.

Despite the moderation of the bill proposed by the Congress, and extensive publicity, few state legislatures were inclined to enact the statute. They were not willing to give up their right to legislate, and so each state decided to keep its own law. This failure meant that uniformity was going to be difficult, if not impossible, to achieve. There was a growing awareness that a unified divorce law was out of harmony with the spirit and tendency of the age. It is difficult to escape the conclusion that there was little real desire to tackle the divorce issue. Most of America had grown used to divorce and were satisfied with the *status quo*. Divorce was simply an accepted part of the American way of life, and nothing was about to change that.

During this attempt to find a uniform divorce law for the whole country, the Christian input was characterised by a lack of agreement. Bishop George Worthington of New York City diocese demonstrated his strong opposition to divorce by signing an agreement that he would never again perform the marriage ceremony for a divorcee and was supported by all but four of the clergy in the diocese.[85] However, the Rev Madison Peters, preaching in the Church of the Epiphany, took the opposite view, believing that divorce should be more easily available. He said, 'Divorced persons who remarry should not be put under the red hot anathema of the Church. I know hundreds of people who have made mistakes in their first marriages, who tried again, and their homes are positively Edenic... I believe that the grounds for divorce should be extended, and among the grounds I would put drunkenness.'[86]

THE REMARRIAGE QUESTION

In the midst of this confusion the rising tide of divorce meant that the various Protestant denominations had to face up to the issue of remarriage. A steadily growing pool of divorced people wanted to know whether they could remarry in church. The dilemma facing the churches was illustrated by the inability of the Interchurch Conference on Marriage and Divorce to find a common policy on remarriage. The fact that the various churches were unable to find an agreed Christian position, which would be understandable to ordinary people who were seeking divorce and remarriage, raised a serious question about their theological position. Why was it that the Church was having such difficulty in agreeing the circumstances for remarriage in church?

In 1904 the Episcopal Church reaffirmed its position of forbidding ministers from remarrying divorced persons unless they were the innocent party in a divorce for reason of adultery. In 1907 this rule was made more restrictive by not allowing a church wedding until at least one year after the divorce. However, the general convention of 1931 agreed a compromise that allowed any person whose marriage had been dissolved by a civil court to apply to a bishop to have the former marriage declared null and void by reason of a marriage impediment. In 1946 the Episcopal Church recognised a list of nine impediments to a valid union that allowed a marriage to be declared null and void, and so permitted another marriage to take place. This list of impediments included 'such defects of personality as to make competent or free consent (to marriage) impossible'. The canon recognised that if one of the impediments existed before marriage, no marital bond was created. Also, if one of the impediments arose during the marriage, the marital bond was broken.[87] This provision meant that a bishop could identify a latent personality defect as a ground for declaring a first marriage null and void, and thereby permit remarriage to take place in church.

The Lutheran Church of America came to the conclusion in 1907 that the innocent spouse in a divorce on legitimate grounds, which included adultery, desertion, impotence, extreme cruelty, conspiracy against life, and habitual drunkenness, should be entitled to remarry in church after waiting at least one year.[88]

THE DIVORCE HABIT

At the pan-Anglican Congress of 1908 the Bishop of Albany, William Croswell Doane, spoke of the shame of the divorce habit in America. 'Here in America we are compelled to strain every nerve in our insistence upon the sanctity of marriage, because, I grieve to say, the country has gained a shameful and sorrowful pre-eminence in what one might call "the divorce habit", the statistics of which are alarming and shocking to the last degree. Slowly and steadily the public conscience is being stirred. Not only in ecclesiastical bodies, but in the Legislatures and in conferences called by the civil authorities, there is a widespread and strong movement towards reducing the causes for divorce *a vinculo*, and toward arresting the possibility of remarriage, if not to the one only possible scriptural exception, at least to only six causes at the outside. Meanwhile the safeguards against hasty and ill-considered marriages are coming to be more carefully defined and in many states increased. With the door of entrance into the Holy Estate guarded and consecrated, it is hoped that the door of exit, "the shameful divorce court", may some day be closed.'[89]

This was an honest assessment of the divorce situation by a prominent bishop. While recognising the shameful state of the divorce situation in the United States, his solution was that the grounds for divorce should be limited preferably to the one scriptural cause, but if that was not possible, then there should be no more than six causes. These comments by an eminent church leader show how Christian thought had failed to see any link between the divorce habit and the Protestant doctrine of divorce. There was no understanding that the Protestant teaching on marriage and divorce, implanted into American culture by the Puritan founders of New England, was now bearing its inevitable fruit. Furthermore, because the Church in America had always been committed to the idea of divorce, it had never taught the people that marriage was an indissoluble union. This failure on the part of the Church meant that the root of secular marriage was firmly established in American culture and the tree of easy divorce was flourishing.

Chapter 13

The 'good' American divorce

The sociological and moral justification of divorce in the 20th century

At the beginning of the 20th century the battleground of American divorce was rapidly changing. The Christian Church disliked divorce but it was unable to offer any coherent biblical grounds for opposing it. Disagreement among the various denominations on the grounds for divorce, and confusion over remarriage emphasised the weakness of the Christian witness. Consequently the Church had no clear message for society and the teachings of Scripture were becoming irrelevant to the argument. Indeed, those who claimed to follow the teachings of the Bible had actually provided the biblical justification for divorce. As divorce numbers escalated at an alarming rate, the Church, unsure of its response, slowly withdrew from the debate, bowing to the superior wisdom of sociological thought. The retreat of the Church left the field open to the social scientists, feminists and liberal clergymen, and others who believed that divorce was a valuable resource. The new experts had plenty to say on the issue and henceforth sociological theories, psychological opinions and feminist ideology would guide the debate.

THE SOCIOLOGY OF DIVORCE

Applying sociological analysis to social problems was a new and growing discipline during the last decades of the 19th century and the early decades of the 20th century. The Rev Samuel Dike, writing the annual report of the National League for the Protection of the Family, placed great faith in the ability of social science to find solutions to the problem of family breakdown. 'If religion must furnish the spiritual power it must have social knowledge for its use. The growth of true Social Science – the term is used here in its most comprehensive sense – supplies that knowledge. The future study of the home in all our higher institutions of learning is well assured. The highly trained professional worker in any portion of the social field will soon have expert knowledge of... the family.'[1] Sociologists were able to use scientific methods, so they claimed, to analyse and interpret social issues and advise society on how to deal with social problems. One of the first issues they turned their attention to was that of divorce. Through their studies into the family they had become 'experts' on the consequences of marriage breakdown. They saw divorce not as a social evil but as the proper response to unsuccessful marriages. Early social scientists tended to argue that divorce was a positive institution, and a number endorsed easy divorce. They also argued that divorce legislation had little effect on the divorce rate. With the development of sociology, divorce was becoming increasingly defined in sociological terms and removed from the field of moral and theological argument.

Sociologist George Elliot Howard, who wrote the three volume *History of Matrimonial Institutions* (1904), used the methods of sociology to justify the need for divorce. The starting point of his analysis was that marriage and the family needed to be liberated from 'the cloud of mediaeval tradition', by which he meant biblical teaching. Once this was achieved, then it followed that marriage and the family were no more than 'the products of human experience, of human habits, and are therefore to be dealt with by society according to human needs. In this regard the Reformation marks the beginning of a social revolution.' Howard identified the Reformation as the start of the social revolution in thinking about marriage and the family. This revolution was continued by 17th century New England Puritans who gave the state 'complete jurisdiction in questions of marriage and divorce, to the entire exclusion of the ecclesiastical authority'.[2] Having underlined the hopelessness of appealing to Scripture in trying to deal with social problems, Howard claimed that the guiding light would come, not from authority, but from a rational understanding of the existing facts. 'Small progress can be expected while leaning upon tradition. The appeal to theological criteria is, no doubt, a matter of conscience on the part of many earnest men. Nevertheless the vast literature which seeks to solve social questions by juggling with ancient texts seems in reality to be largely a monument of wasted energy. Witness the perennial discussion of the "scriptural" grounds of divorce.'[3]

His analysis appeared to uncover a moral quality in divorce that others had missed. The growth of mass divorce, far from being an evil, was just and righteous. There was no virtue in restrictive divorce laws which took no account of the sufferings of the social body. 'Divorce is not immoral. It is quite probable, on the contrary, that drastic, like negligent, legislation is sometimes immoral. It is not necessarily a merit, and it may be a grave social wrong, to reduce the legal causes for a decree to the one "scriptural" ground... Indeed, considering the needs of each particular society, the promotion of happiness is the only safe criterion to guide the lawmaker in either widening or narrowing the door of escape from the marriage bond. The divorce movement is a portentous and almost universal incident of modern civilisation. Doubtless it signifies underlying social evils vast and perilous. Yet to the student of history it is perfectly clear that this is but a part of the mighty movement for social liberation which has been gaining in volume and strength ever since the Reformation. According to the 16th century reformer, divorce is the "medicine" for the disease of marriage.'[4]

Howard argued that there may be occasions when the exercise of the right to divorce becomes a social duty, and it was fallacious to represent the institution of divorce as a menace to social morality. It was just as illogical to assume that the prevalence of divorce in the United States was a proof of moral decadence as compared with other countries in which divorce was prohibited or more restricted. 'To forbid the use of a remedy does not prove that there is no disease.'[5]

Howard saw the divorce movement as an aspect of the mighty process of spiritual liberation, which was radically changing the relative positions of men and women in the family and society. Changing social relations had made the wife more independent and self-supporting, and this emancipated her from the power of her husband. The old patriarchal bonds were being rapidly loosened. 'We are thus confronted by still another phase of the emancipation movement—the divorce problem. In this problem woman has a peculiar interest. The wife more frequently than the husband is seeking in divorce a release from sexual slavery. The divorce movement, therefore, is in part an expression of women's growing independence.'[6]

Howard noted that the manifold social evils associated with marriage had always justly aroused the unsparing criticism of socialist writers. He quoted a number of socialists who were strongly against marriage as an institution and who saw the family as a cause of social problems. He concluded his analysis of socialist writers by claiming that they had rendered an important public service in laying bare the flaws of domestic institutions. The socialists had shown that progress lay along the complete emancipation of women and the absolute equality of the sexes in marriage. 'The liberation of women in every one of its aspects profoundly involves the destiny of the family... This means, of course, a weakening of the solidarity of the family group, so far as its cohesion is dependent on the remnants of mediaeval marital authority. Will the ultimate dissolution of the family thus become the price of equality and freedom?'[7]

Howard's massive work became the standard textbook on the sociology of divorce. A feature of the book was its strong antipathy towards biblical authority. Howard argued that the traditional view had failed and had to make way for the new guiding principle—the promotion of happiness. Divorce was virtuous because it would save people from the disease of marriage. Howard was heavily influenced by the ideology of socialism, and to a large degree he was presenting their views wrapped up in sociological jargon. In effect, sociology was based on little more than the opinion of a group of intellectuals who had a strong political agenda, and an underlying hostility to the biblical view of marriage.

A further contribution to the growing sociological literature was *A History of Marriage and the Family* (1934) by Willystine Goodsell. He observed that the patriarchal household ruled by the father was rapidly disappearing. Wives and mothers had not only achieved political emancipation but also a considerable degree of economic independence. Children had been freed from harsh parental discipline, and 'the family at its best has become democratic in form, a free association of persons bound together by ties of affection, comradeship and mutual help, in which the rights of each member are respected and the future of the individual is not sacrificed, as so often was the case in the past, to the strength and solidarity of the family'.[8] The modern family unity was a spiritual oneness of mutual love and consideration, of common interests and goals, rather than a unity secured by centring all authority in one head. Goodsell noted that the growth of individualism had resulted in the family of the 20th century becoming markedly unstable.[9] 'However beneficial divorce may be as a means of ending intolerable marital relationships, it can hardly be questioned that the legal severance of marriage is itself not rarely a source of unhappiness and maladjustment both to married pairs and to children. Like a surgical operation, divorce may put an end to serious evils but leave in its wake obscure ills that are slow in clearing up.'[10]

Carrol Wright (the first United States Commissioner of Labour, who had produced a report for the USA Congress on divorce in 1889) wrote a book in which he approached the issue of divorce from a sociological perspective. In his *Outline of Practical Sociology* (1898), he observed that the union of man and woman, right from the beginning, has been characterised by 'the complete slavery of women, over which man has all possible rights, and which he may drive away at his will'.[11] At length the right of women to seek divorce in order to escape from intolerable treatment was recognised. According to Wright the divine purpose of marriage was the happiness of the couple. 'If marriage results in happiness, the divine end has been secured; if marriage does not result in happiness, plainly the divine end of the institution has been sadly missed, and few men deny that in some cases divorce more perfectly secures the divine end than a continuation of the contract which may be laying intolerable burdens on entirely innocent people.'[12]

The dominant view among sociologists was favourable towards divorce and they had a significant influence on public opinion. Slowly but surely the public was coming to accept the inevitability of divorce.[13] A significant achievement was their success in altering the framework of the debate. Moral questions surrounding marriage and divorce were no longer considered important as the debate increasingly focused on the social consequences. Furthermore, the social scientists were now the acknowledged experts who claimed divorce was not only inevitable, but also beneficial for women and children who were set free from restrictive marriages. In *Divorce in the Progressive Era*, William O'Neill provided the following perceptive assessment of the situation. 'Once it was conceded that the social effects of divorce were relevant, the opposition virtually disarmed itself. Since no one really knew what the social consequences of divorce were, the whole picture became murkier, while at the same time the moral absolutes which could be wielded by anyone were replaced by lines of reasoning with which sociologists were far more comfortable than their critics. The real victory won by the social scientists involved, then, not reversing public opinion on divorce, but moving the battle to ground of their own choosing, and thereby rendering the largest part of the traditional argument obsolete.'[14] Concluding his analysis of the influence of sociology, O'Neill noted that at the turn of the century the sociologists were simply bypassing Christianity, and if the conservatives proposed to fight they had to attack divorce on the basis of its social inutility. 'But by engaging the enemy on his own terms conservatives made a fatal mistake for they were in no position to challenge the professional credentials and equipment of the sociologists.'[15]

The Protestant tradition, which accepted that divorce was permitted for adultery and desertion, was largely in agreement with the views of the sociologists. This was not surprising, for we have already seen that the Protestant position on divorce was based on the sociological principle of finding a solution for unhappy marriages, rather than on the Scriptures. So the sociological view on divorce was but the natural extension of Protestant thinking. Consequently, the Protestant Church had no grounds for opposing the sociologists' desire to liberate women and children from unhappy marriages. Although the sociologists went much further than the Protestants in their desire to obtain freedom to divorce, the differences between the two positions was a question of degree and not of principle.

REINTERPRETING THE SCRIPTURES

While the social scientists were able to provide convincing theories regarding the necessity of divorce, the moral imperative of the Bible remained as a major obstacle to those pressing for more liberal divorce. Whatever the Protestant theologians might say, the conscience of many Christians was still disturbed by the sayings of Jesus. Almost everyone knew the words of Christ, 'Anyone who divorces his wife and marries another woman commits adultery against her' (Mark 10:11), and the teaching of the apostle Paul, 'A wife must not separate from her husband. But if she does, she must remain unmarried or else be reconciled to her husband' (1 Corinthians 7:10-11). William O'Neill reached the conclusion that for progress to unrestrained divorce to be legitimised it was essential that the teaching of the Bible against divorce be explained away. 'If most liberals came to support divorce because of their feminist sympathies, feminism was far less useful than the Higher Criticism in making a case for divorce. The social scientists may have been more influential in persuading Americans of the need for divorce, but it was essential that the opposition of most church leaders, theologians, moralists, and biblical scholars be undermined if divorce was to become legitimate.'[16]

Liberal theologians, sympathetic to the divorce cause, cast doubt on the teaching of the Bible by showing that it did not actually mean what most people thought it meant. One argument, based on the idea of situation ethics, was that Christ's central doctrine was love and so his words on divorce needed to be interpreted in that context. Christ must have meant that the question of divorce and remarriage should always be decided in a way that produced the most love and happiness in each individual case. Another argument was that Jesus' statements on divorce were only relevant for the context in which he spoke. In the *North American Review* Professor William Ballentine commented that it was wrong to apply a literal interpretation to the Scriptures, for Jesus taught by hyperbole. He argued that most Christians treated a large part of the words of Jesus as figurative, and it was purely a matter of human judgement which should be enforced as practical rules. It followed that the words of Christ concerning divorce could not be used to settle the law of the land. Rather, laws must be fitted to their times. 'The hyperbolical utterances of Jesus… are not looked upon as requiring, or even justifying, a mechanical conformity to the letter of Scripture.'[17]

An article by Norma Jones observed that periodically a wave of virtue swept over the land on the subject of divorce. The response of some Christians was to talk and write about amending the laws so that no divorce could be granted for any cause save one, the so-called scriptural one. But the words of Christ were addressed to those whose customs and circumstances were far different from those of the men and women of today. 'A lot of stress is laid on the text, "What, therefore, God hath joined together, let not man put asunder." But what means have we for knowing whom God really joins together? We have never found any formula laid down in the Bible for a marriage service; so what constitutes true marriage in his sight?' Jones contended that because of human nature honourable divorce was almost a necessity. 'If mutual love and respect do not hold two people together in this closest of all relations, no law, human or divine, will be able to do so.'[18]

Carrol Wright was another advocate of divorce to reinterpret the words of Christ. He argued that Jesus was not a lawmaker but a teacher of general principles. It was never the intention of Christ to lay down a law against divorce. Divorce was a secular institution and therefore the state's responsibility. According to Wright, the sacredness of the marriage contract was destroyed by adultery because happiness has been completely wrecked, and the moral sentiment of society outraged.[19] He observed that those who had insisted on limiting divorce to one cause (adultery), had given up that ground and accepted divorce for any cause which destroyed the purpose of marriage. 'The words of Christ, like many of his sayings, can be applied literally only to the social conditions in which he lived; they are not meant to be a code of law for all later generations.'[20]

The liberal interpretation of the Scriptures added to the confusion on the question of divorce and meant that the Christian position was even more uncertain. The Bishop of New York, William Manning, recognising the confusion within the churches, made a vain plea for them to act together in the matter of divorce. 'At present the influence of religion against divorce and remarriage is weakened immeasurably by the varying standards of different churches and even of different ministers of the same church. Those whom one church refuses to marry go immediately to another and are married without question. In a matter of such vital importance to society, this ought not so to be.'[21] In his book *Divorce in America under State and Church* (1925), Walker Gwynne concluded, 'Even preachers seem to be ignorant of the teaching of their great textbook the New Testament, or else frankly set it aside as out of touch with the spirit of the time... The authority and explicit precepts of him whom the world regards as the greatest of moralists, and others as their divine Master, are for the most part wholly ignored. Jesus Christ, in fact, is the last person to whom appeal is made for either approval or condemnation. And so no solution is offered, and none can be.'[22]

Despite these pleas for a return to a biblical view of marriage, the Christian view was dominated by the Protestant tradition that favoured the sociological grounds for divorce. The edifice of marriage in the USA was now without biblical foundation and at the mercy of every blast from sociological theory. The proposition of liberal theologians that Christ did not actually oppose divorce provided a major boost to the divorce movement, for it finally removed divorce from the arena of moral and theological debate. The liberal interpretation of the New Testament – that the words of Christ did not prohibit divorce – influenced many Christians. Indeed, if Christ did not oppose divorce then there could be no real objection to it. And so a major obstacle, which had troubled the consciences of many people who were familiar with the words of Jesus, was removed. Explaining away the teaching of Jesus allowed the Church to rationalise its position on divorce as appropriate to the social context of the day. It also salved the consciences of those who simply took the line of least resistance.

DIVORCE FOR THE SAKE OF THE CHILDREN

After the Second World War divorce, which had once seemed so flagrantly immoral, was becoming a part of everyday life. This presented a dilemma for it was still widely believed that divorce was detrimental to the well-being of children; to most people it was self-evident that the break-up of the home was deeply damaging for the children. An important factor that helped to change attitudes was the evidence, produced by sociologists, that divorce was not really harmful for children, and sometimes could even be a positive benefit. One of the first challenges to the orthodox view that divorce was damaging to children was the social research of Professor Ivan Nye published in 1957. He tested the hypothesis that the adjustment of children in broken homes, and unbroken but unhappy homes, was not significantly different. A survey of 780 Washington high school children measured, among other things, the level of psychosomatic illness, delinquency, and parental relationships in different family settings. Unhappy unbroken homes were those in which the parents quarrelled a lot and were not very happy, as judged by their children. The study found that the children of divorced parents suffered less from psychological problems, were less inclined towards delinquency and had better relationships with their parents than children whose parents had frequent quarrels.

On the basis of his research Professor Nye concluded that reconstructed families (including a stepparent), or partial families (composed of one parent and children), did better than unhappy but intact families. 'Failure to perceive the good adjustment both of children and spouses in many broken homes may stem from a concentration upon the tensions and adjustments which occur at the time of the break. After a period of adjustment, a new equilibrium is established, complicated, perhaps, by the necessity for each family member to play new and less clearly defined roles, but largely free of the unbearable conflicts of the previous unhappy marriage. The child is often relieved of a parent unable or unwilling to play the role of parent, and, if the remaining parent remarries, may receive one who can and will play the role satisfactorily.'[23] Consequently, Nye believed that an unhappy marriage might be worse for a child than to be reared by a single understanding parent. He admitted that he had always questioned the assumption that divorce made it more difficult for a child to adjust to life, for he believed that the crucial factor in the child's adjustment was whether the family is a success or failure, and not whether the home is intact.[24]

Research findings, which claimed that children benefited from divorce, soon gained wide acceptance and gave parents the justification they needed to end their marriages. Dr Charles McCormick, a psychologist and member of the New School for Sociological Research, supported this view. He informed a meeting of 'Parents without Partners' that those who sought to preserve an unhappy marriage for the sake of the children were often unaware of the substantial benefits these children would derive from the divorce of their parents. The advantages of divorce were that the children finally knew where they stood. Unhappy parents would no longer bury themselves in the routine of their unhappy marriage, but would be compelled to rethink their lives and seek professional guidance. It was claimed that divorced parents sometimes gained a better working relationship with their children than they had enjoyed when they were married.[25]

The idea that children did not really mind divorce was reinforced in 1973 by a large national survey of 20 thousand high school student leaders across the country. The findings of the survey, widely reported in the press, showed that students accepted divorce as a way of solving the problem of a failing marriage. The survey asked a hypothetical leading question as to whether or not students would seek a divorce if their marriage was not working and other means of solving the problem had failed. According to the survey 71 per cent of students said they would.[26] This survey indicates the way in which divorce as the solution to marriage problems was seen as the prevailing orthodoxy. However the findings were misleading for, as we shall see later, children are almost universally opposed to the divorce of their parents.

Review of the effects of fatherlessness: 1973

In the late 1960s there was growing concern about the welfare of the six million American children living in fatherless homes. The fact that the numbers would probably increase as the divorce rate accelerated, led to a major review of the literature on the effects of fatherlessness on children. The review, undertaken by Elizabeth Herzog and Cecilia Sudia, looked at studies published during the last two decades, plus a few earlier studies. Over four hundred studies were abstracted, but the sixty studies that were the most scientifically rigorous formed the core of the review.[27] The results of the review were published in 1973 under the auspices of the Society for Research in Child Development and funded by the National Institute for Child Health. A concern identified by the reviewers was the frequency of adverse comments about the consequences of father absence. The most frequent comment was that fatherlessness was associated with adverse outcomes, such as juvenile delinquency and extramarital pregnancy.[28] The focus of the review was 'to inquire whether growing up in a fatherless home is likely to interfere with the child's achieving his full potential'. The reviewers claimed that it was important to address this question because there was 'a widespread assumption – held by many social scientists, psychologists, and caseworkers as well as the general public – that the answer is unequivocal and affirmative'.[29]

The review concluded that the available research was 'too confused to permit a definite answer to the question whether children in fatherless homes are more likely than others to engage in delinquent behaviour'.

Moreover the evidence suggested that a 'father's absence in itself is less meaningful than are the climate and tone of the home and the kind of supervision given the child'.[30] The reviewers concluded that the absence of a father probably contributed less to juvenile delinquency than socio-economic factors and community traits. Indeed, delinquent behaviour could not be attributed primarily to a father's absence but rather to stress and conflict within the home.[31]

The reviewers comment that 'in our society the one-parent family has been viewed as a form of un-family or non-family or sick family'.[32] However, there were good reasons why the one-parent family should be recognised as a form that exists and functions, rather than an aberration. One reason was that over six million children lived in fatherless families. Thirteen studies produced evidence that some of the adverse characteristics normally associated with father absence were more common among children of unhappy intact homes than among children of less stressful one-parent homes.[33] Despite the ambiguity of the results, the review concluded 'that there is a firm basis for rejecting blanket generalisations about the conse-quences of father's absence'.[34] Moreover, as the 'evidence indicates that discord and conflict in the home can be more detrimental than father's absence, one is forced to prefer a "good" one-parent home for a child'.[35]

This authoritative review of sociological research had a major impact on the way the one-parent family was viewed. Having reviewed over four hundred scientific papers, the authors' conclusion that there was no clear evidence that children were adversely affected by a father's absence was accepted as a vindication for divorce. It was now possible to argue that children were not adversely affected by divorce, and that some would benefit because discord in the home was more detrimental than a father's absence. Undoubtedly this review provided the 'scientific' basis for the claim that a 'good' divorce was better than a 'bad' marriage. Moreover, it was now widely accepted that there was evidence to prove that it was pointless for a couple to stay together for the sake of their children.

Were the findings and conclusions of the social research valid? As we shall see in chapter 17, there is overwhelming evidence of the harm that divorce causes to children, and nowadays most people accept this obvious truth. How then was it possible for 'scientific' research to come up with conclusions that were so misleading? In trying to understand what happened it is important to understand the strong ideological imperative that lay behind much of the research. Many of the social researchers were ideologi-cally in favour of divorce, and were setting out to prove what they already believed. This meant that research studies were designed and results interpreted in ways that would provide the answers that the researchers were looking for. It is surprising how little critical comment there was of this research. Clearly the findings fitted the prevailing ideology of the time.

For those who were promoting divorce as the remedy for unhappy marriages this review was a godsend. The message was clear. Parents had a responsibility towards their children to terminate their unhappy marriages. Divorce was a means of rescuing children from conflict and allowing them a second chance of finding a happy home. Those parents who were divorcing were actually doing their children a good turn and should no longer feel guilty. The message was taken up and spread far and wide by those who were ideologically opposed to marriage. In *Must Divorce Hurt Children?* Ruth Inglis observes, 'The "Don't stay together for the sake of the children" faction was vociferous and campaigning. It was composed of feminists, successful lone parents and radicals who detected sickness in the nuclear family and future health in the new forms of extended family structure that divorce brings.'[36] Some in the mass media felt that they had a public duty to correct the false view that parents should stay together for the sake of their children and so eagerly spread the new orthodoxy. Within a very short space of time the perception of society had changed to accept that parents should divorce for the sake of their children.

In *Divorce – the American Experience* Joseph Epstein observed how ready society was to receive the new wisdom. 'Once upon a time – and not so very long ago at that – people who had a bad marriage often stayed together "for the sake of the children". Today people who have a bad marriage could well as often bust up their marriage "for the sake of the children". Psychologists, marriage counsellors, clergymen (excluding Roman Catholics), lay people, everyone in fact seems to have fallen in step with the new conventional wisdom on the subject of divorce and children. This wisdom holds that a divorce is preferable to bringing up children in a loveless home; that, in other words, a broken home is psychologically healthier for children than a damaged one.'[37]

THE WOMEN'S MOVEMENT

In the second half of the 19th century Mrs Elizabeth Cady Stanton had been a powerful advocate for women's right to easy divorce. In the 1960s feminists were again crusading for divorce liberalisation. An impetus for the growth of contemporary feminism came from the writing of Betty Friedan. She was a psychology graduate who married in 1947 and had three children. She was divorced in 1969 after being married for 22 years. A recent biography claims that while Friedan was unhappy in her marriage, her problems were almost entirely in her own imagination. Worried about her plain looks she was convinced that her husband had a roving eye, and this made her jealous of pretty women.[38] Dissatisfaction with her role as housewife and mother prompted her to write *The Feminine Mystique*, which was published in 1963.[39] The message of her book undoubtedly struck a chord with women, and by 1970 it had sold more than a million copies in the USA and Britain. Excerpts from the book published in popular magazines brought the message to millions more women. According to Rosalind Miles writing in her *Women's History of the World,* 'Friedan's achievement lay in blasting to smithereens the myth of the happy housewife. She thus made it possible for women to break the candy bars of their imprisonment within the domestic sphere and share with one another their frustration and their rage.'[40] A Los Angles lawyer remembered the effect: '*The Feminine Mystique* caused so many divorces you wouldn't believe it.'[41] A feature of the growing divorce numbers was the large proportion initiated by women. During the 1970s the numbers of wives who ran away from the marital home increased dramatically, prompting the President of Tracers Company America to attribute part of the increase to the women's movement. 'Wives usually take off as a declaration of discontent and a lack of personal fulfilment, and with the encouragement of the women's lib movement.'[42]

The world's first conference on marriage and divorce, sponsored by the National Organisation for Women, brought together over a thousand women from every field of endeavour. Women judges, lawyers, legislators, psychiatrists, sociologists and others gathered together because of concern about the divorce situation. The conference was told that women had three main demands. First, they wanted more women judges and lawyers; second, they wanted a uniform divorce law throughout the country so that husbands could not run out on obligations simply by leaving one state; and third, they wanted compulsory disclosure of a husband's finances and enforcement of support awards. 'The dramatic highpoint of the conference came on Saturday when seven women, dressed in white masks (to shield identity) and white choir robes, told about their marriages and divorces. With quivering voices and choking back tears, they told of ex-husbands who earned high salaries but refused to pay alimony or child support; of lawyers who charged outrageous fees; of boorish judges and of long, long court delays, during which time the women's savings were drained and they had to go on welfare.'[43]

A man who attended the conference was astounded at the hostility towards men. 'I never realised before that they had this tremendous anger towards us.' A workshop on marriage concluded with only two out of 175 women saying that they wanted to continue in a traditional marriage. Many opted for alternative lifestyles like living in a commune, lesbianism, and open marriage or raising children as a single parent. The mother of modern feminism, Betty Friedan, made the final conference speech. 'If there's anything that makes a feminist it is growing up and believing that love and marriage will take care of anything, and then one day waking up at 30 or 40 or 50 and facing the world alone and facing the responsibility of caring for children alone. If divorce has increased by a thousand per cent, don't blame the women's movement, blame the obsolete sex roles on which our marriages were based.'[44]

An essential part of the feminist message was that divorce provided independence from the oppressive grasp of men. True liberation for divorced women meant that they needed to be financially independent of their ex-husbands and so the alimony question was seen as a major obstacle in the way of real emancipation. Consequently, there was a majority of feminists who were opposed in principle to alimony following divorce. Joseph Epstein comments, 'As a collectivity women's liberationists are opposed to the principle of alimony – a principle, as they see it, thoroughly bound up with what they construe to be the rolled-out notion of wives as the property of their husbands. In this view, alimony is scarcely more than a continuation of this property relationship even after marriage, and hence doubly despicable.'[45]

Some in the women's movement seemed to have had second thoughts about the wisdom of this strategy. An advisor of the National Organisation for Women said at a seminar that people did not realise what was happening. 'The idea that women are going to be able to go out and support themselves somewhat in the style to which they were accustomed has been an unfortunate myth. I've been working on the correlation between welfare and the liberalisation of the divorce laws, and what is happening is that there has been a great epidemic of divorces, and the judicial system hasn't been geared to cope. The courts have been dumping women on the welfare system, because they don't have the mechanism to enforce their support orders, and the orders aren't adequate anyway. We've been following a policy of instant happiness, and it isn't working.'[46]

Meanwhile divorced men responded to the injustices they saw in the law, which they felt was heavily stacked against them, by forming groups to fight for the rights of divorced fathers. More than 80 such groups across the United States and Canada argued that in the majority of divorces the fathers were deprived of a voice in deciding their children's schooling, religious training or choice of occupation. They also felt that the courts were biased against men, and unduly sympathetic to the needs of their wives. The president of Fathers United for Equal Rights of New York said, 'In the past women have been seen as the victims of divorce and the men as the instigators. This has meant that after the divorce men have been punished by losing their rights to their children. They have been forced to become mere visitors. Many of them complain of feeling like Bozo the clown whose only function is to entertain the children.'[47] Visitation was another area of contention. Fathers wanted the courts to enforce their visitation rights, as they claimed many ex-wives were not allowing them to see their children. Another issue that really upset the fathers was supporting their ex-wife's boyfriend in the marital home. 'The fathers object to supporting another man in the house they built and owned. In most cases, the wife's live-in boyfriend sees more of the children than the father does. Only in extreme cases where the boyfriend is beating the child or otherwise mistreating him do the courts take action.'[48]

In *The Silent Revolution* Herbert Jacob observes that the rhetoric of the feminist movement had an enormous impact on the way in which many Americans viewed the ideal family structure. 'Talk of marriage as a contract between equals became more common and undermined the traditional view of marriage as a special relationship in which the husband dominated by natural right. The new marriage bond between equals had many consequences, including justifying a wife's claim to retain her maiden name, her choice of where she would live, and her right to decide whether she would work outside the home. Feminist rhetoric about marriage as a partnership of equals also helped undermine conventional task assignments within the family according to gender.' Feminist ideas meant that men had to share household chores and child care, and encouraged women to think of themselves as financially independent of their husbands.[49]

PSYCHOTHERAPEUTIC DIVORCE

In the American mind, armed with reassurances from sociological research, mass divorce ceased to be a problem and became, instead, a valuable resource, which offered people freedom from unhappy and restrictive marriages. Psychological theory introduced the idea that marriage, divorce and remarriage might be a better way of life than the traditional Christian ideal of marriage until death. A 'good' divorce offered opportunities for inner renewal and self-expression. Americans were invited to open their minds to the possibility that divorce may be a creative rather than a destructive act, and that it may be a better choice for all concerned, including the children.

Writing in *Divorce as a Development Process,* Judith Gold made the point that divorce, although usually destructive and traumatic, could be a catalyst that eventually resulted in positive growth for the individual. Indeed, further personal development may not occur if the marriage remained intact. 'For men, women and children involved, divorce, so common today—indeed so familiar, can be used to catalyse constructive individual psychological development.'[50]

A consequence of the enormous emphasis on psychological well-being was that people started to believe that they should feel good all the time, and when they did not then someone, often their spouse, was to blame for stunting their psychological growth. The effect on commitment to marriage was catastrophic; couples were led to believe that they should feel committed to their marriage only so long as it provided the 'feel good' factor, with ample scope for psychological growth. Failure to achieve psychological growth meant that the marriage was to blame and should be brought to an end. Psychotherapists were accepted as experts who offered advice to those in unhappy marriages.

Their advice was characterised by a non-judgemental approach that claimed to take a morally neutral stand, although many therapists were ideologically in favour of easy divorce. Unhappy individuals would be told the potential benefits of being freed from a restrictive, stifling marriage. Ministers of religion, who were uncertain how to advise those who were seeking divorce, were captivated by the psychological approach. According to the analysis of Barbara Whitehead in *The Divorce Culture*, 'Mainline religious denominations led the procession into psychotherapy. Pastoral counselling began to take a client-centred approach that required clergy to stay within the client's "value system"… Unlike the mainliners, evangelicals tended to use psychology to support traditional religious teaching on marriage and the family, although over time they too came to view marital dissolution in more psychological terms.'[51]

Increasingly the Christian view of marriage became submerged in psychological theory. The old-fashioned biblical view of marriage was almost embarrassing, and certainly no longer relevant in contemporary society that had access to the latest offerings of psychotherapy. Moreover, the Protestant mind had for a long time been favourably disposed to the idea that the essence of marriage was psychological compatibility. We saw in chapter 3 how the Protestant reformer Martin Bucer argued for a form of marriage where companionship and the emotional love between husband and wife were its primary purpose. When the emotional relationship broke down then 'there is no true marriage' and divorce is the remedy. The happiness and emotional satisfaction of individuals is paramount. Psychotherapists were supposed to be the experts in identifying psychological incompatibility, so they knew when a marriage had ceased to be a 'true marriage', and were able to help the couple separate with the least trauma and even to achieve a 'good divorce'.

Protestant Christianity felt comfortable with the values of psychotherapy and was happy to collaborate with it. Pastors would undoubtedly do their best for couples who were psychologically incompatible, but having no clear biblical advice to offer, they were relieved to be able to rely on psychotherapy for help. Christian pastors became careful not to give judgemental advice that might cause psychological damage to unhappy couples.

It followed that those seeking the psychological benefits of divorce should be aided in their effort to make the break. The feeling was that trying to save crumbling marriages at all costs was an archaic belief that had no place in a modern world. 'Marriage counsellors and psychotherapists,' wrote Morton Hunt in the *New York Times* as early as 1967, 'have been adopting the view that where a marriage seems unlikely ever to become satisfying and reasonably free of conflicts, it is proper to help the client get out of it… Divorce counsellors would be the surgeons of marriage, wielding the knife when necessary, but managing the operation so as to minimise the damage, speed the convalescence, and maximise the chance of the patient's full health.'[52] Morton Hunt went on to remind the readers that those who believe that they should 'stay together for the sake of the children' are mistaken, because the evidence gathered by social psychologists pointed in exactly the opposite direction. According to the evidence, children, however distressed they may be at the time of the break-up of the home, are in the long run less damaged by the divorce than they would have been if their parents had remained together. In Hunt's opinion, divorce counselling would 'avoid much of the misery involved in the actual break-up, shorten the interregnum between the old love and the new, and maximise the chances of success in the second marriage'.[53]

An example of this view is a divorced mother of two who explains why she went through with a divorce. 'In considering the divorce, I thought of my survival, rather than: What am I doing? How could I do this to win? When I went to a shrink, I began to break out of old things. He (her husband) was one of the old things I broke out of. I started dating and felt young again. I got a divorce because I felt it was the only way I could expand and grow as a person.'[54]

Practising clinical psychologist, Dr Lee Salk, who had himself experienced the trauma of divorce, gave his views in *What every Child would like Parents to Know about Divorce* (1978). He explained that divorce, just like marriage, was a development stage in life. Marriages fail for any number of reasons, many of them good reasons for ending a relationship.[55] He believed that as long as two people found contentment built around a happy relationship, they were willing to keep things the way they were. But when this feeling changed because the relationship was frustrating and no longer conducive to happiness, productiveness, and the satisfactory nurturing of the children, then he saw nothing wrong with dissolving the marriage. 'It is not for me to decide whether it is right or wrong for a particular relationship to come apart, but if it does as a result of a "growth process" there need be no lingering over the remains. One can and should learn from the past, but the important thing is to channel one's energies toward the mobilisation of resources so that the next stage in growth can take place. And it will.'[56] Dr Salk claimed that many adult patients told him that they couldn't wait to leave home because of family tensions or the absence of spontaneous affection between their parents. Over and over again his patients had said, 'I wish my parents had divorced and found happiness in another relationship.' Other patients whose parents had been divorced admitted that it was difficult for a while, but in the long run, they were all better off.[57]

NO-FAULT DIVORCE

During the 1960s the legal profession and some state legislatures were becoming increasingly aware of the problems inherent in the divorce laws.

Respect for the divorce laws and procedures had declined. Commenting on the woeful state of the divorce laws, Joseph Epstein points out that the contradictions and casual hypocrisy of American divorce laws goes well beyond the mere liberal interpretation of grounds or easy access to migratory divorce. 'They go beyond and they cut deep, affecting the majority of American divorces. No one state of the United States allows divorce by consent, yet in fact the greatest number of American divorces are precisely that – consent divorces dressed up to appear to be cases of divorce for marital misconduct.' A married couple who wants a divorce is often thrown back on invention. 'If they want the divorce, they must invent grounds, hoke up something the court will accept. One or other of them, then, has to take the fall, to be the patsy, to be for form's sake the guilty party.'[58]

But the need to regulate divorce had disappeared, as most Americans now believed that they had the right to get out of an unhappy marriage, and that it was unhelpful to continue the pretence of a link between divorce and marital offences. Many divorcing couples were outraged at the thought that they had to go before a court and swear that the one marriage partner was at fault. Moreover, the divorce laws had fallen into disrepute for most couples who wanted to obtain a divorce had been able to find a way around the laws. For example, many couples exaggerated or lied outright about the reasons for seeking divorce. The law had long been a legal scandal as lawyers and courts found ways and means of using it in a way that allowed couples to get what they wanted. Those who had mutually agreed to divorce were able to do so by producing evidence that a marital offence had occurred. In fact, divorce on demand had, in practice, been available for a long time.

The main argument advanced by those who supported no-fault divorce was that it made the process easier and less acrimonious, and that it was better for the children not to see their parents involved in a legal battle to end the marriage. Mary Ann Glendon describes how in America the no-fault idea blended readily with the psychological jargon that strongly influenced what people thought about their personal relationships. 'It began to carry the suggestion that no one is ever to blame when a marriage ends: marriages just break down sometimes, people grow apart, and when this happens even parents have a right to pursue their own happiness... Above all, one is not supposed to be "judgemental" about the behaviour and opinions of others.' She also points out that the psychotherapy ideology not only refuses to take a moral stand, it actively promotes distrust of morality.[59]

California was the first state to embrace the concept of no-fault divorce. A law commission appointed by the Governor of California accepted that divorce was justified when marriage had broken down. Publication in 1966 of the Church of England's report *Putting Asunder* gave strong moral support to California's no-fault proposals.[60] Lawyers working on divorce reform felt passionately about the bitterness engendered by the current adversarial divorce process, and felt that much of the conflict they saw in the courtroom would be eliminated by removing the need for one party to provide proof of the grounds for divorce. Their aim was to eliminate the need for one party to perjure themselves in providing evidence to the court, and to make the divorce more humane. The Californian no-fault divorce bill, signed into law by Governor Ronald Reagan, came into effect in 1970. It abolished all grounds of fault and permitted divorce for irreconcilable differences that had caused the irremediable breakdown of the marriage or for incurable insanity.

The main purpose of no-fault divorce was to make a clean break possible. After a divorce there would be no continuing obligation between the spouses. Following the division of the assets of the marriage, support would be provided according to need and only for as long as it took for the dependent spouse, usually the wife, to make herself financially independent by finding employment. Once no-fault divorce was successfully established in California, and with no controversy, many states followed and by the 1980s the majority of states had such a legal provision for divorce. Significantly the Church was silent, offering no opposition to the introduction of no-fault divorce.

A difficulty with the no-fault divorce concept was that it allowed one partner in the marriage to unilaterally divorce the other partner against their will. In other words, a marriage would be finished if one spouse wanted to end it. Either spouse has the right to end the marriage whenever they choose to do so, and without reference to the other partner of the marriage. A husband who is having an affair with his secretary, for example, can decide that he no longer desires to be married, and obtain a legal no-fault divorce to marry his new girlfriend, despite the objections of his wife and children. Another feature of the American scene was the do-it-yourself divorce trend, especially in California, where up to a fifth of divorces were done without the help of a lawyer. Newspapers and popular magazines carried advertisements for easy do-it-yourself divorce kits that contained all the legal forms for handling a divorce without the aid of a lawyer, and cost less than $100. The book *How to do your own Divorce in California* proved a best seller.[61]

ROMAN CATHOLIC USE OF ANNULMENTS

Another disturbing feature of the American scene has been the Catholic Church's increasing use of annulments. We saw, in the previous chapter, how in the 19th century the Catholic Church, true to its doctrinal position, boldly witnessed to the lifelong nature of marriage. Cardinal Gibbons was outspoken in his defence of marriage as an indissoluble bond, and referred to divorce as the deadly enemy of marriage. The Catholic Church stood firm on its teaching that marriage is a lifelong union, despite the growing support for divorce among Protestant denominations.

But the last quarter of the 20th century has seen a remarkable transformation in the attitude of the Roman Catholic Church towards marriage, as it has increasingly used annulments to end long-standing marriages. In the 1960s annulments were relatively uncommon and in 1968, for example, the Catholic Church granted around 500 annulments. A massive increase in the granting of annulments occurred during the 1970s; in the ten-year period between 1984 and 1993 church tribunals granted over 500 thousand annulments.[62] So great is the use of the annulments by the American Church that in the 1990s the United States, which accounts for 6 per cent of the world's Catholics, was responsible for three-quarters of all annulments worldwide.[63] Indeed, so great is the use of annulments that it appears that the Church no longer believes in the permanence of the marriage bond, and has, therefore, *de facto* changed its doctrinal position on marriage.

In his book *What God Has Joined Together* (1998) Robert H Vasoli discusses the factors responsible for the crisis in American Catholicism. He argues that the annulment mentality and the divorce mentality are kindred states of mind, which together pose a grave threat to the well-being and integrity of the family.[64] He refers to a 'new pastoralism' in the Church, heavily based on psychological premises which has influenced the outlook on annulments. Psychological thought supports the contention that to deny annulments would be unpastoral, hardhearted and punitive.[65] Vasoli asserts that canon 1095, which he believes to be one of the most controversial statutes in the history of canon law, is responsible for the growing tendency to grant annulments for defective consent. According to this canon, individuals incapable of contracting a valid marriage are 'those who, because of causes of a psychological nature are unable to assume the essential obligations of marriage'.[66] Guided by canon 1095, and using the latest psychological theories, annulment tribunals have shown great ingenuity in creating defective consent scenarios. Vasoli stresses the role of psychology in enabling tribunals to claim apparent scientific grounds for their discovery of a previously undetected phenomenon; namely, the large number of cases of defective consent among those desiring annulments.[67] Unsurprisingly, defective consent, uncovered by a psychological assessment of the marriage, is the most common ground for annulment.

Vasoli concludes that the tribunal system is dedicated to expediting nullity, and refers to a well-oiled canonical assembly line which is geared to providing apparent ecclesiastical and juridical legitimacy for divorce and remarriage.[68] He argues that by relaxing its standards for nullity, the American Catholic Church has ceded the moral high ground on marriage and divorce that it has held since the first Catholic colonists set foot on the shores of Chesapeake Bay. In his view, the American Church is retreating from its historical role as society's guardian of the sanctity and permanence of marriage. 'Instead of being Christian marriage's last line of defence, this once-formidable redoubt has grown porous, made irresolute by actions of its own tribunals and the silence of its bishops. Devout old-line Catholics refer to easy annulments as an incomprehensible abomination, contrary to practically everything they were taught.'[69] Vasoli claims that the damage inflicted on Christian marriage by the American tribunal system's gamesmanship with marital consent is incalculable. Christian marriage is being threatened with destruction and the threat is systematic and real.[70]

What is particularly alarming about the American Catholic Church's use of annulments is the obvious dishonesty and hypocrisy of the procedure. It is surely dishonest for the Church to declare that the marriage of a couple who have taken their vows in church, in the presence of God, and before witnesses, and whose marriage has endured for many years and has produced children, is no marriage. Everybody knows that the couple is married, that they have lived together as husband and wife, and have been father and mother to their children. To declare that they have never been married is not only nonsense, it is dishonest. How is it possible to declare that a marriage that has borne children has never been a marriage? What are the children involved to believe of such a Church? At least divorce acknowledges that a couple were married.

The hypocrisy of the American Catholic Church lies in the fact that it is not prepared to declare openly that it has changed its mind and no longer believes in the indissolubility of the marriage bond. And so while it goes on paying lip service to its traditional teaching on marriage, in practice it has introduced a system of annulments that effectively supports the American culture of mass divorce and remarriage. It has not had the courage of its convictions to declare openly that it has changed its doctrinal position on marriage, divorce and remarriage.

FRUITS OF THE PROTESTANT DOCTRINE OF DIVORCE

The American experience stands as a monument to the Protestant doctrine of divorce. The divorce story is an illustration of the powerful influence that ideas have on the history of a nation. From the beginning of its history, the American Christian consensus had rejected the traditional biblical view that marriage is an indissoluble union, Luther's statement that marriage is a worldly thing was readily embraced by American thought which placed great stress on the secular nature of marriage and discarded any sacramental or religious notion—the idea of a divine component was rejected as a popish plot. Marriage was a purely human contract. As previously shown, Protestant teaching laid great emphasis on the secular nature of marriage, and for a time even forbade the celebration of marriage in church. A man and woman when they married agreed to a secular contract that was usually intended to be a lifelong relationship, but commitment to the marriage was, by its very nature relative, for it depended on neither partner committing a marital offence. As a result of Protestant teaching the traditional Christian understanding of marriage disappeared and America was left with a low, secular view of marriage.

Constructing a utopian view of marriage upon the foundation of Protestant teaching seemed quite natural for secular thought. Utopian secularism saw 'true' marriage based on romantic love as the perfect union of a man and woman that fulfilled the needs of both. The purpose of marriage was the happiness of the individuals, and 'true' marriage made both partners happy and content. When the partners were no longer in love, marriage was meaningless and divorce became a duty. Nevertheless, this was no bad thing, for divorce offered opportunities for psychological growth and further chances of happiness. This view of marriage was highly susceptible to attacks from feminist ideology, which portrayed marriage as a battlefield in the power struggle between the sexes. Because men were in a position of power in the relationship, they were able to exploit women. Women lacked the economic resources to escape and were often trapped in loveless marriages. Feminists saw this as an outrage that the right to easy divorce could alleviate.

Slowly but surely the concept of secular marriage gained widespread acceptance in the American mentality, and in the eyes of most people marriage was seen as little more than a temporary contract that is terminable at the convenience of either party. This low, secular, view of marriage was both idealistic and trivial, and provided the fertile soil of the divorce culture that has gripped America. The Christian consensus in America was adamant that divorce should be available for those in unhappy marriages. Protestant theology insisted that Christ had allowed marriage to be dissolved for offences such as adultery and desertion, among other things. As there was no question about the legitimacy of divorce, it was simply a matter of identifying the right grounds.

So divorce was seen as the means of cleansing society from the evil of broken marriages. Mr Walter George Smith, Chairman of the National Congress of Divorce of 1906, explained the history of divorce in the USA. 'The changed attitude towards marriage, brought into the religious beliefs of many European peoples by the leaders of the religious revolt of the 16th century, bore fruit in divorce legislation. Since the opinion of the leaders of Puritan thought did not differ essentially from that of Milton, that marriage was entirely devoid of sacramental character, divorce seemed under certain circumstances entirely responsible… While Protestant Christianity had given up the sacramental view of marriage, it retained in practice the same respect, or rather reverence, for marriage as all bodies of Christians have always entertained.' He made the point that 'within a generation, however, this portentous revolution in the attitude of men and women towards the most important status of social life has been gathering force, and probably for the first time since Christianity came into general acceptance among civilised peoples, a school of sociological teachers had the courage to come out and frankly accept the logical consequences of the proposition, so often asserted in the past, that marriage is a civil contract only.'[71]

The result of three and half centuries of Protestant thought was that America became the nation with the most liberal divorce laws in the world, with more divorces than any other country, except Japan. Once Protestant teaching had opened the gateway to divorce upon so-called 'scriptural grounds' it was inevitable that human nature would demand divorce for any and every reason. Almost all the reasons for divorce developed by American legislatures had already been identified as legitimate grounds by the reformers. There is little doubt that Luther, Calvin, Zwingli, Bucer and Milton would have approved of the grounds for divorce in America. The Protestant position, founded on sociological principles, had no difficulty in accepting the arguments provided by sociology that divorce was necessary for the good of society.

At the beginning of the 20th century Bishop Doane, alarmed at the growth of divorce, expressed the opinion that America had gained a shameful and sorrowful pre-eminence in what he called 'the divorce habit'. He expressed some optimism that the public conscience was being stirred and hoped that the door to mass divorce would be closed in America. Unfortunately, his optimism was misplaced. At the beginning of the 1970s the divorce rate escalated at an alarming pace and by 1975 annual divorce numbers reached one million for the first time. Each year since then over one million American marriages have been ended by divorce. The Protestant doctrine of divorce is bearing its fruit in the fertile soil of American secular marriage. The Protestant revolt against the traditional teaching of the Church on the indissolubility of marriage has run its course and the results are obvious to all who have eyes to see.

Chapter 14

The causes of mass divorce

The role of sociology, psychology, feminism and the decline of Christian teaching

---

Having traced the pathway to mass divorce in England and America we must try and understand the underlying causes. Many of the debates and arguments that we have examined provide clues to the most important factors. We have seen bitter disagreement as some have argued that divorce was necessary to allow a chance of future happiness. Sociologists have declared that divorce is a legitimate response to the oppression of the patriarchal family, and psychologists have claimed that divorce offers the opportunity for inner growth. Feminists assert that it provides freedom from repressive marriages. Nevertheless, the reasons for mass divorce are complex because human behaviour and human motives are difficult to understand. There is no doubt that many factors have influenced the growth of mass divorce in England and America.

CHANGES IN LEGISLATION

The progressive liberalisation of divorce laws is certainly one factor that has contributed to the development of mass divorce in England. Those who opposed the Divorce Reform Act of 1857 predicted that once the indissolubility of marriage was breached, it would be the first step in a process that would lead eventually to widespread divorce. They argued that legalisation would whet the appetite for more divorce, and so the demand for changes in the law would become incessant and irresistible. Furthermore they predicted that each extension of the grounds would increase the number of divorces. They also pointed to the educative effect of legalisation and argued that it would change the way society viewed marriage. Once the idea of indissolubility was destroyed, society would regard marriage as a contract that could be terminated to suit human convenience. Couples would reason that if their marriage was not satisfactory, they were not bound for life but had an opportunity, supported by the law, for a second chance of success.

Opponents to the legalisation of divorce have been proved correct in their predictions. In our study of divorce in England we saw how each move to more liberal laws was followed by an increase in the divorce rate. While it is debatable to what degree legislation followed, rather than set, public opinion, every change in the law was accompanied by a substantial increase in numbers. The original Divorce Act of 1857, instead of producing around 20 divorces per year as predicted by the promoters, resulted in many hundreds. After the grounds for divorce were extended in the Act of 1937 to include desertion, cruelty and insanity, the numbers more than doubled. The introduction of irretrievable breakdown as a ground in 1969 was followed immediately by a large rise in numbers. These changes are shown graphically in earlier chapters.

American divorce laws, among the most liberal in the world, undoubtedly influenced the way society thought about divorce. The states with the most liberal laws had the highest rates of divorce. The introduction of more liberal laws after the American War of Independence contributed to a level of divorce that was much higher than in 19th century England. High rates in America at the beginning of the 20th century were due not to the number of real hardships, to the number of cruel husbands or malicious wives, but to the fact that the law, which had opened wide the door for cases of desertion and cruelty, allowed multitudes of people to achieve divorce on demand.[1] In other words, the enormous differential in rates between England and the United States at the turn of the 20th century was due not to the waywardness of American husbands and wives, but to the liberal American laws which provided the opportunity for divorce.

DIVORCE AND SOCIAL FACTORS

Various explanations have been advanced for the rise in divorce, including the increasing employment of married women, the rise of feminist ideology, shifts in sexual morality and changes in attitudes towards marriage and divorce.[2] According to the 1956 Royal Commission, the employment of women during the second half of the 20th century was associated with the increase in divorce numbers. As more women obtained paid employment, they became less afraid of the economic consequences of marriage breakdown. The economic independence of working women made divorce an option that was not available to them before.[3]

In Great Britain state funding of the legal costs brought divorce within the reach of the poorest sections of society. The liberalisation of legal aid in

1949 made divorce more widely accessible and meant that over half the petitions were state funded. The welfare state, which provides financial support for divorced mothers, reduced the dependence of women on the financial support of their husbands. Much of public welfare policy is geared towards providing financial assistance for single women and their children. In many ways the welfare state has taken over the provider role of the man, becoming a surrogate husband and father. The net effect is that some women depend for their income, not upon the father of their children, but upon welfare benefits.

It seems likely that the liberalisation of divorce laws has also contributed to a change in public perception that helped to reduce the stigma attached to divorce. Changes in divorce legislation condoned behaviour that had in the past been considered socially unacceptable. In the debates on divorce, several bishops drew attention to the role of the law in setting standards of public behaviour. While the law withheld divorce, the public accepted that it was wrong, and this negative connotation had a strong restraining influence. When divorce was legalised, the public revulsion against divorce diminished as many came to believe that it was morally acceptable. Changes in the law were associated with changes in the moral climate that made people more tolerant of divorce. The well-publicised divorces of many prominent people, including royalty, leading politicians and popular media personalities helped to produce a climate of tolerance. Moreover, coverage in newspapers, women's magazines, television and films presented divorce in a positive way. On television it has become the subject of light entertainment, and Hollywood comedies present divorce as a laughing matter.

THE SOCIOLOGICAL JUSTIFICATION FOR DIVORCE

For centuries Western Christendom believed that marriage was a divine institution. The Bible laid down the rules for marriage and all the arguments to permit divorce had to contend with biblical truth. In the English parliamentary debates we saw how the Christian view provided a powerful moral obstacle to the legalisation of divorce. For divorce to gain wide public acceptance and develop into a mass movement, the biblical view of marriage as a divine institution needed to be discredited. That is, marriage needed to be secularised, and debate about divorce removed from the arena of biblical morality. Sociological theories played an important role in removing the divorce issue from the domain of Christian teaching.

The great contribution of the social sciences to the divorce movement was to undermine the link between marriage and the family. Sociological researchers made the remarkable discovery that the conventional family of father, mother and children was only one of a number of equally valid family setups. According to their observations there are at least seven quite distinct family types in Western culture, including husband and wife families, single-parent families, changing families, blended families, single-sex families and cohabiting families.[4] Although some of these relationships have nothing to do with marriage, they are portrayed as equally valid family arrangements. From this standpoint it follows that marriage is not necessary for the formation of a family. Indeed, many of the family types identified by the sociologists, such as single-parent families, cohabiting families and same-sex families, exist without marriage. It therefore follows that divorce does not break a family but creates, instead, a single-parent family, and, in the event of remarriage leads to the formation of a reconstituted family. It is claimed that this is no bad thing, for different family types are useful for offering a variety of lifestyle choices that suit different people.

Many influential sociologists have concluded that the traditional family is a major cause of social problems. Academic sociology has described the traditional family as a place of male dominance, oppression of women and denial of children's freedom and individuality.[5] Indeed, the reality of the nuclear family provides a disturbing picture of the exploitation of women and abuse of children. Describing the traditional family of husband and wife as a patriarchal arrangement and a potential cause of women's oppression was another important discovery of the social sciences. Because the family is a potential cause of social problems, divorce is a useful remedy to free couples from unhealthy family situations. So in sociological terminology, divorce becomes the solution for the social problems caused by the patriarchal family. It is not surprising that sociological research produced the 'evidence' that children benefited from divorce.

Sociology successfully removed divorce from the moral arena by presenting it as a pragmatic solution to a social problem. Sociologists derided the idea that divorce had a moral dimension as old-fashioned, superstitious nonsense. Moreover, those who held such views had no right to impose their moral beliefs on other people. They should keep their views to themselves, and not disturb the consciences of others with their outdated morality. The social scientists had provided the evidence of the damage caused by failed marriages, and the message was clear. Marriage is simply one lifestyle choice that suits some people, although potentially dangerous in that it often leads to male domination and exploitation. Divorce is a useful resource for liberating women and children from unsuitable family arrangements.

The sociological views described above can be read in any standard textbook, and are taught to students in colleges and universities. Many Christians have modified their views to take account of the 'evidence' provided by sociological research. Consequently, much of what goes for Christian teaching is an accretion of sociological theory with some biblical texts. Politically correct sociological theories have become the new orthodoxy on family and marriage, replacing the biblical view that held sway in the last century.

The Archbishop of Canterbury (Arthur Ramsey) in his speech in the House of Lords in 1963 acknowledged the influence of sociological thought when he promised that the Church would examine divorce from a sociological perspective.[6] The unthinkable occurred when the Church of England accepted that the theories of sociology, and not the Scriptures, should form the basis for divorce legalisation in England. The Church of England report *Putting Asunder*, discussed in chapter 10, was based on sociological principles and helped open the gateway to mass divorce.

THE PSYCHOLOGICAL JUSTIFICATION FOR DIVORCE

Another major incentive to divorce has come from the teachings of modern psychology. The growth of psychotherapy in the second half of the 20th century has had a major impact on the way people view their marriages. According to psychological theory, marriage should be a relationship which provides opportunities for inner growth and happiness. The focus is on achieving personal fulfilment. Psychotherapy teaches people to focus on their own needs to the exclusion of others, even those of their marriage partner and children. Selfish needs and desires become the centre of an individual's existence, and any idea of duty to other people is anathema. Marriage, because of its restrictive nature, can be a major obstacle to achieving these psychological aims. It follows that when a marriage no longer provides opportunities for inner growth, and becomes an obstacle to an individual's needs, wants, desires and happiness, then it should be ended. Divorce is a resource which protects women from exploitative marriages, offering them opportunities for developing inner strength and psychological growth.

It is not difficult to see how damaging this approach is to marriage. It places personal desires and personal happiness at the centre of life. It denies all reference to moral standards and contradicts Christian teaching that we should consider the interests of other people above our own, and that self-denial, self-discipline and self-control are virtues for which we should strive. Predictably, those who are influenced by this way of thinking place their marriages in great danger. Women in particular have been influenced by the false teachings of psychotherapy. They have been persuaded that when they no longer feel good about their marriages, when they no longer love their husbands, they should consider the opportunities offered by divorce. The falseness of this view becomes easily apparent when it is tested against the light of biblical teaching. Elevating self to the centre of one's life is a form of idolatry.

Associate professor of psychology, Paul Vitz, describes in his book *Psychology as Religion* (1977) how psychology has virtually become a religion in the United States.[7] Schools, universities and social programmes extensively propagate it, and it is deeply anti-Christian in its views and beliefs. He describes how the idea of psychological 'self-growth' emerged as a value of American society in the 1960s and 70s. Paul Vitz shows how practising psychologists and psychiatrists popularised the ideas developed from the theories of Fromm, Rogers, Maslow and May. They emphasised the human capacity for change almost to the point of totally ignoring the reality that life has limits, largely ignoring the realities of duty, denial, inhibition and restraint. According to Vitz, over the years these psychological theories have been destroying individuals, families and communities.

Paul Vitz argues that the 'concepts and values of selfism are not conducive to the formation and maintenance of permanent personal relationships or to values like duty, patience, and self-sacrifice, which maintain commitment. There is every reason to believe that the spread of the selfist philosophy in society has contributed greatly to the destruction of families. It is certainly no accident that many case histories in selfist literature are people in conflict with their spouses or families over some self-defined goal. With monotonous regularity the selfist literature sides with those values that encourage divorce, breaking up, dissolution of marital or family ties. All of this is done in the name of growth, autonomy, and "continuing the flux".'[8] He claims that the social destructiveness of psychotherapy can be attributed to the characteristics of the therapy process itself, although psychologists assume that personality characteristics are to blame when a client's marriage ends in divorce. The therapist strongly identifies with his patients and takes their side. The therapist's presumption is to believe everything that clients say, and then to help them rationalise their behaviour. The anti-family effect of psychotherapy is compounded by the overwhelming theoretical bias against parents in various schools of psychotherapy.

Much marriage counselling is based on the concepts of psychotherapy and is fundamentally opposed to the Christian view of marriage and the family. Because most counsellors no longer support the traditional concept of marriage, and believe that divorce is a useful resource for liberating women from oppressive marriages, they have replaced the term 'marriage counselling' with 'relationship counselling' or 'divorce counselling'. There is little doubt that the majority of counsellors, who have set themselves up as experts in giving advice to couples experiencing difficulties in their marriage, have tended to be ideologically in favour of divorce as the best solution for women in unhappy marriages. Paul Vitz argues that 'psychotherapists should be liable for their contribution to any marital breakdown which results in great emotional pain for the other partner, since this is, in effect, a form of alienation of affection... No doubt most experienced therapists do not rashly encourage the break-up of marriages, but even the best of them frequently place much more value on their judgement of the patient's well-being than on that of members of the family. Social or religious values of the family usually rank very low, even with experienced therapists.'[9]

The basic flaw of the psychological approach is that it is based on a faulty view of human nature. It takes no account of the sinful nature that the Bible teaches is common to all. Because psychotherapy does not acknowledge the existence of mankind's sinful nature, it has nothing to offer that meets the deepest spiritual needs of mankind. By denying the sinfulness of human beings it is unable to meet the spiritual and moral needs of men and women. It fails to understand that the cause of mankind's dissatisfaction with life lies within the heart of man.

The attempts of psychotherapy to explain away moral failure are counter-productive because they only encourage people to escape from the truth about themselves. To blame the institution of marriage for our unhappiness is an attempt to justify our actions and only compounds the problem. To believe that an escape from marriage will solve human problems, and provide an opportunity for inner psychological growth, is the height of folly.

THE CULTURE OF SELF-GRATIFICATION

Attitudes towards marriage and divorce have been influenced by the profound changes in values and norms that have occurred over the last three or four decades. The 1960s were a time of social revolution when the traditional morals of society came under widespread challenge. There was a desire for liberation from what were perceived as repressive sexual moral laws, and freedom from moral restraint, expressed by the cliché 'free love', became the new norm. This sense of freedom encouraged people to express themselves by throwing off their inhibitions. Self-gratification became the dominant value and people were encouraged to indulge themselves provided that they did not hurt others. In their book, *Growing Up With a Single Parent* (1994), McLanahan and Sandefur express the view that the changes in social norms and values, which occurred during the 1960s, contributed to the growth of single motherhood. They argue that the removal of the stigma attached to divorce and to the birth of children outside marriage made single motherhood more acceptable. The revolution in sexual mores played a major role as it allowed young men and women to live together in a sexual relationship without being married. The authors contend that the ideology that emerged during the 1960s, encouraging people to place personal freedom and self-fulfilment above family commitments, caused them to leave bad marriages if they did not fulfil their expectations.[10]

In her book *The Divorce Culture*, Barbara Whitehead analysed the ideas behind the divorce revolution in America. She argued that ideas about an individual's obligations to family and society changed fundamentally in the late 1950s and 1960s.[11] Formerly the moral obligation that parents felt towards their children had been a major impediment to divorce, as parents placed their children's interests in the marital partnership above their own satisfaction. This notion, however, was swiftly abandoned after the 1960s, when influential voices in society claimed that the key factor determining the welfare of children was the happiness of individual parents, rather than an intact marriage. It followed that if a divorce could make one or both parents happy, a likely result would be an improvement in the well-being of the children.[12] Whitehead provides a detailed analysis of various cultural icons – including examples from children's books, greeting cards, the literature of self-help, etiquette and advice – that illustrated the shift from an ethic of obligation to others to the goal of self-fulfilment.[13] She believes that this ethical shift had a profound impact on thinking about the nature and purpose of the family, that became increasingly viewed as a domain for unfettered self-expression.[14] A divorce became an event closely linked to the pursuit of individual satisfaction and psychological growth. Whitehead insists that divorce has come to be seen not only as an individual right, but also a psychological resource. It provides an opportunity for divorcees to express their inner selves, develop a better self-image and learn psychological techniques such as assertiveness.[15] She is not opposed to all divorce, but rather casual divorce that focuses only on the rights and desires of the parents regardless of the consequences for the children. This book is valuable because it shows how changes in ideas and values have profoundly affected society.

FEMINISM'S ENCOURAGEMENT TO DIVORCE

Feminist ideas have undoubtedly had a major influence on the way society in general, and women in particular, think about marriage, and have encouraged the notion that divorce is a vehicle for women's freedom and independence from male domination. The typical feminist analysis portrays marriage as good for men and bad for women. An example of this way of thinking is contained in an article in the *Sunday Telegraph*, entitled, 'In seven years he'll still be happy – but she'll want a divorce'. Historian Rosalind Miles, who has written several books chronicling the intensifying battle of the sexes, is quoted: 'For women, marital bliss has always been a relatively rare event. The difference now is that there is a way out. In the Middle Ages a woman could retire to a nunnery if she got fed up with her husband... In the Victorian era, there were basically two options: you could go mad or you could become an invalid. Quite a lot of wives took permanently to their beds or were shut up in lunatic asylums. But many women were just waiting for their husbands to die. The prospect of becoming a widow was what kept many wives going. Of course, the liberalisation of the divorce laws has changed that. Now, instead of waiting for a dreadful husband to die off, you can divorce him.'[16] The blunt message is that marriage is bad for women for it makes them unhappy and divorce provides the way out. This way of thinking sees the current divorce rates as a triumph for women who are being liberated from the oppression of the male dominated, patriarchal family.

A milestone in the rise of modern feminism was the publication of *The Second Sex* by Simone de Beauvoir in 1949. The book rapidly became a world best seller, and drew attention to the apparent plight of women. De Beauvoir gives a particularly disturbing account of motherhood, which she described as follows: 'The mother... is the one who waits, submits, complains, weeps, makes scenes: as a victim she is looked down on; as a shrew, detested... Her fate seems the prototype of rapid recurrence; life only repeats itself in her, without going anywhere; firmly set in her role as housekeeper, she puts a stop to the expansion of existence, she becomes obstacle and negation.'[17] This is the pathetic view that the founder of modern feminism had of motherhood. It hardly rings true with the experience of the vast majority of mothers who love their home and children and are willing to make considerable sacrifices for the welfare of their family. De Beauvoir asserted in 1975: 'No woman should be authorised to stay at home and raise her children... Women should not have that choice, precisely because if there is such a choice, too many women will make that one.'[18] With this statement de Beauvoir encapsulated one of the fundamental tenets of feminism, that women should be discouraged from staying at home and encouraged into full-time work in order to become financially independent. That is, to be truly liberated, women need to compete with men in the work place. Those women who choose to remain at home were regarded as traitors to the women's movement.

A further impetus for the growth of contemporary feminism came from the writing of Betty Friedan. The basic thesis of her best selling book, *The Feminine Mystique* (1963), was that women had been brainwashed into seeing the roles of housewife and mother as the only desirable goals.[19] Her diagnosis of the problem facing married women was simply that being a housewife was intrinsically boring. Women who were housewives lost their identity, and their potential was crippled by the roles of wife and mother. Friedan claimed that a woman who evades her own growth by clinging to the childlike protection of the housewife role would suffer increasingly severe pathology, both physiological and emotional.[20] In fact, it was no exaggeration to call the stagnating state of millions of American housewives a sickness; indeed, 'the feminine mystique described a living death for women'.[21] Society needed to understand how the very condition of being a housewife could create a sense of emptiness, non-existence, nothingness in women.[22] She criticised the post-war glorification of motherhood, and called the American home a 'comfortable concentration camp'. She succeeded in making the word housewife a term of derision, and like de Beauvoir, one of her key objectives was to encourage married women out of the home and into the workplace. Friedan wanted freedom for women to work so that they could become economically and psychologically independent of men. So influential was feminist thinking that it added new words to the English language. Betty Friedan coined the term 'sexism'. Feminists objected to the terms Miss or Mrs, which were used to denote a woman's marital status, noting that Mr did not indicate the marital situation of a man. Feminists promoted the designation Ms for all women.[23]

Over the last two decades a veritable army of feminist authors have lined up to discredit the idea that a woman can find fulfilment in life as a wife and mother. A few examples will illustrate the point. Elaine Storkey in her book, *What's Right with Feminism* (1985), admits that the position of women as mothers has been the subject of critical analysis by many feminist writers since the late 1960s.[24] Storkey writes, 'It is the way that the modern conception of motherhood has forced women into isolation, and played down their own needs and their own unique identities which has led many feminist writers to challenge the ethos behind it.'[25] The notion of motherhood as a pleasurable and satisfying experience, which gives meaning and enrichment to a woman's life, has been challenged. According to Storkey there is evidence which shows that for many women motherhood is more a time of conflict, exhaustion, the sense of the years slipping away, isolation and lack of personal identity.[26] In her discussion on the role of wives and mothers, Elaine Storkey writes, 'In making the feminist case in the area of marriage and the family I am aware that many who are reading this will feel that the emphasis has been unreasonably negative.'[27]

In providing a Christian feminist analysis she concluded that men constitute a problem for women because they combine to impose attitudes and values to uphold certain interests in society. She writes, 'Modern marriage can easily be seen as a pattern of convenience which especially suits men. Male attitudes combine with male structures and reinforce the superiority of men. Aggression, pride, self-glorification and selfishness often cohere in the way men treat women.'[28] It is sad that an analysis, which claims to be from a Christian point of view, gives such a negative view of marriage and of men.

The eminent sociologist, Jessie Bernard, published *The Future of Marriage* in 1972.[29] This book was immediately acclaimed as a classic contribution to the literature of marriage and sex roles. Bernard writes, 'Some of the shocks that marriage may produce have to do with the lowering of status that it brings to women. For, despite all the clichés about the high status of marriage, it is for women a downward status step.'[30] In discussing the adjustments that women have to make when they become wives, she insists that the psychological and emotional costs of all these adjustments show up in the increasing unhappiness of wives with the passage of time and in their increasingly negative and passive outlook on life.[31] Bernard informs her readers that some of the changes brought about are subtle. For example, at marriage a woman moves from the status of female to that of neuter being. The decline in sexual attractiveness of women is attributable to their role as wife; when they become mothers this neutralisation is carried even further. These changes contribute to the sad picture of the mental health of married women.[32]

According to Bernard the two major goals of the Women's Liberation Movement are 'better, rather than more, sex, and relief from the entire responsibility for childcare and housekeeping chores…'[33] Again we see the insistence of feminism that the wife and mother should be freed from her home and children. Housekeeping and caring for children is seen as the main obstacle to true liberation. The claim that married women present a sad picture of mental health is simply not true. On the contrary, as we shall see when we examine the research evidence in chapter 18, divorce has a significantly negative effect on the mental health of men and women alike.

The well-known feminist author Germaine Greer, in *The Female Eunuch* (1973), adopted a vehemently anti-marriage position, encouraging married women to consider abandoning their marriage if they were not entirely satisfied with their lot. She wrote, 'If women are to effect a significant amelioration in their condition, it seems obvious that they must refuse to marry. No worker can be required to sign on for life…'[34] In her analysis a wife was little more than a slave. She also insisted 'that women ought not to enter into socially sanctioned relationships, like marriage, and that once unhappily in, they ought not to scruple to run away'.[35] She presented a detailed argument why women are foolish to marry. She scoffed at the idea of marriage for love, for why should love be exclusive? She mocked the idea that marriage provides security, for people change and marital happiness is unlikely to last. She warned married women that 'the average family has not proved to be a very good breeding ground for children'.[36] The plight of mothers is more desperate than that of other women, 'and yet women with children do break free, with or without their offspring'. Greer pointed out that many women 'would shrink at the notion of leaving husband and children, but this is precisely the case in which brutally clear thinking must be undertaken'.[37] She blatantly encouraged women to consider abandoning their marriage, 'rejecting out of hand the deep prejudice against the runaway wife'.[38]

Writing in *The Times*, journalist Polly Toynbee confirms that *The Female Eunuch* changed many women's lives. In her opinion, 'it launched an army of Noras who set out from their doll's houses in search of themselves, abandoning marriage and security. I was at university at the time, but I met women who say they read the book and packed their bags… It might still make many married women weep to see themselves brutally nailed like butterflies on a pin, narrow lives circumscribed by promises never fulfilled, rewards never delivered, engaged in subterfuge and warfare, nagging and complaining, as husband and wife drag one another down into lesser lives in search of a security not worth having.'[39]

In *Unholy Matrimony* (1988), Liz Hodgkinson, a freelance British journalist, author, and frequent contributor to magazines and newspapers, argued that marriage was so bad, for both men and women, that it should be abolished. The purpose of her book is to expose the tyranny of marriage, which she sees as a destroyer of individuality, independence, self-confidence and self-respect for both men and women.[40] She maintains that marriage is so patently a patriarchal institution ordained by men for the supposed benefits of men that it has become an anachronism, irrelevant to our society.[41] The traditional idea of marriage is no more than patriarchalism asserting itself, and reaffirming the superiority of men over women. She writes, 'Within marriage women are liable to become dependent, cringing, manipulative and wily. Men are liable to become bullies, overpowering, dominant and quick to show anger. Marriage tends to bring out the worst in both sexes—dependence and passivity in women, arrogance and aggressiveness in men.'[42]

In her book *Housewife* (1974), Ann Oakley, a mainline British sociologist whose books and papers are widely used in British universities and colleges, calls for an ideological rejection of marriage and the family. She highly disparages the role of housewives, whom she sees as subordinate to men.[43] Housework is demeaning, pathogenic, and directly opposed to the possibility of human self-actualisation. Any woman who expresses contentment with her role as a housewife is guilty of anti-feminism.[44] Oakley also opposes the family. She writes that the family's gift to women is a direct apprenticeship in the housewife's role. 'For this reason, the abolition of the housewife role requires the abolition of the family, and the substitution of more open and variable relationships.' She acknowledges that, 'if the family goes, so, of course does marriage'. Oakley believes that the only way for women to achieve the ideological revolution that they desire is to abolish the housewife's role, and therefore, abolish marriage and the family.[45] But even that is not enough. Women must also teach their daughters not to be housewives.

Comment

These examples are representative of the feminist view of marriage. According to the feminist mind, marriage, motherhood and the family are prime causes of unhappiness for women. Motherhood is portrayed in a negative light, for it is a great burden that women have to bear. It limits a woman's ability to compete with men on an equal basis. Moreover, it is unjust to expect the mother to take the major responsibility of caring for the children. Feminism demands that childcare responsibilities are shared equally between husband and wife, for children should not interfere with a woman's right to find work outside the home. The role of the housewife is portrayed as boring, causing depression and loneliness. It also inhibits a woman's psychological growth. To overcome these disadvantages, married women must be allowed the freedom to go out and work.

Feminists maintain that marriage perpetuates male authority, and they regard the family as an institution that keeps women in a subordinate role. It is remarkable how little feeling feminists seem to have for children. They appear either not to understand, or not to care, that their ideology has profound consequences for children. Feminism fails to accept that children need the love and attention of their mother. They ignore the fact that many mothers have an extremely strong desire to be with their children, and actually want to stay at home and care for them. It appears not to occur to the feminist mind that children benefit from having a mother at home to care for them—or that many mothers do not want to place their children into childcare to be looked after by other women.

While many people regarded the claims of the more radical feminists as nonsense, the constant demand for sexual equality in all spheres of life has struck a chord and had a powerful effect on the way society at large has come to view marriage. The Christian teaching that the husband is the head of the family is anathema to the feminist mind, for it is the foundation of the patriarchal family and the cause of women's subjugation by men. The feminists incessantly demand 'equality' in the marriage relationship, for their aim is to overturn the Christian teaching that the husband is the head of the house. According to feminist rhetoric, the only type of marriage acceptable to women, is one in which there is equality in every respect between the sexes, especially in economic matters. The wife should retain her independence, preferably her name, and be financially independent of her husband. For her to achieve this, it is essential that she compete in the workplace. The feminist view of marriage has become politically correct and changes in social policy support it. It has transformed the meaning of marriage.

FLAWS IN FEMINIST IDEOLOGY

However, the feminist movement has not had it all its own way. An increasing number of commentators have drawn attention to the fundamental flaws in the feminist ideology. In an essay that examines the basic assumptions of feminism, David Ayers shows that it has profound implications for the family, the economy, politics, marriage, child rearing and education.[46] He argues that feminist writers 'tend to support theories and agendas that would eliminate such traditions as full-time mothering and male support of women and children, viewing women who live in such conditions as deceived, oppressed and retrograde'.[47] In discussing the influence of feminist ideology on the family, Ayers concludes that the feminist revolution has made an incredible contribution to the soaring divorce rate. He writes, 'This is to be predicted, given feminists' consistently pessimistic evaluations of marriage. Feminists directly promote eased divorce restrictions, a fact usually ignored in the popular media. Indirectly, the kind of practical, often financial independence fostered in the "new woman" has been consistently linked to a heightened risk of divorce. This is aggravated further by the amazing fact, that after having encouraged easy divorce laws (partly to provide a vehicle of escape from "male oppression") and denigrating the institution of marriage, feminists continually stress the need for women to develop the skills and outlook necessary to be able to provide for families on their own.'[48] Ayers concludes that feminism is destructive because it is grounded in a set of false presuppositions regarding the creative order.[49] This idea is examined in the next chapter on the biblical meaning of marriage.

Mary Kenny, a well-known newspaper columnist, has expressed the following criticism of modern feminism. 'Where I do feel that modern feminism has gone wrong is in downgrading aspects of women's lives which belonged traditionally to a women's world; denigrating motherhood, the home and the family and relegating all vocations within the domestic arts to an inferior status. It is wrong to characterise the family as a merely patriarchal system which has to be thrown off... Enormous damage has been done to the family over the past three decades, and this has hurt women, as well as children, older people and indeed men.'[50]

In an essay that discusses the role of a woman as wife and homemaker, Dorothy Patterson, the wife of a Baptist pastor, draws attention to the falseness of the feminist position. She writes, 'Women have been liberated right out of the genuine freedom they enjoyed for centuries to oversee the home, rear the children, and pursue personal creativity; they have been brainwashed to believe that the absence of a titled, payroll occupation enslaves a woman to failure, boredom, and imprisonment within the confines of home. Though feminism speaks of liberation, self-fulfilment, personal rights, and breaking down barriers, these phrases inevitably mean the opposite.'[51]

Babette Francis made the following penetrating comment in an article on feminism: 'One of the consequences of feminist antipathy to marriage has been the advent of the permissive society: alternative lifestyles and no-fault divorce laws. Far from enhancing the status of women, a major consequence of no-fault divorce has been the feminisation of poverty: economic analysis indicates that after divorce, the standard of living of fathers and husbands remains the same or improves, while wives and children slip below the poverty line... Because contemporary feminism is based on false premises, it is extremely wasteful of resources. However, the most destructive aspect of feminism is that it promotes hostility between the sexes and an anti-baby, anti-child mentality among women.'[52]

Sharon James in her essay 'Roles without relegation' argues that the assumptions of feminism are so much part of our culture that they have permeated the Christian Church.[53] Evangelical feminists are demanding that marriage must be an equal partnership where husband and wife submit to each other. She writes, 'The failure of whole sections of the Church seems all the more tragic when now we hear non-Christian commentators saying what we should have been declaring all along: modern feminism is based on a lie. It has caused untold damage. The real victims of feminism are women.'[54] James shows that the biblical language of headship is not accidental, but reflects a relationship between the sexes, which was part of the original design for creation.[55] Yet increasingly women are losing the freedom to choose to spend part of their lives as full-time mothers. She insists that the Scriptures accord great respect to the role of the wife and mother.[56] James reaches the following conclusion. 'Despite all the inner contradictions and tensions within the movement there is a broad consensus that women need to be liberated from patriarchy and all its implications. I would argue that modern feminism is incompatible with biblical Christianity and is to be strongly opposed.'[57]

Two themes emerge from the above criticism. The first is that feminism is based on a false premise. The idea that men and women are equal in all regards is contrary to the truths outlined in the biblical account of creation. The Lord of Creation created men and women to be different, with different roles and functions. This fact is obvious to all, and has been generally recognised by mankind since the beginning of time. Only those who choose to deny the truth blatantly follow this obviously futile way of thinking. The ideology of feminism is foolish and deceptive, and has exchanged the truth of God for a lie. The second theme to emerge is that feminism is a destructive ideology that damages people. Those who follow it must understand that it will damage their marriage, their family and themselves. It does not bring freedom, but bondage. It does not help women live better, more fulfilled lives, but rather empty, futile lives. It does not produce equality between men and women, but distrust and conflict. In particular, feminism is destructive for children, for it teaches mothers to put their own interests above those of their children. At its heart, feminism is an attack on marriage and the family. And worse, it is an assault on human dignity which degrades both men and women.

Despite the flaws in their ideology, the continuous flow of feminist writing has undoubtedly influenced the way many women and men view their marriages. The feminist ideology is now accepted as being politically correct, and its views are widely supported in women's magazines and the popular press. Women are under enormous pressure to conform to the latest, politically correct feminist ideas. Consequently many women feel justified in rejecting a marriage that does not make them completely happy. It is not surprising that women now initiate almost three-quarters of divorces. There is little doubt that feminist ideology has had a major impact on the attitude of society towards marriage and divorce.

DECLINE OF THE CHRISTIAN INFLUENCE ON MARRIAGE

We have seen that for centuries the Christian Church believed the doctrine of the indissolubility of marriage. In essence, the Church believed that marriage was a divine institution, made in heaven, that could be broken only by death. Marriage was, to quote from the Book of Common Prayer, 'for richer for poorer, for better for worse, in sickness and in health, till death us do part'. Because marriage is indissoluble while both husband and wife are still alive, the Church forbade divorce with the right to remarriage. The words of Jesus, 'Anyone who divorces his wife and marries another woman commits adultery against her. And if she divorces her husband and marries another man, she commits adultery' (Mark 10:11-12) were well known and accepted as meaning what they said.

In his book *Untying the Knot*, Roderick Phillips provides a summary of the way in which the early Church viewed the issue of marriage and divorce. He describes how in 17th century England the family was seen as the basic unit of society, and order within the family was believed to be essential for social and political order.[58] A vast literature emphasised the importance of marital and family stability for society and polity. Phillips goes on, 'Fundamental to these considerations was religion, for marriage was ordained by God, so that any behaviour that ran counter to harmony in marriage or the family not only threatened social stability but was also contrary to divine commandments.'[59] Consequently, 17th century commentators regarded conflict within marriage and marriage breakdown with the greatest apprehension. Phillips mentions that although the retention of the principle of marriage indissolubility was a source of great annoyance to many members of the Church, there was no bishop or archbishop in the first half of the 17th century who supported the legalisation of divorce.[60] A characteristic of the anti-divorce literature of the 17th century was that 'it appealed almost entirely to scriptural interpretation'.[61] In other words, those who taught that marriage is indissoluble based their teaching on what they believed was biblical truth.

During the Reformation the doctrine of the indissolubility of the marriage bond was attacked and a new teaching introduced that permitted divorce for adultery and desertion. The ideas of the reformers were extremely influential and led over the passage of time to the legalisation of divorce in Protestant Europe, America and eventually England. The process of liberalisation, which continued gradually during the 18th and 19th centuries, reached a high point in the second half of the 20th century with the introduction of no-fault divorce. Coinciding with the liberalisation process was a gradual, but persistent, decline in Christian understanding of the sanctity and permanence of marriage, and a rise in the notion of secular marriage. The decline in the Christian position reached its nadir in the 1960s with the publication of the report commissioned by the Archbishop of Canterbury, *Putting Asunder*. This report stated clearly that its recommendations for divorce liberalisation were based not on Christian principles but on widely popular, sociological principles.

Overwhelmed by ideas from secular society, teaching in the Church on marriage and divorce has become confused and ambiguous. Increasingly the Church has felt unable to stand by biblical teaching with regard to marriage. Because of this confusion most people do not know what the Christian position is with regard to divorce. The situation has been compounded by confusion around remarriage, as many churches have different rules that are changed from time to time to accommodate the latest popular view. Coinciding with the decline in the Christian view of marriage has been an increasing assault on the meaning and role of the family. We saw in chapter 2 how the report *Something to Celebrate* concluded that it was wrong to assume that a particular shape of family is God-given, and made it clear that, in their understanding, marriage and the family are not necessarily linked, 'for families exist where marriage may not (or cannot) and we should not treat them as if they were one and the same thing'.[62] So at the end of the 20th century the Church no longer teaches that marriage is the foundation of the family. John Stott in his book *Issues Facing Christians Today* (1990) reached the following conclusion: 'The greatest single reason for the growth in the divorce rate is the decline of Christian understanding of the sanctity and permanence of marriage, and the growing non-Christian assault on traditional concepts of sex, marriage and family.'[63]

It is difficult to disagree with the conclusion of John Stott. Mass divorce is the result of the Christian Church rejecting the rock on which marriage stability has been based, namely, the doctrine of the indissolubility of marriage. The seeds of mass divorce were sown when the Protestant reformers used the Bible to justify divorce for a number of reasons. Protestant theology prepared the ground for the harvest of mass divorce that now afflicts Western Christian nations. The great divorce debate of 1857 was a turning point for it was the moment when England rejected divine teaching on the indissolubility of marriage and opened the pathway to mass divorce. There could be no halfway point. Divorce for adultery was simply a pretext to find a way around the divine law. Once the Church accepted that marriage was dissoluble it was open to human wisdom, based on the spirit of the age, to define the grounds according to human needs. Now there was no defence against the human arguments of sociology, psychology and feminism. Once the divine law was set aside, every argument in favour of divorce was bound to succeed. From a human perspective, it was perfectly reasonable to allow divorce for any and every reason. What possible reasons could there be for not allowing people a second chance of happiness? Behind the success of the divorce movement lay the Protestant doctrine which provided the biblical justification for divorce.

Chapter 15

What God has joined together

Biblical teaching on marriage

In tracing the pathway to mass divorce we saw how the debates in 19th century England were dominated by scriptural references to marriage and divorce. On one side were those who held that marriage was a contract that could be dissolved on certain grounds. Those who followed the Protestant doctrine of divorce argued that divorce was permissible for adultery and desertion, while the secular humanists rejected the Scriptures and supported divorce for any and every reason. In the parliamentary debates, the proponents argued that divorce was a remedy that offered another chance of happiness to those in unhappy marriages. They claimed that divorce followed by remarriage offered the hope of happy, stable relationships and would reduce the number of illegitimate children. They also asserted that it would be better for children from unhappy homes if their parents divorced.

Those opposed to the legalisation of divorce believed that the Bible taught that marriage is an indissoluble covenant between a man and his wife. From their knowledge of the Scriptures they understood the ramifications of ignoring God's plan for marriage, and warned of the dire consequences of divorce. The Bishop of Oxford, for example, argued that the legalisation of divorce would weaken the institution of marriage in the eyes of society. Although it might take time, he predicted that slowly, step by step, divorce would change the moral aspect of the nation. He believed that the Divorce Reform Act of 1857 was contrary to the law of God, and fruitful in future crime and misery to the people of England.[1] Lord Salisbury argued that extending divorce would poison the happiness of the home and inflict a curse upon the poor.[2] Viscount Dungannon feared that divorce would be the means of introducing great misery among the poorer classes that was too painful to contemplate. He warned of the consequences that would follow once society let go of the idea that marriage was a lifelong union.[3]

Lord John Manners declared that divorce was against the express declaration of the Scriptures and its legalisation would inevitably loosen the marriage tie, and would have momentous consequences for the nation.[4] Mr William Gladstone said that the indissolubility of marriage was an idea firmly established in the mind of England, and therefore introducing divorce would have the most serious social consequences.[5] Sir William Heathcote claimed that the introduction of divorce into England was a national crisis, for it affected the sanctity of the family home and the purity of women.[6]

The prediction that divorce would damage the fabric of society is coming true during our lifetime, and the experience of millions of people confirms that divorce is the cause of great human suffering. (The evidence presented in later chapters provides overwhelming evidence of the harm that divorce causes to men, women and children). Moreover, many people feel uneasy about divorce for they know that the Bible teaches that it is wrong. When Christ was asked about the reasons for divorce he drew attention to the biblical account of marriage as described in Genesis and, before discussing divorce, he clarified God's law regarding marriage. Clearly Jesus was making the point that it is necessary to understand the meaning and significance of marriage before one can even begin to think about divorce. So Jesus went right back to the creation of man and woman to explain the significance of marriage, emphasising God's plan revealed in the first few chapters of the Bible. In our thinking about divorce we would do well to follow the example of our Lord and first understand God's will with regard to marriage.

MARRIAGE AT CREATION

According to the Bible, God instituted marriage immediately after he created the first man and woman, while Adam and Eve were still in the Garden of Eden. We see that the idea of marriage was in the mind of God from the beginning of Creation. In other words, marriage was no afterthought but central to the purpose for which man was created.

God created male and female

God created mankind as sexual beings and his plan is that men and women should unite in marriage to create families and thereby propagate the human race.

> So God created man in his own image, in the image of God he created him; male and female he created them. God blessed them and said to them, 'Be fruitful and increase in number; fill the earth and subdue it' (Genesis 1:27–28a).

The sexual nature of mankind is fundamental to God's creation plan—sexuality is at the centre of the human condition as created in the image of God. Jesus quoted from the first chapter of Genesis to emphasise this

318

ultimate truth; he said that at the beginning of creation 'God made them male and female' (Mark 10:6). Thus, in the original purpose of God, humanity is complete in man and woman. The human race is divided into two sexes and both are required for procreation. Neither male nor female is complete on their own; they need each other. The first command that God gave to mankind, 'Be fruitful and increase in number; fill the earth...' (Genesis 1:28) can only be fulfilled by a man and a woman joining together in sexual intercourse. For this reason God has placed within human nature a strong sexual attraction between men and women. We are endowed with sexual desires that make it natural for us to be attracted to the opposite sex and to enter a sexual relationship. But we are not free to indulge our sexual appetites as we wish, for God has given us moral laws to control our sexual behaviour. These moral laws are not only right, they are also for our good. Implicit within divine law is the idea that sexual intercourse should take place within the marriage union. The God-given mandate to be fruitful and increase in number is to be fulfilled by the marriage of a man to his wife. So we see that human sexuality, which finds its meaning in the procreation of the human race, and marriage are central to God's plan for men and women.

Not good to be alone

At the time of Creation the Lord God emphasised the need that mankind has for companionship. Men and women are not created to live in isolation, but to live in relationship with each other.

> The Lord God said, 'It is not good for the man to be alone. I will make a helper suitable for him.' ...Then the Lord God made a woman from the rib he had taken out of the man, and he brought her to the man (Genesis 2:18,22).

To provide a suitable partner for the man God created a woman from his rib, thereby highlighting the closeness of the relationship between the sexes, and providing a symbol of the one flesh union that is created at marriage. Notice that it is God himself who gives the woman Eve to Adam, as if he is the father of the bride. The man is overjoyed with the woman, his God-given marriage partner. Adam recognises the closeness of the relationship to his new wife, and describes her as, '...bone of my bones and flesh of my flesh; she shall be called "woman", for she was taken out of man' (Genesis 2:23). By referring to bone and flesh Adam is showing that he understands that his wife is a part of him, that she is his flesh and blood, for she was taken out of him. Indeed, the true definition of woman is one who is taken out of man. Adam then names her woman, signifying the role of the man as the head of the family. Later, after the Fall, Adam names his wife Eve (Genesis 3:20), because she would become the mother of all the living. The significance of the family name is discussed later.

The marriage ordinance

Following the introduction of Eve to Adam, God lays down the principles that are to govern all future marriages.

> For this reason a man will leave his father and mother and be united to his wife, and they will become one flesh (Genesis 2:24).

The Scripture explains the reason for marriage: it is because of the fundamental unity between man and woman. God has created males and females to complement each other. The woman is created to be a suitable partner for the man; she is created from the body of the man, and is of the same flesh and bone as the man. The joining together of male and female in marriage creates the fundamental unity of humanity. By joining together in sexual intercourse, husband and wife create a new life which is the natural fruit of their marriage union. It is God's will that children are born into the family created by the one flesh marriage union. Husband and wife, through the fruitfulness of their marriage union, become father and mother to the children born as a consequence of their one flesh union. Both Jesus, in the gospels of Matthew and Mark, and the apostle Paul, in Ephesians 5:25–33, referred to Genesis 2:24 to explain the mystery of the one flesh union created by marriage.

The sinfulness of men and women

The inherent sinfulness of mankind is widely acknowledged, and the pathway of history is strewn with evidence of mankind's sinful nature. The Bible provides a clear explanation of mankind's tendency to sin. The third chapter of Genesis tells how Adam and Eve disobeyed God's command not to eat of the Tree of the knowledge of Good and Evil. By this act of rebellion against God, sin entered the human race and all became sinners. The Bible tells us, 'There is no-one righteous, not even one' and 'all have turned away, they have together become worthless; there is no-one who does good, not even one' (Romans 3:10,12). This truth, that all people are sinful, is one of the most profound truths of the Bible, for it demonstrates that all mankind need salvation from sin. It also explains that we live in an imperfect world, with imperfect human relationships. The corollary of this is that relationships between men and women are affected by our tendency to sin. It follows that all marriages will have problems, for both husbands and wives are imperfect sinful human beings. There are no perfectly happy marriages.

JESUS' TEACHING ON MARRIAGE

When the Pharisees challenged Jesus about the grounds for divorce, he took the opportunity to re-emphasise God's plan for marriage. He pointed out that the divine blueprint for marriage was given at the time of Creation and quoted from Genesis 2:24, thereby reiterating its importance. Jesus said:

> Haven't you read, …that at the beginning the Creator 'made them male and female' and said, 'For this reason a man will leave his father and mother and be united to his wife, and the two will become one flesh'? So they are no longer two, but one. Therefore what God has joined together, let man not separate (Matthew 19:4–6).

With these famous words Christ endorsed marriage as a divine ordinance established at Creation and highlighted its essential characteristics.

A man leaves his father and mother

At the heart of marriage is the idea that a man leaves the family into which he was born and forms a new family with his wife. This point is of fundamental importance and needs to be clearly understood; marriage creates a new family as husband and wife leave the family of their parents and start a family home together. In an essay on divorce, Carl Laney makes the point that 'a man must let go of his parents, with the view to establishing his own home and family'.[7] In order to cement this unity the man leaves his father and mother so that he can give his full devotion to his wife. The leaving of the parental family is a public event. According to Henri Blocher, 'In biblical times the event the Bible calls marriage involved the whole society. The idea of a purely private marriage is simply a recent aberration, the result of individualism and of the disintegration of traditional communities. The marriage feast assured that the marriage was a public event. For Scripture the marriage bond is a part of those social realities supervised by the civil authority; it is the law which binds a woman to her husband.'[8] It is important for society to know that when a couple start living together they are joined to each other in marriage. This is because the family is the basic institution of a good society. Marriage is good for the stability of society, and for the moral well-being of the nation.

For this reason a good society has always frowned on people living together in a sexual relationship without being married. Those who cohabit have correctly been labelled as living in sin for they are flouting the most basic moral laws of a good society. Children born outside marriage, until a few years ago, were officially referred to as illegitimate, for they were the product of a relationship that was not recognised by society. It is customary for a forthcoming marriage to be announced in public so that society knows that a man and woman are to be joined in a lawful marriage. A prerequisite is that both partners are eligible for marriage and any person who knows of a reason why the marriage cannot lawfully take place has a responsibility to declare it. There is a social responsibility to prevent unlawful, bigamous marriages, and to prevent illegitimate births.

The husband and wife take their marriage vows in front of witnesses and make clear their intention to live together as a family for life. It is public knowledge that the man and woman are committed for life and are not available to others. Marriage rings may be exchanged as an outward symbol of the marriage union. A register records the details of the marriage, and most are celebrated with a ceremony. Many marriages are announced in a newspaper and everybody in the community knows that a couple have become man and wife.

A man is united to his wife

At marriage a man is united to his wife. Their unity is based upon vows to live together as husband and wife and to be faithful to each other, whatever the circumstances, until 'death us do part'. Their vows are made in the presence of God, and he is the divine witness to the marriage. Husband and wife are, in fact, entering into a covenant relationship that cannot be broken, except by death, even should one partner prove unfaithful. In their heart and conscience they know that the bond created by marriage is for life. The marriage union provides the fullest expression of mutual loving companionship that human beings can experience in this world. The union created by marriage is not only physical, but is also an emotional and spiritual unity of profound dimensions, as a husband and wife become one flesh.

The word cleave is used in the older translations of the Bible and means to cling to or keep close to, implying loyalty and affection. According to Laney 'a study of the word cleave suggests that marriage involves a partnership commitment to which the husband and wife must be loyal; the biblical concept suggests the idea of being superglued together – bound inseparably by a commitment to a lifelong relationship'.[9] It follows that a man and woman who have been glued together by marriage cannot be easily separated – indeed, separation is likely to cause great damage.

No longer two, but one flesh

Quoting the verse in Genesis, Jesus says 'the two will become one flesh' and draws the following conclusion, 'So they are no longer two, but one.' The man and woman who enter into the marriage bond become one flesh and are no longer two, but one entity. The apostle Paul develops this concept by teaching that 'husbands ought to love their wives as their own bodies. He who loves his wife loves himself. After all, no-one ever hated his own body, but he feeds and cares for it' (Ephesians 5:28–29). Paul is saying that a wife is actually a part of her husband's body—she is of his flesh and blood. He illustrates this mystery by revealing a profound truth that when a man loves his wife he loves himself, for she is a part of him. It follows that when a man hates his wife he hates his own body. Paul then quotes Genesis 2:24, 'For this reason a man will leave his father and mother and be united to his wife, and the two will become one flesh', acknowledging that it is a mystery. There is something so deep and wonderful in the marriage bond that we need spiritual insight fully to understand its divine significance. The union of husband and wife is used in the Scriptures as a symbol of the unity between Christ and his Church; Christ is the bridegroom and the Church is his bride. Paul says that the Church is a part of Christ; we are members of the body of Christ and Christ is the head of the Church. In the same way, the wife is part of the body of her husband. This union between Christ and his Church is based on the covenant promise, sealed in his blood, that he will never leave us or forsake us (Deuteronomy 31:6). He will remain faithful to his promises even although we are faithless.

After a man and woman become one flesh by marriage they can never again be the same as they were before this transformation takes place. In an essay on divorce William Heth explains the union in this way. 'Something unique and "creational" takes place when husband and wife consummate their marriage covenant: they become closely related (one flesh).'[10] Heth shows that Jesus' interpretation of Scripture implies that God himself is involved in creating this new family unit. 'Thus Jesus explains that marriage involves three persons: a man, a woman, and the One who in the beginning created mankind as male and female.'[11] This union changes the relationship of the man and his wife with other family members. Indeed, the biblical statement 'they become one flesh' affirms that just as blood relations are one's flesh and blood, so marriage creates a similar kinship relation between man and wife. They are as closely related as a brother and sister. In their book, *Jesus and Divorce* (1984), Wenham and Heth express the view that 'the moment a man married a woman she became an integral part of his family in the same way in which children born into that family did'.[12] It follows that a husband is closely related to his wife's female relatives, and should his wife die or he divorce her, he could not marry them, for the family relationship remains intact. For the same reason, the wife will never be able to marry her husband's father even should her husband die, or divorce her.

The fundamental principle is that the one flesh marriage bond is indissoluble and even divorce cannot break it. Moreover, the family relationships between children and their grandparents, aunts and uncles and cousins are not changed by divorce; they remain each other's flesh and blood, and are related for life. So Jesus made a profound statement when he said they are *one*, thereby confirming the indissoluble nature of the marriage bond—the consequences of marriage are for life. As the apostle Paul says, 'by law a married woman is bound to her husband as long as he is alive…' (Romans 7:2). This is why it is so important for husband and wife to be faithful to each other.

The one flesh union is complete when the couple consummate their marriage union by sexual intercourse. Husband and wife lovingly share their sexual life, accepting that their sexual union is likely to be blessed by the birth of children. They accept with joy the children that result, for they are the natural, legitimate products of their union—clear evidence that they are truly one flesh. According to Laney the concept of one flesh is illustrated by the children who are born into the family. By their offspring, husband and wife are indissolubly united into one person.[13] Both parents contribute equally to the genetic make up of their children, and the likeness to their parents witnesses to this fact. The one flesh bond created by parenthood is indissoluble, and a child can have only one set of parents. Divorce does not break the bond between parents and children.

The custom of a woman taking the surname of the man she marries symbolised their oneness as a family, and is based on the biblical truth illustrated when Adam was given the responsibility of naming his wife. The family name is important, for society is able to identify the members of a family by their name. The fact that all the members share a common name illustrates their unity as a family and that they belong together as an entity. All the children born into the family will be known by the family name. The contemporary notion that a married woman can retain her maiden name is fundamentally contrary to the idea of biblical marriage; it denies the reality of the one flesh marriage bond. Furthermore, through marriage the husband and wife become members of a wider extended family, with a host of new family relationships. Both husband and wife acquire many relatives, which may include father and mother-in-law, and brothers and sisters-in-law. Because of the current confusion that surrounds definitions of the family, this point must again be emphasised. Biblical teaching makes it clear that a family is formed by the marriage of a man and a woman. Without marriage, there is no family.

What God has joined let man not separate

Having stressed the importance of the creational ordinance of marriage, Jesus concluded with the words, 'Therefore what God has joined together, let man not separate.' He contrasts the divine action of joining together husband and wife with the human inclination to separate as a matter of convenience. According to Jesus, it is God who joins a husband and wife in marriage. This means that God is the author of the new family created by marriage. And so we see a profound biblical truth— families are created by God, and not by man. Jesus is saying that at the most fundamental level a man and woman are joined by God to become a family in marriage. In his book *Divorce and Remarriage* (1993), Andrew Cornes writes, 'whenever a man and woman marry, whatever the circumstances that have brought them together, it is God who is yoking them to one another'.[14] Therefore those who think correctly about marriage will no longer think of a man and his wife as two separate entities.[15]

Jesus warns of the human inclination to break the marriage bond with the words 'let man not separate'. He knew what was in the heart of men and women; he knew that they would not readily accept the divine institution of marriage but would want to use divorce as the remedy for unhappy marriages. And so he warns them not to separate what God has joined together. A married couple has a moral responsibility before God to maintain the family formed at their marriage. Because God joins a couple in marriage, no human being should attempt to destroy it. This is a warning to the marriage partners themselves; they should not do anything that will endanger their marriage. In particular, they should not form any relationship that would threaten their marriage and the family of which their children are a part. Other people should also be careful not to take any action that could endanger a marriage and thereby break a family. For a third person to form a liaison with someone who is married is fundamentally wrong as it endangers the marriage. Adultery is a grievous sin for it can break a marriage, and cause great harm to the whole family, husband, wife and children.

BIBLICAL TEACHING ON THE MARRIAGE RELATIONSHIP

Because marriage is an essential, indissoluble bond, the Bible gives clear instructions about how a married couple should live together. In the Bible the unity between Christ and his Church is used as a symbol of the marriage relationship—just as Christ and his Church are one, so husband and wife are one. The roles and responsibilities of husband and wife and the way the family should be governed are described in the Bible. The need for husband and wife to have a correct understanding of the significance of their marriage, and the right attitude towards each other is emphasised. Biblical Christianity lays down a clear moral framework for the behaviour of men and women, teaching that sexual activity should be confined to the marriage relationship. All forms of sexual immorality are condemned as sinful and a cause of harm to those involved. The Bible teaches that 'marriage should be honoured by all, and the marriage bed kept pure, for God will judge the adulterer and all the sexually immoral' (Hebrews 13:4).

Two passages in the Bible provide teaching about the behaviour of husband and wife. The apostle Paul in his letter to the Ephesians (5:22–33) and the apostle Peter in his first letter (1 Peter 3:1–7) give clear instructions to Christian believers on the way they ought to behave in marriage.

Wives, submit to your husbands as to the Lord. For the husband is the head of the wife as Christ is the head of the church... Now as the church submits to Christ, so also wives should submit to their husbands in every-thing. Husbands, love your wives, just as Christ loved the church and gave himself up for her to make her holy... In this same way, husbands ought to love their wives as their own bodies. He who loves his wife loves himself... Each one of you also must love his wife as he loves himself, and the wife must respect her husband (Ephesians 5:22–33).

Wives, in the same way be submissive to your husbands so that, if any of them do not believe the word, they may be won over without words by the behaviour of their wives, when they see the purity and reverence of your lives... They were submissive to their own husbands, like Sarah, who obeyed Abraham and called him her master... Husbands, in the same way be considerate as you live with your wives, and treat them with respect as the weaker partner and as heirs with you of the gracious gift of life, so that nothing will hinder your prayers (1 Peter 3:1–7).

The headship of the husband

The Bible teaches that the husband is the head of the family. The headship of the husband is taught explicitly in Ephesians. 'For the husband is the head of the wife as Christ is the head of the church... Now as the church submits to Christ, so also wives should submit to their husbands in everything' (Ephesians 5:23,24). In 1 Corinthians 11:3 we read, 'Now I want you to realise that the head of every man is Christ, and the head of the woman is man, and the head of Christ is God.' According to the Bible there is a hierarchy of authority within the family. The family is not to be leaderless, nor is it to be governed by whim or fancy, nor by the majority view. Instead the husband has been given the responsibility of leadership in the family.

The husband, however, is to exercise his leadership role under the authority of Christ, who is his head and the example he should follow in exercising his role. As the leader, he has a responsibility to provide for and protect his wife and children, and is responsible, together with his wife, for the moral well-being of his family. In an essay on headship Edward Donnelly writes, 'God has established a structure in which "the head of the woman is man". This is evident from creation, witnessed to by "nature" and supported by universal Christian practice. Man's headship is carefully qualified so that it poses no threat to woman's worth, dignity or meaningful role in life. Still, he is head and the woman rejects this authority to her and his shame and to the dishonour of God.'[16] For a husband not to take on his God-given leadership responsibility in marriage is to fail his wife and his family, and lays the seeds of dissension in the marriage. He has a unique leadership role in the family that he should not abdicate.[17]

The concept of male headship is anathema to feminist ideology. As we have seen, it is attacked as the foundation of the patriarchal society, and the cause of women's oppression. According to feminist thinking, marriage must be an equal partnership where each submits to the other.[18] But this is a dangerous teaching for it denies biblical truth. Throughout the Bible it is made clear that the man has the leadership role in the family.

Wives submit to your husbands

The Bible teaches that the wife should accept the authority of her husband to lead the family, and submit willingly to his leadership.[19] According to George Knight, writing in *Recovering Biblical Manhood and Womanhood* (1991), 'this particular exhortation to the wife to submit to her husband is the universal teaching of the New Testament. Every passage that deals with the relationship of the wife to her husband tells her to "submit to" him.'[20] Colossians 3:18 tells wives to 'submit to your husbands, as is fitting in the Lord', and Titus 2:5 instructs wives 'to be self-controlled and pure, to be busy at home, to be kind, and to be subject to their husbands, so that no-one will malign the word of God'. She should not challenge his leadership, but should rather support and help him in this role, accepting that it is God who has vested the leadership of the family in her husband. And the example that is used to illustrate the attitude of the wife, is that she should submit to her husband in the same way as the Church submits to its Lord. There can be no greater example of submission. So the wife should not in any way undermine the authority of her husband, for that would damage the family of which she is an integral part; it would also damage her children. Moreover, not only should she submit with an attitude of complete acceptance, but also in everything (Ephesians 5:24). The Bible leaves little doubt about the importance of submission to the headship role of the husband. It mentions the holy women of the past who were submissive to their own husbands, like Sarah, who obeyed her husband Abraham, and called him her master (1 Peter 3:5–6).

It is not difficult to see why feminist ideology is violently opposed to this Christian teaching. The idea that a wife should actually submit to her husband is unthinkable to the feminist mind, and goes against the most fundamental tenet of feminism. For this reason many feminist writers have attacked marriage as an irrelevant and outdated institution.

Husbands, love your wives

The husband is to show a deep love for his wife. We have seen that God has joined the husband and wife together so that they become one flesh, one entity, and part of each other. The husband should love and cherish his wife as himself, as the Scripture says 'husbands ought to love their wives as their own bodies' (Ephesians 5:28). As Christ loved the Church so the husband must love his wife. Christ's love was unconditional—he loved us although we did not love him. And he showed his love by giving of himself, for 'Christ loved the church and gave himself up for her' (Ephesians 5:25). Following this example, the husband must put the interests of his wife and family above his own. A loving husband will give of himself for the benefit of his wife.[21] By loving his wife, he will bring great blessing on the family of which he is the head. And if he does not love his wife then he damages his family, his children and himself. As the Bible says, 'He who loves his wife loves himself' (Ephesians 5:28).

Wives, respect your husbands

We have seen that the wife must submit to her husband because he is the head of the family. Yet she can submit to her husband without respecting him. But that would be wrong for submission without respect means that the wife submits with a poor attitude, not really understanding why she should do so. She must respect her husband because he is the head of the family, the father of her children, and the provider and protector of the family home. She should respect her husband because God has commanded her to do so (Ephesians 5:33) and because it is the right thing to do. George Knight writes, 'A wife's respecting her husband and his headship therefore implies that her submission involves not only what she does but also her attitude in doing it.'[22] The husband has the major responsibility for maintaining order and discipline within the family; this is no easy task, and he needs the respect of his wife as he strives to fulfil his role. After all, how will the children respect their father if his wife does not do so?

MARRIAGE AND CHILDREN

The action of Jesus following the dramatic encounter with the Pharisees shows why marriage is so important and why divorce is not an option. After issuing his serious warning to married couples not to separate, the gospel of Matthew records,

> Then little children were brought to Jesus for him to place his hands on them and pray for them. But the disciples rebuked those who brought them. Jesus said, 'Let the little children come to me, and do not hinder them, for the kingdom of heaven belongs to such as these' (Matthew 19:13–14).

By his loving attitude towards children Jesus is showing that divorce is not even to be contemplated; that husband and wife, and especially father and mother, are never to separate. Here again we see the action of Christ, which is to love and care for children, and the action of his disciples, who fail to understand the value God places on children. Jesus knew that marriage is the God-given institution in which the divine command to 'be fruitful and multiply' is to be fulfilled. God's intention is that the marriage relationship should be fruitful and produce children. The Bible tells us that 'sons are a heritage from the Lord, children a reward from him. Like arrows in the hands of a warrior are sons born in one's youth. Blessed is the man whose quiver is full of them' (Psalm 127: 3–5). Children are a gift from God and those parents who have many children – or as the Psalmist would say, 'a quiver full of arrows' – are blessed by God. The birth of children brings with it parental responsibilities as husband and wife become father and mother. Parents have a God-given responsibility to care for their children—it is unthinkable that they would not do so. The Proverbs of Solomon make it clear that the father and mother must teach and instruct their children, and so children are advised to 'Listen ... to your father's instruction and do not forsake your mother's teaching' (Proverbs 1:8). Within the family home, children are to be loved, taught, and disciplined by both their mother and their father. This is God's plan. Parents, and especially fathers, have a duty to train and discipline their children. The Bible makes it very clear that all children need parental discipline, and that the father should take the lead in disciplining the children, 'For what son is not disciplined by his father?' (Hebrews 12:7).

Moreover, discipline is for the good of the children, for it teaches them that they cannot always have their own way; they need to develop self-control and self-discipline, and they need to recognise and respect the authority of their parents. Parental discipline warns children of the dangers of immoral behaviour. The discipline that parents exercise over their children is a sign of their love, for while any discipline seems unpleasant at the time, it produces a harvest of good in the long run. Parents are to teach their children the difference between right and wrong, and, by their behaviour, set an example for their children to follow. A major problem associated with divorce is that it separates parents from their children. This makes it difficult for parents to discipline their children and to teach them a moral foundation on which they can base their lives. By divorcing, parents show their children that marriage does not matter; by honouring their marriage vows, parents teach their children the importance of marriage and the family.

The Bible teaches that a fundamental purpose of marriage is to provide a secure family home in which children are to be nurtured as they grow into adulthood. This biblical teaching is an eternal truth, and applies to all people, and for all time. And this point needs to be underlined—God's plan for marriage is not only for Christians, but is for all people. It is part of God's common grace; the Creator designed marriage for the good of all mankind. Those who are not Christian need to recognise the wisdom of the biblical view of marriage; to do so will bring great blessing to their family. Those who accept and follow biblical teaching, and understand the true meaning and significance of marriage, are unlikely ever to contemplate divorce, for they know that a father and mother must protect and love their children when they are at their most innocent and vulnerable. The marital relationship between husband and wife, and the parental relationship between parents and children are inextricably linked, because they are the relationships that make the family home complete. To break either relationship is to harm the family, and when one member of the family suffers the whole family is damaged. This is the reason why divorce is such as disaster for all the members of the family.

Chapter 16

Why God hates divorce

Biblical teaching on divorce

Having examined what the Bible says about marriage, we can now turn to the issue of divorce. We have seen that the Bible teaches that marriage is the lifelong union of one man with one woman. That is God's ideal. What does the Bible have to say on divorce? This remains controversial as we saw in our examination of the parliamentary debates. Although a large theological literature debates the meaning and interpretation of the key biblical passages, there is still uncertainty among Christians as to what the Bible teaches about divorce. The issue at stake is this: does Christ allow divorce with remarriage? In other words, is the marriage bond dissolved by divorce? Those theologians who support the Protestant doctrine of divorce argue that Christ allows divorce for marital unfaithfulness, and some claim that the apostle Paul allows divorce and remarriage following desertion by an unbelieving spouse. On the other side of the debate are those who believe that the Bible teaches that marriage is indissoluble and, therefore, remarriage is not permitted following a divorce. For those who wish to study the detailed theological arguments two books are recommended. *Jesus and Divorce* by Gordon Wenham and William Heth deals in detail with the arguments of those who support the Erasmian view of divorce.[1] They explore the different schools of interpretation, and provide a strong critique of the view widely held by evangelicals today, that allows for remarriage after divorce on the grounds of immorality. Andrew Cornes, in *Divorce and Remarriage*, provides a comprehensive study of singleness, marriage, divorce and remarriage from a biblical perspective.[2]

I believe that the biblical teaching on divorce and remarriage, an issue that effects everyone, is clear and understandable. Those who claim that the Scriptures are unclear on divorce imply that Jesus Christ taught in a way that caused confusion. The confusion does not lie with Christ, but with those who find themselves unable to accept the plain truth of his teaching. It is a serious error to claim that the teachings of Christ are unclear. On the contrary, he did not fail to tell the world God's plan for marriage in clear, understandable language. Indeed, he did so in such plain words that his teaching has caused offence even among those who claim to be his followers. The apparent confusion over divorce and remarriage is entirely man-made. This chapter examines two Old Testament passages and the teachings of Jesus Christ and the apostle Paul.

THE MESSAGE OF MALACHI – GOD HATES DIVORCE

The following passage from Malachi describes God's attitude to divorce.

> Another thing you do: you flood the Lord's altar with tears. You weep and wail because he no longer pays attention to your offerings or accepts them with pleasure from your hands. You ask, 'Why?' It is because the Lord is acting as the witness between you and the wife of your youth, because you have broken faith with her, though she is your partner, the wife of your marriage covenant. Has not the Lord made them one? In flesh and spirit they are his. And why one? Because he was seeking godly offspring. So guard yourself in your spirit, and do not break faith with the wife of your youth. 'I hate divorce,' says the Lord God of Israel, 'and I hate a man's covering himself with violence as well as with his garment,' says the Lord Almighty (Malachi 2: 13–16).

The idea of covenant is a biblical concept used to describe the relationship between God and his people. It has been defined as an unchangeable, divinely imposed legal agreement between God and man that stipulates the conditions of their relationship.[3] There are two parties to a covenant, God and man; but man cannot negotiate with God, or change the terms of the covenant; he can only accept the obligations of the covenant or reject them. The prophet makes it clear that God sees marriage as a covenant between a man and a woman. It is a relationship of personal obligation. Both husband and wife have given their word that they will be faithful to each other; they are committed to live together for life. As John Richardson writes in *Sex, God and Marriage* (1998), 'This helps explain why divorce was so hated by God, since the term "covenant" also describes the relationship between God and his people. Moreover, the covenant between God and Israel in the Old Testament is itself pictured as a marriage.'[4]

According to Malachi, Israel was concerned that God was no longer blessing them. Their prayers were not being answered because of God's displeasure with their attitude towards marriage; they were breaking their marriage covenants and divorcing their wives. God was displeased and said, 'You have broken faith with her, though she is your partner, the wife of your marriage covenant' (Malachi 2:14), thereby highlighting the underlying cause of all divorce. God told his people that unfaithfulness, which is a wider term than adultery, is the root cause of all broken marriages and the sin that leads to divorce. The prophet explains why breaking faith with their wives was such a terrible sin—because they had promised lifelong commitment to their marriage covenant, and God was the witness.

The underlying cause of all divorce is always the result of one or both partners being unfaithful to their marriage vows. In public they promise to be faithful whatever the circumstances, but because of selfishness they fail to keep the promises they made when they entered into the marriage covenant. So human waywardness and unfaithfulness lie at the centre of all marriage failure. According to Laney, 'divorce is not only a violation of God's original plan for marriage, it violates the marriage covenant to which the Lord is a witness. Divorce is treachery against life's most intimate companion and is a grievous sin which God hates.'[5]

Yet contemporary society sees divorce as if no one is at fault; it is no longer fashionable to speak of faithfulness to one's marriage partner. Many people feel little compunction in breaking their vows when it is no longer convenient to keep them. There is no longer a belief that loyalty to a marriage partner through thick and thin, for better for worse, is important. Those ideals are portrayed as old-fashioned and outmoded. Instead when a husband or wife feel they no longer love their marriage partner, or the marriage goes through a difficult time, or they fall in love with someone else, then divorce becomes an option. There is little acknowledgement that human unfaithfulness is at the heart of all divorce. Yet the Bible is quite clear on this point and warns, 'Do not break faith with the wife of your youth' (Malachi 2:15).

God's attitude towards divorce is clearly stated by the prophet Malachi. 'I hate divorce,' says the Lord God of Israel, 'and I hate a man's covering himself with violence...' (Malachi 2:16). The God of the Bible, who instituted marriage for the good of mankind, hates divorce. Faithfulness is central to the character of God, he is faithful to all his promises and is faithful to his people. 'If we are faithless, he will remain faithful, for he cannot disown himself' (2 Timothy 2:13). Even though we are unfaithful, God remains faithful to us. Marriage is a covenant promise to live together as man and wife for life, and faithfulness is the knot that binds husband and wife together. Implicit within the marriage covenant is the promise to be faithful to our children, to love and care for them. Divorce breaks the covenant promise of faithfulness to those who are nearest and dearest. Because it is the ultimate expression of human unfaithfulness, it is repulsive to the divine nature and God *hates* it.

Malachi goes on to explain that in the mind of God divorce and violence are linked. In God's eyes, divorce is violence directed against our own family;

it is violence against our own flesh and blood, violence against our husband or wife, violence against our children. There can be no more brutal act than perpetrating violence against our marriage partner and children who are dependent on our love and protection. The spectacle of the terrible violence unleashed by divorce is clearly visible to all around. Because divorce is violence against the family, it is hateful to God. He hates divorce because of what it does to the families involved; the devastation and suffering that result are highly displeasing to him.

In particular, God *hates* the suffering of the children involved in divorces. God *hates* it when a home is broken and a family shattered. God *hates* it when children are deprived of father or mother by divorce. God loathes the heartbreak of the children, and the loneliness experienced by the divorced husband and wife. It is not good for man to be alone and divorce results in loneliness. It is not good for children to be deserted by their parents, and divorce results in deserted children. It is unthinkable that God could have any other attitude to divorce. The message of Malachi is that God *hates* divorce.

THE MESSAGE OF HOSEA – BE RECONCILED

The prophet Hosea was called by God to live out his message to his people by marrying a woman who would be unfaithful to him, and so his marriage was a symbolic picture of the relationship between God and his people. Hosea was to proclaim Israel's need for reconciliation to their faithful, loving God. The key verse is:

> The Lord said to me, 'Go, show your love to your wife again, though she is loved by another and is an adulteress. Love her as the Lord loves the Israelites, though they turn to other gods...' (Hosea 3: 1).

Hosea's wife had been unfaithful and committed adultery with other men. God saw her behaviour as symbolic of the unfaithfulness of his people who were running after other gods, and being unfaithful to the covenant God had made with them. They promised to love him with all their hearts, and to have no other gods. But they had been disloyal by worshipping man-made idols. Yet God did not cast them aside, even though they had betrayed him. Although he was angry and offended by their unfaithfulness and waywardness, he invited his people to return and repent of their sin. The Lord said, 'I will heal their waywardness and love them freely, for my anger has turned away from them' (Hosea 14:4). Despite their unfaithfulness, God was merciful and offered them the hope of reconciliation.

In the same way as God acted towards faithless Israel, he directed Hosea to act towards his unfaithful wife, who was running after other men. Despite the fact that she was an adulteress, God did not tell Hosea to divorce his wife, but rather to love her again. It is clear that God wanted Hosea to restore the relationship; he wanted Hosea to be reconciled, even though his wife was an adulteress, and the law of Moses permitted him to divorce her.

There is no more explicit message in the Bible regarding God's attitude to divorce. God hates it, and does not want a couple to divorce, even when adultery has been involved. Instead, he wants them to make every effort to be reconciled and save their marriage – yes, even to the extent of forgiving an unfaithful wife or husband. Although divorce is permitted for marital unfaithfulness, the Bible teaches that we should do all we can to achieve reconciliation. The unfaithful partner bears a terrible responsibility for they have sinned against God, against their marriage partner, against their children and against their family. They should repent of their foolish action, change their behaviour and ask for forgiveness from all concerned. Adultery is not the unforgivable sin, and God is able to restore the relationship if there is a true change of heart.

True reconciliation requires a change of behaviour on the part of the unfaithful partner, and that the one who has been sinned against should be willing to forgive and be reconciled. Although this may take a long time to achieve, and sometimes is not possible because of the unrepentant heart of the unfaithful partner, the faithful partner should aim at this rather than allowing their marriage to be broken by divorce. Even after divorce, the possibility of reconciliation should be left open, and, if at all possible, it should be sought actively and encouraged. God's guidance for those who face the possibility of a divorce because of marital unfaithfulness is that they should do all in their power to save their marriage. They should be like Hosea and again show their love to their unfaithful partner, doing everything possible to achieve reconciliation. The example of Hosea illustrates God's ideal in the case of a broken marriage.[6] Wenham and Heth write, 'in the event of marital unfaithfulness we believe that Jesus would surely require the forgiveness of seventy times seven and the goal of restoration exhibited by Hosea'.[7]

JESUS' TEACHING ON DIVORCE

Jesus taught about divorce on two occasions. The first time was during the Sermon on the Mount, recorded in Matthew chapter five, and the second occasion, recorded in Mark chapter 10 and Matthew chapter 19, was toward the end of his ministry when the Pharisees confronted him regarding the causes of divorce. The gospel of Luke also gives a brief summary of Jesus' teaching.

Moral responsibility towards marriage (Matthew 5:31–32)

It is significant that Jesus taught about divorce in his Sermon on the Mount while setting his standards for human behaviour. He was dealing with the question of individual responsibility. The Lord outlined a moral framework that was completely revolutionary in its content. In essence he taught that our inner attitude toward God and other people is the foundation for morality. Jesus taught that we ought to treat others as we would like them to treat us. The attitude of our heart is the essence of morality. By Jesus' standard, to look at a woman with lust is adultery; that is, the inward, lustful desire is of itself sinful. These are the standards of behaviour that God expects from his people; they have to do with attitudes, thoughts and desires, as well as the way we treat others. Above all, the standard is that we should be kind and forgiving. We should not seek revenge when wronged, and should even pray for our enemies and those who persecute us. Applying his teaching to divorce, Jesus shows that divorce is not only wrong, but with the correct attitude to one's marriage partner should not even be contemplated.

While on the Mount, Jesus dealt with divorce in the context of his teaching on adultery. Jesus said,

> It has been said, 'Anyone who divorces his wife must give her a certificate of divorce.' But I tell you that anyone who divorces his wife, except for marital unfaithfulness, causes her to commit adultery, and anyone who marries a woman so divorced commits adultery (Matthew 5:31–32).

Here Jesus sets God's standard for marriage. With the words, 'but I tell you that anyone who divorces his wife, except for marital unfaithfulness, causes her to commit adultery', Jesus says that any man who divorces his wife is causing her great harm, for he is the cause of her becoming an adulteress. It is against God's will and cannot be an option to be used for man's convenience. What Jesus is teaching is that an attitude of the heart that even entertains the thought of divorce is adultery against one's marriage partner. So the principle the Lord is laying down is that in God's eyes even the thought of divorce is immoral—an act equal to adultery. However, he makes an exception to this rule for the man whose wife is guilty of marital unfaithfulness. For a man to divorce an unfaithful, adulterous wife is not equal to adultery on the part of the man for it does not cause her to commit adultery because she has already done so. (The exception clause is discussed in more detail below.)

Having established the principle that to divorce is immoral, unless it is for marital unfaithfulness, Jesus places an absolute restriction on remarriage. He says that a man who divorces his wife causes her to commit adultery, unless of course she has already committed adultery. The assumption is that the divorced wife will remarry and so commit adultery against her husband. The fact that the divorced wife commits adultery when she remarries a single man means that her marriage bond is still intact and therefore was not destroyed by the divorce. And Jesus lays the responsibility squarely at the feet of the husband; it is his immoral action in divorcing his wife that causes her to commit adultery.

Furthermore anyone who marries a woman so divorced commits adultery. That is, the (single) man who marries the divorced woman, whether she is the innocent partner or not, commits adultery against her husband. This is a remarkable teaching for it raises the obvious question: how can a man be guilty of adultery if he marries a divorced woman? The only possible explanation is that in Jesus' understanding the marriage bond is still intact because she is joined to her husband by God—so the divorced woman is still bound to her husband for the marriage bond is indissoluble except by death. Therefore, in God's eyes, her first marriage is still intact even although her husband has divorced her, and so the (single) man who marries her is entering into an illicit sexual relationship with a married (although divorced) woman. For this reason anyone who marries a divorced woman commits adultery, and the divorced woman commits adultery when she remarries.

In evidence to the Royal Commission of 1912, Professor JP Whitney, a church historian, explained that the passage was dealing with the question of human responsibility. 'A man was responsible if by the act of divorcing his wife he put her in the position in which she was almost bound to commit adultery. The question is presented as one of the responsibilities of man and in pronouncing it the Lord, as it were, pulled himself up before condemning the man, because if the man put away his wife for adultery it is clear that he could not be held responsible for her afterwards falling into adultery. The real cause and responsibility (for the adultery) then lay not with the man but with the woman.'[8]

The Lower House of the Convocation of York explained this passage in a report produced in 1896. 'Here the putting away of the wife for fornication is granted, but for no other cause. To put her away for any other cause save this would be to put her into the way of temptation to adultery, and the guilt would lie at the husband's door, he would be the cause if she fell into adultery. If, however, she be put away for fornication, which is a just cause of separation, the guilt of any future sin rests with her, as the separation came about through her own misconduct. But to marry a woman thus separated from her husband for fornication – is adultery. In this passage, then, putting away for fornication is allowed, but for any woman put away to marry again is adultery. Why? It can only be because her husband is alive, and because the bond exists. If it exists for her, it equally exists for him. If a new marriage is adultery for her, so is a new marriage for him.'[9]

No remarriage following divorce (Luke 16:18)

In Luke's gospel Jesus deals with the issue of the remarriage of the divorced husband and the divorced wife. The gospel is written for the Gentile world, which would have been largely ignorant of the Jewish laws regarding divorce. Jesus states the simple truth:

Anyone who divorces his wife and marries another woman commits adultery, and the man who marries a divorced woman commits adultery (Luke 16:18).

Here Jesus warns that both a divorced man and a single man commit adultery by being involved in a remarriage. The first point is that for a divorced man to remarry another (single) woman is adultery. It follows that for the remarriage of the divorced man to be adulterous his first marriage must still be intact in Jesus' eyes, and that is why his sexual relationship with a single woman is adultery. Jesus then speaks about the single man who marries a divorced woman. He is guilty of adultery against the divorced woman's husband, because in Jesus' eyes the first marriage of the woman is still intact. According to Andrew Cornes, this text is concerned principally with remarriage. The first part of the verse teaches that 'legal divorce cannot break the marriage bond because (and this is Christ's point) remarriage after divorce is in fact adultery. The second part of the verse makes the point that it is also adultery for a single man to marry a divorced woman.'[10]

The teaching of Luke is straightforward and clear. It states an absolute position that all remarriage is wrong. Now there can be no doubt that Luke was familiar with Christ's teaching on divorce, and it seems remarkable that he would have written in the way that he did if, in fact, Christ had allowed an exception. Indeed, if that were the case Luke could be accused of causing confusion and misleading the Church. For if Christ had taught that there were grounds for divorce, it would be unforgivable for Luke to have simply ignored the exception which fundamentally alters the teaching. It would be highly misleading for Luke to write in a way that could be construed to support the idea that marriage was indissoluble, when, in fact, Christ was teaching the opposite. But we know that Luke, a physician, was meticulously accurate in the way he recorded the gospel of Christ. It is unthinkable that he would not have qualified his writing to make it clear that there was an exception if that were the case. But he did not do so. There is no doubt that Luke believed that Jesus taught that the marriage bond was indissoluble.

Later in his ministry a group of Pharisees tested Jesus by asking him about the causes of divorce. The encounter with the Pharisees is recorded in Matthew 19:3–12 and Mark 10:2–12. While the two gospels report the same event, there are some differences between the accounts of Matthew and Mark. The record of Matthew, which was written for a mainly Jewish audience, mentions the so-called exception clause 'except for marital unfaithfulness', while Mark omits any reference to an exception. At the time there was a debate among the Pharisees about the legitimate grounds for divorce, which was required by Jewish law when a wife was guilty of adultery. This is important because the exception clause has become the foundation of the Protestant doctrine of divorce, and is used by modern Christians to justify their practice of remarriage following divorce. While many books have been written on the interpretation of this clause, the matter remains controversial among theologians.

Jesus and the Pharisees (Mark chapter 10)

Jesus was travelling through Transjordan on his way to Jerusalem and his final Passover before his trial and crucifixion. While in the territory of Perea, which was ruled by Herod Antipas, the man who had imprisoned and executed John the Baptist because of his comments about Herod's incestuous marriage to his brother's wife, the Pharisees approached Jesus and tested him by asking,

> 'Is it lawful for a man to divorce his wife?' Jesus replied [with a question], 'What did Moses command you?' They said, 'Moses permitted a man to write a certificate of divorce and send her away.' Jesus repied, 'It was because your hearts were hard that Moses wrote you this law,' [and then Jesus quoted from Genesis] 'But at the beginning of creation, God "made them male and female". "For this reason a man will leave his father and mother and be united to his wife, and the two will become one flesh".' [Jesus concluded] 'So they are no longer two, but one. Therefore what God has joined together, let man not separate' (Mark 10:2–9).

The response of Jesus is highly significant. He does not launch into a discussion on the possible grounds for divorce or discuss the lawfulness of divorce. In this dramatic encounter the Lord quotes from the two texts in Genesis (1:27 and 2:24) which form the foundation of God's ordinance of marriage as an indissoluble one flesh union. This tells us that if we wish to know the mind of Christ on divorce then we must take account of these two verses. Essentially Jesus is saying that God created one man and one woman and when God united them in marriage they became one flesh. Jesus then draws the conclusion that husband and wife have been joined together by God to become one. For this reason, man should not separate them. This was the public teaching of Jesus on the issue of the lawfulness of divorce.

Later, when Jesus and the disciples were in the house they asked him to explain this teaching. Jesus answered,

> Anyone who divorces his wife and marries another woman commits adultery against her. And if she divorces her husband and marries another man, she commits adultery (Mark 10:11–12).

Here Jesus is saying that remarriage is wrong, reinforcing the teaching given during the Sermon on the Mount. A divorced man who marries a single woman commits adultery against his first wife. This is because the one flesh bond created by God at marriage is still intact in God's eyes, and so the sexual relationship with another woman is adulterous. Similarly, the woman who divorces her husband and remarries another man commits adultery. This is because the divorce has not freed her from the marriage bond and she is still tied to her husband, although legally divorced from him. Therefore, being still married in the eyes of God, she is required either to be reconciled to her husband or to remain unmarried. For her to marry another man is adultery. The emphatic teaching of Jesus is completely contrary to human expectations. He refers to God's creation ordinance, thereby confirming from the Scriptures that marriage is indissoluble and so remarriage following divorce is always adultery.

Andrew Cornes's comments on Jesus' teaching in Mark are helpful. 'Since Jesus specifically calls remarriage after legal divorce "adultery", he is saying that whatever has taken place legally in divorce, the partners are still married. This means that remarriage is not only wrong, it is impossible at the deepest level. Jesus makes the astonishing statement – astonishing in his own day and just as amazing in our own – that it is not actually possible to marry again during the lifetime of a divorced partner; it is only possible to commit adultery with a third party, even though from a legal point of view this new "marriage" has been properly entered into.

'Jesus' teaching also means that divorce – at least in the sense in which the Pharisees thought of it – is not only wrong but is impossible. Again, it is of course perfectly possible to secure a divorce that is valid from the legal point of view. But it is not possible to undo what God has done… Since even after divorce, to marry someone else is to commit adultery, clearly this marriage bond still remains, even after legal divorce. Therefore full divorce – in the sense of the "dissolution" or elimination of the marriage bond – is not something which any legal process is capable of achieving. Only death dissolves the bond.'[11]

It is noteworthy that Mark's account of this exchange with the Pharisees does not mention the phrase 'except for marital unfaithfulness', but makes it clear that Jesus' teaching on divorce and remarriage apply to husband and wife alike.

THE EXCEPTION CLAUSE (MATTHEW CHAPTER 19)

In Matthew's account of the testing of Jesus, the first question put by the Pharisees was, 'Is it lawful for a man to divorce his wife for any and every reason?' (Matthew 19:3). As we have seen, Jesus did not answer the question directly, but referred to the Genesis account of the Creation, and the institution of marriage. He then said, 'So they are no longer two, but one. Therefore what God has joined together, let man not separate' (Matthew 19:6). The Pharisees persisted with their questioning, 'Why then did Moses command that a man give his wife a certificate of divorce and send her away?' (Matthew 19:7). Jesus corrected the Pharisees by pointing out that Moses did not command divorce, but rather permitted divorce because their hearts were hard. He then reaffirmed his teaching given in the Sermon on the Mount.

> Jesus replied, 'Moses permitted you to divorce your wives because your hearts were hard. But it was not this way from the beginning. I tell you that anyone who divorces his wife, except for marital unfaithfulness, and marries another woman commits adultery' (Matthew 19:8-9).

Does adultery dissolve the marriage bond?

A pillar of the Protestant doctrine of divorce is based on Matthew 19:9. The interpretation is that adultery (marital unfaithfulness) dissolves the marriage bond and therefore allows remarriage following divorce. We saw in chapter 3 that Luther and Calvin claimed that adultery meant that the guilty marriage partner was *as good as dead* [my italics], and therefore they believed that the innocent party was free to remarry. Calvin, for example, wrote that a woman who commits adultery sets her husband free, for she cuts herself off from him as a rotten member.[12] Luther said that whoever commits adultery is considered *as one dead* [my italics], and therefore the other may remarry just as though his spouse had died, if it is his intention to insist on his rights and not to show mercy to the guilty party.[13,14] The Westminster Confession of Faith, which outlines the doctrine of the Reformed Protestant faith, says 'in the case of adultery after marriage, it is lawful for the innocent party to sue out a divorce, and, after the divorce, to marry another, *as if the offending party were dead* [my italics].'[15] Significantly, Luther and Calvin both acknowledge that the marriage union is only broken by death. So the question is whether they are correct in their amazing claim that adultery equates to the death of a marriage partner.

The report of the committee of the Lower House of the Convocation of York commented on the official Protestant position. 'We cannot but express our strong feeling that to refuse to the convicted defendant (adulterer), and to grant to the successful plaintiff (innocent party), a licence to marry is an illogical position. They – both of them – are either married or unmarried. If both are married already, then both should be refused, because they already each have a partner alive, and a licence could only be granted for what would in fact be bigamy and adultery. If they are unmarried, the bond is broken, and the one is as free to be married as the other... The Church of England has in no way sanctioned the idea that the bond has been broken.'[16]

In the book *Divorce in America* (1925), the Bishop of Vermont warned of the inevitable consequences of a divorce law that permitted divorce for adultery. 'Where marriage has been allowed to be dissoluble, it has been found impracticable, first, to restrict this to one cause; or second, in practice to prevent collusion in the furnishing of this cause; or third, to distinguish between the "innocent party" (where such really exists) and the guilty as to the right of remarriage. If the bond of marriage has been broken – either by the act of adultery, or by judicial sentence following upon this – it must have been broken for both parties. It can only therefore be a rule of ecclesiastical discipline which forbids a second marriage to the guilty party. On the assumption that the bond of marriage no longer exists, the imposition of such lifelong penalty can hardly be justified.'[17]

Kenneth Kirk examined the assertion that adultery breaks the marriage bond, allowing the innocent person to remarry, in his book *Marriage and Divorce*. He contended that two questions arise which prove the view to be entirely untenable. 'The first is, why should this power of "dissolving a marriage" be attributed to marital infidelity, and be withheld from sins in every degree as flagrant violations of the duty of husband to wife and wife to husband – persistent cruelty, or neglect, or desertion, for example? Indeed, many of these sins are very often more flagrant than adultery. An isolated act of infidelity may be the result of momentary passion or loss of self-control, but cruelty and desertion are conscious and deliberate. Surely, therefore, they must destroy the marriage bond even more effectively than adultery is said to do? There seems to be no satisfactory answer to this question...

'More important, however, is the second question, even though at first sight it appears pedantic and casuistical. If adultery does indeed dissolve the marriage bond, at what moment does it do so? At the moment it is committed – or at the moment when it is first discovered by the innocent party – or at the moment when it is established as a fact after judicial enquiry? ...It seems then that what must be meant by this statement that "adultery dissolves the marriage bond", is the very different statement, "adultery makes the marriage bond voidable, if the injured party chooses to bring an action for divorce". So stated, we have, in effect the present English law on the subject.... For it is natural to ask once more, "Why should this be asserted only of adultery, and not of other causes too?"'[18]

In his discussion of Matthew chapter 19, Andrew Cornes concludes that Jesus had a different idea of divorce from the Pharisees. While they conceived only of full divorce with the right to remarry, Jesus taught that divorce could take place, but it did not break the marriage bond. He makes this clear by calling remarriage after divorce adultery.[19] Jesus teaches that remarriage is not only wrong, it is impossible, for it is not possible to contract a true marriage while a marriage partner is still living. 'And it is not only wrong to divorce one's partner: it is actually impossible in any full sense. You may be able to break the legal ties, you may be able to live apart, but you cannot destroy the marriage; your unity with your partner still exists in God's eyes; the marriage bond can only be broken by death.'[20]

Supporting this interpretation Wenham and Heth say that the one flesh bond of marriage is not dissolved by legal divorce, nor by sexual relations with a third party. 'Just as we cannot "divorce" our children from being our own blood relations, no matter how disreputable they may be, so a man cannot "divorce" his wife who is his own flesh and blood through marriage.'[21] They believe that when Matthew 19:9 is analysed into its constituent parts that it makes a fitting retort to the catch question of the Pharisees. 'They asked, "Is it lawful for a man to divorce his wife for any cause at all?" Jesus replied: "It is always wrong to divorce what God had joined together: what is more, divorce, except for marital unfaithfulness, is tantamount to committing adultery; and remarriage after divorce is always so".'[22] Wenham and Heth conclude that the Erasmian attempt to harmonise the teaching of Jesus in Matthew with the absolute prohibition of divorce and remarriage in Mark and Luke 'is flawed by modern assumptions that Jesus taught against the wrong of unwarranted divorce (a "breaking" of the conjugal life) and not the wrong of remarriage (an attempt to break the union completely, reversing what God has done). Jesus was against both; but if a divorce today should take place against the Master's will, the faithful disciple must not compound the problem by remarrying. The disciple must above all have that faith which counts his Lord's word as good and perfect. And remarriage, which Jesus calls adultery, cannot be God's best for his children.'[23]

The belief that adultery breaks the marriage bond persists among evangelical Christians who permit remarriage today. Some believe that adultery *per se* breaks the marriage bond and therefore permits remarriage just as if the offending husband or wife was dead. But this belief raises many difficult questions. If adultery does break the marriage bond, and if the innocent party is willing to be reconciled, do the couple need to be married again? And what if the innocent party is unaware of the adultery? Is she divorced from her husband who has secretly committed adultery? According to Heth, the view that adultery dissolves the marriage bond 'not only degrades the conception of marriage by making its physical side the dominant consideration; it involves two absurdities. First, a man may cease to be married and yet be unaware of the fact. Secondly, it makes adultery, or the pretence of having committed it, the one way to get rid of a marriage which has become distasteful, and so puts a premium on adultery.'[24]

Others believe that sexual sin (referred to in the gospel of Matthew by the Greek word *porneia*, and translated as marital unfaithfulness) permits the innocent party to choose between divorce with remarriage, and reconciliation. That is, adultery does not *per se* break the marriage bond, but allows the innocent party the choice of breaking the marriage bond or not. An example of this line of thinking is given by Stephen Clark in his recently published book, *Putting Asunder* (1999). In his discussion of the exception clause, Clark argues that 'where the divorce was on the basis of illicit sexual intercourse, then neither the divorce nor subsequent remarriage by the man whose wife had been the guilty party would involve him in adultery. Jesus was neither commanding nor commending divorce for such a reason, nor was he encouraging remarriage. But neither was he forbidding or discouraging it.' Accordingly, 'we are not to understand divorce as a failure to live up to the teaching that Jesus had given in [Matthew] chapter 18 on the need for forgiveness'. So the exception clause in Matthew 19:9 'permits divorce where the wife has been guilty of behaviour which undermines the marriage'.[25] The implication of this teaching is that it is the choice of the innocent party that breaks the one flesh union created by God, and Jesus does not mind which choice we make. The innocent spouse has the right to choose whether or not to separate what God has joined together, and therefore the authority to choose to break the marriage bond. It is not difficult to see that this approach to breaking up a family appears to be completely against the spirit of Jesus' teaching, who warns us not to separate what God has joined together.

The serious fault with the view that adultery breaks the marriage bond is that it ignores the message of Hosea that a husband should love his unfaithful wife again, and do all in his power to achieve reconciliation. The Bible teaches that God wants husband and wife to go to the extreme of forgiveness in order to preserve the family. All attempts in both England and America to legislate for divorce on the grounds of adultery have proved totally disastrous. Even those who argued for the initial law were not prepared to go on defending a divorce law based on adultery as the only ground. It seems inconceivable that a law based on Scripture should prove unworkable in practice. Moreover, the attempts of various Christian denominations to carry out church remarriage of the so-called innocent party have resulted in confusion and hypocrisy. The arbitrary way in which various Protestant churches have carried out remarriages, with different denominations applying different rules, and with differences even within denominations, undermines the credibility of their doctrine. The Protestant marriage discipline of selective remarriage of the innocent party after divorce remains a mystery to most people. It is now widely acknowledged that it is not possible to establish guilt and innocence in any meaningful way.

THE PROTESTANT DOCTRINE OF DIVORCE AND CHILDREN

A further objection to the doctrine that claims an adulterous spouse is 'as good as dead' is that it fails to understand that marriage consists of both a marital relationship between husband and wife, and a parental relationship between parents and children. It fails to acknowledge that an 'offending husband or wife' is also a father or mother with parental responsibilities. The Protestant doctrine of divorce needs to explain whether the offending man is dead both as husband and father and whether the offending woman is dead both as wife and mother. Up to now the doctrine has singularly failed to deal with this issue. If the offending man is 'as good as dead' does this mean that the relationship with his children is also 'as good as dead'? Take the example of the father who has an affair with his secretary. Because he is 'as good as dead', the 'innocent' mother is entitled to divorce him and remarry. But what are the consequences for the children? If their father is 'as good as dead' as far as the marriage is concerned, is he still their father? Can a man who is 'as good as dead' in the eyes of the Church, fulfil his responsibility as a parent? And when the 'innocent' mother remarries, what is the relationship between her new husband and her children? Is her new husband also a new father to her children? And if not, then what is the relationship between her new husband and her children? Or is the new husband, in the mind of the children and according to the teaching of Jesus, another man who is committing adultery against the children's father? So we see that the Protestant doctrine of divorce fails to explain the implications of its assertion that the offending party is 'as good as dead' to the children involved. It ignores the parental responsibility of husband and wife; it ignores the needs of children for the care, love and discipline of both mother and father; it ignores the need for children to grow up in a stable family environment.

The idea that Christ taught that adultery severs the relationship between parents and their children is absurd. It is unthinkable that Christ taught that children should regard an adulterous parent 'as good as dead'. Yet the Protestant doctrine allows divorce even although one of the essential family relationships is still intact—the relationship between parents and their children. According to this doctrine, either Jesus believed that the role of the father is not really important, or that a father, although excluded from the family, can still fulfil his responsibilities towards his children. The implication is that Jesus taught that adultery is a sufficient moral ground to break a family home and deprive children of the care of either father or mother. This doctrine has a devastating effect on children. It places the happiness of husband and wife above the moral well-being of children, and above the stability of the family. The children's well-being is considered to be of secondary importance compared to the needs of the individual parents. What is more, when a parent leaves the family home because of a marital offence, this is made blatantly obvious to children, although they do not understand it. Children are astounded that their parents can so easily depart from the family home, and that they do so with the apparent blessing of the Church.

Does this doctrine really express the mind and attitude of Jesus towards children? Is Jesus, who received the little children despite the objections of his disciples, the one who is responsible for the doctrine that has led to millions of children growing up without a father? No, it is unthinkable that people should claim that the teaching of Jesus allows children to be deserted by their parents. The express purpose of the teaching of Jesus is to preserve the family and prevent children suffering the consequences of broken homes, even to the extent of stating, as he did, that marriage is indissoluble. It is unthinkable that the teaching of Jesus has made children the innocent victims of divorce. The falseness of the Protestant doctrine is a travesty of the teaching of Christ.

Because Jesus' teaching against divorce was so strong and so opposed to the prevailing view of the time, his disciples responded with the amazing statement, 'If this is the situation between a husband and wife, it is better not to marry' (Matthew 19:10). Clearly even his disciples found it difficult to accept his uncompromising teaching, for they understood it to mean that marriage is for life, and so divorce with remarriage is not an option. This teaching was even stricter than the strictest teaching of the Pharisees. Jesus replied, 'Not everyone can accept this teaching, but only those to whom it has been given. For some are eunuchs because they were born that way; others were made that way by men; and others have renounced marriage because of the kingdom of heaven. The one who can accept this should accept it' (Matthew 19:11–12). With this reply, was Jesus acknowledging that not everyone could accept this word, which is the situation today, where remarriage has become common in some parts of the Church?

Jesus emphasised the seriousness of marital unfaithfulness by teaching that it can lead to a divorce (a separation from bed and board). A husband or wife who divorces his or her marriage partner because of marital unfaithfulness is not guilty of immoral behaviour. Instead it is the unfaithful partner who has been immoral. The shame of adultery is that it can split a family, and be the cause of suffering for all involved. It can therefore never be condoned, even though it may be forgiven. In some marriages, plagued by persistent unfaithfulness, divorce may be the only solution. In effect, adultery can wreck a marriage and damage the family. It is a heinous sin because it affects so many other people; it is a total disaster for all concerned. However, Jesus taught an attitude of forgiveness and reconciliation. 'First go and be reconciled to your brother; then come and offer your gift' (Matthew 5:24). In a marriage in which there is marital unfaithfulness the innocent party should do all he or she can to persuade their unfaithful spouse to a change of heart, and so bring about reconciliation that would save the marriage. Many people, when they face the awful consequences of adultery, come to their senses and repent of their sin. Jesus taught that divorce can only be considered when there is marital unfaithfulness—and even then Hosea's marriage is an example. Everything possible should be done to save a marriage. However, as we have already seen, a legal divorce for marital unfaithfulness does not allow a remarriage because in God's eyes the marriage bond is still intact.

TEACHING OF THE APOSTLE PAUL

The apostle answered a number of inquiries from Christian believers concerning marriage in his first letter to the Corinthian Church. In particular Paul deals with two important questions. The first was—is divorce permitted? Paul writes:

> To the married I give this command (not I, but the Lord): A wife must not separate from her husband. But if she does, she must remain unmarried or else be reconciled to her husband. And a husband must not divorce his wife (1 Corinthians 7:10–11).

Paul is teaching new believers and stresses that he is giving them a command from the Lord. And the command from the Lord is clear and emphatic—a wife must not separate from her husband. However, should circumstances arise which make separation inescapable, then the deserted wife has two options: either to be reconciled to her husband or to remain unmarried. Note that remarriage is not an option. It seems unlikely that Paul would have failed to mention the possibility of remarriage for the divorced woman, if he understood that the teaching of Christ allowed remarriage. But Paul does not do so. Instead, he reaffirms the teaching of no remarriage in the strongest possible way.

According to Andrew Cornes, Paul knew of the one exception that Christ allowed namely, divorce in a case of marital unfaithfulness. 'Paul knows this and includes it in his quotation of Christ's teaching. Christ taught not only that a woman should not divorce her husband and a man should not divorce his wife. He also taught that you may divorce for adultery. Moreover, that exception of Christ's came in a setting where remarriage was being discussed. So Christ also taught (according to Paul here) that if (following Christ's permission) you divorce for adultery, then you must remain single or be reconciled to your partner. This is what Paul is doing: relaying Christ's teaching about the right marital state after the one exception Christ allowed: divorce for adultery. The only difference is that Christ put it negatively (to remarry is to commit adultery) whereas Paul puts Christ's teaching positively (after divorce, you must remain single or be reconciled).'[26] FF Bruce adds the comment, 'For a Christian husband or wife divorce is excluded by the law of Christ: here Paul has no need to express a judgement of his own, for the Lord's ruling on the matter was explicit.'[27]

Paul then deals with the issue of the Christian married to a non-Christian. Can they divorce?

> To the rest I say this (I, not the Lord): If any brother has a wife who is not a believer and she is willing to live with him, he must not divorce her. And if a woman has a husband who is not a believer and he is willing to

live with her, she must not divorce him. For the unbelieving husband has been sanctified through his wife, and the unbelieving wife has been sanctified through her believing husband. Otherwise your children would be unclean, but as it is, they are holy. But if the unbeliever leaves, let him do so. A believing man or woman is not bound in such circumstances; God has called us to live in peace (1 Corinthians 7:12–15).

The essence of Paul's teaching is that a believing husband or wife must not divorce his or her unbelieving marriage partner. He mentions that the unbelieving partner and children have been sanctified through the marriage, indicating that their hope of salvation lies in the witness of the Christian parent. The children love both parents, believer and non-believer, and want their family to remain together. It is unthinkable that the Christian parent would do anything to destroy their family. Therefore the Christian should do all he or she can to preserve the marriage and pray for the conversion of the unbelieving partner which God frequently brings about.

In the situation where the unbelieving partner chooses to leave the marriage, despite the Christian spouse having done all they can to preserve it, the Christian should not resist, but allow the unbeliever to leave in peace. But there is no suggestion that the Christian who is left by an unbelieving partner is permitted to remarry. Should an unbelieving partner leave the family home, the Christian spouse should do all in their power to achieve reconciliation; remarriage, which destroys the hope of reconciliation, should not enter their mind.

The so-called Pauline privilege, which allows remarriage for desertion, is derived from the words 'a believing man or woman is not bound in such circumstances'. According to Stephen Clark in *Putting Asunder* (1999), evangelicals who believe that Jesus allows divorce and remarriage for sexual infidelity have long been divided over the question as to whether Paul allows another ground for divorce in this verse. 'Some have argued that this verse allows divorce for desertion, while others have said that it teaches no such thing. Those who believe that it allows for divorce in cases of desertion differ amongst themselves as to the type of situation with which Paul is dealing.'[28] The *New Bible Commentary* suggests that this verse probably allows divorce for desertion. 'Separation in this case presumably means that the Christian is free to marry someone else—provided he or she is a Christian.'[29] But this interpretation appears to be reading into these words what human nature wishes to find, for a perfectly valid interpretation is that a Christian is absolved from pursuing an unbelieving spouse, because 'God has called us to live in peace'. To interpret the words as overriding the clear command from the Lord (that a separated wife must remain unmarried or else be reconciled to her husband) is perverse. Moreover, such an interpretation is out of sympathy with the instruction that 'each one should retain the place in life that the Lord assigned to him and to which God has called him' (1 Corinthians 7:17). Paul's final summing up leaves no doubt about his teaching regarding remarriage:

> 'A woman is bound to her husband as long as he lives. But if her husband dies, she is free to marry anyone she wishes, but he must belong to the Lord' (1 Corinthians 7:39).

Here Paul mentions the one and only situation in which a woman is permitted to remarry, and that is on the death of her husband; and this is because she is bound to her husband for life. If Paul was teaching that remarriage was permitted for desertion he would surely have said so—he could have written 'but if her husband dies or leaves her' but he did not do so. Like Jesus, Paul taught that marriage was indissoluble except by death.

TWO DOCTRINES ON DIVORCE, BUT ONE IS FALSE

From our study of the history of divorce we have seen that since the time of the Reformation the Christian Church has been split on the issue. Some theologians, building on the work of Erasmus and Luther, claim that Jesus allows full divorce (a divorce that dissolves the marriage bond and allows remarriage) in the case of adultery and desertion. This view has become increasingly popular during the 20th century, and is held by most evangelical Christians and Protestant denominations, and is gaining ground in the Church of England. It underpins the campaign to change the marriage discipline of the Church of England and introduce remarriage in church during the lifetime of a former partner.

On the other side of the doctrinal divide are those who believe that marriage is an indissoluble union created by God; that the teaching of the Scriptures permit separation without the right to remarry because the marriage bond is still intact and cannot be broken by legal divorce. The Roman Catholic Church has always held this position, and it is found in the canon law of the Church of England.

These two positions are, of course, diametrically opposed to each other and they cannot both be right; it follows, therefore, that there is a major error in one section of the Christian Church. All the evidence considered in this book suggests that the Protestant doctrine of divorce is based on a false interpretation of the teaching of Christ. The weight of biblical teaching is that divorce is wrong and against God's will; that it is rebellion against God's divine institution of marriage. From the very beginning, God's intention was that marriage is for life.

Chapter 17

Tears and profound sadness

The evidence that divorce damages children

We now consider the consequences of divorce, examining its effects on children and their parents. In doing so, we shall refer to large national studies, examine the findings of research papers and lifestyle surveys, and hear the views of children on how divorce affects them. We should bear in mind that because two factors are associated does not necessarily mean that the relationship is causal. Indeed, it is seldom possible to prove causal relationships in human behaviour. Instead, we should see each relationship described by the research as a part of a jigsaw puzzle. Taken together, they should produce a picture that will help us to reach our own interpretation of the effects of divorce. We start by examining the effect of divorce on children.

During the first half of the 20th century, it was self-evident to most people that children were better off being brought up in a family by their own mother and father. Common sense shouted from the rooftops that a broken home was bad for children, and so parents felt they had a duty towards their children to maintain the family home. Anyone who suggested otherwise would have been regarded as perverse and blind to the most basic facts of life. That is how things were in the 1950s, before the mass divorce movement had taken root in Western society.

However, within little more than a decade this common sense view had been overturned. We have already seen how in the 1960s the experts produced 'evidence' that children were better off out of a family in which the parents were unhappy. Parents were advised that being removed from family conflict by means of a divorce was better for their children. When the quarrelling parents separated and divorced, so the reasoning went, the children would be more contented as they would not have to endure their parents' rows. The experts claimed that, following the divorce, children would rapidly adjust to their new family circumstances and the effects on them would be short-lived. We saw in chapter 13 that some social commentators asserted that divorce did not harm children, claiming that it might help their development. Sociological research claimed that children, removed from unhappy families by the divorce of their parents, were better off. Herzog and Sudia concluded in their review of social research that as the 'evidence indicates that discord and conflict in the home can be more detrimental than father's absence, one is forced to prefer a "good" one-parent home for a child'.[1] This 'evidence' spread the message that parents in an unhappy marriage should divorce for the sake of their children.

Psychological research conducted in the 1960s and 1970s examined children's beliefs about divorce. A series of papers published in the scientific literature asserted that children did not experience divorce as a negative event. One of the early psychological surveys, published in 1960, was conducted on a sample of 295 Californian university students who were all children of divorce. The survey examined the hypothesis that divorce might be traumatic for some children, but for others the divorce might mean relief from tension and the beginning of the child's emotional recovery. Author of the paper, Judson Landis, observed that a significantly larger proportion of the children who thought the home was unhappy reacted to divorce by thinking it was the best for all concerned. A comparison of two groups of children, according to how happy they saw their home prior to the divorce, showed that 'those from apparently happy homes indicated either no change in feelings of security and personal happiness or they shifted to feeling less secure or less happy'. However, 'those who saw the homes as unhappy report greater security and happiness after the divorce'. Asked about any change in attitude towards the divorce with the passage of time, 28 per cent of those from a happy home and 64 per cent of those from an unhappy home reported the marriage was a mistake in the first place. Two-thirds of the children reported that the divorce did not affect their confidence in associating with friends.[2]

In 1971 a paper was published which reviewed ten years' research on the psychological effects of a child's separation from its parents. The author, Michael Rutter, concluded that while a child's separation from his family caused short-term distress, it was of little direct importance as a cause of long-term disorder. Although separation was associated with antisocial behaviour, this was due, not to the fact of separation itself but rather to the family discord which accompanied the separation. According to Rutter, the child was adversely affected by the tension and disharmony caused by family disruption; the break-up of the family caused by divorce was only a minor influence.[3]

The main conclusion of this type of research was that children, while feeling initially upset and downcast about the news of divorce, on the whole do not have negative feelings towards divorce and sometimes found that it facilitated their development. Indeed, divorce could be the beginning of the child's emotional recovery as a significant proportion of children thought divorce was the best for all concerned. Antisocial behaviour that occurred at the time of the family break-up was due not to the divorce but the discord that preceded it. For this reason, many children from unhappy homes felt greater security and happiness after the divorce of their parents. Much of the research showed what most academics wanted to believe—that it was all right to divorce and that the children did not really mind if their parents did so. Once the research papers were published the findings were soon regarded as 'scientific' evidence, and as such, had an enormous influence on society's thinking. There was now evidence that showed that children did not really mind their parents divorcing.

'EXPERT' ADVICE ON DIVORCE

An article on the women's page of *The Times* provides a typical example of the message that was spread by the popular media in the late 1960s. It aimed to address the question—are the children worse off? 'Parents of their own free will prefer to perpetuate their, at best, negative relationship in order to carry out what they consider to be their inescapable responsibility – that of rearing their young in the accepted home-plus-mother-plus-father syndrome. Why do they think that this almost inevitably strained state of affairs is better for the children? There is no proof that a child of one marriage, later brought up in another, fares better or worse than a child whose parents, though at odds with each other, keep their marriage going.'[4]

Another typical example of advice by the experts is contained in the book *The Courage to Divorce* (1974), written by two social workers. The basic message is that divorce could liberate children and bring them psychological benefits. The authors claimed that if a divorce was handled well, 'it is more likely to be a potentially liberating experience which restructures family life in a healthier way and provides potential emotional gratification for all family members'.[5] The authors insist that because of the very nature of their life experience, children of divorce have particular advantages and opportunities that their peers may not have. A properly handled divorce is a relatively non-traumatic event for children, and children of divorce have a unique opportunity of experiencing a variety of family styles.[6] Divorce is also likely to improve the relationship between non-residential fathers and their children, as they are likely to pay more attention to their children than unhappily married fathers do.[7]

A divorced psychologist, Dr Lee Salk, offered advice in *What every Child would like Parents to Know about Divorce* (1978). He advised that parents considering divorce should give their child the opportunity to be heard, for this would make an unhappy situation far more endurable. While denying that he was saying that divorce was necessarily good for children, Dr Salk was only pointing out that divorce was not necessarily bad for them and need not damage them, if it was dealt with in a manner that protected the children's integrity. He had seen young people who had come through a divorce who were emotionally much stronger and perhaps more stable for having been through it. They had not been traumatised by the experience, nor were they turned off marriage itself. Dr Salk believed that had their parents stayed together 'for the sake of the children', in all likelihood they would not have come away with a positive attitude about marriage. It was impossible to hide from children the disenchantment unhappy parents felt for each other.[8]

Even in the early 1980s conventional wisdom was that children from single-parent families were no worse off than children from two-parent families.[9] In their book *Marriage and How to Survive It* (1983), psychologists Dougal Mackay and Jill Frankham make a strong case against parents staying together for their children. They claimed that although divorce does cause children emotional upset, the reaction with young children can be short-lived. According to the authors, marriage experts are unanimous in rejecting the idea that a marriage should be preserved for the sake of the children. 'Divorce may cause them (children) distress but a bad marriage will have an even worse effect on them psychologically.'[10] Therefore the argument that one should stay together for the sake of the children does not really hold up, for 'a bad marriage can do more harm than a broken home'. The authors claim that research findings indicate clearly that the children whose parents have divorced are much better adjusted in many key aspects than those from unhappy homes. When children of divorce are teenagers they are less likely to develop psychosomatic illness, delinquent patterns of behaviour, or hostile feelings to one or both parents. 'This suggests that if you do what is right for you [get a divorce], you will be doing right by the rest of your family.'[11]

From the 1960s it was widely accepted by marriage experts, social scientists, social workers, psychologists, marriage guidance counsellors and family therapists that parents in an unhappy marriage should divorce for the sake of their children. The professional view was 'better a good divorce than a bad marriage'. This idea was widely proclaimed in the popular media, chat shows and women's magazines. It was the advice given to hundreds of thousands of parents who sought professional counselling for their marital difficulties. In this chapter we examine the effects of divorce on children, and show how misleading this advice was. The aim is to provide an overview of some of the more important research findings that deal with the effects of divorce on children.

THE CALIFORNIA CHILDREN OF DIVORCE STUDY

An important study into the long-term effects of divorce on children is the work of Dr Judith Wallerstein, who has done a longitudinal survey of sixty North California families, following them up for over 15 years. The study, which began in 1971, was one of the earliest to examine the effect of divorce on the psychological well-being of children. The aim was to describe the effects of divorce on a group of children over many years as they grew into adulthood. The children in the survey were drawn from average middle-class American families, and were considered to be functioning within normal developmental limits before the divorce of their parents. In all, the study involved 131 children from sixty families which had divorced, on average after 11 years of marriage. If anything, the sample was weighted towards the higher end of the social scale and 92 per cent of the families were white. The study involved in-depth interviews with the children and parents by trained psychologists. The initial interview occurred within the first year of the marital separation, with follow-up contacts at 18 months, five years, and ten years. The findings of the study have been extensively reported in many scientific papers, and have been written up in two books, *Surviving the Break-up* and *Second Chances*. A summary of some of the more important findings is presented for different groups of children, according to their age at the first interview.

Children aged three to five – the pre-school children

At the initial interview after the divorce the researchers described the children in this group as 'frightened, bewildered, and very sad. Their immature grasp of the events swirling around them, together with their difficulty in sorting out their own fantasy and dream from reality, rendered them especially vulnerable.'[12] Having seen the relationship between their parents fall apart, they were afraid that other relationships might similarly break down, resulting in their being left all on their own with no one to care for them. These young children were especially anxious as night approached, when many 'became fretful, waking frequently, crying, and begging to be taken into the parent's bed'.[13]

As the children tried to understand the disturbing events of the separation, 'they reached explanations that caused great anguish'. For example, many concluded that the departed parent had rejected them, and had decided to replace them with another family.[14] Despite an unbearable sense of rejection, 'the children's loyalty and intense love for their departed father remained unchanged', despite repeated disappointments in the relationship with him after the separation.[15]

Follow-up interviews with pre-school children

A disturbing finding was that at the eighteen month mark almost half of the pre-school children were more troubled than at the initial interview. Indeed, at five years one-third of the children were severely depressed.[16] When these children were interviewed ten years later, almost a third of them regarded 'the divorce as a central aspect of their lives that evoked strong feelings, tears, and profound sadness'. Many felt lonely and had a sense of deprivation within their current situation, and that included those with parents who had remarried. More than half of the children 'spoke wistfully of the intact family', and 'felt deprived because they missed many of the experiences of a "together" family'.[17]

Even among those who were very young at the time of the divorce, the wish for reconciliation was present in half of the sample ten years after the divorce of their parents. One youngster commented: 'I wish my stepfather would go back to his first wife, I wish my stepmother would go back to her first husband, and I would like my mum and dad to get together again.'[18] Almost all children retained 'an intense awareness of their father', and this included those who were living with a stepfather. As the children became older so the need for the absent father increased, and many felt 'a powerful need to make contact with an absent father' they had not seen for many years.[19]

Children aged six to eight

Children of this age suffered intensely at the time of their parents' separation. Their immediate reaction was one of profound and 'pervasive sadness'. The impact of the separation, usually as a consequence of their father leaving the family home, was so 'strong that the children's usual defences and strategies for coping did not hold sufficiently under the stress'.[20] Consequently, 'crying and sobbing were not uncommon, especially among the boys, and many children were on the brink of tears' as they spoke to the interviewers. These children were afflicted with a profound sense of sorrow and had 'great difficulty in obtaining relief'. The interviewers give an example of a seven-year-old boy who was very sad about the split, but maintained that he did not cry because, 'I have to hold it in, cause I'd be crying all the time.'[21] Sometimes the intensity of the child's distress was directly related to the conflict between the parents, but even when there was no conflict some children still suffered an intense feeling of sadness.

Many children were very frightened by the collapse of their family, and worried that they would be 'left without a family, and would end up living with strangers'.[22] Children in this age group yearned for their absent father. Many 'missed their father acutely' and felt he had rejected them. Their longing for their departed father was similar to the grief caused by the death of a parent. One example given by the interviewers was of a boy who prayed every night for the return of his father, and then cried in his sleep. Their despair and sadness was characterised by an 'intense, almost physical, longing for their father'. In the opinion of the researchers, these children were expressing 'inner psychological needs of great power and intensity'. Even fathers who had been verbally and physically abusive were missed just as much as those fathers who had maintained good relationships with their children.[23]

In general, children had difficulty in expressing anger at their father, but some, mostly boys, 'expressed considerable anger at their mother for either causing the divorce or driving their father away'. The children most profoundly hurt by the loss of the father tended to be those who were most angry with their mother. Most children repeatedly expressed the wish that their parents would become reconciled and that the family would be together again. So deep was the desire for reconciliation that some children held on to the wish even after the remarriage of one or both parents.[24]

Follow-up of children aged six to eight

At the ten-year follow-up interview it was estimated that 40 per cent were underachieving to a significant degree at school, to such an extent that several youngsters who could have aimed for professional careers were instead aiming for semi-skilled jobs. Over half regarded the divorce as the central experience of their lives. In their unhappiness, their loneliness and their sense of deprivation, the youngsters who were 16 to 18, ten years after their parents' divorce, suffered more than any other age groups in the study. They 'spoke longingly of their lives in the intact pre-divorce family'. To these children it was 'self-evident that strong, invisible ties between divorced parents had lasted over the years', and many still viewed their parents as a couple. The loss of the father was a recurring theme, and many yearned for their father, even though he had often let them down badly through the years.

These children did not regard 'the divorced family as a new social norm'. Instead they considered divorce as a sign of marital failure, and felt that it should only be contemplated as a last resort when children are involved. The fact that one parent had been unfaithful during the marriage was painful to the children, a cause of real bitterness. Despite the fact that they had spent more than half their lives in a divorced family, mostly with their mother, and half of them with a stepfather, their own father remained a significant psychological presence in their lives. They spoke with some feeling of the lack of opportunity for a close relationship with their own father. Only a quarter of the girls and 30 per cent of the boys enjoyed a reasonably good relationship with their father, and more than half of the group suffered intense feelings of rejection.[25]

Children aged 9 to 12

Children in this age group tried to develop ways of coping with their profound feelings of loss and rejection. The researcher quotes an example of one boy who sat for 'many hours sobbing in his darkened room' after his father had left home. Although the father's visits were infrequent, it was some time before the child would admit that he missed his father intensely and longed to see him daily and was profoundly hurt by his father's behaviour. Most children felt 'ashamed of what was happening to their families' and so did all they could to conceal their troubles from the outside world. Their sense of shame was not really relieved by the high incidence of divorce in the community around them. Many children did not want other people to know that their parents were separated, and felt embarrassed by the behaviour of their parents. They also tried to hide from others their own hurt feelings. Many children in this age group felt intensely angry with their parents, and especially the parent whom they blamed for the divorce. There was also a feeling of 'moral indignation and outrage' that their parents were behaving in a way that they considered to be immoral and irresponsible.[26]

Children aged 13 to 18 – the adolescents

The interviewers tell of the 'profound sense of loss' experienced by these adolescents. Some reacted 'with profound grief' as if a person whom they loved very much had died. They reported feelings 'of emptiness, tearfulness, difficulty in concentrating, chronic fatigue, and very troublesome dreams, all symptoms of mourning. Although no person had actually died, these adolescents appeared to be mourning the family of their childhood.' And as they mourned the passing of their family, a feeling of outgrowing the family of their childhood magnified the sense of loss caused by the divorce. Both sets of feelings fused and produced an overwhelming sense of 'grief for the family that was no longer available to them' because of the divorce, 'and for the family they were leaving because they were growing up'.[27]

Many adolescents conveyed feelings of loneliness, the fear of being isolated, and some equated their parents' divorce with death. Feelings of depression were common, and many were preoccupied with the survival of relationships, wondering whether family relationships would remain alive or would die with the dying marriage.

The interviewers describe how they were 'unprepared for the quality of the anguish' that these children experienced, and particularly for the frantic appeals of the children for them to help restore the parents' marriage. To illustrate this point they cite the example of a fourteen-year-old boy who told them: 'I felt that the rug had been pulled out from under me. I cried and I begged and begged. I tried to talk sense to my mum until I was almost mute.' He even explained to his parents that reconciliation would save the family a great deal of money. He appealed to the interviewers to do something to effect reconciliation on his behalf.[28]

The adolescents as a group often experienced great anxiety; they worried about their present and their future, about how they would be supported and who would send them to school. They were also concerned about whether they would succeed as sexual partners, and about whether they would achieve a better marriage than their parents. The anxiety among some children was so great, according to the interviewers, that at times it 'bordered on panic'.[29]

Another common emotion was a deep sense of anger. Many accused their parents of behaving childishly or immorally and made the point that the divorce represented their parents' unwillingness to address marital problems in a responsible and mature way appropriate to their age. They felt one or both of their parents were putting their own wishes and needs above those of their adolescent children and this selfishness made them angry. Many felt disappointed with the behaviour of their parents, which they thought did not accord with standards of proper conduct, and this led them to worry about issues of right and wrong in general.[30]

Another recurring theme was the conflict of loyalty that these children endured. Most children expressed their love for both their parents, and felt that they were being torn in two by demands to take one side against the other. 'These demands of the parents on the youngsters frequently led to despair, depression, and guilt.' One fourteen-year-old began to sob: 'I am in the middle. It is my struggle. I am loyal to my father and I love my mother.'[31] Because of their unhappiness these youngsters entered actively into a variety of activities which kept them away from home. Some took advantage of the diminished parental supervision they were receiving. 'Perhaps stimulated by the divorce, they became quickly involved in a very hectic social life that included increased sexual activity.'[32]

Follow-up of children aged 9 to 18

Ten years after the divorce a significant number of individuals, who were by now young adults, still regarded it as the dominant influence in their lives. They retained vivid memories of the unhappy events surrounding the break-up of their family. They still had strong emotions as they looked back, feeling sad at the divorce, but retaining some resentment towards their parents and a wistful sense of having missed out on the benefits of having grown up in an intact family. A smaller than expected number was going on to college and a significant number seemed to be drifting with little direction in their lives.[33]

The sleeper effect

A most unexpected finding of the research was that many young people, and especially young women, experienced a delayed effect of divorce. In the decade after a divorce 60 per cent of children felt rejected by one of their parents. The young people stressed to the researchers how much they felt the need for a family structure, and how they wanted moral guidance and protection.[34] Ten years after the divorce a significant proportion of young men and women were troubled, drifting and underachieving. Two-thirds of young women aged between 19 and 23 showed a disturbing pattern of behaviour when they were required to make decisions about the future course of their lives, especially when such decisions meant committing themselves to a relationship with a member of the opposite sex. Many of the young women, who appeared to have done reasonably well in early adolescence, became very frightened of failure as they approached early adulthood. Late adolescence and early adulthood became a time of particular anxiety and stress for them. When they faced up to their need to form a committed relationship, they became extremely anxious and fearful of betrayal, and concerned that they would not be loved. It seems that intense anxieties, which may have been hidden before, came to the fore and caused great suffering among these young women as they struggled to make meaningful relationships with men. More than half of the young women seemed anxious about making commitments and were preoccupied with fears of betrayal. A significant number were involved in a web of short-lived sexual liaisons. Many were fearful of repeating their parents' unhappiness.[35]

THE EXETER FAMILY STUDY: 1994

The aim of this study was to examine the health, social and educational profiles of children who had experienced separation and divorce. The participants in the survey were selected by sending almost a thousand questionnaires to families in the Exeter area. Matched pairs were selected where one child had experienced family breakdown, and the other child still lived with both biological parents—that is, their natural family. The pairs of children were matched for things such as age, sex, social class, and mother's level of education. The design of the study allowed the data to be analysed comparing the groups by family structure, and also by comparing the matched pairs of children.[36]

The study looked at 152 families in all—76 intact families (children living with both natural parents) and 76 families that had been broken by divorce (or occasionally by death), which were designated 're-ordered families' by the researchers. There were in-depth, confidential interviews with both parents and children, and the study was thus able to measure and compare a number of health, educational and social outcomes for children living in different types of family. The intact families were divided into high conflict and low conflict families, according to the level of marital conflict. The study reported the following findings.

Happiness and self-esteem of children

The survey measured a child's sense of well-being and happiness as reported by their parents. A far higher percentage of children from broken

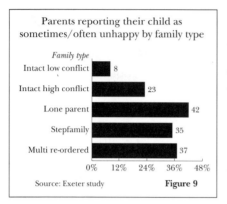

Parents reporting their child as
sometimes/often unhappy by family type

Source: Exeter study   **Figure 9**

families were reported as being unhappy, compared with children from intact families (**figure 9**). This concern extended from children who appeared abnormally quiet or withdrawn, to those with the more obvious manifestations of misery. Significantly, fewer children in intact high conflict families were unhappy than was the case with children from broken homes.[37]

A psychological measure was used to ascertain feelings of self-esteem, and the results show that a higher proportion of children from re-ordered families reported low estimates of their own self-worth. It is again noticeable that the children from high conflict intact families (39 per cent reported low self-worth) did better than those from lone-parent families (57 per cent), stepfamilies (56 per cent) and multi re-ordered families (68 per cent). Taken together, children in re-ordered families were significantly more likely to report lower self-esteem than their matched intact family. For example, negative factors were reported from 44 re-ordered families compared with 23 intact families. It is clear that children who experience divorce tended to have poorer self-esteem than children from intact families.[38]

Psychosomatic health problems

The incidence of psychosomatic symptoms, which included recurrent pains, headaches, stomach aches, feeling sick and other non-specific symptoms of not feeling well were most common among children from multiple re-ordered families. Children from stepfamilies were also more likely to have these symptoms than their matched pairs among the intact families. Moreover, there was little difference between the high and low conflict families. The study also found that children in low conflict families were the least likely to be referred for psychotherapy, while children from re-ordered families had much higher levels of referral. The high conflict intact families had rates that were lower than those of broken families.[39]

Children from broken families reported more problems with their schoolwork than children from intact families. There was no difference between children from high and low conflict families. Parents of children

360

from broken families were twice as likely to report that their children were involved with truancy from school.[40]

Contact with relatives

Parents and children were asked about contact with the child's grandparents, and how contacts had changed over time. While a small number of children from intact families reported reduced contact with grandparents, three times as many children from re-ordered families did so. **Figure 10** shows the children's view of reduced contact with grandparents. Children in lone, step and re-disrupted families were all more likely to report seeing their grandparents less often. On the maternal side, however, there was little difference between intact and re-ordered families, while on the paternal side, re-ordered families were significantly more likely to have infrequent contact than intact families. According to the researchers, 'children often said they found it difficult and stressful to visit grandparents when one or other parent was excluded. Parents also found such situations painful. Children's Christmases were often divided between separate visits to warring sets of relatives.' Children found it very distressing to visit grandparents separately or with just one of their parents. At Christmas time most children from intact families saw both sets of grandparents, whereas just under half of the children from re-ordered families saw their maternal grandparents, and very few saw their paternal grandparents.[41]

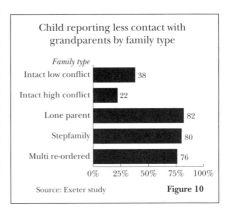

Child reporting less contact with grandparents by family type

Family type	
Intact low conflict	38
Intact high conflict	22
Lone parent	82
Stepfamily	80
Multi re-ordered	76

Source: Exeter study　　**Figure 10**

General points from the study

1. Seventy per cent of non-resident parents described their children as being very upset by their departure from the home, and over half said their children had not wanted the marriage to end.

2. Some resident parents reported strong feelings of regret, waste, devastation and anger at the divorce.

3. In some divorces where the wives had asked their husband to leave the family home the fathers felt bewildered by the rejection, even when it was their own behaviour that was to blame. Many fathers felt that the marriage should not have ended, and they would have liked to try again.

4. Resident parents were more negative about the future than non-resident parents. Almost three out of four non-resident parents interviewed said they regretted the end of their marriage and felt it was a waste.

5. A sizeable minority said that the separation from their children was worse than they had expected. Many had not appreciated the full consequences of separation for themselves or their children. Some resident parents, usually mothers, expressed unexpected feelings of loneliness, as well as a concern for the health of their ex-partners.[42]

6. The experience of many children following the divorce of their parents is of increased conflict, which can last over an extended period, with the child involved to an extent that may not have been the case while the marriage lasted. For some children whose parents are able to co-operate, conflict between parents can, after this initial period, be reduced.[43]

7. Children disliked their comings and goings between their parents. Most children described the transfer between parents as stressful. Children did not find it easy to talk about one parent to the other; some said they never mentioned the absent parent at all. The majority of children whose parents had found new partners were confused and ambivalent towards the relationship. Only 3 out of 27 children felt positive about their mother's and father's new relationships, even though they may have a reasonable relationship with their parent's new partner.[44]

8. Many parents found the process of surrendering their marital relationship while at the same time maintaining their parenting relationship particularly painful.[45]

9. Many children did not understand the reason for their parents' divorce. Children were left confused and bewildered by the divorce, often hoping for reconciliation for far longer than their parents imagine.[46]

An important finding of the Exeter study was that children in the so-called high conflict families did far better than children from families broken by divorce. According to the researchers, 'the most significant factor of those examined was the re-ordering of the family – the loss of a parent on one or more occasion – rather than the presence of serious conflict or violence that was most closely associated with the children's poorer outcomes as measured.' It appears that, in general, children are content to put up with family conflict, and prefer their quarrelling parents to remain together.

A programme on BBC television, which interviewed a number of the parents and children who participated, brought the survey to life. 'The cold statistics were turned into reality by an edition of Panorama last week, which outlined the findings and followed one emotionally disturbed little boy whose parents had divorced through a session with a child psychologist.

His pain and unhappiness were dreadful to watch. He fashioned clay models of his parents together, the family as he would like it to be. The psychologist asked what they were doing. "Cuddling", he replied. As tears took over he said that perhaps they wouldn't argue "if I hadn't been born". This from a 10-year-old boy six years after his parents had split up; parents, moreover, who were kind, thoughtful people who had done everything they could to institute a "civilised" divorce.'[47] No one watching the programme could doubt that children affected by divorce suffer considerable emotional pain.

STUDY OF CHILDREN'S BELIEFS ABOUT DIVORCE: 1984

Children's beliefs about reactions to parental divorce were explored, using a randomly selected sample of 166 school children in the third and fifth grades. The survey sample was divided equally between boys and girls, and included children from both intact families and families broken by divorce. The children were from a middle-class suburban community near Detroit.

The main finding was that divorce was viewed 'as a profoundly negative event that shocks children, upsets and changes children's lives, and contributes to insecurity and lowered self-esteem'. One of the strongest findings was the intense reconciliation wish of children. In this survey, 95 per cent of children expressed the wish that their parents would be reconciled following a divorce. The next most common reaction was that 88 per cent of children felt like crying all the time, and 85 per cent felt that they were all alone. The researchers comment, 'For this group of children, at least, there is virtually a unanimous claim that a child would want their family back and intact rather than split apart.' The authors of this survey concluded: 'The overall consensus of these children quite clearly indicates that divorce is perceived as a highly negative, disruptive event.... The family is central to the child's construction and maintenance of a definition of reality. When the family is shaken, the whole world shakes.'[48] The findings of this survey are remarkably consistent with those of the California Children of Divorce study.

THE CROYDON TEENAGER LIFESTYLE SURVEY

One of the aims of the Croydon study was to compare teenagers in different types of family structure with regard to drug taking and sexual behaviour. The survey of almost three thousand teenagers aged between 16 and 19 years examined a number of lifestyle factors by family structure. Families were divided into those in which the teenagers lived with both natural parents, those where the teenagers lived with one of their natural parents and a stepparent or partner (who was not a parent), and those who lived with a single parent, usually their mother.[49]

Cigarette smoking and illicit drug abuse

Teenagers from stepfamilies (35 per cent) and single-parent families (33 per cent) were more likely to smoke cigarettes than teenagers living with their natural parents (26 per cent). Similarly, there were more adult smokers in the homes of the stepfamilies (48 per cent) than natural families (33 per cent). So both parents and teenagers from stepfamilies smoked more cigarettes than their counterparts in natural families.

Family structure was strongly associated with the use of illicit drugs. Teenagers from stepfamilies were almost twice as likely to use cannabis regularly (38 per cent) compared with teenagers from natural families (19 per cent). The proportion of children from lone-parent families (26 per cent) using cannabis was intermediate between natural families and stepfamilies, as shown in **figure 11**. A similar picture emerged for all the illicit drugs. For example, 5.9 per cent of teenagers from stepfamilies had used amphetamines regularly compared to 1.6 per cent from natural families, and 15.3 per cent of teenagers from stepfamilies had used ecstasy compared with 6.7 per cent from natural families.

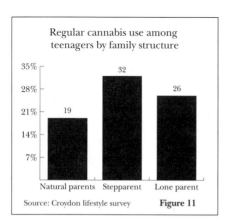

Regular cannabis use among teenagers by family structure

Natural parents   Stepparent   Lone parent

Source: Croydon lifestyle survey   **Figure 11**

Sexual behaviour

Teenagers from broken homes were far more likely to have become sexually active, and at an earlier age, than teenagers from natural families. The survey showed that 55 per cent of teenagers from stepfamilies had become sexually active compared with 35 per cent from natural families. The rate for children from lone-parent families (51 per cent) was just below that of the stepfamilies. Moreover, of those who were sexually active, 63 per cent of teenagers from stepfamilies had their first intercourse before their 16th birthday compared with 50 per cent from natural families. Again we see a significant difference in sexual behaviour between teenagers from different family structures. Teenagers from stepfamilies (66 per cent) were also more likely to have watched a sexually explicit film than teenagers from natural families (55 per cent).

School absenteeism and television

Teenagers from stepfamilies (16 per cent) were nearly twice as likely to have been absent from school for four or more days in the past month than their counterparts from natural families (9 per cent). The finding of the Croydon survey is consistent with that of the Exeter study, which showed that children from re-ordered families (26 per cent) were twice as likely to miss school through truancy, compared with children from intact families (13 per cent).

Another finding was that children from stepfamilies spent a great deal of time in front of TV sets, with 59 per cent watching two or more hours of TV after school each day, compared to 38 per cent of teenagers from natural families.[50]

The findings of this survey show a strong relationship between family structure and teenage behaviour. We have seen that teenagers from stepfamilies are more likely to smoke cigarettes and take illicit drugs, more likely to be sexually active, more likely to have watched sexually explicit films, more likely to have missed school and more likely to spend a lot of time in front of a TV set than their counterparts from natural families. In other words, the findings of this survey provide evidence that as a group, teenagers from stepfamilies are at considerable disadvantage compared with those who live with their natural parents. In each area children from lone-parent families did better than those from stepfamilies. This of course does not mean that all children from stepfamilies do poorly. There are clearly some children in stepfamilies that do well. However, as a group they are more likely to be involved in high risk behaviour compared with those who live with both of their natural parents.

THE BRITISH NATIONAL CHILD DEVELOPMENT STUDY

A national cohort of 17 thousand British children born in one week in 1958 has been followed up for almost three decades. A research paper by Kathleen Kiernan, 'Impact of Family Disruption in Childhood', used data from the national study to describe the effects of marital breakdown as children grow into adulthood.[51] Factors such as the age at which young people leave home, and their reason for doing so, the age at which they start work, and the age at which they form sexual relationships and get married were examined.

Effects of marital disruption on young women

For most risk factors there is a highly significant difference between young women who grew up with both their natural parents and those who did not. Young women who grew up in stepfamilies fared worse in almost every way. For example, young women from stepfamilies are almost four times more likely to leave home because of friction, and three and a half times more likely to be married by age 20, and three times more likely to cohabit by age 20. They are also twice as likely to have left school earlier and entered work sooner, and to have an extramarital birth. Young women from single-parent homes are only twice as likely to leave home early, but four times as likely to be cohabiting at age 20 and three times as likely to have an extramarital birth as their counterparts from intact families. So we see that daughters from stepfamilies and lone-mother families are at great risk of entering into an unstable sexual relationship while they are still in their teens, and at considerable risk of having a baby outside marriage. There is no doubt that divorce during childhood, regardless of whether or not it is followed by remarriage, has serious consequences for young women as they grow into adulthood.

Effects of marital disruption on young men

There were again large differences between young men who grew up in stepfamilies and those who grew up in intact two-parent families. For example, young men from stepfamilies were three times more likely to have left home because of friction, were four times more likely to have entered a cohabiting relationship, twice as likely to have fathered a child outside marriage, and twice as likely to have married as a teenager. Young men from lone-mother families did relatively better than those from stepfamilies, and had a lower relative risk for each risk factor.

The study shows that, in general, children living with a divorced parent who has found a new partner do even worse than children from single-parent families following divorce, when both are compared with natural families. The author of the paper concludes, 'Parents' marital disruption during childhood, regardless of whether or not it results in remarriage, seems to have important consequences for the adult family behaviour of daughters.'[52]

The findings of this survey are consistent with the so-called sleeper effect described by the California Children of Divorce study, referred to earlier in this chapter. Thus research evidence shows that there are enduring effects of marital breakdown, which manifest themselves particularly during late adolescence and early adulthood. Young people who experienced divorce are especially prone to leave home early because of friction, are prone to enter unsatisfactory sexual relationships at an early age and to experience all the problems associated with becoming unmarried parents.

THE USA NATIONAL HEALTH INTERVIEW SURVEY: 1981

The National Health Interview Survey is an ongoing household survey based on a representative sample of the USA population. In the 1981 survey, information was gathered from over 15 thousand children. The data collection method consisted of an interview with the parent or guardian of the child, usually the mother. The survey obtained information on a broad range of physical and mental health problems. The main focus of the study was stepfamilies (although parents with live-in partners were excluded) and single-parent families, who were compared with intact biological two-parent families.[53]

The main findings of the survey were as follows: first, children living in mother-stepfather families were found to have more problems than those living in intact families. Stepchildren were three times as likely to have needed psychological help in the last year, ranked a little lower in their classes at school, and were about 50 per cent more likely to have repeated a grade than the children from intact families.

Second, the survey confirmed the hypothesis that children in stepfamilies have more developmental difficulties than children from intact nuclear families. The overall level of developmental problems was similar among stepchildren and children in single-parent families. The researchers concluded that the stepfamily situation entailed some special problems for the child. This is illustrated by the finding that stepchildren with half-brothers or sisters have a higher level of behavioural problems than those in other sibling situations. The author of the paper offers the following interpretation, 'When the child's biological parent and stepparent produce additional children of their own, the stepchild may be cast out, or may see himself or herself in a less favoured position, as an unwelcome reminder of the earlier, broken union. This may intensify the rivalry that occurs in virtually all sibling relationships and create additional emotional difficulties for the stepchild.'[54]

THE USA NATIONAL HEALTH INTERVIEW SURVEY: 1988

In 1988 the National Health Interview Survey focused on child health, and collected information on a representative sample of 17,110 children.[55] The survey found that family structure was strongly related to academic perform-ance. After controlling for social factors, the survey found that the percentage of children who repeated a grade at school was 21.5 per cent for those living with their divorced mother; 29.7 per cent for those living with a single never married mother; 21.7 per cent for those living with a mother and stepfather, and 11.6 per cent for those living with both biological parents. Clearly, family structure is strongly related to academic performance.

The survey found that children from stepfamilies and single-mother families were twice as likely to have been expelled, or suspended, from school compared with those living with both biological parents. This finding is consistent with the findings reported in the Exeter and Croydon surveys that children from stepfamilies are more likely to absent from school. With regard to behaviour, the survey found that children from the three alternative family types were two to three times more likely to have received treatment for behavioural problems than children living with both their natural parents.

The authors conclude, 'The data revealed an excess risk of negative health and performance indicators among children who did not live with both biological parents. These findings are consistent with the hypotheses that children are adversely affected by the emotional trauma and stress that precede and accompany parental separation and divorce, and by the relative lack of attention, supervision, and opposite-sex role models provided by single parents, regardless of marital status.'[56]

YOUNG PEOPLE AND CRIME IN ENGLAND AND WALES

A House of Commons Home Affairs Select Committee set up an enquiry in 1992 into issues affecting juvenile offenders as a result of public concern about the high level of juvenile crime. The Home Office Research Unit conducted a national survey to examine the extent, frequency and nature of self-reported crime among young people in England and Wales. A random sample of 1,721 young people aged 14 to 25 were interviewed about their background, family life, their school experiences and aspects of their current lifestyle, and respondents were asked whether they had ever committed one of a list of 23 criminal offences. Respondents were classified as an offender if they had committed at least three petty offences or one serious offence.[57]

The survey found that those who lived with both natural parents were the least likely to have reported offences, followed by those living with a lone parent, while those living with one natural parent and one stepparent were the most likely to have done so. These findings are described in **figure 12**, which shows that 57 per cent of males and 34 per cent of females from stepfamilies had reported an offence compared to 42 per cent and 17 per cent respectively from natural families. Indeed, the difference in offending rates between those brought up by two natural parents and those brought up both in single-parent and stepfamilies was statistically significant for both males and females.[58] The higher rate of offenders from single-parent families was found to be statistically associated with less parental supervision, a greater likelihood of a poor relationship with at least one parent and greater poverty. Among the children living in stepfamilies, a poor relationship with at least one parent and lower levels of parental supervision accounted for the higher levels.[59]

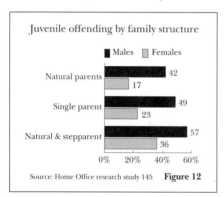

Juvenile offending by family structure

■ Males ▨ Females

Natural parents — 42 / 17
Single parent — 49 / 23
Natural & stepparent — 57 / 36

0% 20% 40% 60%

Source: Home Office research study 145   **Figure 12**

The research also showed a strong association between family attachment and juvenile offending. Those children who had a bad relationship with one or both parents were much more likely to admit having committed a criminal offence than those who had a good relationship with their parents. Among the males, for example, 80 per cent who got on badly with their father had offended compared with 43 per cent of those who had a good relationship with him.[60] Other research has also concluded that the role of the father would seem to be critical in determining the offending behaviour of children.[61]

There has been a debate about the causes of the rising incidence of juvenile crime in Great Britain. Many social commentators have claimed that the main causes are socio-economic factors such as poverty and unemployment.[62] However, some people believe that the breakdown of the family is one of the most important factors. In *Families Without Fatherhood* (1993), sociologists Norman Dennis and George Erdos argue that the breakdown of the family, and father absence is a major factor behind the rising crime rates in Great Britain.[63] In *The Divorce Culture*, Barbara Whitehead reaches the conclusion that divorce 'contributed to the tide of fatherless juveniles filling the courts and jails'.[64] In *Life Without Father*, David Popenoe argues that there is a the strong probability that a key underlying cause of juvenile delinquency and violence is the rapid growth of fatherlessness that has occurred in America over the last three decades. He writes, 'Many people have an intuitive presumption that fatherlessness must be related to delinquency and violence, and based on the research that has been conducted, the weight of evidence strongly buttresses that presumption. Juvenile delinquency and violence are clearly generated disproportionately by youths in mother-only households and in other households where the biological father is not present.'[65] Furthermore, recent research in the USA has shown a strong association between juvenile offending and children born to single mothers. In fact, individuals in the highest risk group – males born to unmarried teenager mothers – have an elevenfold increased risk of juvenile offending compared with males born to married mothers in their twenties.[66] The clear implication of this research is that family structure, and in particular the absence of a father, has an effect on the future behaviour of children.

An article in *The Economist*, which summarises the evidence of the growing problem of uneducated, unmarried, unemployed men, shows that two-parent families are demonstrably better at raising trouble-free children than one-parent families. 'Fatherless boys commit more crimes than those with father at home; a study of repeat juvenile offenders by the Los Angeles Probation Department found that they were much more likely to come from one-parent backgrounds than either the average child or than juvenile criminals who offended once only.' Indeed the relationship between crime and having a father at home is so strong that it holds even after controlling for race and low income.[67]

This hypothesis has been tested by doing a correlation between crime figures and divorce for England. The annual number of crimes reported to the police over the period 1951 to 1996 has been correlated with the number of divorces over the same period.[68] The result shows a remarkable correlation

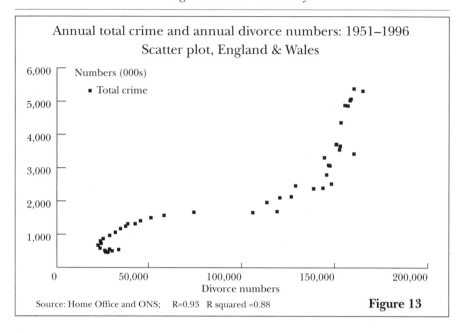

Annual total crime and annual divorce numbers: 1951–1996
Scatter plot, England & Wales

Source: Home Office and ONS;   R=0.93   R squared =0.88   **Figure 13**

of 0.93, which is highly statistically significant, as shown in **figure 13**. (A correlation of 1 shows perfect correlation, which is never found in behavioural factors). We need to be aware of two things; first, that correlations over time should always be interpreted with caution, for they may produce spurious associations between two variables that are clearly unrelated to one another, and second, that a powerful correlation does not necessarily prove cause and effect. So what should we make of the strong correlation between divorce and crime? We know that divorce causes children to lose contact with their father, and we know that crime is related to poor parenting, and especially to the relationship between children and their father; so the variables are clearly related to each other. It would be unwise, therefore, to simply dismiss the correlation—it deserves further study and explanation, for the relationship is unlikely to be spurious. Indeed, it is possible that the breakdown of the traditional family that results from mass divorce is one of the main factors causing the alarming rise in juvenile crime.

CHILD ABUSE AND FAMILY TYPE

A study of the relationship between child abuse and family type has shown a disproportionate concentration of abuse in non-traditional family types. Robert Whelan in *Broken Homes & Battered Children* (1994) writes, 'If our analysis is correct, it would point to a correlation between increases in family breakdown and child abuse. It would also suggest a bleak future for the nation's children unless measures can be taken to re-establish the traditional family, based on marriage, as the normal environment for the rearing of

370

children.'[69] Since 1973 the National Society for the Prevention of Cruelty to Children has collected data on child abuse or children deemed to be at risk. Over the period 1977 to 1990, the number of abused children rose by two and a half times and the number of children at risk by nearly three and a half times. And these increases took place during a period when the child population was falling. An analysis of over five thousand cases of abuse by parental situation shows that children living with a mother and father substitute are almost nine times more likely to be abused than children living with both their married natural parents in a traditional family. Children living with their natural mother alone are over three times more likely to be abused. Whelan concludes that the two-parent family is safe for children compared with households headed by lone mothers or by mothers living with other men.[70]

The Family Court Reporter Survey examined a sample of 141 abused and 'at risk' children between 1982 and 1988. The results of the survey showed that children living with their two natural parents were at far less risk of abuse than any other family set-up.[71] Only 18 per cent of the children were from homes where they were living with their two natural married parents, although 78 per cent of the children of Great Britain live in such homes. The relative risk of abuse is shown in **figure 14**. An odds ratio of 1 indicates that a child's chances of being abused are no greater than the chances of living in that type of family. According to Whelan 'the most important point to make is that the household type of two natural married parents is the only one to give a relative risk of abuse lower than 1. In other words, it is comparatively safe. The further we move from the traditional family, based on marriage, the greater the risk for children.' Note

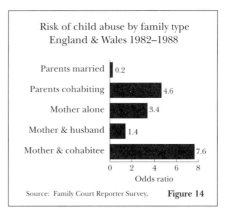

Risk of child abuse by family type
England & Wales 1982–1988

Parents married 0.2
Parents cohabiting 4.6
Mother alone 3.4
Mother & husband 1.4
Mother & cohabitee 7.6

0 2 4 6 8
Odds ratio

Source: Family Court Reporter Survey, **Figure 14**

that children in stepfamilies, which are the next safest option, are six times more likely to be abused. Children with lone mothers are 15 times more likely and children in cohabiting situations 20 times more likely to be abused than the children living with their married natural parents.[72]

An analysis of 35 cases of fatal abuse between 1968 and 1987 examined the relative risk of fatal abuse by family type. The results are presented in **figure 15**. There is a large gap between the traditional family of a married mother and father and all other family types. The natural mother with live-in boyfriend was by far the most dangerous situation for children, being 70 times more

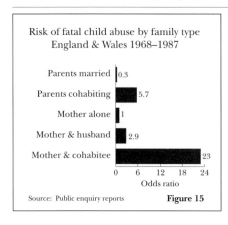

Risk of fatal child abuse by family type
England & Wales 1968–1987

Parents married 0.3
Parents cohabiting 5.7
Mother alone 1
Mother & husband 2.9
Mother & cohabitee 23

0   6   12   18   24
Odds ratio

Source: Public enquiry reports   **Figure 15**

likely to suffer fatal abuse than children in a traditional family. Children in stepfamilies (natural mother and husband) are at 9 times the risk of fatal abuse, while children living in a lone-mother household were relatively safe from fatal abuse.[73]

These studies all point in the same direction and show without any doubt that the safest place for children is to live with their biological father and mother in a family created by marriage. All the alternative households place children at risk. Those households from which the natural father is absent are at the highest risk of child abuse. Indeed, the evidence shows clearly that the child's father is the most important factor in preventing the child from suffering abuse. The greatest danger to children is having a man in the home who is not their natural father. The cohabiting situation, which is becoming increasingly common following divorce, is highly dangerous for children.

CHILDREN RUNNING AWAY FROM HOME

A report published by The Children's Society, *Still Running* (1999), provides information on young people who run away from home. The researchers estimate, from the findings of a survey of schoolchildren, that 'at least one in nine young people run away overnight one or more times before the age of 16'. Extrapolating from this finding, it is estimated that in the UK around 77 thousand children under 16 run away from home for the first time each year. Asked for the reasons why they had run away, 80 per cent mentioned problems at home. According to the researchers, 'The findings indicate that problems at home strongly predominate amongst the reasons for young people running away.' Another key finding was that young people who live in stepfamilies or with a lone parent were significantly more likely to run away than those living with both birth parents. This was true even after socio-economic factors were taken into account. The research found that 'only three out of 17 young people in the purposive sample who first ran away at 16 or 17 were living with both birth parents, and the majority had experienced a parental separation'. In most cases relationships with stepparents were a major issue for the young person.[74]

The findings of this research are consistent with the evidence that we have examined in this chapter. Once again it is clear that stepfamilies are a cause of problems for children and that these problems are long-lasting and profound. It seems that many children are so unhappy with their home situation that they are prepared to run away, and even to sleep rough in order to escape from the conflict.

CONCLUSIONS

We have seen the evidence of the harm that divorce does to children. There is a remarkable consistency in the evidence from the various studies. There can be no doubt that children experience great emotional suffering as a direct consequence of their parents' divorce. They grieve intensely for the loss of their family, and for their departed parent. The vast majority of children do not want their parents to divorce, and would do anything to prevent it happening. Forty-five boys and girls aged between seven and nineteen were interviewed about divorce and its aftermath for a television series. The interviewers found that, with one exception, all the children interviewed had wanted their parents to stay together, even in families where there had been arguments and fights over many years.[75] Almost all children, no matter how bad the marriage of their parents may have been, have an intense desire that their parents would be reconciled, and that the family would be together again. It was startling that many children considered their parents still to be a couple, even long after the divorce. The loss of their father caused children emotional pain of almost unbearable dimensions. Indeed, no matter how much their father had neglected them, almost all children demonstrated a powerful psychological need for their father.

The evidence that we have examined leaves little doubt that divorce has an enormous influence on the well-being of children. We have seen that almost every dimension of a child's life is affected. We have seen that following the divorce of their parents children tend to be less happy, exhibit lower self-esteem, show more psychological problems, do less well at school, are absent from school more, and have high rates of truancy, cigarette smoking, drug abuse and sexual promiscuity, leave home early, have high rates of criminal activity, enter unsatisfactory sexual relationships and become pregnant before they are married, when compared with children living with both their natural parents. While it is not possible to prove that divorce causes these effects (it is seldom possible, as previously stated, to prove cause and effect in human behaviour), our common sense tells us that divorce has an extremely damaging effect on children. This evidence is undoubtedly uncomfortable for some people, and especially those who have promoted divorce as the easy answer. Yet our experience confirms that the picture presented in this chapter is true.

Those who claimed that parents should divorce for the sake of their children have proved to be false prophets. They based their claims on false evidence, often supported by biased research. It seems that research was done with the intention of providing a justification for divorce, and so the results were predictable. Sociological research on the effects of divorce on children had more to do with ideological beliefs than scientific validity. There seems little doubt that research was used as a weapon in the ideological attack on marriage and the family discussed in earlier chapters. So-called experts in marriage and family were really no experts at all. Their 'expert' advice about the effects of divorce on children was seriously misleading. We may also question the liability of those who gave wrong advice and so contributed to a couple's decision to divorce.

The correlation between divorce and crime is an interesting finding, which supports the idea that family breakdown is an important factor in the rising levels of junvenile crime. While saying definitely that there is a causal link is not possible, our common sense again tells us that it is more than likely that the link is not spurious. A strong association between family attachment and juvenile crime has been shown. In particular, boys who have a poor relationship with their fathers are likely to become involved in crime. An experienced magistrate has told me that the vast majority of juveniles who appeared in her court (80 per cent was her estimate following a small survey) were from broken homes.[76] It seems that many children, who, because of the divorce of their parents, have been deprived of parental care and discipline, express their anger and unhappiness by indulging in a life of petty crime. So we see that one of the costs of easy divorce is a rise in antisocial behaviour among young people.

Another important finding was that children in stepfamilies resulting from divorce in general fared remarkably poorly, and did not see their new environment as a suitable replacement for the family that they had lost. In almost every indicator that we have looked at, children from stepfamilies tended to do worse than the children who lived with both their parents, and also usually tended to do worse than children from lone-parent families. From the evidence presented in this chapter, it seems reasonable to conclude that a stepfamily created as a result of divorce provides a poor environment for children. McLanahan and Sandefur in their book, *Growing up With a Single Parent*, comment that stepfathers are less likely to be committed to the child's welfare than their natural father, and sometimes compete with the child for the mother's time, thereby adding to the stress levels in the family. In their view, children may reject their stepfathers because they don't like sharing their mother, or because they feel loyalty towards their biological father, or because they hope their parents will get together again. The negative view of stepfamilies portrayed in some children's books has an uncomfortable ring of truth.[77]

The research into child abuse leaves no doubt that the safest place for children is the family created by the marriage of their parents. The level of child abuse found in other family arrangements is deeply disturbing. It shows that those who claim that all family arrangements are equally valid are wrong. They are certainly not equal when it comes to the probability of children being abused. Those who have made the ideological assertion that marriage does not matter, who have ridiculed and mocked marriage as an irrelevant patriarchal institution that needs to be abolished, must face up to the consequences of their perverted ideas. It seems strange that the sociologists and feminists are not concerned about the obvious link between child abuse and family breakdown.

Another amazing finding was that the majority of children have an intense desire for the reconciliation of their parents. The reason for this is surely because they know that the only way in which their broken family can be restored is for their parents to become reconciled. As we have seen, children know that a stepfamily, which results from the divorce of their parents, is not ideal, for it has come about as a consequence of behaviour that excluded one of their parents from the family home. Consequently they feel alienated and never quite at home in a stepfamily. Surely the reason why children are so against divorce is because they know that their own family – that is, the family formed at the marriage of their parents – has been permanently damaged. This is why children hate divorce and don't like stepfamilies.

Chapter 18

The loneliness of divorce

Evidence of the mental health problems associated with divorce

The proponents of divorce liberalisation predicted that it would increase the sum of human happiness. Time and again, those who promoted divorce claimed that it liberated people from miserable marriages, allowing them a further chance of happiness. Such was the optimism of the divorce movement that Lord Birkenhead declared in the English Parliament that the names of the pioneers of divorce reform would be breathed with unspeakable gratitude by thousands and thousands, and by generations yet to be, because of their humanity and wisdom in supporting divorce reform.[1] Feminists claimed that marriage was bad for the mental health of women. Divorce was portrayed as the remedy for unhappy marriages that would provide women with a second chance of happiness. Psychologists asserted that divorce was no bad thing for it provided opportunities for inner growth. In this chapter we shall look at some of the evidence on the relationship between divorce and mental health.

THE BRITISH NATIONAL SURVEY OF PSYCHIATRIC MORBIDITY

The national survey of psychiatric morbidity carried out in Great Britain in late 1993 is one of the largest surveys of psychiatric illness ever undertaken. The survey population comprised adults living at home in England, Wales and Scotland. It involved 200 trained interviewers collecting information from 10 thousand people. The main focus was to measure the prevalence of neurotic disorders in the population. The survey gathered information on 14 symptoms, such as fatigue, irritability, worry, depression, anxiety and sleep problems, among others. The frequency of these symptoms was estimated for each informant in the last week, and information collected by marital status made it possible to compare the mental health of married, separated, divorced and single people. According to the researchers, 'The prevalence of many symptoms varied considerably among women according to their marital status. Most neurotic symptoms were least prevalent among married women and most prevalent among divorced women.'[2]

Overall neurotic score

The frequency and severity of the 14 symptoms were used to calculate what the researchers refer to as an overall neurotic score. A score of over 12 was designated as the threshold for significant neurotic disorder.[3] The survey found that 14 per cent of the sample were on or above the threshold score of 12 (indicating significant neurotic psychopathology) and almost two-thirds of the sample had an overall score of 6 or less. Women were slightly more likely than men to have a score of 12 or above. Analysed by marital status, the survey showed that the level of neurosis (indicated by the overall neurotic score) in divorced women (29 per cent) was almost double that of married women (15 per cent). Single women (24 per cent) and cohabiting women (18 per cent) also had a higher level of neurosis than their married counterparts. Among men, 29 per cent of those separated from their wives, and 17 per cent of those who were divorced had a significant neurotic score, compared to 11 per cent of both married and cohabiting men, and 10 per cent of single men. According to the researchers, 'Marital status had a marked association with neurotic psychopathology (illness) for both men and women. The groups with the highest scores were divorced and separated women, and men separated from their wives; almost 30 per cent of these groups had a score of 12 or more.'[4] This finding provides convincing evidence that the claims of feminist writers that marriage is bad for the mental health of women is false and misleading.

Prevalence of neurotic disorders

The prevalence of neurotic disorders was based on the frequency and severity of the various symptoms mentioned above. Prevalence is expressed as the rate per thousand population in the last week; that is, a person needed to have experienced the symptoms of the disorder in the week prior to the survey in order to feature in the prevalence rates. The most common neurotic illness was mixed anxiety and depressive disorder, shown in **figure 16**. It can

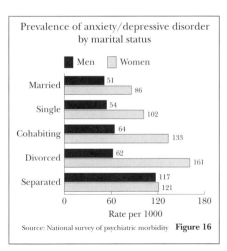

Prevalence of anxiety/depressive disorder by marital status

	Men	Women
Married	51	86
Single	54	102
Cohabiting	64	133
Divorced	62	161
Separated	117	121

Rate per 1000

Source: National survey of psychiatric morbidity   **Figure 16**

377

be seen that divorced (161 per thousand), cohabiting (133 per thousand) and single women (102 per thousand) have higher rates than their married counterparts (86 per thousand). Among the men, those who are separated (117 per thousand) have rates more than double that of married men (51 per thousand).[5]

The authors of the report reach the following general conclusion regarding the level of neurotic illness by marital status: 'The prevalence of every neurotic disorder varied markedly with marital status for both men and women. The rates for any neurotic disorder among women were highest among the divorced (304 per thousand) and lowest among the married (170 per thousand), while among men the highest rates were among the separated (309 per thousand) and lowest among the married and cohabiting (116 and 115 per thousand respectively).'[6] The authors also highlight the fact that in the case of depressive episodes, the rate among separated men (111 per thousand) was almost eight times the rate in married men (14 per thousand).[7] In particular, separated men and divorced women are severely affected, with almost a third suffering from a significant neurotic disorder.

Prevalence of alcohol and drug dependency

The levels of drug dependence and alcohol dependence were also measured. The survey showed that, in general, men have much higher rates of alcohol and drug dependency than women. The national survey found that divorced and separated men were particularly prone to alcohol and drug dependency. **Figure 17** shows that 20 per cent of separated men and almost 10 per cent of divorced men were dependent on alcohol, compared with 4 per cent of married men. Over 14 per cent of single men and nearly 9 per cent of cohabiting men were dependent on alcohol. The pattern for drug dependency shows that a much lower percentage of married men were dependent, compared with all other groups. Among women, prevalence rates for alcohol dependency in the divorced (23 per thousand) and separated (26 per thousand) are at least double that of married women (9 per thousand). Drug dependency among women showed similar variations, with divorced and separated women having much higher rates than married women.[8]

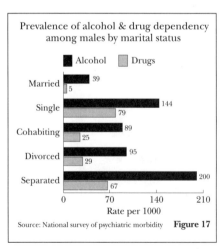

Prevalence of alcohol & drug dependency among males by marital status

Source: National survey of psychiatric morbidity   **Figure 17**

SUICIDE AND MARITAL BREAKDOWN

After the Second World War there was a gradual increase in suicides in England & Wales among both men and women, with numbers peaking in 1963. After 1963, suicides among females have continued to fall, whereas among males, suicides fell until the early 1970s. Since then suicides among males have been increasing due to a rise among young men. This was the first time since 1911 that suicide trends between men and women have moved in opposite directions. There is a strong link between marital breakdown and suicide. An analysis of suicide in England & Wales for the period 1970–72 shows that in each age band the rate

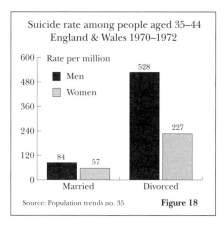

Suicide rate among people aged 35–44
England & Wales 1970–1972

Source: Population trends no. 35   **Figure 18**

is higher among divorced men and women. For example, **figure 18** shows the suicide rate for males aged 35–44 was 528 per million divorced men, compared to a rate of 84 per million for married men in the same age band. The rate among females was 227 per million for divorcees and 57 for married women.[9] So we see that divorced men are at least five times more likely to commit suicide than their married counterparts, and divorced women three times more likely.

Data on suicide rates by marital status for West Sussex and Portsmouth show that those who are separated but not yet divorced are at twenty times the risk, and those divorced at five times the risk, compared to those who are the married, as shown in **figure 19**.[10] This finding is consistent with the mental illness profile of separated men described by the National Survey of Psychiatric Illness.

A worrying trend has been the suicide rate in young men, which has doubled between 1971 and 1991, with the largest rise in those aged between 25 and 34. This trend has occurred while suicide rates in other groups have fallen. One of the factors that has contributed to the increase in suicides is the increase in divorce. It is estimated that the increase in the

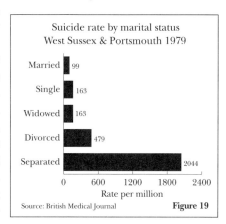

Suicide rate by marital status
West Sussex & Portsmouth 1979

Source: British Medical Journal   **Figure 19**

numbers of divorced and single men accounts for half the recent rise in suicide rates among young men.[11]

This trend has also been observed elsewhere. A Swedish study of suicide among young people found the highest rate among men in the 25–29 age group. Males were two and a half times more likely to commit suicide than females. However, for both males and females there were significantly fewer married and more divorced people among those committing suicide compared with corresponding age groups in the overall population.[12]

UK NATIONAL COHORT STUDY

The findings from the UK National Cohort Study were presented to the Royal College of Psychiatrists Annual Conference in 1997. The study measured levels of anxiety, depression, and potential alcohol abuse in just over two thousand participants, aged 43 at the time of the survey. Divorce and separation were found to be associated with increased anxiety and depression, and increased risk of alcohol abuse. These associations were present after adjusting for a number of social and educational factors and financial hardship. Divorced women were twice as likely as their ex-husbands to drink, and more likely to feel anxious, depressed and lonely after the divorce.[13] The author of the paper, Dr Marcus Richards, was reported in the press as follows, 'Many studies have shown that divorce can be destructive, but a most intriguing finding is that the impact is remarkably tenacious. There is no suggestion that it is something you bounce back from. It is a major stress, a traumatic event, and it doesn't surprise me that women are drinking to get over it. The image comes to mind of women who are vulnerable, perhaps are socially isolated, have lost an intimate contact and are drinking more as a result. The picture of a lone woman working her way through a bottle of sherry is what this data suggests.'[14]

USE OF MENTAL HEALTH SERVICES

The fourth national study of general practice morbidity in England & Wales was carried out in 1991 and 1992 and covered a one percent sample of the population. It presents statistics on the reasons for which people consult a general practice, as perceived by the practitioners themselves. The study showed that divorced people (and a small number of widowed people) were far more likely to consult their doctor with mental health problems than those who were married. The age standardised consultation ratio for divorced men aged 16–64 years was 190 compared to 83 for married men. For women the ratios were 151 and 91 respectively. Moreover, the study showed that the effect of marital status was far stronger than that of social class. Men and women in social class five had consultation ratios of 128 and 122 respectively, which was significantly lower than that of divorced men and women.[15] The information on consulting rates is consistent with the findings of the National Survey of Psychiatric Morbidity and suggests that divorced people have high rates of mental illness.

From these statistics it can be predicted that divorced people are far more likely to be admitted to a mental hospital than the rest of the population. Indeed, divorced men have an admission rate of 1,959 per hundred thousand, which is eight times higher than that of married men (257 per hundred thousand). For divorced women there is a fourfold variation (1,596 per hundred thousand compared to 433 per hundred thousand respectively). The rate of admission for single men was 663 and single women 623.[16] Married men and women have the lowest rates while divorced men and women have the highest.

PARENTAL EMOTIONS AFTER DIVORCE

The California Children of Divorce Study, discussed in more detail in chapter 17, provides some insight into the emotional pain and distress that accompanies almost all divorces. The research showed that at the time of the divorce, around 80 per cent of fathers and an even higher proportion of mothers expressed intense anger and bitterness toward their marriage partner. Women tended to be the more hostile and angry.[17] Divorce unleashed an intensity of hatred and hostility that bordered on the desperate, and was accompanied by fits of rage, in about 20 per cent of men and women. The researchers used the term 'embittered chaotic' to describe the behaviour of this group of parents. Their intense anger was associated with depression and chaotic behaviour. They made no attempt to shield their children from the bitterness and drama caused by the divorce.[18]

About a third of parents were severely depressed following the separation, and in some cases this had a detrimental effect on their ability as parents. A larger proportion – about 30 per cent of men and 60 per cent of women – were mildly to moderately depressed after their divorce.[19] After eighteen months both men and women were coming to terms with the divorce. Nevertheless, about 40 per cent of men had negative feelings about the divorce, and many women looked back wistfully to the marriage they had left. Close to half of the women expressed some negative feelings about their divorce, and 9 per cent were still bitterly opposed to divorce.[20] Depression was a problem particularly among women; almost 50 per cent were depressed to a considerable degree, and some had suicidal thoughts. They felt abandoned—overwhelmed with parenting responsibilities and failure to achieve the better life that they had anticipated when they sought the divorce. Men were also depressed because they felt a profound sense of loss caused by the ending of their marriage, and they especially missed family life and the daily contact with their children. Some men felt abandoned and rejected.[21]

Loneliness was common following divorce. The survey showed that two-thirds of the women and almost half of the men felt a profound sense of loneliness. Both men and women felt the lack of a meaningful relationship with some continuity, and some expressed weariness with the superficiality of their current social scene and contacts with people of the opposite sex that led nowhere.[22] Even after ten years, half of the women and one-third of the men were still intensely angry with their former partners. The researchers were astonished that divorce continued to occupy a central position in the emotions of many adults ten and fifteen years after the event.[23] The hurt and humiliation caused by the divorce seemed to remain embedded in the memory.

The researchers found that about half the men and women in the study were happy with their lives ten years after the divorce, and had no regrets.[24] However, in only 10 per cent of couples were both husband and wife better off following the divorce. The usual picture was for one partner to succeed in reconstructing their life, while the other partner did not. Ten years after divorce half of the women and two-thirds of the men were no better off or had a worse quality of life than before the divorce.[25]

Another important finding was that divorce was associated with a diminished capacity to parent. In the immediate aftermath of the divorce both mother and father, because of the radical alterations in their lives, were inclined to focus on their own problems and unhappiness, and this was associated with a diminished ability to care for their children's needs.[26] The researchers reported that ten years after the divorce, over a third of good mother-child relationships had deteriorated, with mothers less available to their children both physically and emotionally. Among fathers the situation was even worse, with more than half of the good relationships having deteriorated. The researchers warn, 'This erosion of parenting is a serious issue in divorce and one that merits wide attention.'[27]

Comment

The evidence suggests that divorced people, as a group, suffer great emotional pain and a sense of rejection. Undeniably, divorce is associated with high rates of depression, mental illness, and suicide. It produces a deep sense of anger, severe guilt and overwhelming sadness. The breakdown of the family usually results in a profound sense of failure in both partners. Moreover, this sense of failure can be long-lasting, and some people are still aware of the consequences of their divorce many years later. For a small group of people the divorce may bring relief from a situation that was intolerable. There are a small number of marriages in which the abuse and threat of violence is so great that it is no longer possible to live in the same household. While separation in those circumstances can offer relief, there is still a sense of loss, for the family has been split and the children have lost a parent.

As men are more likely to leave the family home, they are especially prone to the loneliness that follows divorce. The evidence also shows that men indulge in self-destructive behaviour, as demonstrated by their high rates of alcohol and drug abuse. Those who have recently separated from their family appear to suffer intensely. They suffer because they have lost the family home where they lived together with their wife and children; the home to which they returned after a hard day's work. Their marital relationship has come to an end—they are no longer a husband and no longer have the comfort and support of their wife. Their parental relationship is severely damaged for they lose daily contact with their children. Undoubtedly divorce is a severe shock to the mental well-being of a man for he has lost his role, his purpose, his home, his wife and his children.

Divorced women are characterised by high rates of mental illness. As they are likely to have custody of their children, the maternal role appears to modify the self-destructive forces that we saw among the men. But there is no doubt that women suffer intense emotional pain, a deep sense of anger and guilt as a consequence of the break-up of their family. They are left to care for the children, often with little or no support from the father. They experience the loneliness of single parenthood, and have to deal with the sadness of the children who mourn the loss of their father and the break-up of the family, on a day to day basis. The new lifestyle of being a divorcee is full of stress and worry, which is aggravated by economic difficulties. She has lost the protection and support of her husband, and in the future will have to fend for herself in a hostile world. Her future, and that of her children, is uncertain as she struggles to cope with the reality of being a divorcee. The claims of feminist writers that marriage is bad for the mental health of women is patently false, and flies in the face of an overwhelming body of evidence. It is divorce, not marriage, which damages the mental well-being of women.

Chapter 19

Destructive associations

Mortality, unemployment and sexual behaviour

Many people agree that mortality figures provide a good proxy measure for health. For this reason public health specialists use mortality rates to compare the relative health status of different groups within a population. For example, mortality figures are routinely analysed by social class to describe differences between the groups. It is well known that people in the more deprived social classes have mortality rates that are significantly higher than rates in the more affluent social classes. An obvious strength of mortality data is that it is collected for all deaths, and therefore is routinely available in large numbers.

DIVORCE AND MORTALITY

National mortality data for England & Wales have been used to examine mortality by marital status. Death rates for different age groups are presented in **figure 20**. In each age group divorced men have higher rates than their married counterparts. Divorced men in their forties and fifties, for example, have death rates double those of married men. The death rate for divorced men in their 60s is about 70 per cent higher than for married men of the same age. Single men under 50 have higher death rates than both married and divorced men, but similar rates to divorced men in the older age groups.

The rates for divorced women are also higher in each age group than for married women, although the mortality differential is smaller—for example, divorced women in their 50s have a rate about 40 per cent higher than that of married women. The death rate for divorced women in their 60s is about 33 per cent higher than for their married counterparts. Single women have

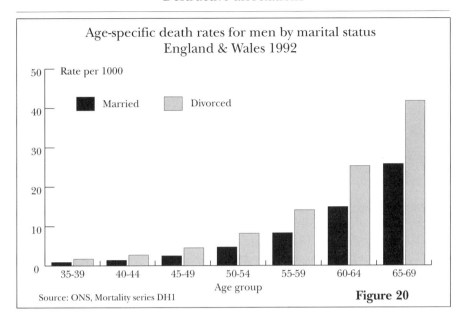

Age-specific death rates for men by marital status
England & Wales 1992

Source: ONS, Mortality series DH1

Figure 20

death rates that are higher than married women at every age. Married women in their 30s, 40s and 50s have death rates half that of their single counterparts.[1]

In order to make an overall comparison of the relative health of married and divorced people, age standardised mortality rates by marital status have been calculated using England & Wales mortality data.[2] This calculation takes account of possible differences in age structure between married and divorced populations. Among relatively young men aged 65 and under (**figure 21**), the death rate for divorced men (80 per thousand) was 70 per cent higher than the death rate for married men (47 per thousand). Among women the death rate of divorcees was 37 per cent higher than the rate of married women. These results are consistent with the age-specific rates shown above. So we see that men have higher mortality rates than women in general, and this difference is magnified by divorce. Of particular interest is the fact that single women have death rates in the younger age groups that are twice those of married women.

DIVORCE AND UNEMPLOYMENT

The General Household Survey is a continuous survey that is based on a sample of the general population resident in households in Great Britain. The 1991 survey obtained information from 19 thousand people living in just under 10 thousand private households throughout the country. It collected information on unemployment by marital status. The data showed that divorced men have age-specific unemployment rates that are more than

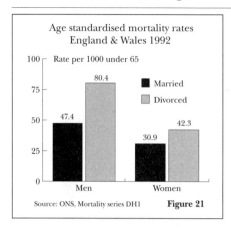

Age standardised mortality rates
England & Wales 1992

Rate per 1000 under 65

Source: ONS, Mortality series DH1   **Figure 21**

double those of married men. For example, in the 35–44 age group, divorced men had a rate of unemployment that was three times higher than the rate among married men; 18 per cent among divorced men compared to 5 per cent among married men. In the 45–54 age group, unemployment among divorced men was twice that of married men (14 per cent compared to 6 per cent respectively). It is significant that there is no difference in unemployment rates between divorced and married women.[3]

TRENDS IN SEXUAL BEHAVIOUR

The British National Survey of Sexual Attitudes and Lifestyle is the largest survey into sexual behaviour ever undertaken. An expert team of epidemiologists designed and carried out the survey – funded by the Wellcome Trust – which collected information from a scientifically chosen sample of 19 thousand representatives of the British population in the age range 16 to 59. Findings of the survey were reported in 1994 in the book *Sexual Attitudes and Lifestyles*.[4]

The survey provided strong evidence of major changes in sexual behaviour in the British population over the last four decades. One of the most important changes was a sharp fall in the age of first sexual intercourse. For example, among women the median age of first sexual intercourse has fallen from 21 years for those born in the early 1930s, to 17 years for those born in the early 1970s, showing a 4 year reduction in the median age over four decades. Among men the median age of first intercourse declined from 20 years to 17 over the same period.[5]

Another measure of sexual activity was the proportion of people who were sexually active before their 16th birthday. Data from the survey showed a large change over the last four decades. Among women aged 55 and over (born in the 1930s) around 1 per cent had their first sexual intercourse before they were 16, compared to 19 per cent of women born in the 1970s, and teenagers at the time of the survey. The authors comment that these changes in sexual behaviour 'seem to have coincided with a period in which the traditional constraints on early sexual expression – social disapproval of sex before marriage, negative attitudes towards teenage sexuality and a fear of pregnancy – have been gradually lifted'.[6]

Another major trend was an increase in the number of sexual partners during the last four decades. The survey found a steady increase in the proportion of people who reported 10 or more partners over a lifetime; an effect that was more marked for women than men. Around 3 per cent of women, for example, who became sexually active in the 1950s reported 10 or more partners, compared with 10 per cent who became sexually active in the 1970s.[7]

Multiple sexual partners

Not surprisingly, marital status has a great influence on sexual behaviour. Divorced and separated men, in particular, are prone to multiple sexual partnerships. Comparing men and women in the 25–44 age group, the survey shows that almost 40 per cent of divorced/separated men (including a small numbers of widowers) reported two or more partners in the last year, compared with 26 per cent of single men, 15 per cent of cohabiting men and 5 per cent of married men. Among the females, 16 per cent of divorced/separated women (including a small number of widows) reported two or more partners, a rate similar to that of single women (15 per cent), but much higher than married women (2 per cent).[8]

The difference in sexual behaviour between married and divorced men is further illustrated in **figure 22**, which shows the number of female sexual partners reported in the last five years. Whereas 82 per cent of married men reported one sexual partner, almost a quarter of divorced men reported five or more partners, and just under 50 per cent report three or more partners in the last five years. Among divorced women, 20 per cent reported 3 or more sexual partners in the last 5 years, compared to 3 per cent of married women. However, one in six divorced women (17 per cent) reported no sexual partner in the last five years.[9] According to the researchers, 'The data presented here suggest that those who are separated, divorced and widowed may be a group with particularly rapid partner change.'[10]

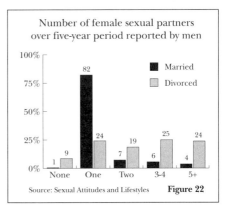

Number of female sexual partners over five-year period reported by men

Source: Sexual Attitudes and Lifestyles   **Figure 22**

An important aim of the national survey was to identify the population at higher risk of adverse outcomes from their sexual behaviour. Accordingly, the survey defined risk-taking behaviour as having two or more partners in the last year, but not using a condom in that time; this was considered to be practising 'unsafe' sex. As expected, marital status had a strong effect. By far the highest rates were reported by divorced/separated men, 17 per cent of whom had practised 'unsafe' sex in the last year, compared to 3 per cent of married men. It is interesting to observe that cohabiting men (10 per cent) were three times as likely to report 'unsafe' sex in the last year compared with married men. The rates of 'unsafe' sex in the last year reported by single, divorced and cohabiting women were 11 per cent, 9 per cent and 6 per cent respectively. Married women (1 per cent) had by far the lowest rate of 'unsafe' sex.[11]

Consistent with the reported rates of 'unsafe' sex, divorced women were more likely to have had a venereal infection than their married counterparts. The survey shows that 4 per cent of divorced women had attended a clinic for venereal disease in the last 5 years compared to 1 per cent of married women. The figures for men are 6 per cent and 2 per cent respectively.[12]

A study by the Centres for Disease Control and Prevention in America has found that during the 1990s the number of over 50s who are infected with AIDS through heterosexual sex has doubled. This increase is explained by the newly divorced throwing themselves into new relationships, and infection rates are especially high among the retirement communities of Florida. In response to this new threat the campaign for 'safe' sex has developed the slogan – 'Sex is not only for the young. Neither is AIDS.'[13]

Abortion by marital status

Divorced women are twice as likely as married women to have had an abortion. The national survey shows that 22 per cent of divorced or separated women have had an abortion at some time during their lives, compared to 11 per cent of married women. For the last five years the figures are 5 per cent and 3 per cent respectively. It is interesting to note that the level of miscarriage in the last five years was virtually the same in married and divorced women (7 per cent and 6 per cent respectively).[14]

Comment

Divorce is associated with a significant increase in mortality, suggesting that it has a profound effect on both men and women. The destructive behaviour associated with divorce is undoubtedly a factor that contributes to the higher death rates. Some people are so disturbed by divorce that they lose their purpose in life, and some even the will to live. The differential in death rates between divorced and married women is smaller than that observed in men. This is probably due to the restraining effect of maternal responsibilities, which modify the self-destructive behaviour so apparent among men. Married women have lower death rates than single women in each age group, showing that marriage has definite beneficial effects. Feminists are wrong when they say that marriage is bad for women.

The higher unemployment rate among divorced men is evidence of their lack of motivation and purpose—they lack the motivation to provide for the family of which they are no longer a part. Women, however, face to face with the economic realities of providing for the children, have little choice but to work in order to support themselves.

The evidence from the national survey of sexual behaviour shows that divorced people are far more likely to have multiple sexual partners, and to suffer the consequences of their unhealthy lifestyle. As we have already seen, divorced men are prone to enter into cohabiting relationships, many of which are of short duration. It is particularly sad for the children of divorce to see their parents behave in a way that they regard as immoral. Moreover, the parents' pattern of sexual behaviour sets an example their children are likely to emulate as they grow older. Casual sexual relationships have consequences and often cause a feeling of frustration and regret. It becomes rather pointless for mature men and women in their late 30s and 40s to be 'playing the field', moving from one sexual encounter to the next. Many divorced people feel guilty because they sense that a lifestyle of uncommitted sex is wrong and sets a bad example for their children. The high rate of abortion among divorced women is particularly sad, for it shows that although they have given themselves sexually, they have been unable to accept the pregnancy that results from the relationship.

Chapter 20

Divorce – the myth and the reality

The inescapable moral imperative surrounding divorce

Society's views towards marriage have undergone a major change during the last few decades, and mass divorce has become part of the way of life in England and America. Much of the literature on divorce presents an optimistic picture about the likely benefits, especially for women, and there is even talk of the good divorce. Some commentators claim that divorce opens the way for a promising future, and suggest that new relationships following divorce are likely to be more fulfilling. Psychologists and marriage counsellors advise that divorce can provide opportunities for psychological growth. Moreover, the idea that an unhappy couple should divorce for the sake of their children, despite all the evidence to the contrary, is still the popular view.

Yet we have seen that the Bible teaches that divorce is wrong, and the evidence shows that it damages people. So there appears to be a gap between contemporary thinking and the reality of divorce. In this chapter we consider the optimistic view of divorce presented by popular divorce literature, and contrast it with the reality of divorce as it affects real people. We shall see that the idea of the good divorce is a myth – generated by self-acclaimed experts – that does not ring true with the experience of those who know the reality for themselves.

THE MYTH OF THE GOOD DIVORCE

Many writers have claimed that the initial bad feelings that follow divorce can lead to good things, and there are numerous books and feature articles in women's magazines that proclaim the benefits that follow divorce. A typical example of this way of thinking is expressed in *The Good Divorce* (1994) by Constance Ahrons.[1] She divulges a tightly held secret that out of many bad marriages come good divorces. She insists that while there are bad divorces, there are also good ones, and millions of people now live with the reality of divorce as a normal passage in their lives. She complains that society glorifies the so-called intact family, while stigmatising divorced families as broken and incomplete.[2] According to Ahrons, about half of all divorced couples end up with a good divorce, in which they part without destroying the lives of those they love. 'Their children continue to have two parents. The divorced parents continue to have good relationships with their children. The families of good divorces continue to be just that—families.'[3] Ahrons argues that if unhappy couples knew their bad marriage was harming their children, and if they knew that the long-term effects of a good divorce on a family were positive, there would be almost nobody left who believed in duty, home and family.[4] She goes on to reassure her readers that there are many good options in divorce, the best-case scenario being to set up an immediate, successful, temporary limited partnership with your ex-spouse.[5]

The Good Divorce argues that current divorce rates should not be viewed with gloom and doom, because divorce is one way for families to adapt to current realities. Instead, we are urged to change our outdated ideals about marriage and family. Because divorce is here to stay and cannot be cured, we should view divorce as intrinsically part of married life, and 'stop loading it with negative judgements and explore ways to improve families' quality of life, post-divorce'.[6] The following statement probably sums up the philosophy of the book: 'Marriage is good – and so is divorce. It all depends to whom each happens, and why, and how—and when.'[7] The author married when she was nineteen; she had two daughters and divorced her first husband when she was 28.[8]

In *Divorce and Your Children* (1990), Anne Hooper argues that the best way of helping our children come to terms with divorce is to accept the reality of the situation.[9] 'We are no longer a "single marriage society" but a "divorce and remarrying society". The sooner we recognise and accept this, the sooner we can begin to make use of what we have got, to help ourselves and our children by extending our families in a modern way.'[10] In discussing the gains of remarriage, she asserts that the new relationship may provide a better model of caring than before. For example, if the natural parent had been suffering from depression, the arrival of a new spouse will remove the bad feelings and lighten the entire household. The stepparent may fit well into the children's interests, and so provide a new dimension. Indeed, 'some people are better parents than others, and it could be that the stepparent is an improvement over the natural parent'.[11] When discussing the divorce with your children Hooper suggests you should admit that it won't be the same without daddy, 'but it will be fun in a different way and we will be able to do different things. One of the things I thought we might do that was different would be to buy a dog. How do you feel about that?' Hooper believes that the new dog is something for the children to direct their confused emotions towards, something to take their minds off their parents' divorce.[12]

The Family Through Divorce (1977) is a book that offers a complete guide to the legal and emotional issues involved in divorce. The authors express the view that 'the family crisis of separation and divorce can indeed be an opportunity for growth and development, rather than simply trauma and pain. Stepfamilies represent new hope, as many achieve fulfilling new lives for their members.'[13]

Psychological theory claims that divorce gives women the opportunity to explore their inner selves and so validate themselves. Professional counsellors even advise that divorce can generate psychological benefits as women gain in self-esteem and self-confidence, and have more control over their lives. A report in *The Times*, under the headline 'Psychologists extol benefits of divorce for all the family', summarised the research findings presented at a conference of the British Psychological Society. Psychologists told the conference that divorce can benefit parents and children by increasing their self-reliance and giving them control over their lives. 'The break-up of the traditional nuclear family is not as big a disaster as it is painted. Although single parents may have more to cope with, they experience greater rewards, mothers have a sense of achievement over doing a difficult job well and children report a feeling of love and security no matter who provides it, according to research in London and Lancaster.'[14]

Another example of the psychological approach is contained in the book *Marriage and How to Survive It* (1983), which is co-authored by a clinical psychologist.[15] Readers are invited to assess the condition of their marriage from a psychological perspective.[16] Having done the psychological tests in the book a couple may conclude that they are psychologically incompatible. Although they may be well matched intellectually and share common interests, one partner feels that his or her development as a person is somehow being arrested by remaining in the marriage. According to the authors, 'This usually comes across in the form of a statement such as "I have to leave in order to be myself".'[17] The authors admit that moving out to be on your own is not the immediate answer to life's problems, but 'if you stick with it and face up to life's new challenges, you will start to change as a person. Many of your fears will start to disappear as you find yourself doing many things you thought you were not capable of... So if you know in your heart that the marriage is over and there are no practical obstacles to your moving out, push aside your doubts and take the plunge. If you do not do it now you will spend your old age regretting the fact.' The book then gives practical hints about how to build a new life after your divorce, and advises that the earlier you move out the more chance you have of being fulfilled in both your career and personal life.[18] The message of the book is that divorce can improve an individual's psychological development.

The Relate Guide to Starting Again is written to help the reader get over a relationship that has finished. The book presents an optimistic view of future relationships after divorce. 'The end of a relationship can be a new beginning. Without the constraints of a partnership you can concentrate on your own needs and take steps to construct a more satisfying way of living and relating to people, which includes any children you might have.'[19]

The books discussed above and many others not mentioned, which present divorce in euphemistic terms, have helped to cultivate the myth of the good divorce. This way of thinking sees divorce as something that is inevitable in a modern society and something that should be viewed as just a normal part of everyday life. Divorce is portrayed as an opportunity for women to achieve psychological growth and development, and something that they should not run away from. Women should not be afraid to admit that their marriage is not working, and should have the courage to take the plunge. If they handle the process well then it can be a good divorce, from which the people involved and even their family will benefit. What is startling about the above accounts from people who claim to be expert in the area is the large gap between their perceptions of divorce, and the reality of what hundreds of thousands of people have experienced for themselves.

THE REALITY OF DIVORCE

We must move beyond the unrealistic claims of contemporary thinking to see the truth about divorce. In doing so we must take account of the teaching of the Bible, bear in mind the evidence that we have examined in previous chapters, and refer to our own experience and common sense. As we noted at the beginning of this book, divorce is an issue which affects everyone in society, from the highest to the lowest, and we all have our own experience to guide us. Many of us have seen the reality of divorce at first hand.

The testimony of two people who have experienced divorce will help to put a sense of reality into the discussion. Two personal accounts of divorce were published in the *British Medical Journal*. The first is by a father who had become alienated from his wife because of a continuing affair with another woman. Despite the fact that they were using separate bedrooms and had discussed divorce, he found the psychological impact of the actual event unexpectedly severe. He writes:

> I suppressed as best as I could the pain of telling the children that I wouldn't be living with them any more – although suppression made the pain no less acute. What I had not expected was a wave of tenderness for my wife, which, very briefly, restored between us a confidence and rapport that had been long lost. In hindsight this was clearly mutual shock; the same kind

of reaction that follows a long awaited death. Soon my wife's mood became more bitter, and mine more depressed, as I realised that, firstly, the triangle in which I had long existed had merely been perpetuated in a different form, and, secondly, the move I had made was irrevocable. In the initial state of shock I had thought it possible that I would return and had even written to my wife about my strong desire to do so. As things settled down my presumably mild depression settled in. The symptoms were early waking, reduced libido, and, above all, apathy, not in my work, which was wholly unaffected by the traumatic events, but in my private life. Going out to a theatre or a film, for example, seemed difficult or impossible, like a heavy unpleasant household chore that you keep putting off. The relationship with my children, fortunately, caused few direct problems, although I found meeting for 'restaurant meals' as poor a substitute for living with them, as I had expected. Where their welfare was concerned I had no difficulty in combining well with their mother. That was virtually the only area of accord and agreement, however. The pressure caused by her continuing alternation between dependence and bitter recrimination has certainly borne heavily on me, so has the pressure from my partner to force a total breach with my wife.[20]

The second account is from a wife who admits that her marriage had not been happy for the past few years. When her husband left her for another younger woman she went into a state of shock that lasted for months. She writes:

It came as a complete surprise, not only to me and the children, but to all our friends and relatives... I made it easier for him by being reasonable and calm while he was around and only breaking down at night in the privacy of my room. I could only think a day at a time; the future meant nothing; I was absolutely numb. The children were devastated. They adored him, and he had not only betrayed me, but he had betrayed them as well – he had left! They felt insecure, frightened, and guilty and did not know whom they should blame, even though I was honest and told them our breakdown in marriage wasn't only one sided and that we should have both tried harder. Their absolute despair and misery nearly broke me; they cried night after night for months. They were ashamed. They couldn't talk to me, their father, or even their close friends. They wanted to hide like animals and lick their wounds. After the first couple of weeks their father persuaded them to see him and 'Mary' frequently and regularly. They withdrew from him to hide their pain. He rarely saw their real distress. I think it would have been better if he had given them longer to adjust. They know that he loves them, but they are no longer the most important people – they come second. It takes time to come to terms with that. I have rarely criticised 'Mary', but two years later the children are still distant and disinterested in her. I think he expected them to accept her too soon. It was lucky we both decided that we had to do the best for the children. Our standard of living has dropped and I am often worried about money, but my husband earns a good salary and, though not generous, he won't let us starve.[21]

These two accounts of the reality of divorce ring true with the personal experience of millions of people. There is no doubt whatsoever that divorce has extremely profound, powerful affects on those involved. Why?

THE MORAL IMPERATIVE

In the vast literature that promotes the idea of the good divorce there is not the faintest hint that divorce is one of the major moral issues of our time. Contemporary thinking on divorce has gone to great lengths to deny the moral dimension. Counselling services usually adopt what they call a morally neutral position, simply helping the individuals decide whether a divorce is in their own best interests. An unhappy wife or husband will be advised to make their decision without any moral consideration. Any suggestion that divorce is a moral issue is seen as judgemental, forcing unwelcome moral views on to other people. So the popular view is that individuals should be encouraged to decide on their divorce free from the restrictions imposed by moral considerations, and especially the teachings of the Bible.

The idea of no-fault divorce is further evidence that society has chosen to ignore the moral dimension. It suggests that no one is morally responsible for a divorce—nobody is to blame. But this is a delusion for the underlying cause of divorce, as we have already seen, is a husband or wife being unfaithful to their marriage vows, as a result of wrongdoing and selfishness. In *Second Chances,* Judith Wallerstein writes that she is yet to meet the man, woman or child who emotionally accepts no-fault divorce. 'In their hearts, people believe in fault and in the loss associated with the decision to end a marriage. Adults almost inevitably blame each other, but rarely blame themselves.'[22] And this is surely evidence of the way divorce afflicts the conscience, a clear indication of the inescapable moral dimension. A further moral dimension is the harm that divorce causes other people, and especially the children. Indeed, the moral aspect is so obvious that many children feel that their parents have failed in one of life's major tasks, which is to maintain a marriage and the family home. Children believe that one of their parents, and sometimes both, put their own selfish desires and lack of self-restraint above the needs of the children, allowing them to suffer the brunt of the divorce.

Despite a fervent campaign to propagate the idea that there is no moral dimension to divorce, most people are aware of the teachings of Christ and know in their heart that divorce is wrong. In the strongest possible language

Christ condemned divorce as immoral, tantamount to committing adultery. The betrayal and violence that are the essence of divorce are so sinful in the eyes of God, that he hates divorce. It is, therefore, impossible for human beings, created in the image of God with a moral conscience, to escape the moral dimension of divorce. Because we live in a moral world where there is a distinction between right and wrong, no matter how much we may try to convince ourselves otherwise, we cannot escape the terrible truth that we are accountable to God for our actions. We know when we have done wrong, our conscience tells us so, and we cannot escape the feeling of shame and guilt that results from our wrongdoing. Men who leave their family for another woman are especially prone to being weighed down by guilt as they witness the sorrow they have inflicted on their wife and children. These men often have difficulty in visiting their children for they are a constant reminder of their wrongdoing. And because divorce is against God's plan for marriage, those involved know in their deepest conscience that they have done a great wrong to their family, to their children and to themselves. This is why those who instigate divorce have profound and enduring feelings of guilt.

We also cannot escape the moral imperative that wrongdoing has consequences—as the Bible says, we reap what we sow. To pretend otherwise is simply to deceive ourselves. The reality is that those who choose to ignore God's moral law with regard to marriage and divorce reap the consequences of their immoral behaviour. This book has provided ample evidence of the consequences of divorce. Personal experience provides further evidence, and few can doubt this obvious truth.

DIVORCE DAMAGES THE FAMILY

Divorce damages the one flesh unity created by marriage; it tears apart two people who not only belong together, but who have in fact become one entity. This tearing apart wreaks havoc with the family created by their marriage. The idea that the destruction of their family will lead to future inner happiness is a delusion, as many people have found out to their cost. The experience of breaking up their family home proves much more painful than either husband or wife ever anticipated. It comes as a crushing blow to the children, who feel afraid, abandoned and ashamed, for they know that they have lost their family through the thoughtless, selfish and careless behaviour of their parents. The public knowledge that their family has been broken by divorce causes disgrace, humiliation and shame for the children. It is widely known that the behaviour of one or both parents has led to the break-up—that they have put their own interests before those of their children. The children are acutely embarrassed by the failure of their parents to solve their problems. They feel humiliated that their parents have not been willing to stay together for their sake. The tragedy of divorce is that it damages relationships within the family. The husband and wife, who are also father and mother to the children, no longer recognise each other as a part of the family. By their actions they have deprived their children of a normal family life; the family which God intended would nurture them as they grew into adulthood.

A key legal aspect of divorce is that it ends a marriage contract and means that both husband and wife are free legally to remarry. In the eyes of the law the legal relationship between husband and wife is broken, and the marriage is dead. The wife, who may also be a mother, has become a divorcee, and is available to other men, while the husband and father can now legitimately entertain his girlfriends. Divorced women often have a reputation of being sexually available. For the children who retain a parental relationship with both parents this is a horrible situation. Their father and mother are now sexually available to others; they can remarry, or, if they prefer, they can simply live with their new partners.

Following their divorce, parents have less time for their children and are less sensitive to their needs. In particular, divorce is associated with diminished contact between fathers and their children; a phenomenon sometimes referred to as 'father loss'. Many fathers feel that they are no longer of central importance to their children's lives and have difficulty in maintaining a meaningful relationship. A further difficulty for divorced fathers is that they are required to make visits to see their children. It proves to be extremely difficult to establish a meaningful relationship with children under these circumstances. Moreover, visits usually arouse complex feelings and emotions within the father. He, of course, misses his children and wants to see them. But each visit brings back painful memories, and often a sense of hurt, jealousy and regret. Each visit reinforces the reality that he is no longer part of the family, and is no longer a significant part of the lives of his children. Many fathers feel sad and humiliated at the thought of having to obtain permission to visit their children—their own flesh and blood. Sometimes the experience of parting after weekend visits can be extremely upsetting for both father and children, as it reinforces the idea that they are not a 'together' family. It is hardly surprising that many fathers are erratic in their visits and some opt out altogether.

Grandparents fulfil an important role in the lives of their grandchildren. Their presence brings a sense of stability and permanence, for it puts the family relationships into a historical context. As we have already seen, divorce leads to less contact with grandparents, and some children lose all contact with one or other set of grandparents. The paternal grandparents usually suffer a feeling of loss for, although they really love their grandchildren, they have fewer opportunities to see them.

We have seen that, in general, children do not thrive in stepfamilies created by the remarriage of one of their parents following divorce. The founder of the National Stepfamily Association expresses the opinion, in a letter to *The Times*, that an overriding factor which pushed people to contemplate divorce in preference to staying together is 'the belief in the existence of a new and perfect partner, either in reality or in the imagination, with whom the divorcee can share a new and better life. This belief is so often shattered as the recently divorced face up to the harsh reality of any new relationship, with the further complications of stepchildren, financial competition from the previous family and the need to arrange and cope with weekend access visits to children.'[23]

One of the sadder findings of the California Children of Divorce Study was that half of the children whose mothers had remarried said they did not feel welcome in the new family.[24] Among the older children in the study more than half resented their stepfathers and 90 per cent felt that having a stepfather had not enhanced their lives.[25] The foreboding that most children have about acquiring a stepfather is psychologically understandable. It is disturbing for children to have a man whom they hardly know, who is in no way related to them, taking the place of their real father. This is no surprise really for a second marriage founded on divorce is against God's plan for the family. Moreover, children know in their heart that a stepfamily created following divorce is built on the failure of their real family. It is predictable that children do not usually thrive in stepfamilies built on the foundation of divorce.

CHILDREN AND DIVORCE

In the 1960s and 1970s the traditional view that parents should stay together for the sake of their children was replaced by a new consensus, which claimed that the primary purpose of divorce was to improve the happiness and well-being of the parents and that this would benefit the children. A number of social commentators claimed that divorce did not cause serious long-term damage to most children and so it was pointless for parents to stay together for their sake. Some social researchers even claimed that children thrived on divorce, for they were better off out of an unhappy home.

These claims have proved to be to disastrously false. We have seen the evidence which shows the suffering that divorce causes for children and the long-term nature of the damaging effects. The reality is that children hate divorce and suffer considerably from the loss of the family home and daily contact with their father. In a feature article, model Laura Bailey, whose parents divorced when she was five, comments, 'When your absolute hero – your father – doesn't come back, it's really frightening, whatever age you are. The danger is that it sets a pattern in relationships. My father's leaving is probably a huge part of all the relationships I have had with men in my life.'[26] Jemma Redgrave made the following comment on her parent's divorce. 'It was the major trauma of my childhood. So huge was the effect on me that I don't remember a lot about it. I blocked it out. I didn't lose my father exactly, but suddenly he wasn't around so much and I missed him terribly. It's something my brother Luke and I found very difficult. Children want their parents to be together.'[27]

Divorce usually leads to a period of considerable instability. Many children move from home to home, experiencing economic deprivation as their single mother, dependent on state benefits, struggles to make ends meet. Parenting skills of the lone mother decline as she spends a great deal of her emotional effort on sorting out her life. A feature article on divorce in the *Daily Mail* tells of the problem a divorced mother had with disciplining her two teenager sons. 'Without a man at home, I found discipline hard. Boys reach a stage when they are taller and stronger than you and won't listen. They played truant, and the school didn't tell me about it for months. No extra effort was made to help me because I was a single parent, and neither boy came out of education with any qualifications.'[28]

In those situations where the mother develops a new sexual relationship, the children have the indignity of sharing their home with the man with whom she chooses to cohabit. It is not difficult to imagine the profound unhappiness caused to children when their mother brings another man into the family home. In some cases the children are exposed to a number of male cohabitees before their mother eventually remarries. Most children know that this is an immoral lifestyle, and are deeply upset. We saw in chapter 17 that these situations are particularly dangerous for the children, who are at high risk of being abused by their mother's current lover. One has only to read the newspapers to see the continuous catalogue of tragedies suffered by children at the hand of their mothers' lovers.

A CAUSE OF LONELINESS

Divorce breaks the bonds of companionship created by marriage and is associated with feelings of intense loneliness. Young men do not do well following their divorce, and have high rates of suicide. Many lose direction, feel alienated and have a diminished sense of purpose in life. Older women are especially likely to feel isolated and lonely, and face old age with a rising sense of anxiety. The reality is a far cry from the optimistic and misleading picture of divorce presented by many feminist writers. Christmas becomes a particularly difficult time because of its focus on the family. Following divorce it is not easy for family members to meet without a lot of tension and anger. It is not surprising that a group like the Samaritans, who provide help for people contemplating suicide, are so busy during the festive season, for it is at these times that the loneliness caused by divorce really strikes home.

A BEGINNING, NOT AN END

Many people believe that divorce brings an end to an unhappy situation and allows them to make a fresh start. The notion of a 'clean break' divorce suggests that the past marriage relationship is wiped away, allowing the divorcee to start again with a clean slate. But the reality is different, for divorce is not an end, but rather the beginning of a new and often difficult relationship with their former marriage partner. While the divorce ends the marital relationship between husband and wife, the parental relationship with their children remains intact. The family created by marriage is not dead, but disfigured, with unpleasant consequences for all its members. Experience shows that for many people the feelings and memories of the divorce are vivid and fresh many years later. In a feature article a woman admits that she still has bad dreams about her ex-husband eleven years after the divorce. In the California study half the women and one-third of the men were still intensely angry at their former partner ten or fifteen years after the break-up.[29] Although the marital part of the relationship is over, the parenting component of the relationship remains very much alive, and continues for a long time. The children remain attached to both parents and are passed to-and-fro between them. Some children have to endure the appalling indignity of being cross-examined by one parent about the lifestyle of the other. The aggravations, bitterness, pain and jealousy that are engendered are debilitating and emotionally exhausting.

So the startling truth is that divorce does not wipe out the family relationships created at marriage—it only distorts them, and divorcees live with this reality for the rest of their lives. The history of their marriage remains; they are forever ex-husband and ex-wife, forever father and mother to their children, no matter what they do in the future. And this reality has profound consequences, for the actions of each still affect the other in a very tangible way. When an ex-husband ill-treats his ex-wife, he is hurting the mother of his children, and that hurts the children. When an ex-husband does not support his ex-wife, then it is his children who suffer financial hardship. When an ex-wife neglects the children, and allows her boyfriends to mistreat them, the ex-husband feels acute guilt and anger, for his children are suffering because he is not there to care for them.

A HUMAN TRAGEDY

So now we know the reality of divorce. Its effect on men, women and children go to the heart of the human condition. It has a profound effect on our spiritual life, challenging our sense of right and wrong, disturbing our conscience. It affects our inner being, damaging our dignity and touching the image of God that is in each man and woman. It deeply affects our emotional life, causing a permanent sense of sadness and loss. It affects our peace of mind. It is forever engraved on the memory, which is never free of the thought of what might have been. It causes an extreme sense of regret and waste. It affects the present and the future. It affects the whole family and everybody that we love. Its effects are permanent and can never be undone. In a sentence, the reality is that divorce is an outrage against our children, violence against our family, and a human tragedy for husband and wife of overwhelming proportions.

There are millions who will testify that this is the reality of divorce. So we see that the idea of the good divorce is indeed a cruel myth. We know from our experience and our conscience that the biblical principle that we reap what we sow is true. Men and women who sow divorce reap its consequences—this is the shocking reality. Those who claimed that divorce was the answer to unhappy marriages, and that it would lead to future happiness have proved to be false prophets; their advice has had appalling consequences. Unfortunately, many people have been misled by these false claims, and are now experiencing the reality of divorce for themselves. Those who through their own selfishness and wrongdoing instigate divorce will inevitably suffer the consequences of their actions. Moreover, divorce demonstrates the biblical truth that the sins of the fathers are visited on their children. God is not mocked; his moral laws for marriage cannot be rejected with impunity.

Chapter 21

The battle over marriage

The failure of the Protestant doctrine of divorce

We have uncovered the ideas that allowed divorce to spread like a plague across the social landscape of England and America. Few can doubt that the secularisation of marriage and the move to mass divorce are among the most important changes that have occurred in these countries during the 20th century. No analysis of the serious social problems so prevalent in society, such as teenager violence, juvenile crime, illicit drugs and extra-marital births, can be complete without taking account of the effects of mass divorce. Yet it appears that in both England and America the easy acceptance of no-fault divorce has settled the controversy and done away with the need for debate. Mass divorce is an accepted part of our way of life.

ENGLAND'S ROAD TO DIVORCE

England occupies a unique position in the history of divorce. It is the only country to have gained the benefits of the Reformation, while at the same time rejecting the Protestant doctrine of divorce and so retaining a belief in the indissolubility of the marriage bond. One of the great triumphs of the Christian faith was its stabilising influence on English family life following the Reformation. Over the centuries the Church of England developed a marriage discipline that brought enormous blessing to the nation. Society was transformed as everyone – believers and unbelievers alike – accepted the biblical truth that marriage was a permanent union, only broken by death. The marriage service, based on the words of Christ, became a part of English culture and a clear witness to the lifelong nature of the marriage bond. The words of the ceremony were ingrained into the national conscience and there was no doubt about their truth. Everyone, with few exceptions, believed that the marriage bond, solemnised in the presence of God, was for better, for worse, until death. Marriage was a serious matter of religious significance – a symbol of the union between Christ and his Church, and therefore indissoluble. The Church taught this belief consistently from pulpits across the land, and most of the country accepted the obvious biblical truth that marriage was lifelong.

As long as the Church witnessed faithfully to this eternal truth its teaching had great authority, helping to sustain family stability even among those who did not follow the Christian faith. Innumerable couples made their marriage vows in the Church of England, accepting that they were married for life, and this brought great stability to the English home. The Church's teaching on the lifelong indissoluble nature of marriage was the salt that preserved family life. The Bishop of Salisbury, in his speech to the House of Lords in 1857, noted that the providential grace of God had preserved England from the curse of divorce.[1] Consequently, in 19th century England divorce did not enter into the thinking of the ordinary man; the people's minds were settled and secure in the idea of one wife for life. Any notion that a man could exchange his wife was unthinkable. This view of marriage was in sharp distinction to that of Protestant Europe where the idea of divorce was inexorably spreading through the population.

The divorce debate of 1857 was a watershed in that it introduced the idea of divorce to the English nation. At this crucial time the difference of opinion among the bishops in the House of Lords was significant. It prevented the Church from speaking with a united voice, some arguing that marriage was indissoluble, others (who accepted the Protestant doctrine of divorce) arguing that divorce was permissible for adultery. So the public witness of the Church against divorce was divided. Those, like the Bishop of London, who believed marriage was dissolved by adultery, felt obliged to side with the secular humanists in the campaign to legalise divorce. The dominant view among the grassroots of the Church of England, however, was firmly against divorce. Nine thousand clergy had signed a petition against the Act and many felt that the bishops had not faithfully represented the views of the Church. The people had no appetite for divorce for they still believed marriage to be a lifelong union. Consequently, the number of divorces that followed the Act was very small. Nevertheless, the fact that divorce was now available placed it on the national agenda, and offered encouragement to those who wanted divorce to become yet more widely available.

A key point to emerge from the debate was the difference in position between the leadership and the grassroots of the Church. The bishops were reluctant openly to support the doctrine of the indissolubility of marriage. On the other hand, the clergy and laity were continually pressing the bishops to speak out clearly so that everyone would know where the Church stood.

On many occasions the clergy and laity pressed for a statement from the bishops to clarify the Church's position on marriage, divorce and remarriage, but the bishops avoided this for they did not want to say anything that might endanger the link between Church and state. They were reluctant to criticise the divorce laws passed by Parliament, and did not want conflict between state and Church. They were also very aware of the sentiment within the liberal establishment that wanted more liberal divorce laws. So the bishops tried to placate the secular world while at the same time remaining faithful to the teaching of Christ. But they could only maintain this balancing act with compromise and fudge. A classic example of the fudge was the statement at the end of the 19th century from the Upper House of Canterbury Convocation that claimed that the teaching of Christ on divorce and remarriage was ambiguous and therefore they were unable to make a clear statement. It said, 'In regard of the question of remarriage, the teaching of Holy Scripture cannot be pronounced to be perfectly clear.'[2] In 1896, although a committee of the Lower House of York Convocation reached a unanimous view that marriage was indissoluble, it received no support from the House of Bishops.

During the first part of the 20th century liberal theologians argued that as the teaching on divorce was so difficult to understand, it was impossible to be sure what Christ really meant. Because Christ's teaching was ambiguous they supported the arguments of the secular humanists for extending the grounds for divorce. They argued that Christ laid down, not a definite law, but an 'ideal' for marriage, that few could attain. They did not agree with the view that the Church must regard marriage as indissoluble. Rather, they believed that the state was right in granting divorce under certain circumstances. They accepted that adultery, desertion and other factors, which caused the purposes of marriage to be defeated, were grounds for divorce. This attack on the indissolubility of marriage by a few liberal theologians undermined the Church's witness, and provided a massive boost to the divorce campaign.

In the 1930s the Church committed the cardinal error of deciding that Christ's teaching on marriage was meant only for Christians. It decided not to try to impose his teaching on the whole of society, and not to oppose any 'reasonable extension' to the grounds for divorce. Underlying this concession was the inference that it would be better for society not to be constrained by the harsh sayings of Christ. This line of reasoning accepted that it was possible for the state to improve the divorce laws for the benefit of the majority by disregarding biblical teaching. The church leadership was behaving in a way that suggested that they were ashamed of the gospel of Christ, and unwilling to take a stand on the truth of Christ's words in the councils of men. The report, *Putting Asunder*, commissioned by the Archbishop of Canterbury (Ramsey) in 1963, contended that the Church's advice to the state should not be based 'upon doctrines that only Christians accept, but upon premises that enjoy wide acknowledgement in the nation as a whole'.[3] The report argued that biblical standards were not applicable to the majority of the nation. Because biblical morality applied only to Christians, and not to the nation, the state was justified in giving the people the divorce laws they wanted, free from any moral restraint. The presumption was that the state, guided by the principles of secular humanism, was able to make more humane laws than a law based on the words of Christ. But the notion that Christ's teaching was only for Christians, and not for all people, failed to grasp the truth of the Church's prophetic ministry to the nation. In his speech to the General Synod, the Rev Henry Cooper reminded the Church of its prophetic ministry. He said the Church did not believe in two standards, one for mere human beings and one for Christians. The gospel was not meant to be preached to Christians only, but to all people.[4] The Bishop of London (Leonard) reminded the Church that the institution of marriage was not merely for Christians, though Christians are given the grace to fulfil it. He said, 'We believe that it is an institution given by God in creation and we therefore have the responsibility in this matter to speak to all men.'[5]

The permissive 1960s saw a major change in the way society at large viewed marriage. It was during this period of increasing moral decline that *Putting Asunder* provided the justification for the irretrievable breakdown of marriage. It claimed that marriages could die – and when a marriage was dead, divorce was the sensible option. During the permissive era cohabitation became increasingly popular and traditional marriage was portrayed as an outdated and oppressive institution. Illegitimate births increased at an alarming rate, and in the late 1970s the British Government removed the stigma of illegitimacy, thereby indicating society's approval of the single-parent family.

The growing acceptance of secular marriage was accompanied by a sharp decline in the proportion of church marriages. In *The Proposal*, a report of the Labour Party's think-tank, Demos, society was blatantly encouraged to think of marriage in purely secular terms. It proposed that the marriage vows should not necessarily express a lifelong intention. The essence of *The Proposal* was that the marriage contract needed to be renegotiated after an agreed period, and that serial marriage should be encouraged.[6]

REMARRIAGE OF DIVORCEES IN THE CHURCH OF ENGLAND

At the dawn of the 21st century the Church of England is engaged in the final great struggle over the marriage question. Divorce is now so widespread, that there is a feeling that the Church should do something to show that it cares for those who have been hurt by it. Accordingly, the Church is seriously considering a change in marriage discipline that will allow divorcees who have a former partner living to remarry in church. Those who oppose the remarriage of divorcees in church are portrayed as lacking in compassion.

The remarriage question is crucial to the public witness of the Church. At stake is nothing less than Christ's teaching on marriage. Without doubt, the most powerful public witness to the lifelong nature of marriage is the refusal of the Church to remarry divorced persons. By this discipline the world knows that Christ taught that divorce is morally wrong and that marriage is a lifelong union. Therefore a person cannot remarry while a former spouse is living. The early Church witnessed faithfully to the truth of Christ's teaching, and the civilised world came to understand that marriage, as ordained by God, was lifelong and remarriage was not permitted. The message was clear, simple, absolute, and easy to understand. It had great authority and exerted a powerful influence on society. Everyone knew that the Church of Christ did not permit remarriages under any circumstances at all, and most accepted the wisdom of his teaching. However, the spirit of the age opposes the teaching of Christ and yearns after temporary marriage and the convenience of remarriages.

When the divorce controversy was at its peak in 1896, an article in the *Church Quarterly Review* argued that the Church of England should retain its law forbidding the remarriage of divorced persons. 'Careful study of the evidence within our reach and a full consideration of the recent controversies in England make us to be unhesitatingly convinced that the law of Christ laid down in Holy Scripture, committed to Christians, and defined and administered by the Church, affirms the absolute indissolubility of Christian marriage. Nor are we less convinced that any recognition by churchmen of the possibility of "marriage" after divorce must have an injurious effect upon Christian morality. Marriage is at the very centre of human life. It cannot be touched without affecting what is of highest importance to the individual and the race. Christian theology has taught us to see in it the creation of an objective bond, the setting up of a relation which no subsequent events can destroy. To overturn this belief is to imperil the safeguards of family life, the protection of woman's honour, the restraints which the best mortals sometimes need. Without it, it is hard to see what may become of distinctions which make the difference between acts that are lawful and gross sins real.'[7]

In 1955 Archbishop Geoffrey Fisher said that the Church was right to exclude from marriage in church all, without exception, who have a former partner still living. He argued that because marriage is a social institution, a church service is an official act of the Church carrying its whole authority. 'The Church has a duty to Christ and to society to bear witness to what he said marriage is. It cannot, least of all in present circumstances, make exceptions in its public solemnisation of marriage without compromising its witness. If the Church were to marry divorced persons there would be no way left in which it could bear effective witness before the world to the standard of Christ, for there is no other official or formal act which would give it the opportunity.'[8]

While Archbishop Fisher did not condemn remarriage outright, he did warn against church remarriages. 'Let me say quite frankly that in some cases where a first marriage has ended in tragedy, a second marriage has, by every test of the presence of the Holy Spirit that we are able to recognise, been abundantly blessed. For this reason I do not find myself able to forbid good people who come to me for advice to embark on a second marriage.' He explained the Lord's teaching to those who approached him seeking remarriage, and told them that it was their duty to decide before God what they should do. He reminded them that if they remarry, they would never again be able to bear a full and clear witness to the Lord's declaration of marriage as an indissoluble bond. 'But that does not mean that the Church should marry them. They would then be asking the Church to compromise the one way in which it can give a clear testimony to our Lord's standard for their sakes.' So it is their private responsibility, and if they seek marriage, it must be by a civil ceremony without trying to involve the Church in the act. 'Thus if they feel denial of a church marriage to be a cross of suffering, they should bear it for the Church, so that it may not, in its official acts of marrying, compromise the standard entrusted to it by the Lord, to defend which is the Church's essential duty. I have hardly ever found anyone who is not responsive to this line of argument and who does not find in it a real spiritual and moral strength and consolation.'[9]

In his book *Divorce and Remarriage*, Andrew Cornes gives a clear explanation of why remarriage is wrong. 'Those who are married have entered into a lifelong union. They promise this solemnly at their marriage. And whether they realise it at the time or not, God joined them together as one flesh. This marriage lasts until death; legal divorce does not undo it. And it is for this reason rather than any other – it is because they are still married – that Christians are unable to support them in any second marriage.'[10] He advises that the Church should explain to those seeking a second marriage that the reason they cannot be remarried in church is because Christ said that marriage is for life. Cornes believes that nothing less than this kind of explanation does justice to Christ's teaching. The Church is called to bear witness to his truth.

At the heart of the remarriage debate is the public witness of the Church. To allow remarriages in church is to damage the witness of the Church to the lifelong nature of marriage. This point cannot be made too strongly – to allow church remarriage is to publicly repudiate the teaching of Christ. The Church would be saying that Christ was wrong when he called remarriage adultery.

Selective remarriage in church

The promoters of church remarriage claim that it will be selective, only for those who are deemed to be 'deserving' cases, or in the old parlance, the 'innocent' party. The sharp logic of Archbishop Geoffrey Fisher identified the problems associated with this approach. He argued that to make exceptions for those who were 'deserving' of a church remarriage would raise a number of unanswerable questions. 'On what principles should the exceptions be made? Only for those where the partner was divorced for adultery? Or for any cause? Only for the innocent? But in this case how shall innocence be judged and what be its standard? Moreover, it would be impossible for the Church to satisfy public opinion that in each case the granting of the exception was justified, and not influenced by weakness, or wealth, or social status, or some other unworthy reason.'[11] Fisher wrote his objections to remarriage before the era of no-fault divorce. How is it now possible to establish the true reasons for divorce when the couple claims that the marriage has irretrievably broken down? Lord Denning said in a debate in the House of Lords that the divorce courts did not even attempt to establish innocence or guilt.[12] How, therefore, could the Church possibly do so?

There is yet another unanswerable question for those who promote church remarriage. How many times can a person be remarried in church? Once, twice or several times? And on what principle is the decision made? A discussion document on remarriage from the working party of the House of Bishops recommends that 'neither of the partners should have been married more than once'.[13] But why only one remarriage? It is well known that remarriages have a greater chance of failing than first marriages. It therefore seems unduly harsh that couples should be denied the possibility of seeking happiness in a third marriage. If a person who has divorced once is allowed to remarry, on what grounds is the person who has divorced twice denied this right? Which of the arguments advanced by those in favour of church remarriage do not apply also to a second remarriage? Surely the argument that the Church should show compassion to divorcees, applies even more to those who have experienced several divorces? The argument of grace must surely mean that a person can be forgiven for any number of divorces, and allowed any number of remarriages. Or is the grace to forgive limited to only one divorce? The rule of 'only one remarriage' is nonsense. It means that the second marriage, but not the first, is seen as indissoluble and therefore no third marriage is possible. The impossible dilemma of how many remarriages in church are permissible is not difficult to see. Clearly, the 'only one remarriage in church' rule is arbitrary and not based on any biblical principle.

So the Church of England is on the horns of a dilemma. It can try to apply the discipline of selective remarriage, a discipline that has proved unworkable in the Methodist and American Episcopal Churches. However, it is well known that such a discipline has been discredited because it leads to widespread injustice and dissatisfaction. For centuries the Protestant doctrine of divorce has sought to find a satisfactory way of dealing with the remarriage of 'deserving' divorcees, but has failed to produce a credible formula. It is unlikely that the Church of England is about to discover some hidden mystery that will justify the remarriage of 'deserving' divorcees that is consistent with the teachings of Christ. Should the Church choose to go the way of selective remarriage, the moral weakness of its position will soon become apparent to all.

It does not take a lot of insight to realise that selective church remarriage, granted only in 'deserving' cases, is but the thin edge of the wedge. Breach the principle and the floodgates will open. The assurances of those who promote remarriage mean nothing. They will certainly not be satisfied with only a handful of 'deserving' cases. Arguments for extension are inevitable, for once the principle of church remarriage is accepted, there will be nothing to stop a move to indiscriminate remarriage. Before long the flaws in the selective approach will become evident, and the cry will be for the unlimited remarriage of divorcees in the Church of England. Already the Methodist Church has demonstrated that selective remarriage is unworkable in practice and moved on to unlimited remarriage. The introduction of selective remarriage is only the first step in the campaign to achieve the remarriage of all divorcees in the Church of England. Should this happen, the Church's witness to the lifelong nature of marriage will be dead.

The fresh start theory

Many who now support remarriage do so because they claim that God's grace allows a divorced person to make a fresh start. The very fact that divorce is so common proves that marriages die, and the Church must respond to the needs of those who have experienced the death of their marriage—it should help those who have met with failure and disappointment and not slam the door in their faces. Fortunately, the Church has finally discovered that God's grace allows divorcees to be forgiven past mistakes, such as marrying the wrong person, and make a fresh start in a new marriage.

The basic flaw in this argument is that it is based on a distorted view of the nature and character of God. While emphasising God's grace and love, it ignores his holy character. The prophet Habakkuk describes the holiness of God: 'Your eyes are too pure to look on evil; you cannot tolerate wrong' (Habakkuk 1:13). And central to God's holiness is his moral law, revealed through the Law and Prophets and through the life of Christ, and implanted in the heart of man. According to the New Testament, 'the law is holy, and the commandment is holy, righteous and good' (Romans 7:12). Because

God cannot tolerate wrongdoing and moral evil, Christian believers will do all they can to keep the moral law of God.

Fresh start teaching, however, implies that God's grace overturns his moral law. The inference is that God – because he is gracious and merciful – will overlook the clear teaching of Jesus that 'anyone who divorces his wife and marries another woman commits adultery against her. And if she divorces her husband and marries another man, she commits adultery.' The idea that God will condone remarriage is fundamentally wrong, for it disregards God's moral law—the standard by which we ought to live and by which we will be judged. We have already seen that the God of the Bible hates divorce because it breaks the marriage covenant of lifelong faithfulness between husband and wife. The suggestion that God's grace condones divorce, and permits a fresh start by remarriage to 'another man' or 'another woman' is anathema to God's moral law. Jesus said, 'If anyone loves me, he will obey my teaching... He who does not love me will not obey my teaching' (John 14:23, 24).

At the heart of the Christian gospel is the message of salvation from sin. The Christian gospel makes it absolutely plain that the sin of the divorcee – like the sin of all those who truly repent and turn to Christ – can be forgiven. The gospel message is for the broken-hearted and the vilest of sinners. But the consequences of the divorce remain, even after the sin that lies behind divorce has been forgiven. As we have already seen, divorce does not break the marriage bond, for the divorced person is still a part of the family created by marriage and has numerous family relationships that, although damaged by divorce, are lifelong. There is no doubt that God wants these relationships to be restored. What, then, is the moral duty of a divorced husband or wife who confesses their sin and receives forgiveness through the grace of God? When a Christian wife is forgiven, her clear responsibility is to put right the wrongs she has done to her husband and children, and to 'be reconciled to her husband' for she knows that the Bible says that 'a wife must not separate from her husband' (1 Corinthians 7:10,11). Likewise the Christian husband should seek to be reconciled with his estranged wife. So the forgiveness of God makes reconciliation possible and restores the family relationships that have been damaged by divorce.

Another problem with fresh start theory is the suggestion that God's grace allows the divorcee to benefit from his or her sin. But this is to profoundly misunderstand the gospel of grace. As an example, take the man who breaks God's moral law by stealing his neighbour's car. Although the thief can be freely forgiven if he repents and confesses his sin, does that mean that he is morally entitled to keep the stolen car? Does God's forgiveness allow the thief to benefit from his sin? Of course not! The repentant thief is required to make restitution, to return the stolen goods to their rightful owner, and to face the legal consequences of his theft. He also wants to make restitution for he knows that it is the right thing to do. He cannot make a fresh start while driving his neighbour's car. In the same way, the forgiven divorcee cannot continue in the sin that led to the divorce. He cannot desert his wife and children to remarry another woman. He is required to restore the family relationships that his actions have broken and to be reconciled to his wife and children.

And finally, how many fresh starts is a person permitted? On what grounds can the fresh start theory deny a person a second, third or fourth remarriage? Indeed, as God's grace is unlimited, surely this theory demands an unlimited number of remarriages for those who wish to start again and again. Moreover, the fresh start theory is open to the most cynical abuse. It provides encouragement to the husband or wife who desires to be rid of a spouse in order to marry another person. How easy it is for a husband or wife to say that their marriage is dead, to divorce, claim forgiveness, and qualify for a church remarriage. And all this, it is claimed, is permitted because of God's grace and compassion.

The real significance of the fresh start theory is that it shows how the modern proponents of remarriage have abandoned the discredited arguments of the Protestant reformers about marital offences and the right of the 'innocent' party to remarry. But at least those arguments had some semblance of scriptural support; the advocates of the fresh start theory make no pretence of scriptural support, but rather base their belief on an incomplete view of the character of God and the vague notion that a gracious God must allow a fresh start. We would do well to remember that the God of the Bible said, 'I *hate* divorce.'

AMERICA AND THE PROTESTANT DOCTRINE OF DIVORCE

The road to mass divorce in America was very different from that taken by England. Throughout most of its history, the English Church has stood for the indissolubility of marriage, while the American Christian tradition has always favoured divorce. The strong Protestant influence meant that from the earliest times the American mindset was sympathetic to the desire for divorce and remarriage. In chapter 3, we saw how great reformers such as Luther, Calvin, Zwingli and Bucer concluded that the Bible permitted divorce for adultery and desertion, among other things. They taught that marriage was a secular thing, and attacked the sacramental view of marriage; their followers were encouraged to see marriage as a purely civil contract. Colonial America provided the perfect opportunity for the Reformation theories on marriage and divorce to be put into practice.

Adherents of the Protestant faith were determined that the traditional view of marriage taught by the Anglican and Roman Catholic Churches would not gain ground in America. The Puritans of New England vehemently opposed the sacramental view of marriage, heavily emphasising the civil nature of the marriage contract. For a time they did not permit church weddings, insisting that the ceremony had to be conducted by a civil magistrate. Marriage, as Luther had said, was a worldly thing. This insistence on the secularisation of marriage had long-term consequences for the way American society came to view marriage. Charles Thwing, in his 19th century analysis of the American family, highlighted the link between Reformation thought and the notion that marriage was a purely secular contract. In his opinion the secularisation of marriage formed the basis of American divorce legislation.[14]

Over the passage of time, Protestant thought allowed divorce for causes other than adultery and most extensions of the grounds for divorce in America were made with the tacit agreement of the Protestant tradition. Even when, in the 20th century, divorce numbers were growing at an alarming rate, the Protestant denominations were not prepared to make any fundamental change to their theological support for divorce. The tragedy of the Protestant position was that it helped to undermine marriage in the eyes of society, and especially American society, where it exerted great influence. It failed to understand the link between marriage and the family, and to acknowledge that divorce breaks families, causing unbearable suffering to children. Protestant teaching made divorce respectable, providing the moral platform for the mass divorce movement. Today the Protestant tradition is helpless in its witness against mass divorce, and is in confusion over the issue of remarriage; each denomination having its own rules, which change from time to time, and are not understood by the average person. Protestant denominations, such as the Baptists, Lutherans, Methodists, Presbyterians and Congregationalists, who teach that Christ allows divorce and remarriage, have failed to recognise the far-reaching consequences of their teachings for society.

The American obsession with secular marriage has meant that many weddings take place without a religious ceremony. The popular view that marriage is a civil contract, not unlike many other contracts, has led to the loss of its religious significance. For many there was no commitment to marriage as a lifelong union—it was something entered into lightly and easily deserted. This low view of marriage encouraged the belief that divorce was necessary to help people achieve further chances of happiness. Accordingly, the American debate has always concentrated on identifying the right grounds for divorce. When the Bishop of Albany, William Doane, spoke of the shame of the divorce habit in America at the beginning of the 20th century, he hoped to reduce the causes for divorce, 'if not to the one only possible scriptural exception, at least to only six causes at the outside'.[15] There was no belief in the Church that divorce was against the teaching of Christ and therefore morally wrong. When the divorce numbers were growing at an alarming rate, the Church was unable to offer any real guidance

412

to society, and was glad to leave the arena to the sociologists and psychologists. It is not surprising that at the turn of the 20th century the American rate of divorce was so much higher than that of England.

THE IDEOLOGICAL BATTLE OVER THE MEANING OF MARRIAGE

The battle over marriage has been a battle between the ideas of biblical Christianity and of secular humanism. While the biblical view was firmly defended by the Church, the secular humanist view, which held that marriage was a man-made contract that lasted only so long as it suited the couple, was unable to make any progress. Those who followed the words of Christ taught that divorce was always wrong, whereas the secular humanists maintained that divorce was a valuable resource for dealing with unsuitable marriages. These opposing arguments were at the heart of the parliamentary debates. As long as the Church of England was clear about what the Scriptures taught about marriage and divorce, and stood firm on these beliefs, then the nation at large was guided by the Word of God and the pleadings of secular humanism were unable to stand against the force of biblical truth. When the Church compromised the teaching of Christ, the ideas of secular humanism were ready to step into the breach created by the retreat of the Church. With each step backwards from the doctrine of marriage indissolubility, the campaign for the promotion of free divorce gained ground. A confounding factor in the struggle was the Protestant doctrine of divorce, which occupied a position halfway between the two views outlined above. The Protestants, in fact, wanted a little bit of divorce. The effect of their teaching was to undermine the absolute position that the marriage bond was indissoluble save by death, and it brought comfort to the secular humanists for it meant that those who claimed to speak for the Christian faith were divided, unable to agree on what Christ had taught about marriage. Consequently, the Christian witness was seriously undermined, leaving the field open to the arguments of the secular humanists.

At a deeper spiritual level, the great divorce controversy has been, in reality, an intense battle over the nature and meaning of marriage. Is marriage a civil contract that can be terminated for certain reasons, or an indissoluble union of which God is the author? Underlying the divorce debate is a spiritual war of immense proportions, which the apostle Paul alluded to in his letter to the Ephesians. 'For our struggle is not against flesh and blood, but against the rulers, against the authorities, against the powers of this dark world and against the spiritual forces of evil in the heavenly realms' (Ephesians 6:12). Behind the divorce controversy are the powers and authorities of this dark world that are seeking to destroy the institution of marriage as ordained by God. As in the Garden of Eden, a subtle question has been asked, 'Did Jesus really say that divorce is wrong?' The importance of the spiritual battle cannot be overemphasised. It is not

413

an obscure theological debate over the indissolubility of marriage, but an attack on the divine institution of marriage. What we have studied is a rebellion against God's plan for marriage that is having enormous conse-quences for the whole of society. The struggle over the meaning of marriage, which has intensified during the last three decades, involves everyone and affects the whole of Western society. Those who follow the gospel of Christ, whether they like it or not, are involved in a spiritual war of immense proportions, and it is no longer acceptable for Christians to sit on the sidelines, avoiding what many see as a controversial and difficult subject. Committed Christians have a responsibility to become involved in the battle over the meaning of marriage. Those who adhere to the Protestant view of divorce need to explain why their beliefs have led them to side with the forces of secular humanism in the campaign to achieve the freedom of divorce. We must challenge the false ideas that have become so prevalent, and witness to the truth of biblical teaching. We need to understand what is a stake, the significance of the battle.

A CRISIS OF FAMILY BREAKDOWN

In the first chapter we saw that the idea that the traditional family was in a state of serious decline was a matter of controversy, with some arguing that the family was simply changing. The evidence shows that millions of children, because of their parents' divorces and because of the increasing numbers of births to unmarried women, are now growing up outside a stable family home. Millions have lost meaningful contact with their fathers, and are growing up without the care, discipline and love that only he can provide. The idea that children do not need a father has proved to be a cruel deception. The hurt for these children is profound, and many still suffer the effects as they grow into adulthood.

Both England and America are rapidly becoming societies in which the numbers of fatherless children are counted by the millions, and both countries are beginning to reap the social consequences. The decline in discipline among young people, the increasing rates of violent juvenile crime, the burgeoning use of illicit drugs, the growth in underage sex and illegitimate teenager births that cause so much despair and concern, are all symptoms of the instability that results from widespread family breakdown. We read daily in our newspapers of human tragedies caused by divorce and broken homes; we read of husbands who assault their former wives and, recently, of a divorced father who burnt himself and his children to death in a car rather than face life without his children; we read of divorced mothers who are abused, assaulted and sometimes murdered by their lovers. There is an enormous growth in violent behaviour among very young children, most of whom come from unstable family situations. We read daily about children from so-called reconstituted families who are abused in the most

414

appalling ways by their mothers' boyfriends. While society has been busy entrenching the right to easy no-fault divorce, it has been indifferent to what divorce is doing to children. Undoubtedly, the shocking behaviour of many young people is a cry for help to an adult world that does not want to hear about their plight and would like to believe that there is no family breakdown crisis.

REAFFIRMING THE CHRISTIAN VIEW OF MARRIAGE

One of the great triumphs of the Christian faith was its influence on marriage and family life. The witness of the early Church to Christ's teaching on the lifelong nature of marriage, by word and deed, had a powerful effect on all who heard the message. The Archbishop of Canterbury, Geoffrey Fisher, explained how the teaching of Christ revolutionised the way society thought of marriage. 'It routed the whole practice of the contemporary world. It created a new belief in monogamous lifelong marriage as a duty to God, and imposed it upon its members and in the end on the civilised world. Surely the impetus for such an assault and victory must have come from our Lord. It could not have happened otherwise. It is not therefore surprising that the Church in the West has put such an emphasis on the lifelong and indissoluble character of marriage. Plainly the thing of lasting importance is to preserve this victory of Christ.'[16]

The question that we must now face is—can the current trend in mass divorce be changed? Is it possible for England and America to turn away from mass divorce? Can marriages be preserved so that children will grow up in families in which they are cared for and disciplined by both their father and mother? Can the Church again influence the way society thinks about marriage? The answer to these questions depends upon the Church's witness on marriage and divorce. If the Church fails to take a moral lead and speak the words of Christ to society without compromise, then it is inevitable that the present situation will continue and England and America will reap the consequences of mass divorce. Let us not make the mistake of believing that God is indifferent to the current situation, for God will judge the nations in righteousness and truth.

If the Church acknowledges its failure to witness to the biblical meaning of marriage, and resolves once again to teach Christ's words on marriage, then society can be transformed. There is no doubt that many people are longing for moral guidance from the Word of God, for they have suffered deeply and know in their hearts that there is a better way. The Church has the responsibility to preach and teach God's truth with regard to marriage. As people come to accept the truth that marriage is a lifelong union ordained by God they will understand why Christ said that divorce is morally wrong. The popular idea that mass divorce is an aspect of modern society that cannot be changed is a cruel deception spread by those who seek to undermine the biblical view of marriage and the family. The trend in mass divorce can be reversed just as soon as the Christian Church returns to sound teaching on the subject. Christians of all traditions have a responsibility to be God's witnesses to the sanctity and permanence of marriage, and to live by these truths. We need to make it clear that God's plan for marriage, instituted at Creation, is for the good of all.

God calls his people to be the salt of the earth and the light of the world. Christians are commanded to proclaim God's gospel to the world, including the moral law by which all people ought to live. We have been entrusted with God's truth, and we must prove faithful. Christian people cannot remain silent in the face of mass divorce that is wreaking havoc with people's lives. We must make a major effort to reaffirm to all in society God's plan for marriage, exhorting all to accept the fundamental importance of marriage and the family. If we do so, then with God's grace and help, the current trend in divorce can be reversed, as society again accepts that marriage is God's plan for the good of men, women and children.

Endnotes

Chapter 1. The phenomenon of mass divorce

1. Mavis Maclean. *Surviving Divorce*. London, MacMillan, 1991, p4.
2. Babette Francis. 'Feminism and the state: The Australian experience', in *Feminism v Mankind*. Milton Keynes, Family Publications, 1990, p20.
3. Office of Population Censuses and Surveys. *Marriage and Divorce Statistics, 1837-1983: England & Wales.* (OPCS series FM2 no.16) (Historical Series), London, HMSO, 1990.
4. Glenda Riley. *Divorce: An American Tradition*. New York, Oxford University Press, 1991, p3.
5. Joseph Epstein. *Divorce, the American Experience*. London, Cape, 1975, p18.
6. Arthur J. Norton and Louisa F. Miller. *Marriage, Divorce and Remarriage in the 1990's.* US Bureau of the Census, Current Population Reports, Special studies, Series P-23, no. 180, Washington D.C., U.S. Government Printing Office, 1992, p5.
7. Patricia H. Shiono and Linda Sandham Quinn. 'Epidemiology of divorce', *The Future of Children, Children and Divorce.* 4:1, Spring 1994, p21.
8. 'It's the values, stupid: next year's campaign theme', *The Economist*, 337, 11 November 1995.
9. Youth risk behaviour surveillance system. Assessing health risk behaviours of youth, US Department of Health and Human Services, Centers for Disease Control and Prevention, 1998.
10. 'National data show drop in homicide and increase in youth suicide', US Department of Health and Human Services. *HHS News*, 23 October 1995.
11. Kate Muir. 'Daddy doesn't live here', *The Times*, 30 June 1992. © Times Newspapers Limited, London.
12. Great Britain. *Report of the Royal Commission on Marriage and Divorce*. London, HMSO, 1956, table 5.
13. Office of Population Censuses and Surveys. *Marriage and Divorce Statistics, 1837-1983.*
14. These statistics appear in the publications of the Office of Population Censuses and Surveys, *Marriage and Divorce Statistics: England & Wales for 1990 to 1996.* (OPCS series FM2 nos. 18, 19, 20, 21, 22), London, HMSO, 1992-1996.
15. S.C. Clarke. *Advance report of final divorce statistics, 1989 and 1990.* Monthly vital statistics report, 43:12, suppl., Hyattsville, Maryland, National Center for Statistics, 1995.
16. Chris Southgate. *Newly Single: an Approach to Life after Marriage.* Berkshire, Cat Publications, 1992.
17. Anne Charlish. *Caught in the Middle*. London, Ward Lock, 1997, p49.
18. James Jones. 'Family values: let's hear it from the children', *Daily Telegraph*, 30 November 1998.
19. Michael Harper. *Equal and Different*. London, Hodder and Stoughton, 1994, p180.
20. 'Unhappy families, broken families, unhappy children', *The Economist*, 25 June 1994.
21. 'Unhappy families: Governments are increasingly unable to ignore the costs of divorce', *The Economist*, March 1993. © The Economist, London.

22. Andrew Yates. 'Divorce puts a strain on the housing chain', *The Times*, 10 February 1991.
23. Barbara Dafoe Whitehead. *The Divorce Culture*. New York, Alfred A Knopf, 1997, p106.
24. Susan Gettleman and Janet Markowitz. *The Courage to Divorce*. New York, Simon and Schuster, 1974, p213.
25. Dougal Mackay and Jill Frankham. *Marriage and How to Survive It*. Loughton, Essex, Judy Piatkus Publishers, 1983, p139.
26. Lawrence Stone. *Road to Divorce: England 1530 to 1987*. Oxford University Press, 1992, p422.
27. Cosmo Gordon Lang, Archbishop of Canterbury. *The Marriage Question*. A sermon at St Paul's Cathedral, 11 October 1908. White Cross League, Westminster Abbey.
28. Arthur C. Hall, Bishop of Vermont. *Church's Discipline Concerning Marriage and Divorce: First Triennial Charge*. New York, Longmans Green, 1896, p4.
29. Melanie Phillips. 'Where are the New Victorians?', in Ruth Lister (ed.), *Charles Murray and the Underclass: the developing debate*. London, Institute of Economic Affairs, 1996, p157.
30. Whitehead. *Divorce Culture*, p182.
31. David Popenoe. *Life Without Father*. New York, Martin Kessler, 1996, p3.
32. Judith S. Wallerstein and Sandra Blakeslee. *Second Chances: men, women and children a decade after divorce*. London, Corgi Books, 1990, pxiii.
33. Bruce Anderson. 'A moral revival: just what can Britain learn from the past?' *Daily Mail*, 26 October 1996.
34. Leo McKinstry. 'The emptiness of Labour's new policy on marriage', *Sunday Telegraph*, 1 November 1998.
35. Harper. *Equal and Different*, p164.
36. Sue Slipman. 'Would you take one home with you?' in Ruth Lister (ed.), *Charles Murray and the Underclass*. p161.
37. John Haskey. 'Families: their historical context, and recent trends in the factors influencing their formation and dissolution', in *The Fragmenting Family: Does it Matter?* London, IEA Health and Welfare Unit, 1998, pp32-3.
38. David Popenoe. 'The national family wars', *Journal of Marriage and the Family*, 55, August 1993, p553-55.
39. Stanley A. Ellisen. *Divorce and Remarriage in the Church*. Grand Rapids, Mich., Zondervan, 1977, p17.
40. Ibid. p21.
41. Norman Doe. *The Legal Framework of the Church of England*. London, Oxford University Press, 1996, p375.
42. Ibid. p376.
43. Ibid. pp377-78.
44. Ruth Gledhill. 'Priest and divorcee to marry in registry office', *The Times*, 26 November 1994. © Times Newspapers Limited, London.
45. Jonathan Petre and Catherine Elsworth.'Bishops want divorcees remarried in church', *Sunday Telegraph*, 17 May 1998. © Telegraph Group Limited, London, 1999.
46. Mary Kirk and Tom Leary. *Holy Matrimony?* London, SPCK, 1994.
47. Methodist Church Division of Social Responsibility, *Preparing for Christian Marriage*. Report received by the Conference of 1996. pp4-5.
48. Ibid. p3.
49. Ibid. p11.
50. Ibid. p14.
51. Ibid. p3.
52. Ibid. p11.
53. Ibid. p13.
54. Ibid. p17.
55. Ibid. pp18-19.

56. Anne Wilkinson-Hayes and Paul Mortimer (eds.), *Belonging: a resource for the Christian Family*. Baptist Union of Great Britain, April 1994, p60.
57. Ibid. p62.
58. Ibid. p64.
59. *Remarriage: URC Practice*. United Reformed Policy on divorce and remarriage.

Chapter 2. Marriage under challenge

1. Jason Burt. 'Why marriage is losing its appeal', *Daily Mail*, 10 May 1997.
2. Office of Population Censuses and Surveys. *Marriage and Divorce Statistics, 1837-1983: England & Wales*. (OPCS series FM2 no.16) (Historical Series), London, HMSO, 1990.
3. These statistics appear in the publications of the Office of Population Censuses and Surveys. *Marriage and Divorce Statistics: England & Wales for 1990 to 1996*. (OPCS series FM2 nos. 18, 19, 20, 21, 22), London, HMSO, 1992-1996.
4. *Population Trends 94*, Winter 1998. London, Office of National Statistics, 1999, table 22, p67.
5. John Haskey. 'Divorce and Remarriage in England & Wales', *Population Trends 95*, Spring 1999, London, Office of National Statistics, 1999.
6. Patricia H. Shiono and Linda Sandham Quinn. 'Epidemiology of divorce', *The Future of Children, Children and Divorce*, 4:1, Spring 1994, p17.
7. S.C. Clarke. *Advance report of final marriage statistics, 1989 and 1990*. Monthly vital statistics report, 43:12, suppl., Hyattsville, Maryland, National Center for Statistics, 1995.
8. United States. National Center for Health Statistics of the United States. *Annual Reports*, 1981 to 1995.
9. Arthur J. Norton and Louisa F. Miller. *Marriage, Divorce and Remarriage in the 1990's*. US Bureau of the Census. (Current Population Reports, Special studies, Series P-23, no. 180), Washington D.C., U.S. Government Printing Office, 1992, p5.
10. Ibid. p6.
11. Ibid. p12.
12. Nena O'Neill and George O'Neill. *Open Marriage: A new lifestyle for couples*. London, Peter Owen, 1972, p54.
13. Ibid. p194.
14. Ibid. p188.
15. Germaine Greer. *The Female Eunuch*. London, Grafton Books, 1986, p320.
16. Ibid. p18.
17. Ibid. p322-23.
18. Liz Hodgkinson. *Unholy Matrimony*. London, Columbus Books, 1988.
19. Ibid. p117.
20. Brenda Hoggett. 'Ends and means: The utility of marriage as a legal institution', in J.M. Ekalaar and S.N. Katz (eds.), *Marriage and cohabitation in contemporary society*. Butterworth, 1980, pp94-103.
21. Clifford Longley. 'Two models of marriage', *The Times*, 16 March 1991.
22. 'How Brown got it wrong over tax and the family', *Mail on Sunday*, 14 March 1999.
23. Richard J. Udry. 'Divorce', in *Encyclopedia Americana*. Grolier, vol. 9, 1993, p214.
24. Morton Hunt and Bernice Hunt. *The Divorce Experience*. New York, McGraw-Hill, 1977, p268.
25. 'I'm Ms not Mrs, officer's wife tells the world', *Daily Telegraph*, 8 January 1999.
26. Judith Woods. 'When new love dares not speak its name', *Daily Telegraph*, 28 July 1998.
27. Helen Wilkinson. *The Proposal: giving marriage back to the people*. London, Demos, 1997, p42.
28. Ibid. p43.
29. Ibid. p44.
30. Ibid. p45.

31. Wilkinson. *The Proposal: giving marriage back to the people*, p51.
32. Catherine Bennett. 'Till disillusion and failure do us part', © *Guardian*, 12 February 1997.
33. 'Take your sleeping partners', *Sunday Times*, 18 November 1990. Quote is from Antony Head of Gold Blend. © Times Newspapers Limited, London.
34. Lydia Slater. 'Mother Madonna', *Daily Telegraph*, 3 February 1998. © Telegraph Group Limited, London, 1999.
35. Nick Gordon. 'No man about the house: Michelle Pfeiffer', *Sunday Times*, 15 August 1993. © Times Newspapers Limited, London.
36. Lucinda Rosenfeld. 'Mock marriage', *Vogue*, 28 February 1998, p51.
37. Sally Ann Lasson. 'Wedded bliss-ters', *Sunday Times*, 26 July 1992.
38. Jenni Murray. 'Why no woman should marry', *Options*, July 1992, pp8-9.
39. 'Profile: Helen Mirren', *Sunday Telegraph*, 4 January 1998.
40. Elizabeth Grice. 'Actress Cherie Lunghi took a gamble for the sake of her daughter – but will it pay off?', *Daily Telegraph*, 7 July 1998. © Telegraph Group Limited, London, 1999.
41. Polly Toynbee. 'A woman's work is never done', *The Times*, 14 September 1991.
42. Sarah Sands. 'Cook's mistress is barred from State Banquets', *Daily Telegraph*, 14 January 1998.© Telegraph Group Limited, London, 1999.
43. Mary Anne Glendon. *Abortion and Divorce in Western Law*. Cambridge, Mass., Harvard University Press, 1987, p108.
44. John Haskey. 'Trends in Marriage and Cohabitation: the decline in marriage and the changing pattern of living together in partnerships', *Population Trends 80*, Summer 1995, London, HMSO, 1995, pp5-15.
45. Office of Population Censuses and Surveys. *General Household Survey. 1993*. (OPCS Series GHS no. 24), London, HMSO, 1995.
46. Lester Middlehurst. 'The real Rosie in my life', *The Mail on Sunday*, 27 December 1998.
47. Office for National Statistics. *Birth Statistics 1995*. (ONS series FM1 no 24), London, HMSO, 1997.
48. Central Statistical Office. *Social Trends 26*. Jenny Church (ed.), London, HMSO, 1996, p54.
49. Shiono and Quinn. 'Epidemiology of divorce', p21.
50. 'The family: Home sweet home', *The Economist*, 336, 9 September 1995. © The Economist, London.
51. Constance R. Ahrons and Roy H. Rodgers. *Divorced Families*. New York, Norton, 1987, p213.
52. Meyer F. Nimkoff. 'Illegitimacy', in *Encyclopaedia Britannica*. London, William Benton, 1963, vol. 12, p83.
53. *Report of the Royal Commission on Marriage and Divorce*. London, HMSO, 1956, p305.
54. Jon Davies. 'The Family: R.I.P? Religion, marriage, the market and the state in Western Societies', in *The Family: Is It Just Another Lifestyle Choice?* London, IEA Health and Welfare Unit, 1993, p2.
55. Christine McMullen. 'What is a family?', *Home & Family*, Autumn 1993.
56. 'Code for schools omits marriage from core values', *The Times*, 29 October 1996.
57. *The Times*, 7 January 1997.
58. 'Return of the family', *Sunday Times*, 28 February 1993. © Times Newspapers Limited, London.
59. Kate Muir. 'Daddy doesn't live here', *The Times*, 30 June 1992. © Times Newspapers Limited, London.
60. *Something to Celebrate – valuing families in Church and Society*. Report of Working Party of Board for Social Responsibility, London, Church House Publishing, 1995, p6.
61. John Drane and Olive Drane. *Happy Families?* Handbook of Pastoral Care, London, Marshall Pickering, 1995, p3.

62. Ibid. p4.
63. Ibid. p6.
64. Malcolm Wicks. *Daily Telegraph*, 11 October 1991.
65. John Muncie and Roger Sapsford. 'Issues in the study of "The Family"', in John Muncie et al. (eds.), *Understanding the Family*. Milton Keynes, Open University, SAGE Publications, 1995, chapter 1, p31.
66. Rudi Dallos and Roger Sapsford. 'Patterns of diversity and lived realities', in John Muncie et al. (eds.), *Understanding the Family*. Milton Keynes, Open University, SAGE Publications, 1995, chapter 4, p165.
67. *Something to Celebrate*, p6.
68. Ibid. p9.
69. Drane and Drane. *Happy Families?* p20.
70. Ibid. pp20-31.
71. Ibid. p35.
72. Ahrons and Rodgers. *Divorced Families*, pp213-14.
73. Clifford Longley. 'What exactly do we mean by a family?', *Daily Telegraph*, 30 January 1998.
74. Janet Daley. 'Why are they afraid of using the M-word?', *Daily Telegraph*, 20 January 1998. © Telegraph Group Limited, London, 1999.

Chapter 3. Divorce and the Reformation

1. St. Augustine. *Treatises on Marriage and Other Subjects*. Roy J. Deferrari (ed.), New York, Fathers of the Church, 1995, p31.
2. Gordon J. Wenham and William A. Heth. *Jesus and Divorce*. Updated edition. Carlisle, Paternoster Press, 1997, p7.
3. *The New Bible Dictionary*. J.D. Douglas (ed.), Leicester, Inter-Varsity Press, 1962, pp1112-13.
4. George Hayward Joyce. *Christian Marriage: an Historical and Doctrinal Study*. 2nd edition, London, Sheed & Ward, 1948, pv (introduction).
5. Ibid. p317.
6. Roderick Phillips. *Untying the Knot: a Short History of Divorce*. Cambridge University Press, 1991, p5.
7. V. Norskov Olsen. *The New Testament Logia on Divorce: a study of their interpretation from Erasmus to Milton*. (BGBE 10), Tubingen, Mohr, 1971, p22.
8. Ibid. p21.
9. Ibid. p23.
10. Ibid. p26.
11. Joyce. *Christian Marriage*, p392.
12. Olsen. *The New Testament Logia*, p26.
13. Ibid. p27.
14. Wenham and Heth. *Jesus and Divorce*, p79.
15. John Calvin. *Tracts Containing Antidote to the Council of Trent*, translated by Henry Beveridge, Edinburgh, Calvin Translation Society, p217.
16. Ibid. p219.
17. John Calvin. *Calvin's New Testament Commentaries. A harmony of the Gospels Matthew, Mark and Luke*. translated by T. Parker, David W. Torrance and Thomas F. Torrance (eds.), Carlisle, Paternoster Press, 1995, vol. 2, p244.
18. Ibid. p244.
19. Ibid. p246.
20. Ibid. p190.
21. Ibid. p247.
22. John Calvin. *Sermons on the Epistle to the Ephesians*. Edinburgh, Banner of Truth Trust, 1973, p565.

23. Martin Luther. *The Christian Society.* Walther I. Brandt (ed.), Luther's Works, vol. 45, Philadelphia, Concordia Publishing House, p17.
24. Ibid. p30.
25. Ibid. p30,33.
26. Ibid. p32.
27. Ibid. p32.
28. Martin Luther. *Sermon on the Mount.* Jaroslav Pelikan (ed.), Luther's Works, vol. 21, St Louis, Concordia Publishing House, p96.
29. Luther. *The Christian Society,* p33.
30. Ibid. p34.
31. Luther. *Sermon on the Mount,* p93.
32. Ibid. p93.
33. Ibid. p94.
34. Luther. *The Christian Society,* p20.
35. J.P. Whitney, in *Report of the Royal Commission on Divorce and Matrimonial Causes.* London, His Majesty's Stationery Office, 1912, p280.
36. Olsen. *The New Testament Logia,* p81.
37. Ibid. p79.
38. Phillips. *Untying the Knot,* p19.
39. Olsen. *The New Testament Logia,* p85.
40. Ibid. p64.
41. Whitney. *Royal Commission on Divorce,* p280.
42. Olsen. *The New Testament Logia,* pp67-8.
43. Joyce. *Christian Marriage,* p398.
44. John Calvin. *The Institutes of the Christian Religion.* London, James Clarke, 1962, pp482-84.
45. Whitney. *Royal Commission on Divorce,* pp274-75.
46. Phillips. *Untying the Knot,* p17.
47. *Divorce.* Report of Lower House of the Convocation of York. Westminster, National Society, Sanctuary, 1896, p48.
48. Eric Josef Carlson. *Marriage and the English Reformation.* Oxford, Blackwell, 1994, pp18-19.
49. Ibid. pp21-2.
50. Ibid. p25.
51. Ibid. p25.
52. Ibid. p42.
53. *Formularies of Faith put forth by Authority during Reign of Henry VIII...* Oxford, Clarendon Press, 1825, p91.
54. Ibid. p92.
55. John Keble. *Sequel of the Argument against immediately repealing the Laws which treat the Nuptial Bond as Indissoluble.* Oxford, Parker, 1857, pp204-5.
56. Ibid. p205
57. *Divorce.* Report of the Lower House of the Convocation of York, p50.
58. *Anglican Canons 1529-1947.* Gerald Bray (ed.), Church of England Record Society, vol. 6, Woodbridge, Boydell Press, 1998, p405.
59. Robert Shaw. *The Reformed Faith: an exposition of the Westminster Confession of Faith.* Inverness, Christian Focus Publications, Reprint 1974, p254.
60. Ibid. p257.

Chapter 4. Divorce in England – the first step

1. Hansard. Commons debate, 31 July 1857, cc825-55.
2. Hansard. Lords debate, 10 March 1920, cc362-76.
3. Hansard. Lords debate, 3 July 1856, cc237-38.

4.   Hansard. Lords debate, 26 June 1856, cc1979-82.
5.   Roderick Phillips. *Untying the Knot: a Short History of Divorce.* Cambridge University Press, 1991, p34.
6.   Ibid. p28.
7.   Eric Josef Carlson. *Marriage and the English Reformation.* Oxford, Blackwell, 1994, p130.
8.   Phillips. *Untying the Knot,* p33.
9.   Haggard's Consistory Reports, vol. 1, p118.
10. Gertrude Himmelfarb. *The De-moralization of Society.* London, IEA Health and Welfare Unit, 1995, p53.
11. Ibid. p54.
12. Ibid. p57.
13. Ibid. p71.
14. Hansard. Commons debate, 3 June 1930, c1267.
15. H.J. Wilkins. *History of Divorce and Remarriage.* London, Longmans, 1910.
16. Lawrence Stone. *Road to Divorce; England 1530 to 1987.* Oxford University Press, 1992, p346.
17. Douglas Bush. 'Milton, John', in *Encyclopaedia Britannica.* London, William Benton, 1963, vol. 15, p509.
18. V. Norskov Olsen. *The New Testament Logia on Divorce: a study of their interpretation from Erasmus to Milton.* (BGBE 10), Tubingen, Mohr, 1971, p132.
19. Ibid. p136.
20. George Douglas Howard Cole. 'Socialism', in *Encyclopaedia Britannica.* London, William Benton, 1963, vol. 20, p879.
21. John Butt. *Robert Owen, Prince of Cotton Spinners.* Newton Abbott, David & Charles, 1929, p45.
22. Barbara Taylor. *Eve and the New Jerusalem.* London, Virago, 1983, p32.
23. Ibid. p45.
24. Phillips. *Untying the Knot,* p165.
25. Taylor. *Eve and the New Jerusalem,* p39.
26. Phillips. *Untying the Knot,* p165.
27. Taylor. *Eve and the New Jerusalem,* p185.
28. Max Lerner. 'Liberalism', in *Encyclopaedia Britannica.* London, William Benton, 1963, vol. 13, p989.
29. J.S. Mill. *The Subjection of Women.* London, Longmans Green, 1869, pp155-58.
30. Colin S. Gibson. *Dissolving Wedlock.* London, Routledge, 1994, p56.
31. Stone. *Road to Divorce,* p369.
32. *The Times,* 22 May 1856.
33. Hansard. Lords debate, 26 June 1856, cc1977-78.
34. Ibid. cc1979-82.
35. Ibid. c1983.
36. Ibid. c1986.
37. Hansard. Lords debate, 3 July 1856, c235.
38. Ibid. c239.
39. Hansard. Lords debate, 26 June 1856, c1984.
40. Hansard. Lords debate, 3 July 1856, cc237-38.
41. Ibid. cc244-45.
42. Ibid. c247.
43. Ibid. c246.
44. Hansard. Lords debate, 19 May 1857, cc 483-94.
45. Ibid. cc494-96.
46. Ibid. cc496-508.
47. Ibid. cc508-9.
48. Ibid. cc509-10.

49. Hansard. Lords debate, 19 May 1857, cc510-11.
50. Ibid. cc511-13.
51. Ibid. cc513-14.
52. Ibid. c515.
53. Ibid. cc516-21.
54. Ibid. cc523-31.
55. Ibid. c533.
56. Ibid. cc533-35.
57. Ibid. cc535-37.
58. Hansard. Lords debate, 23 June 1857, c202.
59. Ibid. cc204-5.
60. Ibid. c227.
61. Ibid. c232.
62. Ibid. cc232-34.
63. Ibid. cc234-35.

Chapter 5.   Yes, it is a Protestant doctrine!

1. Hansard. Commons debate, 30 July 1857, cc718-36.
2. Ibid. cc736-42.
3. Ibid. cc742-47.
4. Ibid. cc747-49.
5. Ibid. cc750-54.
6. Ibid. cc754-56.
7. Ibid. cc756-58.
8. Ibid. cc758-64.
9. Ibid. cc764-67.
10. Ibid. cc767-73.
11. Hansard. Commons debate, 31 July 1857, cc825-55.
12. Ibid. cc856-66.
13. Ibid. c867.
14. Ibid. cc873-86.
15. Ibid. cc886-88.
16. Ibid. cc889-90.
17. Hansard. Commons debate, 4 August 1857, cc1022-33.
18. Ibid. cc1041-45.
19. Ibid. cc1046-49.
20. Ibid. cc1051-54.
21. Ibid. cc1821-26, 1870-80.
22. Hansard. Commons debate, 21 August 1857, c1986.
23. Ibid. cc2055-68.
24. Ibid. cc1992-94.
25. Ibid. cc1994-99.
26. Reginald Wilberforce. *Life of Samuel Wilberforce, Bishop of Oxford and Winchester; by his son.* London, Kegan Paul, Trench, 1888, p207.
27. *The Times* (Letter), 23 November 1858.
28. *Life of Lord John Campbell.* 2nd edition. vol. ii, p361. Cited from G.R. Oakley, *Why We Oppose Divorce.* SPCK, 1913.
29. G.R. Oakley. *Why We Oppose Divorce.* London, SPCK, 1913. Cited from p15.
30. Victoria, Queen. *The Letters of Queen Victoria.* AC Benson & Viscount Esher (eds.), London, John Murray, 1907, Part 1, vol. 3, p482.
31. James Cowan. *Christian Marriage Indissoluble; a plain sermon.* London, William Skeffington, 1857.
32. 'Controversy of Divorce'. *The Church Quarterly Review,* January 1896, p436.

33. Chronicle of Convocation, Canterbury, February 1858, p4.
34. Chronicle of Convocation, Canterbury, February 1859, pp34-5.
35. Ibid. p34
36. Chronicle of Convocation, Canterbury, 1865, pp1895-96.
37. Ibid. pp1901-2.
38. Ibid. pp1889-900.
39. Ibid. pp1897-99; pp1911-12.
40. Ibid. pp1902-3.
41. Ibid. p1907.
42. Ibid. pp1912-13.
43. Chronicle of Convocation, Canterbury, July 1883, p231.
44. Ibid. p231.
45. Ibid. p232.
46. Chronicle of Convocation, Canterbury, 1885, pp81-3.
47. Ibid. p83.
48. Ibid. Report no. 193, p327.
49. Chronicle of Convocation, Canterbury, May 1895. p231.
50. Ibid. pp233-34.
51. Ibid. p238.
52. Ibid. p241.
53. Chronicle of Convocation, Canterbury, 1897. Report of Lower House Committee on the Laws of Marriage.
54. Ibid. Report of Upper House on Laws of Marriage.
55. *Divorce.* Report of the Lower House of the Convocation of York. Westminster, National Society, Sanctuary, 1896, p8 of preface.
56. Ibid. p52.
57. Ibid. pp257-66.
58. *Church Quarterly Review*, 40, July 1895, p6.
59. 'Controversy of Divorce', *The Church Quarterly Review,* January 1896, pp437-38.

Chapter 6. *Discovering more grave matrimonial offences*

1. Lawrence Stone. *Road to Divorce: England 1530 to 1987.* Oxford University Press, 1992, p391.
2. H.W. Hill, Secretary of the English Church Union, in *Report of the Royal Commission on Divorce and Matrimonial Causes.* London, HMSO, 1912, vol. 3, p364.
3. Ibid. p366.
4. William J. Knox-Little. *Holy Matrimony.* London, Longmans Green, 1900, p84.
5. H. Hensley Henson. *Christian Marriage.* London, Cassell, 1907, pp22-3.
6. Ibid. p24.
7. Ibid. p37.
8. Ibid. p39.
9. Chronicle of Convocation, Canterbury, April 1910, pp162-64.
10. Ibid. p164.
11. Ibid. p172.
12. Ibid. p174.
13. Ibid. p171.
14. Chronicle of Convocation, Canterbury, February 1911, pp86-8.
15. Ibid. pp92-4.
16. Ibid. p96.
17. Ibid. p96.
18. H. Hensley Henson, in *Royal Commission on Divorce.* 1912, vol. 2, pp404-26.
19. William Sanday, in *Royal Commission on Divorce.* 1912, vol. 3, pp237-53.
20. Hastings Rashdall, in *Royal Commission on Divorce.* 1912, vol. 3, pp306-16.

21. E.G. Wood, in *Royal Commission on Divorce*. 1912, vol. 3, pp367-73.
22. Charles Gore, in *Royal Commission on Divorce*. 1912, vol. 2, pp347-70.
23. *Royal Commission on Divorce*. vol. 1, 1912, p30.
24. Ibid. p30.
25. Ibid. p37.
26. Ibid. p29.
27. Ibid. p30.
28. Ibid. p95.
29. Ibid. p96.
30. Ibid. p171.
31. Ibid. p172.
32. Ibid. p175.
33. Ibid. p176.
34. Ibid. p177.
35. Ibid. p24.
36. Ibid. p184.
37. Ibid. p185.
38. Ibid. pp185-86.
39. Ibid. p187.
40. Ibid. p188.
41. Chronicle of Convocation, Canterbury, November, 1912, pp549-55.
42. Ibid. pp555-56.
43. Darwell Stone. *Divorce and Re-marriage*. London, Longmans Green, 1913.
44. Lord Halifax. Church Union. *The Times*, 21 November 1912.
45. F.B. Meyer. *Morning Post*, 13 November 1912.
46. J. Moyes. *Morning Post*, 13 November 1912.
47. Chronicle of Convocation, Canterbury, April 1914, pp298-316.
48. Chronicle of Convocation, Canterbury, April 1915, pp260-68.
49. 'Divorce' (editorial), *The Times*, 12 November 1912. © Times Newspapers Limited, London.

Chapter 7. The slippery slope

1. A. R. Winnett. *Divorce and Remarriage in Anglicanism*. London, Macmillan, 1958, p213.
2. R.H. Charles. *The Teaching of the New Testament on Divorce*. London, Wms. & Norgate, 1921, p3.
3. Ibid. p79.
4. Ibid. p80.
5. Ibid. pp81-2.
6. Ibid. p120.
7. Hansard. Lords debate, 10 March 1920, cc342-57.
8. Ibid. cc357-62.
9. Ibid. cc362-76.
10. Ibid. cc376-82.
11. Ibid. cc663-79.
12. Ibid. cc684-91.
13. Ibid. cc694-700.
14. Ibid. cc704-07.
15. Hansard. Lords debate, 4 May 1920, cc104-11.
16. Ibid. cc111-13.
17. Hansard. Lords debate, 22 June 1920, cc699-703.
18. Ibid. cc703-13.
19. Ibid. cc716-21.
20. Ibid. cc721-27.

21. 'Divorce Bill Protest', *The Times*, 30 July 1920. © Times Newspapers Limited, London.
22. *The Times*, 2 August 1920.
23. 'Political notes, the divorce division', *The Times*, 15 April 1920. © Times Newspapers Limited, London.
24. Hansard. Commons debate, 8 June 1923, cc2641-47.
25. Ibid. cc2652-54.
26. *The Times* (Leader), 9 June 1923. © Times Newspapers Limited, London.
27. Hansard. Lords debate, 26 June 1923, cc574-79.
28. Ibid. cc579-85.
29. Ibid. cc592-97.
30. Ibid. cc602-6.

Chapter 8. Increasing the sum of human happiness

1. Hansard. Commons debate, 20 November 1936, c2082.
2. Lambeth Conference, 1920. *Encyclical Letter*, p17.
3. Ibid. Report, p44.
4. Lambeth Conference, 1930. Report, p42.
5. Chronicle of Convocation, Canterbury. 1931, pp217-22.
6. Ibid. pp234-35.
7. *The Church and Marriage*. The Majority Report 1935 of the Joint Committees of the Convocations of Canterbury and York. London, SPCK, 1935, pp2-3.
8. Ibid. p4.
9. Ibid. p5.
10. Ibid. p6.
11. Ibid. p12.
12. Ibid. p19.
13. Ibid. p21.
14. Ibid. p23.
15. *The Church and Marriage*. The Minority Report. pp34-6.
16. Ibid. p37.
17. Ibid. quoted from *Modern Churchman*.
18. Ibid. pp42-5.
19. Chronicle of Convocation, Canterbury, 1935, p254.
20. Ibid. pp334-40.
21. Resolutions of Canterbury Convocation, Canterbury, June 1935.
22. A.R. Winnett. *Divorce and Remarriage in Anglicanism*. London, Macmillan, 1958, p227.
23. *The Times* (Letter: National Council of Women), 20 November 1936.
24. *The Times* (Letter: Mothers' Union), 26 November 1936.
25. Hansard. Commons debate, 20 November 1936, c2115.
26. Ibid. cc2098-103.
27. Ibid. cc2081-93.
28. Ibid. cc2098-103.
29. Ibid. cc2103-7.
30. Ibid. cc2107-10.
31. Ibid. cc2114-19.
32. Ibid. cc2126-28.
33. *The Times* (Letter), 1 December 1936.
34. *The Times* (Letter: Mothers' Union), 26 November 1936.
35. Hansard. Commons debate, 28 May 1937, cc575-80.
36. Ibid. cc580-86.
37. Ibid. cc585-89.
38. Ibid. cc631-33.
39. Ibid. cc643-44.

40. Hansard. Lords debate, 24 June 1937, cc730-38.
41. Ibid. cc738-41.
42. Ibid. cc743-51.
43. Ibid. cc751-54.
44. Ibid. cc761-65.
45. Ibid. cc768-74.
46. Ibid. c781.
47. Ibid. cc781-84.
48. Ibid. cc812-18.
49. Ibid. 28 June 1937, cc818-24.
50. Ibid. cc843-48.
51. Stone. *Road to Divorce: England 1530 to 1987.* p402.
52. *Acts of the Convocations of Canterbury and York*, (eds.) A.F Smethurst and H.R. Wilson. London, SPCK, 1962, p90-1
53. J.G. Lockhart. *Cosmo Gordon Lang.* London, Hodder and Stoughton, 1949, p235.

Chapter 9. A new principle in divorce

1. Hansard. Commons debate, 9 March 1951, cc926-35.
2. Ibid. cc938-41.
3. Ibid. cc941-49.
4. Ibid. cc954-59.
5. Ibid. cc980-84.
6. Ibid. cc990-91.
7. Ibid. cc993-99.
8. Ibid. cc999-1006.
9. *The Times* (Letter, Mothers' Union, Rosamond Fisher), 6 March 1951.
10. *The Times* (Letter, Ethical Union, H.J. Blackham), 8 March 1951.
11. *The Times* (Letter, Edwin Monmouth), 14 March 1951.
12. *The Times* (Letter, S.O. Henn Collins), 17 March 1951.
13. *The Times* (Letter, J.E.S. Simon), 9 March 1951.
14. *The Times* (Letter, Marriage Law Society, Robert Pollard), 9 March 1951.
15. 'New proposals on divorce', *The Times*, 28 March 1951. © Times Newspapers Limited, London.
16. Ibid. *The Times*, 28 March 1951. © Times Newspapers Limited, London.
17. *The Times* (Letter, Eirene White), 2 April 1951.
18. Geoffrey Fisher. *The Problems of Marriage and Divorce*. London, SPCK, 1955, pp6-8.
19. Ibid. p9.
20. Ibid. p18.
21. Ibid. pp20-1.
22. Ibid. p22.
23. Great Britain. *Report of the Royal Commission on Divorce*. London, HMSO, 1956, p9.
24. Ibid. p9.
25. Ibid. p10.
26. Ibid. p12.
27. Ibid. p13.
28. Ibid. p14.
29. Ibid. p15.
30. Ibid. p23.
31. 'What cannot be mended', *The Times*, 21 March 1956. © Times Newspapers Limited, London.
32. 'No remarriage in church', *The Times*, 5 June 1956. © Times Newspapers Limited, London.
33. *The Times*, 8 February 1958.
34. *The Times* (Letter, Marriage Reform Society, L.J. Blom-Cooper), 15 February 1958.

35. *The Times*, 10 November 1958.
36. *The Times*, 9 February 1963.
37. Hansard. Debate in Standing Committee C, 6 March 1963, cc15-30.
38. 'Churches unite against divorce proposals', *The Times*, 3 April 1963. © Times Newspapers Limited, London.
39. *The Times* (Letter, British Council, Free Churches), 4 April 1963.
40. 'Love greater after long marriage', *The Times*, 6 June 1963. © Times Newspapers Limited, London.
41. *The Times* (Letter, John Morris, John Parker, Dick Taverne, Julius Silverman, Llywelyn Williams), 13 April 1963.
42. *The Times* (Letter, Edwin Cambrensis), 17 April 1963.
43. *The Times* (Letter, G.B. Bentley, Canon of Windsor), 17 April 1963.
44. *The Times* (Letter, Mr A.P. Herbert), 30 April 1963.
45. Hansard. Commons debate, 3 May 1963, cc1558-62.
46. Ibid. c1577.
47. Ibid. cc1581-82.
48. Hansard. Lords debate, 21 June 1963, cc1528-35.
49. *The Times* (Letter, Mr Leo Abse), 20 June 1963.
50. Hansard. Lords debate, 21 June 1963, cc1543-47.
51. Ibid. c1548.
52. Ibid. c1550.

Chapter 10. A divorce bill full of tears

1. William Barclay. *Ethics in a Permissive Society*. London, Collins, 1971, p13.
2. *Putting Asunder: A Divorce Law for Contemporary Society*. Report of Group appointed by the Archbishop of Canterbury in January 1964. London, SPCK, 1966, p3.
3. Ibid. p17.
4. Ibid. p18.
5. Ibid. p21.
6. 'A new light on divorce', *The Times*, 29 July 1966. © Times Newspapers Limited, London.
7. 'New basis for divorce', *The Times*, 29 July 1966. © Times Newspapers Limited, London.
8. Church Assembly, report of proceeding. London, 1967, pp230-31.
9. Ibid. pp234-35.
10. Ibid. pp239-40.
11. Ibid. pp250-53.
12. Ibid. pp245-47.
13. Ibid. p271.
14. Great Britain. The Law Commission. *Reform of the Grounds of Divorce: The Field of Choice*. London, HMSO, 1966, pp10-11.
15. Ibid. p14.
16. Ibid. p16.
17. Ibid. p24.
18. Ibid. pp54-5.
19. 'Divorce by consent proposed', *The Times*, 16 January 1968. © Times Newspapers Limited, London.
20. 'Mr Abse criticises Archbishop', *The Times*, 19 January 1968.
21. 'Archbishop denies breach of faith', *The Times*, 20 January 1969. © Times Newspapers Limited, London.
22. 'Breakdown or offences' (editorial), *The Times*, 16 January 1968. © Times Newspapers Limited, London.
23. *The Times* (Letter, Mr Geoffrey Crispin, QC), 27 January 1968.

24. *The Times* (Letter, Phyllis Willmot), 8 February 1968.
25. Hansard. Commons debate, 6 December 1968, cc2033-43.
26. Ibid. cc2043-50.
27. Hansard. Commons debate, 17 December 1968, cc1057-61.
28. Ibid. cc1061-66.
29. Ibid. cc1066-72.
30. Ibid. cc1073-79.
31. Ibid. c1078.
32. Ibid. cc1079-85.
33. Ibid. cc1085-90.
34. Ibid. cc1090-95.
35. Ibid. cc1112-16.
36. Ibid. cc1116-21.
37. Ibid. cc1121-30.
38. Hansard. Lords debate, 30 June 1969, c303.
39. Ibid. cc307-13.
40. Ibid. cc339-42.
41. Ibid. cc358-63.
42. Ibid. cc369-75.
43. Ibid. cc375-80.
44. Ibid. cc380-81.
45. Ibid. cc395-98.
46. Ibid. cc398-400.
47. Ibid. cc402-6.
48. Ibid. cc441-42.
49. 'Divorce on demand', *The Times*, 2 July 1969. © Times Newspapers Limited, London.
50. *Family Law: the Ground for Divorce.* (The Law Commission Report. no. 192). London, HMSO, 1990, p1.
51. Ibid. p5.
52. Ibid. p6.
53. Ibid. p7.
54. Ibid. p8.
55. Ibid. p27.
56. 'Diminishing Divorce Law', *Sunday Times*, 12 December 1993. © Times Newspapers Limited, London.
57. Hansard. Commons debate, 4 August 1857, cc1041-45.
58. Hansard. Lords debate, 22 June 1920, cc699-703.
59. Hansard. Commons debate, 26 May 1937, cc580-86.
60. Hansard. Lords debate, 30 June 1969, cc395-98.
61. Chronicle of Convocation, Canterbury. 20 November 1912, pp549-55.
62. Hansard. Lords debate, 10 March 1920, cc663-79.
63. Hansard. Commons debate, 20 November 1936, cc2098-103.
64. Ibid. cc2114-19.

Chapter 11. Confusion over remarriage

1. Church Assembly, report of proceedings. London, 1967, p268-71.
2. *Marriage, Divorce and the Church.* Report of Commission on the Christian Doctrine of Marriage. (The Root Report 1971), London, SPCK 1971, Introduction, pxi.
3. Ibid. p3.
4. Ibid. p36.
5. Ibid. p38.
6. Ibid. pp71-2.
7. Ibid. p72.

8.   General Synod, report of proceedings. London, Church House, February 1972, p77.
9.   Ibid. p80.
10.   Ibid. pp81-3.
11.   Ibid. pp83-4.
12.   Ibid. p 86.
13.   Ibid. p93.
14.   Ibid. p98.
15.   General Synod, report of proceedings, November 1974, p 814.
16.   *Marriage and the Church's Task.* (The Lichfield Report), report of the General Synod Marriage Commission, London, CIO Publishing, 1978, pp78-9.
17.   Ibid. p85.
18.   Ibid. p90.
19.   Ibid. p90.
20.   Ibid. p100.
21.   Ibid. p110.
22.   Results of the reference to diocesan synods, 1979-1980, p5.
23.   General Synod, report of proceedings, February 1981, p87.
24.   Ibid. p89.
25.   Ibid. p90.
26.   General Synod, report of proceedings, July 1981, p800.
27.   Ibid. p821.
28.   Ibid. p822.
29.   Ibid. p823.
30.   Ibid. p824.
31.   Ibid. pp824-26.
32.   Ibid. pp832-33.
33.   Ibid. p835.
34.   Ibid. p838.
35.   Ibid. p844.
36.   Ibid. p846.
37.   *Marriage – and the Standing Committee's Task.* (GS 571). London, CIO Publishing, April 1983.
38.   Ibid. p4.
39.   Ibid. p53.
40.   General Synod, report of proceedings, July 1983, pp431-36.
41.   Ibid. p446.
42.   Ibid. pp448-49.
43.   Ibid. p453.
44.   *Report from the House of Bishops.* (GS 616), March 1984.
45.   Ibid.
46.   General Synod, report of proceedings, 1984, p291.
47.   Ibid. pp299-302.
48.   Ibid. p303.
49.   *Report of the House of Bishops.* (GS 634), 1984.
50.   *Marriage in Church after Divorce.* (GS 633), 1984.
51.   Diocesan Synods' response to draft marriage regulations, 1985.
52.   *House of Bishops' Report.* (GS 669), 1985.
53.   General Synod, report of proceedings, 1985, pp204-6.
54.   Ibid. pp207-10.
55.   Ibid. pp214-15.
56.   General Synod, report of proceedings, 1994, pp902-3.
57.   Ibid. p913.
58.   General Synod, report of proceedings, 1994. p933.

59.   *Marriage.* A teaching document from House of Bishops of the Church of England, London, Church House Publishing, 1999, p7.
60.   Ibid. p9.
61.   Ibid. pp14-15.
62.   General Synod, report of proceedings, February 1981, p89.
63.   John Keble. *Sequel of the Argument against immediately repealing the Laws which treat the Nuptial Bond as Indissoluble.* Oxford, Parker, 1857, pp204-5.
64.   *Divorce.* Report of the Lower House of the Convocation of York, p50.
65.   Phillips. *Untying the Knot*, p33.
66.   *Marriage.* A teaching document, 1999, pp17-18.
67.   Ibid. p19.
68.   Ibid. pp23-4.
69.   *Marriage in Church after Divorce.* Report from working party commissioned by the House of Bishops of the Church of England, London, Church House Publishing, 1999, p12.
70.   Ibid. p13.
71.   Ibid. p45.
72.   Ibid. pp46-7.
73.   *Acts of the Convocations of Canterbury and York.* (eds.) Smethurst and Wilson. pp90-1.
74.   Geoffrey Fisher, *The Problems of Marriage and Divorce.* London, SPCK, 1955, p21.

Chapter 12.   The American divorce habit

1.   Barbara Dafoe Whitehead. *The Divorce Culture.* New York, Alfred A.Knopf, 1997, p3.
2.   David Popenoe. *Life Without Father.* New York, Martin Kessler Books, 1996, p19.
3.   Charles F. Thwing and Carries F. Butler Thwing. *The Family, an Historical and Social Study.* Boston, Lothrop Lee, 1913, pp87-8.
4.   Nancy F. Cott. 'Divorce and the changing status of women', in Michael Gordon (ed.), *The American Family in Social-Historical Perspective.* 2nd edition, New York, St Martin's Press, 1978, p348.
5.   Glenda Riley. *Divorce: an American Tradition.* New York, Oxford University Press, 1991, p9.
6.   Thwing and Thwing. *The Family*, pp88-9.
7.   William O'Neill. *Divorce in the Progressive Era.* New Haven, Yale University Press, 1967, p11.
8.   Nelson M. Blake. *The Road to Reno: a History of Divorce in the United States.* New York, Macmillan, 1962, p41.
9.   Cott. 'Divorce and the changing status of women', p348.
10.   Roderick Phillips. *Untying the Knot: a Short History of Divorce.* Cambridge University Press, 1991, p38.
11.   Ibid. p40.
12.   Merril D. Smith. *Breaking the Bonds.* New York University Press, 1991, p23.
13.   Ibid. p35
14.   Phillips. *Untying the Knot*, p141.
15.   *The Times*, 25 October 1858.
16.   *The Times* (Letter), 25 November 1858.
17.   Smith. *Breaking the Bonds*, p20.
18.   Robert G. Ingersoll. 'Is divorce wrong?' *North American Review*, 397, November 1889, p531.
19.   Smith. *Breaking the Bonds*, p47.
20.   Ingersoll. 'Is divorce wrong?' p531.
21.   Smith. *Breaking the Bonds*, p74.
22.   O'Neill. *Divorce in the Progressive Era*, p22.
23.   *The Times*, 28 April 1869. © Times Newspapers Limited, London.
24.   *The Times*, 14 December 1869. © Times Newspapers Limited, London.

25. Blake. *The Road to Reno*, pp104-5.
26. Carroll D. Wright, Commissioner of Labour. *A Report on Marriage and Divorce in the United States. 1867 to 1886.* Washington, February 1889, p10.
27. Ibid. p13.
28. Ibid. pp172-78.
29. *The Times*, 26 December 1889. © Times Newspapers Limited, London.
30. *The Times*, 10 October 1891.
31. O'Neill. *Divorce in the Progressive Era*, p26.
32. Ibid. p34.
33. Ibid. p27.
34. Joel Prentiss Bishop. *Marriage and Divorce*. 6th edition, Boston, Little Brown, 1881, vol. 1, p26.
35. Ibid. p27.
36. Ibid. p29.
37. Ibid. p30.
38. Ibid. p31.
39. Carl N. Degler. *At Odds: Women and the Family in America from the Revolution to the Present.* Oxford University Press, 1980, p175.
40. Elizabeth Cady Stanton. *Eighty Years and More 1815-1897. Reminiscences of E.C. Stanton.* London, Unwin, 1898, p216.
41. Rosalind Miles. *Women's History of the World.* London, Collins, 1990, p238.
42. Stanton. *Eighty Years and More*, p224.
43. Ibid. p229.
44. Ibid. p231.
45. Ibid. p232.
46. Mrs Stanton, Letter to the Seventh National Women's Convention in 1856, p 89
47. Blake. *The Road to Reno*, p95.
48. *New York Daily Tribune*, 5 March 1860.
49. *New York Daily Tribune*, 17 March 1860.
50. *New York Daily Tribune*, 28 March 1860.
51. *New York Daily Tribune*, 7 April 1860.
52. Theodore D. Woolsey. *Divorce and Divorce Legislation.* New York, Charles Scribner's Sons, 1882, p59.
53. Ibid. p66.
54. Thwing and Thwing. *The Family*, p91.
55. Ibid. p99.
56. Ibid. p100.
57. Ibid. pp105-6, 107.
58. Ibid. p159.
59. Ibid. pp161-62.
60. Ibid. p172.
61. Ingersoll. 'Is divorce wrong?', pp529-38.
62. Henry C. Potter. 'Is divorce wrong?' *North American Review*, 397, November 1889, pp524-29.
63. James Gibbons, Cardinal. 'Is divorce wrong?' *North American Review*, 397, November 1889, pp517-24.
64. William Gladstone. 'The question of divorce', *North American Review*, 397, December 1889, pp641-44.
65. *The Times*, 19 December 1889. © Times Newspapers Limited, London.
66. J.D. Lawson in *Report of the Royal Commission on Divorce and Matrimonial Causes.* London, HMSO, 1912, vol. 2, p470.
67. Robert Crane in *Report of the Royal Commission on Divorce and Matrimonial Causes.* London, HMSO, 1912, vol. 2, p161.

68. A.R. Winnett. *Divorce and Remarriage in Anglicanism*. London, Macmillan, 1958, p254.
69. Ibid. p255.
70. O'Neill. *Divorce in the Progressive Era*, p42.
71. *New York Times*, 15 November 1904. Copyright © 1904 by the New York Times. Reprinted by permission.
72. *New York Times*, 8 December, 1904.
73. *New York Times* (editorial), 1 February 1905. Copyright © 1905 by the New York Times. Reprinted by permission.
74. Blake. *The Road to Reno*, p139.
75. Ibid. p139.
76. Ibid. p140.
77. O'Neill. *Divorce in the Progressive Era*, p43.
78. 'Uniform Law relating to Annulment of Marriage and Divorce', in *Report of the National Congress on Uniform Divorce Laws*. Washington, February 1906, p2.
79. *New York Times*, 21 February 1906. Copyright © 1906 by the New York Times. Reprinted by permission.
80. Blake. *The Road to Reno*, p141.
81. Ibid. p143.
82. *Report of the National Congress on Uniform Divorce Laws*. Washington, February 1906, p6.
83. Ibid. p7.
84. Ibid.p10.
85. *New York Times*, 17 November 1906.
86. *New York Times*, 19 November 1906. Copyright © 1906 by the New York Times. Reprinted by permission.
87. Frederic Hood. 'The Church's Marriage Discipline', *Church Times*, 30 September 1949.
88. Phillips. *Untying the Knot*, p156.
89. William Croswell Doane, Bishop of Albany. 'The Sanctity of Marriage', in *Pan-Anglican Congress Report*. London, SPCK, June 1908, p4.

Chapter 13. The 'good' American divorce

1. Report of the National League for the Protection of the Family. Everest Press, 1900, p15.
2. George Elliot Howard. *History of Matrimonial Institutions, Chiefly in England and the United States*. London, Unwin, 1904, vol. 3, pp167-68.
3. Ibid. p224.
4. Ibid. pp219-20.
5. Ibid. p252.
6. Ibid. p250.
7. Ibid. p235.
8. Willystine Goodsell. *A History of Marriage and the Family*. New York, Macmillan, 1934, p480.
9. Ibid. p482.
10. Ibid. p488.
11. Carroll D. Wright. *Outline of Practical Sociology*. New York, Longmans Green, 1898, p168.
12. Ibid. p170.
13. William O'Neill. *Divorce in the Progressive Era*. New Haven, Yale University Press, 1967, p194.
14. Ibid. p196.
15. Ibid. pp258-59.
16. Ibid. p212.
17. W.G. Ballentine. 'The hyperbolical teachings of Jesus', *North American Review*, 179, 1904, pp446-56.
18. Norma W. Jones. 'Marriage and divorce: the letter of the law', *North American Review*, 181, 1905, pp597-602.

19. Wright. *Outline of Practical Sociology*, p179.
20. Ibid. p171.
21. Walker Gwynne. *Divorce in America under State and Church*. New York, Macmillan, 1925.
22. Ibid. p20.
23. F.I. Nye. 'Child adjustment in broken and in unhappy unbroken homes', *Marriage and Family Living*, 19, 1957, pp356-61.
24. *New York Times*, 29 March 1958.
25. *New York Times*, 8 October 1959.
26. *New York Times*, 15 November 1973.
27. Elizabeth Herzog and Cecilia E. Sudia. 'Children in fatherless families', in *Review of Child Development Research*, vol. 3, University of Chicago Press, 1973, p141.
28. Ibid. p141.
29. Ibid. p142.
30. Ibid. p153.
31. Ibid. p154.
32. Ibid. p200.
33. Ibid. p208.
34. Ibid. p214.
35. Ibid. p220.
36. Ruth Inglis. *Must Divorce Hurt Children?* London, Temple Smith, 1982, p37.
37. Joseph Epstein. *Divorce, the American Experience*. London, Cape, 1975, p178.
38. Sharon Churcher. 'Betty Friedan: Her Life by Judith Hennesse: The violent passion that made the mother of feminism hate men', *Femail on Sunday, The Mail on Sunday*, 27th June 1999.
39. Betty Friedan. *The Feminine Mystique*. New York, Norton, 1963.
40. Rosalind Miles. *Women's History of the World*. London, Collins, 1990, p274.
41. *New York Times*, 5 January 1974. Copyright © 1974 by the New York Times. Reprinted by permission.
42. *New York Times*, 16 February 1973. Copyright © 1973 by the New York Times. Reprinted by permission.
43. 'Obsolete divorce laws assailed at N.O.W. Conference', *New York Times*, 21 January 1974. Copyright © 1974 by the New York Times. Reprinted by permission.
44. Ibid.
45. Epstein. *Divorce, the American Experience*, p158.
46. *New York Times*, 8 February 1976. Copyright © 1976 by the New York Times. Reprinted by permission.
47. Sharon Johnson. 'Divorced fathers organizing to bolster role in children's lives', *New York Times*, 1 August 1977. Copyright © 1977 by the New York Times. Reprinted by permission.
48. Ibid.
49. Herbert Jacob. *The Silent Revolution: The Transformation of Divorce Law in the United States*. Chicago, University of Chicago Press, 1988, p23.
50. Judith H. Gold (ed.), *Divorce as a Developmental Process*. Washington D.C., American Psychiatric Press, 1988, introduction, p xi and p xiv.
51. Barbara Dafoe Whitehead. *The Divorce Culture*. New York, Alfred A. Knopf, 1997, p29.
52. Morton Hunt. 'Help wanted: Divorce Counselor', *New York Times*, 1 January 1967.
53. Ibid.
54. Steven Roberts. 'But why the epidemic?' *New York Times*, 5 January 1974. Copyright © 1974 by the New York Times. Reprinted by permission.
55. Lee Salk. *What every Child would like Parents to Know about Divorce*. New York, Harper & Row, 1978, p3.
56. Ibid. p5.
57. Ibid. p8.

58. Epstein. *Divorce, the American Experience*, p125.
59. Mary Anne Glendon. *Abortion and Divorce in Western Law*. Cambridge, Mass., Harvard University Press, 1987, pp107-8.
60. Jacob. *The Silent Revolution*, p46.
61. *New York Times*, 5 January 1974. Copyright © 1974 by the New York Times. Reprinted by permission.
62. Robert H. Vasoli. *What God has Joined Together*. New York, Oxford University Press, 1998, p4.
63. Ibid. p5.
64. Ibid. p13.
65. Ibid. p21.
66. Ibid. p72.
67. Ibid. p82.
68. Ibid. p200.
69. Ibid. p211.
70. Ibid. p212.
71. *Report of the Royal Commission on Divorce*. London, HMSO, 1912, vol. 2, p473.

Chapter 14. The causes of mass divorce

1. Hansard. Lords debate, 10 March 1920, cc370.
2. Roderick Phillips. *Untying the Knot: a Short History of Divorce*. Cambridge University Press, 1991, p244.
3. *Report of the Royal Commission on Marriage and Divorce*. London, HMSO, 1956, p9.
4. John Drane and Olive Drane. *Happy Families?* Handbook of Pastoral Care. London, Marshall Pickering, 1995, pp20-31.
5. John Muncie and Roger Sapsford. 'Issues in the study of "The Family"', in John Muncie et al. (eds.), *Understanding the Family*. Milton Keynes, Open University, SAGE Publications, 1995, chapter 1, p31.
6. Hansard. Lords debate, 21 June 1963 cc1543-47.
7. Paul C. Vitz. *Psychology as Religion: the cult of self-worship*. Grand Rapids, Mich., Eerdmans, 1977, p10.
8. Ibid. p83.
9. Ibid. p84.
10. Sara McLanahan and Gary Sandefur. *Growing Up with a Single Parent: What Hurts, What Helps*. London, Harvard University Press, 1994, p142.
11. Barbara Dafoe Whitehead. *The Divorce Culture*. New York, Alfred A. Knopf, 1997, p4.
12. Ibid. p6.
13. Ibid. p4.
14. Ibid. p5.
15. Ibid. p5.
16. Alasdair Palmar. 'In seven years he'll still be happy – but she'll want a divorce'. *Sunday Telegraph*, 7 December 1997. © Telegraph Group Limited, London, 1999.
17. Simone De Beauvoir. *The Second Sex*. London, Penguin, 1972.
18. Nicholas Davidson. *The Failure of Feminism*. Buffalo, Prometheus, 1988, p17.
19. Betty Friedan. *The Feminine Mystique*. New York, Norton, 1963.
20. Ibid. p290.
21. Ibid. p336.
22. Ibid. p305.
23. Elizabeth H. Plech, 'Women's rights movement', in *Encyclopedia Americana*, Grolier, 1993, vol. 29, p111.
24. Elaine Storkey. *What's Right with Feminism*. London, Third Way Books, SPCK, 1985.
25. Ibid. p18.
26. Ibid. p17.

27. Ibid. p21.
28. Ibid. p162.
29. Jessie Bernard. *The Future of Marriage*. London, Yale University Press, 1982.
30. Ibid. p38.
31. Ibid. p41.
32. Ibid. pp41-2.
33. Ibid. p248.
34. Germaine Greer. *The Female Eunuch*. London, Grafton Books, 1986, p319.
35. Ibid. p18.
36. Ibid. p320.
37. Ibid. p322.
38. Ibid. p323.
39. Polly Toynbee. 'A woman's work is never done'. *The Times*, 14 September 1991.
40. Liz Hodgkinson. *Unholy Matrimony*. London, Columbus Books, 1988.
41. Ibid. p117.
42. Ibid. p121.
43. Ann Oakley. *Housewife*. London, Allen Lane, 1974, p237.
44. Ibid. pp222, 224.
45. Ibid. p236
46. David Ayers. 'The inevitability of failure: the assumptions and implementations of modern feminism', in John Piper and Wayne Grudem (eds.), *Recovering Biblical Manhood and Womanhood*. Wheaton, Ill., Crossway Books, 1991.
47. Ibid. p313.
48. Ibid. p328.
49. Ibid. p330.
50. Mary Kenny. 'Feminism and the psychologically masculine', in Christine M. Kelly (ed.), *Feminism v. Mankind*. Milton Keynes, Family Publications, 1990, p10.
51. Dorothy Patterson. 'The high calling of wife and mother in Biblical perspective', in Piper and Grudem (eds.), *Recovering Biblical Manhood and Womanhood*, p365.
52. Babette Francis. 'Feminism and the state: the Australian experience', in Christine M. Kelly (ed.), *Feminism v. Mankind*, p20.
53. Sharon James. 'Roles without relegation', in Brian Edwards (ed.), *Men, Women and Authority*. London, Day One Publications, 1996.
54. Ibid. p229.
55. Ibid. p230.
56. Ibid. p231.
57. Ibid. p244.
58. Phillips. *Untying the Knot*, p28.
59. Ibid. p28.
60. Ibid. p33.
61. Ibid. p34.
62. *Something to Celebrate*, p9.
63. John Stott. *Issues Facing Christians Today*. London, Marshall Pickering, 1990, p286.

Chapter 15. What God has joined together

1. Hansard. Lords debate, 18 May 1857, cc523-31.
2. Ibid. cc516-21.
3. Ibid. cc513-14.
4. Hansard. Commons debate, 3 July 1857, cc767-73.
5. Hansard. Commons debate, 31 July 1857, cc825-55.
6. Hansard. Commons debate, 30 July 1857, cc736-42.
7. J. Carl Laney. 'No divorce and no remarriage', in H. Wayne House (ed.), *Divorce and Remarriage: Four Christian Views*. Downers Grove, Inter-Varsity Press, 1990, p17.

8. Henri Blocher. *In the Beginning*. Leicester, Inter-Varsity Press, 1984, pp105-6.
9. Laney. 'No divorce and no remarriage', p18.
10. William A. Heth. 'Divorce, but No Remarriage', in H. Wayne House (ed.), *Divorce and Remarriage: Four Christian Views*. Downers Grove, Ill., Inter-Varsity Press, 1990, p77.
11. Ibid. p77.
12. Gordon J. Wenham and William A. Heth. *Jesus and Divorce*. Updated edition. Carlisle, Paternoster Press, 1997, p105.
13. Laney. 'No divorce and no remarriage', p20.
14. Andrew Cornes. *Divorce and Remarriage: Biblical Principles and Pastoral Practice*. London, Hodder & Stoughton, 1993, p66.
15. Ibid. p65.
16. Edward Donnelly. 'Headship,' in Brian Edwards (ed.), *Men, Women and Authority*. London, Day One Publications, 1996, p110.
17. Wayne Grudem. 'Wives like Sarah, and the husbands who honour them: 1 Peter 3:17', in John Piper and Wayne Grudem (eds.), *Recovering Biblical Manhood and Womanhood*. Wheaton, Ill., Crossway Books, 1991, p199.
18. Elaine Storkey. *What's Right with Feminism*. London, Third Way Books, SPCK, 1985, p182.
19. Wayne Grudem. 'Wives like Sarah, and the husbands who honour them: 1 Peter 3:17', p196.
20. George W. Knight. 'Husbands and wives as analogues of Christ and the Church: Ephesians 5:21-33', in *Recovering Biblical Manhood and Womanhood*, p168.
21. Ibid. p172.
22. Ibid. p175.

Chapter 16. Why God hates divorce

1. Gordon J. Wenham and William A. Heth. *Jesus and Divorce*. Updated edition, Carlisle, Paternoster Press, 1997.
2. Andrew Cornes. *Divorce and Remarriage: Biblical Principles and Pastoral Practice*. London, Hodder & Stoughton, 1993.
3. Wayne Grudem. *Systematic Theology*. Leicester, Inter-Varsity Press, 1994, p515.
4. John Richardson. *God, Sex and Marriage*. London, MPA Books and St Matthias Press, 1998, p40.
5. J. Carl Laney. 'No divorce and no remarriage', in H. Wayne House (ed.), *Divorce and Remarriage: Four Christian Views*. Downers Grove, Ill., Inter-Varsity Press, 1990, p31.
6. Wenham and Heth. *Jesus and Divorce*, p125.
7. Ibid. p126.
8. J.P. Whitney, in *Report of the Royal Commission on Divorce*. London, HMSO, 1912, p275.
9. *Divorce*. Report of the Lower House of the Convocation of York. Westminster, National Society, Sanctuary, 1896.
10. Cornes. *Divorce and Remarriage*, p196.
11. Ibid. p193.
12. John Calvin. *Calvin's New Testament Commentaries. A Harmony of the Gospels Matthew, Mark and Luke*, translated by T. Parker, David W. Torrance and Thomas F. Torrance (eds.), Carlisle, Paternoster Press, 1995, vol. 1, p246.
13. Martin Luther. *The Christian Society*. Walther I. Brandt (ed.), (Luther's Works, vol. 45), Philadelphia, Concordia Publishing House, p32.
14. Martin Luther. *Sermon on the Mount*. Jaroslav Pelikan (ed.), (Luther's Works, vol. 21), St Louis, Concordia Publishing House, p96.
15. Robert Shaw. *The Reformed Faith: an Exposition of the Westminster Confession of Faith*. Inverness, Christian Focus Publications, Reprint 1974, p257.
16. *Divorce*. Report of the Lower House of the Convocation of York, p46.

17. Cited from Rev Arthur C.A. Hall, Bishop of Vermont, in *Divorce in America* by Rev Gwynne, Macmillan Company, 1925. p133.
18. K.E. Kirk. *Marriage and Divorce.* Centenary Press, 1933, pp107-10.
19. Cornes. *Divorce and Remarriage*, p216.
20. Ibid. p214.
21. Wenham and Heth. *Jesus and Divorce*, p110.
22. Ibid. p120.
23. Ibid. p126.
24. P.P. Levertoff and H.L. Goudge. 'The Gospel according to St Matthew', in C. Gore, H.L. Goudge, A. Guillaume (eds.), *A New Commentary on Holy Scripture.* New York, Macmillan, 1928, p174, cited by William A. Heth. 'Divorce, but No Remarriage', in H. Wayne House (ed.), *Divorce and Remarriage: Four Christian Views.* Downers Grove, Ill., Inter-Varsity Press, 1990, p100.
25. Stephen Clark. *Putting Asunder. Divorce and Remarriage in Biblical and Pastoral Perspective.* Bridgend, Bryntirion Press, 1999, p91.
26. Cornes. *Divorce and Remarriage*, p243.
27. F.F. Bruce. *Paul: Apostle of the Heart Set Free.* Grand Rapids, Eerdmans, 1977, p1676, cited by J. Carl Laney. 'No divorce and no remarriage', in H. Wayne House (ed.), *Divorce and Remarriage: Four Christian Views.* Downers Grove, Ill., Inter-Varsity Press, 1990, p41.
28. Stephen Clark. *Putting Asunder,* p137.
29. Norman Hillyer. '1 and 2 Corinthians', D. Guthrie, J.A. Motyer, A.M. Stibbs, D.J. Wiseman (eds.), *The New Bible Commentary.* London, Inter-Varsity Press, 1970, p1060

Chapter 17. Tears and profound sadness

1. Elizabeth Herzog and Cecilia E. Sudia. 'Children in fatherless families', in *Review of Child Development Research.* vol. 3, University of Chicago Press, 1973, p220.
2. Judson T. Landis. 'The trauma of children when parents divorce', *Marriage and Family Living,* February 1960.
3. Michael Rutter. 'Parent-child separation: psychological effects on the children', *Journal of Child Psychology and Psychiatry,* 12, 1971, pp233-60.
4. Diana Kareh. 'The shaky state of the union', *The Times,* 16 January 1968. © Time Newspapers Limited, London.
5. Susan Gettleman and Janet Markowitz. *The Courage to Divorce.* New York, Simon & Schuster, 1974, p83.
6. Ibid. p86.
7. Ibid. p94.
8. Lee Salk. *What every Child would like Parents to Know about Divorce.* New York, Harper & Row, 1978, p12.
9. Sara McLanahan and Gary Sandefur. *Growing Up with a Single Parent: What Hurts, What Helps.* London, Harvard University Press, 1994, pp12-13.
10. Dougal Mackay and Jill Frankham. *Marriage and How to Survive It.* Loughton, Essex, Judy Piatkus Publishers, 1983, p139.
11. Ibid. p141.
12. Judith S. Wallerstein and Joan B. Kelly. *Surviving the Breakup: How Children and Parents Cope with Divorce.* New York, Harper Collins, 1996, p57.
13. Ibid. p57.
14. Ibid. p60.
15. Ibid. p61.
16. Judith S. Wallerstein. 'Children of divorce: preliminary report of a ten-year follow-up of young children', *American Journal of Orthopsychiatry,* 54:3, July 1984, pp446-47.
17. Ibid. p451.

18. Wallerstein. 'Children of divorce: preliminary report', p452.
19. Ibid. p454.
20. Wallerstein and Kelly. *Surviving the Breakup*, p65.
21. Ibid. p66.
22. Ibid. p67.
23. Ibid. pp68-9.
24. Ibid. pp69-70.
25. Judith S. Wallerstein. 'Children of divorce: Report of a ten-year follow-up of early latency-age children', *American Journal of Orthopsychiatiatry*, 57:2, April 1987, pp199-211.
26. Wallerstein and Kelly, *Surviving the Breakup*, pp73-6.
27. Ibid. p86.
28. Ibid. p81.
29. Ibid. p85.
30. Ibid. p87.
31. Ibid. p88.
32. Ibid. p90.
33. Judith S. Wallerstein, Shauna B. Corbin, Julia M. Lewis. 'Children of Divorce'. in *Impact of Divorce, Single Parenting and Stepparenting on Children*. E. Mavis, T. Hetherington and Josephine D. Arasteh (eds.), N.J. Hillsdale, Lawrence Erlbaun Associates, 1988, p 210.
34. Judith S. Wallerstein. 'Children after divorce: Wounds that don't heal', *Perspectives in Psychiatric Care*, 24:3/4, 1987/88,
35. Judith S. Wallerstein. 'Special Article. The long-term effects of divorce on children: a review'. *Journal of the American Academy of Child and Adolescent Psychiatry*, 30:3, May 1991.
36. Monica Cockett and John Tripp. *Family Breakdown and its Impact on Children: The Exeter Family Study*. University of Exeter Press, 1994, pp6-7.
37. Ibid. pp18-19.
38. Ibid. p19.
39. Ibid. p21.
40. Ibid. pp23-4.
41. Ibid. pp32-3, 57.
42. Ibid. pp42-3, 57.
43. Ibid. p58.
44. Ibid. pp44-5.
45. Ibid. p42.
46. Ibid. p57.
47. Margarette Driscol. 'Don't leave me this; Children', *Sunday Times*, 13 February 1994. © Times Newspapers Limited, London.
48. James W. Plunkett and Neil Kalter. 'Children's beliefs about reactions to parental divorce'. *Journal of the American Academy of Child Psychiatry*, 23:5, 1984, pp616-21.
49. E.S. Williams, D. Kumar, R. Milton, M. Scott, and M. Wallis. *Lifestyle of 16-19 Year Old Teenagers in Croydon*. London, Department of Public Health, Croydon Health Authority, 1996.
50. Ibid. Appendix 2, p40.
51. Kathleen E. Kiernan. 'The impact of family disruption in childhood transitions made in young adult life'. *Population Studies*, 46, 1992, pp213-34.
52. Ibid. p233.
53. Nicholas Zill. 'Behavior, achievement, and health problems among children in stepfamilies: findings from a National Survey of Child Health', in *Impact of Divorce, Single Parenting and Stepparenting on Children*. E. Mavis, T. Hetherington and Josephine D. Arasteh (eds.), N.J. Hillsdale, Lawrence Erlbaun Associates, 1988, pp325-68.

54. Ibid. p365
55. Deborah A. Dawson. 'Family structure and children's health and well-being: data from the 1988 National Health Interview Survey on Child Health'. *Journal of Marriage and the Family*, 53, August 1991, pp573-84.
56. Ibid. p580.
57. John Graham and Benjamin Bowling. *Young People and Crime.* (Home Office Research Study 145), London, Home Office, 1995.
58. Ibid. pp34-5.
59. Ibid. p49.
60. Ibid. p37.
61. R.E. Johnson. 'Mother's versus father's role in causing delinquency'. *Adolescence*, 22:86, 1989, pp305-15.
62. Steve Doughty. 'The great myth of poverty and crime'. *Daily Mail*, 2 January 1997.
63. Norman Dennis and George Erdos. *Families Without Fatherhood.* London, IEA Health and Welfare Unit, 1993.
64. Barbara Dafoe Whitehead. *The Divorce Culture.* New York, Alfred A. Knopf, 1997, p189.
65. David Popenoe. *Life Without Father.* New York, Martin Kessler Books, 1996.
66. Amy Conseur, et al. 'Maternal and perinatal risk factors for later delinquency'. *Pediatrics*, 99:6, June 1997, p785.
67. 'Men: Tomorrow's second sex'. *The Economist*, September 1996, p288. © The Economist, London.
68. Home Office Research and Statistics Directorate. Offences Recorded by the Police 1901 to 1996.
69. Robert Whelan. *Broken Homes and Battered Children.* Oxford, Family Education Trust, 1994, p9.
70. Ibid. p23.
71. Ibid. p29.
72. Ibid. pp27-30.
73. Ibid. pp30-3.
74. *Still Running. Children on the Streets in the UK.* Safe on the Streets Research Team, (research director, Professor Mike Stein), London, The Children's Society, 1999.
75. Gillian McCredie and Alan Horrox. *Voices in the Dark: Children and Divorce.* Based on the Thames Television Series. London, Unwin Paperbacks, 1985, p6.
76. Margaret White, retired Croydon Justice of the Peace. Personal communication.
77. McLanahan and Sandefur. *Growing Up with a Single Parent*, p29.

Chapter 18. The loneliness of divorce

1. Hansard. Lords debate, 10 March 1920, cc663-79.
2. Office of Population Censuses and Surveys. Surveys of Psychiatric Morbidity in Great Britain. *Report 1: The prevalence of psychiatric morbidity among adults living in private households.* Howard Meltzer, Baljit Gill, Mark Petticrew, Kerstin Hinds. London, HMSO, 1995, p34.
3. Ibid. pp1-10.
4. Ibid. p14.
5. Ibid. p78.
6. Ibid. p69.
7. Ibid. p69.
8. Ibid. p78.
9. L. Bulusu and M. Alderson. 'Suicides 1950-82'. *Population Trends 35*, London, HMSO, 1984.
10. Jack Dominian. 'Health and marital breakdown'. *British Medical Journal*, vol. 2, 18 August 1979, pp424-25.

11. J. Charlton, S. Kelly, K. Dunnel, B. Evans, R. Jenkins. 'Suicide Deaths in England and Wales: Trends in Factors Associated with Suicide Deaths'. *Population Trends 71*, London, HMSO, 1993.

12. A. Hulten and D. Wasserman. 'Suicide among young people aged 10-29 in Sweden'. *Scand J Soc Med*, 20:2, June 1992, pp65-72.

13. M. Richards, R. Hardy and M. Wadsworth. 'The effects of divorce and separation on mental health in a national UK birth cohort'. *Psychol Med*, 27:5, 1997, pp1121-28.

14. Gaby Hinsliff. 'Divorce is turning ex-wives to drink'. *Daily Mail*, 1 July 1997.

15. Office of Population Censuses and Surveys. *Morbidity Statistics from General Practice. Fourth National Study 1991-1992.* Anna McCormick, Douglas Fleming, John Charlton. London, HMSO, 1995.

16. R. Cochrane and M. Stopes-Roe. 'Women, marriage, employment and mental health'. *British Journal of Psychiatry*, vol. 139, 1981, pp373-81.

17. Judith S. Wallerstein and Joan B. Kelly. *Surviving the Breakup: How Children and Parents Cope with Divorce.* New York, Harper Collins, 1996, p26.

18. Ibid. p28.

19. Ibid. p31.

20. Ibid. p153.

21. Ibid. pp155, 156.

22. Ibid. p156.

23. Judith S. Wallerstein and Sandra Blakeslee. *Second Chances: men, women and children a decade after divorce.* London, Corgi Books, 1990, p29.

24. Ibid. p29.

25. Ibid. p40.

26. Wallerstein and Kelly. *Surviving the Breakup*, p36.

27. Wallerstein and Blakeslee. *Second Chances*, p187.

Chapter 19. Destructive associations

1. Office of Population Censuses and Surveys. *Mortality Statistics, General, 1993, 1994 and 1995.* (Series DH1 no 28), London, HMSO, 1997.

2. Office of Population Censuses and Surveys. *Mortality Statistics, General.* (Series DH1 no 27), London, HMSO, 1994.

3. Office of Population Censuses and Surveys. *General Household Survey. 1991.* Ann Bridgwood and David Savage. (OPCS Series GHS No. 22), London, HMSO, 1993, p103, table 5.19.

4. Anne M. Johnson, Jane Wadsworth, Kaye Wellings and Julia Read. *Sexual Attitudes and Lifestyle.* Oxford, Blackwell Scientific Publications, 1994.

5. Kaye Wellings and Sally Bradshaw. 'First Intercourse between Men and Women' in Anne M. Johnson et al. (eds.), *Sexual Attitudes and Lifestyle.* Oxford, Blackwell Scientific Publications, 1994, chapter 4, p106.

6. Ibid. p106.

7. Anne Johnson and Jane Wadsworth. 'Heterosexual Partnerships', in Anne M. Johnson et al. (eds.), *Sexual Attitudes and Lifestyle.* Oxford, Blackwell Scientific Publications, 1994, chapter 5, p118.

8. Ibid. p122.

9. Anne Johnson, *Sexual Attitudes and Lifestyle*, Data from appendix 3, table A5.2A p444 & table A5.2B p446.

10. Ibid. p123.

11. Ibid. Data from appendix 3, table A10.2 p492 and p494.

12. Ibid. Data from appendix 3, table A9.1 p482 and p480.

13. Damian Whitworth. 'Love is riskier the second time around', *The Times*, 18 May 1999.

14. Anne Johnson, *Sexual Attitudes and Lifestyle*, Data from appendix 3, table A9.2 p484.

Chapter 20. Divorce – the myth and the reality

1. Constance Ahrons. *The Good Divorce: keeping your family together when your marriage falls apart.* New York, Harper Collins, 1994.
2. Ibid. p9.
3. Ibid. pix-x in introduction.
4. Ibid. p10.
5. Ibid. p124.
6. Ibid. p45.
7. Ibid. p29.
8. Ibid. p11.
9. Anne Hooper. *Divorce and Your Children.* London, Robson Books, 1990.
10. Ibid. p88.
11. Ibid. p129.
12. Ibid. p63.
13. Janet Reibstein and Roger Bamber. *The Family Through Divorce.* London, Thorsons, 1977, p167.
14. 'Psychologists extol benefits of divorce for all the family', *The Times*, 13 September 1996. © Times Newspapers Limited, London.
15. Dougal Mackay and Jill Frankham. *Marriage and How to Survive It.* Loughton, Essex, Judy Piatkus Publishers, 1983.
16. Ibid. p21.
17. Ibid. p36.
18. Ibid. p149.
19. Sarah Litvinoff. *The Relate Guide to Starting Again.* London, Vermilion, p133.
20. C.F. Donovan. 'Divorce'. *British Medical Journal*, vol. 289, 8 September 1984, pp597-600.
21. Ibid. pp597-600.
22. Judith S. Wallerstein and Sandra Blakeslee. *Second Chances: men, women and children a decade after divorce.* London, Corgi Books, 1990, p7.
23. Elizabeth Hodder. 'Measures to reduce divorce', *The Times*, 24 October 1990.
24. Wallerstein and Blakeslee, *Second Chances*, p279.
25. Ibid. p288.
26. Louise France. 'The girl who went in search of a father – and found Richard Gere', *Daily Mail Weekend Magazine*, 9 November 1996.
27. Elizabeth Grice. 'Mother was the rebel – I was the adult. Jemma Redgrave talks to Elizabeth Grice about her unconventional family', *Daily Telegraph*, 6 February 1998. © Telegraph Group Limited, London, 1999.
28. Cassandra Jardine. 'The reality of being on your own again: Cassandra Jardine talks to three divorcees about their experiences'. *Daily Telegraph*, July 16 1996. © Telegraph Group Limited, London, 1999.
29. Wallerstein and Blakeslee, *Second Chances*, p59.

Chapter 21. Battle over marriage

1. Hansard. Lords debate. 19 May 1857 cc516-21.
2. Chronicle of Convocation, Canterbury. 1885. Report no. 193, p327.
3. *Putting Asunder: A Divorce Law for Contemporary Society.* Report of Group appointed by the Archbishop of Canterbury in January 1964. London, SPCK, 1966, p3.
4. Rev. H. Cooper. Church Assembly debate, report of proceedings, London, February 1967, pp246-47.
5. General Synod, report of proceedings, 1984, pp299-302.
6. Helen Wilkinson. *The Proposal: Giving Marriage Back to the People.* Demos, 1997, p45.
7. 'Controversy of Divorce'. *The Church Quarterly Review,* January 1896, p439.
8. Geoffrey Fisher. *The Problems of Marriage and Divorce.* London, SPCK, 1955, p21.

9.   Geoffrey Fisher. *The Problems of Marriage and Divorce*, pp23-4.

10. Andrew Cornes. *Divorce and Remarriage: Biblical Principles and Pastoral Practice.* London, Hodder & Stoughton, 1993, p481.

11. Fisher. *The Problems of Marriage and Divorce*, pp21-2.

12. Hansard. Lords debate, 30 June 1969, cc398-400.

13. *Marriage in Church after Divorce.* Discussion document from a Working Party commissioned by the House of Bishops of the Church of England. London, Church House Publishing, 2000. p47.

14. Charles F. Thwing and Carries F. Butler Thwing. *The Family: an Historical and Social Study.* Boston, Lothrop Lee, 1913, pp105-7.

15. William Croswell Doane, Bishop of Albany. 'The Sanctity of Marriage', in *Pan-Anglican Congress Report (June 1908: London).* London, SPCK, 1908, p4.

16. Fisher, *The Problems of Marriage and Divorce*, p9.

Index

A

Abortion 388
Abse, Leo, MP 193, 197, 208, 213
Acland, Sir Francis, MP 160
Adultery
    breaks the marriage bond? 283, 341,
      343–344
    Bucer, Martin 51
    Calvin, John 45
    Charles, RH 131
    consequences of divorce law 341
    Council of Trent 52
    Erasmus 43
    grievous sin 325, 346
    grounds for divorce 68, 69, 81, 84, 92,
      98, 130, 135, 341
    Hosea's wife 334
    Jesus' teaching 17, 336–338, 345
    Luther, Martin 47, 50
    marital offence 218
    Methodist Church 14
    Milton 65
    no remarriage 62
    on part of husband 73
    Protestant Episcopal Church 268, 271
    Protestant teaching 297, 314, 403
    report of York Convocation 337
    separation from bed and board 62, 253
    Westminster Confession of Faith 59
    Zwingli 52
Ahrons, Constance
    Divorced Families 33
    The Good Divorce 390
American divorce
    after Civil War 257–259
    after War of Independence 255–256
    Catholic use of annulments 295–296
    Congress Report on Divorce 259–261
    during colonial times 252–255
    habit 276
    hypocrisy of divorce laws 293
    monument to Protestant doctrine of
    divorce 296
    no-fault 293–294
    numbers 3–5, 258, 259, 298
    opinions on divorce system 269–270
    part of everyday life 252
    social problems 4–5
    views on divorce problem 261–269

Anderson, Bruce 10
Anderson, Professor James 204
Anson, Sir William 120
Archbishop of Canterbury
    Cranmer, Thomas 56, 57, 58, 62, 80
    Davidson, Randall 114, 124, 136–137,
      138, 140–141, 148, 149
    Fisher, Geoffrey 180, 186, 191, 407
      on marriage 187–188
    Lang, Cosmo 156, 168, 177
    Longley, Charles 104
    Ramsey, Arthur
      198, 205, 208, 214, 233, 234
    Runcie, Robert 238, 244
    Sumner, John 73–74
    Whitgift, John 58, 252
Archbishop of York
    Garbett, Cyril 186
    Lang, Cosmo 9, 61, 120, 133–135
    Ramsey, Arthur 192
    Temple, William 172
Augustine of Hippo 40–41, 77, 79, 80
Austin, George
    Archdeacon of York 13, 246
Awdry, Daniel, MP 212
Ayers, David 311

B

Ballentine, Professor William 282
Baptist denomination
    267, 271, 272, 412
Baptist Union
    Belonging 16
Barclay, William 201
Baroness Emmet of Amberley 216
Bentley, Geoffrey, Canon of Windsor 196
Beresford-Hope, Alexander, MP 94–5, 222
Bernard, Jessie
    The Future of Marriage 308–309
Bethell, Sir Richard
    Attorney General 83
Births outside marriage 32
Bishop, Joel
    *Commentaries on the Law of Marriage and
      Divorce* 261–262
Bishop of Barking
    Inskip, James 155

Select Bibliography

1.   Ahrons, Constance R. and Rodgers, Roy H. *Divorced Families*. New York, Norton, 1987.
2.   Ahrons, Constance. *The Good Divorce: keeping your family together when your marriage falls apart*. New York, Harper Collins, 1994.
3.   Augustine. *Treatises on Marriage and Other Subjects*. (ed.), Roy J. Deferrari, Fathers of the Church, New York, 1995.
4.   Barclay, William. *Ethics in a Permissive Society*. London, Collins, 1971.
5.   Bernard, Jessie. *The Future of Marriage*. London, Yale University Press, 1982.
6.   Bishop, Joel Prentiss. *Marriage and Divorce*. 6th edition, Boston, Little Brown, 1881.
7.   Blake, Nelson M. *The Road to Reno: A History of Divorce in the United States*. New York, Macmillan, 1962.
8.   Blocher, Henri. *In the Beginning*. Leicester, Inter-Varsity Press, 1984.
9.   Butt, John. *Robert Owen, Prince of Cotton Spinners*. Newton Abbott, David & Charles, 1929.
10. Calvin, John. *Calvin's New Testament Commentaries. A Harmony of the Gospels Matthew, Mark and Luke*. vol. 2, translated by T.H. Parker, David W. Torrance and Thomas F. Torrance (eds.), Carlisle, Paternoster Press, 1995.
11. Calvin, John. *Sermons on the Epistle to the Ephesians*. Edinburgh, Banner of Truth Trust, 1973.
12. Calvin, John. *The Institutes of the Christian Religion*. London, James Clarke, 1962.
13. Calvin, John. *Tracts Containing Antidote to the Council of Trent*. translated by Henry Beveridge, Edinburgh, Calvin Translation Society.
14. Carlson, Eric Josef. *Marriage and the English Reformation*. Oxford, Blackwell, 1994.
15. Charles, R.H. *The Teaching of the New Testament on Divorce*. London, Wms. & Norgate, 1921.
16. Charlish, Anne. *Caught in the Middle*. London, Ward Lock, 1997.
17. Clark, Stephen. *Putting Asunder. Divorce and Remarriage in Biblical and Pastoral Perspective*. Bridgend, Bryntirion Press. 1999
18. Clarke, S.C. *Advance report of final marriage statistics, 1989 and 1990*. Monthly vital statistics report, 43:12, suppl., Hyattsville, Maryland, National Center for Statistics, 1995.
19. Cockett, Monica and Tripp, John. *Family Breakdown and its Impact on Children: The Exeter Family Study*. University of Exeter Press, 1994.
20. Cornes, Andrew. *Divorce and Remarriage: Biblical Principles and Pastoral Practice*. London, Hodder and Stoughton, 1993.
21. Cott, Nancy F. 'Divorce and the Changing Status of Women', in Michael Gordon (ed.), *The American Family in Social-Historical Perspective*. 2nd edition, New York, St Martin's Press, 1978.
22. Dallos, Rudi and Sapsford, Roger. 'Patterns of diversity and lived realities', in John Muncie et al., (eds.), *Understanding the Family*. Milton Keynes, Open University, SAGE Publications, 1995.

23. De Beauvoir, Simone. *The Second Sex*. London, Penguin, 1972.

24. Degler, Carl N. *At Odds: Women and the Family in America from the Revolution to the Present*. Oxford University Press, 1980.

25. Dennis, Norman and Erdos, George. *Families Without Fatherhood*. London, IEA Health and Welfare Unit, 1993.

26. *Divorce*. Report of the Lower House of the Convocation of York. Westminster, National Society, Sanctuary, 1896.

27. Doane, William Croswell. 'The Sanctity of Marriage', in *Pan-Anglican Congress Report (June 1908: London)*. London, SPCK, 1908.

28. Doe, Norman. *The Legal Framework of the Church of England*. London, Oxford University Press, 1996.

29. Drane, John and Drane, Olive. *Happy Families? Building Healthy Families*. Handbook of Pastoral Care. London, Marshall Pickering, 1995.

30. Ellisen, Stanley A. *Divorce and Remarriage in the Church*. Grand Rapids, Mich., Zondervan, 1977.

31. Epstein, Joseph. *Divorce, the American Experience*. London, Cape, 1975.

32. Fisher, Geoffrey, Archbishop of Canterbury. *The Problems of Marriage and Divorce*. London, SPCK, 1955.

33. *Formularies of Faith put forth by Authority during Reign of Henry VIII...* Oxford, Clarendon Press, 1825.

34. Francis, Babette. 'Feminism and the State: The Australian Experience', in *Feminism v Mankind*. Milton Keynes, Family Publications, 1990.

35. Friedan, Betty. *The Feminine Mystique*. New York, Norton, 1963.

36. Gettleman, Susan and Markowitz, Janet. *The Courage to Divorce*. New York, Simon & Schuster, 1974.

37. Gibson, Colin S. *Dissolving Wedlock*. London, Routledge, 1994.

38. Glendon, Mary Anne. *Abortion and Divorce in Western Law*. Cambridge, Mass., Harvard University Press, 1987.

39. Goodsell, Willystine. *A History of Marriage and the Family*. New York, Macmillan, 1934.

40. Graham, John and Bowling, Benjamin. *Young People and Crime*. (Research Study 145) London, Home Office, 1995.

41. Great Britain, Central Statistical Office. *Social Trends 26*. (ed.), Jenny Church, London, HMSO, 1996.

42. Great Britain, Office for National Statistics. *Birth Statistics 1995*. (ONS series FM1 no 24) London, HMSO, 1997.

43. Great Britain, Office of Population Censuses and Surveys. *General Household Survey 1993*. (OPCS series GHS no. 24) London, HMSO, 1995.

44. Great Britain, Office of Population Censuses and Surveys. *Marriage and Divorce Statistics, 1837-1983: England &Wales*. (OPCS series FM2 no.16) (Historical Series) HMSO, London, 1990.

45. Great Britain, Office of Population Censuses and Surveys. *Marriage and Divorce Statistics 1990 to 1996: England & Wales*. (OPCS series FM2 nos.18 to 22) London, HMSO, 1992-1996.

46. Great Britain, Office of Population Censuses and Surveys. *Report 1: The prevalence of psychiatric morbidity among adults living in private households*. Surveys of Psychiatric Morbidity in Great Britain, Howard Meltzer, Baljit Gill, Mark Petticrew, Kerstin Hinds, London, HMSO, 1995.

47. Great Britain. *Report of the Royal Commission on Divorce and Matrimonial Causes*. London, HMSO, 1912.

48. Great Britain. *Report of the Royal Commission on Marriage and Divorce*. London, HMSO, 1956.

49. Great Britain. The Law Commission, *Family Law, the Ground for Divorce*. (Report no. 192) London, HMSO, 1990.

50. Great Britain. The Law Commission, *Reform of the Grounds of Divorce: the Field of Choice*. London, HMSO, 1966.

51. Greer, Germaine. *The Female Eunuch*. London, Grafton Books, 1986.

52. Gwynne, Walker. *Divorce in America under State and Church*. New York, Macmillan, 1925.

53. Hall, Arthur C.A. Bishop of Vermont. *Church's Discipline Concerning Marriage and Divorce: First Triennial Charge*. New York, Longmans Green.

54. Harper, Michael. *Equal and Different*. London, Hodder and Stoughton, 1994.

55. Haskey, John. 'Divorce and Remarriage in England & Wales', *Population Trends 95*, Spring 1999, London, Office of National Statistics, 1999.

56. Haskey, John. 'Families: their historical context, and recent trends in the factors influencing their formation and dissolution', in *The Fragmenting Family: Does it Matter?* London, IEA Health and Welfare Unit, 1998.

57. Haskey, John. 'Trends in Marriage and Cohabitation: the decline in marriage and the changing pattern of living together in partnerships', *Population Trends 80*, Summer 1995, London, HMSO, 1995.

58. Henson, H. Hensley. *Christian Marriage*. London, Cassell and Company, 1907.

59. Herzog, Elizabeth and Sudia, Cecilia E. 'Children in fatherless families', in *Review of Child Development Research*. vol. 3, Chicago, University of Chicago Press, 1973.

60. Himmelfarb, Gertrude. *The De-moralization of Society*. London, IEA Health and Welfare Unit, 1995.

61. Hodgkinson, Liz. *Unholy Matrimony*. London, Columbus Books, 1988.

62. Hooper, Anne. *Divorce and Your Children*. London, Robson Books, 1990.

63. *House of Bishops report*. (GS 669), 1985.

64. Howard, George Elliot. *History of Matrimonial Institutions, Chiefly in England and the United States*. vol. 3, London, Unwin, 1904.

65. Hunt, Morton and Hunt, Bernice. *The Divorce Experience*. New York, McGraw-Hill, 1977.

66. Inglis, Ruth. *Must Divorce Hurt Children?* London, Temple Smith, 1982.

67. Jacob, Herbert. *The Silent Revolution: The Transformation of Divorce Law in the United States*. Chicago, University of Chicago Press, 1988.

68. Johnson, Anne; Wadsworth, Jane; Wellings, Kaye and Read, Julia. *Sexual Attitudes and Lifestyle*. Oxford, Blackwell Scientific Publications, 1994.

69. Joyce, George Hayward. *Christian Marriage: an Historical and Doctrinal Study*. 2nd edition, London, Sheed & Ward, 1948.

70. Keble, John. *Sequel of the Argument against immediately repealing the Laws which treat the Nuptial Bond as Indissoluble*. Oxford, Parker, 1857.

71. Kiernan, Kathleen E. 'The impact of family disruption in childhood transitions made in young adult life', *Population Studies*. vol. 46, 1992.

72. Kirk, Kenneth E. *Marriage and Divorce*. Centenary Press, 1933.

73. Kirk, Mary and Leary, Tom. *Holy Matrimony?* London, SPCK , 1994.

74. Knox-Little, William J. *Holy Matrimony*. London, Longmans Green, 1900.

75. Laney, J. Carl. 'No Divorce and No Remarriage', in H Wayne House (ed.), *Divorce and Remarriage: Four Christian Views*. Downers Grove, Ill., Inter-Varsity Press, 1990.

76. Lang, Cosmo Gordon. *The Marriage Question.* Sermon at St Paul's Cathedral, October 1908. White Cross League, Westminster Abbey.

77. Luther, Martin. *The Christian Society.* Walther I. Brandt (ed.), (Luther's Works, vol. 45), Philadelphia, Concordia Publishing House.

78. Mackay, Dougal and Frankham, Jill. *Marriage and How to Survive It.* Loughton, Essex, Judy Piatkus Publishers, 1983.

79. Maclean, Mavis. *Surviving Divorce.* London, MacMillan, 1991.

80. *Marriage – and the Standing Committee's Task.* (GS 571), London, CIO Publishing, April 1983.

81. *Marriage and the Church's Task.* (The Lichfield report), Report of the General Synod Marriage Commission, London, CIO Publishing, 1978.

82. *Marriage in Church after Divorce.* (GS 633), 1984.

83. *Marriage, Divorce and the Church.* Report of the Commission on the Christian Doctrine of Marriage. The Root Report, London, SPCK, 1971.

84. McCredie, Gillian and Horrox, Alan. *Voices in the Dark: Children and Divorce.* Based on the Thames Television Series. London, Unwin Paperbacks, 1985.

85. McLanahan, Sara and Sandefur, Gary. *Growing Up with a Single Parent: What Hurts, What Helps.* London, Harvard University Press, 1994.

86. Miles, Rosalind. *Women's History of the World.* London, Collins, 1990.

87. Mill, J. S. *The Subjection of Women.* London, Longmans Green, 1869.

88. O'Neill, William. *Divorce in the Progressive Era.* New Haven, Yale University Press, 1967.

89. Oakley, Ann. *Housewife.* London, Allen Lane, 1974.

90. Olsen, V. Norskov. *The New Testament Logia on Divorce: a study of their interpretation from Erasmus to Milton.* (BGBE 10), Tubingen, Mohr, 1971.

91. Phillips, Roderick. *Untying the Knot: a Short History of Divorce.* Cambridge University Press, 1991.

92. Popenoe, David. *Life Without Father.* New York, Martin Kessler, 1996.

93. *Putting Asunder: A Divorce Law for Contemporary Society.* Report of group appointed by Archbishop of Canterbury, January 1964. London, SPCK, 1966.

94. *Recovering Biblical Manhood and Womanhood.* John Piper and Wayne Grudem (eds.), Wheaton, Ill., Crossway Books, 1991.

95. Reibstein, Janet and Bamber, Roger. *The Family through Divorce.* London, Thorsons, 1977.

96. *Report of the House of Bishops.* (GS 634), 1984.

97. *Report of the National League for the Protection of the Family.* Everest Press, 1900.

98. Riley, Glenda. *Divorce: An American Tradition.* New York, Oxford University Press, 1991.

99. Rutter, Michael. Parent-child separation: psychological effects on the children. *Journal of Child Psychology and Psychiatry.* vol. 12, 1971.

100. Salk, Lee. *What every Child would like Parents to Know about Divorce.* New York, Harper & Row, 1978.

101. Shaw, Robert. *The Reformed Faith: an Exposition of the Westminster Confession of Faith.* Inverness, Christian Focus Publications, Reprint, 1974.

102. Smith, Merril D. *Breaking the Bonds.* New York, New York University Press, 1991.

103. *Something to Celebrate.* Report of a Working Party of the Board for Social Responsibility. London, Church House Publishing, 1995.

104. Southgate, Chris. *Newly Single: an Approach to Life after Marriage.* Berkshire, Cat Publications, 1992.

105. Stanton, Elizabeth Cady. *Eighty Years and More, 1815 to 1897. Remininiscences of E.C. Stanton.* London, Unwin, 1898.

106. Stone, Lawrence. *Road to Divorce; England 1530 to 1987.* Oxford University Press, 1992.

107. Storkey, Elaine, *What's Right with Feminism.* London, Third Way Books, SPCK, 1985.

108. Stott, John. *Issues Facing Christians Today.* London, Marshall Pickering, 1990.

109. Taylor, Barbara. *Eve and the New Jerusalem.* London, Virago, 1983.

110. *The Anglican Canons 1529-1947.* Gerald Bray (ed.), Church of England Record Society, vol. 6, Woodbridge, Boydell Press, 1998.

111. *The Church and Marriage.* Report of Joint Committees of the Convocations of Canterbury and York, London, SPCK, 1935.

112. The Methodist Church Division of Social Responsibility, *Preparing for Christian Marriage.* Report received by the Conference of 1996.

113. Thwing, Charles F. and Thwing, Carries Butler. *The Family: an Historical and Social Study.* Boston, Lothrop Lee, 1913.

114. 'Uniform Law relating to Annulment of Marriage and Divorce', in *Report of National Congress on Uniform Divorce Laws.* Washington, February 1906.

115. Vasoli, Robert H. *What God has Joined Together.* New York, Oxford University Press, 1998.

116. Wallerstein, Judith S. and Blakeslee, Sandra. *Second Chances: Men, Women and Children a Decade after Divorce.* London, Corgi Books, 1990.

117. Wallerstein, Judith S. and Kelly, Joan B. *Surviving the Breakup: How Children and Parents Cope with Divorce.* New York, Harper Collins, 1996.

118. Wenham, Gordon J. and Heth, William A. *Jesus and Divorce.* Updated edition, Carlisle, Paternoster Press, 1997.

119. Whelan, Robert. *Broken Homes and Battered Children.* Oxford, Family Education Trust, 1994.

120. Whitehead, Barbara Dafoe. *The Divorce Culture.* New York, Alfred A Knopf, 1997.

121. Wilberforce, Reginald. *Life of Samuel Wilberforce, Bishop of Oxford and Winchester; by his son.* London, Kegan Paul, Trench, 1888.

122. Wilkins, H. J. *History of Divorce and Remarriage.* London, Longmans, 1910.

123. Wilkinson, Helen. *The Proposal: Giving Marriage Back to the People.* London, Demos, 1997.

124. Williams, E.S. et al. *Lifestyle of 16–19 Year Old Teenagers in Croydon.* London, Department of Public Health, Croydon Health Authority, 1996.

125. Winnett, A.R. *Divorce and Remarriage in Anglicanism.* London, Macmillan, 1958.

126. Woolsey, Theodore D. *Divorce and Divorce Legislation.* New York, Charles Scribner's Sons, 1882.

127. Wright, Carroll D., Commissioner of Labour. *A Report on Marriage and Divorce in the United States. 1867 to 1886.* Washington, 1889.

128. Wright, Carroll D. *Outline of Practical Sociology.* New York, Longmans Green, 1898.

Acknowledgements

1. Extracts from *The Demoralisation of Society: From Victorian Virtues to Modern Values* published in 1995, and *The Family: Is It Just Another Lifestyle Choice?* published in 1993 by IEA Health and Welfare Unit, The Institute of Economic Affairs, 2 Lord North Street, Westminster, London SW1P 3LB, are used by kind permission of IEA Health and Welfare Unit.

2. Material from *Happy Families?* by John Drane and Olive M. Fleming Drane, published by Harper Collins in 1995, are used by kind permission of the authors.

3. Extracts from *Divorce and Remarriage: Four Christian Views* edited by H.Wayne House 1990, used by permission of Inter Varsity Press, P.O. Box 1400, Downers Grove, Ill., 60515.

4. Extracts from *Broken Homes and Battered Children*, © and published by Family Education Trust, 1994, used by kind permission.

5. Extracts from *The Future of Marriage*, copyright © Jessie Barnard, published by Yale University Press, used by permission.

6. *Young People and Crime*, Home Office Research Study 145, is Crown copyright and extracts are reproduced with the permission of the Controller of Her Majesty's Stationery Office.

7. Extracts from *Understanding the Family* by J Munice et al., copyright © 1995 are reprinted by permission of Sage Publications Ltd.

8. Extracts from *Divorce and Remarriage*, copyright © Andrew Cornes 1993, used by kind permission of Hodder and Stoughton Publishers.

9. Extracts from *Jesus and Divorce*, copyright © Gordon J. Wenham and William A. Heth, used by kind permission of Paternoster Publishing.

10. Extracts from *Something to Celebrate – The Report of a Working Party for the Board for Social Responsibility* (Church House Publishing, 1995) are copyright © The Central Board of Finance of the Church of England 1995 and are reproduced by permission.

11. Extracts from *The Church and Marriage: the Majority Report* (1935) are copyright © The Central Board of Finance of the Church of England and are reproduced by permission.

12. Extracts from *The Church and Marriage: the first Minority Report* are copyright © The Central Board of Finance of the Church of England and are reproduced by permission.

13. Extracts from *Marriage, Divorce and the Church (The Root Report)* (1971) are copyright © The Central Board of Finance of the Church of England and are reproduced by permission.

14. Extracts from *Report on Marriage and the Church's Task (The Lichfield Report)* (1978) are copyright © The Central Board of Finance of the Church of England and are reproduced by permission.

15. Extracts from the findings and recommendation of The Standing Committee on Marriage Discipline *(Marriage – and the Standing Committee's Task)* (GS571) are copyright © The Archbishop's Council, 1999 and are reproduced with permission.

16. Extracts from *Marriage in Church after Divorce: A Report by the House of Bishops* (GS616) are copyright © The Archbishop's Council, 1999 and are reproduced with permission.

17. Extracts from the *Draft Marriage Regulations (Marriage in Church After Divorce)* (GS633) are copyright © The Archbishop's Council, 1999 and are reproduced with permission.

18. Extracts from the *Draft Marriage Regulations 198–* (1984) (GS634) are copyright © The Archbishop's Council, 1999 and are reproduced with permission.

19. *Second Chances,* © Judith Wallerstein PhD & Sandra Blakeslee 1989, published by Corgi, a division of Transworld Publishers Ltd.

20. Extracts from *Surviving the Break – How children and parents cope with divorce,* by Dr Judith S. Wallerstein and Joan B Kelly are reproduced by kind permission of Blackwell Publishers.

21. Extracts from *Sexual Attitudes and Lifestyle* by Anne Johnson & Jane Wadsworth are used by permission of Blackwell Scientific Publications.

22. Extracts from *Equal and Different,* copyright © Michael Harper are used by permission of the publishers Hodder and Stoughton.

23. Material quoted from *Issues Facing Christians Today* by John Stott is used by permission of publishers Harper Collins Publishers.

24. Material quoted from *The Female Eunuch* © 1970 Germaine Greer is reprinted with the permission of Gillon Aitken Associates Ltd.

25. Material from *Divorce and Remarriage in the Church,* by Stanley A. Ellisen, 1977, copyright © by the Zondervan Corporation, used by permission of Zondervan Publishing House.

26. Extracts from *Robert Owen, Prince of Cotton Spinners,* © David & Charles, 1971, used by kind permission of the publishers.

27. Extracts from *Abortion & Divorce in Western Law,* by Mary Ann Glendon, copyright © 1987, by the President & Fellows of Harvard College. Reprinted by permission of Harvard University Press.

28. Copyright material from *The Daily Mail* and *Mail on Sunday* used by permission.

29. Copyright material from the Telegraph Group Limited used by permission as indicated in the endnotes.

30. Copyright material from *The Times* and *The Sunday Times* used by permission as indicated in the endnotes.

31. Copyright material from *The New York Times* used by permission, as indicated in the endnotes.

32. *Divorce – the American Experience* by Joseph Epstein (London, Jonathan Cape 1975). Copyright © Joseph Epstein, reprinted by permission of George Borchardt.

33. *Housewife* by Ann Oakley (Penguin Books, 1974) copyright © Ann Oakley. Reproduced by permission of Penguin Books.

Also published by Belmont House Publishing

Cohabitation or Marriage?

by Declan Flanagan and Dr Ted Williams

This report discusses the increasing trend in cohabitation. It outlines the biblical view of marriage and shows why cohabitation is not a good idea. Exposing flaws in the arguments of those who encourage young people to live together before marriage, the Report goes on to demonstrate many of the negative consequences for those who choose to cohabit. The authors show that marriage is God's intended way, and conclude that cohabitation is morally indefensible. The Christian Church needs to understand the issue to help reverse the current trend. The Report aims to provide information that will be of value to Christian leaders, theological students, youth workers and, of course, concerned parents.

ISBN 0 9529939 0 2

Also available from Belmont House Publishing

Jesus Christ – the King of Glory

This attractive booklet is a devotional aid written to help Christian worship
worship their Saviour and Lord. It uses Scriptures to describe the wonder, glory
and majesty of Jesus Christ. Just under two hundred text are used to build up a
word picture of Jesus – the King of Glory.

ISBN 0 9529939 2 9

Also available from Belmont House

Problems of Marriage and Divorce

by Archibishop Geoffrey Fisher

Reprinted in 1999 by permission from Lambeth Palace Library

ISBN 09529939 2 9